# The Journal Letters and Related Biographical Items of the Reverend Charles Wesley, M.A.

## Second Edition, Enlarged

**Kingswood Books**

Rex D. Matthews, Director

*Candler School of Theology, Emory University*

**Editorial Advisory Board**

Ted Campbell

*Perkins School of Theology*

Richard P. Heitzenrater

*Duke Divinity School*

Henry Knight III

*Saint Paul School of Theology*

Mary Elizabeth Mullino Moore

*Boston University School of Theology*

F. Douglas Powe Jr.

*Wesley Theological Seminary*

Sam Powell

*Point Loma Nazarene University*

Karen B. Westerfield Tucker

*Boston University School of Theology*

Sondra Wheeler

*Wesley Theological Seminary*

Brian K. Milford, ex officio

*Abingdon Press*

David C. Teel, ex officio

*Abingdon Press*

# THE JOURNAL LETTERS AND RELATED BIOGRAPHICAL ITEMS OF THE REVEREND CHARLES WESLEY, M.A.

## SECOND EDITION, ENLARGED

EDITED BY

## FRANK BAKER

## RICHARD P. HEITZENRATER

## AND

## RANDY L. MADDOX

KINGSWOOD BOOKS
An Imprint of Abingdon Press
Nashville, Tennessee

THE JOURNAL LETTERS AND RELATED BIOGRAPHICAL ITEMS OF
THE REVEREND CHARLES WESLEY, M.A.,
SECOND EDITION, ENLARGED

*Copyright © 2023 by Abingdon Press*

*First Edition Copyright © 2018 by Abingdon Press*

All rights reserved.
No part of this work may be reproduced or transmitted in any form or by any means, electronic or mechanical, including photocopying and recording, or by any information storage or retrieval system, except as may be expressly permitted by the 1976 Copyright Act, the 1998 Digital Millennium Copyright Act, or in writing from the publisher. Requests for permission should be addressed to Permissions, Abingdon Press, 810 12th Avenue South, Nashville, TN 37203-4704, or emailed to permissions@abingdonpress.com.

Library of Congress Control Number: 2022949749

ISBN: 978-1-7910-2882-4

This project uses the SBL Greek font, which is available from the Society of Biblical Literature at www.sbl-site.org.

Scripture quotations from The Authorized (King James) Version. Rights in the Authorized Version in the United Kingdom are vested in the Crown. Reproduced by permission of the Crown's patentee, Cambridge University Press.

MANUFACTURED IN THE UNITED STATES OF AMERICA

The following Relation will I trust be matter of Rejoicing to you. G[o]d has lately made bare his arm before us. For some loose past my Brother has attended y[e] Malefactors in Newgate, some of w[ch] hardened, some deeply penitent. I did not visit them till Tuesday last. It pleased G[o]d to melt me into something of softness at y[e] sight of y[m]. After Prayers I spake to y[m] from Mat: 5. 25. 26. & set y[e] Terrors of y[e] Lord in Array ag[t] y[m]. They were so much affected, & shewed such signs of true Compunction (declaring audibly that they did deserve Damnation) that I soon passed from y[e] Law to y[e] Gospell. It w[d] have delighted you to have heard & seen their sighs & Groans & Tears, at hearing of X[t] given for us. At my mentioning a saying of Luther: That if all the Sins of y[e] whole world were laid upon one Man, the Blood of X[t] was suffic[t] to cleanse even Him from all Sin. And asking, w[ch] of you believe this; one of y[m] cried out w[th] y[e] utmost Vehemence, I Do. I Do believe it from my Heart. I proceeded be it unto Thee according to thy Faith, & he repeated a most comfortable Amen.

After Sermon I spake a few words to y[m] exhorting y[m] to spend every Moment that stood betwixt y[m] & Eternity in crying to Jesus for Repentance & Faith. Adding that I nothing doubted, but some of y[m] w[d] know before their Execution (which was to be y[e] next Day) that their sins were forgiven y[m]. These, S[r], some of us know it already (said Barecock, who made y[e] Confession above) but may we not, continued He, expect to know it more & more, y[e] nearer we draw to Eternity? The rest seemed full of Comforts & Trust in y[e] Blood of Jesus, expressed a strong Desire of receiving y[e] H[ly] Sacram[t], & much Affection to me for promising to come again in the Afternoon. From thence I went to the old condemn'd Hole, where four more were confined for attempting to break Goal y[e] Night before. I found them chaked down to the floor. Their Ringleader Thomas (a hardned Villain the once a Gentleman) cried out most audaciously "Ay here am I the Author of the Rebellion. I am the Primum Mobile". I ask'd him whether he had consider'd his Rebellion ag[t] GOD & how to make his Peace with Him. He answer'd more composedly I was all his Thought. The other behav'd better. We went to Prayer, & GOD gave me Power to pray in faith. I claim'd the Promise of a Saviour for whomsoever he was willing to receive Him. After Pray[r] they appear'd much humbled. Thomas's Countenance was fallen, & they rejoiced to hear I w[d] see them again. Accordingly in the Afternoon I pray'd by them & preach'd the Gospel from the 2 Crucified Malefactors. They rec[d] it as might be expected from those who had nothing but the Blood of X[t] to trust to. One now declar'd He had Forgiveness of Sin, Peace with GOD & Joy in the H[ly] Ghost. And so says He, I hope this my Companion has, tho' he is afraid to profess it. Upon my saying to his Companion GOD loves You. He reply'd with great Earnestness & Joy. "does he indeed? Can you doubt of that says the other. Suppose one of them y[t] are passing by should offer to die in your place tomorrow. W[d] not He love you. But It has done this for You?" – So not mend w[t] He said but endeavour'd to enforce it, & left them in a most delightful Frame, broken-hearted, believing & ready to receive the Bridegroom.

The next Morning between 6 & 7 my Brother & I with M[r] Sparks & Bray went to see them. The Keeper was letting them out of their Cells. The first Word we heard was Glory be to GOD. This is the most blessed Day I ever saw. Glory be to X[t]. Glory be to X[t]. We said Amen & went in. Barecock the man that spoke, ask'd who is there? We answer'd the Messengers of X[t]. He knew

# CHARLES WESLEY SOCIETY SERIES

*The Manuscript Journal of the Rev. Charles Wesley, M.A.*, Volume I
*The Manuscript Journal of the Rev. Charles Wesley, M.A.*, Volume II
*The Journal Letters and Related Biographical Items of the Rev. Charles Wesley, M.A. Second Edition, Enlarged*
*The Letters of the Rev. Charles Wesley, M.A.*

# CONTENTS

ACKNOWLEDGEMENTS . . . . . . . . . . . . . . . . . . . . . IX

PREFACE TO SECOND EDITION . . . . . . . . . . . . . . . . . X

SIGNS, SPECIAL USAGES, ABBREVIATIONS . . . . . . . . . . . . . XI

INTRODUCTION . . . . . . . . . . . . . . . . . . . . . . . XIV

SELECT CHRONOLOGY OF CHARLES WESLEY . . . . . . . . . . . . XXI

JOURNAL LETTERS AND RECORDS
    DECEMBER 1716–JANUARY 1717; ACCOUNTS OF "OLD JEFFREY" . . . . . . . . 3
    NOVEMBER 7–8, 1738; ACCOUNT OF DYING MALEFACTORS PENITENT . . . . . 30
    JUNE 1739; PROPHETESS LAVINGTON'S CASE . . . . . . . . . . . . . . 35
    MARCH 28–APRIL 1, 1740 . . . . . . . . . . . . . . . . . . . . . 43
    APRIL 6–8, 1740 . . . . . . . . . . . . . . . . . . . . . . . . 50
    MAY 8–15, 1740 . . . . . . . . . . . . . . . . . . . . . . . . 58
    JUNE 19–21, 1740 . . . . . . . . . . . . . . . . . . . . . . . . 67
    JUNE 23–27, 1740 . . . . . . . . . . . . . . . . . . . . . . . . 72
    JULY 14–18, 1740 . . . . . . . . . . . . . . . . . . . . . . . . 77
    JULY 19–30, 1740 . . . . . . . . . . . . . . . . . . . . . . . . 83
    SEPTEMBER 22–27, 1740 . . . . . . . . . . . . . . . . . . . . . 89
    APRIL 14–25, 1741 . . . . . . . . . . . . . . . . . . . . . . . 94
    JUNE 16–28, 1741 . . . . . . . . . . . . . . . . . . . . . . . 111
    C. 1741–42; SHORTHAND NOTES ON BRISTOL METHODISTS . . . . . . . . . 121
    SEPTEMBER 23–OCTOBER 2, 1742 . . . . . . . . . . . . . . . . . 125
    JANUARY 14, 1743 . . . . . . . . . . . . . . . . . . . . . . . 140
    MAY 17–JUNE 27, 1743; SHORTHAND NOTES . . . . . . . . . . . . . . 142
    MAY 17–25, 1743 . . . . . . . . . . . . . . . . . . . . . . . 144
    JULY 11–29, 1743 . . . . . . . . . . . . . . . . . . . . . . . 153
    MARCH 15, 1744 . . . . . . . . . . . . . . . . . . . . . . . 174
    SEPTEMBER 2–17, 1744 . . . . . . . . . . . . . . . . . . . . . 181
    JULY 28–AUGUST 15, 1745 . . . . . . . . . . . . . . . . . . . . 185
    APRIL 14–MAY 11, 1746 . . . . . . . . . . . . . . . . . . . . . 190
    MAY 12–JUNE 14, 174. . . . . . . . . . . . . . . . . . . . . . 196
    JUNE 15–30, 1746 . . . . . . . . . . . . . . . . . . . . . . . 204
    JULY 1–13, 1746 . . . . . . . . . . . . . . . . . . . . . . . 215

July 14–27, 1746 . . . . . . . . . . . . . . . . . . . . . . . . . . . 220
July 27–August 10, 1746 . . . . . . . . . . . . . . . . . . . . . . . 231
August 11–28, 1746 . . . . . . . . . . . . . . . . . . . . . . . . . . 239
August 24, 1747–February 6, 1748 . . . . . . . . . . . . . . . . . . 245
February 8–15, 1748 . . . . . . . . . . . . . . . . . . . . . . . . . 287
September 26–October 27, 1748 . . . . . . . . . . . . . . . . . . . 295
December 9–20, 1748; Elizabeth Story's Declaration . . . . . . . . . 302
June 29–July 20, 1751 . . . . . . . . . . . . . . . . . . . . . . . . 304
July 22–August 13, 1751 . . . . . . . . . . . . . . . . . . . . . . . 314
August 13–October 3, 1751 . . . . . . . . . . . . . . . . . . . . . . 321
July 28, 1751–January 16, 1752; Notebook on
   "The Preachers" . . . . . . . . . . . . . . . . . . . . . . . . . . 339
March 9–10, 1752; Preachers' Covenants . . . . . . . . . . . . . . . 351
November 29–December 11, 1753 . . . . . . . . . . . . . . . . . . . 355
July 8–31, 1754 . . . . . . . . . . . . . . . . . . . . . . . . . . . 365
July 8–August 13, 1754 (Thomas Jackson source) . . . . . . . . . . . 379
October 17–24, 1754 (Luke Tyerman source) . . . . . . . . . . . . . 391
August 26–28, 1756; Notes on Bristol Conference . . . . . . . . . . 392
August 30, 1756; Preachers' Covenant . . . . . . . . . . . . . . . . 394
September 17–28, 1756 . . . . . . . . . . . . . . . . . . . . . . . . 395
October 1–10, 1756 . . . . . . . . . . . . . . . . . . . . . . . . . 400
October 11–23, 1756 . . . . . . . . . . . . . . . . . . . . . . . . . 407
November 1771; Case of Magdalen Hunter . . . . . . . . . . . . . . . 416
June 1772–April 1774; Case of Edward Davies . . . . . . . . . . . . 422
c. 1784; Notes on Conversation with Lord Mansfield . . . . . . . . . 424
March 29, 1787; Notes on Sarah (Perrin) Jones's Death . . . . . . . 436

Biographical Accounts of his Musical Sons . . . . . . . . . . . 437
   1769–1772; Account of Charles Wesley Jr. and Joseph Kelway . . . . 439
   June 1776; Biographical Account of Charles Wesley Jr.'s Childhood . 450
   November 1776; Charles Wesley Jr. playing for King and Queen . . . 456
   1776–1777; Biographical Account of Samuel Wesley's Childhood . . . 461

Index of Persons . . . . . . . . . . . . . . . . . . . . . . . . 469

Index of Places . . . . . . . . . . . . . . . . . . . . . . . . . 483

Index of Scripture References and Allusions . . . . . . . . . . 487

# Acknowledgements

This collection of materials was begun as part of a larger effort to provide access to the letters of Charles Wesley by Dr. Frank Baker (1910–99). He collected all of the items that he could locate and prepared initial transcriptions, including some expansion of the shorthand. On Baker's death the effort was carried forward by Dr. Richard P. Heitzenrater, aided by his assistant Alicia Pearson. Most recently Dr. Randy L. Maddox joined the team to prepare the text for publication. All three editors undertook this work as professors in Wesley Studies and directors of The Center for Studies in the Wesleyan Tradition at Duke Divinity School. We wish to acknowledge the steady support of Duke for work on both Charles and John Wesley.

We offer a special acknowledgement to Aileen F. Maddox, an editorial assistant for the Center for Studies in the Wesleyan Tradition at Duke Divinity School. Over the past decade she has developed expertise in Charles Wesley's longhand, working carefully through all of his surviving manuscript materials (journals, letters, poetry, etc.). Transcriptions of all of the material in this volume were reviewed for accuracy under her careful eye, and she prepared the transcriptions of items recently located or added to the collection.

One challenge of preparing Charles Wesley manuscript material for publication is his frequent use of John Byrom's shorthand. The leading expert on Byrom's shorthand is Dr. Timothy Underhill, and we wish to acknowledge his assistance in this venture. Drs. Baker and Heitzenrater "expanded" Wesley's shorthand for some of the items in this collection. The initial expansion of most of the remaining material was by Dr. Maddox. But Dr. Underhill generously agreed to review our expansion of shorthand items, providing corrections and solving some of the most difficult passages. While the final form of the shorthand expansion remains our own, it is more accurate due to Dr. Underhill's assistance.

Finally, we are grateful for permission to transcribe and publish the materials from the Methodist collections in the John Rylands Library given by the John Rylands Library, University of Manchester, and the trustees for Methodist Church Purposes, The Methodist Church in Britain; and to Gareth Lloyd for his assistance.

Richard P. Heitzenrater<br>
Randy L. Maddox

# Preface to Second Edition

The decisive impetus for this second edition was my recent discovery of a manuscript in Charles Wesley's hand that filled a gap among the surviving journal letters for April through August of 1746 (see May 12–June 14, 1746). This manuscript was located, oddly enough, in an uncatalogued volume in MARC titled "Portraits and Letters of Presidents of the Wesleyan Methodist Conference."

Contemplating a second edition, I decided that this would be the most logical place to publish as well the accounts of "Old Jeffrey," or the disturbances at the Epworth Rectory in 1716–17, since the only surviving manuscript records of this episode by a Wesley family member are by Charles Wesley, and the episode shaped his life in continuing ways.

While these two items are additions in this second edition, two brief accounts by Charles Wesley in shorthand of the death of Sarah Pearce in 1773 that were present in the first edition have been dropped here. This is because it has become clear that the shorthand records are Wesley's distillation of two letters / accounts sent to him. They can be found now in the collection of Charles Wesley's in-correspondence on the website of the Center for Studies in the Wesleyan Tradition, Duke University.

Finally, I used the opportunity of this second edition to correct a few scattered errors in the first edition, and add a few notes emerging from continued work in Charles Wesley's papers.

Randy L. Maddox<br>
July 1, 2022

# SIGNS, SPECIAL USAGES, ABBREVIATIONS

## SIGNS

[ ]  Square brackets enclose editorial insertions or substitutions in the original text, or (with a query–?) doubtful readings.

⟨ ⟩  Angle brackets enclose conjectural readings where the original text is defective or obscured.

…  An ellipsis indicates a passage omitted by the preparer of the original source—for this purpose Wesley generally employed a dash.

[…]  An ellipsis within square brackets indicates a passage omitted silently by Wesley from a text he was quoting, to which the present editors are drawing attention.

[[ ]]  Double square brackets enclose passages that are expanded from Wesley's use of John Byrom's shorthand.

/  A solidus or slant line, in address or endorsement information, marks the division between two lines of text in the original.

## SPECIAL USAGES

Cf.  Before a scriptural or other citation by Wesley, indicates that he was quoting with more than minimal inexactness, yet nevertheless displaying the passage as a quotation.

See  Before a scriptural citation, indicates an undoubted allusion or a quotation that was not displayed as such by Wesley.

## ABBREVIATIONS

In addition to common abbreviations like c[irca], ed[itio]n, n[ote], orig[inal], and st[anza], the footnotes in this volume utilise the following abbreviated forms for items referred to repeatedly.

| | |
|---|---|
| AM | *Arminian Magazine* (London, 1778–97). |
| BCP | The Book of Common Prayer (London, 1662). |
| Benham, *Hutton* | Daniel Benham, *Memoirs of James Hutton* (London: Hamilton, Adams, and Co., 1856). |
| Bristol Bands (1741) | Photograph of partial list of men's bands in Bristol in 1741; published in Nehemiah Curnock (ed.), *The Journal of the Rev. John Wesley* (London: Epworth, 1909–16), 2:398. |
| CPH (1738) | [John Wesley (ed.),] *A Collection of Psalms and Hymns* (London: Bowyer for Hutton, 1738). |
| Crookshank, *Ireland* | Charles H. Crookshank, *History of Methodism in Ireland*, Vol. 1 (Belfast: Allen, 1885). |
| CW | Rev. Charles Wesley (1707–88). |
| CW, MS Journal | MARC, DDCW 10/2; S T Kimbrough Jr. & Kenneth G. C. Newport (eds.), *The Manuscript Journal of the Rev. Charles Wesley, M.A.*, 2 vols. (Nashville, TN: Kingswood Books, 2008). |
| Foundery Band Lists | MARC, MA 1977/503/2; manuscript notebook containing lists in JW's hand of members of bands and select societies at the Foundery in London between 1743 and 1746. |
| *Funeral Hymns* (1759) | [Charles Wesley.] *Funeral Hymns* (London [Strahan,] 1759). |
| HSP (1739) | John and Charles Wesley, *Hymns and Sacred Poems* (London: Strahan, 1739). |
| HSP (1740) | John and Charles Wesley, *Hymns and Sacred Poems* (London: Strahan, 1740). |
| HSP (1742) | John and Charles Wesley, *Hymns and Sacred Poems* (Bristol: Farley, 1742). |
| HSP (1749) | Charles Wesley, *Hymns and Sacred Poems* (Bristol: Farley, 1749). |

| | |
|---|---|
| Jackson, *CW Journal* | Thomas Jackson (ed.), *The Journal of Charles Wesley, M.A.* (London: John Mason, 1849). |
| JW | Rev. John Wesley (1703–91). |
| JW, *Works* | *The Works of John Wesley*; begun as "The Oxford Edition of The Works of John Wesley" (Oxford: Clarendon Press, 1975–1983); continued as "The Bicentennial Edition of The Works of John Wesley" (Nashville: Abingdon, 1984—); 20 of 35 vols. published. |
| MARC | Methodist Archives and Research Centre, The John Rylands Library, The University of Manchester, Manchester, England. |
| MS Clarke | MARC, MA 1977/561. |
| MS Funeral Hymns | MARC, MA 1977/578. |
| MS Miscellaneous Hymns | MARC, MA 1977/556. |
| MS Nursery | MARC, MA 1977/594/16. |
| MS Preachers Extraordinary | MARC, MA 1977/583/8. |
| MS Richmond | MARC, MA 1977/55. |
| OED | *The Oxford English Dictionary*, 2nd edition (New York: Oxford University Press, 1989). |
| PCWS | *Proceedings of the Charles Wesley Society.* |
| *Redemption Hymns* (1747) | Charles Wesley, *Hymns for Those That Seek and Those That Have Redemption in the Blood of Jesus Christ* (London: Strahan, 1747). |
| WHS | *The Proceedings of the Wesley Historical Society.* |

NOTE: Full transcriptions of all of the published hymn collections above, and of Charles Wesley's manuscript verse, can be found on the website of the Center for Studies in the Wesleyan Tradition at Duke Divinity School: http://divinity.duke.edu/initiatives/cswt.

# INTRODUCTION

This volume is part of a series dedicated to providing a complete and accurate published collection of Charles Wesley manuscript items beyond his sermons and verse. The various items included in the series constitute crucial primary texts for study of Wesley's life, his ministry, and his increasingly contentious position within Methodism in his later years. The first two volumes of the series were devoted to Charles Wesley's Manuscript Journal, a single bound item held at the Methodist Archives and Research Centre.[1] The present volume gathers a number of scattered items (the majority also held at MARC), many of which are earlier—and more complete—drafts of material in the Manuscript Journal. The third major component of the series is publication of all of Charles Wesley's surviving personal correspondence, which are replete with material of biographical and larger historical interest.

## CHARLES WESLEY'S JOURNALING PRACTICES

The items collected in the present volume not only provide historical and biographical information, they offer insight into Charles Wesley's journaling practices. To begin with, we know that Charles kept a spiritual diary for a while as a student and tutor at Oxford, a practice adopted under the encouragement and example of his brother John.[2] Unfortunately, nothing of this diary is known to survive. Indeed, very little survives from Charles Wesley's hand prior to his departing with John in October 1735 on their missionary venture to Georgia—mainly about a dozen personal letters to family members.[3]

From the beginning of their voyage to Georgia, both Wesley brothers sent back letters to friends and supporters in England. These letters were filled with information on the brothers' physical and spiritual state as well

---

[1] MARC is located in The John Rylands Library, The University of Manchester, Manchester, England. The volume's shelfmark is DDCW 10/2. The published version is S T Kimbrough Jr. & Kenneth G. C. Newport (eds.), *The Manuscript Journal of the Rev. Charles Wesley, M.A.*, 2 vols. (Nashville, TN: Kingswood Books, 2008).

[2] See the description of JW's diary in Richard P. Heitzenrater, *The Elusive Mr. Wesley* (2nd edn., Nashville: Abingdon, 2003), 53–63; the diary will be published in JW, *Works*, vol. 17. In a letter to JW finished January 22, 1729, CW requested guidelines for keeping his diary.

[3] It is likely that the autobiographical reflections at the beginning of MS Shorthand Verse (MARC, MA 1977/565) also date from before 1736.

as significant encounters and activities in their ministry. While not formally published in print at that time, these "journal letters" were public, in the sense that recipients were expected to circulate them to other readers, and they were often read aloud at gatherings of supportive friends.[4] Charles and John continued this practice of sending journal letters after returning to England, as they became immersed in the evangelical/pietist revival breaking out in London, Bristol, and beyond.

Given the public nature of their journal letters, one might expect that they were not simply dashed off during spare moments. The evidence in Charles Wesley's case supports this supposition. While only one example is known to survive, Wesley seems to have kept brief daily notes in shorthand of his activities during his preaching tours of the early revival. When a break in his activity allowed, these brief notes were expanded into a narrative journal letter. He then apparently disposed of the shorthand notes (unless, like in the surviving example, they were in a volume he was keeping for other purposes[5]).

The journal letter that was actually mailed (or sent by hand) was itself typically a clean copy of an initial draft. This copy was often made by an amanuensis, with Wesley making small corrections and sometimes adding a personal note to his brother or other recipients (several of the journal letters in 1740 are examples). On occasion additional copies of the same journal letter were made for delivery to other recipients (see, for example, the letter for June 14–30, 1746).

Wesley routinely kept record copies of the journal letters he mailed. Sometimes this record copy was his original draft. But by the mid-1740s he tended to have an assistant accompanying him copy the material in individual journal letters (each covering a couple of weeks) into an extended journal narrative covering an entire preaching excursion. A good example is the long document, mainly in the hand of James Waller, covering Wesley's preaching tour to Bristol and through Cornwall, from April through August of 1746.[6] Another example is the narrative in the hand of Charles Perronet covering Wesley's first preaching tour in Ireland, 1747–48.[7]

---

[4] See CW's description of the circulation of journal letters by Benjamin Ingham and John Wesley among their Oxford friends, the Georgia trustees, and others in MS Journal, Dec. 6–15, 1736. He records reading a journal letter by JW to a group in MS Journal, Feb. 8, 1737.

[5] The surviving example is a set of shorthand notes covering the period of May 17–June 27, 1743 on an unnumbered page in a bound manuscript volume collecting hymns, MS Clarke. The expanded letter is part of the collection below, with annotation of places where the shorthand notes provide additional information.

[6] The casual observer might miss that this is a continuous document, since it has been accessed into MARC as seven separate files. But the pages are numbered consecutively (with one section missing): DDCW 6/11 (pp. 1–3), (missing May 11–June 13), 6/28 (pp. 10–13), 6/29 (pp. 14–15), 6/14 (pp. 16–18), 6/15 (pp. 19–22), 6/16 (pp. 22 [sic]–23), 6/17 (pp. 24–26).

[7] MARC, DDCW 6/88a.

The next logical step was to weave the various extended journal narratives into a single volume—i.e., the Manuscript Journal, which CW produced in September 1755 with the intention (never realized) of publishing it.[8] However, if the potential purpose of this larger volume was public distribution, then (as John Wesley had already realized and modelled[9]) the material in the earlier journal letters needed to be purged of overly personal, confidential, or potentially embarrassing material. Charles's sensitivity to this need is already evident in his journal letters when he places discussion of delicate topics in a form of shorthand that few would be able to read besides his brother John. Much of this delicate material found in the journal letters is not brought into the Manuscript Journal (and when it does appear there, it is again in shorthand!).

In addition to being abridged and somewhat sanitized (in comparison to the journal letters on which it was based), the Manuscript Journal of Charles Wesley omits a few periods for which there is information in surviving journal letters that are included in this collection.

## TYPES OF MATERIAL GATHERED IN THIS COLLECTION

The largest portion of material in this volume, gathered to supplement the Manuscript Journal, are formal "journal letters" composed by Charles Wesley (the holograph mailed to his recipient, or his record copy) and extended accounts of ministry trips built by compiling a series of journal letters. In both cases, of course, we are limited to the materials that have survived in some form. The lack of material for some periods of Wesley's ministry trips indicate that not all journal letters have survived.

One limitation the formal journal letters share with the Manuscript Journal is that they both conclude in 1756, with the end of Charles Wesley's last formal journey through northern England providing oversight to Methodist societies and lay preachers. Laying aside this role from that point, there was little need for Charles to send extended accounts of his ministry to brother John. Charles continued to preach and lead worship in Methodist settings, but mainly in Bristol and London, staying closer to family. For the next two decades, while his family remained in Bristol, the vast majority of Charles's surviving letters are to his wife Sarah, during periods that he is ministering in London. These personal letters were not intended for broader distribution.

---

[8] CW described this process of collation, and the possibility of publication in letters to Sarah (Gwynne) Wesley covering Sept. 13–22, 1755 (MARC, DDCW 7/83 and DDCW 5/73).

[9] See JW, *Works*, 18:37–38.

This is not to say that Charles Wesley stopped keeping accounts of his daily life. One evidence of this continuing practice are items near the end of the present volume, dealing with events after 1756, which Wesley described as "extracted out of my journal." It is unclear what form the larger source for these extracts might have taken. What is clear is that Wesley (or his family after his death) chose to preserve only excerpts dealing with public matters—like Wesley's dispute with Edward Davies over a horse, or with Joseph Kelway over the costs for musical instruction of Charles Wesley Jr.

Among other items included in this volume are Charles Wesley's scattered accounts of specific events in Methodist life, like his meeting with the prophetess Lavington or his record of a conference in Bristol in August 1756. We also include accounts that appear to come directly from Charles Wesley's hand of death stories of Methodist associates.[10]

The final set of items in this volume are Charles Wesley's accounts of the early years in the lives of his musically gifted sons Charles Jr. and Samuel. One learns as much about the father's social connections and approach to parenting from these accounts as about the sons.

## EDITORIAL PRINCIPLES FOR THE COLLECTION

This collection was developed under a set of editorial principles and practices. The first principle was to privilege Charles Wesley's original in journal letters and other items. For example, when both the holograph (the actual letter mailed, in Wesley's hand) and a copy for Wesley's records survive, we privilege the holograph. The only situation where this priority is reversed is when the record copy is a draft in Wesley's own hand, and the letter mailed was a clean copy by an amanuensis.[11] Whichever our favoured source document, we present Wesley's intended clean text; which means that we do not typically record struck out text that Wesley replaced or intended to delete.

---

[10] Among CW's papers in MARC (MA 1977/501/49) is an account titled "Some Few Remarks Concerning the Late Mr. John Davies, by an intimate Friend." The friend who wrote the remarks was not CW, but apparently Ann Sharland. Another item among his papers is CW's (somewhat abridged) shorthand copy of these remarks (MA 1977/597/7). The shorthand copy is titled an "Instrument for Sally," suggesting its purpose was to help his daughter learn Byrom's shorthand. We do not include either item in this collection because the story does not originate from CW's hand. Cf. John R. Tyson, "'An Instrument for Sally': Charles Wesley's Shorthand Biography of John Davis," *Methodist History* 30.2 (1992): 103–8.

[11] This is why we omit from this collection MARC, DDCW 6/88b, a manuscript covering CW's activities from May 28–June 26, 1736. The manuscript is in an unrecognized hand and simply reproduces the account in CW, MS Journal (which is in CW's hand) with no variants, except that it ignores the shorthand sections of this part of MS Journal. Thus it has nothing new to contribute.

The second principle was to include all relevant material for which there is reliable surviving access to its contents. The items easiest to verify were manuscripts in public repositories that are either in Wesley's hand or have annotations (often in shorthand) by him. We include all of these, and consulted the original in each case. In our research we became aware of two published transcriptions where the original manuscript was apparently accessible to a scholar in the past but its current location is unknown. Given the credibility of the scholars providing the transcriptions, we chose to include these two items—indicating clearly their provenance.[12]

A third principle concerns the rendering of Charles Wesley's text. As Frank Baker noted in working on John Wesley's correspondence, editors face a tension between historical accuracy, showing Wesley "warts and all," and modern readability.[13] Adopting Baker's balanced approach to John, we retain Charles Wesley's colloquialisms, contractions, and outdated grammatical usages. But, like Baker, we silently expand Charles's abbreviations (whenever clear), including abbreviated names. We also silently update archaic spellings (though retaining typical British spellings). Likewise we have generally followed Baker's precedent in imposing modern practices of capitalization and punctuation. In his manuscripts Charles usually showed emphasis by underlining; we render this material in *italics* (as the modern parallel). We are parsimonious in making editorial additions to Wesley's text, and clearly identify these additions with [square brackets]. A few of the manuscript sources have been damaged or have obscured text. In these cases we have reconstructed the missing text as much as possible, placing the reconstructed text within <angled brackets>; a query mark (?) is added when the reconstruction is less than certain.

A distinctive challenge of Charles Wesley's manuscript material is his frequent use of a form of shorthand developed by John Byrom.[14] We include all annotations and longer sections of material in shorthand, providing "expansions" in [[double square brackets]]. By their nature, these expansions retain a degree of uncertainty as a whole. One characteristic of the shorthand is that it often gives only the beginning of a word. In most of these cases the intended word is fairly clear and we simply give the full word. In cases where there may be other cogent expansions than

---

[12] See the journal for July 8–August 13, 1754 (given by Thomas Jackson), and the brief shorthand notes for October 17–24, 1754 (drawn from Luke Tyerman).

[13] See Baker's introductory comments in JW, *Works*, 25:123–28.

[14] See Oliver A. Beckerlegge, *The Shorthand of Charles Wesley* (Madison, NJ: Charles Wesley Society, 2002) and Timothy Underhill, "John Byrom and the Contexts of Charles Wesley's Shorthand," *Wesley and Methodist Studies* 7 (2015): 27–53.

the one which we propose, the more hypothetical part of the expansion is placed in s[ingle] s[quare] br[ackets]—to clue the reader that alternatives may be possible. Beyond this type of tentative expansion, there are scattered instances where we identify a plausible expansion of a word or phrase but indicate a greater degree of tentativeness about the proposal by including a question mark in square brackets [?] immediately after the word (sometimes including a note about the shorthand and other options). As mentioned in the Acknowledgements, our confidence in the cogency of the expansions provided for the shorthand sections of Wesley's material is heightened by the assistance of Dr. Timothy Underhill.

At the end of each item in the collection we list its current repository details or source. We also give the following information, when it is provided in the manuscript:

*Address*: Found only on holograph letters. We give the address exactly as written, without expanding abbreviations or correcting spelling.

*Postmark*: Some holographs have only the "Bishop Mark" indicating the month and date (usually of the day the letter departed from or arrived in London). Others have as well a stamp of the town where the letter was posted. A letter may contain more than one listing if it was redirected. All marks that are legible are indicated.

*Endorsement*: Many of the manuscripts have endorsements or annotations by someone other than Wesley. We generally present here only endorsements that appear to be by the recipient or a contemporary. We identify the hand of the endorser whenever possible.

Our final set of practices relate to annotation of the material included. Our goal is to aid in understanding the items. We identify whenever possible both persons and places on their first appearance in the volume. On later appearances of persons, since Wesley tends to give only last names, we add the first name in [brackets] as judged helpful for clarity. The name and place indices can aid in locating the first appearance, with its potential greater information. We privilege original sources in documenting any quoted material in Wesley's documents, in part because these older sources are increasingly available online. In particular, transcriptions of the original editions of the various collections of hymns and poems published by John or Charles Wesley are available through the Center for Studies in the Wesleyan Tradition, Duke Divinity School (http://divinity.duke.edu/initiatives/cswt). Finally, we identify all quotations from Scripture, as well as significant allusions to Scripture, using "cf." and "see" in the specific manner described under "Signs, Special Usages, and Abbreviations."

# Select Chronology of Charles Wesley

| | | |
|---|---|---|
| 1707 | Dec. 18 | born at Epworth |
| 1716 | Apr. | began Westminster school (Saint Peter's College of Westminster) (lived with brother Samuel Wesley Jr. for the first five years) |
| 1721 | | admitted as a King's Scholar at Westminster |
| 1726 | June 13 | elected to Christ Church, Oxford |
| 1730 | | received BA degree |
| 1733 | Mar. 12 | received MA degree; given Studentship at Christ Church |
| 1735 | Sept. 21 | ordained deacon in the Church of England |
| | Sept. 29 | ordained priest in the Church of England |
| | Oct. 14 | sailed for Georgia (landed Feb. 5, 1736) |
| 1736 | July 26 | left Georgia to return to England (landed Dec. 3) |
| 1738 | May 21 | his "evangelical" conversion |
| 1738–39 | Winter | assisted Rev. George Stonehouse at St. Mary's Church, Islington |
| 1739 | May 29 | first field preaching |
| | Oct. 28 | opened his Bristol ministry |
| 1744 | June 25 | first Conference of Methodist preachers |
| 1747 | Aug. | met Sarah Gwynne for first time |
| | Sept. 09 | first visit to Ireland (through Mar. 20, 1748) |
| 1748 | Aug. 13 | second visit to Ireland (through Oct. 8) |
| 1749 | Apr. 08 | marriage to Sarah Gwynne |
| 1751 | | trip to northern England to "purge" the lay preachers |
| 1752 | Aug. 21 | first child (John) born (died at 18 months of age) |

| | | |
|---|---|---|
| 1755 | June 25 | second child (Martha Maria) born (died July 25) |
| 1756 | | last itinerant trip to northern England |
| 1757 | Dec. 11 | third child (Charles Jr.) born (died May 23, 1834) |
| 1759 | Apr. 01 | fourth child (Sarah Jr.) born (died Sept. 19, 1828) |
| 1760 | | fifth child (Susanna) born (died at 11 months of age) |
| 1764 | July | sixth child (Selina) born (died at five weeks of age) |
| 1766 | Feb. 24 | seventh child (Samuel) born (died Oct. 11, 1837) |
| 1767 | | eighth child (John James) born (died at 7 months of age) |
| 1771 | | moved from Bristol to London |
| 1786 | | attended his last Methodist Conference |
| 1788 | Mar. 29 | death |

# Journal Letters and Records

# Accounts of "Old Jeffrey"
## December 1716–January 1717

**Introductory Comment**

The inclusion of the following accounts in a collection devoted to biographical items concerning Charles Wesley requires some explanation. Neither Charles (just turned nine years old) nor his brother John (then thirteen) were in Epworth at the time these "disturbances" took place. John was a student at Charterhouse in London, and Charles had moved in April 1716 to live with his older brother Samuel Wesley Jr., in order to commence his formal education at Westminster. Those present in Epworth were Rev. Samuel and Susanna (Annesley) Wesley, and their seven daughters who survived infancy. Despite their absence, the disturbances became an enduring part of family lore that shaped the entire Wesley family—including the three sons.

At the time of their occurrence Samuel Wesley Jr. solicited a series of reports about the matter from those in Epworth. Like his younger brothers, Samuel Jr. preserved extracts of letters from his family in a notebook.[1] This notebook had a section compiling letters at the time of the disturbances, and a transcription (made in February 1731) of a set of interviews John Wesley conducted with family and neighbours in Epworth about the matter in late summer 1726. On his death Samuel Jr.'s letter notebook passed to his wife Ursula (Berry) Wesley; then his one child who survived infancy, Philadelphia (Wesley) Earle; and finally to his granddaughter, Philadelphia (Earle) Maunsell. When the granddaughter died in 1774 the notebook became part of property given away to help cover debt. It eventually came into the possession of Rev. Samuel Badcock.[2] As he neared death in 1788 Badcock passed it on to Joseph Priestley, who published transcriptions of several items (including those about the disturbances) in 1791.[3] The notebook itself was then either lost or destroyed; there is no evidence of its present survival.

This is where Charles Wesley's surviving papers become important. Sometime after 1731 (when Samuel Jr. inserted John's interviews) Charles transcribed in shorthand the section of Samuel Jr.'s notebook related to the disturbances at the Epworth rectory. It may have been in late 1737,

---

[1] The manuscript notebook in which JW transcribed letters to and from family members between 1724 and 1729 survives in MARC, (MA 1977/157, JW III.2). CW's letter-book was lost during a trip in 1737 (see CW, MS Journal, June 1, 1737).

[2] See Samuel Badcock to JW, Apr. 22, 1780, John Whitehead, *The Life of the Rev. John Wesley, M.A.*, 2 vols. (London: Couchman, 1793), 1:xv–xvi.

[3] Joseph Priestley, *Original Letters by the Rev. John Wesley and his Friends* (Birmingham: Pearson, 1791); see pp. iii–iv, and 119–66. Priestley was the source for these accounts in Adam Clarke, *Memoirs of the Wesley Family* (London: J. Kershaw, 1823), 161–95.

after Charles's return from Georgia, when he spent time recuperating at Samuel Jr.'s home in Tiverton, Devonshire. Whenever made, the shorthand transcription survives in MARC (MA 1977/567/1). A later document also survives, wherein Charles expands into longhand many (but not all) of the accounts (MARC, DDCW 8/15, pp. 8–43). These documents are important in part because they attest to the authenticity of materials in Priestley's volume (and vice versa). Variant readings between Priestley's published transcription and Wesley's shorthand transcription are few, and mainly stylistic in nature. Lacking Samuel's original notebook, there is no way to tell who introduced the variants.

Lacking Samuel's notebook, Charles Wesley's shorthand copy of this material becomes as well the only surviving manuscript record of the "disturbances" by a member of the Wesley family.[4] This is why we include it here. The text which follows is an *expansion* of Charles's shorthand copy. Unlike elsewhere in this volume, we do not remind readers at each new paragraph or section with double square brackets ([[ ]]) that the original is shorthand. That is because the existence of Wesley's own expansion of much of the shorthand, and Priestley's text as evidence of Samuel Jr.'s original, have removed almost all ambiguity about how to expand the shorthand. Any place where there is ambiguity (or where material appears only in shorthand) will be noted. We also annotate variants between the shorthand copy and Charles's longhand version; as well as significant variants between Priestley's published transcription and Charles Wesley's manuscripts.

---

[4] JW published "An Account of the Disturbances in my Father's House," in *Arminian Magazine* 7 (1784): 548–50, 606–08, 654–56. It provides a coherent distillation of the material in CW's documents, not an independent source.

[page 1⁵]             **Letters**

**Concerning some Supernatural Disturbances**
**at my Father's House in Epworth, Lincolnshire**[6]
1716/7

[Susanna (Annesley) Wesley to Rev. Samuel Wesley Jr.[7]]

                                    Saturday, January 12, 1716/7
Dear Sam,

This evening we were agreeably surprised with your packet, which brought the welcome news of your being alive, after we had been in the greatest panic imaginable almost a month, thinking either you were dead or one of your brothers had been by some misfortune killed.[8]

The reason of our fears is as follows: On the first of December our maid[9] heard, at the door of the dining-room, several dismal groans, like a person in extremis, at the point of death. We gave little heed to her relation, and endeavoured to laugh her out of her fears. Some nights (two or three) after, several of the family heard a strange knocking in diverse places, usually three or four knocks at a time, and then it stayed a little. This continued every night for a fortnight. Sometimes it was in the garret, but most commonly in the nursery or green chamber. We all heard it but your father, and I was not willing he should be informed of it, lest he should fancy it was against his own death, which indeed we all apprehended. But when it began to be so troublesome, both day and night, that few or none of the family durst be alone, I resolved to tell him of it, being minded he should speak to it. At first he would not believe but somebody did it to alarm us. But the night after, as soon as he was in bed, it knocked loudly nine times, just by his bedside. He rose and went to see if he could find out what it was, but could see nothing. Afterward he heard it as the rest.

One night it made such a noise in the room over our heads as if several people were walking, then ran up and down stairs, and was so outrageous, that we thought the children would be frighted. So your father and I rose, and went down in the dark to light a candle. Just as we came to the bottom

---
[5] Page numbers are for the shorthand record (MA 1977/567/1).
[6] DDCW 8/15 revised "my father's house" to "the house of the Revd. Mr. Sam. Wesley."
[7] DDCW 8/15 titles "To Mr. S. W. Junr."
[8] DDCW 8/15 revised "had been" to "was." CW was currently living in London with Samuel Jr.; while JW was a student at Charterhouse in London.
[9] Later identified as "Nanny" Marshall.

of the broad stairs, having hold of each other, on my side[10] there seemed as if somebody had emptied a bag of money at my feet; and on his, as if all the bottles under the stairs (which were many) had been dashed in a thousand pieces. We passed through the hall into the kitchen and got a candle, and went to see the children, whom we found asleep.

Next night your father would get Mr. Hoole to lie at our house,[11] and we all sat together till one or two o'clock in the morning, and heard the knocking as usual. Sometimes it would make a noise like the winding up of a jack;[12] at other times, as that night Mr. Hoole was with us, like a carpenter planing deals.[13] But most commonly it knocked thrice and stopped, and then thrice again, and so many hours together. We persuaded your father to speak, and try if any voice would be heard. One night about six o'clock he went into the nursery in the dark, and at first heard several deep groans, then knocking. He adjured it to speak, if it had power, and tell him why it troubled his house. But no voice was heard. It only knocked thrice aloud. Then he questioned it if it were Sammy, and bid it, if it were, and could not speak, knock again. But it knocked no more that night, which made us hope it was not against your death.

Thus it continued till the 28th of December, when it loudly knocked (as your father used to do at the gate) in the nursery, and departed. We have various conjectures what this may mean. For my own part I fear nothing, now you are safe at London hitherto; and I hope God will still preserve you. Though sometimes I am inclined to think my brother is dead.[14] Let me know your thoughts on it.

Susanna Wesley

[page 2]

**To My Father**[15]

[I.e., Rev. Samuel Wesley Jr. to Rev. Samuel Wesley Sr.]

January 19[16] [1716/7], Saturday

Honoured Sir,

My mother tells me a very strange story of disturbances in your house. I wish I could have some more particulars from you. I would thank Mr. [Joseph] Hoole if he would favour me with a little[17] concerning it. Not that

---

[10] DDCW 8/15 reads "one side" rather than "my side."

[11] Rev. Joseph Hoole (d. 1745) was currently serving as vicar of Haxey, near Epworth.

[12] A "jack" was a small signal flag, run up a mast on a ship.

[13] "Deals" is an archaic word for wooden planks.

[14] I.e., Samuel Annesley Jr. (1658–1732).

[15] DDCW 8/15 renders "To Mr. S. W. senr."

[16] Priestley (and Clarke relying on him) date this letter as Jan. 30.

[17] Priestley has "letter" instead of "little."

I want to be confirmed myself in the belief of it, but for any other person's satisfaction. My mother sends to me to know my thoughts of it, and I cannot think at all of any interpretation. Wit, I fancy, might find many; but wisdom none.

Your dutiful and loving son,

S. Wesley

[Rev. Samuel Wesley Jr. to Susanna (Annesley) Wesley[18]]

January 19, 1716/7, Saturday
Dean's Yard, Westminster[19]

Dear Madam,

Those who are so wise as not to believe any supernatural occurrences, though ever so well attested, could find a hundred questions to ask about those strange noises you wrote me an account of. But for my part,[20] I know not what question to put which, if answered, would confirm me more in the belief of what you tell me. Two or three I have heard from others. Was there never a new maid or man in the house that might play tricks? Was there nobody above in the garrets when the walking was there? Did all the family hear it together when they were in one room? Or at one time? Did it seem to all to be in the same place, at the same time? Could not cats, or rats, or dogs be the spirits? Was the whole family asleep when my father and you went downstairs? Such doubts as these being replied to, though they could not (as God himself assures us) convince them who believe not Moses and the prophets,[21] yet would strengthen such as do believe. As to my particular opinion concerning the events foreboded by these noises, I cannot, I must confess, form any. I think, since it was not permitted to speak, all guesses must be vain. The end of spirits' actions is yet more hidden than that of men, and even this latter puzzles the most subtle politicians. That we may be struck so as to prepare seriously for any ill may, it is possible, be one design of providence. It is surely our duty and wisdom so to do.

Dear madam, I beg your blessing on
Your dutiful and affectionate son,

S. Wesley

I expect a particular account from everyone.

---

[18] DDCW 8/15 titles "To Mrs. W."
[19] The date and place appear at the end of the letter in the original.
[20] The shorthand that CW expands as "part" looks more like "opinion."
[21] See Luke 16:31.

### Susanna (Annesley) Wesley to Samuel Wesley Jr.[22]]

January 27, 1716/7

Dear Sam,

Though I am not one of those that will believe nothing supernatural, but am rather inclined to think there would be frequent intercourse between good spirits and us, did not our deep lapse into sensuality prevent it; yet I was a great while ere I could credit anything of what the children and servants reported concerning the noises they heard in several parts of our house. Nay, after I had heard them myself, I was willing to persuade myself and them that it was only rats or weasels that disturbed us. And having been formerly troubled with rats, which were frighted away by sounding a horn, I caused a horn to be procured, and made them blow it all over the house. But from that night they began to blow the noises were more loud and distinct, both day and night, than before. And that night we rose and went down I was entirely convinced that it was beyond the power of any human creature to make such strange and various noises.

As to your questions, I will answer them particularly. But withal, I desire my answers may satisfy none but yourself; for I would not have the matter imparted to any. We had both man and maid new this last Martinmas,[23] yet I do not believe either of them occasioned the disturbance, both for the reason above mentioned, and because they were more affrighted than anybody else. Besides, we have often heard the noises when they were in the room by us; and the maid particularly was in such a panic that she was almost incapable of all business, nor durst ever go [page 3] from one room to another, or stay by herself a minute, after it began to be dark.

The man, Robert Brown, whom you well know, was most visited by it, lying in the garret, and has been often frighted down barefoot and almost naked, not daring to stay alone to put on his clothes. Nor do I think, if he had power, he would be guilty of such villainy. When the walking was heard in the garret, Robin[24] was in bed in the next room, in a sleep so sound that he never heard your father and me walk up and down, though we walked not softly I am sure. All the family has heard it together, in the same room, at the same time, particularly at family prayers. It always seemed to all present in the same place at the same time. Though often before any could say, "It is here," it would remove to another place.

---

[22] DDCW 8/15 titles "Mrs. W.'s Answer."

[23] The feast day of St. Martin, Nov. 11, and the surrounding season.

[24] The familiar name for Robert.

All the family, as well as Robin, were asleep when your father and I went down stairs. Nor did they wake in the nursery when we held the candle close by them; only we observed that Hetty[25] trembled exceedingly in her sleep, as she always did, before the noise awaked her. It commonly was nearer her than the rest—which she took notice of and was much frightened, because she thought it had a particular spite at her. I could multiply particular instances, but I forbear. I believe your father will write to you about it shortly. Whatever may be the design of providence in permitting these things I cannot say. Secret things belong to God.[26] But I entirely agree with you that it is our wisdom and duty to prepare seriously for all events.

S. Wesley

[**Susanna Wesley Jr. to Samuel Wesley Jr.**[27]]

Epworth
January 24 [1716/7]

Dear Brother,

About the first of December, a most terrible and astonishing noise was heard by a maid servant as at the dining-room door, which caused the upstarting of her hair, and made her ears prick forth at an unusual rate.[28] She said it was like the groans of one expiring. This so frighted her that for a great while she durst not go out of one room into another, after it began to be dark, without company.

But, to lay aside jesting, which should not be done in serious matters, I assure you that,[29] from the first to the last of a lunar month, the groans, squeaks, jinglings, and knockings were frightful enough. Though it is needless for me to send you any account of what we all heard, my father himself having a larger account of the matter than I am able to give, which he designs to send you; yet in compliance with your desire I will tell you, as briefly as I can, what I heard of it.[30] The first night I ever heard it, my sister Nancy[31] and I were sat in the dining room. We heard something rush on the outside of the doors that opened into the garden, then three loud

---

[25] Mehetabel Wesley (c. 1697–1750); later Mehetabel (Wesley) Wright.

[26] See Deut. 29:29.

[27] DDCW 8/15 titles "To Mr S. W. Junr."

[28] The material following "which" in this sentence is present in the shorthand, but left out of DDCW 8/15.

[29] DDCW 8/15 elides the opening of this sentence, to this point, though present in the shorthand account.

[30] This long sentence, present in the shorthand, is omitted in DDCW 8/15.

[31] Anne Wesley (b. 1701); later Anne (Wesley) Lambert.

knocks, immediately after [an]other three, and in half a minute the same number over our heads. We inquired whether anybody had been in the garden, or in the room above us, but there was nobody.

Soon after, my sister Molly[32] was up after all the family were abed (except my sister Nancy), about some business. We heard three bouncing thumps under our feet, which soon made us throw away our work and tumble into bed; afterward the jingling of the latch and warming-pan, and so it took its leave that night.

Soon after the above-mentioned, we heard a noise as if a great piece of sounding metal was thrown down on the outside of our chamber. We, lying in the quietest part of the house, heard less of it than the rest for a pretty while. But the latter end of the night that Mr. [Joseph] Hoole sat up on, I lay in the nursery, where it was very violent. I then heard frequent knocks over and under the room where I lay, and at the children's bed-head, which was made of boards. It seemed to rap against it very hard and loud, so that the bed shook under them. I heard something walk by my bedside, like a man in a long nightgown. The knocks were so loud that Mr. Hoole came out of his chamber to us. It still continued. My father spoke, but nothing answered. It ended that night with my father's particular knock, very fierce.

It is now pretty quiet. Only at our repeating the prayers for the King George and prince, when it usually begins—especially when my father[33] says, "Our most gracious sovereign lord, etc."[34] This my father is angry at, and intends to say three instead of two for the royal family. We all heard the same noise, and at the same time, and as coming from the same place.

To conclude this, it now [page 4] makes its personal appearance. But of this more hereafter. Do not say one word of this to our folks, nor give the least hint. I am,[35]

Your sincere friend and affectionate sister,

Susanna Wesley[36]

---

[32] Mary Wesley (c. 1696–1734); later Mary (Wesley) Whitelamb.

[33] DDCW 8/15 changed "my father" to "he."

[34] See BCP, Morning Prayer, "A Prayer for the King's Majesty."

[35] DDCW 8/15 omits this concluding paragraph found in the shorthand, and reduces the closing salutation to "Your affectionate sister."

[36] Susanna Wesley Jr. (c. 1695–1764), called "Suky;"; later Susanna (Wesley) Ellison.

### [Samuel Wesley Jr. to Susanna Wesley Jr.[37]]

Dean's Yard [Westminster]
February 9, 1716/7

Dear Sister Suky,

Your telling me the spirit has made its personal appearance—without saying how, or to whom, or when, or how long—has excited my curiosity very much. I long mightily for a farther account of every circumstance by your next letter. Do not keep me any longer in the dark. Why need you write the less because my father intends to send me the whole story? Has the disturbance continued since the 28th of December? I understand my father did not hear it all along, but a fortnight after the rest. What did he say remarkable to any of you when he did hear it? As to the devil's being an enemy to King George, where I the king myself I should rather old Nick[38] should be my enemy than my friend. I do not like the news of the nightgown sweeping along the ground, not its knocking like my father. Write when you receive this, though nobody else should, to

Your loving brother,

S. Wesley

### [Samuel Wesley Jr. to Susanna (Annesley) Wesley[39]]

February 12 [1716/7][40]

Dear Madam,

You say you could multiply particular instances of the spirit's noises, but[41] I want to know whether nothing was ever seen by any. For though it is hard to conceive, nay morally impossible, that the hearing of so many people could be deceived, yet the truth will be still more manifest and undeniable if it is grounded on the testimony of two senses. Has it never at all disturbed you since the 28th of December? Did no circumstance give any light into the design of the whole?

Your obedient and loving son,
S. Wesley

Have you dug in the place where the money seemed poured at your feet?

---

[37] DDCW 8/15 omits this entire letter.
[38] A common nickname for the devil.
[39] DDCW adds the title "To Mrs. W."
[40] The date is given at the end of the letter.
[41] DDCW 8/15 elides the beginning of this sentence, to this point.

### [Samuel Wesley Jr. to Samuel Wesley Sr.[42]]

February 12 [1716/7][43]

Honoured Sir,

I have not yet received any answer to the letter I wrote some time ago.[44] And my mother in her last seems to say that as yet I know but a very small part of the whole of the story of strange noises in your house. I shall be exceedingly glad to have the entire account from you. Whatever may be the main design of such wonders, I cannot think they were ever meant to be kept secret. If they bode anything remarkable to our family, I am sure I am a party concerned.

Your dutiful son,

S. Wesley

### [Samuel Wesley Jr. to Emilia Wesley[45]]

February 12 [1716/7][46]

Dear Sister Em,[47]

I wish you would let me have a letter from you about the spirits[48] (as indeed from every one of my sisters). I cannot think any of you very superstitious, unless you are much changed since I saw you. My sister Hetty, I find, was more[49] particularly troubled. Let me know all. Did anything appear to her? I am,

Your affectionate brother,

S. Wesley

[page 5]

---

[42] DDCW 8/15 adds the title "To Mr. S. W. Senr."

[43] The date appears at the end of the letter.

[44] DDCW 8/15 omits this opening sentence and the conjunction "And."

[45] DDCW 8/15 adds the title "To M. Emilia Wesley."

[46] The date appears at the end of the letter.

[47] Emilia Wesley (1692–1771); later Emilia (Wesley) Harper. The Wesley family often called Emilia by this short familiar name; she tended to use instead "Emily."

[48] The shorthand is simply the sign for the letter "s." In DDCW 8/15 CW renders it "disturbances."

[49] DDCW 8/15 changed "was more" to "is."

### [Samuel Wesley Sr. to Samuel Wesley Jr.[50]]

Dear Sam,

As for the noises, etc., in our family, I thank God we are now all quiet. There was some surprising circumstances in that affair. Your mother has not wrote you a third part of it. When I see you here, you shall see the whole account which I wrote down. It would make a glorious penny book for Jack Dunton.[51] But while I live I am not ambitious of being famous for anything of that nature.

I think that is all, but blessings from
Your loving father,

Sam Wesley

The following letter I received at the same time though it has no date.[52]

### [Emilia Wesley to Samuel Wesley Jr.]

Dear Brother,

I thank you for your last, and[53] shall give you what satisfaction is in my power concerning what has happened in our family. I am so far from being superstitious that I was too much inclined to infidelity, so that I heartily rejoice at my having such an opportunity of convincing myself, past doubt or scruple, of the existence of some beings besides those we see. A whole month was sufficient to convince anybody of the reality of the thing, and to try all ways of discovering any trick, had it been possible for any such to have been used. I shall only tell you what I myself heard, and leave the rest to others.

My sisters in the paper chamber had heard noises, and told me of them. But I did not much believe till one night (about a week after the first groans were heard, which was the beginning), just after the clock had struck 10:00, I went downstairs to lock the doors, which I always do. Scarce had I got up the best stairs, when I heard a noise like a person throwing down a vast coal in the middle of the fore-kitchen, and all the splinters seemed to fly about from it. I was not much frighted, but went to my sister Suky, and we together went all over the low rooms, but there was nothing out of order. Our dog was fast asleep, and our only cat in the other end of the house.

---

[50] DDCW 8/15 omits this entire letter.

[51] John Dunton (1659–1733) was a London publisher and Samuel Sr.'s brother-in-law; the husband of Elizabeth (Annesley) Dunton (1657–97).

[52] DDCW 8/15 substitutes for this description the title: "The Answer."

[53] DDCW 8/15 reduces this opening to simply "I."

No sooner was I got up stairs, and undressing for bed, but I heard a noise among a many bottles under the best stairs, just like the throwing of a great stone among them, which had broke them all in pieces. This made me hasten to bed. But my sister Hetty, who sits up later to wait on my father going to bed, was still sitting on the lowest step on the garret stairs, the door being shut at her back; when, soon after, there came down the stairs behind her something like a man in a loose nightgown, trailing after him, which made her fly rather than run to me in the nursery.

All this time we never told my father of it. But soon after we did. He smiled and gave no answer, but was more careful than usual to see us in bed, imagining it to be some of us young women that sat up late and made a noise. His incredulity, and especially his imputing it to us or our lovers,[54] made me, I own, desirous of its continuance till he was convinced. As for my mother, she firmly believed it to be rats, and sent for a horn to blow them away. I laughed to think how wisely they were employed who were striving half a day to fright away Jeffrey (for that name I gave it) with a horn. But whatever it was, I perceived it could be made angry. For from that time it was so outrageous there was no quiet for us after 10:00 at night.

I heard frequently, between 10:00 and 11:00, something like the quick winding up of a jack, at the corner of the room by my bed's head, just like the running of the wheels and the creaking of the iron-work. This was the common signal of its coming. Then it would knock on the floor three times, then at my sisters' bedheads in the same room, almost always three together, and then stay [i.e., pause or stop]. The sound was hollow and loud, so as none of us could ever imitate. It would answer to my mother, if she stamped on [page 6] the floor, and bid it. It would knock when I was putting the children to bed, just under where I sat.

One time little Kezzy,[55] pretending to scare Patty[56] as I was undressing them, stamped with her foot on the floor, and immediately it answered with three knocks, just in the same place. It was more loud and fierce if anyone said it was rats, or anything natural.

I could tell you abundance more of it; but the rest [of the family] will write, and therefore it would be needless.[57] I was not much frighted at first, and very little at last—but it was never near me, except two or three times, and never followed me as it did my sister Hetty. I have been with her when it has knocked under her, and when she has removed it has followed, and still kept just under her feet, which was enough to terrify a stouter person.

---

[54] In DDCW 8/15 "or our lovers" is written in shorthand.
[55] Kezia Wesley (1709–41).
[56] Martha Wesley (1706–91); later Martha (Wesley) Hall.
[57] DDCW 8/15 omits this sentence.

If you would know my opinion of the reason of this, I shall briefly tell you. I believe it to be witchcraft, for these reasons. About a year since there was a disturbance at a town near us that was undoubtedly witches; and if so near, why may they not reach us? Then my father had for several Sundays before its coming preached warmly against consulting those that are called cunning men, which our people are given to, and it had a particular spite at my father. Besides, something was thrice seen: The first time by my mother, under my sister's bed, like a badger, only without any head that was discernible. The same creature was sat by the dining room fire one evening, when our man [Robin] went into the room. It ran by him, through the hole under the stairs. He followed with a candle and searched, but it was departed. The last time he saw it in the kitchen, like a white rabbit, which seems likely to be some witch. And I do so really believe it to be one that I would venture to fire a pistol at it, if I saw it long enough.[58] It has been heard by me and others since December.

I have filled up all my room, and have only time to tell you that I am,[59]
Your loving sister,

Emily Wesley

### [Susanna Wesley Jr. to Samuel Wesley Jr.[60]]

March 27 [1717]

Dear Brother Wesley,

I should further satisfy you concerning the disturbances, but it is needless because my sisters Em and Hetty write so particularly about it. One thing I believe you do not know; that is, last Sunday, to my father's no small amazement, his trencher[61] danced upon the table a pretty while, without anybody's stirring the table. When lo, an adventurous wretch took it up, and spoiled the sport, for it remained still ever after. How glad should I be to talk with you about it. Send me some news, for we [are] secluded from the sight or hearing of any versal[62] thing except Jeffrey.

Susanna Wesley

---

[58] Following "white rabbit," DDCW 8/15 abridges and rewrites to read: "which if I saw it long enough, I would venture to fire a pistol at it."

[59] DDCW 8/15 omits this sentence.

[60] DDCW 8/15 omits this entire letter.

[61] *OED*: "a flat piece of wood on which meat was served and cut up."

[62] *OED*: "single."

### A Passage in a Letter from my Mother to Me,
### dated March 27, 1717[63]

I cannot imagine how you should be so curious about our unwelcome guest. For my part, I am quite tired with hearing or speaking of it. But if you come among us you will find enough to satisfy all your scruples, and perhaps may hear or see it yourself.

S. W.

### A Passage in a Letter of my Sister Emily to
### Mrs. Nutty Berry dated April 1 [1717][64]

Tell my brother[65] the spirit was with us last night, and heard by many of our family, especially by our maid and myself. She [page 7] sat up with brewing, and it came just at one o'clock, and opened the dining-room door. After some time it shut it again. She saw as well as heard it both shut and open. Then it began to knock as usual. But I dare write no longer, lest I should hear it.

Emily Wesley

### My Father's Journal or Diary
### Transcribed by my brother Jack,[66] August 27, 1726,
### and from him by me, February 7, 1730/1[67]

### An Account of Noises and Disturbances in My House at
### Epworth, Lincolnshire,
### in December and January 1716[/7]

From the first of December my children and servants heard many strange noises, groans, knockings, etc., in every story and most of the rooms of my house. But I hearing nothing of it myself; they would not tell me for some time because, according to the vulgar opinion, if it boded any ill to me I could not hear it.

---

[63] DDCW 8/15 omits this letter excerpt.

[64] Priestly (and hence Clarke) misread "Mrs." as "Mr." "Nutty" was the familiar name for Ursula (Bentham) Berry (1669–1753), Samuel Jr.'s mother-in-law. DDCW 8/15 titles this: "Extract of another L[ette]r from the same [i.e., Emilia]."

[65] I.e., Samuel Jr., her son-in-law.

[66] "Jack" was the family's nickname for John Wesley.

[67] DDCW 8/15 reduces these three lines to "Mr. S. Wesley's Journal."

When it increased, and the family could not well conceal it, they told me of it. My daughters Susanna and Anne were below stairs in the dining room, and heard first at the doors, then over their heads, and the night after a knocking under their feet, though nobody was in the chambers or below them. The like they and my servants heard in both the kitchens, at the door against the partition, and over them. The maidservant heard groans as of a dying man. My daughter Emily, coming downstairs to draw up the clock and lock the doors at 10:00 at night as usual, heard under the staircase a sound among some bottles there, as if they had been all dashed to pieces; but when she looked, all was safe.

Something like the steps of a man was heard going up and down stairs at all hours of the night, and vast rumblings below stairs and in the garrets. My man[servant, Robin], who lay in the garret, heard someone come slaring[68] through the outer garrets to his chamber, rattling by his side as if against his shoes, though he had none there; at other times walking up and down stairs when all the family were in bed, and gobbling like a turkey-cock. Noises were heard in the nursery and all the other chambers; knocking first at the feet of the bed, then at the head and behind it; and a sound like that of dancing in a matted chamber next the nursery,[69] when the door was locked and nobody in it.

My wife would have persuaded them it was rats within doors, and some unlucky people knocking without. Till at last we heard several loud knocks in our own chamber, on my side [of] the bed. But till, I think, the 21st at night I heard nothing of it. That night I was waked a little before 1:00 by nine distinct very loud knocks, which seemed to be in the next room to ours, with a sort of a pause at every third stroke. I thought it might be somebody without the house, and having got a stout mastiff, hoped he would soon rid me of it.

The next night I heard six knocks, but not so loud as the former. I know not whether it were the morning after Sunday, the 23rd, when about 7:00, my daughter Emily called her mother into the nursery and told her she might now hear the noises there. She went in, and heard it at the bedstead, then under the bed, then at the head of it. She knocked, and it answered her. She looked under the bed and thought something ran from thence, but could not well tell of what shape, but thought it most like a badger.

The next night but one we were awaked about 1:00 by the noises, which were so violent it was in vain to think of sleep while they continued. I rose, but my wife would rise with me. We went into every chamber and downstairs; and generally as we went [page 8] into one room, we heard it in that behind us, though all the family had been in bed several

---

[68] *OED*: "staggering or sliding one's feet."

[69] A "matted" chamber was a room with either mats on the floor or tapestries hanging on the wall. Cf. *OED*.

hours. When we were going downstairs, and at the bottom of them, we heard, as Emily had done before, a clashing among the bottles, as if they had been broke all to pieces, and another sound distinct from it, as if a piece of money had been thrown before us. The same, three of my daughters heard at another time.

We went through the hall into the kitchen, when our mastiff came whining to us, as he did always after the first night of its coming; for then he barked violently at it, but was silent afterwards, and seemed more afraid than any of the children. We still heard it rattle and thunder in every room above or behind us, locked as well as open, except my study, where as yet it never came. After 2:00 we went to bed, and were pretty quiet the rest of the night.

Wednesday night, December 26 (after or a little before 10:00), my daughter Emily heard the signal of its beginning to play, with which she was perfectly acquainted. It is like the strong winding up of a jack. She called us, and I went into the nursery, where it used to be most violent. The rest of the children were asleep. It began with knocking in the kitchen underneath, then seemed to be at the bedstead, then under the bed, at last at the head of it. I went downstairs, and knocked with my stick against the joists of the kitchen. It answered me as often and as loud as I knocked. Then I knocked as I usually do at my door: 1 — 2, 3, 4, 5, 6 — 7. But this puzzled it, and it did not answer, or not in the same method; though the children heard it do the same twice or thrice after.

I went upstairs, found it still knocking hard, though with some respite, sometimes under the bed, sometimes at the bed's head. I observed my children were frightened in their sleep, and trembled very much till it waked them. I stayed there alone, bid them go to sleep, and sat at the bed's foot by them. When the noise began again I asked it what it was, and why it disturbed innocent children, and did not come to me in my study if it had anything to say to me. Soon after it gave one knock on the outside of the house (all the rest were within), and knocked off for that night.

I went out of doors—sometimes alone, at others with company—and walked round the house, but could see or hear nothing. Several nights the latch of our chamber door would be lifted up, very often when all were in bed. One night, when the noise was great in the kitchen, and on a deal [i.e., wooden] partition and the door in the yard (the latch whereof was often lifted up), my daughter Em went and held it fast on the inside. But it was still lifted up, and the door pushed violently against her, though nothing was to be seen on the outside.

When we were at prayers, when we came to the prayer for King George and the prince it would make a great noise over our heads constantly, whence some of the family (himself)[70] called it a Jacobite. I have been thrice pushed by an invisible power, once against the corner of my desk in the study, a second time against the door of the matted chamber, a third time against the right side of the frame of my study door as I was going in.

I followed the noise into almost every room in the house, from the lower story to the garret, both by day and night, with lights and without, and have sat alone for some time; and when I heard the noise, spoke to it to tell me what it was, but never heard any articulate voice, and only once or twice two or three feeble squeaks, a little louder than the chirping of a bird, but not like the noise of rats, which I have often heard.

I had designed on Friday, December the 28th, to make a visit to a friend, Mr. Downes, at Normandy, and stay some days with him. But the noises were so boisterous on Thursday night, that I did not care to leave my family. So I went to Mr. [Joseph] Hoole of Haxey, and desired his company on Friday night.

He came, and it began after 10:00, a little later than ordinary. The younger children were gone to bed, the rest of the family and Mr. Hoole were together in the matted chamber. I sent the servants down to fetch in some fuel, went with them, and stayed in the kitchen till they came in. When they were gone I heard loud noises against the doors and partition; and at length the usual signal, [page 9] though somewhat after the time. I had never heard it before, but knew it by the description my daughter had given me. It was much like the turning about of a windmill when the wind changes. When the servants returned I went up to the company, who had heard the other noises below, but not the signal. We heard all the knockings as usual, from one chamber to another; but at its going off, like the rubbing of a beast against the wall. But from that time till January the 24th we were quiet.

Having received a letter from Samuel [Jr.] the day before relating to it, I read what I had written of it to my family. And this day at morning prayer the family heard the usual knocks at the prayer for the King George. At night they were more distinct, both in the prayer for the king and that for the prince; and one very loud knock at the "Amen" was heard by my wife and most of my children at the inside of my bed. I heard nothing myself. After 9:00, Robert Brown, sitting alone by the fire in the back kitchen, saw something come out of the copper-hole,[71] like a rabbit, but less, and turned round five times very swiftly. Its ears lay flat on its neck, and its little scut stood straight up. He ran away with the tongs in his hands, but when he could find nothing was frighted, and went to the maid in the parlour.

On Friday, the 25th, having prayers at church, I shortened as usual

---

[70] This is marked as an editorial insertion; almost certainly by CW when he made the shorthand copy of Samuel Jr.'s original extract of Samuel Sr.'s journal—since it does not appear in Priestley, and is also present in DDCW 8/15.

[71] *OED*: "a kind of stove."

those in the family at morning, omitting the confession, absolution, and prayers for the king and prince. I observed when this is done there is no knocking. I therefore used them one morning for a trial. At the name of King George it began to knock, and did the same when I prayed for the prince. Two knocks I heard, but took no notice after prayers, till after all that were in the room, ten persons besides me, spoke of it, and said they heard it. No noise at all at the rest of the prayers.

Sunday, January 27, two soft strokes at the morning prayers for King George above stairs.

### My Mother's Account
### August 27, 1726[72]

[Susanna (Annesley) Wesley to John Wesley]

About ten days after Nanny Marshall had heard unusual groans at the dining-room door, Emily came and told me that the servants and children had been several times frighted with strange groans and knockings about the house. I answered that the rats John Maw[73] had frightened from his house, by blowing a horn there, was come into ours, and ordered one should be sent for. Molly was much displeased at it, and said, if it were anything supernatural, it would certainly be very angry, and more troublesome. However the horn was blown in the garrets, and the effect was that, whereas before the noises were always in the night, from this time they were heard at all hours day and night.

Soon after, about 7:00 in the morning, Emily came and desired me to go into the nursery, where I should be convinced they were not startled at nothing. On my coming thither, I heard a knocking at the foot, and quickly after at the head, of the bed. I desired if it was a spirit, it would answer me; and knocking several times with my foot on the ground, with several pauses, it repeated under the sole of my foot exactly the same number of strokes, with the very same intervals. Kezzy, then six or seven years old, said, Let it answer me too, if it can. And stamping, the same sounds were returned that she made, many times successively.

Upon my looking under the bed something ran out pretty much like a badger, and seemed to run directly under Emily's petticoats, who sat opposite to me on the other side. I went out. And one or two nights after, when we were just gone to bed, I heard nine strokes, three by three, on the other side the bed, as [if] one had struck violently on a chest with a

---

[72] DDCW 8/15 titles instead: "Mrs. W.'s Account to Mr. J. W., Aug. 27, 1726."

[73] John Maw (c. 1680–1753) was one of the principal landholders in the Epworth area, numbered among his best parishioners by Rev. Samuel Wesley Sr. (in a letter to Mr. Stephenson, May 14, 1734). See *WHS* 5 (1906): 201.

large stick. Mr. [Samuel] Wesley leapt up, called Hetty, who alone was up in the house, and searched every room in the house, but to no purpose. It continued from this time to knock and groan frequently, at all hours day and night; only I earnestly desired it might not disturb me between 5:00 and 6:00 in the evening, and there never was any noise in my room after during that time.

At other times I have often heard it over my mantletree;[74] and once, coming up after dinner, a cradle seemed to be strongly rocked in my chamber. When I went in, the sound seemed to be in the nursery. When I was in the nursery, it seemed in my chamber. One night Mr. Wesley and I were waked by some one's running down the garret stairs, [then down the broad stairs, then up the narrow ones, then up the garret stairs,[75]] then down again, and so the same round. The rooms trembled as it passed along, and the doors shook exceedingly, so that the clattering [page 10] of the latches was very loud.

Mr. Wesley proposing to rise, I rose with him, and went down the broad stairs, hand in hand, to light a candle. Near the foot of them, a large pot of silver seemed to be poured out at my waist, and to run jingling down my nightgown to my feet. Presently after we heard the noise as of a vast stone thrown among several dozen of bottles which lay under the stairs. But upon our looking, no hurt was done. In the hall the mastiff met us, crying and striving to get between us. We returned up into the nursery, where the noise was very great. The children were all asleep, but panting, trembling, and sweating extremely.

Shortly after, on Mr. Wesley's invitation, Mr. [Joseph] Hoole stayed a night with us. As we were all sitting round the fire in the matted chamber, he asked whether that gentle knocking were it? I told him yes, and it continued the sound, which was much lower than usual. This was observable, that while we were talking loud in the same room, the noise, seemingly lower than any of our voices, was distinctly heard above them all. These were the most remarkable passages I remember, except such as were common to all the family.

### My Sister Emily's Account to Jack[76]

About a fortnight after the time when I was told the first noises were heard, I went from my mother's room, who was just gone to bed, to the best chamber, to fetch my sister Suky's candle. When I was there, the windows

---

[74] *OED*: "a beam across the opening of a fireplace."

[75] CW likely skipped a line inadvertently at this place. The text in brackets comes from Priestley's transcription, and helps CW's shorthand text make sense.

[76] DDCW 8/15 titles: "Mrs. Em. Wesley's Account to Mr. J. W." CW uses "Mrs.," though Emelia was still single, because she was now 34 and older single women were so addressed.

and doors began to jar and ring exceedingly. And presently afterwards I heard a sound in the kitchen, as if a vast coal had been thrown down and mashed to pieces. I went down thither with my candle, and found nothing more than usual. But as I was going by the screen, something began knocking on the other side, just even with my head. When I looked on the inside, the knocking was on the outside of it. But as soon as I could get round, it was at the inside again. I followed it to and fro several times, till at last finding it to no purpose, and turning about to go away. Before I was out of the room the latch of the back kitchen door was lifted up many times. I opened the door and looked out, but could see nobody. I tried to shut the door, but it was thrust against me, and I could feel the latch, which I held in my hand, moving upward at the same time. I looked out again, but finding it was labour lost, clapped the door to and locked it. Immediately the latch was moved strongly up and down. But I left it and went up the worst stairs, from whence I heard as if a great stone had been thrown among the bottles which lay under the best stairs. However, I went to bed.

From this time I heard it every night for two or three weeks. It continued a month in its full majesty, night and day. Then it intermitted a fortnight or more, and when it began again it knocked only on nights, and grew less and less troublesome, till at last it went quite away.

Toward the latter end, it used to knock on the outside of the house, and seemed further and further off, till it ceased to be heard at all.

### My Sister Molly's Account to Jack[77]

August 27, 1726

I have always thought it was in November. The rest of our family think it was the first of December 1716, when Nanny Marshall, who had a bowl of butter in her hand, ran to me and two or three more of my sisters in the dining room and told us she had heard several groans in the hall, as of a dying man. We thought it was Mr. Turpine, who had the stone, and used sometimes to come and see us. About a fortnight after, when my sister Suky and I were going to bed, she told me how she was frightened in the dining room the day before by a noise, first at the folding doors and then overhead. I was reading at the table, and had scarce told her I believed nothing of it, when several knocks were given just under my feet. We both made haste into bed, and just as we lay down, the warming pan by the bedside jarred and rang, as did the latch of the door, which was lifted swiftly up and down. Presently a [page 11] great chain seemed to fall on the outside of the door (we were in the best chamber). The door,

---
[77] DDCW 8/15 revises this first line to: "Mrs. Molly Wesley's Account to Mr. J. W."

latch, tongs, the warming pan, and windows jarred, and the house shook from top to bottom.

A few days after, between 5:00 and 6:00 in the evening, I was by myself in the dining room. The door seemed to open, though it was still shut, and somebody walked[78] in a night-gown trailing upon the ground (nothing appearing), and seemed to go leisurely round me. I started up, and ran up stairs to my mother's chamber and told the story to her and my sister Emily. A few nights after, my father ordered me to light him to his study. Just as he had unlocked it, the latch was lifted up for him. The same (after we blew the horn) was often done to me, as well by day as by night. Of many other things all the family as well as me were witnesses.[79]

My father went into the nursery from the matted chamber, where we were, by himself in the dark. It knocked very loud on the press-bed head.[80] He adjured it to tell him why it came, but it seemed to take no notice. At which he was very angry, spoke sharply, called it [a] deaf and dumb devil, and repeated his adjuration. My sisters were terribly afraid it would speak. When he had done, it knocked his knock on the bed's head, so exceeding violently as if it would break it to shivers. And from that time we heard nothing till near a month afterwards.

September 8 wrote.

### My Sister Suky's Account to Jack[81]

I believed nothing of it till about a fortnight after the first noises. Then one night I sat up on purpose to hear it. While I was working in the best chamber, and earnestly desiring to hear it, a knocking began just under my feet. As I knew the room below was locked, I was frighted, and leaped into bed with all my clothes on. I afterward heard as it were a great chain fall, and after some time the usual noises at all hours of the day and night.

One night, hearing it was most violent in the nursery, I resolved to lie there. Late at night several strong knocks were given on the two lowest steps of the garret stairs, which were close to the nursery door. The latch of the door was jarred, and seemed to be[82] swiftly moved to and fro, and presently it began knocking about a yard within the room on the floor. It then came gradually to sister Hetty's bed, who trembled strongly in her

---

[78] DDCW 8/15 mistakenly omits "walked."
[79] DDCW 8/15 omits this sentence.
[80] "Press bed" is archaic for a bed that folds into a cupboard; see *OED*.
[81] DDCW 8/15 renders the title: "Mrs. Suky W.'s Account to Mr. J. W."
[82] DDCW 8/15 omits "seemed to be."

sleep. It beat[83] very loud, three strokes at a time, on the bed's head. My father came and adjured it to speak, but it knocked on for some time, and then retired to the room over, where it knocked my father's knock on the ground, as if it would beat the house down. I had no mind to stay longer, but got up and went to sister Emily and my mother, who was in her room. From thence we heard the noises again in the nursery. I proposed playing a game at cards; but we had scarce begun when a knocking began under our feet. We left off playing and removed back again into the nursery, where it continued till toward morning.

### Sister Nancy's Account to Jack[84]

September 10 [1726]

The first noise my sister Nancy heard was in the best chamber, with my sister Molly and my sister Suky. Soon after my father ordered her to blow a horn in the garrets, where it was knocking violently. She was terribly afraid, being obliged to go in the dark; and kneeling down on the stairs, desired that, as she acted not to please herself, it might have no power over her. As soon as she came into the room the noise ceased. Nor did it begin again till near 10:00. But then, and for a good while, it made much greater and more frequent noises than it had done before.

She afterward came into the chambers in the daytime.[85] It commonly walked after her from room to room. It followed her from one side of a bed to the other, and back again, as often as she went back. And whatever she did which made any sort of noise, the same thing seemed to be done just behind her.

When five or six sat in the nursery together, a cradle would seem to be strongly rocked in the room over, though no cradle [page 12] had ever been there. One night she was sitting on the press-bed end, playing at cards with some of my sisters. My sisters Molly, Hetty, Patty, and Kezzy were in the room, and Robin Brown. The bed on which my sister Nancy sat was lifted up with her on it. She leaped down, and said, "Surely old Jeffrey would not run away with me."[86] However, they persuaded her to sit down again, which she had scarce done when it was again lifted upward several times successively, a considerable height; upon which she left her seat, and would not be prevailed upon to sit there any more.

---

[83] DDCW 8/15 has "began to be" in place of "beat."

[84] DDCW 8/15 renders the title: "Miss Nancy W.'s Account to Mr. J. W."

[85] DDCW 8/15 omits this sentence.

[86] The shorthand is "her" rather than "me." We follow DDCW 8/15 in replacing the third person with first person, presenting it as a quotation.

Whenever they began to mention Mr. S.,[87] it presently began to knock, and continued to do so till they changed the discourse. All the time my sister Suky was writing her last letter to him it made a very great noise all round the room. And the night after she set out for London it knocked till morning, with scarce any intermission.

Mr. Hoole read prayers once, but it knocked as usual at the prayers for the king and prince. The knockings at those prayers were only toward the beginning of the disturbances for a week or thereabouts.

### Mr. [Joseph] Hoole's Account at Haxey

September 16 [1726]

As soon as I came to Epworth, Mr. [Samuel] Wesley telling me he sent for me to conjure, I knew not what he meant. Till some of your sisters told me what had happened, and that I was sent for to sit up. I expected every hour, it being about noon, to hear something extraordinary, but to no purpose. At supper too, and at prayers, all was silent, contrary to custom. But soon after one of the maids, who went up to sheet a bed, brought the alarm that Jeffery was come above the stairs. We all went up, and as we were standing round the fire in the best chamber something began knocking just on the other side of the wall, on the chimney-piece, as with a key. Presently the knocking was under our feet. Mr. Wesley and I went down, he with a great deal of hope, and I of fear. As soon as we were in the kitchen the sound was above us, in the room we had left. We returned up the narrow stairs, and heard at the broad stair head, some one slaring with their feet (all the family being now in bed beside us) and then trailing, as it were, and rustling with a silk nightgown. Quickly it was in the nursery, at the bed's head, knocking as it had done at first, three by three. Mr. Wesley spoke to it, and said he believed it was the devil, and soon after it knocked at the window, and changed its sound into one like the planing of boards. From thence it went on the outward south side of the house, sounding fainter and fainter, till it was heard no more.

I was at no other time than this during the noises at Epworth, and do not now remember any more circumstances than these.

### Epworth, September 1 [1726]

My sister Kezzy says she remembers nothing else but that it knocked my father's knock in the nursery one night, ready to beat the house down.

---

[87] Likely a young suitor of Susanna Jr.

### Robin Brown's Account to Jack[88]

The first time Robin Brown, my father's man[servant], heard it was when he was fetching down some corn from the garrets. Some what knocked on a door just by, which made him run away downstairs. From that time it used frequently to visit him in bed, walking up the garret stairs, and in the garrets, like a man in jack boots, with a nightgown trailing after him; then lifting up his latch and making it jar, making presently a noise in his room like the gobbling of a turkey-cock; then stumbling over his shoes or boots [page 13] by the bedside.

He was resolved once to be too hard for it, so took a large mastiff we had just got to bed with him, and left his shoes and boots below stairs. But he might as well have spared his labour, for it was exactly the same thing whether any were there or no. The same sound was heard as if there had been forty pairs [of shoes]. The dog indeed was a great comfort to him, for as soon as the latch began to jar he crept into bed and made such a howling and barking together, in spite of all the man could do, that he alarmed most of the family.

Soon after, being grinding corn in the garrets and happening to stop a little, the handle of the mill was turned round with great swiftness. He said nothing vexed him but that the mill was empty. If corn had been in it, Old Jeffery might have ground his heart out for him; he would never have disturbed him.

One night, being ill, he was leaning his head upon the back kitchen chimney (the "jam" he called it) with the tongs in his hands, when from behind the oven's top, which lay by the fire, something came out like a white rabbit. It turned round before him several times, and then ran to the same place again. He was frighted, started up, and ran with the tongs into the parlour.

### Epworth, August 31 [1726]

Betty Massy[89] one day came to me in the parlour and asked me if I had heard Old Jeffery, for she said she thought there was no such thing. When we had talked a little about it, I knocked three knocks with a reel I had in my hand against the dining-room ceiling, and the same were presently repeated. She desired me to knock so again, which I did, but they were answered with three more so violently as shook the house, though no one was in the chamber over us. She prayed me to knock no more for fear it should come in to us.

---

[88] The first name in the shorthand is given simply with the letter "R"; which could be expanded as Robert. We follow Priestly and DDCW 8/15 in using the familiar form of his name. In DDCW 8/15 the title ends "to Mr. J. W." instead of "Jack."

[89] Elizabeth Massey, daughter of Richard and Elizabeth Massey, was baptized in Epworth in 1703.

### Epworth, August 30, 1726[90]

John and Kitty Maw,[91] who lived over against us, listened several nights in the time of the disturbance, but could never hear anything.

### Of the general circumstances which follow
### most, if not all the family, were frequent witnesses:

1. Presently after any noise was heard, the wind commonly rose, and whistled very loud round the house, and increased with it.
2. The signal was given, which my father likens to the turning round of a windmill when the wind changes; Mr. Hoole (rector of Haxey), to the planing of deal boards; my sisters, to the swift winding up of a jack [flag]. It commonly began at the corner of the top of the nursery.
3. Before it came into any room, the latches were frequently lifted up, the windows clattered, and whatever iron or brass was about the chamber rung and jarred exceedingly.
4. When it was in any room, let them make what noise they would, as they sometimes did on purpose, its dead hollow note would be clearly heard above them all.
5. It constantly knocked while the prayers for the king and prince were repeating; and was plainly heard by all in the room but my father—and sometimes by him; as were also the thundering knocks at the "Amen."
6. The sound very often seemed in the air in the middle of a room, nor could they ever make any like it themselves by any contrivance.
7. Though it seemed to rattle down the pewter, to clap the doors, draw the curtains, kick the man's shoes up and down, yet it never moved anything except the latches, otherwise than by making it tremble; unless once, when it threw open the nursery door.
8. The mastiff, though he barked violently at it the first day he came, yet whenever it came afterwards, nay sometimes before the family perceived it, he ran whining[92] or quite silent, to shelter himself behind some of the company.
9. It never came by day, till my mother ordered the horn to be blown. [page 14]
10. After that time, scarce anyone could go from one room into another, but the latch of the door they went to was lifted up before they touched it.

---

[90] DDCW 8/15 omits the heading; Priestley gives the date as Aug. 31.

[91] Catherine Maw was buried in Epworth in 1747.

[92] This word is missing in the shorthand, but present in DDCW 8/15 and Priestley.

11. It never came into my father's study, till he talked to it sharply, called it [a] deaf and dumb devil, and bid it cease to disturb the innocent children and come to him in his study if it had anything to say to him.

12. From the time of my mother's desiring it might not disturb her from 5:00 to 6:00, it was never heard once in her chamber from 5:00 till she came down stairs; nor at any other time when she was employed in devotion.

13. Whether our clock went right or wrong, it always came, as near as could p[ossib]ly[93]
be guessed, when by the night it wanted a quarter of 10:00.[94]

### Addenda to my father's diary[95]

Friday, December 21. Knocking I heard first, I think, this night; to which disturbances I hope God will in his good time put an end.

Sunday, December 23. Not much disturbed with the noises that are now grown customary to me.

Wednesday, December 26. Sat up to hear noises. Strange! Spoke to it, knocked off.

Friday, [December] 28. The noises very boisterous and disturbing this night.

Saturday, [December] 29. Not frighted with the continued disturbance of my family.

Tuesday, January 1, 1717. My family have had no disturbance since I went.

### Memorandum of Jack's[96]

The first time my mother ever heard any unusual noise in Epworth was long before the disturbances of Old Jeffrey.[97] My brother, lately come from London, had one evening a sharp quarrel with my sister Suky—at which time my mother happening to be above in her own chamber, the door and windows rang and jarred very loud; and presently several distinct strokes, three by three, were struck.

---

[93] This word in the shorthand is missing in both DDCW 8/15 and Priestley.

[94] I.e., 9:45 p.m.

[95] The word "Addenda" is in longhand. DDCW 8/15 omits the addenda; Priestley placed it immediately after the longer entry from SW Sr.'s diary (on p. 149).

[96] DDCW 8/15 omits the heading.

[97] DDCW 8/15 abridges to: "... was long before these disturbances."

From that night[98] it never failed to give notice, in much the same manner, against any signal misfortune or illness of any belonging to the family.

*Sources*: CW shorthand transcription from Samuel Wesley Jr.'s letter-book (MARC, MA 1977/567/1); and CW longhand expansion of portions of previous (DDCW 8/15, pp. 8–43).[99]

---

[98] DDCW 8/15 reads "From that time ...."

[99] Compared with Joseph Priestley, *Original Letters by the Rev. John Wesley and his Friends* (Birmingham: Pearson, 1791), 119–66.

## ACCOUNT OF DYING MALEFACTORS PENITENT
## NOVEMBER 7–8, 1738[1]

The following relation will I trust be matter of rejoicing to you.[2] God has lately made bare his arm before us.[3] For some weeks past my brother [JW] and I had attended the malefactors in Newgate, some of them hardened, some deeply penitent. I did not visit with them till Tuesday last. It pleased God to melt me into something of sympathy at the sight of them. After prayers I spoke to them from Matthew 5:25–26, and set the terrors of the Lord in array against them. They were so much affected, and showed such signs of true compunction (declaring audibly that they did deserve damnation) that I soon haste[ne]d from the law to the gospels. It would have delighted you to have heard and seen their sighs and groans and tears, at hearing of Jesus Christ given for us. At my mentioning a saying of Arndt's, that if all the sins of the whole world would be laid upon one man the blood of Christ would suffice to cleanse even him from all sin,[4] and asking "Which of you believes this?", one of them cried out with the utmost vehemence, "I do, I do believe if from my heart." I proceeded, "Be it unto thee according to thy faith."[5] And he repeated a most comfortable "Amen."

After sermon I spoke a few words to them exhorting them to spend every moment that stood between them and eternity in crying to Jesus for repentance and faith, adding that I nothing doubted but some of them would know before their execution (which was to be the next day) that their sins were forgiven them. "I hope, sir, some of us know it already,"

---

[1] The presence of JW and CW at Newgate Prison in London on Tuesday, Nov. 7, and Wednesday, Nov. 8, 1738 is confirmed by JW's diary and *Journal*, and CW's MS Journal. Accounts in *Gentleman's Magazine* 8 (1738): 602; *London Evening Post* (Nov. 4, 1738); and *London Magazine and Monthly Chronologer* 7 (1738): 578 name twelve men executed at Tyburn on Nov. 8: Dean Bryant and George Whatley, for murdering their wives; Jonathan Thomas, for filing of guineas (who was drawn on a sled); Charles Golding and Joseph Upton, for burglary of homes; Edward Barcock and Henry Fluellen, for street robbery; John Fosset, Thomas Jones, Thomas Raby, and William Sylvester, for highway robbery; and John Machell, for stealing two mares. A more detailed description of the men and their crimes can be found in: The Ordinary of Newgate, *His Account of the Behaviour, Confession. and Dying Words, of the Malefactors who* were Executed at Tyburn on Wednesday the 8th of November (London: John Applebee, 1738); available online: https://www.oldbaileyonline.org/browse.jsp?name=OA17381108.

[2] The recipient of this account is not identified. Many are possible (James Hutton, George Stonehouse, George Whitefield, and so on). Indeed, it was likely sent to more than one recipient, and intended to be read aloud (by CW or others, see below on Oct. 27, 1747), which is why it is included in this collection. The copy that survives is not the holograph, but a clean copy for CW's records.

[3] See Isa. 52:10.

[4] Johann Arndt, *True Christianity*, Book II, Chapter 2, sec. 12 (London: Brown & Downing, 1712–14), 1:437.

[5] Cf. Matt. 9:29.

said Barcock (who made the confession above). "But may we not," continued he, "expect to know it more and more, the nearer we draw to eternity?" The rest seemed full of comfort and trust in the blood of Jesus, expressed a strong desire of receiving the Holy Sacrament, and much affection to me for promising to come again in the afternoon.

From them I went to the old condemned hole, where four more were confined for attempting to break gaol[6] the night before. I found them staked down to the floor. Their ringleader Thomas[7] (a hardened villain, though once a gentleman) cried out most audaciously, "Aye here I am, the author of the rebellion, the *primum mobile*!" I asked him whether he had considered his rebellion against God, and how to make his peace with him. He answered, more composedly, it was all his thought. The others behaved better. We went to prayer and God gave me power to pray in faith. I claimed the promise of a Saviour for whomsoever he saw willing to receive him. After prayer they appeared much humbled. Thomas's countenance was fallen and they rejoiced to hear I would see them again.

Accordingly, in the afternoon I prayed by them and preached the gospel from the two crucified malefactors.[8] They received it as well as might be expected from those who had nothing but the blood of Christ to trust to. One now declared he *had* forgiveness of sin, peace with God, and joy in the Holy Ghost. "And so," says he, "I hope this my companion has, though he is afraid to profess it." Upon my saying to his companion, "God love you," he replied with great earnestness and joy, "*Does he indeed?*" "Can you doubt of that," says the other. "Suppose one of them that are passing by should offer to die in your place tomorrow. Would not he love you? But Christ had done this for you." I could not mend what he said, but endeavoured to enforce it and left them in the most delightful frame, broken-hearted, believing, and ready to receive the Bridegroom.

The next morning, between 6:00 and 7:00, my brother and I, with Mr. Sparks[9] and [John] Bray, went to see them. The keeper was letting them out of their cells. The first word we heard was "Glory be to God. This is the most blessed day I ever saw. Glory be to Christ!" We said "Amen" and went in. Barcock, the man that spoke, asked "Who is there?" We answered, "The messengers of Christ." He knew our voice and replied, "O, are you come! You are God's ambassadors. You are his instruments in saving my soul. We went into him. He fell on our necks and kissed us. Then he knelt

---

[6] I.e., jail.

[7] Jonathan Thomas, convicted of filing guineas.

[8] Luke 23:33–43.

[9] Rev. John Sparkes (c. 1713–47) was an ordained Anglican without a regular pastoral post. He had first convinced CW to preach at Newgate Prison a few months earlier (see CW Journal, July 10, 1738)..

down to thank us, and blessed God with so much transport that we could not refrain from tears. "Dear gentlemen, weep not for me. I was never so happy in my life. This is the most joyful morning I ever knew. I am innocent of the fact for which I am to die, but I deserve a thousand deaths for my sins, and bless and praise God for suffering this. He has so ordered it that he might save my soul. I adore his goodness for it and shall do so for all eternity. I am perfectly at ease and have not the least doubt, the least fear of death. For today I shall be with him in paradise."[10] You may imagine how this affected us. We entered one of the cells, where we found six more children appointed unto death. There is no describing their love and joy at the sight of us. They were much altered since our last seeing them—all full of peace and comfort, some of joy and exaltation, and one (innocent) young man only not so triumphant as Barcock. We sang and rejoiced together, and they blessed and prayed for us most heartily. Then we went to the chapel and joined in prayer and the Holy Sacrament. Their earnestness (especially Barcock's) was inexpressible.

Toward nine they were carried down to have their irons taken off and to be tied for execution. I asked them first, "Which of you *knows* his sins are forgiven?" "Sir," says Barcock, "I speak it with humility, *I am sure of it*." To the gaoler he said, "As sure as you knock off these fetters, so surely has Christ knocked off the fetters of sin from my soul." Many like words he spoke, full of joy and confidence, and love to us, the spectators, and officers.

While they were tying them like sheep for the slaughter my brother and I went before in the Ordinary's[11] coach. They followed us soon after (Thomas on a sledge[12]). At Tyburn, Barcock spied us in the coach and made signs of his joy and satisfaction, moving his head and hands, and looking up to heaven with a smiling countenance. Others of them saluted us in like manner. It was a joyful meeting when we came upon the cart. We were all animated at the sight of one another. To prevent the Ordinary's troubling them, I immediately began singing "Behold the Saviour of mankind / Nailed to the shameful tree."[13] They joined with one heart and voice, expressed their full reliance on the death of Christ, and marvelously showed forth the power of his resurrection. Barcock was full of the most triumphant confidence. He had heaven in his look. Observing the sun, he said, "God has approved my prayer. I asked for such a day, and

---

[10] Cf. Luke 23:43.

[11] The "Ordinary" was the Church of England priest appointed as chaplain to Newgate. This was James Guthrie from 1734 to 1746.

[12] That is, while the other convicted men rode to the execution site in a wagon, Jonathan Thomas was tied to a crude wooden pallet and dragged behind a horse (apparently for leading the escape attempt).

[13] A hymn by Samuel Wesley Sr., published by JW in *CPH* (1737), 46–47.

as this sun shines upon my body so the mercy of God shines upon my soul." Three besides him avowed their innocence, and I will believe the testimony of God's Spirit most plainly visible in them before a world of human witnesses. God preserve us from the miserable justice of our fellow worms!

We prayed and sang alternately from 11:00 to near 12:00. Never did I see so much of the power of faith. One of our poor brethren lay at the bottom of the cart half dead, having been distracted ever since sentence was passed. Another had a good hope. The other nine (two of them murderers) were strong in the faith, giving glory to God. Thomas I was particularly pleased with. The evening before, upon my asking on what he grounded his hope, he answered "The alone merits of Christ." I now observed his countenance changed and asked whether he had found peace. "Yes," said he, "perfect peace. Such as I could not have conceived. It is the peace of God that passes all understanding." "Why then," I replied, "You must have experienced a mighty change since I last saw you." "I have so," said he, "though I had not thoughts of dying a few hours ago." "But you now die in the Lord." "I do, in full faith, and an assured, confident hope." Some of the others (and I think the four innocent men) had the full assurance of faith. They were greatly delighted with singing, particularly Watts' "Triumph over Death"[14] and those verses in the *Collection*

>Upon thy gracious promise, Lord
>  My humbled soul is cast!
>O bear me through this shameful death,
>  And raise me up at last!
>
>Low as this mortal frame must lie
>  This mortal frame shall sing,
>Where is thy victory, O grave;
>  And where, O death, thy sting![15]

The last verse we sang was

>A guilty weak and helpless worm,
>  Into thy arms I fall

---

[14] This was not Isaac Watts's hymn on Job 19:25–27 of that title, but another in *Hymns and Spiritual Songs*, 2nd ed. (London: John Lawrence, 1709), 230–31 (Book 2, no. 110); which JW had included in *CPH* (1737), 25.

[15] Sts. 4–5 of "A Thought in Affliction," in *CPH* (1737), 44 (modifying the third line quoted from "O bear me safe thro' life, thro' death").

> Be thou my life, my righteousness
> My Jesus, and my all.[16]

Thomas did not join audibly, but I saw his lips move and there appeared on his face and whole behaviour a calm composure and settled tranquility. Upon my looking at my watch, he enquired with great unconcern what o'clock it was. I told him "Just the time when our Lord Jesus said 'It is finished'."[17] We took our leave of them for a little time and desired them to pray and wait for us in paradise. Thomas's last words (which he spoke with great steadiness) were "Farewell, we shall quickly meet again." All the stories of Roman magnanimity fall short of his contempt of death. Indeed, they all seemed to forget themselves, through their regard and affection for us. They thanked and blessed and prayed for us, kissing our hands (for we could not hinder them), and seeming full of love—the genuine fruit of faith.

While they were dying and for half an hour after we spoke to the spectators, several of whom seemed much affected and came in the evening to hear my brother preach.

I must break off abruptly. — May we tread in the steps of their faith; confess we have just as much merit as they and *no more*; that trusting (like them) *entirely* on the merits of Christ, we may, though condemned malefactors, receive a *free pardon*.[18]

[London]
November 11, 1738

*Endorsement*: by CW, "NB Nov. 11 1738 / [[dying malefactors]] / Acct. of Dying Malefactors Penitent."[19]

*Source*: manuscript copy for records, in unknown hand, endorsed by CW; MARC, MA 1977/501/142.

---

[16] St. 6 of Isaac Watts's "Faith in Christ," *Hymns and Spiritual Songs*, 211–12; as included by JW in *CPH* (1737), 52.

[17] Cf. John 19:30.

[18] The last two words are larger than the prior text, surely to suggest emphasis, which is indicated here by placing them in italic font.

[19] In the upper righthand corner of the outside page CW has also written in shorthand: [[All Sunday or every day from 11:00 to 12:00 we met together / every night from 6:00 to 7:00 either by ourselves or with Mr. Vicks[?]]]. There is a list of last names on lefthand margin of this page—they are *not* the names of the malefactors and either common (like Jones) or difficult to expand with certainty.

## Prophetess Lavington's Case[1]
## [June 1739]

I. N. I.[2]

The first mention I heard made of Mrs. Lavington[3] the prophetess was, if I remember, by a child of God who had received the Holy Ghost while a Quaker but is now baptized into the visible church of Christ.[4] He told me he much feared our brethren would be seduced by her, for he knew her to be a wicked woman, and now to live in adultery with one [Mr.] Wise, a French Prophet; who himself confessed that he had lain with her.

Upon this notice I thought it my duty to inquire farther; "not to believe every spirit, but to try the spirits whether they were of God."[5] His providence, without my seeking it, cast me upon one Anne Graham who has been a child of God these seven years. She informed me that she had been carried to the prophetess, as to a most experienced Christian who knew the state of every one's soul; that she was at first greatly taken with her, as were the strongest of our brethren and sisters who flocked after her, some or other of them, continually, and received her prophecies as uttered by immediate inspiration.

She spoke as in the person of the Most High God, ushering in her prophecies with "The Lord saith"; sometimes singing, sometimes expounding her songs. She flattered a person present most excessively, telling him he should be another Whitefield.[6] Some of her words were, "I

---

[1] In 1685 Louis XIV repealed the Edict of Nantes, subjecting Protestants in France to renewed persecution. Protestants in the isolated Cévennes region of south-central France in particular raised an insurrection, encouraged in part by some prophesying the soon return of Christ to set up a millennial reign. The insurrectionists came to be called "Camisards." As the revolt was put down, many sought refuge in England, where their distinctive practices led to them being called the "French Prophets." This stream intermingled with other continental immigrants like the Moravians and pietists, especially in London and Bristol. Thus both JW and CW encountered them in the initial years of the revival. This document was prepared by CW in the midst of a particular encounter with a colorful prophetess. It was likely the source of, and provides more detail than the description of the encounter in MS Journal. For more background, see Hillel Schwartz, *The French Prophets* (Berkeley: University of California Press, 1980); and Kenneth G. C. Newport, "Early Methodism and the French Prophets: Some New Evidence," WHS 50 (1996): 127–40.

[2] "*In Nomine Iesu*"; "In the name of Jesus."

[3] Newport suggests that her first name was Mary ("Early Methodism," 130), citing this manuscript. CW uses only her family name. Little is known of her beyond the accounts here and in the journals of JW and CW.

[4] George Cawdry, baptized June 4, with CW in attendance.

[5] Cf. 1 John 4:1.

[6] Rev. George Whitefield (1714–70), who preceded the Wesley brothers by three years in his evangelical conversion in 1735. Ordained deacon in June 1736 (and priest in 1739), he began preaching in London in various churches with almost immediate success. This success carried over to Bristol in Jan. 1737, and then across the Atlantic on his first journey there. In

say unto thee, it shall be so. Thou shalt come to Jacob's well and drink. Thou shalt be married to Christ. Thou shalt receive a white stone. The Lord shows me that I should call thee sea-horse. ...."

After every prophecy her audience expressed their approbation by crying out, "The Lord speaketh good things! Glory be to the Lord!"

Several advices she gave them, as: 1) That the men and women should not be separated in the societies (because they were not in the church triumphant), for the Spirit of God would not work till they were brought together again. The men and women must (as she called it) "set shoulder to shoulder." 2) That all should marry at all hazards. "Let them take wives out of the streets, but let them marry." [3)] A third advice was that they should not sing psalms in the societies.

Her advice to Anne Graham in particular was: 1) To dress as fine as she could—that being a part of Christian liberty, and you are now (said she) fit to wear any thing. Her whole discourse to her and all others whom I have as yet spoken with tended to breed and nourish pride. By this mark Mr. [Westley] Hall[7] said he found her out immediately.

2) She bade Anne Graham advise her mistress "not to go so often to the sacrament, which did her hurt." Anne might go—for Anne had still a veneration for our Lord's command, and therefore the prophetess could not speak so plainly to her as she did to others, whom she found better disposed to cast off the means of grace.

John Cheney told me that she expressly dissuaded him from going to the sacrament, which she blasphemously called a beggarly element. She said in the hearing of Anne Ellis and Mary Cades (as themselves informed me) that if they could not yet go without crutches, they must even use them a little longer. But as they grew stronger, they would be called from the means of grace, and in particular the sacrament—concerning which she used this horrid expression, "What, shall I feed upon husks with swine, when I can feed upon the fatted calf?"

---

Feb. 1739, back in Bristol, he turned to field preaching and soon convinced JW and CW to join in this new setting. Despite their shared passion in the revival, the Wesley brothers and Whitefield held divergent theologies (Arminian and Calvinist). These soon caused tensions (and eventual divisions) in the broad Methodist movement.

[7] Rev. Westley Hall (c. 1709–76), a native of Salisbury, became a pupil of JW at Lincoln College on Jan. 26, 1731. Within a year he was closely involved with the "Oxford Methodists." An apparent model of Christian piety, JW gladly introduced Hall to his family; only to find him courting Martha and Kezia at the same time in 1734–35. Hall married Martha on Sept. 13, 1735, days after being ordained both deacon and priest, professedly in order to accompany JW and CW to Georgia. Within a month Hall withdrew from this venture. More importantly, he eventually proved unfaithful to Martha, justifying his actions by appeals to polygamy in Scripture. In addition to fracturing his marriage, this led to an end of his service as an Anglican priest and supporter of the Methodist cause. Hall kept up some correspondence with Martha until his death.

[3)] A third advice which she pressed upon Anne Graham was, "By all means to marry any one she could get." She told her she should know the man she was to marry, should find in herself whom God would join her to; and denounced terrible woes if she did not marry whom God should choose for her. When Anne mentioned St. Paul's advice, 1 Corinthians 7, the prophetess replied, "I do not believe St. Paul there."

She pretends (as Anne farther informed me) to know people's thoughts (which is the incommunicable attribute of God) and boasts that she can call the angels and archangels, and command Christ himself to come unto her. She puts all her followers upon looking for visions and revelations only, says she always sees a little angel with a cap and a feather on the top of a ladder when her prayer is answered. "For I" (says she) "am like unbelieving Thomas; unless I see with my eyes, I cannot believe."[8]

I asked Anne Graham how she came to suspect her for a false prophetess. She answered that God had showed it her. She had heard that Mrs. Lavington was a bad woman and lived in adultery, but it was God convinced her and opened her eyes by his word. The second time of her going she endeavoured to try the spirits, and instead of joining with the prophetess, cried earnestly to God to save her and the others from giving heed to seducing spirits, and that he would send true ministers into his church. She went home in great trouble of spirit, but could not sleep all night. Examined herself and all that had passed. Found her intention was pure, and she in perfect charity. Thought of consulting me, and prayed earnestly for direction when that scripture came strongly into her mind, "Notwithstanding I have a few things against thee, because thou sufferest that woman Jezebel, which calleth herself a prophetess, to teach and to seduce my servants to commit fornication, and to eat things sacrificed unto idols. And I gave her space to repent of her fornication, and she repented not. Behold, I will cast her into a bed, and them that commit adultery with her into great tribulation, except they repent of their deeds. And I will kill her children with death; and all the churches shall know that I am he that searcheth the reins and hearts: and I will give unto every one of you according to your works." (Revelation 2:20ff.) She was immediately filled with joy in the Holy Ghost, had the strongest assurance of faith, and saw through the whole in a moment with conviction that it was all a delusion of Satan.

She was tempted not to tell me, because (thought she) he will not believe me; besides the others will certainly tell him. She prayed again and perceived it was of God that she should communicate it to me, for she clearly saw the imminent danger the societies were in from this woman's getting among them, and the infinite scandal it would occasion, if she was not immediately cast out. She prayed almost continually for my coming,

---

[8] Cf. John 20:25.

sent after, but missed of me, till **Wednesday, June 6**. I providentially went toward the society down the market (a way I never used). She saw, and called me as I passed by, told me of her danger and miraculous escape from this deceiver.

From her I went (not to Fetter Lane as I intended, but) to Mr. [John Bray]'s society,[9] where I unexpectedly found the prophetess. I spoke a few words from Romans 6. Upon my insisting on holiness being the great mark of faith, Mr. Wise asked me whether a man could attain perfection here? I answered, "If we say that we have no sin, we deceive ourselves, and the truth is not in us."[10] The prophetess seemed very uneasy while I expounded, groaning and swelling, I suppose through the operation of the Spirit. I turned upon her and said, "If you have any thing to say, speak in the name of Jesus." She began her outcry with great violence of action, speaking in the person of God. "My children look for perfection, I say for absolute perfection. You may attain to absolute sinless perfection. ....." She went on wresting several scriptures to favour that arrogant doctrine of devils. I was once minded to have rebuked her in the name of Jesus that she should hold her peace. But God repressed me, and gave me uncommon recollection and command of spirit. So I sat quiet and let her go on, replying nothing, but offering to sing when her prophecy was over. "Yea" (said she, still in the person of God) "sing, my children. By all means, I say, sing." We did sing "Creator Spirit, by whose aid...," which I chose for the sake of that verse, "Chase from our minds th' infernal foe."[11] I observed she did not join with us, but continued kneeling from the time she ceased prophesying. Mrs. S[ellers[12]] and others were in raptures while the spirit was upon her. They all knelt down with great devotion. I stood till I should know how I liked it. She prayed with most pompous expressions borrowed (as it should seem) from the mystics, and flattered one present in a gross shocking manner. Her prophecy she concluded with an horrible laugh (as if the devil in her mocked his foolish admirers). She endeavoured to turn it off by saying she "could not but smile at God's marvellous goodness."

---

[9] CW identifies the society in MS Journal, though there he places these events on Thursday, June 7. John Bray (fl. 1738–44), a brazier of Little Britain, London, was one of the founding members of the Fetter Lane society. He was very helpful to CW, who was lodging in his home at the time of his conversion on May 21, 1738. In Dec. 1739 Bray emerged as a leader in the "stillness" controversy, which eventuated in the Wesley brothers leaving the Fetter Lane society in mid 1740. The next three years were marked by Bray seeking leadership roles among the English Moravians, finding those doors blocked, and seeking reconciliation with the Wesleys. Financial difficulties led him to leave London in late 1744, and he receives no further mention by CW.

[10] 1 John 1:8.

[11] John Dryden, "Veni Creator" which JW included in *CPH* (1738), 40–41.

[12] CW gives the full last name in MS Journal; her first name was Lydia.

George Cawdry was there before I came. The prophet and prophetess fell upon him and vehemently blamed him for being baptized,[13] telling him that he was past it. He was quite above it. She highly complimented him upon his gifts, assuring him that he was called to preach, and preach he must. After I was gone, she said in Mr. Okeley's[14] hearing she "would not go by St. Paul, but by the spirit in herself."

I must not forget the behaviour of Anne Graham while I was taking down her relation. She appeared under strong temptation, the enemy labouring with all his power and subtlety to disturb and hinder her. I was forced to bring her back ten times before she could finish any one thing she had begun to say. She cried and prayed and trembled, continuing in an agony all the day, as I imagined she would. The tempter tried all ways to deter her from writing down any more particulars. She told me she now knew what it was to wrestle with principalities and powers and spiritual wickedness in high places,[15] for the devil had been upon her as a roaring lion,[16] filling her with all manner of evil suggestions. He asked what it signified to take down any account. And when she did begin, he caught from her what she was going to write. Then he darted such horror into her, as she had never known before. Her body likewise was full of violent pain, which she believed he inflicted, and which she said explained to her what was meant by St. Paul's thorn in the flesh,[17] the messenger of Satan to buffet him.

One impudent suggestion she often began to tell me, but forgot it again immediately. At last the devil could hinder her no longer. It was, "You see what it is to be a Christian. You had better be still in your natural state, than thus tormented." She had several scriptures brought to her remembrance which strengthened her in her conflict, such as, "Lo, I am with you always."[18] "I have prayed for thee, that thy faith fail not."[19] "Rejoice not over me, O mine enemy: when I fall, I shall rise again."[20] "God shall bruise Satan under your foot shortly."[21]

---

[13] Cawdry, a Quaker, had been baptized by Rev. Scott on June 4; see CW, MS Journal.

[14] CW interacted with both Francis Okeley (1719–94) and his brother John (1721–92); it is not clear which of the brothers is intended. CW spells "Oakly."

[15] Cf. Eph. 6:12.

[16] Cf. 1 Pet. 5:8.

[17] See 2 Cor. 12:7–9.

[18] Cf. Matt. 28:20.

[19] Luke 22:32.

[20] Cf. Mic. 7:8.

[21] Cf. Rom. 16:20.

A farther account of the prophetess I received from one Mrs. Rigby, who has known her these sixteen years. Her behaviour was so scandalous that their people (the French Prophets), she told me, could not bear her. Her business was to join men and women as spiritual spouses. All marriages to any but the spiritual spouses God intended, she declared null and void; and accordingly took upon her to put asunder whom God had joined,[22] taking a man from his wife and children, a woman from her husband and children, and giving them to whom the spirit bid her. Of this she gave instances, particularly that of one Scholey whom the prophetess took from his wife and children, and joined to another woman, with whom he lived in adultery seven years. The prophetess herself, she told me, lived in like manner with the prophet Wise.

This exactly agreed with the account I had first from Cawdry and then from Scholey. This latter had been awakened by Mr. Whitefield's ministry. He informed me that the prophetess had laboured to persuade him he might innocently lie with his own sister, and did actually induce him to leave his family and live seven years in adultery. First of all she brought him off the sacrament and the other means of grace, telling him when he was in deep despair that it was sent by God as a punishment for his going to the sacrament. Whereas he ought to give himself up entirely to her and his spiritual father, the prophet Wise.

The way she took to seduce him was to puff him up with pride, telling him he should be a preacher and do great things. She likewise preached predestination to him. To others of different sentiments, I hear, she preaches free grace, or universal redemption.

**June 11.** I went with Mr. Oxlee[23] to Mrs. Scholey's who confirmed the prophetess's title to the character of a notorious bawd, and named several persons whom she had attempted to join in spiritual wedlock. Some of her words to Mrs. Scholey were, "I am in that standing that I can go to any one" (and so are you). "I am in the very highest standing of any person upon earth."

**June 12.** I had another of our brethren who gave me a correspondent account of her. She foretold in his presence that God would shortly destroy all outward things. The dispensation of Whitefield, she said, would soon be over, God only using him as the forerunner of greater persons. She hinted that he would be lost at sea.

One more testimony I need produce against the prophetess, which is the testimony of the prophetess herself. On **Tuesday evening, June 12,**

---

[22] See Matt. 19:6.

[23] William Oxlee (1713–78), a clog-maker and one of the early members of the Fetter Lane society, became a leading London Moravian layman. CW spells "Oxly."

I called at Mr. [John] Bray's and found Mr. Hutchings,[24] [John] Robson,[25] and several others there. Soon after the prophet Wise came in. I asked him before them all, whether he had not owned to Cawdry that he had lain with the prophetess. He could not deny it. While he was abusing me with much scurrility, the prophetess entered. She flew upon me, as if she would tear me to pieces, and laboured to outsaw[26] the truth with unparalleled confidence. Scholey and Cawdry confronted her, and repeated Wise's confession. She was all rage and fury, raving against them as villains and hypocrites, with the utmost excess of passion and outrage. She was not more lamb-like towards Mr. Hutchings and me, whom she slighted fools, blockheads, blind leaders of the blind, whose only design was to put out the eyes of this people. As for me, she said the devil was in me. And all this by inspiration from God who, she said, had revealed it to her what we were about and spoke in her. That I might not misrepresent her, I asked whether she was immediately inspired? She answered, "Yes." But as immediately as the prophets of old? "Yes." And does God as *really* speak in you as he did in them? "Yes." Was what you uttered last Thursday of sinless perfection by the immediate Spirit of God? She insisted it was, and went on in flat contradiction to the written word, asserting that if we say we have no sin, we *do not* deceive ourselves, but the truth *is* in us.[27]

I repeated to her the most shocking particulars of the forgoing account, which she owned and justified. As that she can call the angels and archangels, and command Christ himself to her in whatever shape she pleases. That God appears to her, sometimes as a dove, sometimes as an eagle. That in prayers she sees a little angel on a ladder with a cap and feather denoting the swiftness of his motion. That she was utterly above the use of means and ordinances. *That the sacrament was a beggarly element*, and God would shortly destroy all outward things, means, ordinances, and churches. Upon our answering her with, "It is written," she fully proved what Mr. Okeley testified he heard her say, namely that she would not go by what St. Paul said, but by the spirit in herself. "Away with your apostles" was one of her expressions; and others she used, equally blasphemous, to the full conviction of her hearers.

---

[24] John Hutchings (b. 1716) matriculated at Pembroke College, Oxford in 1734, where he became involved in the "Oxford Methodists." Receiving his BA in 1738, he became Charles Kinchin's curate at Dummer, Hampshire. He was present at the origins of the revival in London in 1739, but soon sided with the Moravians and stepped out of leadership. CW spells "Hutchins."

[25] John Robson (b. 1714), matriculated at Lincoln College, Oxford on May 17, 1732, where JW became his tutor. Over the next eight years Robson had a vacillating relationship to first the "Oxford Methodists" and the emerging Methodist revival. Robson received the BA in 1735, and the MA from New Inn Hall in 1742; but there is no record of him taking a parish.

[26] To see beyond, or surpass in foresight.

[27] Cf. 1 John 1:8.

Mr. Hutchings asked whether that was the spirit of meekness by which she spoke? "No!" said she, "but it is the lion of the tribe of Judah." That there was a roaring lion in her, seeking whom he might devour, I readily granted, for I never saw the devil so strong in any human soul. She demanded by what authority I taught the societies; said she would come among them in spite of me; and foretold, if she did not, they would all go down. I stayed asking her questions till all were thoroughly satisfied of what spirit she was of, and then asked "Who is on God's side? Who for the old, rather than the new prophets? Let them follow me." They all did so. God was remarkably present with us. Not a soul among us but was sensible of it.

The lesson for the day which I expounded was 1 John 4[:1–2], "Beloved, believe not every spirit, but try the spirits whether they are of God. Because many false prophets are gone out into the world. ... Every spirit that confesseth not that Jesus Christ is come in the flesh is not of God."

By this mark I proved the spirit of Mrs. Lavington not to be the Spirit of God. She doth not confess Jesus Christ. By her mouth she doth, but not in heart and life—unless adultery is a confession of him. This is the test our Lord himself gives us. "Beware of false prophets."[28] "By their fruits shall ye know them."[29] Hereby I know this woman to be a false prophetess. As likewise by her giving God the lie in contradicting his written word. Why therefore seek we farther witness? To the law and to the testimony![30] If they speak not after this word, it is because there is no light in them. Mrs. Lavington speaks not after this word, therefore there is no light in her. Therefore she is a child of the devil. Therefore she is false, if God is true.

*Source*: holograph account; MARC, DDCW 8/12.

---

[28] Matt. 7:15.
[29] Cf. Matt. 7:20.
[30] See Isa. 8:20.

## MARCH 28–APRIL 1, 1740[1]

Bengeworth[2]

**Friday, March 28.** Breakfasted again at Mr. [Benjamin] Seward's.[3] His wife still bore us company, perhaps for some other reason beside mere complaisance. After breakfast he civilly told her we had a little business and would not hazard a dispute. "So then, you would have me go away," said she and left us. My heart ached for her. He told me she had found him reading my letter, which occasioned her much disturbance; that his weakness would not yet allow of his expounding, but he never meant to forsake the society. I encouraged him, as God enabled me, to wait upon God that he might renew his strength; to show himself at the society, though he spoke nothing; to look for greater things which he should do and experience; and to prepare him for which his late sickness was sent.

The Tuesday after I came (he now informed me) it was strongly impressed upon his mind that we were here. He asked his wife whether one of the Mr. Wesleys was not come, and by her confusion saw that the intimation given him was true.

I left him confirmed in the truth and resolved, as God should strengthen him, to keep up the society. Alas poor world! Where are all thy devices now! Indeed I triumph over thee, but it is in the name of the Lord my God.

Passed the afternoon in taking leave, then called again on Mr. [Benjamin] Seward. His wife, you may be sure, would not appear now. However she took care to leave Henry [Seward][4] as a guard. I endeavoured to speak to his heart in all love and plainness, to convince him of sin, but in vain. Never did I meet a man of so little sense with so many evasions. I durst not let him escape out of my hands without telling him my thoughts of him, and therefore declared to him with much simplicity that he was now in his sins and in his blood, not born of the Spirit, not a believer, not a new creature, not a Christian—and if he died in his present condition, he would die eternally. You may guess what effect this had upon him. I told him he raged in vain, my hook was now within him. I had warned the sinner and delivered my own soul. "Your hook," cried he with much

---

[1] This manuscript is entirely in CW's hand. It was the source of, and provides greater detail than, the account of these days in CW, MS Journal.

[2] Bengeworth, Worcestershire; 1.5 miles east of Evesham.

[3] Benjamin Seward (born c. 1705), was the sixth son of John, steward to Thomas, 1st Viscount Windsor of Blackcastle (c. 1670–1738). Benjamin was born in Badsey, Worcestershire, and matriculated at St. John's College, Cambridge, in 1721. Although he took his degree, he decided not to enter ordained ministry and settled in the Evesham area.

[4] Henry Seward (birth year unknown) was the oldest of four surviving sons of John Seward (see Thomas and William below).

reviling, "what do you mean by your hook?" Benjamin answered with great sweetness, "You know, brother, Mr. Wesley is a fisher of men." As a minister, I told him, I now spoke and showed him his transgressions and his sins. He was not now in a state of salvation. It was my office (and charity in me, not want of charity) to tell him so, and that whether he would hear or whether he would forbear.

He could not comprehend how one man could possibly know another. I answered, if he had the Spirit of God and I had not he must necessarily discern me and I could not him. "For he that is spiritual judgeth all things, yet he himself is judged of no man."[5]

Benjamin was at a loss how to account for his having been much more tempted to passion since he was justified than before. I told him that before his corruptions lay undisturbed at the bottom of his heart, the devil let him be quiet, the world and he were friends. But now all the evil in him is brought out and purged away. The devil tempts him with all his force and malice because he belongs to Christ. And because Christ hath chosen him out of the world [the devil] hateth him; and he is exercised continually by the contradiction of sinners, that patience may have its perfect work.[6]

I had intended now to take my leave, but Mr. Seward pressed me to bring brother [Thomas] Maxfield[7] to breakfast with him before we set out tomorrow.

At the society I summed up all I had said and encouraged and exhorted them to stand by and build up one another, promising to see them again when God should direct my way to them. We had a few noisy ἀγοραβοι[8] among us, which much quickened and emboldened me. Our parting was such as I could wish.

**Saturday, March 29.** God having greatly blest my last to Mr. [Benjamin] Seward, I now wrote him another animating letter and carried it [to] him myself. All was civil and smooth till Henry [Seward] came. We knew his infirmity and begged and prayed him to forbear dispute. But we might as well have prayed a hurricane to stop, or begged the tide

---

[5] See 1 Cor. 2:15.

[6] Cf. James 1:4.

[7] Thomas Maxfield (d. 1784), a native of Bristol, was converted by Whitefield in 1739 in the earliest stages of the revival. Maxfield began assisting JW with pastoral duties there, and followed JW to London, where he became a trusted leader at the Foundery. During one of JW's absences, Maxfield ventured to preach, though a layman. JW initially resisted this innovation, until his mother Susanna convinced him in 1741 that Maxfield was "a son in the gospel." He then embraced Maxfield as the first lay traveling preacher. Maxfield was later ordained at Bath by the Bishop of Derry, to assist JW. Maxfield was trusted by JW and central to deliberations in Conference for two decades. But in the early 1760s he took the side of the perfectionist party in London. This led to a break from JW, with Maxfield setting up an independent chapel.

[8] Those of the market place, or "rabble"; cf. Acts 19:38.

to turn back. He had received a letter from Tom Seward,[9] informing him that the good Bishop of London entirely approved of their management of Benjamin. Benjamin smiled and said, "But you see God has defeated all your contrivances and brought good out of them, for it was your opposition which kept Mr. Wesley here. And as to your pleading the doctor's authority, is it to be imagined that a physician who is a Papist would advise his patient to send for a Protestant priest?" Here I said, "The very sight of you, Mr. Seward, has done me good. As iron sharpeneth iron, so doth a man's countenance his friend."[10] He replied, "And my seeing you, I am sure, has done me good; for I have slept better these three nights than ever and sensibly gather strength every day."

This Henry could not bear, but fell upon me for advising his brother to keep up the society. "I do indeed," said I, "advise him to keep it up, and you to drop it. His advice will prevail who has God on his side." Here poor Henry was quite gone. "Rogue," "rascal," "villain," "pickpocket," were all the titles he could afford me. He acknowledged his putting the pistols into his pocket (only to frighten me he said), but now he justified it and insisted I ought to be shot through the head. Mr. Benjamin with great meekness answered, "If I acted by your principles, I should use them upon you, for my friend is myself. But we know that in your state you *must* act and speak as you do." He was going on to vindicate Mr. [William] Morgan[11] and me, but I stopped him and desired him to leave that to God—never to dispute in our defence, at least not till he was stronger in body. Then it might sometimes be well to answer a fool according to his folly.[12] *Henry started up and most courageously pulled me by the nose.* The cries of Mrs. Seward stopped any farther violence. I was immediately filled with inexpressible comfort. Sat still and felt the hand of God upon me. Had not the least temptation to anger or fear. Said with perfect calmness to Mrs. Seward, "Be not disquieted, madam, upon my account. I have learned to turn the

---

[9] Thomas Seward (1708–90), the youngest son of John Seward, matriculated at St. Johns College, Cambridge in 1727. After taking his degrees and ordination, he served as rector of several parishes and ended his career as prebend of both Lichfield and Salisbury.

[10] See Prov. 27:1.

[11] William Morgan (born c. 1715), a native of Merthyr, Glamorgan, matriculated at Christ Church in 1734, received his BA in 1738 and was ordained deacon by the Bishop of Oxford in May 1738. He was appointed as curate at Idbury and Nether Westcote, Oxfordshire, and began some field preaching among the colliers of Kingswood (preceding Whitefield!). He welcomed CW in his parishes Mar. 1740. His openness to the revival likely led to him being removed from his curacy, as later that summer he was in London, participating in the Fetter Lane society, and soon drawn to join the Quakers. There is some evidence he then left ministry and trained for medicine.

[12] Cf. Prov. 26:5.

other cheek." Opened a testament[13] upon those words, "Jesus wept,"[14] and broke out with brother Maxfield into "Praise God from whom all blessings flow ...." Poor Henry was as the troubled sea which cannot rest, whose waters cast up mire and dirt. Benjamin was perfectly composed. Said to me, "You have now received one mark of Christ"; to his brother, "Was I what you are, I should turn you out of my house this moment." I would not let him proceed. Begged Mrs. Seward's pardon for the disturbance which I had been the innocent occasion of and offered to go. Benjamin stayed me a little, to see if Henry could recover himself, but in vain. I then took my leave of my dear friend (Henry refused to shake hands with such a rascal), confirmed my love to Mrs. Seward and wishes of her happiness, and departed, rejoicing that I was counted worthy to suffer shame for the name of Christ.

Henry followed me, like Shimei,[15] crying "Get ye out! Get ye out!" I missed my whip and sent brother Maxfield back for it. This little circumstance occasioned the delivery of my letter, which I had forgot before but now remembered to send to Mr. Benjamin. Took a turn and offered myself up to Christ to suffer whatsoever he should please to lay upon me. If this light suffering bring so great comfort, how shall we triumph in the fiery trial! Surely the spirit of glory shall then rest upon us!

After returning hearty thanks to our Lord, we set out by 11:00 for Westcote.[16] Never did we feel such joy and comfort before. We gloried in the cross of Christ and esteemed his reproach greater riches than the treasures of Egypt. We saw we had been led by the Spirit to Evesham, had finished the work which God gave us to do, and prospered in the thing whereto he sent us.

Found Mrs. Morgan hungering and thirsting after righteousness—the last was become first.[17] They desired me to expound the lesson. It happened to be St. Paul's Epistle to Philemon. I preached the gospel to a few neighbours from those words, "Grace to you, and peace from God our Father, and the Lord Jesus Christ."[18] In speaking to v. 15, "For perhaps he therefore departed for a season, that thou shouldest receive him forever," the Spirit was present with his demonstration and power. Brother Maxfield felt it and told me Mrs. Morgan had received forgiveness. She went up

---

[13] This is the first of several instances scattered through CW's journal letters where one sees his practice of bibliomancy—or seeking God's direction by opening a bible randomly and reading a passage.

[14] John 11:35.

[15] See 2 Sam. 16:7.

[16] Nether Westcote, Oxfordshire; 3.5 miles east of Burton-on-the-Water.

[17] Cf. Matt. 19:30.

[18] Philem. 3.

to prayer, informed us (but not till Sunday evening) that she had been filled with inexpressible joy and comfort, arising from an assured sense of pardon. That while she was praying in the dark a sudden damp came over her, for her having blasphemously thought her sins were forgiven. She knew not then from whom this fear proceeded but we did. Mr. Morgan had judged of her as Miss J. did of Miss Perrot[19] and laughed at us for fancying her not far from the kingdom of heaven. But hath not God chosen the things which are despised?

**Sunday, March 30.** I was greatly distracted by an unusual unnecessary premeditating what to preach upon. My late discourses had worked different effects. Some were wounded, some hardened and scandalized above measure. I hear of no neuters. The word has turned them upside down. In the pulpit, I opened the book and found the place where it was written, "The Spirit of the Lord is upon me, because he hath anointed me to preach the gospel to the poor ...."[20] I explained our Lord's prophetic office and described the persons on whom alone he could perform it. I found, as did others, that he owned me. We returned home from the altar with the voice of praise and thanksgiving among such as keep holiday. Mrs. Morgan felt every word we sang. I saw and felt it too, as did brother Maxfield. We hasted from dinner to that meat which the world knoweth not of.[21] Idbury church and churchyard were full.[22] I showed them wherein that holiness consists, without which no one shall see the Lord,[23] as described in the Beatitudes.[24]

Answered all their objections and divided to them the word of truth,[25] both law and gospel.[26] He whose word it was made it sharper than any two-edged sword. Several, I trust, were pierced to the dividing asunder their soul and spirit and joints and marrow.[27] One woman the commandment plainly slew. She fell down and was carried off *in a fit*. O that all hardened sinners were so wounded in spirit!

We hasted to Westcote—the poor people having, some of them, several miles to go after church. One told me he came from Buckland.

---

[19] Anne Perrot (b. 1705) of Bristol, mentioned in letters of Mehetabel (Wesley) Wright in 1744–45; and possibly Miss Jeffreys of Bristol, mentioned in CW, MS Journal.

[20] Luke 4:18.

[21] See John 4:32.

[22] Idbury, Oxfordshire; 4 miles east of Burton-on-the-Water.

[23] See Heb. 12:14.

[24] Matt. 5:1–12.

[25] See 2 Tim. 2:15.

[26] CW repeatedly uses this phrase to indicate he both sought to awaken them to their sin (through the law) and open them to the assurance of forgiveness (in the gospel).

[27] See Heb. 4:12.

I read prayers and preached the *pure gospel* from the Good Samaritan.[28] Surely he was in the midst of us pouring in his oil. Some seemed ready for him, and it cannot be long before he binds up their wounds and brings them into his inn and takes care of them. He gave money to me the host, that I too might take care of his patients. I was greatly concerned for their recovery. Brother Maxfield was full of power and hardly ever found so much of Christ before.

We adjourned to Mr. [William] Morgan's. His house was crowded as a minister's ought to be. I had thoughts in the morning of expounding Romans 7 and now a woman told me she had read that Mr. William Seward[29] had been convinced by my explaining Romans 7, which she therefore begged me to expound it now. I did so with great power (yet not I). The woman (I found by her tears) heard her own state (and not St. Paul's) described. Another good Dissenter was deeply affected. Mrs. Morgan thanked God through Jesus Christ our Lord, who hath delivered her. I appointed them to meet here again next Sunday evening, Mr. Morgan having yielded to the tempter and let the society drop.

**[Monday,] April 1.** Breakfasted with brother [Richard] Viney[30] at Mr. Bully's.[31] Found I could not dispatch my affairs this morning, and agreed to stay here till tomorrow. Encouraged [[Charles Graves[32]]] against the fear of man, which had almost separated him from the despised followers of Christ.

'Tis time to leave off. My love to all our dear brothers and sisters. Let us never forget to make mention of one another in all our prayers. I long to hear that *their soul* prospers, their one soul in all. [[What news from dear

---

[28] Luke 10:29–37.

[29] William Seward (1704–40), the fifth son of John Seward, was a gentleman of Badsey, Worcestershire when he was converted under CW's preaching. He became a strong supporter of Whitefield's evangelistic and philanthropic project in Georgia, accompanying Whitefield there on one trip. Seward died Oct. 22, 1740, from a blow struck by detractors while touring South Wales to raise support for Whitefield.

[30] Richard Viney (fl. 1738–44) was an early member of the Fetter Lane society, and interpreted for Peter Böhler, a German Moravian missionary, when he passed through London. Viney joined JW in visiting the Moravians in Germany in 1738. He stayed after JW returned, and aligned himself with the Moravians. Viney returned to England in 1739 and gave leadership to the Moravian continuation of the Fetter Lane society.

[31] Mr. Bully was a local supporter of the Methodists in Oxford in the late 1730s.

[32] Rev. Charles Caspar Graves (c. 1717–87), of Mickleton, Gloucestershire, matriculated at Magdalen College, Oxford in Oct. 1736, where he was drawn into the "Oxford Methodists." Graves was ordained deacon in 1740, at which time he formally disavowed the Methodists. He was reconciled to the Wesley brothers in 1742 and traveled with them for a time. In the early 1750s he was ordained a priest and became perpetual curate of the chapel in Tissington, Derbyshire, while continuing to offer support to surrounding Methodist societies as a clergyman.

Kitty?[33] Not so dear neither, but I could part with her for her good. O pray that I may be always likeminded.

Adieu!]]

[P.S.] Brother Cennick[34] has not [sent[35]] the letter he promised me. My best and heartiest love to his and my colliers.

Heard that a church living was vacant which probably I might have the refusal of, or rather which I might be refused. Had a sudden thought whether I ought not to be refused it, to demonstrate it is no fault of mine that I do not preach within stone-walls? Brother Maxfield, before I communicated my thoughts, had had the very same and himself first mentioned them to me. In all probability neither will the canons present me nor the bishop give me institution and induction. Should I not for this very reason offer myself, that they may be without excuse? What the living is, or where, I know not. I care not. Commend the matter to God and send me your advice to London.[36]

*Address*: "To / The Revd. Mr Wesley / at the School-house[37] / Bristol."
*Postmark*: "OXFORD."
*Endorsement*: by JW, "C[harles] March 31, 1740 / a[nswere]d Ap 5."
*Source*: holograph letter; MARC, MA 1977/503, Box 5, file 9.

---

[33] This may be Kitty Hargreaves, a friend of the Wesley family in Epworth who sent greetings to CW frequently in the early 1730s through letters of his sisters. More likely is a Kitty Davis in Bristol (mentioned once in JW's diary in 1741), but nothing more is known of her.

[34] John Cennick (1718–55) was a native of Reading, Berkshire. His grandparents had been Quakers, but his parents were loyal Church of England members. He experienced a religious transformation on Sept. 6, 1737, and sought out the Methodists in Oxford in late 1738. In 1739 JW employed him to teach at the Kingswood school, but he also preached occasionally and helped administer the society there. Within two years, however, he broke with JW, aligning first with Whitefield, and then throwing in his lot with the Moravians—for whom, in 1745, he became a pioneer preacher in Ireland. CW spells "Senwick."

[35] Orig., "promised"; almost certainly a mistake.

[36] This addition is written vertically in the left margin of the first page.

[37] I.e., the "New Room" which functioned as a school too, not the Kingswood school.

## APRIL 6–8, 1740[1]

London
April 1740

**Easter-day [April 6].** Rose at 5:00 and joined[2] with some of our brothers and sisters in praises to him who died and is alive again. The Foundery[3] was more than full at 7:00. I strongly preached Christ and the power of his resurrection from Philippians 3:9–10. My intention was not to mention one word of the controverted points till I had spoke with each of those who had troubled Christ's little ones, but God ordered it better. He led me, I know not how, *in ipsam aciem et certamen*.[4] How or where it came in I cannot conceive, but my mouth was opened and the Spirit gave me utterance as I never before experienced. I asked who hath bewitched you that you should let go your Saviour,[5] that you should cast away your shield, and your confidence, and deny you ever knew him? Somewhat like this (I don't well know what) I said, and there followed such a burst of sorrow as you never saw. Brother [Thomas] Maxfield had the full strong witness in himself. Near 1,000, he says, were melted into tears. I called them back to *their* Saviour, even *theirs*, in words which were not mine. Strongly pressed obedience to the divine ordinances and prayed my Saviour to stay his hand—and not set to his seal—unless I speak as the oracles of God.[6]

After preaching he sent me a witness of his truth, which I had delivered. A sister long in darkness through doubtful disputations came and declared Christ has again appeared unto her and confirmed his love, and reimprinted forgiveness on her heart. My heart for the time was as hers. Brother Maxfield was in the full triumph of faith.

We went to the house of God as friends, to his altar. I earnestly desired a token for good, and that if it was his truth I was defending I might defend it in his Spirit. I opened the Scripture upon Jeremiah 16:19, "O Lord my strength and my fortress and my refuge in the day of affliction." Asked him that I might not be moved this evening and believed I *had* the petition

---

[1] This manuscript (other than the first phrase and closing paragraph) is in the hand of Thomas Richards. It was the source of, and provides greater detail than, the account of these days in CW, MS Journal.

[2] These first six words are in CW's hand.

[3] A building on City Road, previously used for making cannons, that JW had leased in Jan. 1740 for meetings of his growing community (and housing for himself and CW, when they were in London).

[4] "Into the field of battle and contest"; cf. Cicero, *Epistulae ad Familiares*, XV.iv.16.

[5] See Gal. 3:1.

[6] See 1 Pet. 4:11.

I asked. Dined at Mrs. Hilland's.[7] Our brothers Bell,[8] Simpson,[9] and others, when the bell rung for church, said it is good to be here. "Well then," said I, "I will go myself and leave you to your antichristian liberty." Upon this they started up and bore me company. One of them told a poor man (as he owned in my hearing), "That comfort you received in the sacrament was given you by the devil." I should less blasphemously have called it the drawings of the Father.[10]

The Foundery in the evening was full within and without. I showed them their natural state, and the way to come out of it, in blind Bartimaeus who sat by the wayside begging.[11] I could not have so spoken of the ordinances, had not God instituted them. Every word came with power to our brother Maxfield, and I think he hath the Spirit of God. Not unto me, O Lord, not unto me.[12]

Walked with brother Maxfield (which I need not say) to Bower's,[13] where the bands were to meet. But the door was shut against us. I asked not wherefore, but carried the few sisters to John Bray's. He was out, hearing [Philip Henry] Molther.[14] Several others came afterwards. We joined in hearty prayers and praises. God blessed my words to their comfort and edification, and enlarged all our hearts in love to one another. The poor scattered sheep "knew my voice," and a stranger they will not follow, for they know not the voice of a stranger.[15]

---

[7] John Hilland (or Hyland, d. 1749), a hog butcher, of Old Street; and his wife Martha (d. 1767). See Benham, *Hutton*, 91. The scribe spells "Hiland" throughout the letter.

[8] Richard Bell, a watch-case maker of Vine Court, Bishopsgate Street, was active early in the Fetter Lane society and sided with the Moravians in the split within the society over "quietism." See Benham, *Hutton*, 89.

[9] John Simpson (born c. 1710) of Gainsborough, Lincolnshire, was admitted to Lincoln College, Oxford, in 1728, where in 1730 JW became his tutor. On graduation in 1731 Simpson was ordained and served as curate in Grayington, Lincolnshire for a while. JW's diary records several letters to him, as "Sympson" from 1733–38, but from 1739–40 as "Simpson." By 1739 Simpson was in London, and became one of the leaders in the Fetter Lane society advocating "stillness" or "quietism"; cf. JW, *Journal* Apr. 19, 1740 (*Works*, 19:146).

[10] See John 6:44.

[11] See Mark 10:46–52.

[12] See Ps. 115:1.

[13] Orig., "Bows's." George Bowers (1691–1757), a wholesale dealer in clocks in George Yard, Little Britain, was active early in Fetter Lane and emerged as a leading Moravian in the early 1740s. His last name is sometimes spelled "Bowes." See Benham, *Hutton*, 89, 97.

[14] Rev. Philip Henry Molther (c. 1714–80) was ordained by Count Zinzendorf in 1739 and appointed to missionary work in Pennsylvania. Arriving in London in October, Molther was faced with a three months' delay before his vessel sailed. James Hutton introduced him to the Fetter Lane society, where he was distressed with the popular charismatic phenomena. In reaction he encouraged a type of quietism, nearing complete separation from all church-related activities. This would lead to the disruption of the society on July 20, 1740.

[15] See John 10:4–5.

Within an hour John Bray and John Edmonds[16] came. I had thoughts of leaving them, but God would not suffer me. Let the hireling flee, whose own the sheep are not.[17]

John Bray took me aside and desired my brother Maxfield might be turned out. I submitted it to the women, who unanimously desired he might stay. Then (without losing an hour in dumb show) I gave out an hymn and prayed *according to God*. For an hour I spoke freely to our sisters, no one forbidding me. Confirmed my love to them, my disinterestedness, my success. Told them what God had done for my soul, and others through me. Gloried in the cross of Christ. Lamented their having been so troubled. Exhorted them to hold fast whereunto they had attained and never to forsake the holy ordinances, to be still in the use of means, to reverence the Moravians, to avoid all reasonings and disputes about their faith, and to go on to perfection.

Many close things God enabled me to speak concerning those that troubled them and would exclude us that they might affect them, yet all in the spirit of meekness. Once Satan thrust at me, but in vain, upon my mentioning brother Maxfield's leaving us or staying as they thought fit. They said, if I judged it proper, both Bray and Edmonds and the other men should all be excluded. I was going to declare this their determination when Bray and Edmonds came in, but was restrained when John Bray demanded why I had brought brother Maxfield. I asked a question or two of him: Whether he denied the ordinances to be commands? He answered indirectly, "I grant them to be great privileges." (Edmonds confessed more frankly that he had cast them off.) Whether he had not denied George Whitefield to have faith? This question he answered by begging to be excused. He denounced grievous woes against the women for suffering brother Maxfield to be present contrary to order.[18] They said that order had been imposed upon them when no minister was present, and they were threatened to be turned out unless they consented to it. I put my brother Bray in mind of his respect to the prophetess Lavington,[19] who was for having the men and women brought together again—that they "might sit shoulder to shoulder," as she called it. I did not mention because

---

[16] John Edmonds (1710–1803) was a founding member of the Fetter Lane society, and became one of the oldest surviving members of the English Moravian community. See Benham, *Hutton*, 33, 90, etc. The scribe spells "Edmunds" throughout the letter.

[17] See John 10:12.

[18] The group of men who organized the Fetter Lane society adopted guidelines on Sept. 26, 1738 that allowed for a meeting of a group of women, under the stipulation that no men would be present except their respective husbands, and the (clergy) persons who pray and expound the Scriptures. Since Maxfield was neither ordained nor married at that time, his presence violated this rule.

[19] Mary Lavington was associated with the "French prophets"; for CW's earlier encounter with her, see his MS Journal, June 7–12, 1739.

*I* approved her advice, but only to show him he was not infallible. To his question about brother Maxfield I replied I had brought him because two are better than one, "and because he can as easily discern your spirit, as you can mine."

Brother Maxfield did plainly see that his stillness was ruffled. He *showed* it by threatening to renounce all care of the bands till they refused Maxfield admittance. I mildly told him, and plainly, that I did not see what good he had done them since our leaving London, and desired to know if he could charge us with preaching another gospel. As to Molther, whom he accused me of slighting, I confessed I was not worthy to unloose the latchet of his shoes. Yet would I not give place to him or any other by subjection, no not for an hour. They slandered him indeed, who pretended his authority for casting off the ordinances. But whosoever *did* so, I would cast off him, although my own brother.

We concluded our conference with thanksgiving.

Below,[20] John Bray asked whether I should come to my band on Monday. I answered no, without having time to give the reason. He replied with equal charity, moderation, and humility, "Then you shall be expelled."

We returned home rejoicing. O when shall the temper I this evening enjoyed for ever rule in my heart.

**Monday, April [7].** Before preaching this morning I was greatly straitened,[21] and had I judged by feelings should not have preached at all. But no sooner had I begun than Christ was with my mouth, even Christ made unto us of God wisdom and righteousness.[22] The power of God was in the midst of us and the people flocked as doves to the windows. All love, all glory be to him!

In the hours of conference I was much assisted, but my time was too scanty for my business. Carried Maxfield and D.[23] to our sister Soane's.[24] Thence Mrs. Blund took me away in a coach to Kennington Common.[25] Brother Maxfield was full of the spirit of supplication. I called upon about

---

[20] I.e., the band meeting had been in an upstairs room.

[21] *OED*, includes the meaning "hampered or impeded."

[22] See 1 Cor. 1:30.

[23] Likely Charles Delamotte, whom CW had been with two days earlier; cf. MS Journal, Apr. 5, 1740. Delamotte had accompanied the Wesley brothers on their voyage to Georgia, in principle as his father's business agent. He was soon serving as schoolmaster and assisting JW in various pastoral duties. On his return to England, a few months after JW, he found that many of his family had been converted to the emerging Methodist revival. But Charles Delamotte was more drawn to the Moravian stream of the renewal.

[24] JW mentions being in the home of Mrs. Martha Soane in London several times between Mar. 1739 and Apr. 1740.

[25] A large park in Kennington, Surrey, about 1 mile south of London, across the River Thames.

8,000, "Ho everyone that thirsteth, come ye to the waters."[26] The love and esteem which this dear people bear me requires the counterbalance of our stronger brethren's contempt. It rained hard, but none were washed away. The strong man is disturbed,[27] I find, by a warning I have since received from my old friend [Richard] Goter[28] demanding £10 more, under pain of an arrest. Thou fox, thou fool, the bridle is in thy mouth!

My companions in the coach had been Quakers, but scandalized at their worldly-mindedness, had left them and cleaved to us. They begin to feel themselves sinners. We drank tea together at the Foundery. Thence I was called to supply Mr. [John] Simpson's place at [John] Hilland's society. [I] spoke affectingly from "the Spirit helpeth our infirmities [...] with groaning which cannot be uttered."[29]

Came from writing above to my brother Maxfield's assistance, who was engaged in dispute with Bell—but an overmatch for him, and much wiser in the things of God than his teacher, who now graciously allows him to be a child of God, although never brought into confusion by the still brethren. Brother Maxfield says that as often as any of them sets upon him, he is filled with the Spirit of faith working by love.[30] He could even die for those who by their vehemence and unloving eagerness give the lie to their own professions of stillness. Him they cannot bear, whom they look upon as the only hindrance to my conversion, and very unquiet they are, because the hope of [converting] me is in vain.

**Tuesday, April 8th.** At six met [John] Simpson and [William] Oxlee at the Foundery. Simpson told me plainly if I recommended the ordinances he must preach against me. I avowed my resolution never to give them up, as he and our poor deluded brethren had done. He tried all his Moravian questions on brother Maxfield.

*Illidens solido.*[31]

---

[26] Isa. 55:1.

[27] See Mark 3:27.

[28] On July 13, 1739 a legal writ was prepared against CW by Richard Goter, claiming damages from CW trespassing on his land two days earlier, on his way to preach on Kennington Common. The writ survives (MARC, DDCW 4/3). See also CW, MS Journal, July 29, 1739 and Oct. 18, 1739. CW paid the original fine of £20 (£19.16s.8d. after taxes) on Feb. 29, 1740 (MARC, DDWes 7/30A), inscribing the receipt, "I paid them the things I never took. To be re-judged in that day." Goter appears to be seeking a penalty for late payment.

[29] Rom. 8:26.

[30] See Gal. 5:6.

[31] "Remained resolute under the attack."

He that is spiritual judgeth all things, but is himself judged of none.[32]

Preached to a still crowded audience from Mark 2:10,[33] "The Son of man hath power on earth to forgive sins." Anne Young (one who has been brought into confusion) testified that power, having now received the witness into herself. Several others come out of darkness daily and recover their comfort.

James Hutton[34] called and spoke a few words of expostulation with mildness and love. He is the only still one whom I have not seen ruffled.

Breakfast with Maxfield at Bell's junior,[35] who returns to his confidence which he let go when he dropped the ordinances. His whole household allows that there *are* means of grace, and wait for the Spirit *in* them not *from* them.

Many poor sinners came to confer with me today about their souls. Two hours is full little for this work of the ministry.

At 1:00 the women's bands met by my appointment. I began praying and was quite melted down. So were all. God owned me though man will not. I spoke largely of their being brought into the wilderness, of their folly and ingratitude in giving up not his ministers only but their Saviour himself. My love and sorrow ran through them all. A sister whom Molther had recommended first bore her testimony, that she received the atonement by my ministry and the witness of the Spirit by Molther's, who himself advised her to go to the sacrament. I hence took occasion to vindicate the Moravians from the slander of their preaching against the ordinances. Showed the women that their forsaking them sufficiently accounting for their being forsaken of Christ. Earnestly dissuaded them from reasoning and disputing, from vindicating me, from saying I am of Paul and I of Apollos,[36] from the double extreme of trusting in the means or slighting them—but above all from ever resting till they were in the full and glorious liberty of the sons of God, and so born of God that they could not commit sin.

---

[32] See 1 Cor. 2:15.

[33] Orig., "2:9"; a mistake.

[34] James Hutton (1715–95) was the son of Rev. John Hutton (1676–1750), a nonjuror who had resigned his living, and whose wife was the former Elizabeth Ayscough, second cousin to Sir Isaac Newton. The Huttons boarded scholars at Westminster School, and lived in a house adjoining that of Samuel Wesley Jr. in Dean's Yard, Westminster. Like CW, James Hutton was educated at Westminster. James was converted by JW's sermon "One thing is needful," preached on the eve of JW's departure for Georgia in 1735. Hutton saw the party off at Gravesend, but was dissuaded by his parents from accompanying them. He followed their progress with keen interest, and the Hutton home became a clearing-house for letters to and from Georgia. On the Wesley brothers' return to England, Hutton co-operated in their religious activities, and published many of their early works. When JW and CW split with the Moravians, however, Hutton parted company with them and became a key English leader of that movement.

[35] Apparently the married son and namesake of Richard Bell, also of London.

[36] See 1 Cor. 1:12; 3:4.

Mrs. Jackson[37] also, and others, witnessed a good confession of what God had done for their souls through our ministry. If Christ be not with us, who hath begotten us these? The witnessing Spirit was amongst us now, therefore our hearts danced for joy and in our song did we praise him.

I drank some tea at Mr. \_\_\_,[38] in the borough, who keeps a boarding school. His wife, himself, and sisters seemed not far from the kingdom of God. I spake of the love of Jesus to the Misses.[39] They were all affected, as they showed by their tears. O how easily might children receive Christ, if he were truly preached to them. Mrs. Seaton[40] took me to the Common in a coach. There could not be fewer than 10,000 present. My hoarseness was suspended while I preached the gospel from Luke 14[:13ff.] and compelled the poor, the maimed, the halt, and the blind to come in. Glory, all glory be to Christ Jesus, who is with his ministers always!

In the coach was Mrs. Gardner. My soul immediately took acquaintance with her, and had the same kind of impression which I felt at first sight of Miss P.[41] and Mrs. Morgan.[42] I told her I should soon rejoice over her with singing. We drove to Mr. Crouch's.[43] A violent persecutor was at the society. The book I found opened upon Philippians, and spoke powerfully from those words, chapter 1:25ff., "And having this confidence, I know I shall abide and continue with you all, for your furtherance and joy of faith, that your rejoicing may be more abundant in Jesus Christ, for me by my coming to you again. Only let your conversation be as [it] becometh the gospel of Christ, that whether I come and see you, or else be absent, I may hear of your affairs, that ye stand fast in one spirit, with one mind, striving together for the faith of the gospel and in nothing tempted[44] by the adversaries ...."

[Tuesday,] April 15. Expect more in my next. Write soon and largely. I do not forget my dear brothers and sisters and trust they do not forget me. How go they on at Kingswood?[45] My best and heartiest love to you. My

---

[37] CW, MS Journal identifies as "Jane Jackson."

[38] CW, MS Journal fills in the name: "Hawthorn's."

[39] I.e., the girls in Mr. Hawthorn's school.

[40] Orig., "Eaton"; likely a mistake. Mrs. Seaton appears repeatedly in CW, MS Journal at this time.

[41] This may be Sarah Perrin (1708–87), a Quaker woman with evangelical leanings whom CW met in Bristol sometime in 1740. See Gareth Lloyd, "Sarah Perrin," *Methodist History* 41 (2003): 79–88.

[42] The wife of William Morgan, earlier curate at Westcote Barton, Oxfordshire.

[43] Mr. (Timothy?) and Mrs. Crouch, of Dowgate Hill, hosted a society meeting in their home.

[44] The scripture reads "terrified."

[45] Originally a royal hunting preserve (the "King's Wood"), this Gloucestershire area about four miles east of Bristol was the site of several coal pit mines. William Morgan had pioneered field preaching in this area, joined soon by Whitefield and the Wesley brothers.

brethren George and John Reynolds must write to me. It will do good. Get them a secretary. Let prayer be made without ceasing by the church for me. My soul is among lions. Who is sufficient for these things. Be strong.[46]

*Address*: "To / The Revd Mr Wesley / at the School-house / Bristol."
*Postmark*: "15 / AP."
*Endorsement*: by JW, "C[harles] April 15, 1740 / a[nswere]d 19 +."
*Source*: original letter by amanuensis; MARC, MA 1977/503, Box 5, file 8.

---

Whitefield initiated the plan in Apr. 1739 of building a school there for educating the children of the coal miners, leaving this project in JW's hands when he departed for North America.

[46] This last paragraph is added in CW's hand.

## MAY 8–15, 1740[1]

[London]
1740

**Thursday, May 8.** The power of God was with us greatly in the morning exposition, but much more while we prayed with some of our sisters. Brother [Westley] Hall was just returned. Howell Harris[2] joined us. The Spirit of supplication was poured out and enlarged our hearts with love inexpressible. Our hearts, I say, for even mine was affected as I have seldom or never before experienced. Sister Millar sunk under the power of love and received a second benefit. Christ sent no one of us empty away.

Breakfasted at Elizabeth Spring's. Her sister[3] who had been delivered on Monday evening was waiting in calm confidence for the fullness of the promise. Another (who had likewise received forgiveness under my ministry), while I was turning her to her own heart, had such a sight of it as quite overpowered her. They sent after us to Hilland's, where we were confirming our love to poor dear cold Mr. [John] Simpson. We prayed by her and she recovered the sense of her justification, and is now looking to Jesus the author, that he may be the finisher of her faith.[4]

Met the band upon trial in the afternoon and found them all come forward and *truly still*[5] in the means. My brother Hall preached most explicitly on pure simple believing. Howell Harris declared his experience to the society. O what a flame was kindled in all our hearts! Never man spake (in my hearing) as this man spake. What a nursing-father hath God sent us. He has indeed learned of the Good Shepherd to carry the lambs in his bosom and gently lead them that are with young. Such love, such power and simplicity have I never known. O we have no man like-minded, English or Moravian. The lambs dropped down on all sides into their shepherd's arms. He spoke with the greatest demonstration of the Spirit, especially on the ordinances. Those words broke out like thunder, "I now find a commission from God to invite all poor sinners, justified or unjustified, to his altar, and I would not for 10,000 worlds be the man that should keep

---

[1] This manuscript (other than the last sentence and initials) is in the hand of Westley Hall. It was the source of, and provides greater detail than, the account of these days in CW, MS Journal.

[2] Howell Harris (1714–73), a Welsh schoolmaster, began to preach and found societies in Wales within a few months of his conversion in 1735. With Daniel Rowland, he was the founder of Welsh Calvinistic Methodism. Although on doctrinal grounds he was more attracted to Whitefield, Harris sought to avoid theological rivalries, and had generally friendly relations with the Wesley brothers. His first name is often spelled "Howel."

[3] Lucy Spring; see CW, MS Journal, May 7, 1740.

[4] See Heb. 12:2.

[5] Emphasis shown by capitalized initial letters in original.

any from it. There I first found him myself. That is the place of meeting." He went on with irresistible power. God called forth his witnesses to the truth. Several declared they had found Christ in the ordinances, some had received forgiveness of sins, some on the witness of the Spirit.

Poor Simpson stood by hardening his heart (as afterwards appeared) against conviction. I trust he was the only one whose eyes God did not at this time open. We could not part before 11:00 [p.m.] Scarce any from Fetter Lane were present.[6] Too good care had been taken to prevent them.

**Friday, May 9.** Went to Islington[7] intending to baptize Bridget Armsted.[8] Satan hindered by his churchwardens. They were ready to tear Mr. [George] Stonehouse[9] to pieces for letting me profane the church by baptizing in it last week, and threatened me with a prosecution on that account. Can any one forbid water? Not unless they can dry up the Thames. Christ will quickly show us[10] what river is to be consecrated into a font. At the time of conference Mrs. Dupee[11] informed me she had received the atonement last week while I was preaching it. Is his hand shortened at all that he cannot save;[12] or because we are weak, hath he no power to deliver?

Met at 1:00 with near 100 of the society to keep the fast. Christ met us wonderfully in this his ordinance. Howell Harris, that son of consolation, was present. We were melted down in prayer. The Spirit helped our infirmities, and made intercession with groanings that cannot be uttered.[13] A great power of faith was among us, and reached some who I believe had never experienced it before. Glory be to God that I find the small seed grows, the little leaven spreads, and am persuaded that he who is the

---

[6] JW and Peter Böhler had co-founded a new religious society on Fetter Lane in London on May 1, 1738. In Oct. 1739 Philip Henry Molther, a Moravian who had recently arrived in London while JW was in Bristol, convinced some members of the society of a type of "spiritual stillness" or abstinence from sacraments and devotional practices *until* after one has faith, which was now splitting the society in two—the Moravian-inclined members would remain at Fetter Lane while those aligned with the Wesley brothers moved to the Foundery.

[7] Islington, Middlesex; 3 miles northeast of Charing Cross.

[8] Bridget Armsted (b. c. 1716), a single woman raised a Quaker, appears repeatedly in the Foundery Band Lists (1742–46). CW spells "Armstead"; we follow the spelling in the lists and in JW's *Journal*.

[9] George Stonehouse (1713–93), a native of Hungerford Park, Berkshire, matriculated at Pembroke College, Oxford, in 1729, receiving his BA (1733) and MA (1736). Ordained deacon in June, and elder in September 1737, Stonehouse was appointed vicar of St. Mary's, Islington. He was part of the Oxford Methodists during his student years, and opened his pulpit and churchyard to the Wesley brothers and Whitefield at the outset of the revival, until his churchwardens ended this practice.

[10] Orig., "up."

[11] Margaret Breckley had married John Dupee in March 1738. She was a member of a married women's band at the Foundery in 1745 and died in 1750.

[12] See Isa. 59:1.

[13] See Rom. 8:26.

author will likewise be the finisher of *my* faith.

Went to give the sacrament to a dying woman; found an old subtle pharisee. Could have no access in speaking and betook myself to prayer. The sin-convincing Spirit came mightily upon her, so that she roared for very disquietness of spirit. The strong man armed, who had peaceable kept [in] his house for above seventy years was now disturbed, bound, tormented, cast out.[14] She broke out into strong cryings, and soon after into blessings and thanksgivings. As far as I can discern she is set at liberty. We showed forth our Lord's death and I am sure he was with us of a truth.

At Wapping I spoke to the hearts of many from those words of Isaiah, "Ye have sold yourselves for nought, and ye shall be redeemed without money."[15] Went thence to Rag Fair[16] intending to expound, but found Mr. Simpson there and heard instead of speaking. My presence was a great check upon him, so that I was under no necessity of contradicting him. I did him honour in the presence of the people and confirming his saying with singing and prayer.

**Saturday, May 10.** Spoke strongly to those who trusted in their faith of adherence and insisted largely on that lowest mark of the new birth, forgiveness of sins.

After sermon, my back was scarce turned when [William] Oxlee took his opportunity to draw away Howell Harris to deaf [Richard] Bell's. I came [in] time enough to break off their conference and disengaged my unwary friend, who now, without distrusting God, resolves to go nowhere without me. Two are better than one. He loves dispute just as I do. Our brethren may keep it all to themselves. Their words doth eat as doth a canker, especially Oxlee's. O that viper whom you have cherished in your bosom! God help me to love him! I abhor his principles and practices.

Joined at brother Hall's with him and Howell Harris in reading George Whitefield's journal.[17] We found him present in spirit. God is humbling me. I feel he is. When I am tried, I shall come forth as gold. Met sister Hamilton's band and left them more confirmed in the truth as it is in Jesus. Thought of speaking of [George] Bower's[18] society upon that of Elijah, "How long halt ye between two opinions."[19] When I came there, Bell was just beginning to present. John Bray, James Hutton, [William]

---

[14] See Mark 3:27.

[15] Isa. 52:3.

[16] An infamous street market in east London.

[17] It is not clear whether they are reading a recent manuscript journal, or the journal extracts covering 1737–39 that were now in print.

[18] Orig., "Bowe's."

[19] 1 Kings 18:21.

Oxlee, [William] Holland,[20] [Richard] Ridley[21] and others of the same class sat by. I withstood them to their face because they were to be blamed, and appealed to God that answereth by fire[22] for the truth of my doctrines that the ordinances bind all, both justified and unjustified. Read some verses on false stillness,[23] which James Hutton was much displeased at and ignorantly asked which of the prophets ever wrote verses! A woman testified that the last time I had expounded here and bade them who had been confounded [to] ask Jesus Christ whether they had faith, she did ask in our prayers and immediately the love of God was shed abroad in her heart by the Holy Ghost which was then given her.

The Foundery was crowded. Ridley, etc., followed me thither, for whose sakes I preached on [1] John 2:12ff., "I write unto you, little children, because your sins are forgiven you for his name's sake. ... I have written unto you, young men, because ye are strong, and the word of God abideth in you, and ye have overcome the wicked one." Hence I showed the three particulars which differentiate[24] a child of God from a young man. The young man is strong; the child is weak. The young man hath overcome the wicked one; the child is overcoming him. In the young man the word of God abideth (i.e., he hath the constant witness of the indwelling Spirit); in the child the word of God abideth not (i.e., he hath not [the[25]] constant witness of the indwelling Spirit, but only visits from him now and then, as pledges and tokens that he will shortly come and make his abode with him forever). I never spoke with like power. Ridley could not stand it, but went out again and again, yet still returned. I kept the society after sermon. Several from Fetter Lane desired admittance. Howell Harris spoke most excellently of good works, searching the scriptures, and loving one another. I enforced his advice and prayed them to avoid all disputes. "Then you should not give matter for disputing in your sermons," said Knight most modestly. I thanked him for his kind admonition, but gave all warning that before any could be admitted into the society he must first come to me and

---

[20] William Holland (d. 1761), a painter of Basinghall Street, London, was a devout member of the Church of England who in 1738 introduced the Wesley brothers to Luther's commentaries on Galatians and Romans. He was a founding member of the Fetter Lane society. When the Wesley brothers withdrew in 1740, Holland and his wife Elizabeth (née Delamotte, a sister of Charles and William) remained in this now solidly Moravian society.

[21] Richard Ridley was a member of the Fetter Lane society; cf. JW, *Journal*, May 8, 1742, *Works*, 19:261–62.

[22] See 1 Kings 18:24.

[23] CW was surely reading *The Means of Grace*, an extended hymn he published as a broadsheet in Apr. 1740; cf. *HSP* (1740), 35–39.

[24] Orig., "difference"; an archaic use as a verb.

[25] Orig., "been."

enter his name. I fear this rule will exclude my friend Knight and all his disputatious fraternity.

**Sunday, May 11.** Preached forgiveness of sins to a very numerous audience from Isaiah 43:25ff., "I, even I, am he that blotteth out thy transgressions for mine own sake and will not remember thy sins. Put me in remembrance. Let us plead together. Declare thou that thou mayest be justified." I showed the damning sin of unbelief which makes God a liar continually, and spoke (I trust) searchingly to the hearts of many.

Met the woman leaders for the first time and, after a comfortable prayer, led them to the Lord's Table at St. Paul's.

Dined with a good Dissenter (I know not of what denomination) and went thence to the Common. My brother Hall preached at the same time at [the] Foundery, which made me wonder to find above 30,000 waiting to hear me. The hand of the Lord was upon me, and I prophesied, "O ye dry bones, hear the word of the Lord."[26] Truly there were very many in the open valley, and lo they were very dry. But as I prophesied there was a noise, and behold a shaking, which we saw and heard. Into some of them, I am confident, the breath came and they lived. Ascribe ye unto the Lord the honour due unto his name.[27] I feel I am nothing—worse, infinitely worse than nothing. But Christ is all in all!

Had a delightful love feast[28] at the Foundery and invited our brothers and sisters in Bristol and Wales to be spiritually present with us.

**Monday, May 12.** Was much rejoiced this morning with the sight of my dear brother Benjamin Seward. Howell Harris and Mr. Hall completed our band. We read one of George Whitefield's journals and drank into his spirit. Employed three hours most profitably in conferring with the poor people. Hear of several who daily receive forgiveness or the witness of the Spirit. Three or four were now set at liberty in immediate answer to prayer.

Drank tea at Miss Branford['s] who has been in almost continual darkness ever since her eyes were first opened (two years ago at St. Helen's [church][29]) to see her sins forgiven. In prayer the love of God was shed abroad in her heart and she found herself translated into his marvellous light.

An aged gentlewoman here testified that she had long denied that article of her creed, "I believe [in the] forgiveness of sins," but was experimentally convinced of it yesterday under my brother Hall's ministry. I have also the frequent satisfaction of meeting sinners who have passed

---

[26] Ezek. 37:4.

[27] See Ps. 29:1.

[28] A service in which participants share non-consecrated bread and water with one another. JW had adapted the service from Moravian practice. In both settings it focused on praise and fellowship.

[29] See CW, MS Journal, July 11, 1738.

from death unto life in hearing our brother Whitefield. Our still strong brethren of Fetter Lane deny the fact that any soul has been justified by our ministry since no one gives what he has not himself. "These men have not faith, have not the Spirit; how then can they confer it?" I answer, not at all—yet as much a[s] St. Peter could, or St. Paul. The Holy Ghost is the gift of Christ, and is not communicated by or *from* but *through* the ministers. But some of our more sober brethren allow he hath been received by the hearing of faith, while we were the preachers. Here then they are under a necessity of granting either that George Whitefield hath the Spirit of faith or that a minister can give (that is transmit) the grace he hath not himself. They will rather allow the latter (though our church teaches it). And here we join Jesus with them, so God be the more magnified. "Give God the glory. We know that these men are sinners."[30]

Met the women, who grow in the spirit of peace, unity, and concord. Endeavoured to convince a thronged audience of unbelief. I think God is more and more with me and desire to give him all glory.

**Tuesday, May 13.** Cut off some from their confidence in the flesh. Their resting in a desire of forgiveness without forgiveness. Met a band as usual to our mutual comfort, and proceeded in George [Whitefield]'s journal.

Sarah Redford (justified under the word on Sunday last), Mary Barraby, Ann Broad[31] (a few days since), and others were with me today, testifying the work of God upon their souls.

Dined at Mr. Wilkinson's with Mr. Ball,[32] [Mr.] Buckmaster, and the others that had been concerned in getting us the Foundery. I trust the time was well bestowed upon them.

Met Mrs. [Elizabeth] Witham's[33] band at her house and took Mrs. Ricard in upon trial. When in the depth of despair Christ had given her rest, Satan came in by means of our brethren and gained such advantage over her that she even denied the faith and its author. "Woe unto the man by whom the offence cometh."[34] Our Lord has confirmed his love unto her by me, a worm and no man, the very scorn of men, and outcast of the still ones.

Expounded first at the society in Hare Street,[35] then at Mr. Crouch's

---

[30] Cf. John 9:24.

[31] Mary Barraby is still active in a married women's band at the Foundery in 1745; Ann Broad, in a single women's band. See Foundery Band Lists.

[32] Likely John Ball, who was a member of the select society for married persons, and leader of a married men's band at the Foundery in 1745.

[33] Elizabeth (Harrison) Witham was an early supporter of the Wesley brothers and remained active at the Foundery until her death on Nov. 29, 1747; see CW's elegy "On the Death of Mrs. Elizabeth Witham," *HSP* (1749), 1:282–86.

[34] Matt. 18:7.

[35] It is unclear whether this is a religious society or the "friendly society" that met at the White Horse, on Hare Street, in Bethnal Green.

upon, "The Spirit and the bride say, Come. ..."[36] Met the men leaders with brother Hall at Bray's. Was surprised to find between 20 and 30 of the brethren, and more [surprised] to hear that they constantly meet every Thursday and Sunday evening, the while[37] I preach at the Foundery. The reason is too obvious.

I bore my testimony for the ordinances and weak faith.[38] Asked whether they did not teach: 1) that the means of grace are neither means nor commands; 2) that forgiveness of sins is never given but together with the constant witness of the Spirit. James Hutton would not have them give me an answer. I said if they durst not stand and avow their principles, I should take their silence for confession and warn the people of God to beware of them. Our brother Hall spoke in much meekness and love, but they refused to hear the voice of the charmer. [Joseph] Hodges[39] bore testimony to the power of God accompanying the word preached, which [William] Stanton[40] and most of them deny. We came to no conclusion, only (we trust) our presence prevented some mischief.

**Wednesday, May 14.** 7:30 [[Foundery]], Howell [Harris] expounded this morning. We afterwards met a band. Spoke with a woman to whom Jesus lately appeared but immediately vanished out of her sight. Never did I see [a] soul more inconsolable. Esther Owen[41] was also with me—pierced, melted, overpowered with love. Toward noon took coach with Howell Harris, etc., and were exceedingly comforted in reading John Gambold's extract of the martyrs.[42] Came to Mrs. [Jane] Sparrow's.[43]

---

[36] Rev. 22:17.

[37] I.e., "at the same time."

[38] CW's concern to defend the validity of *degrees* of faith led to publishing on May 24 another broadsheet hymn titled *The Life of Faith;* cf. *HSP* (1740), 6–20.

[39] Joseph Hodges (1710–78), a smith, was one of the members of the Fetter Lane society who aligned with the Moravians and became a much-valued member of the community. See Benham, *Hutton,* 93, 411.

[40] William Stanton (1704–54), a butcher and brewer, also aligned with the Moravians. He and his wife moved to Broad Oaks to care for the children in the school. See Benham, *Hutton,* 90.

[41] Esther Owen's name is listed in the 1745 Foundery Band List in one of the married women's bands.

[42] John Gambold (1711–71), son of a Pembrokeshire vicar, matriculated at Christ Church, Oxford in 1726, receiving his BA in 1730 and MA in 1734. In 1730 he also became part of the "Oxford Methodists." Ordained in 1733, Gambold was appointed vicar of Stanton Harcourt. Over the next decade he grew increasingly estranged from the Wesley brothers and drawn to the Moravians. In 1742 he left the Church of England and became minister of the Moravian congregation in London. In 1754 he was consecrated the first English Moravian bishop. He was writing a tragedy, *The Martyrdom of Ignatius,* at that time and consulting both Wesley brothers on it; the work was published only posthumously in 1773.

[43] Jane Sparrow (d. 1748), a widow and supporter of the Wesley brothers, owned a manor house in Lewisham called The Limes.

Preached at Blackheath[44] from Ephesians 1:7, "In whom we have redemption through his blood, for forgiveness of sins, according to the riches of his grace." God gave me power, I humbly hope, "to sound the unbelieving hearts."[45] A woman screamed out so loud that I could not be heard and was therefore forced to have her removed, but not out of hearing. To the scoffers I spoke with much contention and power. Many were driven off and others constrained to stay. I am sure the word did not return void. Ascribe unto the Lord worship and praise.

We found Mr. Hall in the society, asking whether they were for trying their spirits by the word, or the word by the spirits. I enforced the question, which they would fain evade. Rabbi Hutton[46] forbad their answering me. I accepted the opportunity and warned the few remaining brethren to beware of the leaven of stillness. I showed them the delusion of our other poor brethren that had cast off the ordinances and confined the faith to those only of their own opinions. Foretold the dreadful consequence of their enthusiasm. Set the case of Gregor[47] before their eyes. Besought, entreated, conjured them not to renounce the means, or deny the Lord that bought them. The longer I spoke, the stiller I was—that is, the more tenderly concerned for their souls.

Many reflections, you may suppose, and accusations followed, of which I took little notice. Read a letter from one that had been strongly tempted to leave off the sacrament, but in receiving fully and powerfully convinced that her dissuader was the devil. Hodges's testimony, which he gave me to read, was I believe of great use; so [also] Howell Harris's and my brother Hall's. Others were heartily emboldened to bear their testimony to the divine ordinances. By the strength of God we trust we have stood between the living and the dead, and the plague is stayed.

Poor James [Hutton] was all tergiversation.[48] O how unlike himself! The honest plain undesigning Jacob is now turned a subtle close ambiguous Loyola.[49] [Richard] Bell was more frank, whom I therefore put upon speaking. He expressly denied the sacrament to unjustified sinners—that

---

[44] Blackheath, Kent; 1 mile northeast of Lewisham. Both Whitefield and the Wesley brothers preached on a small open hill in the area.

[45] Cf. "Hymn on the Descent of the Holy Ghost at Pentecost (altered from Henry More)," st. 8, *HSP* (1739), 186:
> The Spirit of convincing speech,
> Of power demonstrative impart,
> Such as may every conscience reach,
> And sound the unbelieving heart.

[46] CW is using the title in a derogatory sense.

[47] Spelled "Greger" in CW, MS Journal; the intended reference is unclear.

[48] *OED*: "The action of 'turning one's back on,' i.e., forsaking, something in which one was previously engaged, interested, or concerned."

[49] I.e., Ignatius Loyola (1491–1556), founder of the Jesuit order.

is, in effect, to all but [Philip] Molther, Mary Ewsters,[50] and himself, for these three are all the church Christ has in England. I mentioned a late information of Mrs. Seaton that Simpson had promised her if she would but leave off the sacrament, prayer, and reading the Scriptures for one week, she should then find what she never found before in her life. He too confessed and justified his advice, which he had given to several, to lay aside the Scriptures because (thought he) they trusted in them. He spoke more moderately than ever I heard him before. The rest seemed to abate somewhat of their stillness and much desired me to preach Christ the foundation, meaning that I should not recommend the ordinances but let them trample upon them unmolested. I did not say that I understood them.

**Ascension Day. Thursday, May 15.** At the Foundery, as Howell Harris had done expounding, prayed with two bands who had much of the love of God abroad in their hearts and earnestly longed for his appearance. Stood godfather with Howell Harris to my brother [Westley] Hall's child,[51] and passed an hour or two at the Christian christening.

Brethren pray for your poor weak brother.

C. W.[52]

*Address & Postmark*: none; likely hand delivered.
*Source*: original letter by amanuensis; MARC, MA 1977/503, Box 5, file 10.

---

[50] Orig., "M. Eusters." Mary Ewsters (b. 1723) was made Warden of the Single Sisters' Choir when the London Congregation of the Moravians organized in 1742. See Benham, *Hutton*, 95, 97.

[51] According to the parish records of St. George's in Bloomsbury, Samuel Westley Hall, the son of Westley and Martha (Wesley) Hall, was baptized on May 2, 1740. It is unclear whether the date was recorded incorrectly there, or if this is a second christening service for their Methodist family. Samuel did not survive to adulthood.

[52] Only the last line and the signature are in CW's handwriting.

## June 19–21, 1740[1]

[Oxford / Bristol]

[June 19, Thursday.] By 12:00 [noon] we came to Oxford, and were much refreshed by our dear brother [John] Robson. As I entered the city (doubting whether I should attempt in my short stay to bring those whom [John] Simpson had been beforehand with me in perverting), I opened my Testament upon Hebrews 10:9, "Then he said, behold, I come to do thy will, O God. He taketh away the first, that he may establish the second." Read my journal to Robson, who vehemently longs to join hand in hand with us.

Called on Mrs. Ford[2] and saw the still ones had been with her by the change of her countenance. She was not the person I left her, but straitened and shut up in Moravian closeness. I found who had been her teacher, by her immediately beseeching me *not to speak* in the society, not to make disturbances and divisions, etc. She could not (upon my asking it) give me any reason for her apprehensions. I had preached the truth from the beginning, I told her, and spoke no other words now. Whence then this unusual suspicion of me? She could or would not explain it, but Mr. Simpson's presence abundantly accounts for it. Wherever he comes, his first business is to supplant us; and this he does by gradually insinuating himself under the appearance of our friend. This gains him admittance. Then he allows God has used us for awakening souls, but as to aught farther, *Nemo dat quod non habet*.[3] If they would be built up, they must come to him. We pretend to speak against works, he says, but no one trusts in them more. He has not yet expressly spoken against ordinances, only in private to Mrs. Fox,[4] [Mrs.] Ford, Charles Graves, and a few others. These he has laboured hard to set against their old ministers, and I bear him record that Satan himself, that great sower of tares, is not more successful in alienating hearts and separating chief friends.

When I come to speak to any whom he has touched the same words which I have spoken from the beginning, their jealousy and fears are alarmed and they desire me not to dispute—that is, when he has given them the poison he sets them against the antidote.

Mrs. Ford had found out now that there are no means of grace, no ordinances or duties. Hearing my journal and expounding afterwards half

---

[1] This manuscript (other than a couple of notes in the margins) is in the hand of Thomas Richards. It was the source of, and provides greater detail than, the account of these days in CW, MS Journal.

[2] Mrs. Ford, of Oxford, had frequently entertained the Wesley brothers since at least Oct. 1738 (see JW, *Works*, 19:357).

[3] "No one can give what he does not have."

[4] Mrs. Fox and her husband, of Oxford sponsored a society at their house and were closely aligned with the Wesley brothers since early 1738 (see JW, *Works*, 18:228).

brought her back again. She confessed she did not love me, having been so prejudiced against me by Simpson. Lord, lay not this sin to his charge! I described the stillness of the first Christians from Acts 2:42ff., who continued in the apostles' doctrine, and in fellowship, and in breaking of bread, and in prayers. I pressed them from their example to a constant use of the means of grace and to continue together daily with one accord in the temple. I vindicated the Moravians and our brother [Richard] Viney from that aspersion of their speaking against the ordinances. Viney sat silent by, but not able to dissemble his want of love towards me. That, alas, is restrained, if not lost!

Called on Charles Graves and, not finding him in his room, was returning home when Robson motioned our looking into the chapel. We did so. Prayers was just done and I caught my poor stray most seasonably. He was not quite gone, so that I trust he will be easily delivered out of the mouth of the *still* lion.

**June 20, Friday.** Carried him with us to Malmesbury,[5] and by the way discovered Satan's devices. In the evening we found out hearty Mr. Line. At the desire of some Baptists, I expounded Romans 7 but not at all to their satisfaction. They could not see any higher state of perfection than what is there described. A pharisee flew out after her manner. I had not time to enlarge upon my declaration to her—namely, that she was still a lost sinner, a damned unbeliever.

Supped at Mr. Ponting's, a man of a better spirit. His faith works by love and not by rage and fury. The Lord hath not left himself without witness in this place. Mr. Line is a sweet, humble soul and will quickly, I trust, come into the gospel-liberty without Simpson's unsettling.

**June 21,[6] Saturday.** Preached at 6:00 this morning to a few hundreds both law and gospel from, "If any man be in Christ, he is a new creature: old things are passed away, and all things are become new. And all things also of God, who hath reconciled us to himself through Jesus Christ."[7] The Baptists and their teacher, I am sure, could not bear the test. But their old resolution must help them out: *Non persuadebis, etiamsi persuaseris*.[8] The rich were sent empty away, but I humbly hope, God filled the hungry with good things.

On the road such an unaccountable heaviness came over me that I feared every moment I should drop off my horse. I was forced to light and lay down for a quarter of an hour. Refreshed with this little sleep I went

---

[5] Malmesbury, Wiltshire, 14 miles west of Swindon.

[6] Orig., "July 21."

[7] 2 Cor. 5:17–18.

[8] This was a Latin translation, common in CW's day of an aphorism (in Greek) in Aristophanes, *Plutus*, l. 600. JW rendered it in English as "Thou shalt not persuade me, though thou dost persuade me," in Sermon 83, "On Patience," §11, *Works*, 3:177.

forward, till we met a poor old man whom we had probably missed of but for my delay. I thought as I waked, God had some end to answer by it. The poor old sinner of 80 years was hereby delivered into my hands. I was enabled to preach the gospel to him with power, and he seemed to receive it with all readiness. We left him looking up to Jesus, and went on praying and praising God.

My first greeting in the Wood[9] was from a collier's daughter. 'Tis hard to say which most rejoiced at the meeting. Mrs. [Elizabeth] Hooper[10] was from home, but her son and Hannah[11] rejoiced over me and I over them. Called on Mrs. Gregory,[12] deeply humbled under the hand of God. He enlarged my heart in prayer for her and poor despairing Nanny Smith.[13] Dined at Mr. Darby's[14] and was refreshed with the sight of them, but more, much more so at Mr. Labee's.[15] There I saw the captive of the mighty taken away, and the prey of the terrible delivered. God had avenged his own elect of their adversary and rescued from his oppression the soul of our dear sister Smith. Lucretia Smith[16] was last Wednesday filled with the spirit of power, and spe<aking[17]> with such wisdom as none of God's enemies can gainsay or resist. "Jesus Christ is strength. As such," she told me, "I find him continually." Glory be to God on high, etc. My brother [Westley] Hall, much strengthened in body, was here, and brother [Thomas] Richards[18] and others. They glorified God on my behalf, even the God by whom we

---

[9] I.e., Kingswood, as CW expands it in MS Journal.

[10] Elizabeth (Brown) Hooper and her husband John (a maltster) lived in Old Market Street, Bristol and were members of the society. When CW got sick in August, he was nursed back to health at their house (see CW, MS Journal, Aug. 6, 1740); and on her death in May 1741 he led in singing a hymn he had written for the occasion (ibid., May 8, 1741).

[11] William Hooper and Hannah Cennick, according to CW, MS Journal.

[12] Likely the Mary Gregory whom CW baptized the preceding fall (see MS Journal, Oct. 30, 1739).

[13] See JW, Diary (Oct. 27, 1739), Works, 19:413.

[14] William Darby appears on a 1741 list of bands in Bristol.

[15] Francis Labee (d. 1755) was a surgeon/midwife in Bristol. He and his wife Sarah appear repeatedly in JW's diary from Apr. 1739 through June 1741. JW spells the name "Labbè." CW and his amanuensis typically spell it "Labbee." We follow the spelling in his will.

[16] A Quaker gentlewoman of Bristol, Lucretia Smith was converted by JW and baptized in Apr. 1738; see JW, *Journal* (Apr. 18, 1739), *Works*, 19:49–50.

[17] A small piece of the manuscript is ripped away.

[18] Thomas Richards (1717–84), son and namesake of the vicar of Ferwig and Cardigan, Wales, matriculated at Trinity College, Oxford, in 1734, but did not graduate. JW listed Richards as the second of his lay traveling preachers. He taught languages at Kingswood School between 1748–51, with his main accomplishment being marriage to Mary Davey, the housekeeper there, in 1749. In 1750 Richards obtained ordination by the Bishop of Lincoln (with the support of Lord Northampton) and an initial placement as curate under George Baddeley in Markfield. Over the years he distanced himself from Methodism, ending his career as vicar of Westbury.

escape death.

From thence I was *led* to Mrs. [Elizabeth] Hooper and Mrs. [Mary (Oxford)] Norman's,[19] where we prayed *after* God and rejoiced for their consolation. She is strong in the Lord and in the power of his might. Poor Portrees gives her over to Satan.

Brother [Thomas] Maxfield asked me to call in upon [John] Haydon.[20] He had quitted his house, but God directed us to sister Purnell.[21] Our poor sister Bradshaw was frightened away by my approach. I followed and found her in the agony. Prayer was torment to her, but we did pray and that fervently. You will quickly hear, we trust, of her deliverance.

Bristol
Saturday, 10 o'clock

My Dear Brother,

Mrs. Grevil[22] says the letter is burnt. Mr. [Felix] Farley[23] agreed with the carrier for 6 shillings per hundred. He has promised to write himself. The orders, etc., will be sent as soon as possible. I will get the experiences as soon as I can. Mr. Hall's coming here has been greatly blessed. I begin to be convinced in some measure of the evil of unbelief. O pray that the Lord would perfect his work in my soul! My love to all.

I am your very unworthy brother,
Thomas Richards

Rem[ember] the index.[24] In my last hymn, put "tost" instead of "racked."[25] The lion is easier kept out than turned out; therefore discard [[Acourt[26]]]. *Sero sapiamus Phryges.*[27] And follow you after our lapsed

---

[19] Mary (Oxford) Norman (1695–1779) was the wife of John Norman (d. 1744). They lived on St. Philip's Plain, and he owned the brickyard on which both JW and CW preached in Bristol.

[20] John Haydon, a weaver, was drawn into the Methodist movement in Bristol in May 1739; see JW, *Journal* (May 2, 1739), *Works*, 19:54.

[21] Mrs. Elizabeth Purnell, who would die on Oct. 22, 1740 (see CW, MS Journal).

[22] Elizabeth (Whitefield) Grevil (fl. 1735–40), the widowed sister of George Whitefield, who boarded the Wesley brothers at her house in Bristol in the earliest years of the revival.

[23] Felix Farley (1708–53), son of a printer and pioneering newspaper proprietor, started his own printing business in Bath in 1732 and moved to Bristol in 1734. He printed several items for the Wesley brothers and became a devout Methodist.

[24] CW is almost certainly referring to the second volume of *Hymns and Sacred Poems*, which JW was in final stages of preparing for publication; it would appear in print on July 14, with an index.

[25] Neither of these words appear in any hymn in *HSP* (1740), so another replacement might have been chosen.

[26] John Acourt was an ardent Calvinist, whose resolve to argue all the early Methodists into his Calvinist view set the societies in confusion. See JW, *Journal*, June 19, 1740 (*Works*, 19:152–53).

[27] Rendering a common Latin proverb (*sero sapiunt Phryges*) in the first person plural,

brethren and allow more time for confirming those that stand. Look after [Richard] Bell junior. Be passive as to the cryings out, neither discouraging nor encouraging. The little flock here grow daily. My love to all with you. Duty to my mother.[28]

*Address*: "To / The Revd Mr John Wesley / at the Foundry in / Upper
    Moorfields / London / Single Sheet."
*Postmarks*: "23 / IV" and "Bristol."
*Endorsement*: by JW, "b[rother] Richards—June 21, 1740 / w[ith]
    C[harles]'s Journal / a[nswere]d in C[harles]'s, 24."
*Source*: original letter by amanuensis; MARC, MA 1977/503, Box 5, file 5

---

present tense: "We Phrygians (Trojans) become wise too late."

[28] This is a personal note written by CW along the left margin of page 2 of the journal letter. Susanna (Annesley) Wesley was now living at the Foundery in London.

## JUNE 23–27, 1740

[Bristol]
June [28,] 1740

Has the numb-fish touched you?[1] Are you *still*,[2] that I have no account how things are carried on in London?[3] You do not sure expect any more journal from *me*? I believe this will be the last.

On Monday [June 30] I propose returning to Oxford, where I am to read a lecture.[4] It may be I shall be here again in the latter end of the week.

You should immediately inform sister Lambert[5] that Jacky[6] is (much to his satisfaction) at Farley's.

Two rules are wanting: 1) That every person, before he can be admitted into the united society, *be in* business; [and] 2) allow of and use the means of grace.

How could you ever, *you yourself*, incline to admit Mary Stretton? You shall be called Jesuit indeed when any man, woman, or child may impose upon you as often as they please. I expect to hear in your next (if[7] you ever write again) that [John] Simpson has persuaded you to let him preach at the Foundery.

I can't find out William Worly, and forget whose 7 shillings it was which I have to pay him, but shall leave it for him with brother [Thomas] Richards.

Mitchell[8] is coming about again, but I desire he may be no more trusted. Neither the generous, disinterested Anthony Williams,[9] although I think he begins to see a little of his heart.

Your sending me no account of things confounds me so that I know not how or what to write—to William Seward especially. What did you mean

---

[1] Referring to an electric ray, which stuns its prey with an electrical shock.

[2] I.e., has JW accepted the false teaching of the Moravians?

[3] Actually JW had written June 24, but the letter appears to have been delayed.

[4] The lecture was on Psalm 130, as part of the requirements for the Bachelor of Divinity degree that CW was pursuing (see CW, MS Journal, Nov. 2, 1739 and July 30, 1740). He soon abandoned this attempt.

[5] Anne (Wesley) Lambert was born to Samuel and Susanna (Annesley) Wesley in Epworth on May 16, 1701. She married John Lambert of Wroot on Dec. 2, 1725. They lived at first in Wroot, then in the London area. Little is known of Anne's fortunes after the death of her husband in 1743.

[6] CW had just escorted John Lambert (b. 1726), son of John and Anne (Wesley) Lambert, from London to apprentice with the Bristol printer, Felix Farley. Little is known of John Jr.'s later life, but among his grandchildren was John Wesley Jarvis (1781–1839).

[7] Orig., "in."

[8] This is likely Thomas Mitchell, who was an early supporter of the revival in Bristol, but sided with Whitefield in the growing tension over the doctrine of predestination.

[9] The husband of Anne Williams, both early band members in Bristol; see JW to James Hutton, July 2, 1739, *Works*, 25:666.

by sending me the £200?[10] Might not you have better received it in town than send the bills to me, to be sent back again? The mortgage, I hear, is [£]250.[11] You must make up the sum, or you do nothing. I know not what to do with your bills, which are left at present in Mr. Lab<ee's[12]> hands.

My duty to my mother, and love to Mrs. Seaton, etc.

I have strange things to tell you, but you are not very fond of my correspondence.

Saturday Noon

Mrs. Ryan[13] (or many beside) will look to Jacky's clothes. The *Journals* are no longer called for here.[14] [Felix] Farley promises to send his bill on Monday. Whence is the printing and binding to be paid? We shall be ruined by printing unless we first and beforehand have money to defray the charge. I intend to receive what we have to receive at Oxford next week.

N. Bath (herself gone wrong) makes great and just complaints of her light, lazy, scandalous lodgers. I know not what to do with them. They give great occasion to the enemy to blaspheme. [[What say you to Kitty?[15] A fair riddance, say I!]]

Could not William Seward muzzle that wild ass's colt? [John] Acourt, I mean; who, if the devil has any apostles, is one. For God and his gospel's sake let us learn a little incredulity and not so hastily give countenance to any man.

The noises and outcries are over.[16] I have not spoke one word against them, nor two *about* them. The devil grows sullen and dumb because we take no notice of him. Yet the work of God goes forward (as many testify) since my coming hither.

# JOURNAL[17]

[**Monday, June 23.**] I forgot mentioning the remarkable effect which the word preached yesterday had upon Chrysy Smith.[18] For a long time

---

[10] See CW's accounting of this money in a journal letter below, for June 27, 1741.

[11] Whitefield and Seward raised the initial monies toward building the Kingswood school house, but it was finished and now controlled by the Wesley brothers. This transaction was apparently to buy out Whitefield's interest in light of the growing split over predestination.

[12] A small part of the manuscript is torn away.

[13] Elizabeth Ryan, a member of the Bristol bands.

[14] JW published the first extract of his *Journal* through Felix Farley in June 1740.

[15] See note on April 1 letter above.

[16] I.e., the unusual emotional demonstrations that had occurred at some earlier Methodist meetings in Bristol.

[17] The journal portion of this manuscript is in the hand of Thomas Richards. It was the source of, and provides greater detail than, the account of these days in CW, MS Journal.

[18] This is likely the shortened friendly name for Lucretia Smith.

after she could do nothing but cry out, "Praise God! Give glory to God! See! He writes in stones!" Out of the abundance of her heart her mouth spoke, but such words, so powerful and full of love, I never heard uttered before.

**Tuesday, June 24.** My brother [Westley] Hall returned to London, and God sent me Howell Harris and John Gambold. Met some of the bands. Began 1 John at the Malt-room.[19] Dined with Gambold and [Thomas] Maxfield at the Cupolas[20] and carried the company to Kingswood. Preached "Christ the way, the truth, and the life"[21] to 1,000 little children. Returned and proceeded in St. John at the New Room.[22] Some were present who *fancy* themselves elect, and therefore (I write what I know) sink into all their old tempers. Full of anger are they and wrath and bitterness and dispute. They no longer work out their own salvation with fear and trembling.[23] They give no diligence to make their calling and election sure.[24] Sure it is already, because they are of such an opinion. They have secured the one thing needful[25] for they believe pr[edestination]. At the head of these is the unhappy sister of my friend.[26]

Without meddling in the dispute, I rebuked them sharply, yet in much love. Howell Harris told me he should have spoken the very same words.

Read my journal to the bands with great reluctance. I trust it will be a seasonable antidote.

**Wednesday, June 25.** Breakfasted at Mrs. Labee's and wrote a few words on the sand.[27]

In great heaviness, met the leaders at 1:00. Nevertheless I found great freedom in prayer. Passed the afternoon chiefly in visiting the bands, whom I met all together at 6:00, and was enabled to speak plainly and

---

[19] A large room near Weavers' Hall in Bristol which the Wesley brothers used for meetings when they could not meet in the latter.

[20] The Cupolas was a village surrounding a copper-smelting works 3 miles east of Bristol city center, just south of Kingswood, overlooking the River Avon (now Troopers Hill nature reserve). See JW to James Hutton (July 2, 1739), *Works*, 25:666.

[21] John 14:6.

[22] In May 1739 JW purchased land near St. James's churchyard in central Bristol, in an area called the Horsefair, and built a room large enough to contain the two societies that had been meeting at Nicholas and Baldwin Streets, including for preaching services. It also housed for a while a school for poor children and a medical dispensary; cf. JW to George Whitefield, Apr. 28, 1741, *Works*, 26:58. This "New Room" (CW will often refer to it just as "the Room" and at times initially as the "school room" or "school house") quickly became the center of operation for the Wesley brothers in Bristol.

[23] See Phil. 2:12.

[24] See 2 Pet. 1:10.

[25] See Luke 10:42.

[26] CW is probably referring to Elizabeth (Whitefield) Grevil.

[27] See John 8:6.

searchingly. Some afterwards confessed they had deceived themselves and fancied they had new hearts before they had.

Never had I so comfortable a meeting with the men before. The presence of God was among us in an extraordinary manner, and his Spirit *with* us testified he should soon be *in* us.

**Thursday, June 26.** Found [[Mrs. Turner[28]]] this morning at the Room under strong buffetings of Satan. For the time, she seems delivered over to him, being as truly out of her senses as anyone in Bedlam.[29] Spiritual pride and envy at [[Betty Bond[?]]] have given the enemy this advantage over her, so that he has now cast her down from the pinnacle. For some days past she has made such disturbance at the society that I could not believe her actuated by the Spirit of God, who never interrupts or destroys his own work. O that all of us might hereby learn that hard lesson, "Be not high-minded, but fear."[30] "He that thinketh he standeth, let him take heed lest he fall."[31]

That she had the grace of God is indisputable. And it is as evident that she trusted in it, and thereby fed the corruptions of her nature. Whatever grace or state she heard described, she must straightway work herself up to. Accordingly when she received any fresh comfort, she set herself to find some new name for it. This must pass for forgiveness (perhaps it was truly such), this for the witness, and that for the seal of the Spirit. I do not know whether she did not tell me last that she was entered into the rest, but I hope she will henceforth think soberly and learn not to blaspheme by taking the work out of God's hand and being her own sanctifier.

In the evening, I farther explained Ezekiel 16, and the secrets of many hearts were revealed. When some cried out I bade the people be quiet, that Satan might lose his end. Those souls I believed sincere, but he therefore tormented them to make them confound the work of God and prevent the hearing his word. Immediately hereupon, as if his device was discovered, the enemy withdrew and the outcries ceased.

I gave an exhortation to the united society that they should adorn the gospel of Christ in all things,[32] especially diligence in their callings. It was well received and, I trust, blest to them.

Found Mrs. [Elizabeth] Hooper very ill and in great pain,[33] which upon our joining in prayer immediately left her.

---

[28] The wife of Capt. Joseph Turner; both were band members in Bristol at the time.

[29] The Hospital of St. Mary of Bethlehem in London, an asylum for the mentally ill.

[30] Rom. 11:20.

[31] Cf. 1 Cor. 10:12. Orig., "least."

[32] See Titus 2:10.

[33] Elizabeth Hooper was drawn to the Methodist movement in Bristol in 1739. In August 1740 she took an ill CW into her home, to nurse him back to health. When she died in 1741, CW wrote a funeral hymn for the occasion. See CW, MS Journal, May 8, 1741; and *HSP* (1742), 124–25.

**Friday, June 27.** Breakfasted at Mrs. Hooper's, who (as far as I can discern what I have no experience of) *is* entered into that rest and ceased from her own works. One (if not both) of her sisters seems in the same state. "They are in Christ new creatures. Old things are passed away; behold all things are become new."[34] Sin is in them, but cannot so stir as to trouble them, no not for a moment. *All* their desires are to God. They pray without ceasing and without wandering. They have no [will], rather no will of their own, in anything great or small, temporal or eternal. Mrs. Hooper, although in great pain, cannot wish it shortened one moment, but entirely acquiesces and rejoices in the divine will. O my soul, be not thou content to live by any lower instance. I believe there remaineth such a glorious rest for the people of God.[35] Lord, help thou my unbelief.[36]

God helped us to keep the fast.

We seem convinced that all the hindrance is in us. We *will* not "come unto him that we may have life."[37] Never Moravian spake as Chrysy Smith speaks upon these things. Out of the mouth of babes and sucklings doth God perfect praise. I believe I shall soon be like her, though I am a devil.

How is the rent of the house to be paid? There is no one besides sister Bath who is able to raise any money.

*Address*: "To / The Revd Mr John Wesley / at the Foundry in / Upper Moor Fields / London. / Single Sheet."
*Postmarks*: "30 / IV" and "Bristol."
*Endorsements*: by JW, "C[harles's] Journal / June 30, 1740." Also two sets of notes for the London membership lists, by JW: "… / f[or] trial / Frances Reynolds, w[idow] / Sus. Jeffreys, u[nmarried], Eagle Court, Strand / Eliz. Dorrel, u[nmarried], D[itt]o[38]"; "m[en] / m[arried], Will[ia]m Standex, Chandler[39] / Kings Str[eet], Bloomsbury / u[nmarried], Will[ia]m Chad, Taylor / King street, 7dials."
*Source*: holograph, with journal section by amanuensis; MARC, MA 1977/503, Box 5, file 4.

---

[34] Cf. 2 Cor. 5:17.
[35] See Heb. 4:9.
[36] See Mark 9:24.
[37] Cf. John 5:40.
[38] I.e., also of Eagle Court, Strand.
[39] A shopkeeper.

## JULY 14–18, 1740

[Bristol]
[July 19, 1740]

[[Dear Brother,]]

You will weary out my constancy in writing by your not being as constant as I.

What need of that idle question, "How many *Hymns* shall be sent down?"[1] As many as you will or as few, rather than none at all. You seem to ask merely to excuse your delay. 300, I suppose, may be sent at a venture; and by the very first carrier, directed to Mr. [Ebenezer] Wigginton[2] with a letter of notice.

Brother Davis does not go to Georgia.

Tell me that you give no countenance to [John] Simpson. Be not so much as seen with him. They complained of me too soon at London. I was only not so tardy in prevention as you.

Is the weekly sacrament for my mother settled?[3] And *my* band? And those at the Foundery? Pray let no more be admitted into the society till I come. We shall be overlaid. Why don't you send Jacky's age?[4] You take no notice of the orders for our society. I forgot to pay Mr. [Joseph] Humphreys[5] the half-crown I borrowed. Will you remember it. N. B., we give away NO hymn-books till our debts are paid.

My love to all the brethren. Make mention of me and Mr. [John] Robson in all your prayers.

My mother may be dead for any notice you take of her. Give my duty.

## Journal[6]

[**Monday, July 14.**] Dined at Mrs. [Rachel] England's and prayed over brother B. and brother S. Once again the unclean spirit was rebuked and ceased from troubling her.

---

[1] *HSP* (1740) had just been printed.

[2] CW had baptized Ebenezer Wigginton, head of a significant Quaker family in Bristol, on Oct. 26, 1739 (see MS Journal).

[3] Susanna (Annesley) Wesley was now living at the Foundery.

[4] John Lambert's birth-date was apparently needed for finalizing apprenticeship papers.

[5] Joseph Humphreys (c. 1720–85), son of a zealous Dissenting minister, was converted by Whitefield in 1738 and became friends with JW and CW in 1740, serving for a short time as JW's pastoral assistant in London. Within the year he would align with Whitefield and the Calvinist Methodists over against the Wesley brothers.

[6] The journal portion of this manuscript is in the hand of Thomas Richards. It was the source of, and provides greater detail than, the account of these days in CW, MS Journal.

Sent for to Miss [Sarah] Perrin at Mrs. [Elizabeth (Whitefield)] Grevil's. I passed an hour or two wondering at the goodness of God towards her. He had answered her by his own mouth and taught, while she was confined from hearing the word. The Scripture was her delight and her counsellors. She had been wonderfully strengthened against all opposition, and grew and flourished under the cross, but now complains she has less of sensible comforts and sees herself worse than ever. I told her of God's method in dealing with man: first humbling him in some measure, then showing him a saviour, and *then* his own heart—which, when it is broken, he binds up and the chief of sinners enters into rest; even that second, perfect rest which remaineth for the people of God.[7] She heard me gladly and, I am persuaded, will soon be free indeed and cease from her own works as God also is ceased.

Spoke a few mild words to poor Porthouse,[8] whom I met here. I held him by the hand and expostulated his railing on us as deceivers of the people. He trembled and could not resist the love wherewith I spoke. Held forth the word of life, the promise of the Father,[9] at the school-room.[10] I bless God, we all seem more and more confirmed in our expectation of that Comforter whom the world cannot receive.

Lay at the Room[11] for the first time and know not when I have had more comfort in finding myself within the everlasting arms.

**Tuesday, July 15.** Breakfasted at Mrs. [Elizabeth (Whitefield)] Grevil's (after an hour well spent with Felix [[Farley]]) and met her pattern and oracle Mrs. Jenny.[12] She justified her saying, "John Wesley will assuredly go to hell when he[13] dies, if he does not publicly recant his sermon."[14] God be praised, who kept me surprisingly calm so that she could not be angry if she would. We parted with prayer and much seeming mutual pity. Mine, I think, was real.

At Temple-backs[15] I was much assisted to expound Revelation 19:12ff. Dined at Mr. [John] Wayne's[16] and lost my way to the school. Met a poor

---

[7] See Heb. 4:9.

[8] The spelling is clear in the text, but this may be Mr. Portrees mentioned in other letters.

[9] See Acts 1:4–5.

[10] I.e., the New Room.

[11] CW is referring to a lodging room that had apparently just been completed near or connected to the New Room; cf. JW to George Whitefield, Apr. 28, 1741, *Works*, 26:58.

[12] She is called "Mrs. Jane" in the letter covering Oct. 24, 1740 below.

[13] Orig., "she."

[14] The sermon *Free Grace*, which comprised a stringent critique of unconditional election.

[15] The street behind Bristol's Temple Church.

[16] John Wayne (1696–1747) was the eldest son and heir of Gabriel Wayne (1653–1722), who had established a major copper smelting operation in Conham. CW often preached at a chapel built and endowed by Sir Abraham Ellison for the workers in this smelt works. CW consistently spells the last name "Wane."

blaspheming harlot who, instead of directing, railed on me most bitterly, I suppose for spoiling her trade.

Preached to the colliers (what many of them have experienced) religion a participation of the divine nature.[17] Returned to the Room and explained the description given of the primitive Christians, Acts 2. Their spirit was sensibly with us. O that it was always so, both with and in us and all mankind.

We had a remarkable proof of his presence while I was convincing the natural man of sin, from his not eating his meat with gladness and singleness of heart,[18] and speaking of those enemies of the cross of Christ whose God is their belly.[19] A poor sinner, being too nearly concerned, cried out most vehemently, "What do you mean by looking at me? And directing yourself to me? And telling me I shall be damned?" I did then address myself to him, but he broke out into curses and hurried away as fast as he could lest our prayers and blessings should overtake him.

**Wednesday, July 16.** Was carried out in the morning exposition to enlarge upon those words, "God so loved the world."[20] I afterwards heard that [Jonathan] Wildboar[21] was present and laid hold of Mary Bosher, telling her, "God hath sent me for you. I must have one of the bands." A sister rescued her out of his hands. I went and settled her with sister [Esther] Highnam, being resolved to join issue with Satan for this soul. Her heart seemed more inclinable, after prayer, to take part with God and us against the devil and herself.

At the time of intercession the Spirit greatly helped our infirmities. We began with particulars, but were at last enlarged in prayer and thanksgiving for all men.

Called upon poor E[dy] Hollaster and prevailed upon her not to leave the bands, as she was strongly tempted to do. The devil knows what he does: *divide et impera*[22] will carry the world before him.

I was never in a worse frame than when the bands met. But we had prayed at noon that God would open my mouth to stir them up, and now the answer came. As soon as I began speaking the Spirit was with me as I never before experienced. The words were not mine in which I rebuked, reproved, exhorted. We all trembled before the majesty of God, excepting Mrs. Davis,[23] whom I rebuked most sharply. But her God hath given up to

---

[17] See 2 Pet. 1:4.

[18] See Acts 2:46.

[19] See Phil. 3:18–19.

[20] John 3:16.

[21] Orig., "Wildbore"; JW gives the full name in his letter to John Smith, July 10, 1747, *Works*, 26:245.

[22] "Divide and conquer."

[23] Mrs. Anne Davis, drawn into the Methodist society in Bristol, was the housekeeper for

a strong delusion, so that she believes the lie of predestination. She never saw her heart. She is the servant of sin and yet confident, diabolically confident, that she shall be saved *because she is elected*. She laughed at God's threatenings, being hardened through the deceitfulness of sin and plainly given over to a reprobate mind.

John Calvin, thy work shall suffer loss; and if thou thyself art saved, it shall be as by fire.

I sent for the men and continued my discourse to all, convincing them of their abuse of mercy. My God humbled me among them and I bewailed many which have sinned already and have not repented, particularly A. W.[24] I plainly and calmly set before him the things which he had done: his envy, malice, evil-speaking, pride, obstinancy, deceit, treachery. He hardened himself as heretofore, rejecting my reproof with anger, bitterness, and reviling. I repeated and confirmed my charge against him and his wife, who have basely betrayed all which has passed in the bands, even from the beginning. "But why, if you so rail at them and say no good is to be got among them, do you not leave them," said Mrs. [Sarah] Labee. "I do not care," answered A., "to put myself out, but should be glad if they would."

Upon his violent behaviour I now thought this the last remedy, and therefore told him he was no longer a member of our society and desired him to withdraw. I left him to inform his wife that neither did she belong to us any longer. We could have no fellowship with them till they acknowledged their fault. He did not behave on the occasion otherwise than I expected, but stayed, urging and reviling, till I said if he would not go we would. He hardly left us, crying out with all the fierceness and sullenness of pride, "God give you a better spirit."

I said amen to his prayer but found it was the good spirit by which I had spoken—for such a love and pity overflowed me as humbled me in the dust. I saw myself in that poor railer, only far worse than him or any I reproved. O what regret did I feel in cutting off this dead member! It was as if one criminal was made to execute another. We betook ourselves to fervent prayer for him and the society. The spirit of supplication was poured out abundantly and we returned to the Lord our God in weeping and mourning and prayer. On all sides were heard the sorrowful sighing of such as are in captivity. Chrysy's[25] mouth was opened to call upon us with divine vehemence, "Give him all your hearts. He will not accept of part. Give him all your hearts, and he will give himself unto you!" His spirit did now strive powerfully with us, and I humbly hope will make us all willing to be saved.

---

the New Room. Within six months she would be removed from that job because of siding strongly with those insisting of predestination and eternal security.

[24] This is almost certainly Anthony Williams (and his wife Anne).

[25] Lucretia "Chrysy" Smith?

**Thursday, July 17.** Found Mrs. [Sarah] Labee deeply mourning and almost despairing at the sight of her heart, which God last night discovered to her at home while we were praying.

The presence of a predestinarian at the Malt-house exceedingly helped me in the exposition. In the evening this note was put up:

> A person desires to declare before this congregation that while the minister was appealing to God for the truth of universal redemption and desiring a token thereof upon some soul there present, the Spirit of the Lord did then bear witness with her spirit that the doctrine there delivered was the truth of God, and she could have gladly staked her eternal salvation thereupon.

After visiting sister [Mary] Hill and leaving her full of peace and ready for the bridegroom, I went after that which was gone astray: B. H.[26] I mean, and A. O.,[27] who have long gone on frowardly in the way of their own heart. The first of these I found, but she told me she was sorry to see me. I spoke notwithstanding what God put in my mouth and, after a long resistance, she was melted down. He clave the hard rock and the waters gushed out. May he carry on in her the work he has now begun and give her repentance never to be repented of.

Received the following note after expounding:

> God showed me under your preaching tonight that he died for me and every man, but that I would not come unto him that I might have life. O pray for me that I may be made willing in the day of his power.
>
> Elizabeth Baddeley

We had a comfortable meeting of the society which was increased with forty-five new members. It was 10:00 when we parted. I then laid me down in peace.

**Friday, July 18.** Overtook my other stray this morning, A. O. Farther from God she could not have wandered, unless she had been in hell. Upon her also he showed that he is greater than the heart. She had been most outrageous against him, but an impression seems to be made upon her and I trust it will sink deeper and deeper. She employed yesterday in reading Romans 9, being so instructed, I suppose, by [Jonathan] Wildboar, whom she has been to hear. That poor weak instrument of the devil stands ready to receive those that are out of the way and by disorderly walking and forsaking the fellowship give themselves over to Satan. When any

---

[26] This may be Elizabeth ("Betty") Hardy, who would correspond critically with JW twenty years later; cf. JW to Elizabeth Hardy, Apr. 5, 1758, *Works*, 27:119–23.

[27] Likely Ann Oldfield (b. 1724), the daughter of Thomas and Mary (Franklin) Oldfield.

has so grieved the good spirit that he departs from them, the evil spirit comes and draws them into the whirlpool of predestination. He teaches them (when they themselves will not be saved) to lay the blame upon God and say he *will* not save them. They then make him a liar and forsworn by blasphemously ascribing their damnation to him.

Predestination is the devil's two-edged sword, but I find he generally tries the side of election first. This is the surest way to persuade his own that they are God's elect children, and thus he seals them his by presumption and makes their damnation sure. When their sins are too gross and they cannot but know they are of the devil, then reprobation steps in and they are swallowed up in despair.

In speaking to Sarah Rutter I was likewise enabled to pull down her strongholds and humble her under a deep sense of her ingratitude. The terrors of the Lord, which I set in array against her on Wednesday night, had no effect. But the love of Christ overbore her obstinate resistance.

Edy Hollaster held out longer against God, doing such despite to his Spirit as I have seldom seen. She had hardened her heart again since my last talking with her, and now flew out with such violent outrage as if she would have torn[28] God out of his throne. We prayed down the spirit of rebellion in her, not leaving her till she had left off fighting against God.

I am even astonished at the full possession which Satan seems to have of some souls here. They are led captive by him at his will, working his works and giving all diligence to make their reprobation and damnation sure. Our Lord was with us in the evening, not in the work of the ministry only but in every work, and word, and thought.[29]

*Address*: "To / The Revd Mr John Wesley / at the Foundry in / Upper Moor Fields / London. / Single Sheet."
*Postmarks*: "21 / IV"[30] and "Bristol."
*Endorsement*: by JW, "C[harles] July 21, 1740 / a[nswere]d 24.
*Source*: holograph, with journal section by amanuensis; MARC, MA 1977/503, Box 5, file 4.

---

[28] Orig., "tare."

[29] The last paragraph is written alongside the left margin.

[30] The London postmark should have read "IY" for July, rather than "IV" for June. The error was corrected by someone writing "IY" next to the postmark.

## JULY 19–30, 1740[1]

[Bristol]
1740

**Saturday, July 19.** After the morning exposition [I] prayed with the poor returning prodigals, who will—all of them, I trust—once more escape out of the snare of the devil.

From 9:00 to 12:00 employed in reading the letters. When I see what God has done by me, it even confounds me [[but in the next moment I found I am proud of my humility[2]]]. Dined at Mr. [Thomas] Willis's[3] and read a sermon of Tobias Crisp's.[4] Whether he be an antinomian as supposed, I know not. But this I know, that he denies Christian holiness, as do all the Puritans (whom I have met with) to a man. This does not make me anything readier to swallow their blessed doctrine of predestination.

Carried two of our London brethren to the bands at Kingswood, with whom they were much delighted and owned that fame for once had lessened truth. Lay at the Cupolas.

**Sunday, July 20.** The lives and railing of some that sit in Moses' chair[5] had well-nigh driven some of our colliers from Church, even before its doors are shut against them. (They were repelled long ago from the sacrament by most of the Bristol ministers.) I exhorted them from Acts 2:42ff. to continue daily with one accord in the temple, where the wickedest administrator can neither spoil the prayers nor poison the sacrament. *These* poor sinners *have* ears to hear.

Gave the sacrament to Mary Hill, who seemed full of a loving confidence in *her* Saviour, although I plainly saw a mixture of nature in her. If God fulfills her heart's desire and now takes her to himself, he will doubtless purge out all the old leaven, though it be at the last moment.

Preached at Rose Green[6] to a numerous <au>dien<ce[7]> and returned to the men's love-feast. I had no life in me till I borrowed it of them. God increase this little spark into a flame.

---

[1] This manuscript (other than one paragraph) is in the hand of Thomas Richards. It was the source of, and provides greater detail than, the account of these days in CW, MS Journal.

[2] This shorthand comment was added by CW between the lines of text.

[3] CW was a frequent guest during this time of Thomas Willis, who apparently owned a coal mine in Hanham, about 4 miles east of Bristol city center. See CW, MS Journal, Sept. 22, 1740.

[4] Tobias Crisp (1600–1643) was a strong Calvinist member of the Church of England clergy; a collection of his sermons was published on his death under the title *Christ Alone Exalted* (1643).

[5] I.e., the clergy who preach / teach biblical law; see Matt. 23:2.

[6] Rose Green was "a plain on top of a high hill," about 2 miles northeast of Kingswood; cf. JW letter to James Hutton, Apr. 1, 1739, *Works*, 25:628.

[7] Some small tears along a crease line in the manuscript; the missing letters are obvious.

**Monday, July 21.** Called on Mary Norman and met a predestinarian, whom I quickly discovered by her full assurance *of unbelief* and denial of Christian liberty. I rebuked her sharply. *"But she had Abraham for her father,"*[8] being so entrenched in her decrees that she defied any less than an almighty power to pull down her strongholds. Indeed I put her by her meekness and showed her to everyone but herself.

Pursued poor Mary Bosher to sister [Elizabeth] Purnell's and besought her (as I had before done today in vain) not to harden her heart and destroy her own soul. God, who has showed such patience and long-suffering towards me, enabled me to persist in my importunity. We prayed but still could make no impression. We were all of us in tears, and so continued weeping over her in silence; till at last her hardness relented and she begged us to pray for her that Christ would make her willing to forsake all for him. Glory be to him, who shows us he is able to subdue all things to himself. After the evening exposition (in which I found much assistance), prayed with Mary Bosher and four or five others who have been most wanton against Christ. They were all melted down and groaned for the hardness of their own hearts. I do not despair but the last will be first.[9]

**Tuesday, July 22.** Met some bands this morning instead of going to church (which I mention to show my disapprobation of it). But it could not be helped. I would always in this thing differ *toto caelo*[10] from our *still* brethren.

Breakfasted at brother Oldfield's with several of our mourning sisters and found it good to be there.[11] At Mr. [John] Wayne's dined with Mr. and Mrs. Ford,[12] who accompanied me to the school. "If any man be in Christ, he is a new creature"[13] was my subject, and God gave me great power to search the heart. He continued it to me in the evening, which concluded in prayer with our lapsed sisters and then with a dying woman.

**Wednesday, [July] 23.** Talked half an hour with Mrs. Turner,[14] who has been strongly solicited by her carnal relations to return to the world. She justifies God and the wisdom of his children, taking shame to herself and confessing that spiritual pride was the sole occasion of her fall.

---

[8] Cf. John 8:39.

[9] See Matt. 19:30.

[10] "The span of the heavens" or "as far apart as possible."

[11] Thomas Oldfield was an apothecary in Bristol, married to Mary (Franklin) Oldfield. He was part of the Calvinist cohort in Bristol that would soon leave the Wesleyan society; see John Cennick to JW, Aug. 16, 1740; and below, Sept. 24, 1740.

[12] Likely James Ford, a surgeon in Bristol. He was at a dinner with JW at John Wayne's on Dec. 30, 1740 (see JW, diary, *Works*, 19:446).

[13] 2 Cor. 5:17.

[14] The wife of Capt. Joseph Turner; both were band members in Bristol at the time.

Met a few of us to keep the fast, and tasted something of the blessedness of mourning.

Stole an hour to walk by myself and enjoyed the solitude. O how pleasing to flesh and blood is this self-indulgence. How does the spirit of slumber or *stillness* lull the soul and quiet its restlessness after God!

*Hic gelidi fontes, hic mollia prata, Lycori;*
*Hic nemus; hic toto tecum consumerer aevo!*[15]

God put a word in my mouth this evening also, and it alight[ed] on my sisters' hearts. I exhorted them with much freedom to give him their whole heart, and convinced them of their unwillingness so to do. The secrets of many hearts were revealed by the stubbornness and blindness of one—sister [Anne] Holton, I mean, who was fallen fast asleep again, full of anger, full of the world; dead, twice dead; yet horribly confident she was in a good way and should go to heaven, was she to die this moment. She was as sure of it as a wicked predestinarian. I tried the weapons of our warfare upon her stronghold and pulled them down to the conviction of all but herself. But last Wednesday this exquisite self-deceiver had complained that I did not speak to her. Now that I do, she strengthens herself in her wickedness and reviles the ministers for listening to others and not showing respect to the old members. I told her (as I had before intended) that she could have no fellowship with us till she better knew her own spirit, but might be upon trial with her own band. God then enlarged my heart towards all, and I drew *them* with the cords of love.[16]

As the women were leaving us, God owned the truths I had spoken and delivered Anne Holton to the messenger of Satan to be buffeted. She cried out like a mad woman, and raged and tore exceedingly. She, who the last moment was sure of going to heaven, talked of hanging herself this [moment]. Me she reviled and threatened hard. Brother [John] Cennick suffered by going too near her. She raved as if possessed by Legion,[17] this child of God with her full assurance of faith! I called the sisters back and spoke suitably to the occasion, showing them as the deceitfulness and desperate wickedness of the heart, so the power of Satan over those that are separated from us. With *us*, the Spirit of our head continued all the evening.

---

[15] Virgil, *Eclogue*, x. 42–43; "Here are cool springs, here soft meadows, Lycoris; here a grove; here with you could I pass my whole life."

[16] See Hosea 11:4.

[17] See Mark 5:15.

**Thursday, [July] 24.** I went to see her, lest[18] Satan should get *irrecoverable* advantage over her. She was still in the false assurance of faith, although she owned she was as far from the mind that was in Jesus as darkness from light. I left her somewhat more moderate but infinitely short of what she takes herself for. What an exertion of omnipotence does such a soul require for its re-awakening! To recover one whose confidence has outlived her innocence is of all spiritual miracles the most extraordinary.

**Friday, [July] 25.** Began talking with the members of the united society, many of whom I do not know by face. One came in crying out, "I am born of God," "I have the indwelling of the Spirit," "I have a new heart," and what not. Upon my examining her, she could give no account or proof or reason for her pretensions. But yet she was sure of it, and all the world should not persuade her to the contrary. One pretty good proof I have of her being a self-deceiver—the witness in her, she says, testifies that he abides in *me*. Yet I fear nothing, but her falling into gross sin, will be sufficient to open her eyes.

I cannot but observe here how exceeding cautious we should be, and backward, to receive the witness which persons bear of themselves. The universal rule should be, *nil admirari*;[19] and the general, not to take notice of such as think themselves justified *till* self be subdued in them and brought into subjection, or at least till they have seen their hearts, which lie hid under that first joy.

Lost half an hour in conversing with one who <mu>ch wants our still brethren to unsettle her. She has received forgiveness and power over outward sin, does not love the world *as* she did, is not so passionate *as* she was, has *partly* a new heart as she fancies, and therefore there she rests and stops short of the promise. I laboured to stir her up and make her restless once more. The Spirit gave her a late violent shake, but she has pacified herself. O how plainly does this show the reason why almost everyone loses the fir<st[20]> comfort: it is expedient for them that it should go away, for <if it go> not all away, the Comforter will not come.[21] Till nature <is quite> dead, it will feed upon the gifts of God instead of the <giver, and> strengthen itself in the grace which is in itself and not <in Christ Jesus.>

Had some talk with Jenny Lloyd, who has left the ba<nd, and gone over to> the devil, or rather is found of him, upon his o<wn ground>

---

[18] Orig., "least."

[19] "Let nothing astonish you."

[20] Starting here a portion of the right hand side of the manuscript page up to about an inch wide is torn away, affecting nearly thirty lines of text. For the remainder of this first paragraph, the missing text can be reconstructed by comparison to the abridged form in CW's MS Journal. Many of the remaining lacunae have probable reconstructions suggested, based on the context.

[21] See John 16:7.

and claimed as his own goods. She gloried at first in <saying Christ has> forsaken us. But there is no temper which we read of <characterizing the> devil which she has not since then both felt and exp<ressed:> self-will, envy, malice, anger, hatred, and revenge. <And all> within the space of a few minutes. Nay, and wha<t seems more> impossible, the height of Calvinistical presump<tion and the> depth of diabolical despair. Every other wo<man she says> either justified herself or condemned God; no<...> those who he knew would not believe. This minut<e she is not> so bad as in her carnal state; the next, such a rep<robate that> God (for it is his fault) *will* not have mercy up<on her. The> devil is not in her, that she is sure of; yet thr<eatens in the> same breath to make away with herself. Notw<ithstanding> all this, she is resolved not to humble herself o<r return to> old comforts and pretensions, *till she is in hell.*

At night I took occasion from Acts 7 to disco<urse on> the sin of resisting the Holy Ghost.[22] The word was as a <fire and an> hammer.[23] I prayed God to apply it home to tho<se ...> and will not believe it; and spoke as comfortably as <I could to> the poor broken-hearted mourners <concerning> it. But who is sufficient for these things? God <applied> his own word aright. The strangers, I trust, many <of them felt> its edge; but so did those also who had more need of healing than wounding. Almost all our lapsed sisters were smitten asunder as with a sword, particularly poor Lucy [Shute]. She gave place to the strong man, and he made his re-entrance. God gave me power to wrestle with him for her deliverance. I asked it as a token of my own. How often has he condescended to this request and not counted it a tempting of him? Anyone that had seen and heard her could not, I think, have any doubt whether those horrid laughters and violent distortions were involuntary and preternatural. I was in an agony for her till the answer came. She received power to call upon Jesus, and the tempter fled before her. I can no more doubt of her being possessed and dispossessed in the self-same hour than of our being alive.

I went thence in the greatest bodily weakness to sister [Esther] Highnam's, where Mary Bosher and Hanna W. was under the same temptation. Commended them both to God's grace, and calling at Mary Hill's, found Jenny Lloyd, convinced (as it should seem) by the word this evening, threatening God that she would destroy herself, sullen and full of the blasphemy of despair. Spoke to her with all mildness and prayed over her. Then between 10:00 and 11:00 returned to the [New] Room. Lucy Shute was rejoicing in God her Saviour and called upon us to join

---

[22] See Acts 7:51.

[23] See Jer. 23:29.

with her. At present she is clean escaped out of the snare of the fowler.[24] But I have learned (at least am learning) not to trust to any present frame, either of my own or others. When a soul has fallen from grace and given itself over unto Satan, it does not so easily or suddenly recover its first estate.[25]

The people who have brother Cook's child desire me not take her away till they had wrote once more to him. I consented the rather because you have sent me no directions where to place her. He must send a second order. They required it £1-5s-0d for keeping her. Brother [Thomas] Richards has borrowed £5-15s-0d, not of Mrs. G.[26] (how *could* you ask it?) but of Mrs. [Elizabeth] Hooper, and paid Cotton in full; the rest being abated on account of the outside quires. 'Tis time to [ap]prentice Jacky Lambert. Ask yourself where is the money.[27]

A third or fourth time I ask whether you think of the orders, that there should be any addition or alteration. I suppose you have laid aside my letters mentioning such a thing, and so clean forgot it. Peter Brown is the bookseller [Felix] Farley has employed to sell your journals.[28]

*Address*: "To / The Revd Mr Wesley / at the Foundry / London."
*Postmarks*: "1 / AV" and "Bristol."
*Endorsement*: by JW, "C[harles] July 30 1740 / a[nswere]d 2, Journal."
*Source*: original letter by amanuensis; MARC, MA 1977/503, Box 5, file 4.

---

[24] See Ps. 124:7.

[25] This paragraph is in CW's handwriting.

[26] Almost certainly Elizabeth (Whitefield) Grevil.

[27] This note is written horizontally in the left margin of page 2. While in the hand of Thomas Richards, this and the following note are clearly from CW to JW.

[28] This note is written horizontally in the left margin of page 3.

## SEPTEMBER 22–27, 1740[1]

[Bristol]

[[Dear Brother,]]

I [[must write a]] second [[letter to excuse the hardness of the first. My manner in blaming is not always the most engaging. But as to the matter, I think my present advice is good and according to the best light God has given me.]]

Here follows[2] a piece of journal, but the last in order of time.

**Monday night, [September 22,]** half hour past 10:00. Mr. [Thomas] Richards disturbed me with news of William Seward's arrival, who had seen and desired him to let him preach at the Room. Richards answered he could not do it without my leave. While he was speaking to me another messenger came with "my son's" duty to me, and the repetition of his request if I did not preach in the morning myself. I sent word back that I did, and would then talk with him farther.

**Tuesday, September 23.** Twas past 11:00 before I slept last night. And waking in a sweat near 5:00, I durst not venture out, not having rose before till near 7:00. Richards' reading prevented Seward's preaching.

Rose at 6:00 and met the women's bands here. At 7:00 Mr. Seward came, and was exceeding loving. Our hearts were united. We prayed and gave thanks and rejoiced till 8:00. Between 11:00 and 12:00, joined in prayer again and set out with Mr. Matthews[3] for the Cupolas. We sang with much love and enlargement of heart in spite of John Calvin. If I did not love him the better for his erroneous opinion, I am sure it made me more industrious to confirm and show my love towards him. Our traveller was a little overbearing at Mr. [John] Wayne's. I preached to the colliers (my sermon and the subject of it, more in my next[4]). Seward desired leave to speak a few words to them. I consented and heard him with pain. It was not so bad as I feared, nor so good as to make me believe him called to the work. In our return he told me that Mrs. [Elizabeth (Whitefield)] Grevil and a band of our discarded members had urged him to claim the pulpit: "he should insist upon it as his right, so great a benefactor,

---

[1] This manuscript (other than the first two and last two paragraphs) is in the hand of Thomas Richards. It was the source of, and provides greater detail than, the account of these days in CW, MS Journal.

[2] Everything up to this point is in CW's handwriting. The remainder of the sentence and the journal that follows are in Thomas Richards' handwriting.

[3] This may be William Matthews, who appears on the Foundery Band Lists for Apr. 1742 (p. 3). A few months later CW was encouraging JW to call Matthews from London to Bristol to provide help; CW to JW, Jan. 10, 1741.

[4] This subsequent letter is not known to survive.

so gifted, etc., as he was." We equally disapproved the baseness of such mischief-makers.

I rode to the Room, through the hard rain, and expounded at 6:00. Seward stood silent by. God magnified his strength in my weakness.

**Wednesday, September 24.** Rose soon after 4:00. Walked to the Horsefair[5] and expounded Acts 13 in course. Barnabas and Saul sent forth with the double call (that is, both outward and inward) gave me occasion to speak against men's going *before* they are sent; Elymas,[6] of the false-hearted and insincere. Poor vicious Oldfield in the desk, I turned upon and applied what was spoken to him by name. He has not ceased to pervert the right ways of the Lord and to speak and do all the wickedness that lay in his power. He has made sport at the word preached, as he was able, and came now on the Pharisees' errand. He asked me, "What sin do I commit while I have the show of sincerity?" I answered, "The sin of uncleanness," and named the place and other circumstances. He confessed it before the whole congregation.

Met the leaders again at 6:00 and was assisted to speak searchingly to some of their hearts. At 7:00 Mr. Seward joined us. He told me he was in a mist—the Baptists last night had laboured hard to make him oppose me and told him I had publicly forbad the reading [of] his journal. Before we parted all was set to rights again. He expressed much abhorrence of Mrs. Jane's[7] so uncharitably sentencing you to hell merely for your opinion. By 1:00 he promised to get from her Mr. Stedder and the party, to join in our intercession.

He failed then, but met me at Mr. Martin's by 2:00.[8] Mr. [Francis] Labee called. He told me abruptly, "I must divide from you. You and your[9] brother are the devil's instruments to stop the work of God. Your two doctrines of universal redemption and perfection are doctrines of devils. I believe the devil is in you. I can call you 'brother' no longer, nor have any fellowship with you." This and more to the same purpose he repeated to our no small astonishment. God gave me great calmness and love. I reasoned with him *against* his hasty resolution and *for* union. The rest joined me. Mr. Matthews asked whether a man could not be saved unless he held predestination. He plainly answered no. I said, notwithstanding his dividing from us, we should never, while we lived, divide from George Whitefield, and heartily wished for George to moderate him now. I told

---

[5] I.e., the New Room, on Horsefair.

[6] See Acts 13:6–9.

[7] She is called "Mrs. Jenny" in the letter covering July 14, 1740 above.

[8] William Martin, a carpenter, was a member of a band for married men in 1741; cf. *WHS* 19 (1934): 163.

[9] Orig., "Your and your."

him I should always love him as my brother. I might say "son," for he owed me his own self. This he confessed, but said I was used like Judas to call him, when I myself was a son of perdition, but soon after he got to a true child of God, George Whitefield. On my asking when we should meet again, he refused any farther conference; remembered he was to dine with me at Mrs. [Rachel] England's, but flew back and said he was commanded "with such an one no not to eat."

After all, he *could* ask me to let him preach. I showed the consequence, but in vain; and therefore at last told him, "I would not suffer him, though it would hinder my brother's dying in a gaol." Notwithstanding which he will speak, he says, and declare us to be false prophets. I told him, smiling, our singing would be louder than his preaching.

Mr. Labee blamed me for charging the Baptists with reprobation,[10] whereas no man could be so absurd as to believe it. Yes, said Seward, I believe it, for hereunto they were appointed. God made all the reprobates to be damned. This stopped Mr. Labee's mouth, and almost opened his eyes.

At night I sharply reproved the bands for their negligence and deadness, recommended in as strong words as I could the much neglected duty of watching unto prayer, and cautioned them all concerning Mr. Seward—that they should never mention him but with love and respect.

Mr. Matthews took his leave of me with tears, being thoroughly awakened and convinced he has lived a Pharisee for three-score years. I trust his visit will be the saving of his soul.

**Thursday, September 25.** This morning, Seward's man gave notice in the Room that his master would preach at 3:00 at Rose Green. Calling a second time at Mrs. [Elizabeth (Whitefield)] Grevil's, I found my friend— but so altered, so embittered! He would hardly let me touch his hand. I accosted him in much love and meekness. I laboured hard for peace. But when I spake to him thereof, he made himself ready to battle. He might be sure, I told him, that I should never separate from him, but always love and acknowledge him for my brother and friend. He could not call me brother (he said) but looked upon me as he did upon the rest of the world. I was a servant of Satan, a fighter against God, a child of the devil, a son of perdition. So was my brother. Both damned, for no man could be saved unless he was a predestinarian. Mr. Portrees looked at him, but he stood to his saying, "All who do not believe reprobation are reprobates!" Indeed, he complained that he did not intend to say it; but we, as it were, betrayed him into it.

---

[10] Francis Labee appears to have been active in the Broadmead Baptist church in Bristol.

Captain [James] Whitefield,[11] calling in, tried to moderate him. Put him in mind of his rashness, and the many letters he had sent him by the American clergy to check it. He declared that his brother George Whitefield would utterly condemn him, for he knew it was his most determinate resolution never to divide from the Mr. Wesleys. That as to the doctrine of reprobation, George no more believed it than we do. Poor Seward still repeated the words which those who now hold his leading-strings taught him. When I pressed him that we might be at peace with one another, he answered, "There is no peace for the wicked. You have no saving faith. The devil is in you. He is in every natural man, and he was never cast out of you." The Captain asked how he was sure of that. He replied that the Holy Ghost moved him to call us children of the devil. The Captain was so shocked that he said at last, "I will not suffer you to go over in my ship. You will use my brother as you do Mr. Wesleys. 'Tis enough to make me throw off all religion. If you are a Christian, I will be a heathen or a Turk."

Finding no good could be done by talking (as to speaking to me alone, he absolutely refused it), I proposed going to prayers; which we did, but could not get him to join with us. Now and then he had some momentary relentings, but the poison he has drank so deeply of is not easily to be expelled. His friends (for they have the modesty so to call themselves) have commended him into madness. I perceived at first sight that he was, but waited my opportunity to set him right. More in my next, if not his sermon, which he preached this afternoon.[12]

I have had a glorious day of it. God has comforted me on every side. Let prayers and thanksgivings be offered him on my behalf.

Ἔρρωσο.[13]

Saturday Night

Mr. Seward lifts up his voice concerning the building. Don't you be surprised by an arrest. Ungodly men are now rulers over him, and Satan stands at his right hand. You collect with all diligence both in public and private. Try every one who is likely to contribute. The £100 must be made up forthwith. We grasped at too great matters here and should have taught fewer boys and paid fewer masters, till the debt was cleared. How shall we retrench expenses? It must be done some way or other. I don't expect £100 bill by next post but pray don't let it be long first.

Send me your journal. Hide our dear brother Seward's infirmity all you can, by not showing this, etc., unless to particular friends. His friends,

---

[11] Captain James Whitefield (1709–66) was a brother of George.

[12] This subsequent letter is not known to survive.

[13] "Farewell" (lit., "be healthy").

such as Mr. Mason,[14] etc., should see by all means. May the Spirit of God direct you in all things.

*Address*: "To / The Revd Mr Wesley / at the Foundry / London."
*Postmarks*: "29 / SE" and "Bristol."
*Endorsement*: by JW, "C[harles] Sept. 27, 1740 / of W[illiam] S[eward]'s part[ing] fr[om] us / C[harles]—a[nswere]d Sept. 29, 1740."
*Source*: original letter by amanuensis; MARC, MA 1977/503, Box 5, file 4.

---

[14] Samuel Mason, a London publisher particularly connected to George Whitefield and William Seward.

## April 14–25, 1741[1]

[Bristol]

**Tuesday, April [14[2]].** At 2:00 our Lord opened my mouth to call all to him in the words of Hosea 6, "Come and let us return unto the Lord. For he hath torn, and he will heal us. He hath smitten, and he will bind us up. After two days will he revive us, in the third day he will raise us up and we shall live in his sight. Then shall we know, if we follow on to know the Lord."[3] I found the same enlargement in the evening, especially in prayer for the malefactors who are to die tomorrow. I am sure some present had faith for them.

**Wednesday afternoon, [April 15].** I preached at Westerleigh[4] (Isaiah 52[:1], "Awake, awake, put on thy strength, O Sion!") to a little flock who invited me thither. Neither in this place hath God left himself without witness.

Had much of the power of God among us in the evening. None of the bands seem inclined to swallow the Horrible Decree.[5] Sin, only wilful sin, can dispose us for that doctrine. But when we put away a good conscience, no wonder if concerning the faith we make shipwreck.

**Thursday, [April 16].** One of our old men in the Wood[6] complained to me that the separatists[7] had got from him the treatise against predestination and burnt it.[8] In like manner John Cennick *answers* all my brother's sermons on *Free Grace*[9] which he can lay hands on. His brethren are great friends to burning, and so, when God permits, will they treat

---

[1] This manuscript is entirely in CW's hand. It contains scattered mark-outs and corrections by CW, but it also contains extensive mark-outs and revisions in the hand of JW, who was preparing for publication an extract titled *A Short Account of the Death of Hannah Richardson* [London: Strahan, 1741]. The transcription that follows ignores JW's revisions, reproducing CW's more complete final text. The text is the source of, but much more extensive than the account of these days in CW, MS Journal.

[2] Orig., "15"; CW misdates by one day throughout.

[3] Hosea 6:1–3.

[4] Westerleigh, Gloucestershire; 7 miles northeast of Bristol. CW spells "Westernly."

[5] CW had just published in March 1741 *Hymns on God's Everlasting Love; To Which is Added the Cry of a Reprobate and the Horrible Decree*; the "horrible decree" was unconditional reprobation (or predestination more generally).

[6] I.e., Kingswood.

[7] Over the last few months a split had emerged among Bristol Methodists around John Cennick's vigorous advocacy of unconditional election or predestination; see JW, *Journal*, Dec. 16–26, 1740 (*Works*, 19:174–75) and Feb. 21–Mar. 14, 1741 (*Works*, 19:181–87).

[8] JW had extracted a relevant portion of the Quaker Robert Barclay's *Apology for the True Christian Divinity* and published it mid-March 1741 in Bristol (Felix Farley), titled *Serious Considerations on Absolute Predestination*.

[9] JW had published his sermon *Free Grace* (*Works*, 3:544–61) in Bristol in May 1739.

the writer of those books. But they do nothing unless they could burn one more book—the Bible.

Heard at Kendalshire[10] that John Cennick had been there the evening after I preached and was greatly withstood by a young man (James Harding[11]) for an hour in the midst of his followers. He asked, "Do you hold reprobation?" Cennick was forced to answer yes. "Then," said Harding, "I will no more come to hear you than I will come to hear the devil, whose doctrine you preach." Last Sunday he likewise met with a severe rebuke from a boy whom he had perverted, but who after hearing me sought out Cennick and said in the midst of the congregation, "You have damned me by your doctrine. I am reprobated. I shall go to hell, and there I shall meet you." This he uttered with many tears, and so *left* him.

God gave me words to maintain his cause. I showed them the end of messiah being cut off,[12] namely "to finish the transgression, and to make an end of sin, and to bring in everlasting righteousness."[13] The Spirit of supplication was poured out, and one soul (as I since heard) was translated into the glorious liberty.

Called on sister [Anne] Williams, who has been long hunted by the predestinarians and buffeted by those messengers of Satan. Before she saw me, or was told of my coming, "she knew in herself that deliverance was at hand." Asked whither they had not sent for me, and was sure I was not far off, just as I entered. In that instant the snare was broken and she was delivered. Satan departed from her for a season and she again trusted in the living God, who is the Saviour of all men.

Instead of expounding, I read the *[Serious] Consideration[s] on Absolute Predestination*. The fire which Christ came to bring upon earth was kindled in many hearts,[14] which bore witness to his universal love.

**Friday, [April 17].** Was much affected in prayer with our dear colliers. A remnant shall be saved from the roaring, reprobating lion. And I doubt not but they will yet take root downward and bear fruit upward.

For the sake of the poor soldiers (of whom I counted above a dozen at the Room this evening) I enlarged upon the faithful saying that Christ Jesus came into the world to save sinners.[15] God forgive those who make

---

[10] Kendalshire (now Kendleshire), Gloucestershire; 7 miles northeast of Bristol.

[11] Harding would later teach for a while at Kingswood school; cf. JW, *Journal*, Mar. 14, 1749, *Works*, 20:265. He may be the James Harding baptized in 1714 in an Independent congregation in Bristol.

[12] See Dan. 9:26; CW spells "Messias."

[13] Cf. Dan. 9:24.

[14] See Luke 12:49.

[15] See 1 Tim. 1:15; and also CW's hymn of this passage from the time period, *HSP* (1742), 93–94.

it *necessary* for us even to mention aught else. I desire to know, and speak, and think of nothing but Christ Jesus, and him crucified.

**Saturday, April [18].** Spoke to four of the society who walked disorderly, making a mock at the word preached, talking, and laughing, and reviling. I put them upon trial, till their behaviour should be more becoming the gospel of Christ.

Just [as] I was going into the society, to read the letters,[16] I was hastily called away to one that was a-dying. It was Hannah Richardson, a young woman of the bands.[17] She had long been a sincere mourner for Christ—a true Hannah, a woman of a sorrowful spirit.[18] God had awakened and drawn her from her infancy, and she heartily laboured to establish her own righteousness, seeking acceptance (as we did all) "not by faith, but as it were by the works of the law."[19]

When it pleased God to send the gospel of his free grace to this city, she gladly parted with her own righteousness and submitted herself unto the righteousness of God. She was a constant hearer of the word, but received no benefit by it—no comfort, no peace, no life. Yet she continued waiting for several months till it pleased our Lord, who sends by whom he will send, to make use of my ministry and apply the word of reconciliation to her soul. Jesus gave her a token for good, and she went home to her house justified. She rejoiced in God *her* Saviour, and testified, "In him I have redemption through his blood, the forgiveness of sins."[20]

But alas, the Comforter was "as a guest that tarrieth but a day."[21] She soon gave place to the reasoning devil, who asked "How can these things be?"[22] How can you be justified, so vile a sinner as you? You only deceive yourself. Hath God for Christ['s] sake forgiven you? He hath not surely forgiven you. By such suggestions he well-nigh tore away her shield. All the comfort of her faith, all her peace and joy in believing, he did entirely spoil her of; God so permitting it, to try her and prove her and show her what was in her heart, that he might do her good in her latter end. He hid his face from her and she was troubled. "I will allure her," said God, "and bring her into the wilderness."[23] Here she long wandered out of the way in

---

[16] Early Methodists wrote regularly to one another about God's work in their lives and their communities, and they often read these letters aloud in society meetings.

[17] "Hannah" may have been her familiar name; her burial record reads "Ann Richardson."

[18] See 1 Sam. 1:15.

[19] Rom. 9:32.

[20] Eph. 1:7; Col. 1:14.

[21] Wisd. of Sol. 5:14.

[22] Cf. John 3:9.

[23] Hosea 2:14.

a barren and dry land where no water was.[24] The poor and needy sought water and there was none, and her tongue failed for thirst.[25] She could truly say with the prophet, "Verily thou art a God that hidest thyself."[26] Or with the patient man, "Behold I go forward but he is not there, and backward but I cannot perceive him; on the left hand, where he doth work, but I cannot behold him; he hideth himself on the right-hand, that I cannot see him."[27] Her bones were smitten asunder as with a sword, while the enemy said unto her, "Where is now thy God? Where is now thy faith? Thou art a thousand times worse than ever."

So indeed she seemed to herself when sin "appeared"[28] sin. God was now uncovering her heart and convincing her of original sin. The old "man of sin" was more and more "revealed,"[29] till at last she saw that her "inward parts were very wickedness"[30] and "every imagination of the thoughts of her heart only evil continually."[31] She had no power to pray, or praise, or so much as to think one good thought, and at the same time was so torn and distracted with doubts and fears that she despaired even of life. That thought above all tormented her: What would become of me if I should die in this darkness? Without holiness no one shall see the Lord.[32] At other times she had a faint persuasion that God would finish his work before he called her hence.

She durst not say she had faith or any interest in Christ, and yet she could not give it up. One little spark of hope lay as at the very bottom of her heart, which was Christ's hold of her. He would not quit his purchase or let her go.

It was often a great trouble to her that she could not fear death as formerly. But this fear was entirely cast out the first moment she was sensible of her justification. Whenever she had the least comfort or peace, she started back as it were and feared to take hold of it, suspecting that she was falling asleep again and resting without Christ. She went mourning all the day long and refused to be comforted because he was not.

For many days and months she walked on still in darkness and had no light, but against hope believed in hope—staggering ofttimes,

---

[24] See Ps. 63:1.
[25] See Isa. 41:17.
[26] Isa. 45:15.
[27] Job 23:8–9.
[28] Cf. Rom. 7:13.
[29] Cf. 2 Thess. 2:3.
[30] Ps. 5:9.
[31] Gen. 6:5.
[32] See Heb. 12:14.

but not falling, through unbelief. Still she bore up under her continual fears of being a castaway. She waited in a constant use of all the means of grace. Never missed the communion or hearing the word, though all was torment to her for she never found benefit. Nothing, she said, affected *her*. There was none so wicked as her. I am a witness to her many complaints and wailings, which always comforted my heart and filled me with joy and faith for her. She persisted with a glorious obstinacy, and "followed on to know the Lord, walking in all his commandments and ordinances blameless."[33] She went on steadily in the way of her duty, never intermitting it on account of her inward conflicts. Not slothful in business, but working almost continually with her own hands. Most strict was she and unblameable in all her relative duties. Those who lived with her never heard a light or trifling word come out of her mouth. She did not sit *still* till she should be pure in heart, but redeemed the time and bought up every opportunity of doing good. To do good she never forgot, but spoke to all and warned all, both children and grown persons, as God delivered them into her hands. She was exceeding tender-hearted toward the sick, whether in body or soul. She could not rejoice with those that rejoiced. But she wept with those that wept and encouraged them to wait upon God (who hid his face from her), to be never weary of well-doing, for in the end, she said, they should reap if they fainted not.

See here a pattern of true mourning! A spectacle for men and angels! A soul standing up under the intolerable weight of original sin! Troubled on every side—perplexed but not in despair: persecuted by sin, the world, and the devil, but not forsaken. Cast down but not destroyed.[34] Walking on as evenly under that load of darkness as if she had been in the broad light of God's countenance. Whosoever thou art that seekest Christ sorrowing, "go thou and do likewise!"[35]

In this agony she continued till it pleased God to visit her with her last sickness. For the two or three first days she could not be kept from the word, but was then constrained to take her bed. She had early notice of her departure and told one of her band that she should not recover. She had expressed great earnestness to see me, but I could not visit her till the Thursday before her death. I found her, to her own sense and feeling, in utter despair. "I am dying," she cried, "without pardon, without a Saviour, without hope." I prayed in full assurance of faith and then testified the love of Christ to her, a lost sinner, assuring her that he would fulfil in her all the good counsel of his good pleasure and the work of faith with power. "My soul for yours," I told her, "if you depart hence before your

---

[33] Cf. Hosea 6:3 and Luke 1:6.
[34] See 2 Cor. 4:8–9.
[35] Luke 10:37.

eyes have seen his salvation. 'Yet a little while and he that shall come will come, and will not tarry.'[36] 'The word of our God shall stand forever.'[37] Every one that seeketh findeth.[38] Fear not. Behold he comes quickly, and one moment of his presence will make you abundant amends for all the pain of absence."

When I was gone she expressed great satisfaction in having seen me. But, said she, it has done me no good. I am still the same. Her sufferings rather increased, and Satan raged the more because he had but a short time. The lion tore her, as it were, to pieces. She was in a mighty conflict and said, "None knows what I have gone through in this sickness. My enemy triumphs over me. It is the hour of darkness. It is more than I am able to bear."

"The captive exile hasteneth that she may be loosed, and that she should not die in the pit, nor that her bread should fail."[39] This trial, as it was the last, so it was the severest of all. "The devil," she said, "besets me sorely. I shall never hold out. I shall perish at last. But if I am lost, I am content. Though I go down to hell, let but Christ be with me and I will go without fear." Here she seemed to be strengthened to endure a greater agony. She drank of the cup which her Lord drank of and had fellowship in those sufferings which made him cry out, "My God, my God, why hast thou forsaken me!"[40] To complete her distress, the angel of death came. She was struck and changed on a sudden (so that one came and told me she was just a-dying). Then, as man would judge, she let go her hold of God, and "the spirit failed before him and the soul which he had made,"[41] which he also purchased and redeemed of old.

In this dreadful moment, this last extremity, this deepest distress that the human soul is capable of, the Comforter came. The Lord her Saviour came suddenly to his temple. "As lightning shineth from one end of the heaven unto the other, so was the coming of the Son of man."[42] He took away the veil from her heart and revealed himself in her in a manner the world knoweth not of. But she broke out, "Now I know that Christ died for me. He has washed me from all my sins in his precious blood. I have eternal life abiding in me."

**Saturday morning, 11 o'clock, [April 18].** Soon after she had found redemption I called and saw her in the full triumph of faith. O how

---

[36] Heb. 10:37.
[37] Isa. 40:8.
[38] See Matt. 7:8.
[39] Isa. 51:14.
[40] Matt. 27:46; Mark 15:34.
[41] Cf. Isa. 57:16.
[42] Cf. Matt. 24:27; Luke 17:24.

unlike what she was at my last visit. "If any man is in Christ, he is a new creature."[43] This is the work which despisers will not believe, though a man declare it unto them.[44] Her soul was passed from death unto life, an hidden everlasting life in God. After we had prayed she witnessed a good confession. "I believe in Jesus Christ. I feel the truth of those words of his, 'I am the resurrection and the life.'[45] I have no fear, no doubt, no trouble. Your words were true, he has fulfilled his promise."

I was hastened back to the society, but found her present with us in spirit, though absent in body. Many tears of joy were shed at my relating of her deliverance. God showed himself a God hearing prayer and greatly manifested his power in the midst of us.

I returned to see a Christian indeed! Never, never did I behold a soul so filled. Some of her words were, "Now indeed he has made me amends for my waiting. Blessed be God! All my pain is nothing. I have suffered nothing. I smell the sweet odour of the name of Jesus. His smell is as the smell of Lebanon.[46] Who is so sweet as my beloved? 'My beloved is mine and I am his.'[47] I love Jesus Christ with all my heart. I desire to be dissolved and to be with Christ. But his will be done. I have no will of my own." While I was saying, "Doubt not, but be persuaded that neither life, nor death, nor things present, nor things ...,"[48] she interrupted me with, "No, no, I cannot doubt, although I did doubt. I cannot fear now. Perfect love hath cast out fear.[49] I have full redemption in the blood of Jesus."

To her sisters she had said, just before I came, "Heaven is open! I see Jesus Christ with all his angels and saints in white. And I am joined to them. I shall never be parted more. I see what I cannot utter or express! Cannot you see Jesus Christ? There, there he stands, ready to receive you all! O do not doubt of the love of Jesus. Look on me! If he has taken me into his bosom, who needs despair. Fear not, fear not. He is loving unto every man. *I believe Christ died for all!*"

Her first words after I first left her were, "Liberty, liberty! This is the glorious liberty of the sons of God! I know it. I see it. I feel it. Believe, believe there is such a liberty, and he will give it you. *I am sanctified wholly, spirit, soul, and body!*"[50]

---

[43] 2 Cor. 5:17.
[44] See Acts 13:41.
[45] John 11:25.
[46] See Hosea 14:6.
[47] Song of Sol. 2:16.
[48] Cf. 1 Cor. 3:22.
[49] See 1 John 4:18.
[50] See 1 Thess. 5:23.

She had spent the time while I was absent in fervent prayer, and at my third visit told me, "I have whatsoever I ask. I have asked life for my mother and sisters, and have obtained it." I took the opportunity and put her upon praying for the peace of Jerusalem; for union; for the preachers of reprobation, that God might open their eyes; for my brother; and for the lambs of this fold, that they might not be turned out of the way; [[for myself that our Lord would give me a h[umble] h[eart].[51] I put them all out, and confessed my sins to his dying saints, and I was under p[ain] of them, and feared lest after having preached to others, I myself should be a castaway.[52] I prayed with many tears, her faith holding up my hands. She assured me that prayer was answered, bid me be of good cheer,[53] and tarry the Lord's leisure.[54]]].

The fourth time I came to see her they told me she had been in a great conflict of faith, oft times repeating, "I will wrestle with thee for a blessing. I will not let thee go unless thou bless him.[55] Bless that soul! Give him the thing I ask." At last she said, "Now I am more than conqueror. I have the petitions I ask. Not one is unanswered. [[He will have the grace of heaven poured upon him in an abundant measure. He shall have it. It is his, I know it. I am sure of it.]]"

To me she said, "I have power with God and with man, and have prevailed.[56] [[You shall, I know, you shall be humble, holy beyond all that I can express. I am assured by God's verse[?]. I now see the glory in which you shall shine with me till eternity.]]"

From expounding at the Malt-room, I returned the last time and found her ready for the bridegroom. Her every word was full of power and life and love. It was the Spirit of her Father which spoke in her. He had been wrestling again and making intercession for the saints and all mankind, particularly our own church and nation. Some of her words were, "Thy judgments are abroad in the earth, O that the inhabitants of this land may learn righteousness! Grant me, sweet Jesus, that they may repent and live." She prayed fervently for the society, that they[57] might abide in the word, keep close together, and be all of one heart and mind. "There is a curse upon them," said she, "a curse of unthankfulness. But I have prayed my dear Lord to remove it, and he will remove it."

---

[51] The shorthand is simply "h h"; this expansion seems likely from the context, but others are possible.

[52] See 1 Cor. 9:27.

[53] See John 16:33.

[54] Cf. Ps. 27:16 (BCP).

[55] See Gen. 32:26.

[56] See Gen. 32:28.

[57] Orig., "that that."

When one of her sisters in band came to see her who was deeply mourning for Christ, she laboured much to comfort her, bade[58] her look at *her*, so miserable and hopeless an unbeliever lately, and assured her the Comforter should quickly come. At sight of her sister's tears, oh how sweetly did she lament over her. I never saw such sympathy! The Spirit in her mourned like a turtledove, and made intercession with groanings that cannot be uttered.[59]

All the time of her sickness she never once complained or showed the least sensibility of pain, or that she had any body at all. When one asked her if she did not feel her pains, being then in strong convulsions, she answered, "My pain is great, but I do not feel it. It does not trouble me. I choose it rather than ease, for my Lord chooses it. Pain or ease, life or death—'tis all one. The Spirit beareth witness with my spirit that I am a child of God.[60] I have the earnest of mine inheritance in my heart. I have no will. I am made perfect in love." [[She caught hold of both my hands and spoke her last words to me, "I am sure, I am sure of our salvation! Amen and amen!"]]

I asked whether that peace which she tasted above a year ago was the same she now enjoyed. She answered, "It was of the same kind, in the lowest or first degree. It surely was justification."

After I went she said, "This day I shall be with him in paradise.[61] Within twenty-four hours I shall be with my beloved."

She continued all night in the labour of love, making powerful supplication for all men. About three on Sunday morning, she said, "It is finished."[62] All suffering for others ceased from that moment, and she began the new song which shall never end. Her whole employment now was the same with theirs to whom she was come, the innumerable company of angels, the church of the first-born. She sang to the harpers' harps, without any intermission till two in the afternoon. Even while they were giving her cordials she sang. Her hope was full of immortality, her looks of heaven, till while with smiles of triumph she resigned her spirit into the hands of her dear Redeemer. Death wanted all its pomp and circumstances of horror. She went away without any agony, or sigh, or groan. She only rested, and sweetly fell asleep in the arms of Jesus.

Let me die the death of the righteous and let my last end be like hers.

[[After her first fervent intercession for me, I opened Daniel 12:12[–13], "Blessed is he that waiteth and cometh to the 1335[63] days. But go thou

---

[58] CW consistently spells the past tense of "bid" as "bad."

[59] See Rom. 8:26.

[60] See Rom. 8:16.

[61] See Luke 23:43.

[62] See John 19:30.

[63] Orig., "3335"; a mistake.

thy way, till the end be, for thou shalt rest and stand in thy lot at the end of the days."

[[In the moreover[?[64]] strongest assurance to me that God shall make me humble, holy, a partaker of his glory, etc., I opened Esther 9:29[-32], "Then Esther the queen, the daughter of Abihail, and Mordecai the Jew, wrote with all authority to confirm this 2nd letter of Purim. And he sent the letters unto all the Jews, ... with words of peace and truth. To confirm these days of Purim in their times appointed, ... the matters of the fastings and their cry. And the decree of Esther confirmed these matters of Purim, and it was written in the book."]]

**Sunday, April [19].** Encouraged the mourners by that sure word of promise, Isaiah 40:31, "They that wait on the Lord shall renew their strength." And again at Kingswood spoke comfort to many from Isaiah 42:3[-4], "A bruised reed shall he not break, and the smoking flax shall he not quench. He shall bring forth judgment unto truth. He shall not fail nor be discouraged, till he hath set judgment in the earth, and the isles shall wait for his law."

In the afternoon proceeded to explain the same chapter and showed the free grace (as they call it) of reprobation. The people were much affected, and several began to find they were only deluded with the sound of free grace by the reprobating preachers, whom they would in no wise hear if they durst avow their principles and honestly preach out what they think.

Rode directly to Baptist Mills[65] and, as it were, *took the field* before the enemy. Though I will not trust in my bow, it is not my sword that shall help me. I found unexpectedly near 3,000 hearers but had no strength either of soul or body till I began. Then my mouth was opened to maintain the truth and mercy and justice of God, who never rejects any that do not *first* reject him. The scripture which [I] offered was Acts 28:[27-]28, "The heart of this people is waxed gross, ... and their eyes have *they* closed, *lest*[66] they should see .... Be it known *therefore* unto you, that the salvation of God is sent unto the Gentiles, and that they will hear [it]."

The author of that great yet common salvation was with us, and by the sharp two-edged sword, which went out of his mouth,[67] did great execution. To him, and him alone, be all the glory!

Returning to the Bristol society, I heard that our sister Hannah had finished her course. My soul was immediately filled with strong consolation and struggled, as it were, to go out after her—as heavenward

---

[64] The shorthand appears to be "mfr."
[65] An area of Bristol half a mile northeast of city center.
[66] Orig., "least."
[67] See Rev. 1:16.

endeavouring. O Jesus! My time is in thy hand; but let me so follow her, as[68] she hath followed thee.[69]

The voice of joy and thanksgiving was in the congregation while I spoke of her death. Our sister Purnell has proved a true prophet that many of the society would quickly follow her,[70] but God would first finish his work and cut it short in righteousness.[71]

**Monday, April [20].** After expounding at Kingswood, called on Mr. W.,[72] who told me Mr. [John] Cennick had preached as strong a sermon against reprobation as my brother ever did. "Are you sure of that?" I asked again and again. "Yes." "Why then," I replied, "Mr. Cennick is not an honest man, for he preaches one thing and believes another. He himself declared to me with his own mouth that he believed reprobation."

The hand of the Lord was upon me at Downend,[73] while I explained that universal call, "Look unto me and be ye saved all the ends of the earth!" Isaiah [45:22]. An extraordinary power was in the midst of us. Many felt the earthquake which precedes the coming of the Son of man.[74] We prayed and sang alternately for two hours. I warned them in strong words of love against the horrible doctrine. God enlarged and bowed and, I trust, established their hearts.

The same sweet power was with the bands at Kingswood. God endued our souls with much strength. O may we always strengthen ourselves in the grace which is in Christ Jesus!

**Tuesday, April [21].** Was much comforted to hear Mr. [George] Whitefield is coming down breathing out threatenings against *me*. Hitherto my brother has been the mark of their displeasure, but now they have also given *me* over to the devil. "For therefore we both labour and suffer reproach, because we trust in the living God, who is *the Saviour of all men*, specially of those that believe."[75]

Spoke comfortably to God's afflicted ones from Isaiah 49:15: "Can a woman forget her sucking child, ..." and hastened to the joyful funeral of our sister Richardson. The room was crowded within and without. My text was Job 19:25, "I know that my Redeemer liveth ...." Spoke searchingly to the hearsay believers, and then largely of her whose faith they might safely follow. Great was my glorying and rejoicing over her. She being

---

[68] Orig., "and."

[69] See 1 Cor. 11:1.

[70] Elizabeth Purnell died on Oct. 22, 1740 (see CW, MS Journal).

[71] See Rom. 9:28.

[72] Likely Anthony Williams.

[73] Downend, Gloucestershire; 5 miles northeast of Bristol. CW spells "Downing."

[74] See Rev. 16:18.

[75] 1 Tim. 4:10.

dead, yet spoke[76] in those words of faith and love which ought to be had in remembrance. I doubt not but she was present with us in spirit; for we were in a measure partakers of her joy, a joy unspeakable and full of glory.[77]

The whole society followed her to the grave, which was through all the city.[78] Satan raged exceedingly in his children, who compassed us in on every side like so many ravening predestinarians. They threw dirt and stones at us and, but that the bridle was in their mouths, would have torn us to pieces.

Still the devil roared for having lost his prey, and made such a disturbance at the grave that the minister seemed frightened, especially when he turned and saw me at his elbow. I could not but smile to hear him say, "There is some design in this." After the burial we joined in the following thanksgiving:

1. Come let us who in Christ believe
   With saints and angels join,
   Glory, and praise, and blessing give,
   And thanks to grace divine.

2. Our friend in sure, and certain hope
   Hath laid her body down,
   She knew that Christ will raise her up,
   And give the starry crown.

3. To all, who his appearing love
   He opens paradise,
   And we shall join the hosts above,
   And we shall grasp the prize.

4. Then let us wait to see his day,
   To hear the welcome word,
   To answer, Lo! we come away,
   We die, to meet our Lord.[79]

**Wednesday, April [22].** Warned the bands once more before the time of trial and sharply rebuked three or four inflexible Pharisees. Then

---

[76] See Heb. 11:4.

[77] See 1 Pet. 1:8.

[78] Ann Richardson was buried Apr. 21, 1741 in the cemetery of St. Augustine's church, on the northwest corner of Bristol.

[79] CW published with minor variants as "After the Funeral," *HSP* (1742), 131.

prayed that God would give me words of consolation, and immediately my mouth was opened. The power filled me and broke out as a mighty torrent. Let him take all the glory who wrought wonderfully in me and by me. All our hearts caught fire, as in a moment. And such strong cryings and tears followed as quite silenced my voice. I sat still while the prayer of the humble pierced the clouds; it entered into the ears of the Lord of Sabbaoth. The sorrowful sighing of such as were in captivity came before him, and according to the greatness of his power, those that were appointed to die. Almost all present found the Spirit making intercession for them, and many received an answer of peace. As soon as the love of God was shed abroad in their hearts the Spirit bore witness, and they witnessed a good confession that Christ died for all.

The spirit of Jesus is the spirit of prophecy.[80] Such words were spoken by some that prophesied as pierced my soul. At last I lifted up the book and cried, "The spirits of the prophets are subject to the prophets. Bow to the written word." Immediately there was a profound silence while I read Elijah['s] contention with the priests of Baal. The God that answereth by fire received my appeal. And at those words, "Then the fire of the Lord fell, and consumed the burnt sacrifice,"[81] a prisoner of hope broke loose from the bondage of corruption and cried out, "Christ died for all." She was filled with faith and the Holy Ghost. Scarce a soul of us was sent empty away. We were all amazed and glorified God, the Saviour of all men, saying, "We never saw it on this fashion."[82]

I thought this triumph was to prepare us for future conflicts, and as soon as I went out a poor collier's wife brought me notice that the elect had a design to get the Kingswood school into their hands. The mistress[83] they had made sure of. A bold confident Pharisee. A vessel of sin fitted for predestination. One who had deceived my brother and crept in, in my absence. But whom I have proved to be a backbiter, a liar, a swearer, a drunkard, and if not a whore it is because others have more grace than her. One who had secretly undermined us, stealing away the children and others, full of all guile and hypocrisy—in a word, worthy to go as a beloved sister and shake hands with John Cennick.

She had taken much pains to get the other mistress out of the house, and very outrageous was she because her labour was lost. The devil owed her a shame, or she would never have said in the rage of disappointment, "What? Has Mr. Wesley set you to watch the house? Are you afraid I should go over to the predestinarians? Do you think I want to take possession?" A

---

[80] See Rev. 19:10.

[81] 1 Kings 18:38.

[82] Mark 2:12.

[83] CW identifies as Hannah Barrow in MS Journal.

woman who heard of these words immediately left her small family and gave me notice that if the separatists got possession of the house, we could in no wise recover it.

I thought it no distrust of God to immediately take horse for the Wood. My heart was calm and full of comfort. George Whitefield was expected every hour and, if our suspicions concerning his friends are ill-grounded, would do well to declare that none of them ever mentioned to him any such design of getting the house (fraudulently or violently) into his hands. As yet I do not think him capable of it. Between 10:00 and 11:00 I came thither and slept in peace.

**Thursday, April [23].** After preaching, told the mistress we should have no farther occasion for her, paid her above her wages, gave her a crown myself, and dismissed her without upbraiding. She was very urgent for a reason and complained much. But, not having taken her for better [or] for worse, I did not multiply words, nor added to the few and kind ones which I had first spoken.

In the evening returned to Bristol, gathered up a stray sheep and carried her to hear the word, which for some time she had forsaken. Strongly exhorted the people to take to them the whole armour of God, that they might be able to stand in this evil day, and having done all, to stand.[84] Seldom, if ever, have I preached with like demonstration of the Spirit. God doubly confirms his word when it is denied.

**Friday, April [24].** Spoke to the colliers from the first scripture that presented, Isaiah 50:7[–8], "For the Lord will help me, therefore shall I not be confounded. Therefore have I set my face like a flint, and I know that I shall not be ashamed. He is near that justifieth me. Who will contend with me? Let us stand together. Who is mine adversary? Let him come near to me." (Just then, as I afterwards heard, George Whitefield passed by the school.) I could not but observe how God casts off the imputation of man's damnation, v. 1., "Thus saith the Lord, Where is the bill of your mother's divorcement, whom I have put away? Or which of my creditors is it to whom I have sold you? Behold for *your iniquities have you sold yourselves*, and for your transgressions is your mother put away."[85] After prayers I was constrained to begin again, I know not why, and pray after the Spirit in a particular manner for myself, that our Lord would give me power over the nations, even as he had received of his Father.

Overtook the principal man of our poor departed brethren and asked, "Now, my brother [Thomas] Bissicks[86] are you ready, as you once said, to

---

[84] See Eph. 6:11–17; and the hymn CW wrote about this time, based on this passage: *The Whole Armour of God* [Bristol: Farley, 1742?].

[85] Isa. 50:1.

[86] See JW's accounts of Thomas Bissicks' in *Journal*, Feb. 24–28, 1741 (*Works*, 19:182–85) and Oct. 16–17, 1741 (*Works*, 19:232). CW spells "Bissick."

go with me to the stake?" I added no more but "Is Christ divided?"[87] and rode quickly to Mrs. [Elizabeth] Hooper's. Here I had resort to the oracle, which gives clear and unambiguous answers to all that consult it. The first word that struck me was Job 30:1, "But now they that are younger than I have me in derision, whose fathers I would have disdained to set with the dogs of my flock." Then I was directed to Daniel 9:25, "The street shall be built again, and the wall, even in troublous times." And then to 1 Corinthians 1:25, "Because the foolishness of God is wiser than men, and the weakness of God is stronger than men." And yet again to Isaiah 52:10, "The Lord hath made bare his holy arm in the eyes of all the nations, and all the ends of the earth shall see the salvation of our God." [[After fervent prayer for myself, opened Psalm 77:15,[88] "Thou hast with thine arm redeemed thy people."]]

At 1:00, met to keep the fast. I never had greater faith in prayer and cannot doubt but that all shall happen for the furtherance of the gospel. The power of the Lord was present to heal, but one predestinarian it wounded deeply. She was struck as with the pangs of death and earnestly desired my prayers. May he who maketh sore, bind up. Some who intended to hear Mr. Whitefield tonight were now by the grace of God restrained from tasting poison *to try if it would hurt them.*

Spent the afternoon chiefly in confirming the weak, whom Mr. [John] Cennick and [Joseph] Humphreys have set upon, without loss of time. Prayed with one strong in the Lord and in the power of his might,[89] or rather lent words to her faith. She said Jesus had shown her what great things my brother should suffer for his name['s] sake[90] that while she was offering him up in prayer, the answer of God said unto her, "And devout men carried Stephen to his burial and made great lamentation over him."[91] I took the more notice of this because, as I remembered, he himself had opened upon the self-same words just as he was setting out the first time for Bristol.[92]

The usual congregation came to the Room at 6:00 (the time of George Whitefield's preaching) instead of 7:00. I left God to choose me a text and opened the book where it is written, "And now I beseech thee, let the power of my Lord be great, according as thou hast spoken," (Numbers

---

[87] 1 Cor. 1:13.

[88] Orig., "Psalm 77:5."

[89] See Eph. 6:10.

[90] Orig., "name-sake."

[91] Acts 8:2.

[92] Humphreys had been drawn into the revival by JW and CW in London in 1740, and sent by them to help in Bristol; but now had aligned with George Whitefield and the Calvinist Methodists.

14[:17]), that famous history of the spies who brought up an evil report of the promised land. I said, "Let us go up at once and possess it, for we are well able to overcome it."[93] God inclined their hearts to listen unto me rather than "the men that went up with us, who say we are not able to go up against the people, for they are stronger than we."[94] We can never conquer all sin; we *must* sin *sometimes*.

Rode directly to Kingswood in (it may be too great) confidence of finding the same extraordinary power. Opened the book upon Solomon's prayer at the dedication of God's house.[95] Many were come from far and near to spend the night in watching unto prayer,[96] and had much of the divine presence. I myself remained like Gideon's fleece, till "at midnight behold a cry! The bridegroom cometh!"[97] A flame was kindled in most hearts and we found the Lord God was among us as in the holy place of Sinai. A little before 1:00 [a.m.] we parted.

**Saturday, April [25].** Found Mr. Humphreys at Mrs. Hooper's and could truly tell him my heart was just the same towards him as ever. Was at sister [Rachel] England's when George Whitefield called. I went down to him and he began complaining of my brother's perverting the money collected for Kingswood school by first finishing Bristol school.[98] Indeed he owned that himself, George Whitefield, consented (when the first collection of about £30 was made) to their joining both in one and thereby, I thought, returned himself an answer. I told him those money matters I was unconcerned in. He must talk with my brother about them.[99] Then he asked if I would let him preach there. I replied, "Would you let me preach universal redemption in your orphan house?" At last he answered, "Yes." "Why then," said I, "we shall be even. For once I have suffered you to preach at the Foundery and contradict all that was ever taught there before. But to be plain, I will sooner die than consent to your preaching false doctrine to my flock." He rose up hastily and said, "Well, I will not stay to stir up your zeal, but your brother loses ground daily in London, and I will stay in England all winter." With those words he went, I waiting upon him to the door. Sims,[100] Humphreys,

---

[93] Num. 13:30.

[94] Num. 13:31.

[95] 1 Kings 8:22–61; or 2 Chron. 6.

[96] I.e., they were holding a watch-night service. These services of prayer, praise, and thanksgiving began about 8:00 p.m. and ran to about midnight. See JW, *A Plain Account of the People Called Methodists*, III, *Works*, 9:264.

[97] Matt. 25:6.

[98] I.e., the "New Room," which initially housed a school for poor children.

[99] See JW's letter to Whitefield on these matters, Apr. 27, 1741, *Works*, 26:58–61.

[100] Likely Peter Sims, of London, who had become a close associate of John Cennick and was instrumental to Cennick's emerging alignment with the Moravians. See JW, *Journal*, Oct. 24, 1750, *Works*, 20:365.

and Cennick were with him. The latter asked me if I had called him hypocrite. "I do call you hypocrite now," said I, "for *not* preaching predestination. And I have found you to be a notorious liar by what you told Mr. A." He justified it and said I *had* promised him never to preach against predestination. "Well then," I replied, "here let the matter rest. Either you or I must be false and liars. If you have wronged *me*, I pray God forgive you, and do myself as freely forgive you as he has forgiven me."

The word at night was very refreshing to my own and others' souls. Our thanksgiving notes multiply—more and more being "convinced of judgment," or that *dreadful* perfection and living without sin. One wrote thus, "There was not a word came out of your mouth last night but I could apply it to my soul and witness it is the doctrine of Christ. I know that Christ is a whole Saviour. I know the blood of Christ hath washed away all my sins and am sure the Lord will make me *perfect* in love before I go hence and am no more seen. 'O for a thousand tongues to sing my dear Redeemer's praise!'[101] Sir, it is under your doctrine that I feel there is such a state as living without sin. I am willing to have it known for the strengthening of others."

Kept the bands and spent half an hour with them in delightful prayer.

*Address & Postmark*: none; likely hand delivered, or CW's copy for records.
*Source*: holograph; MARC, MA 1977/503, Box 5, file 5.

---

[101] CW, "For the Anniversary of One's Conversion," st. 7, *HSP* (1740), 121.

## JUNE 16–28, 1741[1]

[Bristol]

**Tuesday, June 16.** Went to visit a sick man somewhere near Hanham,[2] whose name I had forgot, and therefore called at some of the huts to seek direction. At last a child informed me of one in the neighbourhood who lay a-dying. It was not the man I meant, but whom God meant and sent me to preach the gospel to him. It was good news indeed, and came at the eleventh hour. But I trust he will be saved by it as the penitent thief.[3] When I was going, the woman asked me how Thomas Reed did—the man whom I wanted to find and now got directed to. He had been one of those that drew back,[4] but was now ready to say, "Blessed be he that cometh in the name of the Lord."[5] No *dying* man is grieved to hear Christ died for all.

Spoke with one of the bands who is most cruelly used by her husband because she will not forsake God and his people. A hundred times, she says, he has carried a knife up to bed with him to murder her but was still restrained. Her soul is always in her hand. She sleeps in the region of the shadow of death and fears no evil,[6] as knowing he can have no power over [her] unless it be given him from above. She continually ventures her life upon that word, "How knowest thou, O woman, but thou mayest save thy husband?"[7]

Preached in the Wood on those dreadful words, "Sell all."[8] Never, I think, with more assistance from our Lord. How has the devil baffled those teachers who, for fear of setting men upon works, forbear urging this first universal duty! If enforcing Christ's own words be to preach works, I hope I shall preach works as long as I live.

**Wednesday, June 17.** Gave the sacrament to sister Brimble, dying in such strong agonies as I have not seen before—no, not in Hannah Richardson. She had no fear of hell, but was so deeply convinced of original sin as made all who heard her tremble. She would not let go her confidence that God would finish his works, although there could not be many hours betwixt her and eternity.

---

[1] This manuscript is entirely in CW's hand. It is the source of, and provides greater detail than, the account of these days in CW, MS Journal.

[2] Hanham Mount, Gloucestershire; meadow on small hill 4 miles east of Bristol. CW spells "Hannum."

[3] See Luke 23:42–43.

[4] I.e., one of those convinced of predestination that had separated from the circle of Methodists connected to the Wesley brothers.

[5] Ps. 118:26; Matt. 21:9; 23:39; Mark 11:9; Luke 13:35.

[6] See Ps. 23:4.

[7] See 1 Cor. 7:16.

[8] Luke 18:22.

Met, many of us, at noon in Kingswood to humble our souls with fasting and deprecate the national judgments.[9] In the evening, God gave me words to stir up many that were settled upon their lees. How long have we called him "Lord, Lord," and not done the things that he bids us, not denied ourselves, and took up our cross daily.[10] Deepen, O Lord, the conviction thou hast now given us! If we are dead with thee, we shall also live with thee.[11]

**Thursday, [June] 18.** Visited our brother Haskins's father at Siston,[12] whom God has shown that he is a sinner, but not yet that he is the chief of sinners. Left him desirous to know even as he is known.[13] Soon after, he entered upon his last agony. By his vehement prayers to the Saviour of sinners, and by the faith which God gave his son for him, I trust God made a short work in his soul and received it without spot to himself.[14]

Prayed by another under the strongest convictions of sin, yet nothing doubting but that Jesus will be both the author and finisher of her faith.[15] Several of the poor people joined with us, and among them one of almost Anna's age, who longed to see the Lord's salvation.[16]

Exhorted them of Kendalshire with much earnestness not to receive the grace of God in vain.[17] I never speak there but I find what manner of spirit they are of.[18] Went at their request to pray by a woman who had separated from them. Poor deluded soul! After being elect so long, when she came to die all her cry was, "I am damned, I am damned!" God forbid, say I. But if she perish in her iniquity (her former presumption and final despair), her blood shall God require at *their* hands. Woe, woe unto the preachers of reprobation, except they repent! They pave the way to hell by their doctrine—as many thousands, I fear, have found when it was too late.

At Bristol spoke on the first words that presented, "Thou shalt call

---

[9] The British navy and army had suffered a major defeat at the hands of Spain in March, at Cartagena de Indias (Columbia). This contributed to the decision to dissolve Parliament in April. The election was held Apr. 30–June 11, and the leading Whig party (CW's favoured party), led by Robert Walpole, suffered significant losses.

[10] See Matt. 7:22; Mark 8:34.

[11] See Rom. 6:8; 2 Tim. 2:11.

[12] Henry Haskins was buried June 20, 1741 in Siston, Gloucestershire; 7 miles east of Bristol. CW spells "Sison."

[13] See 1 Cor. 13:12.

[14] See Rom. 9:28.

[15] See Heb. 12:2.

[16] See Luke 2:37.

[17] 2 Cor. 6:1.

[18] See Luke 9:55.

his name Jesus, for he shall save his people from their sins."[19] The Spirit convincing of sin and righteousness was in the midst of us, detecting those who call themselves his people and are not his people. Many of us, I trust, are resolved not to think ourselves his people till we are saved from our sins.

**Friday, [June] 19.** At night I opened the book upon the walls of Jericho falling down,[20] and felt the truth of every word I spoke. O that men would no longer shut their eyes against the light. Then would they see that Jericho is sin, and when Joshua bid them shout it should fall down flat before them. Towards the end of my discourse I was told Howell Harris was present and deeply affected. This he afterwards confessed to me, and that he found the power by which I spake restraining him from denying the truth and filling him with desires of its accomplishment.

My heart yearned towards him, so that I could scarce contain myself, but found three several times my forwardness checked when I was for laying aside all fear and carrying him with me to Kingswood. The treachery of poor George Whitefield was brought to my remembrance, and I was (next to irresistibly) restrained from trusting in man. Went without him to the watch-night in Kingswood and spoke again on the fall of Jericho, with double power. It was a glorious night indeed. We followed the ark, and the shout of a king was in the midst of us.[21] Thine is the kingdom, the power, and the glory![22]

**Saturday, June 20.** Lost two hours in conference with Howell Harris and John Cennick. They may more easily make me believe a lie than I can make them believe the truth. Such power belongeth unto God. However the old man was kept within bounds—Howell Harris only once threatening to renounce and preach against me. John Cennick frankly confessed his hypocrisy; namely, that he had preached what he did not believe, merely to please us. If this be false, he is a foolish liar against himself; if this be true, he is a liar against God and not the servant of Christ.

The colliers having desired a monthly thanksgiving day among them, I went and read the letters and joined with them for three or four hours in praising God with thankful lips.

**Sunday, June 21.** Explained that glorious promise of sanctification, Isaiah 35[:9], "No lion shall be there" (in that high way of holiness) "nor *any* ravenous beast shall come up thereon, it shall not be *found* there." Then showed at Kingswood the true mark of God's (not man's) elect, Isaiah 4:3[–4], "It *shall* come to pass that he that is left in Sion, and he that

---

[19] Matt. 1:21.
[20] Josh. 6.
[21] See Num. 23:21.
[22] See Matt. 6:13.

remaineth in Jerusalem, shall be called" (i.e., shall *be*) "holy, even everyone that is written among the living in Jerusalem. When the Lord *shall have* washed away the filth of the daughters of Sion, and *shall have* purged the blood of Jerusalem from the *midst* thereof by the Spirit of judgment and by the Spirit of burning." Showed hence with the demonstration of that Spirit that all they who deny holiness deny election, and strongly exhorted those who could receive my saying to labour after holiness—which whosoever *hath* attained, he and he only, *hath* made his calling and election sure.

In the afternoon I urged upon all the example of Abraham in offering up his son, his only son, his son Isaac whom he loved.[23] And again at Baptist Mills, with renewed strength, I enforced the universal command of our Lord, "If *any* man *will* come after me, let him deny himself and take up his cross and follow me."[24]

After the society I got an hour by myself in the fields and received strong consolation from the word of God.

**Monday, June 22.** Visited one of the society on her death-bed (as is most probable). God sent me to her that she might preach to *me*. The searcher of hearts suited her words to mine. She conjured me not to depart from the work. "The ministers will endure a great fight of afflictions. All the world will be against you, but go on," said she, "to preach Christ the Saviour of all men, whose blood cleanses from all sin. Christ died for all. None can resist this truth. I have faith for Mr. Whitefield that God will open his eyes. I have not yet attained, but know that Christ shall fill up that which is lacking of my faith." [[3:30 [Francis and Sarah] Labee's, paid her by his consent three guineas for physic.]]

Met the Kingswood bands and the Lord in the midst of them, who bore witness to his own doctrine of the cross. Now we know this is the way. O that we all may walk in it![25]

**Wednesday, June 24.** Asked the woman I saw on Monday, "Have you a new heart now?" "No," she answered, "but I shall receive it, in receiving the sacrament from you." After administering it I repeated my question and she bore witness to the truth, "Everyone that is perfect shall be *as* his master."[26] God, she said, had taken away the evil heart and she had no sin remaining in her. I told her time and temptation would show. Farther she told me, "Mr. Whitefield will be convinced and converted before he leaves England, if he does not wilfully resist the Holy Ghost. But be not you discouraged. Preach you, to all, Christ who died to save all. Tell men that they *may* perfect holiness, and never, never leave off."

---

[23] Gen. 22.

[24] Matt. 16:24.

[25] See Isa. 30:21.

[26] Luke 6:40.

Went at the person's earnest desire to talk with one who had been suborned by the predestinarians to bear an abominable testimony against Christ's minister. The informant was self-condemned and under all the agonies of a guilty conscience. The mystery of iniquity shall be discovered in that day.

Met and warned (I fear for the last time) a poor self-deceiver who, by leaning to his own understanding, is fallen into predestination. From the beginning I always warned him against that death in the pot, spiritual pride, but he would [hear] none of my reproof. His false Ahab-like humility[27] deceived others and himself, so that my fears and jealousy over him were fatally disregarded. Blessed be God for this testimony of my own conscience that I have delivered my own soul!

God gave me searching words, by which many of the bands were deeply wounded. My heart showeth me the wickedness of the ungodly. Never was the Lord more evidently among us. The accursed, I trust, is discovered and will be removed.[28]

**Thursday, June 25.** Found our dying sister still the same, having felt no motion of evil or self-will since the occasion of stumbling (as she thinks) was taken away.

Declared to the little flock at Downend, "Ye are bought with a price. Therefore glorify God in your body, and in your spirit, which are God's." [[Talk of the day of the Lord.]]

At night, in the woman healed of her bloody issue by touching Christ,[29] I showed the way how our fountain of blood, original sin, may be dried up. I find God *owns* the advice which an holy woman gave me from him—namely, to drop all controversy (now I had as their watchman warned them of the sword) and preach only the love of Christ crucified. Virtue did indeed proceed out of him at this time. Many thronged, some touched him, and several, I hope, received faith *to be healed*.

**Friday, June 26.** Alas, poor John Calvin, that ever thy followers should prove followers of Ignatius Loyola and adopt in their practice his principles! "No faith to be kept with heretics. Trust not every man his brother, for they will utterly supplant. The most upright of them is sharper than an hedge-stake," etc.

Howell Harris (who would believe it of Howell Harris?) after his fair professions to me, nay and express confession of the power of God with me, now thinks and speaks little better of me than did William Seward

---

[27] See 1 Kings 21–22.

[28] See Josh. 7.

[29] In the MS Journal entry for June 28, 1738, it is clear that CW was looking at the account in Matt. 9:20–22; but other sermons on this topic may have focused on the parallel passages in Mark 5:25–34 and Luke 8:40–56.

and George Whitefield. Suky H[arding][30] tells me that with many bitter reflections he said to her, "You are under a strong delusion to think you can live without sin. If you are elect, God will bring you out of it; if you are not, then for this past year he has been hardening your heart. You have learned your Jesuitical evasions from the Wesleys. And if you follow them and their doctrine, [you] will infallibly go to hell," etc.

This was after he had been among the elect; for before, while left to his own or rather God's leading, he had showed a better spirit. Coming from the Room that night to Mr. [Francis] Labee's, he stopped their railings against us, said he would hear nothing against his dear brother Wesleys for they were true ministers of Christ and children of God. He confessed before the whole company that he found such a power under the word that his soul seemed lifted up to the third heaven. He longed to be free from sin, which he hated, and oh that it might be. He lay open to the light; and if, said he, the Scriptures say Christ died for all, I will say so too! By these and many like words he utterly confounded the predestinarians. But who can touch pitch and not be defiled. My good friend Labee has given us another cast of his office, and at length prevailed. Tonight at 9:00, he came with honest Howell, but I would enter into no expostulation with my friend while Satan stood at his right hand.

**Saturday, June 27.** Waited at 3:00 for Howell [Harris], who did not come till after the time appointed, and then sent word to me at sister [Mary] Norman's that he would call again in the evening. I sent him word that then I should be engaged. He behaved very fiercely indeed, threatening how to declare against me, for I was a deceiver, and what not; nay, now I was a downright knave. William Hooper spoke a few words in season,[31] that I should not be undone if Howell [Harris] did renounce me, and put him in mind of his late honourable testimony of me. He answered that it was not any power among us which he felt at the Room, but what he often found in walking the streets and, in a word, seemed quite metamorphosed by Labee.

After 9:00, he came with Labee and Mr. Morris.[32] I took him aside and mildly told him of his double dealing. He said he had heard most shocking things of me, inconsistent even with common honesty, and read me half a sheet of lies, which he had from Mr. Labee. I desired a copy of my indictment (which he gave me) and said I would join issue with Labee as to my dishonesty. The case was thus. William Seward *ex mero*

---

[30] CW supplies the last name in MS Journal.

[31] William Hooper (b. 1725) was the son of John and Elizabeth (Brown) Hooper.

[32] Likely Daniel Morris, a corkcutter, who appears on the band list for Bristol in 1741; see *WHS* 19 (1934): 162.

*motu*[33] sent down £200 to pay the mortgage and debt upon the school, and my brother an order to pay £100 to sister [Rachel] England, £40 to Mr. Blatchley, the interest money, and several other smaller matters. I left the £200 in Labee's hands and ordered Mr. [Thomas] Richards to receive and pay it away. Meantime God visited me with a fever, which confined me for six weeks. While I was recovering William Seward came down and, calling with Labee, asked to have his money again. I innocently said it was paid away to the creditors—before Labee, who knew (though I did not) that Mr. Richards had called for but one of the two bills and left the other still in Mr. Labee's hands. My long sickness was the occasion of my ignorance. Mr. Labee immediately went home and represented me as a knave who designed to cheat Seward of £100. A foolish knave indeed! To tell a gross lie before one who could disprove me to my face. But this story has Labee told— *as a secret—only to some particular friends*; and Howell [Harris] assures me he could *hardly get it out of him. Hic niger est, hunc tu, Romane caveto!*[34]

When Howell informed me of this, for one moment I confess I felt the pride of virtue, but recovered myself the next and with great temper asked Mr. Labee concerning it. He behaved himself now like himself, like a coward *forced* to fight. Being dragged out of his lurking hole, he fought most desperately, laying about[35] him in such a manner as might surely have convinced any unprejudiced person. My dear friend, as he has appeared to this very hour, now laid aside the mask of respect and love. "You are a notorious liar, a cheat, a deceiver. Your heart is hardened, your conscience seared, and unless you repent of your wickedness, you will go to hell. Your brother and you quarrelled with Mr. Whitefield, only to prevent his getting any share of the houses." These were some of his expressions, but a sample may suffice. He spoke to prevent my speaking. Only he now said that to my face which for many months he has said behind my back. I told him I freely forgave him, or I knew I could not be forgiven myself. After all, he forgot[36] himself and returned to his natural hypocrisy, testifying his desire to have the two societies united. "How," said I, "could you be united to a liar, a thief, and one whose life you say[37] is directly contrary to his doctrine." "Oh no," he replied readily, "not till you repent and are converted. That is my meaning."

After their departure, we joined in thanksgiving and hearty prayer,

---

[33] "Of his own accord; voluntarily and without prompting or request."

[34] Horace, *Satires*, I.iv.85. "who cannot keep a secret—that man is black of heart; of him beware, good Roman" (Loeb).

[35] *OED*, "to strike out with vigour."

[36] Orig., "forget."

[37] Orig., "so."

particularly for poor Mr. Labee; and about 11:00 slept in peace.

**Sunday, [June] 28.** A day much to be remembered. Preached at Bristol in great weakness on repentance, then at Kendalshire on temptation with more life. My strength increased with my labour, so that in the afternoon I was filled with power, and yet more so at Baptist Mills. Our congregation increases greatly, for the Lord is with us. Passed accidentally by Howell Harris while he was preaching in the Wood, and honoured him before the people. He told me last night he would come to our society; I bid him come in God's name but feared it would be in the name of Calvin. However, I durst not take the matter out of God's hands, or do aught by way of prevention.

Tempted to dismiss the society when there before he came, but checked my own self-help and left it to God. About 8:00, while we were singing,

> Thee[38] triumphantly we praise,
> Vie with all thy hosts above,
> Shout thine universal grace,
> Thine everlasting love,[39]

Howell Harris came, brought according to my order by William Hooper and attended by trusty Mr. [Francis] Labee. I prayed *according to God*, and gave out a hymn which we might all join in. The hand of the Lord, I found, was upon me. I then asked Howell whether he wanted to speak, and sat by for half an hour while he gave an account of his conversion *by irresistible grace*, mixing his poison with his experience—such as the impossibility of his being damned, final perseverance through God's unchangeableness, the praises of George Whitefield, and such insinuations and secret reflections as were to make way for barefaced predestination. I could not but observe the baseness, treachery, and ungenerousness of my friend (that was)—to come, as his friend George before him, for no other end than to draw away disciples after him and pervert them by that very influence which we had given him over them.

After hearing him long and patiently, I was moved to rise up and ask, "In the name of Jesus I speak to you that are spiritual. Doth that Spirit which is in you suffer me still to keep silence and let my brother go on? Can I do it without bringing the blood of these souls upon me?" Many cried out, "No! No! No!" Others, even a whole cloud of witnesses, rose and declared "Christ died for all!" I asked yet again, "Would you have my brother Harris proceed, or would you not? If you would hear him, I will

---

[38] Orig., "the."

[39] They were already singing a short hymn CW would publish the following year: "Gloria Patri, IV," st. 4, *Hymns on God's Everlasting Love*, 2nd series (London: Strahan, 1742), 56.

be silent all night." Again they forbad me in strong words, upon which I gave out, "Break forth into joy, [Your Comforter sing] ...."[40] And we did break forth as mighty thunderings. O what a burst of joy was heard in the midst of us. The God and Saviour of all men was provoked to jealousy and magnified his universal love.

Howell Harris would have entered into dispute but was stopped. "Then," said he, "you thrust me out." "No," said I, "we do not thrust you out. You are welcome to stay as long as you please. We acknowledge you for a child of God." Yet again he began, "If you do not believe irresistible grace ...." And I cut off the sentence of reprobation, which I foresaw a-coming, by:

> Praise God from whom pure blessings flow,
> Whose bowels yearn on all below,
> Who would not have one sinner lost,
> Praise Father, Son, and Holy Ghost.[41]

Here the man who is ruler over him, Mr. Labee, pulled him away and carried him from us. We betook ourselves to prayer, in which the Spirit wonderfully helped our infirmities. Great was the company of mourners and rejoicers. We found God had taken the matter into his own hand and was arose out of his place to maintain his own cause. My mouth and many hearts were opened. I spake as I never spake before, and all agreed in our concurrent testimony. Brother [John] Doleman received forgiveness of sin; and all that knew Christ, an increase of faith and love. I acknowledged the grace given to our dear brother Harris and excused his estrangement from me by the wickedness of that bad man, Mr. Labee, who would, if possible, deceive the very elect. I said, I know not what words of exhortation and instruction. The Spirit of their Father spoke in many. And this I have found since, that just when I began to stop Howell several felt in themselves that the time was come and would themselves have rebuked the madness of the prophet.[42]

Blessed be God who caused us to put our trust in him.[43] O trust in the Lord forever, for with the Lord Jehovah is everlasting strength.[44] Who is so great a God as our God![45] Who would not commit the keeping of their

---

[40] CW, [Hymn 17], *Hymns on God's Everlasting Love* (Bristol: Farley, 1741), 33.

[41] Another instance of singing a song prior to publication; see CW, "Gloria Patri, V," *Hymns on God's Everlasting Love*, 2nd series (London: Strahan, 1742), 55.

[42] See 2 Pet. 2:16.

[43] See Ps. 2:12.

[44] See Isa. 26:4.

[45] See Ps. 77:13.

souls to him![46]

Some put their trust in chariots and some in horses, but we will remember the name of the Lord our God.[47] He hath given a token to them that fear him that we may triumph because of the truth.[48] Thanks be to God who giveth us the victory through our Lord Jesus Christ![49]

*Address & Postmark*: none; likely hand delivered.
*Endorsement*: by JW, "C[harles]'s Journal / Jul[y] 16."[50]
*Source*: holograph; MARC, MA 1977/503, Box 5, file 5.

---

[46] See 1 Pet. 4:10.

[47] See Ps. 20:7.

[48] See Ps. 60:4 (BCP).

[49] See 1 Cor. 15:57.

[50] JW is apparently marking the date he received this journal letter; a later hand adds, incorrectly, "1740."

# c. 1741–1742
## Shorthand Notes on Bristol Methodists[1]

[In the upper left-hand corner is a small box of shorthand notes that are too faded to be reliably expanded.]

[Just right of this box is another small box of shorthand notes, as follows:]

Mrk[2] truly / in love with Betty / Mason refuses to meet / will hdri[?] bngsn[?]

[The remainder of the shorthand runs across the page, starting from the top:]

All sister Williams[?] band[3] offended; Cradock,[4] <u>Winsor</u>[5] *raged* exceedingly
Said she had the js[?6] of God. "Come let us go, and let the believers pray
    by themselves.["]
Mary Jenkins, <u>Rigby</u>,[7] etc.
Sister <u>Swail</u> *fine believers!* Rails, almost blasphemes, witness her leader
    Morgan[8]
Says she finds[?] the love of God, yet full [of] vile bitterness. The secrets
    of many hearts will be revealed
<u>Blanch</u> Walters rails on Sarah Smith so you are strong in faith

---

[1] These notes are not dated. Shorthand copies of a couple of letters from 1743 appear on the inside back cover of the same volume. Many of the names are of early Methodists in Bristol. Rebecca Morgan is described as a band leader, which was not the case yet in 1739, so we have dated the notes around CW's extended stationing in Bristol in 1741–42. The shorthand notes are interspersed with names in longhand. Rather than numerous instances of [[square brackets]], we have chosen to <u>underline</u> the names (and one number) that are in longhand. Everything else on this cover is in shorthand. Since there is little narrative context, the shorthand is more difficult to expand with confidence. In some instances we give simply the letters clearly conveyed in the shorthand. Most new lines start a new topic, but shorthand lines can expand to more than one longhand line. Hanging indents indicate the continuation of a line (and in a couple of places the clear continuation of a topic over more than one shorthand line).

[2] Possibly Thomas Meyrick.

[3] Ann Williams was an early band leader in Bristol; cf. JW letter to James Hutton, Apr. 16, 1739, *Works*, 25:631.

[4] CW refers to "my very good old friend Mrs. Cradock," in Bristol, in MS Journal, May 28, 1751.

[5] Remember that the underlining indicates that the name is written out in longhand. The name is in *italics* to indicate that it was underlined in the original (showing emphasis). All other instances of *italics* in this document were also underlined in the original for emphasis.

[6] Likely two words, beginning with "j" and "s," joined by "and" or "of."

[7] JW mentions a Sarah Rigby in Bristol in a 1749 letter, *Works*, 27:176.

[8] JW lists Rebecca Morgan in 1739 as a member (but not leader) of a band, *Works*, 25:636.

*Rowdon*[9] *tells[?]* [Felix] *Farley we were going to overturn the Church. And there was several in an hour st[?]. Ten now here[?].* [John] Haydon proud, must not meet leaders
Sister[s] Witton[10] *and Morgan very inquisitive who? saith[?] she was a believer*
Elis[abeth] Barber *of society on Turl[?] bands offended at the bands staying[?], threatens never to come. Sennet*[11] *drunk, Bernard[?] struck his wife*
Your ungratefulness to Richards,[12] your senselessness, unprofitableness, what better than the w[orldly?], three q[uarters?] if you dead, no more faith than the devil's, What defense[?] have you had? You let this lot feud, we all four will leave you to[gether?]. Who have they believed at London in your absence? Who mocks[?], who p[ ]! I am weary to bear you.[13] I have spent my strength in vain.[14] Think ye we want numbers? Not us 20 believers. Ye are settled again upon your lees.[15] The first are become last.[16] I verily believe that not one in five were ever judged.
*Bernard chose with wrath[?]. I turn from door.*
Sister Vicary[17] *sorrow[?] better. Sister Morgan told the next band all she had told me, and stopped their speaking their foul complaints.*
*Sister Stevens*[18] *cannot come being* counted an unbeliever, will not come to her band. So Jane Williams.[19] *It will be the turning many out of the way, Mr. Charles* [Wesley] *must answer it.*
Sister[s] Norton,[20] King *accuses sister Taylor*[21] *as a spy;* Gee,[22] *the same Sister Morgan spoke out what passed in the leader's band of sister Sheen's Sister* Hathy *very outrageous*

---

[9] John Rowdon appears on list of Bristol Bands (1741).

[10] Possibly CW's spelling for Elizabeth Wooten—spouse of Michael, who was in a married men's band in 1741; see Bristol Bands (1741), and *WHS* 19 (1934): 162.

[11] John Sennet appears on the list of Bristol Bands (1741).

[12] Likely Thomas Richards, itinerant.

[13] See Isa. 1:14.

[14] See Isa. 49:4.

[15] See Zeph. 1:12.

[16] See Luke 13:30.

[17] John Vicary appears on Bristol Bands (1741).

[18] JW includes a "Kath. Stephens" in a list of women members in Bristol on the address portion of a letter he received from CW on March 16, 1741 (MARC, DDCW 1/12).

[19] Possibly the familiar name for Judith Williams of Bristol; see CW, Manuscript Journal, Sept. 26, 1739.

[20] Sarah Norton, of Bristol; see CW, Manuscript Journal, Sept. 10, 1739.

[21] Mary Taylor, of Bristol; see CW, Manuscript Journal, Oct. 8, 1739.

[22] Possibly Mary Gee; see CW, Manuscript Journal, April 24, 1746 (and below).

They say it is all wrong[?] of Mr. Charles [Wesley]; Mr. John [Wesley] would not have done so.

There are a great many more sincere souls out than in.

What is become of your false show of humility? How are you ch[ildren] of s[atan], How do you prefer others in honour to ourselves.

What wrong[?] have we done you? Your whole ground of offense is that we think better of others than of you.

Ye have lost all faith, but not all pride; you are for posing for believers still, and affronted that we cannot allow.

Your faith stands in the words of man.[23]

If you of<fer[24]> the leaders encourage[ment] and better support, if you increase the togetherness[?] amongst men, have we not set the wolf to keep the sheep?

What r<eason?> have you to be offended who have declared yourselves unbelievers?

You reject us from being your ministers. May we not unite or combine you as we judge most for your good? Ye are wiser than your teachers.[25]

Think not to say with [regard to] ourselves we are Abraham's church. We were the first, the first are become last.[26]

Threaten not us with going to predestinarians or Purdy[27].

<[28]>no if you hang by a single thread, even our good opinion of you, now that is broke you drop back into the w[orld?], and return to an[ything]

<Judg>ment must begin at the house of God.[29]   We are called to Cornwall [and] Newcastle

Ed[ward] Jones offended bitterly at first but soon pacified.

*Mary Smith much disturbed*, thought it not right.

Sister Page[30] irreprovable. *Esth[er] Whitehead* did not like my choice, says I took the worst and left the best behind

*Sarah Dickson went to Molly Thomas*[31] and told all. Wedmore[?] a witness [of the] whole

---

[23] See 1 Cor. 2:5.

[24] An apparent crease on the page obscures part of the word.

[25] See Ps. 119:99.

[26] See Luke 13:30.

[27] John Purdy, of London, had ministered with JW in Bristol in 1739.

[28] A small portion of the page is torn away, possibly removing a letter or two.

[29] See 1 Pet. 4:17.

[30] Marieanne (Deschamps) Page, wife of Isaac Page and sister of Esther Deschamps; see JW to James Hutton, Apr. 16, 1739, *Works*, 25:631.

[31] Mary Thomas (d. 1745); see JW, *Journal*, June 6, 1745, *Works*, 20:82–83.

<[32]> led says it is not of God but man, She could not lead a band as an unbeliever.

[There is a single line of shorthand written vertically along the left hand side of the page; but it is not distinct enough to be legible.]

*Source*: CW shorthand notes; MARC, MA 1977/561 (MS Clarke), inside front cover.

---

[32] A small piece of the page is torn away.

## September 23–October 2, 1742[1]

Newcastle[2]
September 23, [1742]

Several of our Dissenting brethren would needs speak with me after the company was gone. Most of them were open hearted, and ready to part with their idol adherence.[3] But one was much disturbed that I should differ from the Church of Scotland.[4] This cursed devilish national faith! How inaccessible is a man of Satan's *election*! There is more hope of a deist than of him.

**Thursday, September 23.** Expounded the woman of Canaan to a vast multitude this morning.[5] Glory be to God, who still ministers seed to the sower and bread to the eater. We had many women of Canaan among us who, I trust, will never cease crying after him, till Jesus answers, "Be it unto thee, even as thou wilt."[6]

The morning would not suffice to speak with those who came to me. By 12:00 I got to Swalwell,[7] a populous town 3 mile[s] from Newcastle. Found about 1,000 people gathered in a meadow made almost for the purpose. I stood under a large tree, on the top of a green hill of an easy assent. I could not help asking as the people flocked from all sides, "Who are these that fly as a cloud, and as doves to their windows?"[8] Before we had done the hymn I think there could not be fewer than 8,000 poured in upon us. I showed them (God being my strong helper) their damnable estate and the only possible salvation from Hosea 13:9, "O Israel, thou hast destroyed thyself. But in me is thy help." I am sure it was glad tidings to the poor colliers from whom the word shall not return void. Promised to see them again next Wednesday, and rode back to Newcastle.

---

[1] This manuscript is entirely in CW's hand. It covers a period missing in CW, MS Journal.

[2] Newcastle upon Tyne, Northumberland.

[3] I.e., adherence to the doctrine of predestination.

[4] There were at least four Scotch Presbyterian congregations in Newcastle in 1742: at Sandgate (Wall Knoll Meeting House), Garth Heads (above Sandgate, near the Keelmen's Hospital), Groat Market, and Castle Garth. See Eneas Mackenzie, *A Descriptive and Historical Account of the Town and County of Newcastle-upon-Tyne* (Newcastle: Mackenzie and Dent, 1827), 384–92.

[5] Matt. 15:22–28.

[6] Matt. 15:28.

[7] Swalwell (Co. Durham) is on the south side of the Tyne, and on the eastern bank of the river Derwent not far from its junction with the Tyne. It was the site of one major part of the great ironmaking complex established around 1690 on both sides of the Derwent by Sir Ambrose Crowley (d. 1713). Coal mining was also carried on here.

[8] Isa. 60:8.

Having sent away my transcriber this morning, commended to the grace of God, I was employed all the afternoon in writing out my journal myself. Just called at Newgate,[9] whence the prisoners had sent me a petition to visit them, and appointed Tuesday. Drank tea with our brother Robinson's mother. Saw a dancing-room which we have thoughts of taking for our society,[10] and met them for tonight at brother Jackson's.[11]

It was a meeting indeed! For our Lord was in the midst of us. Never have I felt stronger faith for others. My tongue was loosed to proclaim the love of Christ crucified. I called upon "the poor, and lame, the halt, and the blind," and even "compelled them to come in."[12] Every time we prayed, some [person] or other received forgiveness. Two of them gave glory to God before all. Two more declared to *me* that they have found the peace which passeth knowledge.[13] All rejoiced in hope of the grace which shall be brought unto them at the revelation of Jesus Christ.[14]

**Friday, September 24.** Began our Lord's discourse with the woman of Samaria,[15] but could not get half through it. Never have I seen a more deeply attentive audience—no not in Kingswood. Breakfasted at Mrs. Robinson's, one of the 99 righteous persons who (as they imagine) need no repentance.[16] I related the experiences of myself, my parents, and others who have profited in the Jewish religion beyond our equals, and she was by a miracle of grace convinced. A young woman who lay a-dying at the next door, but would not hear of having me [visit her], was now overruled to send for me and we all adjourned thither. She hoped to be saved (as they all tell me on their death beds) because she had done no harm. God gave me convincing words (to strip her of her own righteousness), which struck them at the rebound. The mother and both her daughters are now, I trust, poor publicans.

Conferred with several others who earnestly desired to be taken into our society. I could not reject them, for they see themselves fit for nothing but hell.

---

[9] Site of the major jail or prison for Newcastle.

[10] The dancing room appears to have been on Lisle Street, opposite to the site where the Orphan House was built in 1743; see W. W. Stamp, *The Orphan House of Wesley* (1863), 10.

[11] Henry Jackson (1666–1766) was one of the earliest converts in Newcastle and would be made a trustee of the Orphan House in 1745; see Stamp, *Orphan House*, 113–15.

[12] See Luke 14:15–24.

[13] See Phil. 4:7.

[14] See 1 Pet. 1:13.

[15] See John 4.

[16] See Luke 15:7.

Rode to Tanfield[17] and preached the gospel from that most comprehensive word, "It is finished!"[18] I trust some found it applied to their hearts. Described his sufferings again at the public house from Isaiah 63[:1], "Who is this that cometh from Edom in dyed garments from Bozrah?"

Slept in peace at my colliers.

**Saturday, [September] 25.** Expounded the paralytic healed,[19] and spake searching words to the unredeemed. Accepted the repeated invitation of a neighbouring farmer[20] and passed the morning at his house. There were three or four families lived together in an old county seat. One of the women had been a constant hearer of us in Moorfields, and tasted that the Lord is gracious. She received us gladly, as they did all. An old Dissenter desired me to tell him the meaning of 1 John 3:9, "Whosoever is born of God doth not commit sin, for his seed remaineth in him, and he cannot sin, because he is born of God." I expounded the whole chapter but gave not the least license to sin. He took it with marvellous patience. In discourse he brought the old plea for sin that St. Paul was carnal, and sold under it.[21] I showed him that the apostle could not possibly speak of himself in that chapter. He was convinced and gave up that stronghold likewise. I have not met with his fellow among all the men of adherence: he is a prodigy of tractableness, and surely not far from the kingdom of heaven.

My host made me promise to come to his house myself and send my brother or whosoever of our friends should visit this country. We took sweet counsel together. After dinner I visited a poor sick man, who hopes to be saved for his repentance, but gladly heard of a free and better way, even faith in the blood of Jesus. At 2:00 met by appointment an house more than full of colliers and others, and joined in prayer and singing till it was time to preach. There was a vast concourse of people whom I laboured to convince of sin and of righteousness from 1 Corinthians 6:9[–11], "Know ye not that the unrighteous shall not inherit the kingdom of God? Be not deceived. Neither fornicators, ... nor adulterers, ... nor thieves, nor covetous, nor drunkards ... shall inherit the kingdom of God. And such were some of you. But ye are washed, but ye are sanctified, but ye [are] justified in the name of the Lord Jesus and by the Spirit of our God."

---

[17] Tanfield, Co. Durham, about seven miles southwest of Newcastle, was the center of another early coal mining community.

[18] John 19:30.

[19] Matt. 9:1–9.

[20] Likely John Brown of Tanfield Lea, 1 mile south of Tanfield; cf. JW, *Journal*, Nov. 28, 1742, *Works*, 19:303–4.

[21] See Rom. 7:14.

My mouth was opened to preach both law and gospel. Two ministers were to hear me at the house where I lodged. Some in their room laughed and made great disturbance for a time. After preaching sister Jackson[22] spake to them very plainly and by her rebuke stopped their mouths. By 6:00 we got back to Newcastle.

At 7:00 met the society at my lodgings (now increased to 70). The great power of God was among us as I have seldom known. I had just received strong consolation from the letter of a friend,[23] whom I now commended to the constant prayers of our infant society. John Kitchin, just before we met, had come desiring to be (as he said) "with the Christians." I asked him concerning his state and he only answered me "I am a poor sinner!" This he spake in great simplicity, without that gross affectation of the *still Brethren*.[24]

After the society [meeting] he came and told me he had been struck blind, as he expressed it, in the room so that for a quarter of an hour he could see nothing in it, when in a moment the Sun of righteousness arose upon him with healing in his wings.[25] His gesture explained his words, for he appeared full of all peace and joy in believing.[26]

**Sunday, September 26.** Met a still larger congregation, I think, than ever. Thousands and thousands listened to my exposition of Ezekiel's vision of dry bones.[27] There were many in the open valley, and they were very dry, but the breath of the Lord was present to quicken them. Lord, open the graves of all thy people and put thy Spirit within us, and bring us into our own land. Visited three sick women who received my saying, one of them above 90 years old.

Received the sacrament at St. Andrew's [church]. Dined with our brother Wilkinson, the first-fruits of Newcastle. His wife also grows in the knowledge of our Lord Jesus Christ. 'Tis very remarkable that in this place the husband and wife are generally called together.

Walked to Sandgate.[28] But such a sight mine eyes have never beheld. The usual congregation at Kennington was an handful in comparison. I stood on the highest point of the hill so as to command the whole assembly,

---

[22] Apparently the wife of Henry Jackson.

[23] Likely the letter of Thomas Maxfield, dated Sept. 15, 1742, which CW endorsed "T. Maxfield—ready to lay down his life—for me." MARC, DDWes 2/6.

[24] CW shows emphasis by capitalization.

[25] See Mal. 4:2.

[26] See Rom. 15:13.

[27] See Ezek. 37.

[28] A suburb (consisting of one long street) which had grown up on the banks of the Tyne, outside the medieval walls, and taking its name from Newcastle's south-easterly gate. It was the home of the keel men. CW consistently spells "Sangate" in this letter.

which was extended in a semicircle on either hand the hill. And the area below was so thronged, yet so quiet, that my soul was filled with awe at the sight. The sun shone in all his brightness, but without his strength and fierceness. God opened my mouth so that I verily believed the very most of them heard. 'Tis hardly to be believed, but that with God all things are possible.[29] I preached the law and gospel, about half an hour each, from 1 Corinthians 6:9ff., "Know ye not that the unrighteous shall not inherit the kingdom of God? ... and such were some of you: but ye are washed, ...." The word was as a fire, and as an hammer.[30] Ascribe unto the Lord worship and power.[31] After speaking an hour to the utmost extent of my voice I felt no more pain or weariness than if I had said nothing, but walked or rather ran quite round the town as it were to Mr. [Henry] Jackson's. "It is God that girdeth me with strength of war! He maketh my feet as hart's feet, and setteth me upon high. He teacheth mine hands to fight and mine arms shall break even a bow of steel."[32]

Went with my old friend (who is become a little child) to his society of Pharisees.[33] Their spokesman, a schoolmaster, made me a bow and a speech, wherein he gave me to know as soon as I came in that they were not unanimous about it, and therefore could not receive me; so (in effect) I might go about my business. I told them I did not mean to obtrude myself upon them but only came to join with them in prayer. But if they refused to let a minister of the Church of England pray with them, I had no more to do but to take my leave. They answered I might pray, if I would pray by a form. I replied that was my design, for I know no prayers and no Church like our own. That I was a true son and servant of the Church, and such should live and die. That I had baptized many into our communion, and it was my constant business so to do. But that I could meet with exceeding few Church of England men anywhere, most of her children having forsaken their mother, both in principle and practice, and turned back to popery— even its worst error, justification by works—and refusing all obedience to her injunctions. "You who call yourselves of the Church," I added "do you not hear the Church? She commands you to fast every Friday in the year. Do you obey her? If not, ye are no true members of the Church of England. She teaches that we are justified by faith only, without works; that we are to expect the inspiration of the Holy Ghost, yea and to be filled with the Holy Ghost. Do you agree to these fundamental doctrines? If not, ye are no

---

[29] See Matt. 19:26.
[30] See Jer. 23:29.
[31] See Ps. 96:7 (BCP).
[32] Ps. 18:32–34.
[33] A society that pre-existed the Wesleyan revival in Newcastle.

Church of England men." Mr. Steward[34] answered he had heard and read our most famous divines, and they never taught any other than I said. "As to their preaching," I answer, "I myself, since I came hither, had heard one of their preachers say we were saved by the merit of our repentance." And as to our writers, I asked if he had ever heard of Archbishop Tillotson? "Yes sir. We have his works." "Then you have never read them, for he has ten sermons to prove the popish doctrine of justification by faith *and* works, and their title is Regeneration the Condition of Justification.[35] Our Church calls all that teach such doctrine antichrists and enemies of Christ and his gospel. Her homilies on salvation are the most excellent writings of any but the inspired, and I earnestly recommend them to your most serious perusal.[36] Her definition of faith is ..."

Again Mr. Steward interposed, to mend her definition by taking in good works. I told him I found he had not so much as read our homilies and knew nothing of the doctrines of our Church, or he would have remembered she had sufficiently guarded her meaning concerning the consequent necessity of good works. Yes he had read them, he said, for they had the very best edition of them, Mr. Nourse's.[37] I asked him to show me there the homilies on salvation by faith. He brought the book, but to his great surprise found his edition had clean left them out; which I knew, though he did not. "Well, sir," said I, "you see your famous divines do not all preach justification by faith. No, they have no occasion for faith. They can build without a foundation." When he had taken breath, he fell abruptly upon my holding assemblies contrary to the Church. I asked why he fancied religious societies contrary to the Church, or how then he could vindicate his own? "O but," said he, "you do not use the prayers of the Church." "Sir, you are mistaken. We *do* use some of them." "But why not the whole service?" "Because that would be contrary to an order of our Church, namely that this service be only used in consecrated places. That would be giving occasion to them that seek occasion, and would immediately cry out that we had set up a separate communion." He then talked of some of the canons, which he said I broke. But I cut him short by desiring him first to prove that these canons bound *me*. Again he was stuck on an heap, hearing me deny first principles. I begged him to tell me

---

[34] Likely a title, not a name; that is, the steward of the society.

[35] CW is surely referring to a set of five sermons titled "Of the Nature of Regeneration, and its Necessity in order to Justification and Salvation" (and others in the collection with similar emphases) in John Tillotson, *Several Discourses*, edited by Ralph Barker (London: Richard Chiswell, 1700).

[36] Both JW and CW turned to the Anglican *Homilies* to defend their new-found emphasis on assurance of salvation by faith. In 1738 JW published an abridgement of the first few homilies as *The Doctrine of Salvation, Faith, and Good Works* (see *Works*, 12:31–43).

[37] Peter Nourse, *Practical Discourses on Several Subjects, being some Select Homilies of the Church of England put into a new method and modern stile*, 2 vols. (London 1708). CW spells "Nurse."

by what act of Parliament they were ratified. And yet, I added, because they have the show of authority, my brother and I have observed and do observe *more* of them than any two clergymen in England. I exhorted them all to learn and practice the doctrines of their own church, and parted civilly. Three or four of their pillars came out from among them and desired to be admitted into our society, finding we *are* what their brethren *pretend* to be in a manner, the only true Church of England men.

While I rested at brother Jackson's, several came to speak with me about their souls, some who have found rest and more who are sincerely seeking it. Of the former were Margaret Stirt (an old believer), John Bowmen (Mr. Jackson's son-in-law), W. Todd, and Jane Dent. This last informs me she has been seeking Christ above 30 years, being the strictest professor but never able to find rest. God by his word, which I minister, concluded her in unbelief and then had mercy upon her. "On Thursday night," she said, "I was waked out of sleep by those words, 'My Spirit beareth witness with thy spirit that thou art a child of God.'[38] From that time I have been filled with peace and joy unspeakable. Such inexpressible pleasure I have in reading, praying, and hearing as I thought was not on this side [of] heaven. My eyes are strangely enlightened, so that all things appear quite different to what they did before. I am full of consolation. And yet I find there is something behind. I have fears now and then that I shall not hold out, or shall not be so always. I want that *'perfect love* which casts out fear.'"[39]

Met the society at my lodgings and the great power of God was with us. I asked again and again who had found it present to heal? Several bore witness of the increase of their faith and one that she had now received the unspeakable gift. We had most *sensible* fellowship with our absent brethren and rejoiced as if we had seen them all before us. I marvelled at the power of his grace. How does he finish his work and cut it short![40] A short work does he make with this people. Indeed I never saw such simple, childlike souls. We prayed most earnestly for labourers, and surely the Lord will not leave them as sheep without a shepherd.[41]

**Monday, September 27.** Finished my discourse on the woman of Samaria.[42] The hoar-frost did not lessen my audience. I trust we shall quickly have among us many hardy soldiers of Christ.

Rejoiced this morning with more who have now received the atonement. Elisabeth Shafto, Ann Wanlas, Christian Gibson, Elisabeth

---

[38] Rom. 8:16.
[39] Cf. 1 John 4:18.
[40] See Rom. 9:28.
[41] See Matt. 9:36 and parallels.
[42] John 4.

Coldwall are added to the little children whose sins are forgiven. Isabel Johnson received faith last night at the society, and all her language now is "My soul doth magnify the Lord, and my spirit rejoiceth in God my Saviour."[43]

My audience at Teams[44] was twice as large as before. I opened the book on Isaiah 43:25–26,[45] "I, even I, am he that blotteth out thy transgressions for mine own sake, and will not remember thy sins. Put me in remembrance. Let us plead together. Declare thou, that thou mayest be justified." Received great power to preach the gospel to the poor. Some of the rich of this world stood at a distance from the vulgar, and *seemed* to listen to the truth. Squire Bowes[46] stayed some time; but when I mentioned hell to ears polite, the honourable Wortley Montague[47] took his leave abruptly. Returned to town and called (at the Keelmen's Hospital[48]) in the name and words of the universal Saviour, "Look unto me and be ye saved all the ends of the earth."[49] Employed all the evening in conference.

**Tuesday, [September] 28.** Preached again at the hospital. It rained hard in the night and so continued till I began. Then God stayed the bottles of heaven.[50] The weather hitherto has been so remarkably favourable that it is almost a proverb here, "There will be no rain this evening, for Mr. [Wesley] is to preach." How pitiable are those who exclude the particular providence of God from such little things, as they call them. In all my ways I will acknowledge thee and thou shalt direct my paths.[51]

Preached repentance toward God and faith in Jesus Christ from Acts 3:19, "Repent ye therefore, and be converted, that your sins may be blotted out, when the times of refreshing shall come from the presence of the Lord."

---

[43] Luke 1:46–47.

[44] The villages of High and Low Team, about 1 mile southeast of Swalwell, were known locally as the "Teams" which CW, no doubt following local pronunciation, spelled as "Tames." There were iron works here.

[45] Orig., "43:23."

[46] Orig., "Bows." George Bowes, M. P. (1701–1760), inherited in 1722 the estates of Streatlam (near Barnard Castle) and Gibside (in the Derwent Valley six miles southwest of Gateshead), the latter containing considerable coal reserves. He was one of the group known as the Grand Allies, a cartel dominating the local coal trade.

[47] Orig., "Worthley M." Edward Wortley Montague, M. P. (1678–1761), was not "honourable" as CW seems to have believed. (He is to be distinguished from Edward Wortley Montague (1713–1776) son of Lady Mary, of inoculation fame.) The Wortley Montagues owned or leased various collieries in northwest Durham at Tanfield, Stella, Causey, et al.

[48] The "keel men" used small boats (keels) to carry coal from shore out to waiting ships in Newcastle. For a description of the Keelmen's Hospital, see Mackenzie, *Newcastle-upon-Tyne*, 550–52.

[49] Isa. 45:22.

[50] See Job 38:37.

[51] Prov. 3:6.

Near 2,000 heard me patiently. Visited the sick in the hospital. Received at my lodgings more names for the society. Called on Mr. Bruce, the most moderate of the Dissenting preachers,[52] and went with him to Newgate. Preached there to the debtors and felons from Isaiah 61[:1], "The Spirit of the Lord God is upon me ...." That Spirit was mightily among us, and shook the foundation of their prisons. O that every one's bonds might be loosed!

Dined at Mr. Bruce's and came to a nearer agreement. I rejoiced in his uprightness of heart. Related my conviction of unbelief and the manner in which faith comes. His heart seemed knit to us. Lord, what we know not show thou us.[53]

At 3:00 met all the family of near 200 in their large room at the hospital and exhorted and prayed with them till preaching-time. They received me gladly; spake with much affection of my brother [Westley] Hall, whose memory is dear to them. I was quite spent by speaking to them when I went out to preach on the hill. The congregation was vastly increased by our nearness to the town. But my body for once failed me, having been speaking or preaching almost without intermission from 5:00 in the morning. Yet our Lord could not fail of his promise ("Lo, I am with you always"[54]), and directed me to Ezekiel 16:1. Preached in great weakness. Yet my hearers, I believe, were not so sensible of it as myself, for my voice held out three quarters of an hour. Visited one in the hospital. Then walked (but sprained my foot by the way) to Mr. Jackson's. Thence to my inn, where a servant of Squire Bowes came to confer with me, who fights my battles against the whole fami<ly.>[55] He rejoiced exceedingly in the glad tidings I brought, that Jesus Christ hath purchased for us <power> over all sin. I sent by him a few of our treatises to the young ladies. Walked with his help and brother Jackson's to our dancing-room where the society was met, now increased to 200. It was excessive hot, all the windows being shut. But I received extraordinary strength to exhort and pray for two hours. The enemy raged without (and not without provocation) that Christ should be preached in his school and synagogue. His children broke the windows and attempted to break open the door. Our Lord was greater and wrought more mightily among us. One was quite overpowered through vehemence of desire, as she told those who thought her in a fit. By 9:00 we parted, and I dragged to brother Jackson's a body only not so weak as my soul.

---

[52] George Bruce (1701–95) was minister of the Wall Knoll Meeting House at Sandgate. In 1745 he moved to Minto, Scotland, and ended his career at Dunbar, Scotland (see Mackenzie, *Newcastle-upon-Tyne*, 384). He had apparently moderated his earlier response to JW's preaching in Newcastle; cf. JW, *Journal*, Mar. 28, 1743, *Works*, 19:320–21.

[53] See Jer. 33:3.

[54] Matt. 28:20.

[55] A small rip on the right margin of the MS affects two lines.

**Wednesday, [September] 29.** I live by the gospel, and renewed my strength to preach it this morning. Many poor people stood like lambs in the rain (the first we have had) while I declared my mission to "Turn them from darkness to light, and from the power of Satan to God, that they might receive forgiveness of sins, and an inheritance among all them that are sanctified."[56] Breakfasted with a constant hearer of the word, and several of the poor keelmen ("keelwomen" I should say) flocked to us. They related some instances of their zeal, which pleased them more than me. As that a gentleman happening to say, while I was preaching, that I ought to be sent to Bedlam,[57] a stout young woman collared and kicked him down the hill. More of her fellows joined in the pursuit so that he was forced to fly for his life. Another poor scoffer they put into the pound. I do indeed believe that, were any to offer me violence, the people would stone them. But by and by I trust they will learn to suffer wrong and turn the other cheek.[58]

Already there is, I am told, a visible alteration at Sandgate. Swearing and drinking is no more. They bring forth fruits meet for repentance.[59] O that they may adorn the gospel in all things.[60]

Conferred with more candidates for the society, which is now augmented to 250. Margaret English gives God the glory and informs me that while[61] I was speaking last night in the society of the blood of Jesus the Spirit bore witness with that blood and applied it to her heart. She felt her sins forgiven and is now in her first joy.

Rode in the hard rain to Swalwell for my word's sake, not expecting a congregation, but many were gathered together and waited quietly for my coming. They would not go, they said, but stay all day in the rain, if I would but preach at last. I put them under the trees, stood upon some steps myself, and preached "Through this man forgiveness of sins."[62] The rain gave over and near 2,000, I believe, heard me patiently—and among them a gentleman, an officer. They all stood like men that awaited for the salvation of God.

Returned to town and preached at the hospital. It rained hard when I began, but none stirred while I urged our Lord's invitation, "Come unto me, all ye that labour, and are heavy laden, and I will give you rest."[63] The power of the Lord was mightily among us. To him be all the glory.

---

[56] Acts 26:18.

[57] The Hospital of St. Mary of Bethlehem in London, an asylum for the mentally ill.

[58] See Matt. 5:39.

[59] See Matt. 3:8.

[60] See Titus 2:10.

[61] Orig., "that I, while I."

[62] Cf. Acts 13:38.

[63] Matt. 11:28.

Called at his desire on Mr. W., one who had been with my brother in Georgia, and carried him to our society. Several strangers had broke in, so that I thought of going away. But it was immediately suggested to me I ought rather to stay and preach. I did so and set the terrors of the Lord in array against them.[64] Never had I received more strength from God. Many a Felix trembled,[65] I more than hope, and the poor, mournful sinners were more disposed for their Comforter. To them I divided the word of grace, and expect to hear that some of them *are* come to Mount Sion.

**Thursday, [September] 30.** The rain did not lessen my congregation, to whom I cried, "Verily, verily, the hour cometh and now is, when the dead shall hear the voice of the Son of man, and they that hear shall live."[66] My morning visitants so increase upon me that I have scarcely time to eat; "but man doth not live by bread alone."[67]

Mary M. informs me that while I was speaking against robbing the king of his custom she found herself under condemnation, and cried out of the deep to Jesus till she received forgiveness of that and all her other sins. Catherine Hales on Monday night sunk in self-despair and immediately Jesus Christ was evidently set forth before her eyes as crucified.[68] And the same time those words were inspoken to her soul, "Thou hast chosen the better part."[69] Margaret Kilpatrick tells me that for some time she was struck blind. Then the scales fell from her eyes and she saw the Lamb standing before her clothed with his vesture dipped in blood.[70] In the same view she beheld all her sins as laid upon him. I cannot doubt but our Lord has on this manner manifested himself to them, but their fruits will more evidently show it. Among those that came this morning to seek the law at my mouth were four soldiers, who appear deeply convinced of sin and groaning for redemption.

Half hour past 11:00 set out for Ryton.[71] Four several times,[72] as I was taking the wrong way, some called after me and set me right. I preached in the street on the first words that offered, "Peace I leave with you, my peace I give unto you."[73] The Lord gave me convincing words. I was surprised

---

[64] See Job 6:4.
[65] See Acts 24:25.
[66] John 5:25.
[67] Matt. 4:4; Luke 4:4.
[68] See Gal. 3:1.
[69] Cf. Luke 10:42.
[70] See Rev. 19:13.
[71] Ryton, Co. Durham; a village with an elevated position on the southern side of the Tyne some 6 miles west of Newcastle. CW spells "Righton."
[72] I.e., four different times.
[73] John 14:27.

to see several ladies stand all the time in the rain. While I was returning home, Mr. Humble sent after me.[74] It was at his (supposed) desire I had come, some telling me he had promised to bring all his colliers to hear me. I drank tea at his house. His wife seemed of a Lydia-like spirit. They told me my old Christ Church friend, John Lloyd,[75] was minister of the place and would be glad to see me. I was overpersuaded at last to preach here again on Saturday.

As soon as I got to town the church-warden of our parish[76] came to see me, an honest orthodox convincible Pharisee, full of good will and good wishes toward me and very inquisitive after the truth.

At 4:00 preached in the hospital on the Pool of Bethesda,[77] never with more assistance. The water was troubled and some I know must have stepped into the pool. Mr. Bruce was of my audience. I am pleased with him more and more. O that all predestinarians were like him! My strength was still continued (or rather restored) to exhort and comfort the society of mourners. One of my soldiers found power to lay hold on his Saviour, and bore witness by the truth. Elisabeth Biggot is also enlightened to see her interest in Christ. She was (like some others) struck blind, as she called it, for half an hour, and then suddenly a great light shined into her heart. There are diversities of operations, but the same Spirit.[78]

[Friday,] October 1. At 5:00 this morning began family prayers in the hospital. The whole house was present and received me for their chaplain. I told them in sincerity that I had rather be the keelmen's chaplain than the king's. There is no expressing their love for me. They would even pluck out their eyes and give them me. *I am so canny a creature!*[79] The very Titus of the colliers![80]

Preached in the Square on the grand promise of the Father.[81] Breakfasted in haste at Mrs. Hall's, a sincere follower of our Lord, and then proclaimed at Newgate, "Liberty to the captives and the opening of

---

[74] The Humble family were long-established land owners in Ryton, who had begun to exploit the coal on their estates. The person who entertained CW may have been John Humble, to whose wife Frances there is a memorial in Ryton Church.

[75] John Lloyd (1709–65), rector of Holy Cross, Ryton, 1738–65, entered Christ Church a year earlier than CW, receiving his BA in 1729 and his MA in 1732.

[76] All Saints parish, where JW took the society members to sacrament a couple of months later; see JW, *Journal*, Nov. 14, 1742, *Works*, 19:301.

[77] John 5:1–15.

[78] See 1 Cor. 12:6–9.

[79] CW showed emphasis by writing in larger letters.

[80] Apparently alluding to Titus Flavius Caesar Vespasianus Augustus (39–81 AD), emperor of Rome (79–81), who was renowned for his cunning military conquests.

[81] Acts 2:38–39.

the prison to them that are bound."[82] God made bare his arm before them.[83] His righteousness did he openly show in the sight of these poor heathen.

Called with my old friend on poor Mr. Y., whom his blind leader, the steward of their society, has again turned out of the way. I spake strong words, which I pray God he may never forget. Got an hour and an half for conference and rejoiced with Catherine Brown, whose heavy burden our Lord removed in private prayer. Now she fears neither sin, death, nor hell.

At noon preached at Whickham[84] on "Beware of false prophets ... by their fruits ye shall know them."[85] The curate last Sunday preached on the same text a sermon prepared by the rector[86] (the only man that has lifted up his voice against the truth). The other clergy soon disposed to take Gamaliel's counsel.[87] I gave the scriptural marks of false and true prophets ("by their fruits ye shall know them,"[88] their doctrines and lives) and then declared my doctrine and manner of life. I know not when our Lord has so opened my mouth. "What is the chaff to the wheat? saith the Lord. Is not my word as a fire, and as a hammer that breaketh the rock in pieces?"[89] There was a vast concourse of people, it being a bright sunshiny day. Toward the end of my discourse the curate, who is also schoolmaster, sent all his boys to make as much noise as they could. But they did not (I believe) hinder one person from hearing. Drank tea at Mr. Rawlins, the churchwarden, and returned to town in great tranquillity of spirit.

Visited a poor sinner of fourscore [years] who, when I asked a reason of the hope that was in her, answered as usual: she hoped to be saved because she had never wronged anyone. Another I found patiently waiting for the salvation of God through faith in Jesus Christ. Called on my towardly churchwarden and walked with him to Sandgate. One informed me that a minister out of the country was among my hearers. I had thought of explaining the Beatitudes, but my book opened on John 3, and I saw immediately that was my subject. I never yet found greater—hardly so great—freedom. The word was sharper than a two-edged sword.[90] Lord beget us all again by the word of thy truth.[91]

---

[82] Luke 4:18, citing Isa. 61:1.

[83] See Isa. 52:10.

[84] Whickham, Co. Durham; 3 miles west of Gateshead, another site of heavy coal mining. CW spells "Wickham."

[85] Matt. 7:15–16.

[86] Robert Tomlinson (d. 1748) was rector, with Edmond Lodge serving as curate.

[87] See Acts 5:34–36.

[88] Matt. 7:16.

[89] Jer. 23:28–29.

[90] See Heb. 4:12.

[91] See James 1:18.

Another minister heard me lately (I am told) and wept all the time. Glory be to thee O Lord! Teach me to cast the net on the right side and I shall catch the fishes.[92]

The society, when I came, was excessively crowded. No door nor window could be opened for the howling of wolves without. Such heat I never felt, neither in Georgia nor under the tropic. The candles went out for want of air. I knew none except myself could bear that intense heat for many minutes, and therefore spake a few words (in the name of Jesus and therefore not in vain) and used a short prayer and was pronouncing the blessing, when some without blew in fire and smoke among the people and others within cried out "Fire." In the same moment the windows were all mashed to pieces, the stones poured in on all sides, the people screamed out, and the room was like a sacked city. Many caught hold of me to save themselves or me, so that out of pure love I was almost torn to pieces. My soul was full of peace and power. I laboured to quiet them for some time in vain. But with much ado I beat down their fears and clamours, and made my way to the door, where I stood and put them all out before me. The enemy quitted the field. We sang a verse and gave thanks to God who giveth us the victory.[93]

Spake at Mr. [Henry] Jackson's with a poor young creature, bred a genteel Quaker, and now a confirmed deist. So far I gained upon her that she desired to talk with me again.

**Saturday, October 2.** Prayed with and exhorted my family at the hospital. Then began expounding the Beatitudes,[94] in which our Lord assisted me greatly. Dined at my new friend's, Mr. Humble, and waited upon my old one of Christ Church.[95] But the sword of division, I found, has quite cut him off! He laid many things to my charge, which I defied him and all mankind to prove. My soul was grieved but not disturbed. Through the extraordinary power of God, and his strength, went on into the streets and lanes of the city to bring in the poor and maimed and the halt, and the blind.[96] Twice as many as before, both poor and rich, were assembled whom I called to the gospel-feast, "Come, for all things are now ready."[97] My tongue was loosed, and my heart. I besought and urged them with many tears to accept of the invitation. They were much affected, as well as myself. Even the rich could not refrain from tears. I expected extraordinary assistance, and that God would take me up because my friend had cast me off. Did ever anyone trust in the Lord and was confounded?

---

[92] See John 21:6.

[93] See 1 Cor. 15:7.

[94] Matt. 5:1–12.

[95] John Humble and John Lloyd. CW is obviously at Ryton, fulfilling the promise made two days earlier.

[96] See Luke 14:21.

[97] Luke 14:17.

Returned to the hospital and finished the Beatitudes. Rejoiced with my landlady, now a confessor of Christ. The minister of Tanfield[98] and her wicked husband set upon her with Pharaoh's accusation, that she neglected her worldly affairs.[99] She stopped the minister's mouth with "It is better to be dead to the world than to God." Again when he blamed me for preaching in his parish, she silenced him with "If you laboured *more*, he need not labour so much." Out of the mouth of babes and sucklings hast thou ordained strength![100]

The poor people were not disheartened from meeting in the usual place, and for an hour and an half we had sweet fellowship in speaking, and praying, and praising God.

Sunday Afternoon [October 3, 1742]

Dear Brother,

This people whom our Lord has gathered will be scattered again if left in their infancy. Tomorrow I am bound by my word to set out for Yorkshire. Our brethren Lee[101] and Errington[102] I shall station here till brother [Thomas] Maxfield or [Thomas] Richards can relieve them. London requires two, but Bristol I could look after alone for a month. On my return we must forthwith extract a second hymn-book out of each of the three volumes.[103] Two thousand [copies] I could just now dispose of here. Neither London nor Bristol will yield such a harvest of souls as the rude populous north. Maxfield might come by ship. Write to me under cover to our friend. I shall return by Leicestershire. The Lord strengthen us for the work whereunto he hath appointed us.

My love to all.

Adieu.

*Address & Postmark*: none; likely hand delivered.
*Source*: holograph; MARC, DDCW 6/1.[104]

---

[98] Robert Wilson held the perpetual curacy of Tanfield from 1729 to 1751.

[99] See Exod. 5:4–5.

[100] See Ps. 8:2.

[101] Joseph Lee (d. 1768) was an initial member of the Fetter Lane society who came over to the Foundery with the Wesley brothers. He worked in the same shop with Matthew Errington. JW described him as "for several years a burning and shining light" (*AM* 5 [1782]: 580). But he eventually left the Methodists; cf. JW, *Journal*, Jan. 31, 1786, *Works*, 23:383–84.

[102] Matthew Errington (1711–88), a tailor converted in 1741 in London, helped care for the Foundery for a while. He moved to Newcastle in 1749 and served as JW's book steward at the Orphan House until his death.

[103] This appeared in November as *A Collection of Hymns published by John Wesley ... and Charles Wesley* (London: Strahan, 1742).

[104] Transcriptions were published in *Methodist History* 25.1 (1986): 41–61, and *WHS* 47 (1990), 202–20. The text here corrects scattered misreadings in these earlier attempts.

## JANUARY 14, 1743[1]

Newgate [Prison, London]
January 14, [1743]

[[I came here this morning to see my brethren in the cells and the gaoler has locked me in. It would be no trouble to me, I believe, was I confined here in good earnest[?] for a good cause. For I despair of finding the blessing of retirement except in a grave or a prison.

[[The poor creatures in their agonies are grieving for me. I doubt not but our Lord will bring their souls out of prison.

[[1. Why (in the dust I ask) O why,
  Good God, hast thou my soul forsook?
Suffer'd me in my sins to die,
  Blotted my name out of thy book,
Cast out my unavailing prayer,
And left me to extreme despair?

[[2. How oft have I besought thee Lord,
  To snatch me from the evil day,
To slay me with thy mercy's sword,
  To sweep me far from earth away,
To hide me in the quiet tomb,
Where sin could never never come!

[[3. Yet O! mine enemy hath found,
  And forc'd his slave again to yield;
My spirit feels the mortal wound,
  And all my hopes of death are kill'd,
In sad despair of rest I grieve,
And still I sin, and still I live.

[[4. Why did I not resign my breath
  Before this last and foul offence?
Sin hath defrauded me of death
  While God delay'd to snatch me hence,
O God of love, the doubt explain,
Why have I liv'd to sin again?

---

[1] This brief comment and initial draft of a hymn are written in shorthand, likely while CW was confined at Newgate. It appears in MS Clarke, p. 229, and provides additional detail to the brief account of this event in CW, MS Journal.

[[5. In judgment dost thou here reprieve,
   That I may all my sin fill up,
A mon'ument of thine anger live?—
   Why do I then constrain to hope,
   Why do I still for mercy groan,
   And trembles still my heart of stone?

[[6. O this inexplicable doubt!
   My prayer was heard, and yet I fell;
Thy judgments are past finding out,
   Thy ways are all unsearchable,
   This only do I know, 'tis mine
   To sin, to pardon sin is thine.

[[7. Assist me then to come once more,
   And take the freely proffer'd grace,
Me to thy favour, Lord, restore,
   Me in thine arms of love embrace,
   And hear me in thy bosom breathe
   My passionate desires of death.

[[8. Still do I urge my sole request,
   In horror of offending thee,[2]]]

*Source*: CW shorthand account; MARC, MA 1977/561 (MS Clarke), p. 229.

---

[2] A more polished and complete version of this hymn (running nine stanzas) appears in MS Clarke, 202–4; and was published by CW in *HSP* (1749), 1:115–17. The shorthand version does not show line indentation or CW's typical elision of letters to shorten words. The version given here adopts those from his longhand version in MS Clarke. But this transcription shows the actual words in the shorthand; comparison will show several changes in the longhand (and published) version.

## May 17–June 27, 1743[1]
## [[Shorthand Notes[2]]]

Bristol, May 2

On Tuesday sennight[?], May 16 [i.e., 17[3]].]] D[eo]V[olente].[4] [[preach in Painswick [at] 6:00. Met society at Wynn's

Wednesday [May] 17 [i.e., 18] 5:00 Wynn's. Society. 9:00 Stroud marketplace. 8 in the evening Evesham preach society.

Thursday [May] 18 [i.e., 19]. 5:00 preach society 11:00 Quinton Mr Taylor's 8:00 Evesham

Friday [May] 19 [i.e., 20]. 5:00 Evesham society 6:00 in the evening Wednesbury, the old parks. Society.

Saturday [May] 20 [i.e., 21]. 5:00 Wednesbury. 12:00 Walsall. 6:00 old parks. Society.

Sunday [May] 22. 5:00 Wednesbury. 8:00 Birmingham. 5:00 old parks. Society.

Monday [May] 23. 5:00 Wednesbury 6:00 Melbourne

Tuesday [May] 24. 6:00 Melbourne 12:00 Nottingham Cross met smsn[5] 6:00 again.

Wednesday [May] 25. 5:00 Nottingham 6:00 Edward Bennet[6] Sheffield preach. Society.

Thursday [May] 26. 5:00 Sheffield. 8:00 in the evening again

Friday [May] 27. 5:00 Sheffield 9:00 call at Thorpe Barley Hall Johnsons[7] 6:00 Birstall

Saturday [May] 28. 5:00. 12:00. 6:00. saw Mrs Holmes[8]

Sunday [May] 29. 7:00 Leeds. 1:00 Leeds. 5:00 Birstall

---

[1] This is the single surviving evidence that CW at least on occasion took basic journal notes in shorthand, then wrote the journal letter out more fully later. A journal letter that expands May 17 through May 26 survives and is given next in this collection. No journal letter survives covering May 27 to June 27, but material on these dates does appear in CW, MS Journal.

[2] Everything but the numbers and the words "Barley Hall" in this document are in shorthand. For ease of reading we have chosen not to begin each new line with double brackets.

[3] CW misnumbers by one day until Sunday, May 22.

[4] "God willing."

[5] The journal letter that follows suggests this was a woman; the name could be expanded by: Samson, Simson, Simpson, Sympson, etc.

[6] Edward Bennet, a sugar baker, was an early supporter of the Wesley brothers in Sheffield, but he later joined the Calvinists. Cf. James Everett, *Historical Sketches of Wesleyan Methodism in Sheffield and the Vicinity* (Sheffield: Montgomery, 1823), 1:34, 43.

[7] Barley Hall was a farmhouse near Thorpe Hesley, owned by [John?] Johnson; cf. JW, *Journal* (June 15, 1742), *Works* 19:278.

[8] Elizabeth Holmes (1712–85), of Lightcliffe, near Halifax, Yorkshire.

Monday [May] 30. 5:00 Birstall, by Knaresborough,[9] at Sandhutton, the Crown[10] and consubstantiation[?] question[?], ask for Mr. Meglow[?]
Tuesday [May] 31. Ferryhill, the Swan.[11] 15 miles short of Newcastle
Wednesday June 1.
Wednesday June 8.
Wednesday June 15 and till Tuesday June 21, at Newcastle
   Saturday June 18. my brother at Newcastle
Tuesday June 21. set out
Wednesday June 22. Epworth
Friday [June] 24. Nottingham
Saturday June 25 [Sun 26]. Wednesbury
Sunday [June 26]. Birmingham
Tuesday [June] 27 [i.e., 28] London

*Source*: CW shorthand account; MARC, MA 1977/561 (MS Clarke), p. [219].[12]

---

[9] Knaresborough, Yorkshire, about 12 miles north of Leeds; it would be near here that CW fell off his horse, as recorded in MS Journal.

[10] Sandhutton, a small chapelry in the parish of Thirsk, 3 miles west of Thirsk. Methodist preachers were housed here at the Sign of the Crown, kept by John Pickering, a Quaker.

[11] An inn in Ferryhill Yorkshire; about 15 miles south of Newcastle.

[12] These shorthand notes are on an unnumbered page of MS Clarke that would be 219 counting from the front, or 228 according to numbering that begins from the back on the bottom of pages.

## May 17–25, 1743[1]

1743

Tuesday, May 17. Set out [from Bristol] for the north with Mr. Gurney.[2] At 6:00 in the evening walked from our brother Wynn's to Painswick.[3] Stood in the street and invited sinners to the gospel feast, "Come, for all things are now ready."[4] Some of those dead souls seemed to receive the word with joy. Returned with the society to our brother Wynn's. We went on our way rejoicing and singing "Hosanna to the Son of David."[5] Continued in prayer and the word of exhortation for an hour or two afterwards, and the Lord comforted us greatly by each other.

At 5:00 next morning [**May 18**] we met again and I admitted a dozen new members, who received and brought a blessing with them. The confirming grace of God was upon all. Walked to Stroud, and delivered my message at the marketplace to a very quiet, attentive congregation. In our way back made up a difference between two of the brethren, and in order to complete their union carried them both with me to Evesham.[6]

Here we found the storm of persecution a little blown over. He that letteth,[7] at present, is a Quaker. The mayor likewise keeps off the sons of violence. O that every other magistrate were a terror to evil doers and a praise to them that do well. The church in this place hath rest. God grant they may be edified and walk in the comforts of the Holy Ghost!

Preached in great bodily weakness, and again on Thursday morning [**May 19**].[8] Then took horse for Quinton,[9] where I was (by mistake) expected yesterday. Mr. Taylor the minister[10] was just gone to the visitation, but left his house and church at my service. I read prayers and exhorted

---

[1] This manuscript is entirely in CW's hand. It expands significantly the shorthand notes in the entry immediately above. It is the source of, and provides greater detail than, the account of these days in CW, MS Journal. CW made corrections to the text in a darker ink (and quite possibly at a later time). These include adding the heading "Sheffield House pulled down. Journal from May 17 to May 25."

[2] Nothing more is known of Gurney; this is the only time he is known to accompany CW.

[3] Painswick, Gloucestershire; 3 miles northeast of Stroud.

[4] Luke 14:17.

[5] Matt. 21:9, 15.

[6] Evesham, Worcestershire; 13 miles southeast of Worcester.

[7] In the BCP and the AV, "letteth" is used in the sense of "hindering." Cf. 2 Thess. 2:7.

[8] The shorthand notes (MS Clarke, 219) make clear this preaching was to the society.

[9] Quinton, Worcestershire; 3 miles northeast of Halesowen.

[10] Rev. Samuel Taylor (1711–72), the vicar at Quinton, was a Methodist sympathizer. He was present at both the 1744 and the 1746 conferences that JW and CW held with their fellow preachers.

several wild, starring people "to repent and believe the gospel."[11] They had heard strange stories of those monsters, the Methodists, and seemed much disappointed when they came to hear with their own ears. I could not refuse their pressing invitation for me to stay and preach again in the evening. The lesson was, "And I, brethren, when I came to you, came not with excellency of speech or of wisdom, declaring unto you the testimony of God. For I determined not to know any thing among you, save Jesus Christ, and him crucified."[12] And Mr. Taylor came just as I began my sermon, in which God gave me extraordinary strength and plainness of expression. Some of the bitterest opposers were brought over and confessed they had had things misrepresented [to them]. The word was sharp and two-edged.[13] Many I trust were wounded and some healed. Among the former was Mrs. Taylor, now deeply convinced of unbelief.

I hastened back to Evesham and left Mr. Gurney talking with the minister and people. All the time I am not preaching, he is (according to his measure of faith), and that to all he meets with. He rode the footmen's pace[14] for the sake of some young men from Stratford,[15] whom he fastened upon and much strengthened to bear their daily cross of persecution.[16]

At Evesham I dwelt upon that all-comprehensive promise, "Whatsoever ye shall ask in my name, that will I do,"[17] and our Lord applied it to the comfort of many hearts.

Got half an hour with the society, who walk circumspectly and labour to adorn the gospel.[18] One only person I reproved and silenced, not suffering her any longer, notwithstanding her great gifts, to speak in the church or usurp authority over the men.[19]

**Friday, May 20.** After preaching, took leave of our Evesham friends, and in the afternoon God brought us to our dear colliers of Wednesbury.[20] Here the seed has taken root, and many are added to the church. A society of above 300 are seeking full redemption through the all-cleansing blood of Jesus.[21] Several have received the first knowledge of salvation by the

---

[11] Mark 1:15.

[12] 1 Cor. 2:1–2.

[13] See Heb. 4:12.

[14] I.e., moderate pace, about two miles an hour.

[15] Stratford-upon-Avon, Warwickshire.

[16] See Luke 9:23 and parallels.

[17] John 14:13.

[18] See Phil. 1:27.

[19] See 1 Tim. 2:12.

[20] Wednesbury, Staffordshire; 2.5 miles northwest of West Bromwich. CW spells "Wensbury."

[21] See 1 John 1:7.

remission of their sins.[22] The enemy rages exceedingly and *preaches* against them. Some few have given occasion to them that seek it, by returning railing for railing.[23] But the generality have behaved surprisingly well. Let God have all the glory.

At 6:00 I preached in a garden[24] on the first words that offered, 1 Corinthians 2[:1–2], "And I, brethren, when I came to you ... determined not to know any [thing] among you, save Jesus Christ, and him crucified." While I spake of his sufferings for us miserable sinners, he looked upon us and made us look upon him. My heart was melted, and many mourned with me and wept bitterly. I then met the society, and in many words exhorted and instructed them. The power of the Lord we found present to heal. Surely among this people I have not run in vain or laboured in vain.[25]

**Saturday, May 21.** At 5:00 expounded the woman of Canaan,[26] and strongly commended her example of prevalent importunity. A young man who had been grievously vexed of the devil was now set at liberty, and saved from the guilt of sin.

Spent the morning in conference and found several who had received the atonement in hearing my brother, or Mr. [Thomas] Williams,[27] or Mr. [Charles Caspar] Graves.[28] Went to see a piece of ground that an honest Dissenter gave us to build an house upon, and consecrated it by an hymn.

Walked to Walsall[29] with a great number of the brethren singing. The people were ready with the old complaint, "Behold they that turn the world upside down are come here also."[30]

---

[22] See Luke 1:77.

[23] See 1 Pet. 3:9.

[24] The shorthand notes (MS Clarke, 219) identify the location as "the old parks." On May 23 below CW refers to it as "the orchard."

[25] See Phil. 2:16.

[26] Matt. 15:22–28.

[27] Thomas Williams (c. 1720–87), a native of Llanishen, Glamorgan, Wales, matriculated at Oxford in Oct. 1739, but did not complete his university education. In 1741, back in Llanishen, he was converted under the preaching of CW. Soon after he became one of the Methodist lay preachers, often traveling with CW. In 1744 he sought ordination in the Church of England. Rather than support this attempt (which was not successful), CW in particular chastised Williams for being "too hasty," in part because he lacked a university degree. Resentment over this matter inclined Williams to accept and publicize some (unfounded) allegations of immoral conduct by CW. In response, JW expelled Williams from itinerancy in Aug. 1744. By Dec. 1744 Williams recanted the charges and was reinstated, though only as a probationer. He served in both Ireland and England under JW until he was expelled again in 1755 for an unknown offence. He was later ordained into the Anglican ministry, through the advocacy of Lady Huntingdon.

[28] CW recorded a list of the people he spoke with that morning in MS Clarke (MARC, MA 1977/561), p. 223 (numbered from the back of the volume).

[29] Walsall, Staffordshire; 4 miles north of West Bromwich.

[30] Cf. Acts 17:6.

I was advised to preach on a plain adjoining to the town where the famous Mr. Ball had preached before.[31] But I did not much care to tread in his steps. He had profaned the place and made it his own. I therefore sent some of the brethren to look out a convenient stand nearest the market-place, and took a walk meantime with my sacred counsellor. The book returned me that answer and direction, "Then said I, Lo, I come to do thy will, O God!"[32] Another word of encouragement was given me, "For the Holy Ghost shall teach you in the same hour what ye ought to say."[33]

I asked a farther sign, that if it was the will of God I should proclaim my message at the market-place, the hard rain might give over when I began. We walked through the town amidst the noisy greetings of our enemies, and the moment I set my foot upon the steps of the market-house the rain was stayed and the heavens clear! An host of men was laid against us. The floods lift up their voice, and raged horribly.[34] I opened the book and read the first words, Acts 20:24, "But none of these things move me, neither count I my life dear unto myself, so that I might finish my course with joy, and the ministry which I have received of the Lord Jesus to testify the gospel of the grace of God."

The street was full of Ephesian beasts,[35] some of the fiercest I have ever seen. The principal men set on the rabble, who shouted and roared out, and threw dirt and stones incessantly. Many struck, but none hurt me. I besought them in calm love to be reconciled to God, through Christ Jesus.[36] When I had delivered my message and was just departing, a stream of ruffians were suffered to bear me and my friends down from the steps. A second time we rose, and having given the blessing, were beaten down again. So the third time, when we had returned thanks to the God of our salvation, I then bade them (from the steps) depart in peace, and walked quietly through the thickest rioters, who feebly reviled but had no commission to touch an hair of our head. By this and one thousand proofs we find that "greater is he which is in us, than he which is in the world."[37]

Preached out at Wednesbury, and rejoiced with the society in hope of the glory of God.

**Sunday, May 22.** Rode to Birmingham and exhorted nearly 2,000 sinners "to repent and believe the gospel."[38] These were more noble

---

[31] John Ball (c. 1338–81) gained fame as a roving preacher expounding the doctrines of John Wycliffe, particularly his insistence of social equality. Ball's preaching helped foster the Peasants' Revolt of 1381.

[32] Heb. 10:9.

[33] Luke 12:12.

[34] See Ps. 93:4 (BCP).

[35] See 1 Cor. 15:32.

[36] 2 Cor. 5:20.

[37] 1 John 4:4.

[38] Mark 1:15.

than they of Walsall, in that they received the word with all readiness of mind, and will take my counsel, I trust, and search the scriptures if these things are so.[39] No one made the least disturbance, but stood like men that listened after the truth. Their behaviour put me by my design of returning immediately, and I appointed to meet them again after the eve morning service. Heard a miserable sermon, to disprove the promise of the Father,[40] which was only (said the poor preacher) for the apostles. Offered myself and was not refused the sacrament. Went thence to the people. Many thousands were waiting, on whom I called in the words of Peter, "Repent and be baptized every one of you in the name of Jesus Christ for the remission of sins, and ye shall receive the gift of the Holy Ghost. For the promise is to you, and to your children, and to all that are afar off."[41] Several gentlemen stood among the people with great signs of attention. My mouth was opened and (I believe) their hearts. I expect a great door will be opened in this place.

I thought it a good omen that one of my own name accosted me after preaching, and carried me to another namesake, a tradesman in the town. Some of my well-wishers came soon after to the house to tell me my host was little better than an atheist. I immediately thought of what was said of our Lord, "He is gone to eat with a man that is a sinner,"[42] and stayed with greater liking of my company.

Returned and preached at Wednesbury on the same words[43] to many thousand, and surely the Spirit was present with his demonstration and power. The brethren afterwards suffered the word of exhortation gladly, and I hope will henceforth learn "to turn the other cheek."[44]

**May 23. Monday** prayed with the society and preached for the last time at the orchard. The word I had given me was Acts 14:22, "Confirming the souls of the disciples, and exhorting them to continue in the faith, and that we must through much tribulation enter into the kingdom of heaven." For about an hour I was strengthened to enforce this. And then with many tears and blessings they sent me away, commended to the grace of God.

Between 7:00 and 8:00 set out for Melbourne with some of our Wednesbury brethren. Met on the road a well-disposed gentlewoman who thankfully received my saying and books.[45] In the afternoon God brought us to Melbourne,[46] and I found in preaching forgiveness of sins to

---

[39] See Acts 17:11.
[40] See Acts 1:4–5.
[41] Acts 2:38–39.
[42] Cf. Luke 19:7.
[43] I.e., Acts 2:38–39.
[44] Cf. Matt. 5:39.
[45] The shorthand notes (MS Clarke, 219) say "met smsn."
[46] Melbourne, Derbyshire; 7 miles south of Derby.

*May 1743*

the society they were much affected, and seem many of them just ready to receive the atonement. Near 20 of my congregation were from Coleorton.[47] Passed an hour with poor Mr. R., who appears not far from the kingdom of heaven. Met two young men from Nottingham who clave to me, and sent them away rejoicing in hope.

**Tuesday, May 24.** Between 6:00 and 7:00 preached the gospel to the poor of Coleorton from those words, "The blind receive their sight, ... the deaf hear, ...."[48] They heard with the utmost eagerness, asked in tears after Mr. [Charles Caspar] Graves; and would many of them be soon added to the church, was there any to come and teach them.

My heart was filled with thankfulness in passing by an house where they told me a friend of mine was born. I prayed God in faith, that thousands may have the same cause of rejoicing with me.

Rode to [the] Donington society[49] and asked, "Have ye received the Holy Ghost since ye believed?"[50] Here also I doubt not but a seed shall serve him, now the stumbling block of *stillness*[51] is removed.

At 2:00 I proclaimed my master, the Saviour of all men, at Nottingham Cross. Going to the place I found it written, "Whosoever shall confess me before men, him shall the Son of man also confess before the angels of God."[52] A great multitude was gathered together, whom I invited to our Lord in his own words, "Come unto me all ye that travail and are heavy-laden."[53] Surely the sin-convincing Spirit was mightily among us and overruled all opposition. Here also, I am persuaded, the fire is kindled, which many waters shall not quench.[54]

In the evening I was pressed to expound to Mr. [John] How's society,[55] and called to a crowded audience, "Ho! every one that thirsteth, come ye to the waters."[56] For the present I seem to be in high favour with all parties. I go through good report; therefore evil report is not far off.

---

[47] Coleorton, Leicestershire; 2 miles east of Ashby-de-la-Zouch.

[48] Matt. 11:5.

[49] Castle Donington, Leicestershire; 7 miles northwest of Loughborough. Lady Huntingdon's home, Donington Park, was nearby, but she was not in residence at the time.

[50] Acts 19:2.

[51] CW showed emphasis by capitalization.

[52] Luke 12:8.

[53] Cf. Matt. 11:28.

[54] See Song of Sol. 8:7.

[55] John How (or Howe) was a merchant hosier who had come in contact with JW while on business in London and subsequently started a society in Nottingham. CW was exploring their possible connection, but discerned that How was moving toward the Moravians and a month later started a distinct Methodist society in Nottingham (see MS Journal, June 24, 1743).

[56] Isa. 55:1.

God hath indeed renewed my strength this day, for in the morning I could hardly speak, but riding twenty miles and preaching four times has cured my hoarseness. My strength do I ascribe unto thee![57]

**Wednesday, May 25.** Again at the [Nottingham] Cross by 6:00. Pressed all to receive the "faithful saying, that Jesus Christ came into the world to save sinners."[58] Still there is no breath of opposition, but a storm must follow this calm.

Several followed me to my inn, being desirous to confer with me. One gave me a good caution, for which I sincerely thanked him. "Mr. Rogers,"[59] said he, "did run well and preached the truth as you do here, but what a sad end has he made of it! Take care you don't leave the Church like him."

In the afternoon I came to the little flock at Sheffield who are as sheep in the midst of wolves,[60] the preaching of the ministers having so stirred up the small [and] vulgar against them that they are ready to tear them in pieces. Most of them have tasted that the Lord is gracious,[61] and are just brought through the fire of *stillness*, chiefly by Mr. Graves's ministry. I was much edified by their simplicity,[62] and at 6:00 went with them from our brother [Edward] Bennet's[63] to the society house, which is next door. Hell from beneath was moved to meet us. As soon as I was in the desk with David Taylor,[64] the floods began to lift up their voice.[65] An officer (Ensign Gordon, they called him) contradicted and blasphemed, but I took no notice of him and sung on. The stones flew thick about us, hitting the desk

---

[57] See Ps. 59:9 (BCP).

[58] Cf. 1 Tim. 1:15.

[59] Jacob Rogers (1715–79) was ordained in the Church of England in 1737 after receiving his BA at Cambridge, and appointed a curate in Bedford. He was drawn into the early Methodist revival by Francis Okeley and Benjamin Ingham, and at Ingham's urging had preached at Nottingham Cross in July 1739 and helped found a society there. But Rogers soon after joined Ingham and Okeley in formally joining the Moravians.

[60] See Matt. 10:16.

[61] See 1 Pet. 2:3.

[62] CW again recorded a list of those he met with in MS Clarke, p. 222 (as numbered from the back of the volume).

[63] Edward Bennet, a sugar baker, was an early supporter of the Wesley brothers in Sheffield, but he later joined the Calvinists. Cf. James Everett, *Historical Sketches of Wesleyan Methodism in Sheffield and the Vicinity* (Sheffield: Montgomery, 1823), 1:34, 43.

[64] David Taylor (1715–83) underwent a spiritual awakening in the mid-1730s while a servant in the household of Lady Huntingdon. With her encouragement he was soon preaching and gathering societies in the Sheffield area, in some association with Benjamin Ingham. Taylor was instrumental in the conversion of John Bennet in 1742. While ever an itinerant, Taylor was independent of mind and fluctuated in his alliances, between Methodists, Moravians, and even Quakers for a while.

[65] See Ps. 93:4 (BCP).

and people. For their sakes and the house, I gave notice I would preach out and look the enemy in the face.

The whole army of the aliens followed me. The gentleman laid hold on me, and began disputing and railing. I heard him patiently, and gave him for answer *A Word in Season, or Advice to a Soldier*,[66] then prayed with particular mention of His Majesty and preached the gospel with much contention. Several times the stones struck me on the face, but had no commission to hurt me. One came with great violence against my book, which now proved to me a shield as well as a sword.[67] God endued my soul with much strength, and at the same I felt continually that I had no help or courage in myself. Upon my speaking of sinners as serving their master the devil,[68] our Captain ran at me with great fury, threatening revenge for my having abused, as he said, "his master the king." He forced his way through the passive resistance of our brethren, drew his sword, and presented it to my breast. My breast was immediately steeled, and I threw it open and stood still with my eye fixed upon his. I smiled in his face, and calmly answered to his slander, "I fear God, and honour the king."[69] His countenance fell in a moment. He fetched a deep sigh, put up his sword, and quietly left the place.

I was afterwards informed he had said to one of the brethren, "You shall see, if I do but hold my sword to his breast he will faint away," which was very true according to his principles. And if I did not fear at that time, no thanks to my natural courage.

We returned to the house and gave ourselves unto prayer. The rioters followed and exceeded in their outrage all I have hitherto met with. Those of Walsall, Moorfields, and Cardiff were mere lambs to them. As there is no king in Israel, no magistrate or justice in the town, every man does as seem[s] good in his own eyes.[70] Satan had now put it into their hearts to pull down the society room, and they set to work while we were praying and praising God. It was a glorious time within. Every word of exhortation sunk deep, every prayer was sealed, and many found the Spirit of glory rest upon them. One sent for a constable, who came up desiring me to leave the town—since I was, he said, the cause of all this riot. (It is always the lamb [who] troubles the water.[71]) I thanked him for his advice but

---

[66] This tract had just been published by JW (Newcastle: Gooding, 1743).

[67] See Eph. 6:17.

[68] See Matt. 6:24.

[69] Cf. 1 Pet. 2:17.

[70] See Judg. 17:6, etc.

[71] This is possibly an echo of a comment attributed to Luther when he was summoned to a Roman tribunal for complaining about the practices of Tetzel. "I was the lamb that troubled the water the wolf was drinking." See again on July 25, 1743.

assured him "I should not go one minute sooner or later for this uproar." He said he could do[72] nothing. "I was sorry for their sakes," I answered, "that they had no law nor justice among them. But as for myself, I *had* my protection, and knew my business, as I supposed he did his." In proof whereof, he went from us and encouraged the rioters. They pressed hard to break into the house. I would have gone out to them but the brethren would not let me. They laboured hard all night for their master, and by the morning had pulled down one end of the society room. I could compare them to nothing but the men of Sodom,[73] or those dwelling among the tombs exceedingly fierce.[74] Their outcries often waked me in the night; and yet, I believe I got more sleep than any of my neighbours.

**Thursday, May 26.** I expounded the Pool of Bethesda.[75] The society were all present, with whom I continued till 8:00 in conference. Breakfasted at a sister's with several of the Yorkshire, Derbyshire, Cheshire, and Lancashire brethren who were come to hear me. We took sweet counsel together and encouraged each other to press toward the mark.[76] Dined at our brother Pearce's[77] and met a daughter of affliction, one who had long mourned in Sion.[78] God gave me immediate faith for her, which I made proof of in prayer, and in that hour she received the atonement. The scripture I opened farther confirmed it, "Where they had nothing to pay, he frankly forgave them both."[79] I read the whole passage, and she owned "She ought to love much because she had much forgiven."[80] Again I found a word of comfort for myself, John 3:29, "He that hath the bride is the bridegroom. But the friend of the bridegroom, which standeth and heareth him, rejoiceth greatly because of the bridegroom's voice. This my joy therefore is fulfilled."

*Address & Postmark*: none; likely CW's copy for records.
*Endorsement*: by CW in shorthand, [[Journal—Sheffield house pulled down 1743[81]]].
*Source*: holograph; MARC, DDCW 6/3.

---

[72] Orig., "no."
[73] See Gen. 19.
[74] See Mark 5:1–13.
[75] John 5:1–15.
[76] See Phil. 3:14.
[77] CW possibly meant George Pearson, whose name is on the list in MS Clarke.
[78] See Isa. 61:3.
[79] Cf. Luke 7:42.
[80] Cf. Luke 7:47.
[81] This shorthand phrase is written upside down, at bottom of page four.

## July 11–29, 1743[1]

**Monday, July 11.** Set out [from London] at 2:00 this morning in the hard rain, from which the coach sheltered me till I left that and my company at Colebrook, and rode on to Hungerford.[2] It rained all day incessantly.

**Tuesday, [July] 12.** At 1:00 in the afternoon found three of the brethren waiting for me at Marshfield.[3] Changed my horse and by 5:00 reached Bristol, whence I had been commended to the grace of God for the work of the ministry in the north.[4] Without intending it, I was compelled to search the hearts of those who call themselves believers and are not believers. Both my preaching and exhortation was to convince of unbelief and a great shaking it occasioned. I left most of them, I hope, examining themselves whether they be in the faith.[5]

**Wednesday, [July] 13.** Captain [Joseph] Turner and another accompanied me as far as Exeter, where we found the door shut for the present and rode on. On Thursday eve [**July 14**], brother Turner and I [came] to Bow, sixteen miles farther.[6] I had sent word to St. Ives that they might expect me on Saturday, not thinking it had been so far. But at Exeter they informed me it was above a hundred miles from thence instead of sixty.

**Friday, [July 15,]** at 4:00. Set out alone and by wandering made it three score miles to Bodmin.[7] My horse and his rider were quite worn out, so that I fairly slept till 5:00 next morning without waking. I then found it had rained hard from 3 o'clock, the time I intended to have set out. I had but forty miles, they told me, to St. Ives, but I made it fifty at least. It cost me four hours to reach Mitchell.[8] My violent looseness and colic made them seem four days. I could not stand when I came in, but was forced to lay down, and wait upon the Lord to renew my strength.[9] An hour after the answer came, that as my day, so should my strength be.[10] By 2:00 my

---

[1] This manuscript consists of 14 pages of text, numbered consecutively, though it clearly contains two installments. The majority of the manuscript is in the hand of one or more scribes, but CW writes some sections and makes corrections throughout the whole. The P.S. at the end suggests that this journal letter was sent to Newcastle, for the edification of the society there. CW significantly abridges this material in his MS Journal, including largely removing mention of Thomas Williams from the latter.

[2] Hungerford, Berkshire; 7 miles west of Newbury.

[3] Marshfield, Gloucestershire; about 12 miles east of Bristol.

[4] See the journal letter for May 17–25, 1743.

[5] See 2 Cor. 13:5.

[6] Apparently the Bow, Devonshire, to the northwest of Exeter.

[7] Bodmin, Cornwall.

[8] Mitchell, Cornwall.

[9] See Isa. 40:31.

[10] Deut. 33:25.

153

good guide brought me to Redruth, which I left at 4:00 and wandered toward St. Ives. Passed the River Hayle just before the sea came in. Two tinners met me first, and wished me good luck in the name of the Lord. My next greeting was the devil's children. A company of them shouted as I passed by, and pursued after me like men out of the tombs.[11] I found the bridle was in their mouth. Met brother [Thomas] Williams and brother Shepherd,[12] and rejoiced together in the Lord our comforter.

Between 7:00 and 8:00 entered St. Ives, saluted by the boys and others, as usual. They continued their compliments for some time after at my lodgings (our brother Nance's[13]) but was too weary to regard them. My day and strength ended together. Blessed be the name of the Lord.

**Sunday, July 17.** I rose this morning and quite forgot I had travelled from Newcastle.[14] Spake with some of this loving simple [people], who are as sheep in the midst of wolves. The whole country round about us are coming in to our Lord. Only in this place Satan still keeps his seat, and the little flock stands in jeopardy every hour. The priests[15] stir up the people and make their minds evil affected towards the brethren, saying all manner of evil against them falsely,[16] and railing with such bitterness in their pulpits as to make men even abhor the offerings of the Lord. Nay, even their friends are weary of it and say, "It is enough, when will you preach something for us?" They take true devilish pains, I bear them witness, and pray God forgive their restless implacable malice. Notwithstanding which the sons of violence are greatly checked by the mayor, an honest Presbyterian,[17] whom the Lord hath raised up. He does not interpose so far as to punish the offenders. Neither does he give them the least encouragement. But "he that is not against us is for us."[18]

Preached at 8:00 in the society room on "Thou shalt call his name Jesus, for he shall save his people from their sins,"[19] and found his presence sensibly among us. The hearers likewise were affected with the

---

[11]  See Matt. 8:28.

[12]  Little is known of William Shepherd other than he traveled with JW and other Methodist preachers, assisting them, between 1743–48.

[13]  John Nance (c. 1717–85), an early Methodist in St. Ives, and later churchwarden there.

[14]  CW had left Newcastle upon Tyne on June 21, with short stops in London and Bristol, on his way to St. Ives. He had promised to come to St. Ives in a letter dated May 7, 1743.

[15]  Rev. William Symonds (c. 1684–1776) was rector of St. Ives, Lelant, Towednack, and Zennor, where much of the persecution that follows takes place. He was assisted in these parishes by his curate, Rev. William Hoblyn (1723–59).

[16]  See Matt. 5:11.

[17]  The mayor of St. Ives in 1743 was Richard Harry (d. 1750), an owner of tin and copper mines.

[18]  Luke 9:50.

[19]  Cf. Matt. 1:21.

joyful news, even some who had been opposers of this way, which is every where spoken against. Went to church,[20] where the rector preached from Matthew 5:20, "Except your righteousness shall exceed the righteousness of the scribes and Pharisees, ye shall in no wise enter into the kingdom of heaven." The discourse supposed his congregation to be all believers. His application was very woeful, being nothing but railing at the new "sect," as he called us: "those seducers, enemies to the Church, troublers of Israel, scribes and Pharisees, hypocrites." And I had the Lord to give me a quiet heart and a steady countenance, and he showed himself a God hearing the prayer. My calmness was succeeded by strong consolation, and I rejoiced that I was counted worthy to suffer shame in these low degrees for Christ's sake.

Rode to Towednack[21] (two miles from St. Ives) with brother [Thomas] Williams and almost all the brotherhood. The minister[22] kept us in the church from 3:00 to half an hour past 4:00 waiting, as he knew I was to preach when he had done. The lesson, 1 Timothy 1[:3–11], I believe, a little shocked him, being but too applicable to one who is still a blasphemer, and a persecutor, and injurious. His text was, "Beware of false prophets, which come to you in sheep's clothing, but inwardly [they] are ravening wolves; ye shall know [them] by their fruits."[23] I stood up within two yards just over against him, and heard the most inveterate piece of railing that Satan ever suggested, such horrid foolish self-inconsistent lies as the devil might be ashamed of. I prayed God my countenance might not alter, and was kept in perfect peace. The poor people behaved with great decency and all followed me to hear the word of God. I stayed and spoke a word to the preacher in meekness and love, that he was misinformed. "No," he answered, "it was all truth." "Sir," said I, "if you believe what you preach, you believe a lie." "You are a liar," he replied. To which I readily assented, because all men, I told him were liars. I put him in mind of that great day,[24] to which I cited him to make good his charge. Checked Mr. Williams for answering him, testified my good will towards him, and left him for the congregation.

The scripture I found was, "Come unto me, all ye that labour and are heavy laden, and I will give you rest."[25] God opened a door of utterance to preach the gospel of Jesus Christ, and I know they found the difference

---

[20] The parish church in St. Ives is the Church of St. Ia.

[21] Orig., "Tywednock." CW also often refers to it as "Wednock," a slight misspelling of a common shortened version of the name. We standardize to the current spelling.

[22] CW, MS Journal identifies the preacher on this day as the curate, Rev. William Hoblyn.

[23] Matt. 7:15–16.

[24] I.e., the day of judgment.

[25] Matt. 11:28.

between the true prophets and the false. "Is not my word as a fire, saith the Lord, and as an hammer that breaketh the rock in pieces?"[26]

Returned and met the society, and others with whom the room was crowded. The enemies of our Lord melt away like wax, more and more being convinced that we speak as the oracles of God.[27]

**Monday, July 18.** At 5:00 preached justification by grace from our Lord's words by the mouth of the prophet Isaiah, "I, even I, am he that blotteth out thy transgressions for mine own sake, and will not remember thy sins. ..."[28] Many there present were ready to put him in remembrance, and plead, and declare the promise that they may be justified.

Having sent word to the friendly mayor that I intended to preach at the market-house for my word's sake, and to pay my debt of the gospel, I went forth at 10:00 with brother Williams and Shepherd. They breathed out threatenings against us. But we knew they could have no power over us, unless it was given them from above.[29] A brother came running to stop me, and began, "I am afraid that ...," but I cut him short and bade him keep his fears to himself, telling him, "If the Lord sent us out, he could bring us in again in safety." When I came to the place of battle, the enemy was ready, set in array against us. I began the 100th psalm,[30] and they beating their drum and shouting. I stood still, and silent for some time, finding they would not receive my testimony. Then [I] offered to speak to some of the most violent ones, but they stopped their ears and ran upon me, crying out I should not preach there, and catch at me to pull me down. I saw the great restraining power of God. My soul was calm and fearless at which I much wondered. They had no power to touch an hair of my head. I shook off the dust of my feet[31] and walked leisurely through the thickest of them, who followed like romping and roaring lions, but the lion's mouth was shut.[32] I thought of that promise now fulfilled, "For ye shall go not with haste, nor go by flight, for the Lord shall go before you, and the God of Israel will be your reward."[33] We met the mayor in our way home, who saluted me very courteously and threatened the rioters. Called in at the poor reviling curate's and testified my hearty good will toward him, then passed unmolested with my usual attendant, the mob, to my

---

[26] Cf. Jer. 23:29.

[27] See 1 Pet. 4:11.

[28] Isa. 43:25ff.

[29] See John 9:11.

[30] CW typically began with a hymn, so he likely means that he began singing a setting of Psalm 100.

[31] See Matt. 10:14 and parallels.

[32] See Dan. 6:22.

[33] Cf. Isa. 52:12.

lodgings—where we rejoiced in our Protector and gave thanks to the God of our salvation.

Preached at 3:00 on Kenneggy Downs[34] (five miles from St. Ives within sight of Penzance). About a thousand (many of them tinners) came through the stormy weather to hear the word, and received it, I am persuaded, into honest and good hearts. I bade them, "Behold the Lamb of God, that taketh away the sin of the world."[35] The constraining love of Christ crucified was amongst us. Several wept, and one in particular—as hardy a ruffian as ever was bred in Kingswood, the captain-general of the tinners, famous in his generation for acts of valour and violence and his usual challenge to fight any six men with his club. He is known throughout the west by the title of "the destroyer." This leopard too shall lie down with the kid.[36]

Rode back and expounded at the society, blind Bartimaeus.[37] The power of the Lord overshadowed us, so that the very opposers (many of whom were present) trembled and wept.

**Tuesday, July 19.** From those words of Isaiah, "Surely, shall one say, in the Lord have I righteousness and strength,"[38] showed the two inseparable marks of justification, namely constant peace and power over all sin, and strongly exhorted my hearers to look unto Jesus and be saved.[39]

Set out in the morning for Pool, a little village ten miles off, which is the very heart of the tinners. As I was going towards the congregation, one came and would have stopped me, for the chief men of the parish, he said, forbade my preaching. I sent them a short answer that it was not in the power of all the men upon earth, or all the devils in hell, to hinder my preaching the gospel, as a door was opened to every creature.

Another feeble effort the enemy made by means of a drunkard, and some others who were sent, I doubt [not], on purpose to make a quarrel, that the tinners might strike them. Their drunken champion got within two or three yards of me, intending I suppose to throw me down the hill. He made such disturbance that I was forced to break off my prayer and warn him to shift for himself. He attempted to lay hold on brother Williams and me, upon which a tinner cried out, "Down with him!" In a moment the Philistines were upon him. I strove hard to rescue him, and besought them not to hurt him, otherwise I should go away and not preach at all. They were entreated for him, and taking him by the legs and arms, quietly

---

[34] CW spells "Cannegy Downs."
[35] Cf. John 1:29.
[36] See Isa. 11:6.
[37] Mark 10:46–52.
[38] Isa. 45:24.
[39] See Isa. 45:22.

handed him down from one to another till they had put him without the congregation and he was heard no more.

I declared the "faithful saying, and worthy of all acceptation, that Jesus Christ came into the world to save sinners."[40] About 2,000, most of them tinners, listened to the strange things I brought to their ears. My mouth was opened and my heart enlarged. Theirs also was bowed, as the heart of one man. For God gave us favour in their sight, and we nothing doubt but he will call them a people who were not a people, and them beloved, who were not beloved.[41]

Our prayers for the scoffers also begin, as it should seem, to be answered. For the fiercest of them came to the room this evening and behaved with great decency. They appeared much affected and some wept, while I discoursed on Micah 7:18[–19], "Who is a God like unto thee, that pardoneth iniquity, and passeth by the transgression of the remnant of his people? He retaineth not his anger forever, because he delightest in mercy. He will turn again, he will have compassion upon us. He will subdue our iniquities, and thou wilt cast all their sins into the depths of the sea."

**Wednesday, [July] 20.** After preaching, spoke with more of the society, most of whom I find have the first knowledge of salvation by the remission of their sins. A. G. confessed that faith came by hearing yesterday morning. He has been a sinner above other sinners, most notoriously lewd and wicked, till within this fortnight that God called him and hath now made him equal with those that have borne the heat and burden of the day.[42]

Went to church at 11:00 and heard that terrible[43] scripture, Jeremiah 7. Enough, one would think, to make this most hardened people tremble. Never were words more applicable than those, "Stand in the gate of the Lord's house and proclaim there this word, and say, Hear ye the word of the Lord, all ye of Judah, that enter into these gates to worship the Lord. Thus saith the Lord of hosts, the God of Israel, Amend your ways and your doings, and I will cause you to dwell in this place. Trust ye not in lying words, saying, The temple of the Lord, the temple of the Lord, the temple of the Lord, are these! ... Behold, ye trust in lying words, that cannot profit. Will ye steal, murder, and commit adultery, and swear falsely, and burn incense unto Baal, and walk after other gods whom ye know not; and come and stand before me in this place, which is called by my name, and say, We are delivered to do all these abominations. Is this house, which is called by my name, become a den of robbers in your eyes? Behold, even I have seen it, saith the Lord. ... Seest thou not what they do in the cities

---

[40] Cf. 1 Tim. 1:15.
[41] See Rom. 9:25.
[42] See Matt. 20:12.
[43] I.e., terrifying.

of Judah and in the streets of Jerusalem? The *children gather wood*, and the fathers kindle the fire, and the women knead their dough, to make cakes to the queen of heaven, and to pour out drink-offerings unto other gods, that they may provoke me to anger. ... Since the day that your fathers came forth out of the land of Egypt unto this day, I have even sent unto you all my servants, the prophets, daily rising up early and sending them. Yet they hearkened not unto me, nor inclined their ear, but hardened their neck. They did worse than their fathers. Therefore thou shalt speak all these words unto them, but they will not hearken to thee. Thou shalt also call unto them, but they will not answer thee. But thou shalt say unto them, This is a nation that obeyeth not the voice of the Lord, their God, nor receiveth correction. Truth is perished and is cut off from their mouth."[44]

The second lesson, John 8, was as remarkable, showing the servants' treatment in that of the Master. I was much comforted and strengthened thereby, but warned withal to expect all manner of evil in this place.[45]

The two ministers are continually labouring to inflame the people, saying like those of old, "These men do exceedingly trouble our city."[46] They beat their drum, the pulpit, twice a Sunday and blow the trumpet in the streets every day, setting on the children to insult us, and training them up betimes in the devil's service. I pray God lay not these sins to their charge![47]

At 2:00 rode part of the way, and walked the rest, to Zennor,[48] a little town four miles from St. Ives. About 700 poor country people, with sincerity in their faces, received my saying, "The kingdom of God is at hand, repent ye and believe the gospel."[49] The place is one of Mr. [William] Symonds' four parishes, and is come in, to a man, at the joyful sound. Many wept at calling their sins to remembrance, and seem not far from the kingdom of heaven.

Began at 8:00 expounding the Good Samaritan[50] but could not proceed for pity to the poor mockers. Many of them were present, but their mocking is over. I urged and besought, and with tears even compelled them to come in.[51] The Spirit made intercession for them, and God who knoweth what is the will of the Spirit shall surely grant them repentance unto life.[52]

---

[44] Cf. Jer. 7:2–28.
[45] See Matt. 5:11.
[46] Cf. Acts 16:20.
[47] See Acts 7:60.
[48] CW spells "Sunner."
[49] Mark 1:15.
[50] Luke 10:29–37.
[51] See Luke 14:23.
[52] See Rom. 8:27.

**Thursday, [July] 21.** Rose, and went on describing the signs of the coming of the Son of man.[53] Some felt their souls pierced asunder as with a sword. The prisoners of hope lifted up their heads, and found the kingdom even at the door.

Walked with my friends to the house of God, as I would earnestly advise all who have opportunity to do.[54] The lessons were Jeremiah 9 and John 9. I prayed the Lord to apply them to the reader's heart, some afterwards observed to me that poor Rabsheka was daunted.[55] O that he may have no rest in his flesh by evasion of his sin till he obtains mercy, and preaches the faith which now he persecutes.

Preached the law and the gospel near St. Hilary Downs[56] (seven miles from hence) to about 1,500 as dead, unawakened souls as any in the nation, but simple and willing to be taught the way of salvation. They were mostly tinners, on whom I called in the name and words of my Master, "O Israel, thou hast destroyed thyself. But in me is thy help."[57] None complained of my plainness of speech, and several, I would hope, begin to be stirred up to lay hold on the Lord.

At St. Ives expounded the Good Samaritan,[58] but my voice and strength failed me, so that I was forced to go to bed and leave Mr. Williams to meet the society.

**Friday, July 22.** Set out in the rain at noon and preached at 2:00 in Morvah, a settlement of the tinners between seven and eight miles from St. Ives. The weather did not hinder near 2,000 of those poor outcasts from hearing the word with all readiness. I could preach nothing but gospel to them. My text was Luke 7:41[–42], "There was a certain creditor which had two debtors: the one owed 500 pence, and the other 50. And when they had nothing to pay, he frankly forgave them both." As far as I can hitherto conjecture or discern, this will be the Kingswood of Cornwall.

At the room I began speaking from Isaiah 40[:1], "Comfort ye, comfort ye my people, saith our God." When the armies of the aliens broke in upon us, in like manner as their brethren of Cardiff, Sheffield, and Wednesbury,[59] they began most outrageously threatening to murder all the people if they did not go out that moment. They broke the sconces, dashed the windows in pieces, tore away the shutters, benches, and everything but the stone walls,

---

[53] See Matt. 24:30–33.

[54] CW was attending morning prayers at the parish church.

[55] See 2 Kings 18:17–37 and Isa. 36:1–37:13.

[56] An open chalk upland near St. Hilary, Cornwall.

[57] Cf. Hosea 13:9.

[58] Luke 10:29–37.

[59] On these earlier episodes see CW, MS Journal, Nov. 18, 1740 (Cardiff); May 20, 1743 (Wednesbury); and May 25, 1743 (Sheffield). The latter two are also treated in journal letters.

being armed sufficiently for the purpose. I stood with brother Williams looking on, but my eye of faith was unto the Lord. They carried away the poor's box[60] and the little that was in it. Swore bitterly I should never preach there again, which lie I immediately disproved by telling them Christ died for them all. Several times they lifted up their hands and clubs to strike me, but a stronger arm than theirs restrained them. My brother Williams they struck several times, but their blows, he said, were feeble and could not hurt. They beat and dragged the women about, and trampled upon them without mercy. One very aged woman and several others they knocked down, and threatened to murder us all. The longer they stayed, and the more they raged, the more power I found from above. I bade the people stand still and see the salvation of the Lord,[61] resolving to continue with them and see the end. In about an hour the devil's servants were weary, or rather forced to obey the word, "Hitherto shalt thou come and no farther, and here shall thy proud waves be stayed."[62] At last they fell to quarrelling among themselves, broke their captain's head (the town clerk[63]), and drove one another out of the room. Having kept the field, we gave God thanks for the victory, and in prayer the Spirit of glory rested upon us.

Going home we met the mayor (with another justice of the peace) and went back to show him the havoc of the mob and gentlemen rioters. He said all that a magistrate should say on such an occasion. Commended the society people as the most quiet inoffensive subjects His Majesty has. Encouraged us to sue for justice, as all the laws of God and man were broke through by our persecutors. Told us he himself was no more secure from such lawless violence than we (and by the way, the mob have threatened after they have pulled down our society room to pull down his meeting house). Wished us prosperity and success. And left us rejoicing in our strong helper, who never yet failed them that trust in him. 'Tis a very particular providence that this man is raised up to favour us just so much, and no more, least we should trust in an arm of flesh. Our people behaved just as they ought—none striking or answering again, but turning the other cheek and suffering all things.

Pray for your persecuted brethren (who stand in jeopardy every hour) and for the weakest of them,

Your faithful minister,
C. W.

St. Ives
July 21, 1743[64]

---

[60] A collection box for gifts of money or other articles to be distributed to the poor.

[61] See Exod. 14:13.

[62] Cf. Job 38:11.

[63] CW identifies below as a Mr. Naul.

[64] Across the bottom of p. 6 on the manuscript, written upside down in shorthand: [[My journal in Cornwall July 1743]].

## JOURNAL CONTINUED.

[Saturday, July 23.] We stand in jeopardy every hour. Neither our lives nor properties are secure. And yet I can find no one that fears them who can kill the body only.[65] Great grace is upon all the brethren. If they suffer with Christ, they know they shall also reign with him.[66] I see more and more of the guardian hand of God overruling the opposition of men and devils. Last night's uproar, it seems, was a concerted thing. The gentlemen had resolved to destroy all within doors. They came upon us like roaring lions, headed by the mayor's son,[67] and one of the rabble almost as drunk as him. He struck out the candles with his cane, and began most outrageously beating the women. I laid my hand upon him and said, "Sir, you appear like a gentleman. I desire you would show it by restraining those of the baser sort. Let them strike the men or me if they please, but not hurt poor helpless women and children." He was turned into a friend immediately, and laboured the whole time to quiet his associates. Much mischief and violence he did prevent. Some not of the society were likewise provoked to stand up for us, and put themselves between us and our enemies. Nay, some of them forcibly withheld the ruffians, and did not, like our people, turn the other cheek, but made use of the arm of the flesh.

Some of our bitterest enemies were now brought over by seeing the meekness of the sufferers and the malice of their persecutors. It was a stranger woman, it seems, that broke Mr. Naul's head. They had sworn to drive us all out and then take possession of the house, but their commission did not go so far. All they were suffered to do was to break all the windows, sconces, shutters, and benches, hurt and bruise several of the people, mostly women, steal the poor's money, and several of our books. [I] spoke with some of the sufferers, and particularly Florence Williams, who was beat and her arm very much bruised by Mr. Naul (lawyer and town clerk) who with most of his company had made himself sufficiently drunk for the purpose. Willmot Williams interposed when Naul fell upon her father, and begged him not to strike a feeble old man, "but strike me" (she said) "as long as you please." He gave her a violent blow on the back and left her. William Harry he struck on the head, and kicked and trampled upon Eleanor Launder. Who likewise received a blow on her head with a whip by Thomas Paul, who bruised her hand very much and dragged her out of the room. But she rose, came in again, and stayed till all was over. Joan Nance received an heavy blow on her head by W. Kempthorn. Thomas Paul struck Edward May in the face, and James

---

[65] See Matt. 10:28 and parallels.

[66] See 2 Tim. 2:12.

[67] Richard Harry had one surviving son in 1750, William Harry.

Woolcock upon the head with a whip. John Nance was struck in the face by Charles Worth, the lawyer, who signalized himself by breaking most of the windows. Whether it was the lawyer or some other of the rabble that stole his hat, he cannot say. Many others were beaten. And it is astonishing that no more mischief was done by men so fully qualified for the service of the devil. But the bridle was in their mouth. This one of them confessed, whom a brother overheard say as they were going home, "I think the *desk was insured*. We could not touch it, nor come near it."

Proved the devil a liar once more at least, and preached in the room at 5:00 this morning. Those words first struck mine eyes, "For thou shalt break forth on the right hand and on the left, and thy seed shall inherit the Gentiles, and make the desolate cities to be inhabited. Fear not, for thou shalt not be ashamed. Neither be thou confounded, for thou shalt not be put to shame."[68] I expounded the whole chapter (Isaiah 54) and dwelt upon that glorious promise wherewith it concludes: "Behold, I have created the smith that bloweth the coals in the fire, and that bringeth out an instrument for his work, and I have created the waster to destroy. No weapon that is formed against thee shall prosper, and every tongue that shall rise against thee in judgment thou shalt condemn. This is the heritage of the servants of the Lord, and their righteousness is of me, saith the Lord."[69] I remember the same promise was given us after the first grand riot in Cardiff. Now also the Lord hereby administered strong consolation to our souls. We stand fast in one spirit, and with one mind, striving together for the faith of the gospel, in nothing terrified by our adversaries.

Preached in the afternoon at Gwennap, beyond Redruth to between 2,000 and 3,000 sincere souls who devoured the word of grace and reconciliation, and seemed, all of them, ready to cry out (with the prodigal, whose history I explained), "I will arise and will go to my father."[70] An hour I was in speaking, but the time seemed short to me and to them. Surely the Lord hath a great work to do among this people. About a thousand of my audience were tinners from about Redruth. They and their brethren, I hear, are taken as one man. God has given us their hearts, and if any one speak against us (say they) he deserves to be stoned. We have the favour with all the people. Let God have the glory and their poor souls the benefit.

In our return a poor man came to me with a complaint that while he was hearing me last Tuesday someone stole his goods. I thought he wanted me to give him something towards his loss, which I did with a book. But he said that was not it. He wanted me to help him to his things

---

[68] Isa. 54:3–4.

[69] Cf. Isa. 54:16–17.

[70] Luke 15:18; cf. Luke 15:11–32.

again, for surely such a man as I could know who took them. I comforted him with a word of advice, but told him I was no cunning man, as he took me to be.

Expounded in the room (in spite of Satan and all his host) the woman with the issue of blood.[71] And afterwards spoke a word in season to the society, that they should possess their souls in patience,[72] not threatening nor even speaking of the late uproar, but suffering all things, that the gospel be not hindered.[73] Our enemies are daily in hand to swallow us up. They swear bitterly they will have the house down. But they shall first have God's leave. Till then, it is as safe as our house not made with hands, eternal in the heavens.[74]

**Sunday, July 24.** Expounded at 5:00 and met the society at 8:00, whom in many words I exhorted to save themselves from this perverse generation by rejecting all their good and suffering all their evil.[75] Surely this cluster shall not be destroyed, for there is a blessing in it! Being to preach at Wednock[76] between 1:00 and 2:00, I durst not trust the minister, least he should serve me this Sunday as his curate did the last; and so make me disappoint the congregation. It was near 11:00 before he began prayers. I found much comfort at home, and saw how easily a soul may fall into stillness from God's supplying immediately the word of means where means cannot be had. The brethren informed me that the poor curate had laboured again with all his might to stir up the people, yet at the same time charging us with his own virtues, such as railing mobs, occasioning mutterers, doing violence, and everything wicked and diabolical. Walked with my brother [Thomas] Williams and [John] Nance to Wednock, and waited till half hour past 2:00 for the people, whom Mr. [William] Symonds kept as long as he could from the word, by not beginning the morning service till noon. This did not hinder a large multitude from listening to the history of our Lord's sufferings, as described by the prophet Isaiah (chapter 55). The word did not return empty.[77] I promised, if the Lord permitted, to finish my discourse at a place something nearer St. Ives after evening service. The curate's not beginning it last Sunday till near 5:00 frightened me from venturing to church, by which I found Satan got an advantage. I ought to have gone at all hazards. We called in at a neighbour's and got a dish of tea, and then walked to the place appointed.

---

[71] Mark 5:25–34.
[72] See Luke 21:19.
[73] See 1 Cor. 9:12.
[74] See 2 Cor. 5:1.
[75] See Acts 2:40.
[76] I.e., Towednack.
[77] See Isa. 55:11.

A friend came riding up to us with tidings of danger, which I durst not stay to hear of, and therefore run into it for safety. I find on all such occasions our safety is in looking unto Jesus with a fixed and single eye, and not thinking of consequences for one moment. Otherwise we are apt to take counsel with flesh and blood, and seeing the wind boisterous, we are afraid and begin to sink.[78]

Some would have had me preach in the stony road, but I went farther off into a field, and began giving out the hymn. This drove the little flock from the midst of the ravening wolves, who now stood by themselves, the confessed instruments of Satan. They soon fell upon us, threatening and reviling, and striking all they came near. They swore bitterly they would be revenged upon us for *our* making such a disturbance on the Sabbath day, taking away the people from church and doing so much mischief as *we* do continually. They came near with stones and sticks and endeavoured to pull me down. I bade them strike me, and spare the people. Many lifted up their hands and weapons, but were not suffered to touch me. My time is not yet come.[79] Brother Williams got all the honour of several blows, but no harm by any of them. We were encompassed by an host of men, with no visible way of escape. But the Lord hath many ways. He touched the heart of one of our bitterest persecutors, who had formerly struck Mr. Williams, but now came up to me most affectionately, took me by the hand, and besought me to depart in peace, assuring me he would protect me from all violence. Another gentleman also said the same, whom I thanked for their good will but told them that I *had* a Protector. But I saw there was no door opened and therefore should not preach there at this season.

Ten cruel, cowardly ruffians I saw upon one poor unarmed man, striking him with their clubs till he fell to the ground. Another they pursued who narrowly escaped by the swiftness of his horse. My friend they set upon for offering to interpose, and forced him and his horse to fly in their own defence. Brother Williams and I were walking slowly home when his old enemy Thomas Paul ran after us, took him by the throat, and struck him with great violence. He was repeating his blow when the other amicable gentleman laid hold on him and took him off. We went on our way, rejoicing in God our continual Saviour. We heard the blasphemy of the multitude, but fear was not on every side. Our eyes were unto the Lord, who hid us in the hollow of his hand and kept us in perfect peace.[80] I thought of the march of the Israelites, when the pillar of the cloud came between the Egyptians and the camp of Israel so that the one came not near the other all the night.[81]

---

[78] See Matt. 14:30.
[79] See John 7:6.
[80] See Isa. 49:2; 26:3.
[81] See Exod. 13:21–22.

At about 6:00 our guard conducted us safely to our lodgings. A troop of the enemy followed. I went out and looked them in the face, and they pulled off their hats and slunk away. We ascribed unto the Lord worship and power.[82] The right hand of the Lord hath still the preeminence.[83] He hath again made bare his mighty arm in the sight of all the heathen.[84]

The society came to me at our brother Nance's where we gave ourselves unto prayer. Never yet have I found a greater blessing in the exercise. Our hearts danced for joy and in our song did we praise him. We longed for his glorious appearing and by the eye of faith saw the Captain of our salvation, as coming in the clouds of heaven to confess us before his Father and the heavenly angels.

**Monday, July 25.** Exhorted them at the room to consider him who endured such contradiction of sinners against himself.[85] As yet, blessed be God, none appear wearied or faint in their minds; but all grow under the cross, and increase in number as well as in faith and patience. The two who were so cruelly beat last night we find are not of the society, but hearty well-wishers to it—two fiery disciples, who lately beat the opposers. The minister's mob (it now appears) intended much more mischief than they were permitted to do, and it is amazing that they should have been so far restrained. A little inconsiderable incident God sometimes makes use of to blast all the counsels of his enemies. In which case we should ascribe the whole work to him, as much as if he had visibly stopped them by twelve legions of angels. Their captain (a lawyer) was damped and disarmed by one word from an old man, to whom he owed money, and who cried on sight of him, "Ay, ay! tomorrow I shall send you to prison." They also hindered one another, some being for more mischief and some for less. Our people behaved as followers of the Lamb, God wonderfully withholding them from resisting evil. Even "the destroyer" stood calmly looking on, who but a few days ago had beat a troop of men that molested Mr. Williams. They did not yet care to meddle with him, fearing least they should rouse the leopard, but wisely fell upon those who they knew would suffer all things. But with his favourable loving kindness did the Lord defend them as with a shield,[86] so that none of them are dangerously hurt.[87]

---

[82] See Ps. 96:7 (BCP).

[83] See Ps. 118:16 (BCP).

[84] See Isa. 52:10.

[85] See Heb. 12:3.

[86] See Ps. 5:13 (BCP).

[87] Along the left margin of this paragraph is written some Greek that appears to read: "Πυρσοελθε Βεαις σοφαλλον" (though there is a looping line drawn through it that may be meant to indicate a reordering of parts of it). In any case, this is not a standard Greek phrase and the meaning is very unclear.

*July 1743*

The ministers (as the mayor told one of them) are the principal authors of all this sin, by continually representing us in their sermons as popish emissaries, and urging the enraged multitude to *take all manner of ways* to stop us. Their whole preaching is of cursing and lies, *dolus, an virtus, quis in hoste requirit?*[88] And yet (such is their great modesty) they say, "Mr. Williams and I are the cause of all." 'Tis always the lamb that troubles the water.[89] However, they have gained their point, by making the rabble of St. Ives (including the gentry) like-minded with themselves; and all the cry, both of the great vulgar and the small, is "*Ad leones!*"[90] It is now that I begin to be a minister of God! O that we may approve ourselves such in all things! "In much patience, in afflictions, in necessities, in distresses, in stripes, in imprisonments, in tumults, in labours, in watchings, in fastings; by pureness, by knowledge, by longsuffering, by kindness, by the Holy Ghost, by love unfeigned, by the word of truth, by the power of God, by the armour of righteousness on the right hand and on the left, by honour and dishonour, by evil report and good report. As deceivers, and yet true. As unknown, and yet well known. As dying, and behold we live. As chastened, and not killed. As sorrowful, yet always rejoicing. As poor, yet making many rich. As having nothing, yet possessing all things."[91] Yesterday we were to be stoned for popish incendiaries. Today it was our turn to have favour with all the people.

I preached the pure gospel on Kenneggy Downs, to a great multitude of simple hearty tinners. Many, I believe, felt these words: "Who is this that cometh from Edom, with dyed garments from Bozrah? This that is glorious in his apparel, travelling in the greatness of his strength? I that speak in righteousness, mighty to save."[92] They received the word with all readiness and gratitude, wondered at the wickedness of St. Ives's people that could endeavour to hurt or murder us for telling them the truth, in which they so greatly rejoiced. Perhaps it is so permitted, that we may be thrust out to the tinners altogether. The will of the Lord be done, as he shall make it known to us. Passed a comfortable hour in the afternoon at our brother May's in singing and prayer, that we may be able to withstand in [the] evil day, and done all to stand.[93]

Went home and wrote my journal, but was as it were dragged away from it, and even compelled, to pray. Never did that Spirit more evidently show me things to come and warn me to prepare for an approaching trial.

---

[88] Virgil, *Aeneid*, 2.390, "Trickery or courage, what does it matter against an enemy?"

[89] See note above on May 26, 1743.

[90] "To the lions!"

[91] Cf. 2 Cor. 6:4–10.

[92] Isa. 63:1.

[93] See Eph. 6:13.

I was led to ask that at this time the fierceness of men might be refrained. We had scarce begun at the room when news was brought me that all the gentlemen were coming to pull it down. I opened the book upon 1 Thessalonians 2:4, "But as we were allowed of God to be put in trust with the gospel, even so we speak; not as pleasing men, but God, who trieth our hearts." For some minutes my mouth was opened, and the word was with great power. The hard rain, I believe, delayed our enemies, whom we looked for every moment. About half a dozen of them came first, and threw eggs in at the window where brother Williams and I stood, but could not touch us. Others cast great stones to break the shutters. Others struck one or two of the women, and cursed and swore as usual that they would have the house down. I continued praying for them with the congregation, and then bade our own people "depart in peace."[94]

Our brother Nance was gone to the mayor and the ruffians retreated for a while, I suppose to call their fellows. I thought it more expedient to stop the mayor, and walked down the town and met him at the head of the posse. At first hearing of the uproar he started up, charged all he met in the king's name to come and assist him to keep the peace—even some of the rebels, whose feet were swift to do evil,[95] he turned back and forced along with him. I came up to him and thanked him for his readiness to defend the innocent, but said I was come to save him the trouble of a walk in the rain. He behaved with great civility and resolution, declaring before all that none should hurt us—but hoped I should soon go to preach in some other place. "That," I answered, "I should certainly do when I had delivered my message here, for I was come from Newcastle and going everywhere to preach the gospel to every creature." By means of this interview God scattered the people that delight in war.[96] The aliens disbanded and I met the society at the room, no one molesting us. Glory be to God that we are once more delivered out of the mouth of the lion.[97] I make no doubt but they thought to have accomplished their design this night, had not the Lord beheld their threatenings and stilled the raging of the sea, the noise of the waves, and the madness of the people.[98]

**Tuesday, July 26.** Showed my brethren their calling from Matthew 10:16[–22], "Behold, I send you forth as sheep in the midst of wolves … and ye shall be hated of all men for my name['s] sake: but he that endureth to the end shall be saved." I wonder, and give *God* thanks, for their steadfastness. It is the Lord's doing.

---

[94] Luke 2:29.

[95] See Prov. 6:18.

[96] See Ps. 68:30.

[97] See 2 Tim. 4:17.

[98] See Ps. 65:7.

In our way to Pool, a man met us as a messenger of Satan to discourage us. I durst not stay to hear *how much* the gentlemen were displeased at my speaking to the poor tinners that they may be saved. Another stopped us near the place and demanded my letters of orders. I marvelled at Mr. churchwarden's ignorance and self-sufficiency; gave him my Oxford sermon,[99] and rode on. He followed me with another gentleman and vowed I should not preach in their parish. When I began, he came up to me and began shouting and hallooing, and reading, and putting his hat before my face. We went to another place. He walked after us all the way, like Shimei,[100] often asking when did any true minister preach among hedges and ditches? I named my text, "And the Lord said unto the servant, Go out into the highways and hedges, and compel them to come in."[101] I feared the people's zeal, but they stood quiet as lambs. When I asked if it was their desire to hear the word, they cried out all, "Yes, yes, by all means." "Then," said I, to him who stood on my right hand, "I shall surely preach here, unless your master is stronger than mine." After much contention, I walked away with 2,000 or 3,000 people after me (most part tinners) to the next parish, as my wise churchwarden supposed. He followed us a mile (and a warm walk he had of it), then left us on the borders of the neighbouring parish. However, to take my leave of his [parish], I preached in what he called "his," and called to the poor, and maimed, and halt and blind, "Come for all things are *now* ready."[102] In spite of the world and the devil, the poor had the gospel preached unto them and heard it gladly. Great was the zeal and affection they expressed towards me. I do not wonder at Satan's opposition. He will surely fight for his kingdom, which I believe was never so shaken in this place before.

All was quiet this evening at St. Ives, the mayor having declared his resolution to swear twenty new constables and suppress the rioters by force of arms. All the time I was preaching he stood at a little distance to awe the rebels. Their drum he sent for and seized, and shows by all his words and actions that the Lord hath answered our prayers. After giving a word of exhortation to the society, walked with my brother Williams to his house. He received us with the utmost civility. Told us he had engaged another justice of [the] peace to join with him in suppressing the rioters, and was resolved to prevent all farther violence. He has set the whole town against him, by not giving us up to their fury. He plainly told Mr.

---

[99] CW, *A Sermon Preached on April 4, 1742 before the University of Oxford* (London: Strahan, 1742).

[100] See 2 Sam. 16:5–6.

[101] Luke 14:23.

[102] I.e., he preached on Luke 14:15–24.

Hoblyn (the fire and faggot[103] minister) that he would not be perjured to gratify any man's malice. That he had sworn to keep the peace and prevent all mobs. That if murder should be committed, as they threatened, and he expected daily, he should have our blood upon his head, and never be *at peace* as long as he lived. He told us that he has often heard Mr. Hoblyn say "that they ought to drive us away by blows, not arguments." They would have carried us away, that is certain, alive or dead, but the Lord hath raised one up to stand in the gap.[104] And in spite of the old murderer, he that letteth is not yet taken out of the way.[105] He offered to go with us and guard us home, but we would not suffer him.

Four of our persecutors lay in wait for us with their weapons (as we were informed the next day), but *our God* directed us a way to escape them. We looked through all second causes and saw the providential hand of God overruling all things to his glory and our salvation. It was time for him to lay to his hand.[106] The enemy cried so, and the ungodly came on so fast and more so maliciously set against us, that a little bloodshed would not have satisfied them. For the present we are delivered out of the mouth of the lion, and still continue in *his den unhurt*.[107] O that men would therefore praise the Lord for *his* goodness and declare the wonders which he doth for the children of men.

**Wednesday, July 27.** Now that our temptation is abated at least, if not ended, the angel of the covenant comes *himself* and ministers unto us. In declaring his promise this morning, "*Whatsoever* ye shall ask in my name, I *will do it*,"[108] my heart was hot within and the flame broke out and spread to all around. Strong faith did the Spirit work in us, and refreshed and comforted us on every side. All the psalms in the morning service were written for our instruction and encouragement, and we could say from *our hearts,* "If the Lord himself had not been on our side, when men rose up at us, they had swallowed us up quick when they were so wrathfully displeased at us. Yea, the waters had drowned us, and the stream had gone over our soul. ... But praised be the Lord, who hath not given us over for a prey unto their teeth. Our soul is escaped even as a bird out of the snare of the fowler. The snare is broken, and we are delivered. Our help standeth in the name of the Lord, who hath made heaven and earth."[109] Those words also in the second lesson gave us great comfort (but we wondered Mr.

---

[103] OED: "With special reference to the practice of burning heretics alive."

[104] See Ezek. 22:30.

[105] See 2 Thess. 2:7.

[106] Cf. Ps. 119:126 (BCP).

[107] See Dan. 6:22.

[108] Cf. John 14:13.

[109] Cf. Ps. 124:1–7 (BCP).

[William] Symonds could bear to read them), "If the world hate you, ye know it hated me before it hated you. Remember the word that I said unto you, The servant is not greater than his lord. If they have persecuted *me*, they will also persecute *you*. If they have kept *my* saying, they will keep *yours* also. But all these things will they do unto you for my name['s] sake, because they know not him that sent me. If I had not come and spoken unto them, they had not had sin. But now they have no cloak for their sin. But this cometh to pass that the word might be fulfilled which is written in their law, 'They hated me without cause.' But when the Comforter is come, he shall testify of me. And *ye* shall also bear witness, because ye have been with me from the beginning."[110]

Walked with brother Williams to Zennor, which is *all our own*, and the whole country beyond it, even to the Land's End. It rained almost continually till I began preaching "through this man forgiveness of sins,"[111] then held up till I commended them, at parting, to the pardoning grace of God. I do not remember when the word has had greater effect. The whole multitude, I strongly believe, will be added to the church.

Still we find the lion's mouth stopped at St. Ives. I met the society and did not once hear the enemy roar. O that in this short calm we might prepare for the next storm. O that *now* the church hath a moment's rest, it may walk in the comforts of the Holy Ghost, and be edified. The Spirit of grace and supplication was largely poured out this night, and we had fellowship with our absent brethren, especially our poor fellow-sufferers in Staffordshire.

**Thursday, July 28.** Expounded while our Lord applied, "There is none like unto the God of Jeshurun, who rideth on the heavens in thy help, and in his excellency on the sky. The eternal God is thy refuge, and underneath are the everlasting arms. And he shall thrust out the enemy from before thee, and shall say, 'Destroy them.'"[112] Afterwards I found myself led away into the mountain. Between these two, the mountain and the multitude, my desire is to spend and to be spent. Who can declare the loving kindness of the Lord or show forth all his praise?[113] Is he not a very present help in time of trouble?[114] Doth he not compass us about with songs of deliverance?[115] Never have I found him more than in this trial, which drives us all closer to him than ever. Once when I was almost wearied and faint in my mind, he lifted me up by that scripture which I opened upon, "And God is faithful,

---

[110] Cf. John 15:18–27.

[111] Cf. Acts 13:38.

[112] Cf. Deut. 33:26–27.

[113] See Ps. 106:2.

[114] See Ps. 46:1.

[115] See Ps. 32:7.

who will not suffer you to be tempted above that ye are able."[116] So indeed I have found him, and can set to my seal that God is true. He never failed them that seek him. "Call upon me," he saith, "in the time of trouble, so will I hear thee, and thou shalt praise me."[117]

I do give him the praise of my deliverance. He shall have all the glory, for I have no pretence to take the least part of it to myself. Natural courage I have none. What was formerly thought such was mere pride and vainglory, and I am feeling convinced every moment that of all those that ever denied Christ there is not a greater coward than myself. Therefore is his strength made perfect in weakness.[118] Therefore is the excellency of the power not of me but of God.[119]

God hath made great use of his ministers, the magistrates, to restrain at this time the madness of the people. They will not (as some of them have openly said) to disgrace their office, as to be heads or ringleaders of a mob. (Would to God the magistrates in Staffordshire would follow their example!) They cannot but see (and some of them I have heard confess) that we are quiet inoffensive men. Who suffer wrong from most, but do it to no man. Who speak not evil of dignities, nor meddle at all with our betters. But submit ourselves to every ordinance of man for the Lord's sake, and honour the powers that be as ordained of God.[120] Who render unto Caesar the things that are Caesar's,[121] and exercise ourselves herein to keep a conscience void of offence toward God and toward man.[122]

Dined at our brother Chillew's[123] (a confessor of the faith which once he persecuted) and rode on to St. Hilary Downs. Here they told us how our enemies threaten to interrupt us by hurling (as they called it) to drive away the people, and do I know not what to us. They have used all means to deter the poor tinners from the word, telling them they shall be turned out of their business, etc. To the man that receives us they sent word that they will prosecute him, will starve his children, pull down his house, and so forth. But he was not at a loss for an answer, God having touched

---

[116] Cf. 1 Cor. 10:13.
[117] Cf. Ps. 50:15 (BCP).
[118] See 2 Cor. 12:9.
[119] See 2 Cor. 4:7.
[120] See Rom. 13:1.
[121] See Matt. 22:21 and parallels.
[122] See Acts 24:16.
[123] CW was clearly uncertain of this name; in MS Journal it appears as "Mr. Mitchell." He likely means William Chenhall, an inn-keeper of St. Just, who was converted by JW around this time. See Richard Treffery Jr., *Memoir ... with some Account of Methodism in St. Just* (London, 1837), 16.

his heart. I cannot doubt now but the Lord hath a great work to do in this place. The noisy careless hearers were kept away by the enemy's threats, but about a thousand of our beloved tinners listened to the joyful tidings with sincere desires of salvation. The first time I could not preach the gospel to the mixed multitude, but mostly the law. Today my charge was "Comfort ye, comfort ye my people."[124] That word of grace, "Thine iniquity is pardoned" quite melted them down. They wept on all sides, and showed by all possible marks of affection towards us that they thought our saying worthy of all acceptation.[125]

Began explaining the Beatitudes[126] to our own society, and a delightful hour we had afterwards by the blessings of God, none lifting up his hand or voice against us. I do not despair but some of our persecutors themselves may, before we depart, receive that *damnable popish doctrine* (as Mr. Hoblyn judiciously calls it) of justification by faith only.

**Friday, July 29.** Went on with the Beatitudes, and showed the necessity of labouring after that holiness or poverty, mourning, hungering, etc., *after* we have tasted that the Lord is gracious. The remnant, I trust, begins to take root downward, and will *see their hearts*, without either casting off the ordinances or denying the faith. From Germans[127] and predestinarians, good Lord deliver us!

P.S. My dearest brethren of Newcastle, stand fast and close together. Fear not, only believe.[128] Pray always, and particularly for

Your loving servant and brother,<br>C. W.

*Address & Postmark*: none; likely hand delivered.
*Source*: CW record copy, mainly by amanuensis; MARC, DDCW 6/4–6/9.

---

[124] Isa. 40:1.
[125] See 1 Tim. 1:16.
[126] Matt. 5:1–12.
[127] I.e., Moravians.
[128] See Mark 5:36 and parallels.

## March 15, 1744[1]

March 1743[/44[2]]

### Wakefield—Journal Continued.[3]

[Thursday, March 15.] Hearing that many of our poor brethren from Heaton[4] were summoned hither by the malice of their constable, I sent about the town and got them to our inn. Not one of them knew what Jacobite or nonjuror meant.[5] I explained to them the nature of the oaths, which they might safely take I said, and no honest man could refuse. Exhorted them to fear God and honour the king. They were much comforted and confirmed.

At 11:00 waited upon Justice Burton at his inn (with two other justices: Sir Rowland Winn,[6] and Mr. Zouch a clergyman[7]). Told him I had seen a warrant of his to summon witnesses to some treasonable words said to be spoken by "one Westley." That that was not my name, neither had I ever spoken such words. Yet as I supposed I was the person meant, I had therefore put off my journey to London to wait upon him, and answer whatsoever should be laid to my charge. He answered he had nothing to say against me and I might depart. I replied that was not sufficient without clearing my character, and that of many other innocent men whom their neighbours were pleased to call Methodists. "Vindicate them," said my brother clergyman, "that you will find a very hard task." I answered, "Hard as you may think it, I engage to prove that they all to a man who are called by the name are true members of the Church of England, and loyal subjects to His Majesty King George." I then desired they would [be] pleased to administer to me those oaths and added, "If it were not too much trouble, I would wish you to send for every Methodist in England, and give them the same opportunity of declaring their loyalty upon oath."

---

[1] This manuscript is entirely in CW's hand. It is the source of, and provides greater detail than, the account of these days in CW, MS Journal.

[2] While CW dates "1743," his MS Journal makes clear this is "old style," and the date is 1744.

[3] The earlier portion(s) of this journal letter do not appear to survive.

[4] Heaton, Yorkshire, on the northwest outskirt of Bradford; CW spells "Haton."

[5] The Wesley brothers and their followers were being accused of not supporting King George II [of Hanover], in favor of the Stuart family that was removed from the throne in 1688. "Jacobite" was the name given to supporters of the exiled James II and his descendants. The clergy who refused to take an oath of allegiance to William and Mary when James II was exiled were called "nonjurors." The accusations were fanned in the context of a threatened French invasion in support of Prince Charles Edward Stuart (the grandson of James II). The accusations led JW to write King George on March 5, affirming the loyalty of Methodists to George and the Church of England (see JW, *Works*, 26:104–6).

[6] Rowland Winn (1706–65), 4th Baronet of Nostell Priory, just outside Wakefield. CW spells "Wynn."

[7] Rev. Charles Zouch (1694–1754), vicar of Sandal Magna, Yorkshire.

Justice Burton said he was informed that we constantly prayed for the Pretender[8] in our societies (or "nocturnal meetings," as Mr. Zouch termed them). I answered, "The very reverse is true. We constantly pray for His Majesty King George by name. These are some hymns we sing in our meetings,[9] a sermon [I] preached before the university,[10] another my brother preached there,[11] his *Appeal*,[12] and a few more little treatises containing our principles and practices." Here I gave them our books, and was bold to say, "I am as true a Church of England man, and as loyal a subject as anybody in the kingdom." "That's impossible," they cried all. But as it was not my business to dispute, and as I could not answer till the witnesses appeared against me, I withdrew without reply.

While I waited at a neighbouring house one of the brethren brought to me the constable of Birstall,[13] whose heart God hath touched. He begged me to give him some of those hymns and books I had sent by him to the justice. Told me he had summoned the principal witness, Mary Castle, on whose information the warrant was granted and who was setting out on horseback when the news came to Birstall that I was not gone forward to London but back to Wakefield. Hearing this, she turned back and declared to him that she did not hear the treasonable words herself, but another woman *told her so*. Three more witnesses who were to swear to our words, now retracted in like manner, and *knew* nothing of the matter. The fifth, good Mr. Woods (the alehouse keeper who had threatened to swear away my life), is forthcoming it seems in the afternoon (by which time *'tis probable* I shall leave Wakefield, as a friend at his elbow whispers).

Now I plainly see the consequence of my not appearing here to look the enemy in the face. Had I gone on my journey, here would have been witnesses enough and oaths enough to stir up a persecution against both me and all the people of God. I took the witnesses' names: Mary Castle, W. Walker, Lionel Knowls, Arthur Furth, Joseph Woods—and a copy of the warrant as follows:

West Riding of Yorkshire

To the Constable of Birstall in the said Riding or Deputy.

These are in His Majesty's name to require and command you to summon Mary Castle of Birstall aforesaid, and all other such persons as

---

[8] James Stuart (1688–1766), the son of James II, who asserted his claim to the British throne against the house of Hanover, especially in the Jacobite rebellion of 1715.

[9] One or more of *HSP* (1739), *HSP* (1740), and *HSP* (1742).

[10] CW, *A Sermon Preached on April 4, 1742 before the University of Oxford* (London: Strahan, 1742).

[11] This was likely JW, *Salvation by Faith* (London: Hutton, 1738).

[12] JW, *An Earnest Appeal to Men of Reason and Religion* (Newcastle: Gooding, 1743).

[13] Birstall, Yorkshire; 2 miles northwest of Batley. CW spells variously "Burstal" and "Bristal."

you are informed can give any information against one Westley, or any other of the Methodist speakers for speaking any treasonable words or expressions, as praying for the banished, or for the Pretender, etc., to appear before me, and other [of] His Majesty's justices of the peace for the said Riding at the White Hart in Wakefield on the 15th of March instant, by ten of the clock in the forenoon, to be examined and declare the truth of what they and each of them know touching the premises, and that you likewise make a return hereof before us on the same day. Fail not. Given under my hand, the 10th of March 1743.[14]

E. Burton

I opened the book upon my own commission, 2 Timothy 4:5, "But watch thou in all things, endure afflictions, do the work of an evangelist, make full proof of thy ministry."

Between 2:00 and 3:00, honest Mr. Woods came—and started back at sight of me, as if he had trod upon a serpent. One of our brethren took hold of him and told me he trembled and shook every joint of him. The justice's clerk had bid the constable bring him to him as soon as ever he came, as the friendly constable himself informed me. But notwithstanding all the clerk's instructions, Woods frankly confessed to one of our brethren that now he was come he had nothing to say, and would not have come at all had they not forced him.

I saw the clerk take him aside and at the same time cast my eye on Isaiah 54:4, "Fear not, for thou shalt not be ashamed. Neither be thou confounded, for thou shalt not be put to shame." We found all day long that God standeth at the right hand of the poor,[15] particularly in the case of our Heaton brethren. When their constable was called for to give in his report, the justices asked him what those thirteen men were. He could not say they were Papists, or Jacobites, or nonjurors, or indeed anything—for he was taken speechless, and so confounded that he fell upon one of the justices, and behaved in all appearance as quite drunk, though his companions all declared he was quite sober. The justices turned against him and in great anger threatened him with the stocks, reproved him severely for bringing those men to them and drove him out of the room. He was hardly out of the door when he fell down as dead. The brethren took him up and took care of him till he came to himself. And then he declared to brother Shent,[16] "God struck me with blindness, so that I could

---

[14] I.e., 1744 (Burton is also using Old Style dating, where the new year begins March 25).

[15] See Ps. 109:31.

[16] William Shent (1714–88) was a barber and wigmaker of Leeds. His wife Mary (née Musgrave; married in 1737) was converted by John Nelson and brought her husband into the fold soon after. Shent's shop in Briggate became the initial home of the Leeds society, and he became its leader. He also served for a few years as a regional itinerant, until business failure and problems with alcohol led to his removal from these roles.

not find the door. It is the hand and judgment of God upon me!" Our brethren were dismissed unsworn, only with the loss of a day's business, but with a large increase of faith.

Sent a note to Justice Burton desiring I might have an hearing now the witness was come. He came out to me and promised I should. However, I waited, mostly at their door, till near 7:00 at night. While I stood there a brother of Mr. Ingham's[17] was for breaking into the room and bailing the Germans[18] (there under examination) and standing up for the gospel of Christ—when he was so drunk he could neither stand up nor go. With much ado I kept him out, and saved my old friend's and his friends' credit. Ockershausen,[19] the German teacher, I took public notice of him and hoped "he would appear a true man." He refused the oaths, told the justices he owned no king but King Jesus, and so provoked them that they agreed to send him back to his own country, as they design to deal by all his fellows. Poor Mr. Kendrick[20] they were some hours examining and at last agreed, instead of making his mittimus[21] (as was first intended), to send him and his wife to the place from whence he came—from constable to constable, as a vagrant. The reason of their severity was one of his friends abusing Justice Burton, challenging him to fight, etc., which all went to the account of the Methodists.

When all their businesses were over, and I had been insulted at their door by boys and men from 11:00 in the morning to 7:00 at night, I was last sent for and they asked what would Mr. Wesley desire?

**Wesley**: "I desire nothing but want to know what is alleged against me."

Justice Burton made a slight excuse for making me wait so long and then said, "What hope of truth from him? He is another of them." And then addressing to me, "Here are two of your brethren: one so silly it is a shame he should set up for a teacher, and the other has told us a thousand

---

[17] Rev. Benjamin Ingham (1712–72), a native of Ossett, Yorkshire, matriculated at Oxford in 1730, and became involved with the Wesley brothers in the "Oxford Methodists." He was ordained in June 1735 and accompanied JW and CW to Georgia, meeting the Moravians on ship as they did. When Ingham returned to England, he accompanied JW in 1738 to Herrnhut and Marienborn. Ingham's initial labors in the evangelical revival were focused in the West Riding of Yorkshire. As the Wesley brothers and Moravians parted ways in the early 1740s, Ingham sided with the Moravians. About a decade later, Ingham separated from the Moravians, leading about 80 congregations into a connexion of "Ighamites" that he guided. By "brother of Ingham" here, CW almost certainly means a "follower" rather than a sibling.

[18] CW again means Moravians in general, only some of whom were of German origin. He changes to "Moravian" in the MS Journal extract.

[19] John Ockershausen, of German ancestry, had joined the Moravians in London in 1739 and was now active in Yorkshire. CW spells "Okerhause."

[20] William Kendrick, a native of London, had joined with the Moravians after CW expelled him from the Foundery society in 1741. He had since moved repeatedly.

[21] *OED*: "A dismissal from an office or situation; a notice to quit."

lies and equivocations upon oath. He has not wit enough or he would make a complete Jesuit."

[**Wesley:**] I looked round and said, "I see none of my brethren here, but those gentlemen," pointing to Mr. Zouch, who looked as if he did not thank me for claiming kindred.

**Burton**: "Why, do not you know that man (showing me Kendrick)?"

**Wesley**: "Yes, sir, very well. For two years since I expelled him out of our society in London for setting up for a preacher." To this, poor Kendrick assented, which put a stop to all farther reflections on the Methodists.

**Justice Burton** then said I might depart, for they had nothing against me.

**Wesley**: "Sir, that is not sufficient. I cannot depart till my character is fully cleared. It is no trifling matter, even my life is concerned in the slander."

**Burton**: "I did not summons you to appear."

**Wesley**: "I was the person meant by 'one Westley'; and my (supposed) words were the occasion of the order, which I read, signed by your name."

**Burton**: "I will not deny my order. I did send to summon the witnesses."

**Wesley**: "Yes sir, and I wrote them down from the constable's paper. The principal witness, Mary Castle, was setting out, but on hearing I was here turned back and declared to the constable she only heard another *say* that I spoke treason. Three more of the witnesses recanted for the same reason. And Mr. Woods, who is here, says *now* he is come he has nothing to say, and he should not have come neither if he had not been forced. Had not I been here, he would have had enough to say; and ye would have had witnesses enough and oaths enough. But I suppose *my* coming has prevented theirs."

One of the justices added, "I suppose so too!" They all seemed fully satisfied, and would have had me so too. But I insisted on their hearing Mr. Woods.

**Burton**: "Do you desire he may be called as an evidence for you?"

**Wesley**: "I desire he may be heard as a witness against me, if he has aught to lay to my charge."

Then Mr. Zouch asked Woods what he had to say, what the words were which I spoke. Woods was as backward to speak as they to have him, but was at last constrained to say,

[**Woods:**] "I have nothing to say against the gentleman. I only heard him pray that the Lord would call home his banished."

**Zouch**: "But were there any words before or after which pointed to these troublesome times?"

**Woods**: "No, none at all."

**Wesley**: "It was on the 12th of February, before the earliest notice of the invasion. But if folly and malice may be the interpreters, any words which any of you gentlemen speak may be construed as treason."

**Zouch**: "It is very true."

**Wesley**: "Now, gentlemen, give me leave to explain my own words. I had no thought of praying for the Pretender, but for all those who confess themselves strangers and pilgrims upon earth; who seek a country, and know that this is not their place. The scripture, you sir know (to the clergyman), speaks of us as captive exiles who are absent from the Lord and from their home while in the body. Our home is no other than heaven."

**Zouch**: "I thought you would so explain your words, and it is a fair interpretation. They plainly mistook you."

I asked if they were all satisfied. They said they were and cleared me as fully as I desired. I then asked them again to administer to me the oath. Mr. Zouch looked on my sermon and said with the rest it was quite unnecessary, as I was a clergyman of the Church of England, and student of Christ Church, and preached before the university, and had taken the oaths before.[22] Yet I motioned it again, till they acknowledged my loyalty unquestionable. I then presented Sir Rowland and Mr. Zouch with the *Appeal*[23] and took my leave.

After 7:00 we set out for Birstall, and a joyful journey we had. Our poor brethren met us on the road, and we gathered together on the hill and sang praises lustily, with a good courage. Their enemies were rising at Birstall, full of the Wednesbury devil,[24] on presumption of my not finding justice at Wakefield, in which they were the more confirmed by my delay. They had begun pulling down John Nelson's house,[25] but our singing struck a damp into them and scattered the people that delight in war.[26] Now I see if I had not gone to confront the enemy or had been evil entreated at Wakefield, it would have occasioned a general persecution here, which the Lord hath now crushed in the birth.

---

[22] The Oath of Allegiance and Supremacy signed by CW on June 13, 1726 is still extant, held in MARC (DDCW 6/82); as is his subscription to the Articles of Religion (DDCW 6/83).

[23] JW's *Earnest Appeal to Men of Reason and Religion* (1743), *Works*, 11:44–101.

[24] See the account of the unrest in Wednesbury above (May 20–21, 1743).

[25] John Nelson (1707–74) was a stonemason from Birstall who heard JW preach while working on buildings in Moorfields, London in 1739, and was converted. On his return home he became an evangelist in the area around Birstall. In 1742 JW enrolled him as a regular traveling preacher, and he remained under appointment until his death.

[26] See Ps. 68:30.

I carried back the society and joined in hearty thanksgiving to the victorious Captain of our salvation.[27] "No weapon that is formed against thee shall prosper; and every tongue that shall rise against thee in judgment thou shalt condemn!"[28]

*Address & Postmark*: none; likely CW's copy for records.
*Endorsements*: by CW on wrapper, "Mar. 1743 / Trial at Wakefield / before the Justices." [[My Journal with the Justices, March 1743/4.]]
*Source*: holograph; MARC, DDCW 6/2.

---

[27] See the hymn that CW wrote upon completing this interrogation at Wakefield, in *HSP* (1749), 2:240.

[28] Isa. 54:17.

## September 2–17, 1744[1]

**Sunday, September 2.** Received the sacrament at the College.[2] Preached repentance and redemption of sins at Baptist Mills in the hard rain.[3] Met the society, and Jesus was assembled together with us. Scarce a soul among us but what was moved, as their tears and rejoicings witnessed. Most could say truly, "our fellowship is with the Father, and with the Son."[4] I have not been more refreshed these many months past. Blessed be the God of all consolation.

**Tuesday, September 4.** Waited most of the day at the New Passage[5] for our sister [Mary] Jones and her little ones.[6] They got to our side by 5:00 in the afternoon, through perils of water, for the boat struck against a rock and stuck fast. The man laboured to get her off, till they must all have sunk if they had stayed in her a few minutes longer. Then they got to shore in a small boat, and the passengers came over in another vessel.

**Thursday, [September] 6.** In answer to a letter from Wales, wrote as follows,

> My desire of reconciliation with poor Mr. [Thomas] Williams flows, I think, from true love and pity to his soul, and more to his father[7] whose grey hairs I told him, he will bring down with sorrow to the grave. I never trusted the younger with any thing of consequence, for I saw through him from the beginning. But charity hopeth all things.[8] Therefore I bore with him, and still I know not how to give him up.
>
> My lot has been to meet with treachery and ingratitude from almost every one I ever loved. I can *forgive* such, but not *trust* them. In returning them good for evil I find no difficulty. But to humble myself before them,

---

[1] This manuscript (one long page, with text on front and back) is entirely in CW's hand. It is the source of, and provides greater detail than, the account of these days in CW, MS Journal.

[2] That is, Bristol Cathedral, on College-Green. This seat for the Bishop of Bristol was commonly referred to as "Bristol College."

[3] His sermon on Acts 2:37–39.

[4] Cf. 1 John 1:3.

[5] This is the ferry across the mouth of the River Severn to Wales, departing east of Pilning, Gloucestershire and landing near Black Rock, just north of Sudbrook, Monmouthshire. CW would have been on the Pilning side, about 10 miles northeast of Bristol.

[6] Mary Forrest (1712–88) of Minehead, Somerset, married Robert Jones (1706–42) of Fonmon Castle near Cardiff, Glamorganshire in 1732. Robert came under the influence of Howell Harris in 1741, became a Methodist, and a warm friend of JW and CW. When Robert died unexpectedly in June 1742 both brothers kept up a close relationship with her and her three surviving children: Mary (1733–81), Robert (1734?–93), and Catherine (1735–68).

[7] Thomas Williams Sr. (c. 1697–1783) of Llanishen, Glamorgan, Wales, who welcomed CW to Wales and accompanied him in his first preaching tour in November 1740; see CW, MS Journal, Nov. 7, 1740.

[8] See 1 Cor. 13:7.

to follow them up with kindness so as even to seem *afraid* of them, this does much violence to my pride. That I compel myself to submit to it, and take up the cross my nature soul most abhors, whom my nature would soonest tear to pieces, those I labour first to put first into my bosom.

**Friday, [September] 7.** Was our watch-night at Kingswood. God never sends us away from thence without a blessing.

**Sunday, [September] 9.** After administering the sacrament to the whole society, took horse with Mr. [William] Shepherd and others for Churchill,[9] where he had desired me to preach after the funeral of his relation. At 5:00 we met the corpse being brought[10] out of the house with the minister[11] and justice before it. The latter took Mr. Shepherd aside and threatened him with terrible things in case I preached. They went to church and I sunk down in the house, quite spent and wearied out with the heavy rain and hard riding. Before 6:00 the brethren returned—and the congregation, notwithstanding Mr. Justice's[12] public warning them in the churchyard, and abusing Mr. Shepherd in great variety of foul language, and pulling him by the chin, etc.

Many poor people listened with great attention while I called, "Behold the Lamb of God that taketh away the sin of the world."[13] Out of the abundance of my heart my mouth spake,[14] for the love of God in Jesus Christ constrained me.[15] When I had finished my discourse Mr. Justice called out and bid them pull me down. He had stood at a distance some time, striving in vain to raise a mob, for not a man would stir at his bidding. Only one behind struck me once with a stone. While I was in my prayer the captain cried again, "Pull him down." I told him I had nothing now to do but pray for him. He answered, "I have nothing to do with prayer." "I suppose so, sir," said I, "but we have." Then he came up and laid hold of my gown, but I stepped down to save him trouble. He told me he was a justice of peace. "I reverence you sir," I answered, "for your office['s] sake; but must not neglect my own, which is to preach the gospel." "H[ell] on the gospel," he replied. And I said, "Sir, you are a blasphemer, and was you a king, I would tell you so." "I say," said he, "it is an unlawful assembly." "Be so good sir, then," I replied, "to name the law or Act of

---

[9] Churchill, Somerset; 3 miles south of Congresbury.

[10] Orig., "bringing."

[11] Rev. Blinman Gresley (c. 1716–73) was vicar of nearby Banwell and perpetual curate of Churchill.

[12] I.e., the Justice of the Peace; not a last name.

[13] Cf. John 1:29.

[14] See Luke 6:45.

[15] See 2 Cor. 5:14.

Parliament which our assembly is contrary to." He answered (unhappily enough), "It is contrary to the Waltham Act."[16] "How so, sir," said I? "I am in my proper habit, and see none among us in disguise." He did not urge the unlawfulness any more, yet insisted I should not preach there. I told him I had licence to preach throughout England and Ireland by virtue of my degree. "That I know sir," said he, "and am sorry for it. I think you are fellow of a college too."[17] "Yes sir, and a gentleman; and as such would be glad to wait upon you, and have a little conversation with you yourself." He should be glad of it too he answered, for "I had behaved more like a gentleman than any of them." I charged the people to say nothing, but go home quietly, and so Mr. Justice and I parted tolerable friends.

By this little trial my body as well as soul was greatly strengthened. We took horse, and went on our way rejoicing three miles farther to Mr. Star's,[18] where I preached next morning to an house full of serious sinners, and urged them to come weary and heavy laden to their friend.[19] It was a word of comfort to our souls. They seemed all affected much, and pressed me to come and speak to them again the words of this life.

**Tuesday, [September] 11.** At Bath[20] our Lord applied his own words to our hearts, "Is it nothing to you, all ye that pass [by]? behold, and see if ever sorrow was like unto my sorrow, ...."[21] In the society also he manifested his power, and comforted us on every side.

**Thursday, [September] 13.** Rejoiced to hear of the triumphant death of a sister in London, whose last breath was spent in prayer for me.[22] None of our children die without leaving their fathers a legacy. The word in the evening was as a fire and as an hammer. The rocks were broken in pieces,[23] particularly a poor, hardened sinner who for sometime withstood me before his mouth was stopped, and very many were melted down. Some testified their having at that time received the atonement.

---

[16] The "Waltham Black Act," passed in 1723, was directed against poaching and related offenses. It detailed a list of property offenses which, if committed while armed or disguised (as with blackened faces), could carry the death penalty. The Act was often interpreted to mean that being disguised could be considered a crime in itself.

[17] After receiving his MA, CW was elected to a Studentship at Christ Church, Oxford (their equivalent of a Fellow). While he only taught for a couple of years, he held this position until he married.

[18] Mr. Star lived in Way Wick, Somerset; 4 miles east of Weston-super-Mare. CW spells "Starr"; we follow the spelling in JW's *Journal* (see *Works*, 20:142).

[19] Matt. 11:28.

[20] Bath, Somerset; 11 miles southeast of Bristol.

[21] Lam. 1:12.

[22] CW identifies the woman in MS Journal as Elizabeth March; cf. JW's account of her death in his *Journal*, Sept. 6, 1744, *Works*, 20:38.

[23] See Jer. 23:29.

**Friday, [September] 14.** Was comforted at the sight of my beloved brother Thomson.[24] Our Lord himself welcomed him among us, for both in the word preached and in the midst of the brethren afterwards his power was remarkably present, and we rejoiced together as men that divide the spoil.

**Sunday, [September] 16.** Displayed from Isaiah 35 the glorious privileges of the gospel to our colliers—and the wilderness and the solitary place was glad for them.[25] Even my stammering tongue spake plainly of the great sanctifying promises, which were mixed with strong faith in those that heard. My brother Thomson assisted me to administer the blessed sacrament to all the society, and was (as he afterwards expressed it) on the highest round of Jacob's ladder. It was a passover much to be remembered. We saw the felicity of his chosen, and rejoiced in the gladness of his people, and gave thanks with his inheritance.

Took horse with brother Shepherd for Mr. Star's. The justice's behaviour last Sunday has done us good service, being generally disapproved of. The minister likewise was so kind as to send me many hearers (by his seasonable discourse this morning on "Beware of false prophets"[26]), who knew nothing of my coming till he gave them notice. And then they said, "It is but fair to go and hear what he has to say for himself." Near 3,000, I believe, attended patiently while I cried with great enlargement, "Ho, every one that thirsteth, come ye to the waters."[27] They expressed much satisfaction in the joyful tidings, and seemed willing to receive the Saviour from sin.

**Monday, [September] 17.** Read, it being our thanksgiving day, John Nelson's case[28]—a plain accomplishment of that promise, "I will give you a mouth and wisdom, which none of your adversaries shall be able to resist."[29]

*Address & Postmark*: none; likely CW's copy for records.
*Source*: holograph; MARC, DDCW 6/10.

---

[24] Rev. George Thomson (1698–1782), vicar of St. Gennys, who had given strong support to CW in Cornwall a couple of months earlier; cf. CW, MS Journal, July 13, 1744 and following.

[25] See Isa. 35:1.

[26] Matt. 7:15.

[27] Isa. 55:1.

[28] Nelson had been impressed to military service against his will (see CW, MS Journal, May 4, 1744). CW was reading Nelson's summary of how he was freed to return to preaching, which was published as *The Case of John Nelson* (London: Strahan, 1745).

[29] Cf. Luke 21:15.

## JULY 28–AUGUST 15, 1745[1]

**July 28, Sunday evening.** Took my leave of the flock at the Foundery in the words of Isaiah 35:1–10 with strong desires of their accomplishment, "And the ransomed of the Lord shall return, and come to Zion with songs and everlasting joy upon their heads: they shall obtain joy and gladness, and sorrow and sighing shall flee away."[2] Lay at Brentford.[3] Next morning found our brothers Larwood[4] and Meyrick[5] at Slough, and with them and Thomas Butts[6] and Thomas Witham[7] came safe to Bristol by 3:00 on **Tuesday afternoon.** My brother has been here since Thursday.

I preached on the first (seasonable) words that offered, "Be patient therefore, brethren, unto the coming of the Lord. ....." James 5:7. The God of all consolation was present.

**Wednesday, July 31.** Began visiting the classes. Mr. Gwynne[8] of Garth accompanied us and rejoiced greatly in the grace given them.

**[Thursday,] August 1.** Began our conference with Mr. Hodges,[9] six of our own assistants, and Herbert Jenkins,[10] and Mr. Gwynne. Continued therein five days and parted, as we met, with great love.[11]

---

[1] This manuscript (one long page, with text on front and back) is entirely in CW's hand. It is the source of, and provides greater detail than, the account of these days in CW, MS Journal.

[2] Isa. 35:10.

[3] Brentford, Middlesex; 8 miles west of Charing Cross.

[4] Samuel Larwood (d. 1755) first appears as a traveling preacher this year (see JW, *Works*, 10:159). He left the Wesleyan itinerancy in early 1754, settling as an independent minister in Southwark, where he died Nov. 1, 1755.

[5] Thomas Meyrick (d. 1770) was a member of a band for single men at the Foundery by 1742. He seems also to have been JW's business manager or "steward" at the time. He became a traveling preacher for several years, serving in various parts of the country.

[6] Thomas Butts (1719–78) was looking after JW's book-concern at the Foundery as early as 1742, when he was still "on trial" as a member of a single men's band. On May 19, 1746 he married Hannah Witham (1720–62), with JW officiating. By 1755 Butts was replaced as JW's book steward by Robert Windsor, and set up on his own as a music publisher.

[7] Thomas Witham (1724–1809), son of Thomas and Elizabeth (Harrison) Witham of London, was active in the Foundery society and would soon be brother-in-law to Thomas Butts.

[8] Marmaduke Gwynne (1692–1769), a wealthy landholder of Garth, Wales, and loyal member of the Established Church, was drawn into the evangelical revival in 1737 through the preaching of Howell Harris, and began offering support to the leaders of the revival. He had met the Wesley brothers during their visits to Wales, and would eventually become CW's father-in-law. Interestingly, CW spells the name "Gwyn" throughout this journal letter.

[9] Rev. John Hodges (1700–77), rector of Wenvoe, was one of the Welsh clergy most sympathetic with the Wesley brothers' early work in Wales.

[10] Herbert Jenkins became a Methodist in 1743 but later joined Whitefield and his friends, often preached for Andrew Kinsman in Plymouth, Bristol, and South Wales, and was later apparently a Dissenting minister in Maidenstone. See *WHS* 6 (1907): 141.

[11] This was the second annual meeting the Wesley brothers held with their lay "assistants" and sympathetic clergy; the six assistants present were Larwood, Meyrick, Richard Moss,

**Friday, August 2.** I called on our watch-night to a multitude of poor maimed, halt, blind souls, "Come; for all things are now ready."[12] God confirmed the word of his messenger. Many, I am persuaded, were in that hour compelled to come in. Till midnight our souls were satisfied as with marrow and fatness while our mouth praised God with joyful lips.

**Sunday, August 4.** Found the never-failing presence of God in his ordinance at Kingswood. The cup of blessing which we bless, is it not the communion of the blood of Christ?[13] O that all the world might *so show forth* and partake of his death till he come to judgment![14]

At Conham chapel[15] I read the service and preached repentance and faith for the remission of sins.[16] Then declared at the Mills, "One thing is needful."[17] The hard rain did not scatter any of the hearers who listened with deepest attention as to words whereby they might be saved.

Our Lord was mightily with us in the society, confirming the souls of his disciples and animating us through much tribulation to enter into the kingdom of heaven.

**Wednesday, [August] 7.** While I was speaking from those words, "The end of all things is at hand,"[18] the Spirit demonstrated them to our hearts, and we felt with solemn joyful concern the weight of things eternal!

In the bands he passed by us again and showed us his goodness. It was a time of blessed sorrow and love. For near two hours we tasted the powers of the world to come[19] in solid serious joy and humility. Our brethren and companions in tribulation were brought to our remembrance, and surely the Lord heard *his own* prayer, both for them and for all this guilty nation.

**Friday, August 9.** In reading the letters, we received faith to pray for the revival of God's work and the propagation of his gospel. Neither can we doubt but that all things that happen shall happen for the furtherance thereof.

---

Thomas Richards, John Slocombe, and James Wheatley. The minutes of this conference can be found in JW, *Works*, 10:147–68.

[12] Luke 14:17; preaching his sermon on Luke 14:15–24.

[13] See 1 Cor. 10:16.

[14] See 1 Cor. 11:26.

[15] A chapel built and endowed by Sir Abraham Ellison for the workers in the smelt works owned by CW's friend John Wayne in Conham, Gloucestershire, 3 miles east of Bristol. CW spells "Connum."

[16] Acts 2:37–39.

[17] Luke 10:42.

[18] 1 Pet. 4:7.

[19] See Heb. 6:5.

**Saturday, August 10.** Took horse between 11:00 and 12:00 with John Trembath[20] for Shepton Mallet,[21] where a great door seems to be opening, and there are not yet many adversaries. Soon after 4:00, we came to our host's[22] at the farthest end of the town. Near 7:00 we walked back through the town and a mile farther to the place of preaching. Many attentive souls were assembled, to whom I explained, "The poor have the gospel preached unto them."[23] At the beginning, one of the devil's drunken champions attempted to disturb us, being sent for that purpose by his master and fellows at the alehouse. My voice prevailed, and he soon quitted the field and left me to deliver my message to those that had ears to hear.[24]

They desired me to meet the little society, but at an unusual place, to disappoint the mob who they apprehended would follow and be troublesome. I walked a little way forward toward the town, then turned back over a field to drop the people, and springing up against a rising ground, sprained or broke my leg, I know not which, but fell down when I offered to set it to the ground, having quite lost the use of it. While the brethren were carrying me in their arms the owner of the field met us and with much bad language was for turning us back, but was disarmed by two words speaking, and permitted them to carry me to a hut of one of the society. It was quickly filled by the poor people. I immediately bathed my leg in cold water, but found no relief of the great pain. It was soon noised about the town that I had broke my leg, some said my neck, and that it was a judgment upon me. The principal man of the place, Mr. P——[25], sent me a kind message that his bath-chair[26] was at my service, to bring me to his house. I returned thanks but declined his offer on account of my pain, which unfitted me for any company except that of my best friends, *the poor*. With these I continued praying, singing, and rejoicing for two hours, and observed in all their words and looks the love and simplicity of the gospel. Happiest they that could come near to do anything for me. When my strength was all exhausted, they laid me on their bed (the best they had), but I could not sleep for pain.

[**Sunday, August 11.**] Met the society at 6:00 next morning and took in

---

[20] John Trembath (fl. 1740–60) was a native of St. Gennys, Cornwall, who became one of JW's traveling preachers as early as 1743. But he proved disinclined to study and self-discipline, drifting in and out of the itinerancy from 1750 onwards.

[21] Orig., "Shippenmallard." Shepton Mallet, Somerset is 18 miles south of Bristol.

[22] Apparently William Stone, at whose home CW stayed again on June 3, 1746; see below. JW also stayed with Stone in Shepton Mallet in Feb. 1748; see JW, *Works*, 20:206.

[23] Cf. Matt. 11:5ff.

[24] See Matt. 11:15 and parallels.

[25] Likely Strode Poyntz (1705–66), a well-to-do clothier in Shepton Mallet.

[26] *OED*: "a large chair on wheels, for invalids." I.e., a wheelchair.

near twenty new members. About 8:00, the surgeon we had sent for from Oakhill[27] came, and found in dressing my leg that it was not broke, only violently sprained. Many poor people being come from far to hear the word, I got the brethren to carry me out in a chair, which they set on a table, and I preached kneeling upon it. I thought of Halyburton's best pulpit,[28] which alone seemed preferable to this. I explained the end of our Lord's mission from his own words, Luke 4:18, "The Spirit of the Lord is upon me, because he hath anointed me to preach the gospel to the poor; ....." They received it with all readiness of mind, and shall surely find it the power of God unto salvation. For near an hour I forgot my maim, and believed I should be enabled to preach at Oakhill also, at noon as had been appointed.

Accordingly, I sent and borrowed the friendly Mr. P—'s chair, in which the brethren carried me to Oakhill, about 3 measured miles. I found a large congregation, of Dissenters chiefly—not wise and rich and opinionated[29] as the generality, but poor and simple and longing to be taught the first elements of the doctrine of Christ. I did not perceive one of them go away (though for the first quarter of an hour it rained as hard as it could rain) while I pointed them to "The Lamb of God, which taketh away the sin of the world."[30] The word was not bound, like me, but ran very swiftly through their hearts. For almost an hour I spake kneeling as before and felt no pain or weariness till I had done. Then my flesh shrank at the twenty measured miles I had to ride, which seemed next to impossible. However, they sat me on the horse, and by 9:00 at night I was brought to Bristol, but in such extreme pain as I have not felt with all my broken bones and sicknesses. I could not help glorying meanwhile in his strength which is made perfect in weakness,[31] and wished, depending on his help, that every day of my life might be like this!

**Monday, August 12.** Was a close prisoner all day, but in the evening borrowed a chair belonging to the poor-house and was carried out to hear my brother's farewell sermon.

**Tuesday, August 13.** Preached myself on, "They that wait on the Lord shall renew their strength,"[32] and then, confiding in the promise, went in my chair and lay at Mr. Wigginton's[33] by the waterside.

Between 4:00 and 5:00 next morning [**August 14**], I was carried to

---

[27] Oakhill, Somerset; 3 miles north of Shepton Mallet. CW spells "Okel."

[28] Thomas Halyburton used this term for his death bed. CW spells "Halliburton."

[29] Orig., "opiniated."

[30] John 1:29.

[31] See 2 Cor. 12:9.

[32] Isa. 40:31.

[33] Ebenezer (d. 1745) and Ann (Bundy) Wigginton (d. 1757) were supporters of the Wesley brothers in Bristol. Ebenezer would die in November of this year.

*July–August 1745*

Captain Philips's vessel, which was filled mostly with our own people from Wales. We passed the day in singing and reading, and by 6:00 on **Thursday morning [August 15]** landed safe at Cardiff.

At night most of the gentry in town were at the room. I called to the convicted sinners, "Strengthen ye the weak hands, and confirm the feeble knees,"[34] and laboured to trouble the careless, as well as to comfort the troubled hearts. The word was a two-edged sword.[35] I afterwards exhorted the society to pray always and build up one another, which thing they also do.[36] Blessed be God, that we have not here spent our strength in vain.[37]

*Address & Postmark*: none; likely CW's copy for records.
*Source*: holograph; MARC, MA 1977/503, Box 5, file 5.

---

[34] Isa. 35:3.

[35] See Heb. 4:12.

[36] See 1 Thess. 5:11.

[37] Three names, in another hand of undetermined date, appear after letter: "Dr. Rob. / Mich. Watkis. / S. Mack."

## April 14–May 11, 1746[1]

**April 14, 1746.** At 10:00 in the morning set out with James Waller[2] in a chaise for Bristol. Our young fiery horse took to it beyond expectation, yet started so and flew out at first that we were often in great danger. But the Lord brought us safe to sister Hardwick's in Brentford.[3] I preached at night on the "blood of sprinkling,"[4] and we were all melted down by it. I never fail of a blessing in this place.

**Tuesday, April 15.** We drove to Woolhampton.[5]

**Wednesday, [April] 16,** to Sandy Lane[6] and by 11:00, a **Thursday morning,** came safe to Bath. At 1:00 set out again and by 5:00 saluted our friends in the Horsefair, Bristol. I found the Spirit of supplication as soon as I entered our house. Preached on "Hosanna to the Son of David: ...."[7] Met the society and was comfortably assured that the power of God was among them.

**Friday, April 18.** Found more life among the men['s] bands than I ever remember. "Can these dry bones live?"[8]

**Saturday, April 19.** We had a great blessing at Weavers' Hall.[9] God gave testimony to the word of his grace,[10] and many were deeply affected under it.

---

[1] This manuscript is in the hand of James Waller, with CW inserting scattered words that had been overlooked. It was the source of, and provides greater detail than, the account of these days in CW, MS Journal.

[2] James Waller (c. 1723–1802) first appears on the Foundery Band Lists (p. 47), on trial, in March 1743. This is the earliest known example of him traveling with CW as an assistant, to drive the carriage and the like. Through these trips Waller met Elizabeth Gwynne (1730–95), the sister of CW's wife Sarah, and in Dec. 1750 CW joined James and Elizabeth in marriage. Waller became a successful lace merchant in London and provided support to Sarah (Gwynne) Wesley after CW's death.

[3] Thomas Hardwick (1681–1746), originally of Herefordshire, had moved to Isleworth, Middlesex, where in 1711 he married Jane Garding (d. 1762). Thomas was a stonemason/architect, and the family eventually settled in Brentford, Middlesex. They were friends of CW and supporters of his Methodist cause. Thomas had died in mid-March of this year, so CW names only the wife. Also in the home would have been their son Thomas Hardwick Jr. (1725–98), another stonemason/architect, who would marry Sarah Witham (d. 1787) on Dec. 31, 1748, with CW officiating the service.

[4] Heb. 12:24.

[5] Woohampton, Berkshire; about 9 miles west/southwest of Reading.

[6] Sandy Lane, Wiltshire; about 4 miles southeast of Chippenham.

[7] Matt. 21:9.

[8] Cf. Ezek. 37:3.

[9] A hall in the Temple Meads section of Bristol that was a regular preaching point for CW and JW.

[10] See Acts 14:3.

**Sunday, April 20.** Was a day of salvation. We had a comfortable sacrament at Kingswood. I preached with great severity at the Conham, and "the stones cried out"[11] on every side, and the Pharisees were offended. I thought of our Lord's direction, "Let them alone."[12] They too may have a wounded spirit by and by. For the evening I spoke (yet not I) to many hearts from those words, Hebrews 9:12, "Neither by the blood of goats and calves, but by his own blood he entered in once into the holy place, having obtained eternal redemption for us." God stood in the midst of the congregation, but in the society he was more sensibly present. The Lord came down in his great convincing, comforting power, and bowed all our spirits before him. A loud cry was heard at first, but it sunk lower and lower, and turned into the groans that cannot be uttered.[13] This most blessed mourning continued above two hours. The Spirit of the Lord was upon me, as a Spirit of prayer and love.[14] I could, at that time (I think I could, and was forced to declare it) have laid down my life for their salvation. The backsliders were most upon my heart, to whom I seem principally sent. One such caught hold of me at going out, and cried with great earnestness, "I have found my Saviour again. He has wrote forgiveness upon my heart." Such a night we have hardly had for some years past.

**April 21, Monday.** Expounded Revelation 3:2–3, "Be watchful, and strengthen the things which remain, that are ready to die. ... Remember how thou hast received and heard, and hold fast, and repent." Again the power of the Lord was present to wound and heal. Many cried after him in bitterness of spirit. One that had fallen from grace and lay in the pit of despair above three years was lifted up again, and the new song, as she informed me, put in her mouth. (I afterwards recollected that this was the day on which I first received forgiveness.[15]) I called at Newgate [prison] at the request of the condemned malefactor but was refused admittance to him. The poor wretch having, as they *told* me, altered his mind.[16]

In the evening the word was again as a "two-edged sword."[17] Enjoyed an hour of solemn sorrow among the penitents.

---

[11] Cf. Luke 19:40.

[12] Matt. 15:14.

[13] See Rom. 8:26.

[14] See 2 Tim. 1:7.

[15] CW is likely confusing April 21 with May 21. May 21, 1738 was his "Pentecost" experience recorded in detail in his MS Journal. But if he does mean May 21, this is the only place where he explicitly identifies that day as the time when he first received forgiveness of sins (as compared with assurance, or the like).

[16] This was 19 year-old Matthew Henderson, convicted of murder; see The Ordinary of Newgate, *His Account of the Behaviour, Confession, and Dying Words of Matthew Henderson, Who was Executed on Friday the 25th of April, 1746* (London: M. Cooper, 1746). Available online: https://www.oldbaileyonline.org/browse.jsp?name=OA17460425.

[17] Heb. 4:12.

**Wednesday, April 23.** Passed an hour with some of our *first* children, and found the Spirit of God among us as in the former days. It continued at Weavers' Hall. But in meeting the women's bands I was carried above things temporal. The cloud rested on the tabernacle.[18] The Spirit of supplication was given. I broke out again and again into fervent effectual prayer, their faith bearing me up. In the midst of strong cryings one was suddenly brought to me, whom I offered up to the throne [of grace]. It was one that "did run well,"[19] and had often strengthened my hands in the Lord. Immediately followed such a burst of divine power as broke all our hearts. All members suffered with that one member, and God who knoweth what is in the mind of the Spirit[20] shall surely bring back that wanderer to his fold.

**Thursday, April 24.** In the society I declared the promises to backsliders[21] and many rejoiced for the consolation. Mary Gee in particular was released and again laid fast hold on eternal life.

**Sunday, April 27.** "This is the day which the Lord hath made; we will rejoice and be glad in it."[22] After sacrament he poured out upon us the never failing Spirit of intercession. At Conham likewise, he met us in his own house. A vast quiet congregation listened at the [Baptist] Mills while I preached on "Wisdom crieth without; she uttereth her voice in the streets: she crieth in the chief place of concourse, in the openings of the gates: ...."[23] Again my heart was comforted with our dear children of the society. We were with him on the mount (a bright cloud overshadowing us), and said "it is good for us to be here!"[24]

**Monday, April 28.** Preached before setting out for the country society, and the Lord left a blessing behind him. Drove to Bath and rejoiced with the little increasing flock there.

**Tuesday, [April] 29.** Through many perils and almost impassable ways, got at last to Rode.[25] At the Cross declared the end of our Lord's coming, "that they might have life" (or pardon) and that they might know it more abundantly (or holiness and heaven).[26] Urged the hearers in close,

---

[18] See Exod. 40:35; Num. 9:18.

[19] Gal. 5:7.

[20] See Rom. 8:27.

[21] See Hosea 14:4.

[22] Ps. 118:24.

[23] Prov. 1:20ff.

[24] Matt. 17:4 and parallels.

[25] Rode, Somerset; 4 miles northeast of Frome. Spelled "Rhodes" here; corrected in MS Journal.

[26] John 10:10.

convincing words (which did not fall to the ground[27]) and then the society to lay hold on the Lord, their life eternal.[28] Left them mourning for him, refusing to be comforted. Lodged at Mr. Node's a clothier, whose large family are, I trust, becoming an household of faith.

**Wednesday, April 30.** Preached with a double power and blessing. A poor mourner had been crying for mercy all night in the society house. Yet still he answered her not a word. Read a few letters which were greatly blest to their souls. Conversed at my lodgings with many which have tasted the love of Jesus since I was here last, mostly under the preaching or prayers of our lay-helpers. How can any man dare deny their being sent of God? O that they who have the outward call might be provoked to jealousy, and by making full proof of their ministry take the matter out of our weak hands. Set out in our chaise. Broke it in a slough on the common, and made an hard shift to reach Bradford[29] by noon. Rode thence to [South] Wraxall,[30] (Mr. Sumpsion's) and returning to Bradford in the evening, preached on our Lord's words, "If any man enter by me, he shall be saved."[31] Spake close and searching to their hearts. Prayed by a sister who had been much abused by a wild, wicked man, yet who pretended great love to us and zeal for the work of God. Out of pure devilish envy and malice he knocked her down, bruised her all over, and broke four or five small bones, and continues to say all manner of evil of her falsely. She answers him only by her prayers and love. The society room being quite open and exposed, I was hindered by the great confusion without from meeting the people.

Lay down but got little sleep, with our worse than Cornish accommodation.

**Thursday, May 1.** I endeavoured to strengthen the weak hands and confirm the feeble knees.[32] Many received a sure and comfortable hope that their God will come and save them. The poor disconsolate soul (at Rode that was) here found peace and pardon, and now rejoices with joy unspeakable. Advised the society to walk as becometh the gospel.[33] Hardly prevailed upon the violent man that had so evil entreated our sister, to allow her some small relief till she should recover. Gave her the sacrament and received a blessing with her. Called on a little church in the house of a

---

[27] See 1 Sam. 3:19.
[28] See 1 Tim. 6:12.
[29] Bradford-on-Avon, Wiltshire.
[30] South Wraxall, Wiltshire (CW spells "Rexal"); about 2.5 miles north of Bradford-on-Avon.
[31] John 10:9.
[32] See Isa. 35:3.
[33] Phil. 1:27.

brother on the road and spent a few blessed moments in prayer. At night preached at Bath on "Jesus shall save his people from their sins."[34] We rejoiced in steadfast hope of full redemption.

**Friday, May 2.** Returned to Bristol and heard the news of our late victory in Scotland.[35] Spake in the evening from the first words that offered, "He that glorieth, let him glory in the Lord,"[36] and read some letters. I hope we did rejoice unto him with reverence and thankfully receive the answer of that prayer:

> All their strength overturn, *overthrow,*
>     Knap their spears, and break their swords,
> Make the daring rebels know
>     The battle is the Lord's![37]

And oh that in this farther reprieve, before the sword returns to our land, we might all know the time of our visitation!

**Sunday, May 4.** Our Lord gave us his blessing in the word, but a far greater in the sacrament. From preaching to the Conham stocks and stones,[38] hastened to Baptist Mills and called to many thousands, "Come, and let us return unto the Lord. For he hath torn, and he will heal us; he hath smitten, and he will bind us up."[39] My heart and mouth were opened to invite lost sinners to Christ. The word I know should not return void,[40] but many shall follow on till they know the Lord.

At the society, continued in my proper office exhorting backsliders to come again to the fountain. We heard the general cry of fear and grief and joy in answer to our prayers, and sweetly felt the most sensible presence of God.

**Monday, May 5.** Comforted them again who did run well and are groaning to recover their peace. Met the smaller society whose prayer of faith was answered, both upon them and me.

---

[34] Matt. 1:21.

[35] The Jacobite forces threatening England were defeated at the battle of Culloden on Apr. 16.

[36] 1 Cor. 1:31.

[37] "For his Majesty King George," st. 2, lns 5–8, *Hymns for Times of Trouble and Persecution*, 2nd ed. (London: William Strahan, 1745), 55.

[38] I.e., lifeless or unawakened listeners.

[39] Hosea 6:1.

[40] See Isa. 55:11.

Went to seek the sheep that were gone astray. Found sister Cox[41] desirous again to return. Then called on poor J. H.,[42] one of our first and dearest children in Bristol, but the cares of this life and the spirit of offence had choked the word, and he had gone back to the world, more than three years ago. He was ready to sink into the earth at sight of me, but after prayer his spirit revived and he seemed resolved, with his wife, to set their hand to the plow again. So did Mr. J. and his wife. After all their revolting, I trust they will all escape safe to land.

**Tuesday, May 6.** Met my brother at Kingswood, with many others, in the evening.[43] Heard him gladly.

**Wednesday, May 7.** Breakfasted with some that were grown slack (brother Rogers and S.) but are stirred up again to lay hold on the Lord, and I think more in earnest than ever. Dined with one who had been so bitterly offended with the singers that he quite forsook both the word and people of God. We left him in a better mind. Spent an hour with a moderate drunkard, warning him to flee from the wrath to come.[44] After we were gone the fear of death fell upon him, and the same instant he received power over his sin, which has continued ever since.

**Sunday, May 11.** Showers of blessings we received at the sacrament and were wonderfully carried out in prayer for the ministers. I preached at Kingswood in the afternoon, the Lord assisting me much, and yet more in my exhortation to the society.

At 5:00 my brother preached "the death of the righteous"[45] to as large and quiet a congregation as I have ever seen at Bristol. I added a few words in confirmation of his, and the Lord, I trust, gave them his blessing. The day was well concluded with a primitive love feast.

*Address & Postmark*: none; CW's copy for records.[46]
*Source*: CW record copy, by amanuensis; MARC, DDCW 6/11.

---

[41] Apparently Hannah Cox, one of the early converts in 1739; see JW, *Journal*, Apr. 26, 1739, *Works*, 19:52.

[42] Possibly James Harding (see Apr. 16, 1741 above), or John Haydon, a weaver, who was drawn into the Methodist movement in Bristol in May 1739 (see JW, *Journal*, May 2, 1739, *Works*, 19:54).

[43] JW had joined CW in Bristol because they were preparing for their third annual conference with their assistants, May 12–15, 1746; see JW, *Works*, 10:168–85.

[44] See Matt. 3:7 and parallels.

[45] Num. 23:10.

[46] The pages are numbered 1–3, and are part of a continuous document that is now missing the next six pages (covering May 11–June 13), but includes 6/28 (pp. 10–13), 6/29 (pp. 14–15), 6/14 (pp. 16–18 ), 6/15 (pp. 19–22), 6/16 (pp. 22 [sic]–23), and 6/17 (pp. 24–26).

## May 12–June 14, 1746

[[a primitive love feast.]][1]

**Monday, May 12.** Began our Conference with Mr. [John] Hodges, [Samuel] Taylor, etc., and continued therein four days.[2] Then my brother returned to London.

**Friday, May 16.** One of the things agreed upon was that the preachers should attend the public worship on Wednesday and Friday at all opportunities. This morning I went for a walk with Mr. Hodges to St. James [church], and waited for the loving kindness of the Lord in the midst of his temple.[3] The 80th Psalm, which was read in course, confirmed us in our judgment that this was the will of God concerning us. He did not at this time send us away without a blessing; and surely he will turn us again. He will show the light of his countenance, and we shall be whole.[4]

**Whitsunday, May 18.** We had asked in prayer last night a double portion of the Spirit and today the answer came![5] Met at 4:00, and continued singing or speaking till 6:00. Rode to Kingswood and preached the second time, through our Lord strengthening me. At the sacrament the skies, as it were, poured down righteousness.[6] Mr. Hodges assisted me at Conham by reading prayers. Then I preached a fourth time to a great quiet multitude at the [Baptist] Mills, and met and exhorted the society to walk worthy their holy calling.[7] This might properly be called the Lord's Day.

**Monday, May 19.** Rode over the Downs and preached at a meeting house four miles from Bristol,[8] to a thronged attentive audience. It had not been used for some years. But now one of our colliers preaches there constantly, and a great door seems to be opening in the country round about. It rained all day till 5:00 in the afternoon, then cleared up till the preaching hour was over. A drunkard disturbed us at first, till I ordered him to be taken away, and we then had a blessed opportunity among the penitents. Our Lord was present and made us know it, for we sunk down under an awful sense of his greatness and love.

---

[1] Written in shorthand at the top left corner of the page, these are the concluding words of the previous journal letter.

[2] The minutes of this third annual Conference of the Wesley brothers with their helpers can be found in JW, *Works*, 10:168–85.

[3] See Ps. 48:9.

[4] See Ps. 80:3, 7, 19.

[5] See 2 Kings 2:9.

[6] See Isa. 45:8.

[7] See Eph. 4:1.

[8] The Downs are just north-east of Bristol centre.

**Tuesday, May 20.** Found a great revival in my own soul in reading that strangest of all writers, Dr. H–.[9]

**Wednesday, May 21.** My soul continued all desire and prayer. The power reached whomsoever I spoke with, especially the congregation in the evening and the women's bands, who were all filled with the spirit of love and supplication.

**Thursday, May 22.** Many heard his voice while I explained these his words, "Behold I stand at the door and knock."[10] But in the society we all seemed bowed down before him, and were even constrained to open the door.

**Friday, May 23.** Passed two hours with a young clergyman, who seems determined to know nothing but Christ crucified.[11] His name is cast out already in his own parish, for endeavouring to do all the good he can among them. It seems as if our Lord was answering our long-continued prayer, and thrusting out more labourers into his harvest.[12]

Prayed by a dying man, a forgetful hearer of the word in his health, but who now has all the marks of true repentance, and waits for the Comforter in full assurance of hope.[13]

Rode to Conham by 6:00, and after reading prayers and preaching, hastened back to the watchnight at Bristol. Expounded the ten virgins.[14] But my body by 11:00 at night could hold out no longer.

**Sunday, May 25.** Received the usual blessing in the sacrament. Let the world (the Quakers and the Orthodox) *dispute* about the ordinance—our Saviour satisfies us a shorter way.

At 5:00 my subject was "Repent and be converted, that your sins may be blotted out, when the times of refreshing shall come from the presence of the Lord."[15] We felt the power of God's word as a fire and as a hammer.[16] Between 5,000 and 6,000, by computation, listened with great attention. O that they might all be doers of the word.[17] Our children, whom I exhorted afterwards, seemed resolved to take the kingdom of heaven by force.[18]

---

[9] This was likely the "mystic doctor," John Heylyn (c. 1684?–1759). Both CW and JW were familiar with Heylyn's edited volume, *Devotional Tracts Concerning the Presence of God* (London: Joseph Downing, 1724).

[10] Rev. 3:20.

[11] See 1 Cor. 2:2.

[12] See Matt. 9:38.

[13] See Heb. 6:11.

[14] Matt. 25:1–13.

[15] Acts 3:19.

[16] See Jer. 23:29.

[17] See James 1:22.

[18] See Matt. 11:12.

**Monday, May 26.** Rode to Bath, preached and met the classes.

**Tuesday [May 27] evening.** Preached at the cross in Rode[19] on "He shall save his people from their sins.[20]" Found more and more of the society under deep convictions.

**Wednesday, May 28.** Preached Christ the prophet, priest, and king from his own words, Isaiah 61: "The Spirit of the Lord God is upon me because the Lord hath annointed me to *preach* good tidings to the meek; he hath sent me to *bind up* the broken hearted, to proclaim liberty to the captives, etc." Many felt the truth and comfort of his saying. Visited the classes.

Rode by [South] Wraxall to Bearfield,[21] where I reasoned with a numerous congregation on "righteousness, temperance, and judgment to come."[22] The Judge stood at the door, and applied his own awful words, "The trumpet shall sound, and the dead shall be raised, ...."[23] It was a solemn season in the society also. Many trembled before him and lamented after him. All appeared in some degree affected, and stirred up to lay hold on the Lord.

**Thursday, May 29.** Discoursed on Matthew 7:7, "Ask and it shall be given you, ...," with great effect. Spake severally with our children and found them in a thriving condition. Of the many that are justified, not one dreams that he is sanctified at once and wants nothing. All are pressing toward the things before, and labouring after holiness of heart.[24] Received a little abusive language from the warm gentleman that half-murdered our sister, and washed my hands of him.[25]

Breakfasted at my old host's Mr. P—, the first that received me into his house six years ago.[26] God has given him yet another call. O that it may prove effectual! Returned and read the letters at Bristol.

**Friday, May 30.** In great deadness was revived by praying with one of a fearful heart.

Rode in the afternoon to [Wick[27]], and preached forgiveness of sins to several simple souls.[28] Mrs. Haynes and her family were present, and

---

[19] CW again spells "Rhodes."

[20] Matt. 1:21.

[21] Bearfield, Wiltshire, village just outside Bradford-on-Avon.

[22] Acts 24:25.

[23] 1 Cor. 15:52.

[24] See Phil. 3:14.

[25] See CW's account in his journal letter above covering Apr. 30, 1746.

[26] This was likely Richard Pearce, landlord of the Cross Keys and a pillar of the society at Bradford-on-Avon; cf. *WHS* 6 (1908): 116.

[27] A blank space is left in the journal letter; the name is supplied in CW, MS Journal.

[28] Possibly on Acts 13:38; see CW, MS Journal, Sept. 28, 1743.

carried me home to her house. The justice came soon after.[29] The large house and gardens, the five little children, the sweet behaviour of their mother, and above all the open, generous, amiable temper of Mr. Haynes, made me think I was got to Fonmon Castle and conversing again with my friend come back from paradise.[30]

**Sunday, June 1.** In the sacrament found the usual power, and blessing in prayer. It rained most part of the day. At the [Baptist] Mills I was told that the child of a papist had much displeased his father by saying, "I believe it will be fair because Mr. Wesley is to preach here." But so it was. About 5:00 the clouds dispersed, the rain ceased, and we had a blessed opportunity. My word was afterward blessed (I have reason to hope) to the society.

**Monday, June 2.** Between 5:00 and 6:00 set out with James Waller in the chaise, Mr. [John] Meriton accompanying us. Stayed an hour at Publow, where the vice of one and the enthusiasm of another has quite scattered the flock and destroyed the work of God. Mr. Meriton gave private baptism to a child of our host, whose eyes again are opened and he no longer makes the spirit swallow up the letter.

At 1:00 preached the necessity of repentance and conversion to many serious seekers at Oakhill. Then prayed with the society, and went on to Shepton Mallet. Called to a wild, confused multitude, "Ho, everyone that thirsteth, come to the waters!"[31] The word did not return void,[32] although many continued wholly unconcerned. Got by night to Coleford.

**Tuesday, June 3.** My morning's congregation were of a better spirit, and drank in every word. I then spoke with each of the society and was surprised at their growth in grace. Scarce a man among them was justified when I saw them last; and now there are near fourscore that have tasted the pardoning love of God. We had sweet fellowship together in fervent prayer.

Baptised a Baptist woman, and all her fears and doubts fled away in that moment.

Preached at 1:00 in the shell of their society room. The hearers without were near as many as those within, and were not hindered by the rain from giving diligent heed to the words which were spoken, "Lift up the hands that hang down, your God shall come and save you."[33] Seldom

---

[29] Thomas Haynes (1699–1776) had an estate in Abson, Gloucestershire, just north of Wick, and was a justice of the peace. Thomas and his wife Sarah (c. 1702–88; maiden name unknown) were married about 1733. At this point CW identifies only as "Mrs. H."; but he gives the full surname later in the MS Journal.

[30] I.e., Robert Jones (1706–42) of Fonmon Castle.

[31] Isa. 55:1.

[32] See Isa. 55:11.

[33] Isa. 35:3–4; read incorporating Heb. 12:12.

have I seen souls so hungry for the bread of life, and in due season they shall be filled.[34]

Hastened back in the hard rain to Shepton [Mallet]. Spent an hour with the principal gentleman of the town (one of my hearers on Monday evening).[35] Preached to many sincere souls from that best of prayers, if rightly used, "His blood be upon us, and upon our children!"[36] And our hearts were much enlarged and comforted. Met the classes at my host [[Stone's]], and slept in peace.[37]

**Wednesday, June 4.** Encouraged the society by the promise "Be thou faithful unto death and I will give thee the crown of life."[38] Soon after 6:00 set out for Portland. But could drag our chaise with both horses no further that day than Sherborne.[39] Called on Dr. R[obertson] at Pitcomb[e], but he was from home.[40] However our labour was not in vain, for we then saw the deliverance of God. Driving down the steep hill our horse stumbled and threw me out of the seat. I fell on my back upon the wheel, which must have bruised or maimed—perhaps killed—me if the horse had stirred a step farther. My feet were entangled in the chaise, while my head hung down over the wheel. But neither foot, nor back, nor head were any hurt, only I was pretty much stunned and dirtied.

Four hours it cost us to go five miles. It rained incessantly, and blew an hurricane all the day following, so that we were right glad to reach William Nelson's house in the island by 9:00 at night.[41]

Preached on **Friday morning, June 6,** to a houseful of staring, loving people, on the words I first met, Jeremiah 50:20, "In those days and in that time, saith the Lord, the iniquity of Israel shall be sought for and there shall be none; and the sins of Judah, and they shall not be found. For I shall pardon them whom I reserve." A few (I hoped by their tears) had need of a physician, but most of them seemed unawakened. At noon preached

---

[34] See Lev. 26:4–5.

[35] On Aug. 10, 1745 (above) CW identified this man as Mr. P— (likely Strode Poyntz).

[36] Matt. 27:25.

[37] William Stone, at whose home JW stayed when in Shepton Mallet in Feb. 1748; see JW, *Works*, 20:206.

[38] Rev. 2:10.

[39] CW spells "Sherburn."

[40] John Robertson (c. 1691–1761) was educated at Marischal College, Aberdeen and was awarded his M.D. at King's College, Aberdeen in 1730. Born at Wells, Somerset, he married a widow, Jane Webb, of Pitcombe and settled down on her beautiful estate there to the leisurely pursuits of a devout and very scholarly gentleman. In 1747 he had published under a pseudonym *The True and Antient Manner of reading Hebrew without Points,* and in that same year wrote to CW suggesting some emendations to the AV—mostly from Johann Bengel (see Robertson to CW, Sept. 23, 1747).

[41] For more on William Nelson (d. 1770), see Robert Pearce, *Methodism in Portland* (London: C. H. Kelly, 1898).

on a hill in the midst of the island,[42] on the faithful saying; and at night from "Wash ye, make ye clean, put away, ...."[43] Most of the island came to hear, and gave a dull, stupid attention to the word. But few as yet felt the burden of their sins, and the want of a Saviour.

**Sunday, June 8.** Mr. Meriton preached morning and evening. I on the hill at noon, and after evening service to all the islanders (I believe) that were able to come. I called, "Is it nothing to you, all ye that pass by?"[44] About half a score answered "It is nothing to us"—by turning their backs. But the rest hearkened and heard with greater marks of sincerity than I had before observed. I found faith at this time that our labour would not be in vain in the Lord.

**Monday morning, June 9.** Explained at Southwell (the farthest village, where there never was preaching before) the words of good old Simeon, "Lord now lettest thou thy servant depart in peace."[45] Some very old men were present and seemed, as did most of the rest, to have ease to hear. I distributed a few books among them, rode round the island, and returned by noon to the hill; preached there, and in the evening at my lodgings for the last time. Now the power and blessing came. My mouth was opened, and their hearts. The rocks were broken in pieces.[46] They were in tears on every side, especially at hearing some of the letters read. I continued exhorting them to save themselves from their untoward generation from 7:00 till 10:00.[47] We could hardly part. The little society of twenty members was much comforted and confirmed. The whole people were desirous to hear the words of this life again. I promised to send them Mr. [John] Trembath in his way to Cornwall and commended them to God and the word of his grace.[48]

**Tuesday, June 10.** By 8:00 in the evening came to Axminster, not expecting any work there, when a brother unknown found us out at our inn and pressed us much to stay and preach to them the next morning. At the same time an officer came in and courteously saluted us. I found in conversing with him that he was one of my first friends and schoolfellows at Westminster. We soon renewed our acquaintance, although it had been interrupted for near 30 years; and the sooner because I took knowledge of him that he had been with Jesus. He knew our fellow labourer Haime and

---

[42] Portland is on a peninsula that could be cutoff from the mainland at high tide.
[43] Isa. 1:16.
[44] Lam. 1:12.
[45] Luke 2:25–32.
[46] See Jer. 23:29.
[47] Acts 2:40.
[48] See Acts 20:32.

the little flock with him,[49] and was not ashamed of Christ or his servants. We took sweet counsel together, and the Lord was in the midst of us.[50]

**Wednesday, June 11.** Preached in the bowling-green to about 1,000 well-behaved people, from "Come unto me, all that travail and are ...."[51] They seemed to receive the word with all readiness of mind. I could not help saying within myself on leaving them, "Surely God was in this place and I knew it not!"[52] Got to Exeter by night.

**Thursday, June 12.** Spoke with some of the poor shattered society here, and was grieved by the havoc Satan has made of the flock.[53] That restless antinomian wolf leaves all in pieces but those who keep close to the word of their shepherds. I did not find any call or inclination to preach there, so went on in the afternoon toward Tavistock. At 4:00 in the morning set out for Crockernwell[54] and called at Sticklepath on our old friend A. B.[55] If thou art she; but oh how changed! The spirit of bigotry has scoured(?) and swallowed them up. We *did* not dispute, because I *would* not, resolving through the grace of Christ to part friends.

Mr. Meriton had left us at Exeter, and Mr. [William] Shepherd came in his place. We designed to bait[56] at a small village but overshot it, so were forced (or rather, sent) to a small farmhouse for the sake of the woman and her poor neighbour. We preached Christ to them, and utterly astonished them. Left some books to enforce our sayings and went on our way rejoicing. By 6:00 came to Tavistock, not knowing why—only my brother Meriton had desired me to call on his friend and host Mr. Kinsman.[57] Put up at an inn and sent for him from over the way. He came, received us gladly, and carried us to his house. Me he said he knew, or his heart misgave him it was I, as he saw me coming down the street. The two that had gathered the little flock there, he informed me, were Mr. Adams and Mr. [Herbert] Jenkins, men with whom I have always found the closest fellowship in heart. I would have declined meeting their society, but they

---

[49] John Haime (1710–84), of Shaftesbury, first heard CW preach in 1742, while serving as a soldier. He soon organized a religious society for his fellow soldiers. Upon his discharge from the army in 1747 he served as a travelling preacher. See Vickers, *Dictionary*, 146.

[50] See Ps. 55:14.

[51] Matt. 11:28.

[52] Cf. Gen. 28:16.

[53] See John Cennick, *An Account of a Late Riot at Exeter* (London: J. Hart, 1745).

[54] CW spells "Croakendon Well."

[55] CW had previously been favourably received in Sticklepath by Hannah Bidgood (possibly she went by "Ann") and other Quakers; see CW, MS Journal, July 13, 1744. See his similar comment on June 24, 1746, below.

[56] I.e., stop for a meal.

[57] Andrew Kinsman (1724–93), a native of Tavistock, was converted by George Whitefield and became the leading supporter of Calvinist Methodism there.

would take no denial. I therefore passed half an hour with them in prayer and perceived we had all drank into the same Spirit.

**Saturday, June 14.** Prayed again with them and gave a short word of exhortation. Went to church as usual, but did not send (according to my custom) to ask the pulpit, the minister having so lately refused it to Mr. Meriton for fear of displeasing his parish. I knew it was not displeasing to God my preaching in the field, and therefore went forth in the evening to call sinners to repentance. A large herd of wild beasts were got together, and very noisy and tumultuous they were. But the bridle was in their mouth. At first I stood under a wall, but the violence of the multitude forced me thence. I then walked to the middle of the field, and began calling, "Wash ye, make you clean, ...."[58] The waves of the sea raged so horribly that few could hear.[59] But all might see the restraining hand of God. I continued half an hour (in prayer mostly) and quietly walked through the thickest and fiercest of the king's enemies to my lodgings.

*Source*: CW record copy; MARC, Portraits and Letters of Presidents of the Wesleyan Methodist Conference, Vol. 1, ff. 11–12.[60]

---

[58] Isa. 1:16.

[59] See Jude 1:13.

[60] This volume has not yet been assigned a shelf number.

## June 15–30, 1746[1]

**Sunday, June 15.** At 5:00 joined with the society in prayer that the Lord would set before us an open door, which none might be able to shut.[2] At 8:00 went forth again to the highways and hedges.[3] Found my audience greatly increased, but they did not seem like the same people. All were quiet and attentive while I declared, "The poor have the gospel preached to them."[4] The Lord was present in his convincing power. I endeavoured to strip them of all show of good, and insisted that the natural man has absolutely nothing of his own but pure evil:[5] no will or desire to good (till it be miraculously infused), any more than the devils in hell. They looked like men overawed[6] and confounded. The followers of Jesus were immediately satisfied I was no free-willer, Arminian, etc., as I had been represented. Their hearts clave to me. The partition wall was broken down at once, and we all discovered Satan's devices to keep us asunder by those hard suspicious thoughts of each other.

Went from evening service to the field. Most of the congregation followed, besides multitudes that seldom or never came near a church. Several thousands hearkened to their own history in the prodigal son.[7] Many seemed cut to the heart, and resolved to arise and return to their Father.[8] He had compassion on us, and ran (we trust) and fell on the neck of many. The mouths of gainsayers were stopped, their opposition ceased, and their hearts seemed turned as the rivers of the sea. I took a compass and walked with some of the brethren quite through the town. We were surprised by the general civility.

But my greatest joy and matter of thanksgiving was my reception by the weak, sincere children of God who *followed not with us*.[9] They complained

---

[1] CW's journal letter for these two weeks survives in four manuscripts. This transcription follows DDCW 6/12, which is the only one in CW's hand. DDCW 6/28 is a careful copy of CW's original, mostly in the hand of James Waller (with sections likely by John Meriton), even correcting the text in one place (noted below). DDCW 6/30 introduces several variants (noted below), most of which are echoed in the copy found among Lady Huntingdon's papers (Leicestershire Record Office, 14D32/573; probably forwarded to her by James Erskine, since she and CW were not corresponding at this point). The other scribes are unidentified. CW's journal letter was the source of, and provides greater detail than, the account of these days in his MS Journal.

[2] CW was in Tavistock, Devonshire at the moment; 13 miles north of Plymouth.

[3] See Luke 14:23.

[4] Matt. 11:5.

[5] Leicestershire 14D32/573 substitutes "sin" for "evil."

[6] DDCW 6/30 and Leicestershire 14D32/573 substitute "overpowered" for "overawed."

[7] Luke 15:11–32.

[8] DDCW 6/30 and Leicestershire 14D32/573 substitute "Father's house" for "Father."

[9] In MS Journal CW identifies this as "Andrew Kinsman's society." Kinsman (1724–93),

to me of a brother who had made a division and carried away fifteen of the flock into a separate society. I went and talked with him and each of his company. They told me they were convinced (by reading my brother's books) of universal redemption, and *therefore* met by themselves to avoid dispute, and hearing such books read as they did not agree to,[10] and to confirm one another in what they thought the truth. I told them that was not a sufficient reason for separating. They were not so many but one society might hold them all. That our common enemies would triumph in our dissensions. That charity was more than[11] true opinions, and they ought to go back to their brethren and continue with them to the end. They yielded to my persuasions[12] and I carried them with me to the society, who received them with open arms and hearts. I exhorted them all to love and unity and mutual forbearance; warned them in many words against pride and idolatry; read them the deaths of some of our children, and set them on fire; beat down the party spirit, and every temper contrary to love; and in fervent prayer commended[13] them to the confirming grace of God in Christ Jesus.

**Monday, June 16.** Some of the society from Plymouth had come to hear me and much importuned me to go thither. I had no thought nor desire of ever seeing that place, having too much condemned some who have entered into our labours to follow their example.[14] But the brethren so urged that they even compelled me. I went with the utmost reluctance,[15] resolving however only to preach in the streets or fields. Took a delightful leave of our Tavistock friends. Prayed by the wife of one of the lately-separated brethren and found great union[16] of spirit with both. Rode on to sister Morgan's,[17] one of our own Bristol children, who was overjoyed to receive us, and thence to Plymouth. The first house I entered was full

---

a native of Tavistock, was converted by George Whitefield and became the leading supporter of Calvinist Methodism there and in Plymouth (where he had settled). His group was complaining to CW about a cohort of their followers who had separated after becoming convinced through JW's writings of the universal offer of salvation (not doctrinaire universalism).

[10] Only DDCW 6/28 includes "not"; but this is clearly the intended reading.

[11] DDCW 6/30 substitutes "now their" and Leicestershire 14D32/573 substitutes "now the" for "more than."

[12] DDCW 6/30 and Leicestershire 14D32/573 substitute "instructions" for "persuasions."

[13] DDCW 6/30 and Leicestershire 14D32/573 substitute "committed" for "commended."

[14] The society in Plymouth was started by and aligned with George Whitefield. CW is hesitant to "proselytize" as he believed some Calvinist Methodists had in Wesleyan circles.

[15] Leicestershire 14D32/573 substitutes "regret" for "reluctance."

[16] DDCW 6/30 and Leicestershire 14D32/573 substitute "unity" for "union."

[17] DDCW 6/12 reads "S. Morgan"; DDCW 6/30 and Leicestershire 14D32/573 misread this as an "I." or "J." This may be the Rebecca Morgan who was admitted to the society in Bristol on Apr. 18, 1739 (see JW, *Journal*, Works, 19:50).

of the society people. We prayed and sang together, and our hearts were knit[18] in the love of Christ crucified.

They desired me, with their steward, who had come for me, to preach in their society house. I rather chose the street, having sent to the minister to desire the use of his church, which he civilly refused. A confused multitude were got together, and tolerably quiet, while I showed them the necessity of repentance and conversion.[19] One blow I received on my head with a stone, for which my zealous friends, the mob, were ready to tear the poor man in pieces. Many were come to hear me in hopes of my opposing Mr. Whitefield, but were not a little disappointed at my confirming his saying, and bringing none other doctrine than salvation by grace through faith in Jesus. I gave notice of my intention to preach next evening in the same field where that faithful minister of Christ, my beloved brother George Whitefield, had first showed them the way of salvation. The people immediately took it in their heads that I was his brother in the flesh as well as in the Lord.

The stewards and many of the society pressed me to give them a word of exhortation in their Tabernacle as the society room is called. But I could not consent; nor yet to preach there in the morning. Nay, it seemed almost an intrusion my lodging at the sister's to whom their house belongs. But they had provided a bed for me there, which I was forced to accept of.

**Tuesday, June 17.** Breakfasted at Mrs. St—, whose husband, one of the stewards, is greatly taken with the *still* Brethren and is gone to London to visit "the only church upon earth." I found my heart much enlarged towards her and a few simple souls with her, and honestly told them what I thought right and what wrong in the English Moravians. The good in them (or any others) I hope always to acknowledge; the evil always to reject.

In the evening preached repentance and faith from Isaiah 1:16. A numerous congregation encompassed me, and a whole army of soldiers and sailors stood behind—shouting and blaspheming.[20] I was constrained to tell the people, "They shall not at this time hinder my delivering my message." It was according to my faith. Still the floods lifted up their voice,[21] but were forced to keep their distance. A wall of brass and pillar of fire were between us.[22] They raged and stormed and threatened, but could not come beyond their bounds or hinder the attention of any that came to hear. I then[23] gave notice that I should not depart on the morrow

---

[18] Leicestershire 14D32/573 substitutes "united" for "knit."

[19] CW's typical brief title for his sermon on Acts 2:37–39.

[20] DDCW 6/30 and Leicestershire 14D32/573 substitute "blasphemies" for "blaspheming."

[21] See Ps. 93:3.

[22] See Jer. 1:18 and Exod. 14:19–20.

[23] DDCW 6/30 and Leicestershire 14D32/573 substitute "there" for "then."

as I purposed,[24] but stay a few days with them, seeing the enemy was so alarmed. And [I] warned the opposers not to be too violent, least I should stay to live and die with them.

The society were now so exceeding urgent with me to go to their room that I could hold out no longer but went and prayed with them there, and provoked them to love and good works.[25] Our hearts were strangely opened and warmed. For my part I found no manner of difference betwixt them and our colliers, or tinners, or children at the Foundery. And they embraced *me* as a younger brother of George Whitfield. Satan's accusations were turned to good, and the doctrine of free grace was doubly welcome to them from *so strong an Arminian*!

**Wednesday, June 18.** Began at 5:00 explaining at the Tabernacle Zechariah 13:6, "What are these wounds in thine hands? ...." We looked on him we have pierced and mourned, but with a blessed not a bitter mourning. Most of the society followed me into the house and we continued singing and conferring[26] till 8:00. Went to church, and in the afternoon to the Dock,[27] where[28] I expounded Isaiah 35 to about 2,000 most simple, hungry[29] souls, who devoured every word. The power wherewith God accompanies the word is generally proportioned to the disposition of the hearers. Many hands were lifted up and knees strengthened, and the men of fearful hearts believed he will come and save <the>m.[30]

**Thursday, June 19.** Preached again at 4:00 on the sufferings <of our> Lord,[31] and again we had fellowship with him therein. In the evening at Plymouth, invited the weary burdened sinners to Christ.[32] Our adversaries had quitted <the> field. Many of the rich heard (or seemed to hear) me gladly. Our own people, I am sure by their behaviour and confession afterwards, were comforted. We spent another hour in the room, and I warned them in much love against the antinomian errors which they were blindly running into. Some few had drank the deadly thing, but I trust it shall not hurt them, Many, nay most, were on the brink of that pit. One had preached the doctrine among them—but too grossly, not having learned his lesson of dissimulation perfect. Some of his hymns they had got concerning the salvation of the devils (a doctrine of *mine* as

---

[24] Leicestershire 14D32/573 substitutes "proposed" for "purposed."

[25] See Heb. 10:24.

[26] DDCW 6/30 and Leicestershire 14D32/573 substitute "confirming" for "conferring."

[27] Plymouth Dock (now called Devonport), Devonshire; 2 miles northwest of Plymouth.

[28] DDCW 6/30 and Leicestershire 14D32/573 substitute "when" for "where."

[29] DDCW 6/30 and Leicestershire 14D32/573 substitute "hungering" for "hungry."

[30] A small portion of DDCW 6/12 is torn away but can be reconstructed with confidence.

[31] Likely his sermon on Lam. 1:12, which he would preach the next day in Plymouth.

[32] His sermon on Matt. 11:28.

these simple souls were persuaded), and his life and conversation was too agreeable to his principles. But others were labouring to bring in the *still* doctrine,[33] or antinomianism refined. The righteous God shall hew all their snares in pieces.

**Friday, June 20.** Discoursed in the morning on that *legal* saying of our Lord's (as some would call it), "If ye love me, keep my commandments."[34] They received it with gladness, and appear more and more established in the present truth.

Went a second time to my dear friends at the Dock. Passed an hour with Mr. Hyde and his family, who seem all sincere seekers. One of the daughters that had been a great persecutor desired me (as did others) to take her into the society. I knew not well what to do but said I would speak with the stewards, and if they approved of it, receive her in my brother Whitefield's name.

Drank tea at Mrs. Stephens, one who had heard Mr. Whitefield but none since him. She told me, on my inquiry,[35] the reason of her not joining the society was because she could not believe particular redemption.[36] I answered her that she might notwithstanding have the benefit of Christian fellowship, and keep her private opinion to herself. I am persuaded several would have entered into the society if I had stayed and given them a little encouragement, but I was fearful of stretching myself in another man's line.

Preached Christ crucified to about 3,000 from Lamentations 1:12, "Is it nothing to you, all ye that pass by? behold, and see if there be any sorrow like unto my sorrow, ...." The word was as a fire and melted down all it reached. For above an hour we mourned and rejoiced together in him who loved us. I have not had a time of so great refreshment since I left Bristol.

**Saturday, June 21.** Preached at 4:00 once more and took my leave of the loving society; then of my hostess, Mrs. Wheatly, Mrs. Earl, and others, whom I greatly love, not only for their Christian kindness to me but my brethren also—[Charles] Graves, [Edward] Greenfield, [and Thomas] Maxfield—whose bonds they had compassion on. The Lord recompense them in that day!

Spoke with several at Plymouth who had found comfort under the word, and encouraged them to be faithful unto death. One young woman that received forgiveness in hearing clave to me as Ruth to Naomi[37] and would have gone to any of our societies I should advise. But I advised

---

[33] DDCW 6/30 and Leicestershire 14D32/573 substitute "principals" for "doctrine."

[34] John 14:15.

[35] DDCW 6/30 and Leicestershire 14D32/573 substitute "inquiring" for "inquiry."

[36] I.e., limited atonement.

[37] See Ruth 1:16.

her to continue in her calling till she had a plainer direction. Instead of preaching, I let our departed[38] children preach this evening;[39] and being dead they yet spake to many hearts. The hearers[40] were in tears on every side and, I trust, will so follow them as they followed[41] Christ.

**Sunday, June 22.** Preached repentance and faith from Hosea, "O Israel, thou hast destroyed thyself; but in me is thy help."[42] After public prayers, thought it necessary to write to the minister as follows:[43]

Reverend Sir,

I am informed that one has been with you to ask liberty for me to sit in your pew. I knew nothing of it till she told me you had granted the favour. As such, I humbly acknowledge it, although I should never have troubled you on such an occasion. The meanest place in the church is good enough for me.

If that same person, at her first waiting upon you, spoke anything disrespectful (which by her own account I fear she did), give me leave, sir, to assure you it was utterly against both my judgment and practice. I abhor the thought of rashly censuring any man, especially a minister. Neither do we ever suffer it in any under *our* care. My general aim and design, I trust, is the same as yours, and many [of] my superiors—even the glory of God and the salvation of sinners.

Permit me, reverend sir, to subscribe myself with unfeigned respect,
The least and meanest of your brethren,

C. W.

Sent this with the *Rules* of our society[44] and a few other books by James Waller. Then went to church and because I would not slight his civility sat in his pew. One effect at least it had, the drawing several of the curious gentry after me to the field. I preached upon a hill under Stoke churchyard. It was quite covered with the surrounding multitude, upwards of 5,000 by computation. Expounded the good Samaritan,[45] with great assistance from my Master. Some reviled at first, on whom I turned

---

[38] Leicestershire 14D32/573 substitutes "departing" for "departed."

[39] I.e., he read the death stories of Methodist children.

[40] Orig., "They" changed to "The hearers"; DDCW 6/28 reads "They."

[41] DDCW 6/30 and Leicestershire 14D32/573 substitute "follow" for "followed."

[42] Cf. Hosea 13:9.

[43] As becomes clear immediately after this letter, CW was in Stoke Damerel, a western district of Plymouth, near Plymouth Dock, the site of St. Andrew's church. The vicar of St. Andrew's was Zachariah Mudge (1694–1769).

[44] *The Nature, Design, and General Rules of the United Societies* (1743); see JW, *Works*, 9:69–75.

[45] Luke 10:29–37.

and by a few severe words silenced them. The congregation behaved[46] as men seeking God. O that none of them might rest till their wounds are bound up. They followed me with their blessings and prayers. One only curse have I heard in Plymouth, from one who with great bitterness called me "Whitefield the Second!"

Till past 10:00 I continued praying and speaking with the society, and now I plainly saw the end and design of my mission hither. Never have I felt greater love to any souls than these. I could no more dispute with or speak one word to grieve or trouble them than I could cut their throat. But I strongly exhorted them to peace and love, humility, and heavenly mindedness. I gave them the history of the still Brethren and us.[47] Warned them against their errors and those many others which beginners are liable to. Strengthened my brother Whitefield's hands and charged them so to follow him as he followed Christ—for though they had many instructors, not many fathers. The Lord was with us of a truth and made us all drink into the same Spirit of love. They adored the goodness of our Shepherd in stopping them, when in such imminent danger of being scattered like their poor brethren in London; besought me to visit them again and send our preachers; promised through the grace of Christ to stand in the old paths and make his word their rule and never receive any that <wou>ld bring another doctrine.

Our own children in the gospel could not express greater love. They could have plucked out their eyes and given them [to] me. Several offered me money, but I told them I never accepted[48] it and desired them to keep it for their own preacher Mr. \_\_\_, which they promised to do. Others would have persuaded James Waller to have accepted[49] their presents, but their love was sufficient for him likewise.

Parted next morning in the words of our Lord, "Let not your hearts be troubled: .... In my Father's house are many mansions: ...."[50] He blessed our going out. We left a blessing behind us and carried[51] away, we hope, a large increase of love.

**Monday, June 23.** Dined at sister Morgan's with several of the brethren from Plymouth. Preached once more at Tavistock and took leave of the brethren there, but found I had them still in my heart to live and die with them.

---

[46] DDCW 6/28 substitutes "seemed" for "behaved."

[47] *A Short View of The Difference between the Moravian Brethren lately in England and the Rev. Mr. John and Charles Wesley* (1744); forthcoming in JW, *Works*, vol. 14.

[48] DDCW 6/28 substitutes "excepted" for "accepted."

[49] Leicestershire 14D32/573 substitutes "excepted" for "accepted."

[50] Cf. John 14:1–2.

[51] DDCW 6/30 and Leicestershire 14D32/573 substitute "came" for "carried."

**Tuesday, June 24.** Our brothers [Andrew] Kinsman and Davis left us at Launceston, whence we drove on heavily to Mr. Bennet's,[52] through ways impassable (as we should have thought) if our guide had not brought us through. I got an hour or two for the employment I should choose to spend my life in, if my Disposer were so pleased. But solitude was never made for man, though every man so pines after it.

At night Mr. Bennet returned, and John Trembath from preaching. I was much troubled that he had not called at Portland,[53] and *had* called at Sticklepath,[54] where our poor friends (that were) engaged him in vain janglings, showed him a letter wrote by Mr. [Benjamin] Ingham against my brother, railed at those things in his *Appeal*[55] which they had commended[56] to me, and quite laid aside the mask and stood confessed bigots.

**Wednesday, June 25.** Read prayers and preached Christ in Tresmeer church, which was crowded with earnest seeking souls. All appeared to feel the word of reconciliation. My spirit[57] was much refreshed among them.

**Thursday, June 26.** Cuz. Reed[58] conducted us to his house where I preached the blood of sprinkling[59] to a few listening sinners. Next morning I pointed them again to the Lamb of God, and found their hearts bowed down before him. Before noon we came to our brother Hitchens'[60] in Gwennap,[61] wet and weary enough with the continual storms that have waited upon us from our entrance[62] into Cornwall. At night encouraged the poor persecuted sheep by the promise Zechariah 13: 7–9. They were much affected both under the word and afterwards in the exhortation. The Lord smiled upon our first meeting.

---

[52] Rev. John Bennet (c. 1670–1750) was curate of churches in Laneast, Tresmeer, and North Tamerton, Cornwall. He lived in Tresmeer, which is 4 miles north of Trewint.

[53] A quarry and village about 2 miles southwest of Glastonbury, Somerset.

[54] Sticklepath, Devonshire; 4 miles east of Okehampton. DDCW 6/30 and Leicestershire 14D32/573 read "Mr. Sticklepath."

[55] JW, *Earnest Appeal to Men of Reason and Religion* (1743), *Works*, 11:44–101.

[56] DDCW 6/30 substitutes "commanded" for "commended."

[57] DDCW 6/30 and Leicestershire 14D32/573 substitute "soul" for "spirit."

[58] It is quite possible the "Cuz." is an abbreviation for "cousin," but if so it is an extended (and unidentified) relationship.

[59] See Heb. 12:24.

[60] James Hitchens was a "tinner" or blacksmith in Gwennap. His son Samuel would die in Aug. 1746; see CW's "Hymn on the Death of Samuel Hitchens," *HSP* (1749), 2:74–75. A month later James would lose his son Thomas.

[61] Gwennap, Cornwall; 3 miles southeast of Redruth.

[62] DDCW 6/30 and Leicestershire 14D32/573 substitute "entering" for "entrance."

**Saturday, June 28.** Preached in the afternoon at Ludgvan[63] to about 1,000 (tinners mostly), "Repent and be converted ...."[64] There is the promise here of a great harvest. Returned to Gwennap and strongly urged the hearers to "come boldly to the throne of grace"[65] for pardoning mercy and confirming grace.

**Sunday, June 29.** After preaching, examined the society and found them in a prosperous way. Their sufferings have been[66] for their furtherance and the gospel's. The opposers behold and wonder at their steadfastness and good conversation in Christ and, for the present, forebear to persecute. Most of them have tasted the grace of God, as their lives show. Were all who *profess* the truth like-minded, this nation would soon be re-converted to God.

Preached the gospel to the poor at Stithians.[67] The poor received it with tears of joy. The persons most[68] affected were, I believe, from Gwennap. Went to church[69] and heard a good sermon upon "Watching," supposing the hearers had been all awakened.

My evening congregation was computed upward of 8,000. My mouth was opened to preach the pardoning God from the history of the returning prodigal.[70] I felt (as it were) the people sink under the superior power of him that sent me. Their hearts seemed given me, as their behaviour showed. Not one inattentive (hardly one unaffected) person could I observe. All stood uncovered, and knelt at the prayers, and hung *narrantis ab ore*.[71] Scarcely have I seen such an audience in England. For an hour and an half I invited them to return to their Father.[72] Surely the word of God shall not return void.[73] I felt no weariness or hoarseness after speaking, but spent an hour and an half more with the society, warning them against pride and the love of the creature, and stirring them up to universal obedience.

**Monday, June 30.** Both shepherds and sheep had been scattered in the late cloudy day of persecution. But the Lord gathered them again and kept

---

[63] Ludgvan, Cornwall; 2 miles northeast of Penzance. CW spells "Luggon."

[64] Acts 3:19.

[65] Cf. Heb. 4:16.

[66] DDCW 6/30 and Leicestershire 14D32/573 substitute "here being" for "have been."

[67] Stithians, Cornwall; 3 miles northwest of Penryn.

[68] DDCW 6/28, DDCW 6/30, and Leicestershire 14D32/573 substitute "mostly" for "most."

[69] Apparently St. Stithians church in Stithians, whose vicar was Rev. Thomas Hearle.

[70] DDCW 6/28 reads "returning prodigal son"; Leicestershire 14D32/573 reads "prodigal returned."

[71] "On the speaker's lips."

[72] Leicestershire 14D32/573 substitutes "Father's house" for "Father."

[73] See Isa. 55:11.

them together by means of some of the brethren who began to *exhort* their companions, some one or more in every society. No less than four of them sprang up in Gwennap. I talked closely with each this morning, and found no reason to doubt of their having been used by God *thus far*. Advised and charged them not to stretch themselves beyond their measure by speaking *out* of the society, or fancying themselves ministers or public teachers. If they keep within their bounds, as they promise and I believe, they will be useful in the church. And I would to God all the Lord's people were such prophets as these!

In the evening preached to our dearest children at St. Ives from Isaiah 35, last [verse], "The ransomed of the Lord shall return, and come to Sion with songs."[74] He brought us some steps forward on our journey, I hope, by this very meeting and comforted us together on every side.

[July 15, 1746]

[[Dear Brother,

[[I should not suddenly trust Mr. [William] Shep[herd ]. It is a bold venture, your sending [Samuel] Larwood[75] to Yorkshire. Send me to Newcastle, Ireland, anywhere but London. I am in terribly good humour just now, but I shall never love verjuice. Hang me on a crab-tree[76] if you catch me there again while my friend Sarah [Clavel][77] holds her station at the Foundery. I have hazarded my peace and my soul too much already.

[[I want a *genesis thematica*[78] upon bigotry, not forgetting catholic love.[79] I rejoice that Molly Francis[80] is from Kingswood while a friend of ours is at

---

[74] Isa. 35:10.

[75] While the letter is in shorthand (except for "Mr. Green"), this is the first of eight instances where CW added longhand expansions, apparently to aid JW in reading awkward outlines; namely "Larwd," "verjuice," "crabtree," "Genesis," "Thematica," "Catholic," and "rebuffs."

[76] Cf. Samuel Wesley, Jun., "The Bondsmen," ll. 139–40 (*Poems*,1736, p. 251):
But dogs, the proverb says, by cruel fate
Hang'd on a crab-tree, will the verjuice hate.

[77] Sarah Clavel (bap. Aug 26, 1705), of Deptford/Greenwich, was a band leader for single women at the Foundery as early as 1742 (see Foundery Band Lists, pp. 5, 25, 39; and JW, *Journal*, Sept. 6, 1742, *Works*, 19:295). By 1744 she was also serving as the lead housekeeper for the Foundery; see *WHS* 14 (1923): 27.

[78] An initial essay.

[79] This request may have contributed to JW publishing in 1750 Sermon 38, "A Caution Against Bigotry," *Works*, 2:63–80; and Sermon 39, "Catholic Spirit," *Works*, 2:81–95.

[80] Mary ("Molly") Francis would return to Kingswood, serving as mistress of the school for girls that was lodged in the "old house." In 1751 she married John Maddern, one of JW's traveling preachers. The couple served together at Kingswood for a few years, then moved to London, where John became a respected local preacher. When John died, Molly returned to Bristol, to serve as housekeeper at the New Room 1770–82. See A. G. Ives, *Kingswood School* (London: Epworth, 1970), 40, 50.

it.]] Mr. Green[81] [[is in great danger if left alone in London. Whose hands can you leave him in? I would as leave the Germans[82] snapped him up as Sarah Clavel.

[[I find it is utterly in vain to write to you upon anything whereon we are not already agreed. Either you set aside the whole by the short answer that I am in an ill humour, or you take no notice at all of my reasons but plead conscience. You are now purging the church without fear of favour. Here is one says she is a new creature and slanders her neighbour. Will not own her fault, yet must she be screened and kept, both in the bands and in your house.[83] I have so little success in my remonstrances that I have many times resolved never to contradict your judgment as to any thing or person.

[[I like your proposals for amendment. As to rising, what should hinder, but allowing the first hour to prayer? As to renouncing tea, etc.,[84] what must I do for food in Cornwall? It is my beer some days in the week, and the only one I can get. I have some things upon my mind on this head, but meet with so many rebuffs I have no heart to tell them to you. Now I suppose you will answer you speak that is in your heart by all means—and at the first touch of blame, knock all on the head again.

[[Bring a stock of franks to Bristol.

Adieu.]][85]

*Address*: "To / Mrs Elis. Cart / at Mr Edw. Nowyers / at the Golden Anchor / Bishopsgate street / London / Single Sheet."
*Postmark*: "16 / IY."
*Endorsement*: by JW, "Jul. 15, 1746 / a[nswere]d 19."
*Sources*: MARC, DDCW 6/12 (holograph); compared to DDCW 6/28 (likely CW's record copy, in another hand), DDCW 6/30, and Leicestershire Record Office 14D32/573 (the latter two being copies in another hand to send to readers; the second to Lady Huntingdon and found in the Hastings family papers).

---

[81] Possibly the John Green who served a year as curate of Thurnscoe, Yorkshire in 1745, was present at the 1748 Conference in London, and would side with the Calvinist side of the Methodist movement; see JW, *Journal*, May 12, 1754, *Works*, 20:486.

[82] I.e., the Moravians.

[83] Sarah Clavel is listed as a band leader and member of the select society at the Foundery through Feb. 1745 (see Foundery Band Lists, pp. 70, 85, 92, 142). She is absent from the select society lists after that point (see ibid, pp. 105, 118, 132, 135), and in Nov. 1745 is listed as a member of a band for single women, but is *no longer* the leader (p. 128). So something happened in early 1745 (which CW calls "slander") that led to her change of status. It is possible that she condoned or passed on Elizabeth Story's (false) accusation of CW for sexual impropriety in early 1745; see Randy L. Maddox and Timothy Underhill, "Untwisting the Tangled Web: Charles Wesley and Elizabeth Story," *Wesley and Methodist Studies* 8 (2016): 175–83.

[84] The agreement to cease drinking tea is recorded in JW, *Journal*, July 6, 1746, *Works*, 20:125. CW's attempt to do so was not successful; see MS Journal, July 28, 1746.

[85] The shorthand letter was expanded by Frank Baker and published in *Works*, 26:207–8.

## JULY 1–13, 1746[1]

**Tuesday, July 1.**[2] In the evening we were again refreshed by that promise, Zechariah 12:10, "I will pour upon the house of David, and upon the inhabitants of Jerusalem, the spirit of grace and of supplications." We received a foretaste as it were, the drops before the shower.

**Wednesday, July 2.** Encouraged them again to cry day and night, by the example of the importunate widow.[3] My evening congregation at Crowan,[4] about 1,500, received the word as sinners waiting for redemption, "All we like sheep have gone astray; we have turned every one to his own way; and the Lord hath laid on him the iniquity of us all."[5]

**Thursday, July 3.** At our lodgings, preached Christ crucified.[6] Spake with the classes, who all seem much in earnest. Spent the day at Mr. Thomas's at Sithney[7] and showed about[8] 2,000 sinners the love and compassion of Jesus toward them from Matthew 9:36. Many that came from Helston, a town of rebels and persecutors, were struck and convinced and so far converted that they acknowledged their sin, and declared they would be no more found fighting against God.

**Friday, July 4.** My subject this morning was "I am the door; if any man enter in by me, he shall be saved."[9] Spake with the few that desire to meet in society. Sixteen they are at present, who wait for the promise. I admitted four or five more. Preached repentance and forgiveness again at noon.[10] The opposers at Helston heard and were farther convinced. God grant that all who now persecute[11] may come to preach the faith by their lives.

---

[1] CW's journal letter for these two weeks survives in three distinct manuscripts, none of which are in CW's hand. While catalogued separately, DDCW 6/28–29 are parts of a single consecutively numbered manuscript (which continues in DDCW 6/14–15) that CW likely kept for his records (much of it in the hand of James Waller, the rest likely by John Meriton). In the case of the immediately preceding journal letter, the text in DDCW 6/28 was found to reproduce most faithfully CW's copy; so DDCW 6/28–29 is the text followed in this transcription. Variants in the other two distinct manuscripts which were surely sent to readers (DDCW 6/13 and the continuation of Leicestershire Record Office 14D32/573) will be noted. These materials were the source of, and provide greater detail than, the account of these days in CW, MS Journal.

[2] CW is still in St. Ives, Cornwall.

[3] Luke 18:1–8.

[4] Crowan, Cornwall; 3 miles south of Camborne. Orig., "Crowen."

[5] Isa. 53:6.

[6] CW's usual title for his sermon on Lam. 1:12.

[7] Sithney, Cornwall; 2 miles northwest of Helston.

[8] DDCW 6/13 and Leicestershire 14D32/573 substitute "to above" for "about." Interestingly, in MS Journal CW revises down to "above 1,000."

[9] Cf. John 10:9.

[10] Almost certainly his sermon on Acts 2:37–39.

[11] DDCW 6/13 and Leicestershire 14D32/573 substitute "pursueth" for "persecute."

Rode to Wendron[12] and preached[13] to a great multitude, "Ho, every one that thirsteth, come ye to the waters."[14] A poor drunkard lift up his voice, which helped me much, and I had double strength given me to invite and compel sinners to come in. Spake to the infant society and explained the end and design of their meeting. Found great faith and love for them. They appeared like-minded. Our[15] hearts were knit together in the love that changeth not.

**Saturday, July 5.** Pointed them to the Son of man lifted up, as Moses lifted up the serpent in the wilderness.[16] Exhorted the society again. The Lord was with us. Preached repentance and remission of sins[17] (in the afternoon near Mr. Probis's[18]) to near 2,000 serious hearers. At night after preaching again in the house at Gwennap, my voice quite failed me.

**Sunday, July 6.** Rode in the heavy rain to Stithians, the proudest deadest people in all Cornwall. Rebuked them sharply. Refused to examine the society. Gave them a fortnight to know their own minds, whether they would serve God or mammon. Spake privately with their exhorter, who seems modest and humble and fearful of reaching beyond his measure. The woman who keeps the society could not be satisfied without acquainting me how rich and strong she was in grace, that she could not be afraid of pride, [that][19] she could not fall nor err, etc. I assured her a common harlot was in a far better state, but she is above all reproof or conviction. "A wild ass, used to the wilderness, that snuffeth up the wind at her pleasure; in her occasion who can turn her away."[20] God deliver us from these[21] saints of the devil's making. One of them hinders the work of God more than a hundred drunkards.

We were wet through in our return to Gwennap, yet the Lord gave us a fair hour in the evening. Upward of 3,000[22] listened to the gracious words that proceeded out of his mouth, "Come unto me all ye that labour

---

[12] Wendron, Cornwall; 2 miles north of Helston.

[13] DDCW 6/13 and Leicestershire 14D32/573 substitute "cried" for "preached."

[14] Isa. 55:1.

[15] DDCW 6/13 reads "them. They appeared our"; Leicestershire 14D32/573 reads "them, as they appeared. Our."

[16] See John 3:14.

[17] Acts 2:37–39.

[18] Richard Provis, of Brea, Cornwall; 1 mile east of Camborne. See JW, *Journal*, Sept. 13, 1746, *Works*, 20:141.

[19] Orig. in all copies, "not."

[20] Jer. 2:24.

[21] DDCW 6/13 substitutes "the" for "these."

[22] Once again, in MS Journal CW revises down to "near 2,000."

and are heavy laden and I will give you rest."[23] Above a third of them were of Redruth,[24] which seems on the point of surrendering to the Prince of peace. They are convinced of the truth more than rationally. Some of the gentry I have conversed with who are stripped of all, waiting for the gift of Christ's[25] righteousness. I do not remember to have seen a better behaved audience. The whole country feels the benefit of the word. Hundreds who follow not with us, neither are joined to our society, have broke of their sins, are outwardly reformed, and though violent persecutors once will not suffer a word to be spoken against this way.[26]

Many of those who have here fallen off in the late[27] persecution desired to be present at the society. I addressed myself mostly to the backsliders. God touched their hearts. Several followed me to my lodgings and begged to be admitted again. I received them back upon trial.

**Monday, July 7.** Found much the same congregation in the evening to whom I preached pure gospel from Isaiah 61[:1], "The Spirit of the Lord [God] is upon me ...." The Redeemer came to many who turn away from iniquity. It was a season of love, pardoning love, in Christ Jesus! The Spirit of supplication was poured upon us in the society. O that we may live in the Spirit and walk in the Spirit till the days of our pilgrimage are ended.

**Tuesday, July 8.** From Genesis 32:26, "I will not let thee go, except thou bless me," encouraged them at St. Ives to turn to God, to keep mercy and judgment, and wait upon him continually in prayer and all the commandments and ordinances.

**Thursday [July 10]** evening. Preached at Ludgvan, not without a blessing, and returned to St. Ives.

**Friday, July 11.** Paid our old friend Mr.[William] J[ohn][28] a visit and rode from thence to Gulval.[29] A few attended the word preached and were deeply affected under it. Returned and lodged with our friend at Trewidden.

**Saturday, July 12.** In the evening at Morvah enforced the obedience of faith from Matthew 11:29, "Take my yoke upon you, and learn of me; for I am meek and lowly in heart, and ye shall find rest unto your souls."

---

[23] Matt. 11:28.

[24] DDCW 6/13 and Leicestershire 14D32/573 read "of G. Redruth."

[25] DDCW 6/13 changes "Christ's" to "Christian."

[26] Manuscript DDCW 6/28 ends at this point; the transcription follows from this point DDCW 6/29.

[27] DDCW 6/29 reads "great"; in this instance we follow DDCW 6/13 and Leicestershire 14D32/573, because they agree with CW, MS Journal.

[28] William John, a J.P., owned a manor named Trewidden near Heamoor, Cornwall (1 mile northwest of Penzance). JW had visited similarly on Apr. 13, 1744 (*Journal, Works*, 20:24).

[29] Gulval, Cornwall; 1 mile northeast of Penzance.

Here also they were growing rich and fancying the work finished as soon as begun. I showed them the farther rest that remaineth for the people of God,[30] and inculcated on them this first, great lesson of humility.

**Sunday, July 13.** From 5:00 till 8:00 was speaking with the leaders and classes,[31] and found them better than I expected. Most of the poor scattered sheep from St. Just[32] attended the preaching at Morvah, and I was directed to those seasonable words of our Lord, "And will ye also go away?"[33] Spake with much severity and love to their hearts, showed them the only hindrance of God's work, and strongly besought them to cast up the stumbling block of sin out of their way. Advised them to turn again to the Lord in weeping and wailing and mourning—on Friday, especially the church fast—to humble themselves under the judgments of God, through which they (of St. Just) have lost the gospel for the present. Promised to engage all their brethren to meet them that day at the throne of grace and join in prayer that all which letteth[34] may be taken out of the way and the gospel have free course among them. Warned them against receiving any other gospel, and expostulated with them on their unfaithfulness, unprofitableness, covetousness, idolatry, pride. Told them I knew not whether my Lord has any further work for me in that part of the vineyard, but he would show me by their fruits if I was to minister to them any more. It pleased him to apply my words to the breaking of their hearts. All the outward signs of sorrow and repentance and humiliation, lest the candlestick should be totally removed. Their fears and vehement promises of amendment and eager requests of my coming to them again convinced me there is a seed among them, a remnant, a blessing which shall not be destroyed.

Went to church at Zennor.[35] As soon as it was over, preached to the same congregation and many strangers from all parts of the twofold rest of pardon and holiness.[36] Talked with their young exhorter[37] and advised him to practice the gospel before he preached it. He promised, as did two more this morning, to observe my brother's directions and never exhort out of his own society. His offer to leave off speaking entirely, I did not judge[38] it expedient immediately to accept of.

---

[30] See Heb. 4:9.

[31] Leicestershire 14D32/573 reads "leaders of classes."

[32] St. Just, Cornwall; 3 miles southwest of Morvah.

[33] Cf. John 6:67.

[34] I.e., "hindereth."

[35] St. Senara's is the parish church in Zennor.

[36] CW's typical name for his sermon on Matt. 11:28–30.

[37] This was John Maddern, who would become a Methodist itinerant the next year (and marry Molly Francis in 1751).

[38] DDCW 6/13 and Leicestershire 14D32/573 omit "not."

Rode to St. Ives, having lost both strength and voice. Yielded to their importunity and rose from the bed to preach. The room was crowded with hearers. I had preached once or twice before. Since it was covered it holds, I think, upward of 500, and was full within and without. I discoursed with much pain and straining on that great day,[39] whether with any success God knows only. The people behaved with uncommon decency. No one, either of the great vulgar[40] or the small, offered to make the least disturbance and indeed the whole place is outwardly changed. None have I seen or heard lift up his hand or voice against us since I came. I walk the street with astonishment, hardly believing myself in St. Ives. It is the same throughout all Cornwall. All opposition falls before us, rather is fallen, and not yet suffered to lift up its head again. This also hath the Lord wrought. O that we may walk in the fear of God while we have this short rest and in the comforts of the Holy Ghost and be edified.

Exhorted the society to do their first works.[41] Blamed some for their slackness, pride, love of the creature, and covetousness; and stirred them up to repentance and zeal, and every good word and work. Minded them of observing the following Friday as a day of solemn prayer and humiliation unto the Lord, that he may remove every stumbling block out of the way from our hearts and make us all patterns to them that believe.

Put one disorderly person (the first of the kind) out of the society. O that the Son of man would thoroughly purge his floor,[42] take away all things that offend,[43] and make us a glorious church without spot or wrinkle.[44]

*Endorsement*: by CW, "Journal / at Plymouth, &c. / June, July" (on DDCW 6/13).

*Sources*: MARC DDCW 6/28 and DDCW 6/29 (CW's record copy, by amanuensis, covering July 1–6 and 6–13 respectively); compared to two copies by amanuenses for others that were apparently hand delivered: MARC, DDCW 6/13 (July 1–13) and Leicestershire Record Office 14D32/573 (the portion covering July 1–13).

---

[39] I.e., the day of judgment.

[40] DDCW 6/13 and Leicestershire 14D32/573 reduce "either of the great vulgar" to "either vulgar."

[41] See Rev. 2:5.

[42] See Matt. 3:12, Luke 3:17.

[43] See Matt. 13:41.

[44] See Eph. 5:27.

## July 14–27, 1746[1]

**Monday, July 14.** Last night I had recommended the rebuilding of the [preaching] house to their charitable consideration, and this morning many came to set down their names and contributions. The people offered willingly, to their power and above their power. O that they might be fruitful as in this, so in every good work. But still there is a bar, an hindrance, a cursed thing which I cannot get at. They are not the same people they were when first I ministered to them. My God humbles me among them. I know not why, but trust he will discover it.

Breakfasted the second time at a brother's who had lost his love and faith together, through causeless anger at his wife. Satan had got such advantage over both that they had not spoke to each other for three weeks, till I came. It pleased the Author of Peace to reconcile them before we parted, and make them of one heart again. Immediately the Comforter returned as a Spirit of love, and I believe they are more in earnest than ever.

Just before I set out on the eastern round John Trembath came and refreshed my spirit with his account of the brethren in Tavistock and Plymouth. He was received with great love and much blessed among them. Their earnest request both by him and near twenty letters for my return, I know not how to deny. But the Lord will show me plainer if I am to see them again.

Picked up in my way a stray sheep who had followed at the beginning but was frightened by persecution and turned back. Preached at Penponds[2] to about 2,000 people, "They that be whole have no need of a physician, but they that are sick."[3] The power of the Lord was present both to wound and to heal.

**Tuesday, July 15.** Rode from Mr. Harris's[4] to Gwennap. Continued all day in great deadness and aversion to the work. But in going forth to the congregation I felt a sudden faith springing up in my heart and made proof of my ministry on about 2,000, *really* not *verbally poor* sinners, "Comfort ye, comfort ye my people, saith your God. Speak comfortably to Jerusalem,

---

[1] The only surviving copy of CW's journal letter for these two weeks is a continuation of the long consecutively numbered manuscript (that began with DDCW 6/11, continued in DDCW 6/28–29, and carries on here in DDCW 6/14–15), that CW likely had made for his records. The manuscript is mostly in the hand of James Waller (and some sections likely by John Meriton, with CW making a few corrections (mainly adding words overlooked in the copying). This material was the source of, and provides much greater detail than, the account of these days in CW, MS Journal.

[2] Penponds, Cornwall; about 1 mile west of Camborne.

[3] Mark 2:17.

[4] Harris lived in Rosewarne, Cornwall; about 3 miles southwest of Penponds; see *Wesleyan Methodist Magazine* 126 (1903): 504.

and cry unto her, … that her iniquity is pardoned."[5] I *did cry*, and their hearts answered. An extraordinary blessing, I believe, was upon all.

**Wednesday, July 16.** Breakfasted at Mrs. B— in Redruth, who seems resolved with her whole house to serve the Lord. The town is greatly alarmed and troubled that the plague (as they call it) is come almost as far as the market-house. At Crowan enlarged on the promise to them that fear the Lord, namely that on them the Sun of righteousness shall arise.[6] I set the terrors of the Lord in array against the careless and secure, and then in strong words exhorted the society to walk worthy of their calling.[7]

**Thursday, July 17.** Made a strict inquiry into the behaviour of each member of the society. Put out two or three of a doubtful character. Left them, I trust, much stirred up and confirmed in Moses' and Mary's choice.

Preached in the evening at Stithians on "They that be first shall be last,"[8] and severely reproved the proud, careless people who call themselves the society. I spake to each and asked not whether they were justified, but whether they were awakened. They *promised* better fruit. And I felt hope for them after I had purged out the most careless and the "new creature," as she calls herself. I look for no blessing on my labours if I suffer such real enthusiasm among us, that horrible pride, that abomination of desolation standing where it ought not![9]

**Friday, July 18.** Found a great blessing with a few in prayer at Wendron—a few present in body but surely all our brethren were present with us in spirit. Got some hours by myself, and yet I was not alone. Lord, if it be thou that sayst, "Be not afraid," bid me come unto thee on the water.[10]

The rain ceased only while I was calling, "O Israel, thou hast destroyed thyself; but in me is thy help."[11] The numerous congregation drank in every word, and the Lord opened my mouth and heart toward them. A poor drunkard exclaimed for a few minutes and turned his back. I did not wonder when I heard he was an alehouse-keeper. Men of his craft are always our sworn enemies. The people in general were, I believe, awakened and resolved to work out their salvation.[12]

**Saturday, July 19.** I had a visit from Captain Trounce, the man who hindered my brother's preaching here and threw him over the wall.[13] He

---

[5] Isa. 40:1–2.

[6] I.e., he preached on Mal. 4:2.

[7] See Eph. 4:1.

[8] Matt. 19:30.

[9] See Matt. 24:15 and parallels.

[10] See Matt. 14:27.

[11] Hosea 13:9.

[12] See Phil. 2:12.

[13] JW, *Journal*, July 7, 1745 (*Works*, 20:78–79), provides an account of this incident in Tolcarn, but does not highlight Captain Trounce as the main instigator.

complained of one of the society who had forced him to pay a debt twice over. I examined and found it so, laboured to persuade the man to do justice, and on his refusal put him out of the society. Our old adversary that was behaved with great civility and affection, appeared hugely obliged, and promised to vindicate us wherever he came. Twice he has been to hear me—the first night *unseen*, but last night he showed himself boldly in the face of people. I found great faith and love for him. Sent him a letter of thanks with some of our books, for which he expressed great satisfaction.

At one preached "Jesus Christ the same yesterday, today, and forever."[14] The people of Ludgvan seem to be more and more convinced, and promise a rising church.

Rode to Sithney, where the word begins to take affect. The rebels of Helston threaten hard, and Satan rages at the shaking of his kingdom. All manner of [evil] they uttered concerning us. Papists we all are, that is certain, and are for bringing in the Pretender.[15] Nay, the vulgar do believe I *have brought* him with me, and James Waller is the man! But a law is to come tonight from London (they are told) to put us all down and set £100 upon my head, etc. We had, notwithstanding, a numerous congregation, and many of the fiercest persecutors. I declared my commission, "To open their eyes, and to turn their darkness to light, and from the power of Satan unto God, …."[16] Their hearts *were* turned by the word of his power. I spake largely and familiarly with them and *saw* them all convinced—*rationally* convinced, I mean, they all appeared. And many were pricked in their hearts and ready to ask "what must we do to be saved?"[17]

[Sunday, July 20.] Our Lord was in the midst of the little society, whom I met again in the morning and then expounded blind Bartimaeus.[18] The seals fell fast from their eyes. Their open opposition is all over, they are caught in the gospel net. Near 100 of the most violent rioters were present, who a few months since had cruelly abused and beat the sincere hearers, not sparing women or children. Much blood was shed through the zeal of the pious minister,[19] who hired the mob for their purpose. But now these very men come (expecting a disturbance) to *fight for me* and vowed they would lose their lives in my defence. There was no occasion, indeed, of their service; all was quiet, as it generally is when the devil threatens most.

Rode cross the country to Redruth. Walked through the town a mile to church. Was surprised at the general civility. Some time since it was as

---

[14] Cf. Heb. 13:8.

[15] James Stuart (1688–1766).

[16] Acts 26:18.

[17] Cf. Acts 16:30.

[18] Mark 10:46–52.

[19] Rev. William Newton was vicar of Sithney.

much as his life was worth for a Christian to appear in this place, at least a Christian preacher. But the leopards are laid down with the kids.[20] In the church, while the eyes of all were upon me, I cast mine on Jeremiah 1:8, "Be not ashamed of their faces, for I am with thee to deliver thee, saith the Lord."

I returned to Gwennap the same way, and drew the congregation after me. Near 10,000 by computation were waiting for the word of life. Upwards of 9,000, I believe, there might be. Thomas Meyrick gave out the hymn. But in the midst [of singing], the table fell in and let us sink softly to the ground. Neither were hurt, nor I at all surprised, having three minutes before the idea of myself falling exactly in that manner. This I the more observed, because I had just the *same notice* of a like accident on Thursday at Crowan. While I was speaking to about twenty of the society in the chamber, I had the preapprehension (but without fear or any visible reason) of the floors sinking, and within a few minutes the main beam broke, and we expected all to fall to the ground. It was as if something had happened which I had just before heard of. I went on singing at Gwennap without any interruption. Then expounded the Good Samaritan,[21] and God set to his seal. For about an hour I was enabled to call sin-sick souls to Christ. Surely he had a multitude of patients there. Permitted several strangers from Redruth, etc., to be present at the society, where we rejoiced like men that divide the spoil.

**Monday, July 21.** Returned to St. Ives and immediately found *their* burden. John Trembath informed me that almost the whole society are slaves to snuff or tobacco. Those that stood like a rock in time of persecution are well-nigh subverted now by so base a lust. Their pipes they could not so conveniently use. But as to their snuff, they take it continually in the midst of singing, preaching, and praying. Yet such is the deceitfulness of the heart, they could see no harm in it. They would not acknowledge it to be an idol, but said, "Why, if God convince us it is contrary to his will, we will leave it off." I was too much weighed down this evening to speak. But on Tuesday night **[July 22]** I declared and disburdened my whole mind. I laid down the Christian's rule, "Whether ye eat, or drink, or whatsoever ye do, do all to the glory of God."[22] Then asked, "Do ye take snuff or smoke to the glory of God? If not, it is contrary to the written word and therefore sin." Again, "Do you take snuff to please God or yourselves? If to please yourselves, it is contrary to Christ's example, for Christ pleased not himself; contrary to his command, 'if any man will come after me, let

---

[20] See Isa. 11:6.

[21] Luke 10:29–37.

[22] 1 Cor. 10:31.

him *deny* himself.'[23] To do anything merely to please yourself is to deny Christ." Again, "Can ye do this in faith? If not, whatsoever is not of faith is sin. Can you offer it up to God as a spiritual sacrifice acceptable through Jesus Christ? If not, it is a sacrifice to the devil and the flesh." With many other words I urged and reproved them and showed them what was in their hearts. I reminded them of their first zeal and love, and the Lord gave weight to my sayings. Their hearts were broken and made obedient to the yoke of Christ. They judged themselves for their self-indulgence, slackness, neglect of prayer and a long train of evils which this cursed idolatry had drawn after it. I gave notice of my design to talk with each of the bands again, and put all out of that society who could not say either, "I take snuff to the glory of God, to please God by preserving my health," or "I promise through his grace to take it no longer." Several of them threw away their boxes before they left the room. One, I found in examining them, used it out of real necessity; and one chose rather to part with Christ than her idol. All the rest appeared willing and determined to forsake all for his sake.

Before I came to Cornwall and since, I have heard on all hands miserable recounts of the St. Just people. That being scattered by the persecution and left as sheep without a shepherd, they had wandered into by-paths of strange and erroneous doctrine. That now they said they were in rest, sanctified wholly as soon as justified, could never fall nor err, and needed no more grace or teaching. That their preacher, John Bennetts,[24] a tinner of themselves, had led them into and confirmed them in these and many other errors, being full of pride and covetousness. Yet to this man they all gave heed, and declared if their old teachers and fathers in the gospel disallowed him, they would hear and follow him notwithstanding. The brethren at Gwennap and St. Ives durst not go near St. Just for fear of infection, so that they were cut off, as it were, from us and quite fallen away and come to nothing.

I looked upon them as such, yet appointed John Trembath in his western round, to make full inquiry and bring me his report, that I might know if there was any hope of my doing them any good. The answer of prayer on our fast day, and his account, encouraged me to go at least and try. On Tuesday therefore I sent Mr. [William] Shepherd before to appoint the society (what remained of it) to meet me at John Bennetts' on Wednesday, 1 o'clock, that we might humble ourselves before the Lord, if haply he might renew us to repentance.

On **[July 23]** Wednesday noon I came to John Bennetts' at Trewellard, a village belonging to St. Just, about a mile and a quarter from the church

---

[23] Luke 9:23.

[24] On hearing of his death in 1765, JW described John Bennetts of Trewellard as "a wise and a good man, who had been about twenty years a father" to the society at St. Just; see *Journal*, Sept. 12, 1765, *Works*, 22:20–21.

town. Found about a dozen of the shattered society, who quickly increased to 50 or 60, and perceived as soon as we knelt down there was a blessing in this cloister. The Spirit of supplications was with us, and we wrestled with God in his *own* strength from 1:00 till 9:00, with only the hour for preaching between. No such prayer have I felt since I came into Cornwall. It constrained me to acknowledge that God was with them of a truth. My hope revived, my faith returned for them, and I asked, nothing doubting, that the door might again be opened among them. And that their fiercest opposer might be taken out of the way, as God knew best. But if it were his will, that he might be disarmed and converted at once! This man was once a gentleman of fortune, but *is* a poor drunken spendthrift, brother to Dr. Borlase,[25] and retained by that lover and dispenser of justice to supply the defective laws—being kept drunk almost continually for the service. This champion out of the camp of the Philistines they send forth on all occasions to defy the armies of the living God. This was the man that pressed my brother for a soldier, dragged away Edward Greenfield[26] from his business and family when past age, to be a soldier, sailor; assaulted Mr. Meriton[27] on the king's high road, and tried to serve him in the same way; seized on Mr. [Charles Caspar] Graves, the third clergyman, in bed and hurried him on board a man-of-war, who after some days through fear put him on shore half dead and destitute of all things. In a word, he seems raised up by the devil (to say nothing of the doctor) to stop and destroy the work of God, and swears continually that there shall never be any more preaching about St. Just.

For a year and a half, Satan has seemed to triumph in his success. So much good will one sinner hinder, if armed with the sins of God's people! In praying for this poor soul, I thought the heaven and earth would meet. The Spirit made intercession and bowed all down before him. We believed the door *should* be opened for preaching the gospel at this time, and it was unto us according to our faith. Between 6:00 and 7:00 I took the field, or rather the street, and cried to about 1,500 hearers, "If God be for us, who can be against us? He that spared not his own Son, but delivered him up for us all,

---

[25] Rev. Dr. Walter Borlase (1694–1776), vicar of Madron and Kenwyn, was a major persecutor of Methodists in Cornwall, particularly around St. Just; cf. JW, *Journal*, June 19 – July 2, 1745 (*Works*, 20:69–74). The "brother" was actually a brother-in-law, Stephen Ustick (1700–54) of Botallack, who married Catherine Borlase in 1724 and was a constable for the area.

[26] Orig., "Greenfell"; cf. JW, *Journal*, June 25, 1745, *Works*, 20:72–73.

[27] Rev. John Meriton (1698–1753) was educated at Gonville and Caius College, Cambridge, and ordained deacon in 1723 to serve as curate to his stepfather, the rector of Oxborough, Norfolk. In 1740 he served as a hired clergyman in the Isle of Man, arousing some opposition because of his evangelical preaching. He was befriended by JW and Whitefield. By 1744 Meriton was closely associated with the Wesley brothers, and attended their first Conference that year. For a few years he accompanied one or other of them on their preaching itineraries.

how shall he not with him freely give us all things?"[28] We experienced the truth in this hour. The Lord surrounded us as a wall of brass.[29] None opened his mouth or appeared on Satan's side. The little flock were comforted and refreshed abundantly, and rejoiced in so speedy an answer to their prayers.

An hour or two I spent afterwards in speaking with each of the society, and was amazed to find them just the reverse of what they had been represented. Most of them were clearly justified and had kept their first love, even while men rode over their heads and they were passing through water and fire. All acknowledged the necessity of a farther work and groaned for full redemption. Their exhorter I had much conversation with, and was pleasingly disappointed in him also. He appears a solid, humble Christian, raised up to stand in the gap and keep our trembling sheep together in the cloudy, dark day. God put a word in his mouth, which with the utmost natural reluctance he delivered to them from time to time, and many seals were given him. He seemed, as far as I can discover, free from all error and self-seeking, a father of the people, a repairer of the breach, a restorer of paths to dwell in.

I was ready for rest before 10:00. But no rest could I find all night, for the multitude of my bedfellows. At 4:00 [July 24] spoke with more of the society, and adored the miracle of grace that has so kept these few sheep in the midst of ravening wolves. Well may the despisers stand and wonder! Behold a bush in the fire, burning yet not consumed![30] What have they not done to crush this rising sect? But lo, they prevail nothing. *Non hydra secto corpore firmior vinci dolentem crevit in Herculem!*[31] For one preacher whom they cut off, twenty spring up. Neither threatenings nor persuasions, flattery nor violence, dungeons nor persecutions of various kinds can conquer them. Many waters cannot quench this little spark, which the Lord hath kindled, neither can the floods of persecution drown it. *Merses profundo; pulchrior evenit!*[32]

Our enemies are utterly confounded. They cannot find instruments for their purpose. Their former tools desert them so fast and say, "If they will persecute, let them do it themselves. As for us, we will fight against God no longer." I much doubt whether in a little time the reverend and worshipful [Walter Borlase[33]] will be able to raise a mob, although like the worthy justice and minister at Grimsby, he heads it himself.

---

[28] Rom. 8:31–32.

[29] See Jer. 1:18.

[30] See Exod. 3:2.

[31] Horace, *Odes*, IV.iv.61–62. "No, the hydra, as its body was hewn, grew mightier against Hercules."

[32] Horace, *Odes*, IV.iv.65. "Plunge it into the depths; it emerges all the fairer."

[33] A blank is left in the journal letter, but the reference is fairly obvious.

Rode with a merry heart to Ludgvan and was enabled to call many sin-sick sinners to the Physician of Souls.[34] Made what haste we could to Zennor to meet their society. O how unlike them of St. Just!

**Friday, July 25.** Examined their classes—dead, senseless, trifling most of them; full of leaves but no fruit. Such they have been from the beginning to this day. I told them plainly they would soon be stirred up and be in earnest or fall away and come to nothing. The subject of my discourse was our Lord's warning to the Church of Laodicea.[35] O that they may yet have ears to hear. Silenced another of their exhorters and returned to St. Just. By 1:00 the flock were got together. For two hours we poured out our souls in prayer for a nation loaded with iniquity. After a short rest I went down to them again, it being their design to spend the whole (holy) day in their employment. I was led undesignedly to pray for one poor drunken persecutor, and the Spirit came pouring down like a flood. We were filled with the divine presence.

I had left my hymn-book in the chamber, told them I would stop up for it, and be with them immediately. One came after me with news that Mr. Ustick[36] was just coming to take me up. I opened the book on Acts 27:22ff., "And now I exhort you to be of good cheer, for there shall be no loss ...." Next I was directed to Joshua 22:6, "So Joshua blessed them and sent them away, and they went unto their tents." I made up my letters and went to the congregation with a quiet heart, but my friend Ustick was gone. He did not beat either man, woman or child as was his constant custom, but asked if Mr. Wesley was there, for he had a warrant to apprehend him. Went out at the other door and told those he met that he had been searching all the house for Wesley but could not find him. We supposed he had not yet got sufficient courage (that is, drink) for his purpose, and expected his return. I thought it best to make the devil a liar and began preaching an hour before the time appointed, on the scripture just now given me. O what a flame was kindled in a moment by the bare reading of the words! I had only to speak and leave God to apply. He filled us up to the brim with faith and power and joy. The Spirit of the Lord lifted up a standard. Such an half hour I have hardly ever known. He caused us to triumph indeed, and tread upon all the power of the enemy. In full confidence of faith I promised them this very thing should work together for good and the furtherance of the gospel. Some steps I am sure we are hereby brought on our journey already.

After an interval of half an hour, I received strength to preach again in the courtyard to about 2,000 earnest souls. My subject was "Saul, Saul, why

---

[34] Likely his sermon on The Good Samaritan, Luke 10:29–37 (see above, July 20).

[35] Rev. 3:14–16.

[36] I.e., Stephen Ustick (1700–54) of Botallack; CW spells "Eustick" both times in this paragraph.

persecutest thou me?"[37] The word was a two-edged sword and did great execution. Glory to whom glory is due! I observed at dismissing them what a sore disappointment the adversary had today, who by his attempt to hinder their hearing one sermon had occasioned their hearing two. Concluded by singing the following hymn with the voice of joy and thanksgiving:[38]

1. Glory, and thanks, and praise
   To him that hath the key!
  Jesus, thy sovereign grace
   Gives us the victory,
  Baffles the world, and Satan's power,
  And open throws the gospel-door.

2. Sin, only sin could close
   That door of pard'ning love;
  But spite of all our foes
   Thou dost the bar remove,
  The door again thou openest wide
  And showest thyself the crucified.

3. Thy miracles of grace
   We now repeated see,
  The dumb sets forth thy praise,
   The deaf attends to thee
  Leaps as a bounding hart the lame,
  And shows the power of Jesu's name.

4. The lepers are made clean,
   The blind their sight receive,
  Quicken'd the dead in sin,
   The humble poor believe
  The gospel of their sins forgiven,
  With God himself sent down from heaven.

5. Thankful again we hear
   The all-restoring sound,
  Again the Comforter

---

[37] Acts 9:4.

[38] This is the first record of this hymn, which CW would later publish (with a few revisions) in *HSP* (1749), 1:323–24.

> Within our coasts is found,
> The Saviour at the door is seen,
> Lift up your hearts, and take him in.

6. Lord, we the call obey,
   In thee alone confide,
   Rejoice to see thy day
   To feel thy blood applied,
   Our faith hath made us whole, we know,
   And in thy peace to heaven we go.

At my first coming hither I left James Waller behind, expecting warm service. But he begged so hard to go with me now that I could not refuse him. At midnight we were alarmed with the noise of horses and loud voices, and expected no other than Mr. Ustick and his Myrmidons.[39] Rose and after a short prayer that if they did come, God would smite the Syrians with blindness. Betook ourselves to rest again—such rest, I mean, as a strange Cornish bed could afford.

**Saturday, July 26.** Gladly rose to meet the congregation, whom I encouraged "to run with patience the race set before them. Looking unto Jesus ...."[40] We had a glorious opportunity, such as the last triumphant evening with the society. I doubt not but many of these souls, if occasion required, would be strengthened to resist unto blood.

Rode to Trewidden to see sick Mrs. Barnes, probably for the last time on this side eternity. In the evening met many of our St. Just children again at Morvah, and strongly exhorted them to persevere in our Lord's words, "He that endureth to the end, the same shall be saved."[41]

**Sunday, July 27.** Met the society and then discoursed from Isaiah 35[:1], "The wilderness and the solitary place was glad and rejoiced even with joy and singing." I had thought of crossing the country to Gwennap, but a letter from Plymouth received this morning stopped me and a sudden thought came into my heart that I should go show myself at St. Just church.[42] Several lies beginning already to sprout up, such as Ustick's having put me to flight, which my appearance would immediately confute. Accordingly I told the people my design, and set out with my trusty friend, John Bennetts. He confirmed me in my hope that God put the thought into my heart by telling me he had that very

---

[39] See Homer, *Iliad*, ii.684; a warlike people inhabiting ancient Thessaly, whom Achilles led to the siege of Troy.

[40] Heb. 12:1–2.

[41] Matt. 10:22.

[42] Rev. William Borlase (1695–1772), brother of Walter, was vicar of the church at St. Just.

morning, *as it were, seen himself going before me into his own pew*. But that he could not then see how that could happen. We went gladly together into the house of the Lord. The first words I met in my book were, "O let not the simple go away ashamed, but let the poor and needy give praise unto thy name. Arise, O God, maintain thine own cause; remember how the foolish man blasphemeth thee daily. Forget not the voice of thine enemies: the presumption of them that hate thee increaseth ever more and more."[43] The psalms and scriptures for the day were most apposite and animating.

I went from the church to the large round stone near brother Chenhall's door,[44] our old pulpit. The whole congregation followed. I preached from Matthew 22:1[ff]. All was quiet till I came to those words, "And the remnant took his servants, and entreated them spitefully, and slew them."[45] Then one began throwing dirt, etc., and setting on his faithful allies, the dogs. Another screamed out like one just come from the tombs, but her sweet voice was so loud and ill managed that it quickly broke. This woman, it seems, was a Papist and mother to the rioter. He continued casting stones and cursing like Shimei,[46] but half a dozen tall tinners rearing themselves up around me so entrenched and covered me that only my face appeared for his mark. Not being able to get one soul to second him, he made a shameful retreat with his dogs and mother, and not a dog after him wagged his tongue against us. For near two hours I invited and exhorted them to save themselves from this untoward generation.[47] Showed them the evil of their doings, particularly their persecuting Christ in his members. Besought them to lay down their arms and be reconciled to God. Spake much of the laws of the land which they had violated in abusing us and showed them the consequence. Here my discourse was as mixed as the multitude: law, gospel, threatenings, promises, which I trust the Spirit applied to their several cases. They seemed all subdued at last, and I verily believe will be no more found fighting against God.

*Source*: CW record copy, by amanuensis; MARC, DDCW 6/1

---

[43] Ps. 74:22–24 (BCP).

[44] William Chenhall, an inn-keeper in St. Just, had been converted by JW's preaching; cf. *WHS* 8 (1912): 190.

[45] Matt. 22:1–6.

[46] See 2 Sam. 16:5–6.

[47] See Acts 2:40.

## July 27–August 10, 1746[1]

[**Sunday, July 27, continued.**] Rode to St. Ives and expounded the woman bowed together with a spirit of infirmity.[2] The word was not bound, though it has been hitherto, and their souls I trust begin to be loosed. In the society I found the bar removed (as to many or, I would hope, most of them) and the Lord returned in his power and love. We rejoiced in the consolation of Israel; and the language of our heart was, "What have I to do any more with idols?"[3]

**Monday, July 28.** Begun my week's experiment of leaving off tea, but my flesh protested bitterly against it. I was but half awake or half alive all day, and my headache so increased toward the evening that I could not preach nor speak nor think, but was forced to go to bed in my own defence. I continued the same for the two following days; only my milk-diet threw me into a violent purging, which so weakened me that I could hardly sit my horse. However, [**July 29**] I made a shift to ride to Gwennap and received (supernatural) strength to point near 2,000 sin-sick souls to their physician. After exhorting the society likewise, I was led to brother [James] Hitchens's, weary and faint enough. I would have eat but could get nothing.

**Wednesday, July 30.** Made almost a day's journey of it to St. Ives and found the place full of rejoicings. The preposterous occasion was a poor prodigal's returning again to his husks—one who *did* belong to the society a 12-month ago but forsook us and his own mercies. His wife was married to him yesterday and brought to bed today.[4] That one who formerly belonged to us should relapse into sin was such a comfort to the good people of St. Ives that they could not tell how to express their joy. The bells they set a ringing all day. They shouted, and cursed, and blasphemed like their friends *beneath*, threw dirts and stones at such of our people as they could find, and rejoiced over the poor unhappy sinners as he who set them at work will one day rejoice over them, except they repent. The happiest man of them all was Mr. [William] Hoblyn the curate. He gave a loose to joy and reviling. His beastly expressions will not bear repeating, being unbefitting the mouth of a man, much more of a Christian man and

---

[1] Two manuscripts of CW's journal letter for these two weeks survive. The first (DDCW 6/16) is in his own hand, with pages numbered as a continuation of DDCW 6/14–15. The second manuscript (MA 1977/503, Box 5, file 11) is in the hand of Charles Perronet, who was copying CW's original (and accidentally omitted a full line). We present the text of CW's original and note significant variants in Perronet's copy. This material was the source of, and provides much greater detail than, the account of these days in CW, MS Journal.

[2] Luke 13:11–17.

[3] Hosea 14:8.

[4] I.e., they were married just before she gave birth to a child.

a minister.—I did not know till now that[5] an holiday in hell is always an holiday in St. Ives.

**Thursday, July 31.**[6] Took the occasion of strongly warning[7] the society against known sin and showed them what welcome they must expect if they went back to the world. I trust they are much stirred up to watching and prayer, through the over-hasty triumph of Satan and Mr. Hoblyn.

**Friday, August 1.** Left out of the society three or four of a doubtful character, not daring to trust them with the honour of God and his people. At the hour of intercession our hearts were somewhat moved, and we desired to turn to God in weeping and fasting and mourning. As many as can promised henceforward to meet the true members of the Church of England at the throne on this day.

Pointed them at Gulval to the Lamb of God who taketh away the sins of the world.[8] They shed many delightful tears of love, or desire. My spirit was much relieved after its sore exercise at St. Ives, whither I got back by 10:00 at night.

**Saturday, August 2.** Preached for the last time (as I thought) but still without life or power. Took my cold leave of these languid souls and rode to Ludgvan. Thence, after preaching with effect, to Sithney. Here one spake with me who had been set at liberty from the guilt of sin the first time he heard me— I think as soon as I named my text. I preached Christ crucified[9] in the evening and next morning [**Sunday, August 3**] to many who seem truly desirous to know him.

Met and laboured to confirm the souls of the disciples, and hastened to Gwennap. From evening service at Redruth, rode back to my own church, the valley by our society-house, and found at least 10,000 sinners waiting for the glad tidings of salvation. I bade them to the great supper and in my Master's words even compelled them to come in.[10] It was a glorious opportunity. Not unto me but unto thy name be the praise![11]

**Monday, August 4.** Dined at brother Harris's;[12] preached at Penponds from, "O Israel, thou hast destroyed thyself; but in me is thy help."[13] A great multitude listened to the word. Many, I trust, were both condemned

---

[5] MARC, MA 1977/503 shortens "know till now that" to "know that."

[6] MARC, MA 1977/503: "July 21"; a mistake.

[7] MARC, MA 1977/503: omits "strongly."

[8] John 1:29.

[9] CW's usual title for his sermon on Lam. 1:12.

[10] Luke 14:15–24.

[11] See Ps. 115:1.

[12] Mr. Harris, of Rosewarne, see July 15 above.

[13] Cf. Hosea 13:9. MARC, MA 1977/503 reverses to "in thee is my."

and made willing to receive their Saviour. Passed the night at Mr. T's, who seems once more resolved to set his hand to the plough and never more look back.

**Tuesday, August 5.** Spake plain and strong words to my friendly host and a young lawyer, his nephew, who received my saying beyond expectation. They followed us to Mr. Harris's and appeared quite hearty and affectionate. Rode to Gwennap and rejoiced over those blessed mourners who even devoured the word, "Blessed are the poor in spirit ...."[14] I heard afterwards that several of them received forgiveness in that hour. In the society found more life than ever. The power of the Highest overshadowed us and filled our hearts with joy and love.

**Wednesday, August 6.** I had designed as on this day to set out for Bristol, but many providences concurred to show me it was the will of my Lord that I should stay a few days longer. Accordingly, I returned to St. Ives, but with an heavy heart. Enforced with a little life, the necessity of constant prayer.[15] Met the society and was forced, in spite of myself, again to rebuke them sharply.

**Thursday, August 7.** Preached again in the spirit of heaviness. Put out two more of the society, re-examined all, and charged them to walk as becometh the gospel.[16]

Rode to brother [John] Bennetts's and lost my burden among our dear children of St. Just. The courtyard was crowded with listening souls while I said in the words of the prophet Zechariah,[17] "What are these wounds in thine hands? ...."[18] Our Lord himself answered and made himself known to us by the marks of his sufferings. It was a time of great refreshing. Before preaching I read them the late act against swearing,[19] one of a hundred which had been sent my brother by a justice of peace. I thought that magistrate's design best answered by reading it before our largest congregations. Last Sunday I read it to 10,000 at Gwennap; and both there and here I believe it was greatly blessed and convinced the hearers that we are hearty friends to Caesar and to all who under him are a terror to evildoers, a praise to them that do well.

I found by the whole behaviour of this people that our Lord hath got himself the victory. Satan is fairly beaten out of the field. His drunken champion is no more heard of, but disabled and bound by the prayer of

---

[14] Matt. 5:3.

[15] See 1 Thess. 5:23.

[16] See Phil. 1:27.

[17] CW spells as "Zechary"; MARC, MA 1977/503 omits the name.

[18] Zech. 13:6.

[19] *An Act more Effectually to Prevent Profane Cursing and Swearing* [London: Thomas Baskett, 1746].

faith. The door is wider opened than ever and all opposition falls before the gospel, or power of God unto salvation.

How doth our Lord take the wise in their own craftiness! Hoping thereby to hinder John Bennetts's preaching, the righteous Dr. [Walter] Borlase made him constable. But he preached so much the more, and the mob were so awed by his office that they gave him no interruption at Trewellard. And in spite of sober Mr. [Stephen] Ustick's[20] breaking open their locks and doors now and then, his house has been a sanctuary to the flock of Christ. Toward the expiration of his office, the doctor turned him out of it—and just then my Lord sent me.

I rejoiced over them, seeing their steadfastness and love. Near 150 are gathered again and knit together in the name of Jesus. We drank into the same Spirit, and with one mouth and heart magnified the God of our salvation.

After the society, rode with brother [William] Shepherd to brother [William] Chenhall's at the church town [St. Just] and slept very quietly in the bed whence they had dragged away poor Charles Graves to the man-of-war.

**Friday, August 8.** Met the congregation at 5:00 and more of the power of God than ever. I *thought* he would give us a double blessing at parting. We more than tasted the powers of the world to come[21] while the Spirit applied those words to our hearts, "These are they which came out of great tribulation, and have washed their robes, and made them white in the blood of the Lamb!"[22] Such an hour of triumph I have seldom known. In this employment let me live and die!

Got back to St. Ives by 1:00, and humbled ourselves under the hand of our offended God. He did now begin to lift us up. A great spirit of mourning ran through our hearts. In the evening likewise the word was with power while I explained, "The Spirit and the bride say, Come!"[23] He did call and the sincere ones answered. A cry followed, which was music to God and man. The dead branches were not suffered at this time to clog the living, but both under the word and among the society our Lord humbled and comforted our hearts.

**Saturday, August 9.** We had sweet consolation again from that word, "The marriage of the Lamb is come, and the bride hath made herself

---

[20] MARC, MA 1977/503 omits "were so awed by his office that they gave him no interruption at Trewellard. And in spite of sober Mr."; demonstrating he is copying from DDCW 6/16 where this comprises one full line that was skipped.

[21] See Heb. 6:5.

[22] Rev. 7:14.

[23] Rev. 22:17.

ready."[24] I took my leave of the flock, trusting that the Good Shepherd will care for them still and keep them faithful unto death and set them on his right hand in that day!

Preached my farewell sermon to the dear people at Ludgvan, and in the evening comforted many mourners at Gwennap by the glorious privileges of the gospel displayed in the 35 of Isaiah.

**Sunday, August 10.** Enforced the duty and promise, Matthew 7:7, "Ask, and ye shall receive; seek, and ye shall find," upon a people that *have* ears to hear. My evening audience was larger, I believe, by 2,000 than any I have seen in Cornwall. Near 12,000[25] by computation listened with all the marks of sincerity while I commended them to God and to the word of his grace.[26] For near two hours I was enabled to preach repentance toward God and faith in Jesus Christ.[27] Broke out again and again into prayer and exhortation. The Lord, I saw, had given me their hearts, and believed not one word would return empty.[28] Seventy years' sufferings were infinitely overpaid by one such opportunity. Lord, what am I, and what is my father's house that thou should use *me* for the salvation of souls?[29] O that my lips, my heart, my life may thank thee! O that I may spend and be spent in the service of thy church!

Never had we so large an effusion of the Spirit as this night in the society. I could not doubt (at the time) either their perseverance or my own and still am I humbly confident that we shall stand together among the multitude which no man can number and say, "Worthy is the Lamb that was slain to receive power, and riches, and wisdom, and strength, and honour, and glory, and blessing!"[30]

### After Preaching the Gospel
### in Cornwall 1746[31]

1. All thanks be to God
   Who scatters abroad

---

[24] Cf. Rev. 19:7.

[25] In MS Journal CW revised the number down to about 9,000.

[26] See Acts 20:32.

[27] His sermon on Acts 3:19.

[28] See Isa. 55:11.

[29] See 2 Sam. 7:18.

[30] Rev. 5:12.

[31] CW published this hymn (with scattered revisions) as "Thanksgiving for the Success of the Gospel," *Redemption Hymns* (1747), 3–5.

>        Throughout every place
>    By the least of his servants his savour of grace!
>            Who the victory gave
>            The praise let him have,
>            For the work he hath done
>    All honour and glory to Jesus alone!

2.       Our conquering Lord
         Hath prosper'd the word,
         And made it prevail
     And mightily shaken the kingdom of hell.
             His arm he hath bar'd,
             And a people prepar'd
             His glory to show,
     And witness the power of his goodness below.

3.       He hath open'd a door
         To the penitent poor,
         And rescued from sin,
     And admitted the harlots and publicans in:
             They have heard the glad sound,
             They have liberty found
             Thro' the blood of the Lamb,
     And plentiful pardon in Jesus' name.

4.       The opposers admire
         The hammer and fire,
         Which all things o'ercomes,
     And breaks the hard rocks, and the mountains consumes.
             With quiet amaze
             They listen and gaze,
             And insensibly join
     Constrain'd to acknowledge—the work is divine!

5.       And shall *we* not sing,
         Our Saviour and King.
         Thine heritage we
     With rapture ascribe our salvation to thee.
             Thou, Jesus, hast bless'd,
             And the faithful increas'd,

Who thankfully own
We are freely forgiven thro' mercy alone.

6. Thy Spirit revives
His work in our lives,
His wonders of grace
So mightily wrought in the primitive days.
O that all men might know
His tokens below,
Their Saviour confess,
And embrace the glad tidings of pardon and peace.

7. Thou Saviour of all,
Effectually call
The sinners that stray;
And O! let a nation be born in a day!
Thy sign let them see,
And flow unto thee
For oil and for wine,
For the blissful assurance of favour divine.

8. Our heathenish land
Beneath thy command
In mercy receive,
And make us a pattern to all that believe:
Then, then let it spread
Thy knowledge and dread,
Till the earth is o'erflow'd,
And the universe fill'd with the glory of God!

## [LETTER ADDED TO MA 1977/503, BOX 5, FILE 11]

Plymouth
Sunday Night, [August 17, 1746]

[[Dear Brother,

[[Satan is indefatigable[32] to alienate the hearts of this people from me, but I defy him. His chief instrument is poor Herbert Jackson, that mere tool of the Dissenters. My stay here will be the shorter. You must

---

[32] CW also wrote "Indefatigable" in longhand beneath, so that it would not be misread.

take no notices of this to any. My journal likewise, when it comes, keep to yourself. John Trembath is given over with the spotted fever.[33] Against hope I believe he will recover. [Thomas] Richards is not yet come. On Tuesday or Wednesday I think of returning to Tavistock, and St. Gennys.[34] On Tuesday sennight I hope to see Exeter, but know not how to get thither. My horse has got the]] fashions,[35] [[I expect to leave him behind me.

[[Brother pray for me. The peace of God be with you.

Farewell]]

*Address*: "To / The Revd. Mr Wesley / at the Foundry / London / single sheet."
*Postmarks*: "PLYMOUTH" and "20 / AV."
*Endorsement*: by JW, "C[harles] Aug. 17, 1746 / a[nswere]d 22 / Journal."
*Source*: MARC, DDCW 6/16 (holograph); compared to MARC, MA 1977/503, Box 5, file 11 (record copy in hand of Charles Perronet).

---

[33] CW also wrote "fever" in longhand beneath, so that it would not be misread. "Spotted fever" was a common name at the time for typhus.

[34] St. Gennys, Cornwall; 7 miles southwest of Bude.

[35] *OED*: "'Fashions' is the 15th–17th century spelling for the obsolete word 'farcin.' The modern spelling for this word is 'farcy,' which is defined as 'a disease of animals, esp. of horses, closely allied to glanders.'"

## August 11–28, 1746[1]

**Monday, August 11.** Set out at 4:00 with brother [James] Waller and [William] Shepherd. Preached in the evening at St. Tudy's[2] to many listening souls on "Repent and believe the gospel."[3] Mr. Bennet and Thomson[4] were of my audience. Just as I was concluding, a gentleman rode up to me very fiercely and bade me come down. We exchanged a few words, and after I had dismissed the people, talked together in the house till the poor drunken lawyer went away in as good a temper as he was then capable of. I had more difficulty to get clear of another sort of antagonist, one Adams, a poor old enthusiast, who travels throughout the land as "overseer of all the ministers."[5] Such he is confident God has made him, and such he everywhere proclaims himself. His nonsense, lies, and blasphemies the devil makes good use of among the simple and unawakened. His message at present to the ministers (he says) is "that they should all unite and my brother he has persuaded to it already." To keep him quiet, I spake kindly to him. But immediately after my preaching, he got among the people scattering his firebrands. I saw nothing was to be done by fair words, and therefore resolved to wash my hands of him all at once.

Exhorted the people for an hour in the house and my labour was not in vain in the Lord.

**Tuesday, August 12.** Setting out for Mr. Bennet's, found the prophet cleaving to us and determined to wait upon me as long as I stayed in the country. He fell upon me *after his manner*. I accepted the challenge and resolved to have a fair trial of skill with him. Mr. Shepherd I set sentinel over him to take care he did not come within 200 yards of me. He was forced to keep his distance till we came to Tregeare.[6] There, with our host's leave, I instructed the servants *not* to listen to his journal, nor put into his mouth. "This kind goeth not out but by fasting."[7] According to expectation he flew into a violent rage, denounced his judgments against us, and left the house.

---

[1] CW's journal letter for these two weeks survives in one manuscript (DDCW 6/17), in his own hand, with pages numbered as a continuation of DDCW 6/14–16. This manuscript was the source of, and provides much greater detail than, the account of these days in CW, MS Journal.

[2] St. Tudy, Cornwall; 5 miles northeast of Wadebridge. CW spells "St. Eudy's."

[3] Cf. Mark 1:15.

[4] Rev. John Bennet, vicar of Tresmeer; and Rev. George Thomson, of St. Gennys.

[5] This is the John Adams, of Tresmeer, who was eventually confined as a madman; cf. JW, *Letter to the ... Bishop of Gloucester*, I.29, *Works*, 11:493.

[6] Trageare, Cornwall; 1 mile southeast of Tresmeer.

[7] Cf. Matt. 17:21.

At night, Mr. Bennet read prayers. I preached, "They that be whole have no need of a physician, ...."[8] The church was full of our Lord's patients, and greatly were we comforted together.

**Wednesday, August 13.** Got to Tavistock by 2:00. Mr. Adams came in a few minutes after us. I repeated my prescription to our host, "Give him no attention, and nothing to eat and he will never stay with you." *Probatum est*[9] again. He waited till the evening, and then marched away for Plymouth.

I preached in the field as before, but such stocks and stones I have not seen, no not at Conham. The words rebounded as from a wall of brass.[10] So great a bar I have never felt, and was therefore forced in a quarter of an hour to dismiss the congregation. The society made me some amends. Several of these are thoroughly in earnest and received me as at the first. Our meeting was not in vain.

**Thursday, August 14.** Many letters I had received in Cornwall from Plymouth urging me to visit them in my return, and so much the more because they expected Mr. [Herbert] Jenkins at the same time. In hopes of meeting him, I had hurried from Mr. Bennet's although expected to preach there for some days. Mr. [Andrew] Kinsman accompanied us to Plymouth. A faithful brother met us on the road, and informed me of what I expected, the indefatigable pains Satan has taken to make the minds of the brethren evil affected towards me. Letters after letters have been sent them from London and Bristol warning them against me as a designing, wicked man, who came to subvert their faith and steal their tabernacle from Mr. Whitefield. Mr. Jenkins himself (he told me) was carried away by their lies, and so deeply prejudiced as to threaten to expel out of the society those who had invited me. As soon as I came to Plymouth, I took my old friend apart and gave him a true relation of what had passed, offering, if he was not thoroughly satisfied, to leave the place immediately without preaching at all. At the same time I observed the different treatment we had received from *his* friends, particularly at Bath, where they had set up a society in the same street in direct opposition to ours. (To say nothing of the Tabernacle in London and every other place where they *could* enter into our labours.) But I too much condemned *their* practice to follow it, or to stir up dispute among *their* children. He *now* saw clearly that *they* had done wrong and owned it was contrary to the will of God. Their rival society in Bath, as is plain, said he, be its coming to nothing. He believed my assurances, seemed fully satisfied, and insisted upon my preaching this evening in the Tabernacle and as long as I should stay.

---

[8] Mark 2:17.

[9] "It has been proved."

[10] See Jer. 15:20.

The family and others joining to desire it, I preached in their house (Mr. Jenkins first praying) from Hebrews 4:14ff. The Lord was with my mouth and confirmed his own word. Many confessed the comfort they received. A very few who heard with prejudice, cavilled at and wrested my sayings to their own hurt. These laboured to prejudice Mr. Jenkins and my host. The former (I observed) was quite altered both in his behaviour and looks, as often as had been conversing with those bigoted persons, who haunted him continually to keep him out of my company.

To save him farther uneasiness I resolved to preach no more at the Tabernacle, and to leave them on Monday, a week sooner than I intended. This I acquainted him with **Friday, August 15**; and followed him in the morning and sat under his preaching unobserved.

Walked in the afternoon to the Dock and my spirit revived among that simple, loving people. Preached to a large audience, "the blessedness of mourning" and "hungering after righteousness."[11] Many, I believe, tasted it in that hour. I gave notice that my brother Jenkins would preach in the morning.

**Saturday, August 16.** Spent the morning in conversation with Mrs. Patrick, Mrs. Stephens, Mr. Hyde's family, and other sincere followers after Christ. Baptized a young woman, who in that moment lost her burden of sin, and was soon after filled with peace and joy in believing.

Herbert Jenkins asked me to preach in the evening at Plymouth, but I feared it might give occasion of cavil and dispute, and therefore chose to sit in the desk and hear him. I concluded his discourse with a collect.

**Sunday, August 17.** Took the field and discoursed on Zechariah 12:10. We had a foretaste of the promise, the first-fruits of that spirit of grace and supplications. Many looked upon him that had pierced, and partook of the blessedness of mourning, as they afterwards told me. Yet some were offended at my "preaching up free-will," as they called my inviting all to Christ, yet at the same time most explicitly declaring it must be by a supernatural divine power they came—otherwise they could not possibly feel a good desire or think a good thought. Equally impossible, I acknowledge it now, to speak without giving offence to those who are resolved to take it.

Declared after evening service to a numerous audience in the field, "They that be whole have no need of a physician, but they that are sick."[12] The word did not return empty. The number of the sick, I hope, increases. We went back with the voice of praise and thanksgiving.

**Monday, August 18.** Called on several of a right spirit, and laboured to confirm them in the faith and love *unfeigned*. At noon took boat for the

---

[11] Matt. 5:4–6.

[12] Matt. 9:12 or Mark 2:17.

Dock with sisters Gregory, Veal, Poppelstone, and Herbert Jenkins. In perils by water, in perils among false brethren! The sea was so rough that it tried our faith. A little supernatural courage I had given me for the rest, or I should have been the most fearful of the company. Their fear was kept within bounds, so that none stirred. If they had, we must have been overset. In two hours our invisible Pilot brought us safe to land, thankful I trust to him for our deliverance, humbled for our littleness of faith, and more endeared to each other by our common danger.

Dined at M[rs]. Dawson's with many of our friends, and took sweet counsel together. At Mr. Hyde's our company was increased to upwards of twenty. And to complete all, Mr. Bennet came—a good man and with good tidings, which rejoiced my heart.

At 7:00 we found thousands waiting in the street for the word of life. Just before I began speaking, Mr. [John] Adams ran after me with "The Lord hath sent me to forbid your preaching; and if you dare preach, he will execute judgment upon you." The *brutum fulmen*[13] of an enthusiast could not hinder my delivering my message. One or two of the brethren locked themselves up with him in the society-room while I took my leave of these delightful souls, the Lord comforting us on every side. The word was as fire and melted down all before it. I spake and prayed alternately for two hours. The moonlight added to the outward solemnity of our meeting. Our eyes were filled with tears and our hearts with love. Scarce a soul but was affected either with grief or joy. We drank into one Spirit and trod upon all the powers of the enemy, being fully "persuaded, that neither life, nor death, nor things present, nor things to come, shall be able to separate us."[14]

**Tuesday, August 19.** At 4:00 in the morning, spake to as many as the room could hold, from "Be thou faithful unto death, and I will give thee a crown of life."[15] God again gave testimony to his word, and our hearts were one in him.

After communing with several who cleave to our Lord and us, we returned to Plymouth. Here honest Herbert [Jenkins] and I came to a full explanation, and he desired *we might not think of uniting yet*, the *people* (as he said) not being ripe for it. I offered him again and again liberty to preach to any of our societies wherever he came, but now he thinks *it might not be so proper*. He must not complain then (I told him) of *our* want of catholic love or lay the blame of *not* uniting to *us*. We agreed there could be no thorough coalition till each party gave up the thoughts of *drawing over* the other and consented to lay aside the dispute entirely. I left one advice with

---

[13] "Mere noise."

[14] Cf. Rom. 8:38–39; and 1 Cor. 10:12.

[15] Rev. 2:10.

*him*—that is in no wise to set up for himself or draw George Whitefield's children into a meeting house and separate congregation, but keep them together both from Germans and antinomians till his friend's return.

At 4:00 set out for Tavistock, and came thither with the night. Here we heard what made our ears tingle. A young man has given the adversary occasion to speak reproachfully. The whole town was full of it, and the minister quite transported with joy, running about (like poor beastly Mr. [William] Hoblyn) and crying, "They are all alike!" The society was broken up and fled every man to his tent, for they heard the blasphemy of the multitude and fear was on every side. Mr. Rattenbury and the most solid, gracious persons were for leaving the town. So was I at first, hearing of the scandal, and talked of departing early in the morning. But the Lord taught me better, even that I was to stay and bear part of their burden. Accordingly I took up my cross (the heaviest I ever bore) and stayed to pray with and comfort my poor host and his wife.

I spent all **Wednesday [August 20]** there. Sent for and talked to each of the society and gave them advice suitable to the occasion. The young man frankly told me the first occasion of his falling was *his opinion* that it was impossible. He had been the forwardest of all in insisting on the perseverance of the saints, and easily slid from pride into slackness and lust. Great things he had spoken of himself and his experience, had gone and reproved the minister for false doctrine, and so distinguished himself as if he had been trained up by the enemy on purpose to destroy the work of God.

At 8:00 the poor scattered society ventured to meet me, and my God humbled me among them. We cried unto him, as out of the deep, and he heard our prayer. Their steward had forsaken them, and they had all resolved to meet no more. I told them I had no authority to exclude any from their society, but they had themselves and I would be witness to their proceedings. Then I asked whether they still acknowledged the two offenders members of their society, or whether they rejected them. They all with one consent rejected them. Then I told them they were free from the reproach, and no more blameable than St. Paul and the Corinthian church *after* that wicked person was put out from among *them*. I warned them against Satan's devices or the double extreme of either tolerating or showing too great severity toward a lapsed brother, against spiritual pride, and all manner of sin to which it leads. Spoke comfortably to them and promised to send our preachers among them when their orderly walking had opened the door again. They were greatly encouraged, and resolved through grace to stand together and preach the gospel by their lives. Strong faith the Lord gave us in prayer that he would bring good out of evil, and in spite of the powers of darkness plant a glorious church in this place.

**Thursday, August 21.** Set out at 6:00 for Mr. Bennet's. In the evening preached Christ crucified[16] in Tresmeer church. The words came close to their hearts. Next morning (**Friday, August 22**) enforced the duty and promise [of] Matthew 7:7 and pleaded it in prayer with full assurance of faith. Mr. Bennet's house was full of earnest souls, whom our Lord did not send empty away. The sight of our brother [George] Thomson refreshed me much. I preached at night in Laneast church,[17] to a people ready prepared for the Lord.

**Sunday, August 24.** Preached morning and afternoon at St. Gennys[18] with the demonstration of the Spirit and of power. But lost my voice so that, when I came to Mr. Bennet's, I could not be heard. However, for a quarter of an hour I strained to speak to the crowds in his house, many of whom believe that Jesus shall save his people from their sins.

Here I received news from brother [James] Hitchens that John Trembath (whom we left ill of a fever) was still alive, but Samuel Hitchens departed in peace and triumph.[19] His last word was "The chariots of Israel are come!"[20]

**Monday, August 25.** Set out in our chaise and by Tuesday noon [**August 26**] got with much difficulty to Exeter. Found the little flock miserably divided into three parties or societies—Mr. Jenkins's, Mr. Goodwin's, and the Germans. They had been informed that I was opposing Mr. Jenkins at Plymouth with all bitterness of contention—and they believed it. I had neither time nor inclination to meddle with their quarrels, nor faith for composing them, and therefore hastened forward to Bristol, where on Thursday night [**August 28**] I met my brother returned from Wales.

*Source*: CW record copy in his own hand; MARC, DDCW 6/17.

---

[16] CW's usual title for his sermon on Lam. 1:12.

[17] Laneast, Cornwall; 7 miles west of Launceston; another of John Bennet's churches.

[18] The parish of George Thomson; CW spells "St. Ginnys."

[19] Samuel Hitchens, James's son, died on Aug. 16. JW assisted Hitchens in writing an account of the death, published as *A Short Account of the Death of Samuel Hitchens* (London: [Strahan,] 1746). See also CW's "Hymn on the Death of Samuel Hitchens," *HSP* (1749), 2:74–75.

[20] Samuel was singing st. 7 of "Hosannah to God," in CW, *Funeral Hymns* ([London: Strahan,] 1746), 23.

## AUGUST 24, 1747–FEBRUARY 6, 1748[1]

[Monday,] August 24, 1747. Upon my brother's earnest instance for me to hasten to Ireland, after reading the letters and taking leave of the society [at the Foundery, in London], took coach with Charles Perronet,[2] Thomas Hardwick,[3] and two others. It was past midnight when we got to Brentford.[4] I lay down for an hour, but could not sleep.

[August 25, Tuesday.] Set forward between 2:00 and 3:00 in the morning. Passed two hours very comfortably with sister R. Reached Wycombe by 11:00,[5] where Mr. Hollis[6] stopped and carried us to his house. Preached at 12:00 to a few serious people on "Lift up your eyes, and look on the fields; for they are white already unto harvest. And he that reapeth receiveth wages, and gathereth fruit unto life eternal: that both he that soweth and he that reapeth may rejoice together."[7] Took horse again at 3:00 and by 8:00 got safe to Oxford, to our old host and friend and brother Evans.[8]

August 26, Wednesday. Set out at 5:00. Wandered an hour out of our way. Came to Burford[9] by 9:00. Parted again at Frog Mill[10] and came with the night to Huntley, seven miles beyond Gloucester.

---

[1] CW made his first excursion to Ireland, to minister among the budding Methodist community there, through the fall and winter of 1747–48. As was his practice when on the road, CW mailed journal letters every week or two over this six month period, reporting on his work. Only five of these letters have survived (DDCW 6/18–DDCW 6/22), covering less than half of CW's time in Ireland on this trip. But it was also CW's practice to keep a connected record, copied from the journal letters before they were mailed. This record copy (DDCW 6/88a), most of it in the hand of Charles Perronet, has survived and provides access to the material in most of the missing journal letters. Comparison of Perronet's copy to surviving letters demonstrates his general (though not perfect) accuracy in copying. We transcribe here the whole of the longer copy document, noting where surviving individual journal letters pick up and leave off. In cases where there is variance between Perronet's copy and a surviving letter in CW's hand, we privilege CW's text (noting significant variances). This combined material was the source of, and provides much greater detail than, the account of these months in CW, MS Journal.

[2] Charles Perronet (c. 1719–76), was a son of Rev. Vincent and Charity (Goodhew) Perronet of Shoreham. When his family aligned with Methodism in the mid-1740s, Charles became a traveling preacher. By the mid-1750s, he became estranged from the Wesley brothers, through his advocacy of separation from the Church of England.

[3] This would be Thomas Hardwick Jr., who appears briefly in the Minutes as a possible assistant between 1746 and 1747 (*Works*, 10:183, 186, 190, 205).

[4] Brentford, Middlesex, the home of Thomas Hardwick Jr.

[5] I.e., High Wycombe, Buckinghamshire; 28 miles northwest of London.

[6] CW had known Isaac Hollis of High Wycombe since at least 1738; see MS Journal, Dec. 11, 1738.

[7] Cf. John 4:35–36.

[8] He appears repeatedly in JW's *Journal*, but his first name is never given.

[9] Burford, Oxfordshire; 7 miles west of Witney.

[10] Frog Mill Inn, about half way between Burford and Huntley (Gloucestershire) at a fork in the road. "on the right [running] to Cheltenham and Gloucester; and on the left—the Old Gloucester Road—to Gloucester over the Cotswolds." C. G. Harper, *The Oxford, Gloucester and Milford Haven Road. Vol 1 : London to Gloucester* (1905).

**August 27, Thursday.** Before 5:00 we renewed our strength and our labour. Overtook an hearer of Howell Harris, who conducted us within ten miles of Builth.[11] For the rest of the way the river was our guide. Between 9:00 we found our brother [Edward] Phillips[12] at Builth, and were glad soon after to betake ourselves to rest.

**Friday, August 28.** My brother [JW] not being come from Dublin, according to the appointment, we concluded he was detained by cross winds, and had the opportunity thereby of resting ourselves and our weary beasts.

At 9:00 I preached in the street, "Repentance toward God, and faith in Jesus Christ."[13] The people behaved with great decency. We were afterwards much refreshed with the sight and conversation of Mr. Gwynne.[14]

At noon I preached in Maesmynis church, Mr. Phillips reading prayers. Mr. Williams[15] preached afterwards in Welsh. Met the congregation again at 4:00 in the street and explained the Good Samaritan.[16] He was present, binding up our wounds. Rode with Mr. G[wynne] and two of his family to Garth and preached the fourth time from Isaiah 40[:1], "Comfort ye, comfort ye my people, saith your God." The family received us as messengers of God. If such we are, in us they received him that sent us.

**[Saturday,] August 29.** Rode to the Wells,[17] and called the labouring, burdened sinners to Jesus.[18] He gave me to speak searchingly and comfortably. Three ministers were of my audience. Two of them with all the people received the word and seemed affected by it. Returned to Garth rejoicing. Still no tidings of my brother. While we were talking of him, whether he would come or no, he came and brought life and a blessing with him. Heard him in the evening declaring that eternal life.

**Sunday, August 30.** I preached at 9:00 on a tombstone in Builth churchyard; my brother at 11:00 in Maesmynis churchyard, the church

---

[11] Builth Wells, Brecknockshire.

[12] Edward Phillips (1716–76), a graduate of Jesus College, Oxford (1734–38), was ordained in 1740 and served first as curate, then rector of St. David's church, Maesmynis, Brecknockshire, until his death. He retained Methodist sympathies all his life.

[13] Cf. Acts 20:21.

[14] In MS Journal, CW specifies that Marmaduke Gwynne came to see him at Rev. Phillip's, with two of his family.

[15] Rev. Rice Williams (1704–84), of the nearby parish of Llansantffraed-in-Elwell, Radnorshire (4 miles northeast of Builth Wells), who was now actively supporting the Wesley brothers.

[16] Luke 10:29–37.

[17] CW, MS Journal specifies that this was Llandrindod Wells, Radnorshire; about 8 miles north of Builth Wells.

[18] Matt. 11:28.

being too small. After 2:00 I discoursed on the Prodigal Son,[19] and the Lord bowed the hearts of all that heard. Rode to Garth and gave the marks of the Messiah from Matthew 11:5, "The blind receive their sight, the deaf hear, ...." My mouth was opened and, I believe, their hearts. By 8:00 my brother returned (with Mr. Gwynne) from preaching in Llansantffraed church.[20] It was now agreed that I should stay in this country till Wednesday.

**Monday, August 31.** After preaching once more on the tombstone, my brother set out for Bristol. I preached there again at 3:00, and bid a multitude to the Great Supper.[21] Rode to Garth and explained the woman that *was* a sinner, and Simon the Pharisee.[22]

**Tuesday,[23] September 1.** Preached again at Maesmynis, and in Builth, on Lamentations 1:12, "Is it nothing to you, all ye that pass by? ...." Now the great blessing came, and the love of Christ crucified constrained us. All were melted down as wax before the fire. I took a sweet leave of the weeping flock, and found that if we never met again upon earth, yet can we never be parted.

Returned to Garth, and preached happiness in Christ Jesus from Acts 3:26,[24] "God, having raised up his Son Jesus, sent him to bless you, in turning away every one of you from his iniquities." We continued rejoicing in the Lord till past 11:00.

**Wednesday, September 2.** Met the whole family, both children and servants, at 6:00, and in strong words declared the end of Christ's coming, namely "that they might have life, and might have it more abundantly."[25] All seemed to receive my saying, and were grieved at our departure. We took our leave, commending them to the grace of God and knowing that our labour hath not been in vain in the Lord.

Between 10:00 and 11:00 took horse with Mr. [Marmaduke] Gwynne, Mr. [Edward] Phillips, and a brother from Anglesey who undertakes to be our guide. Found the seven Welsh miles to Rhayader[26] [a] good four hours' ride. Preached in the church to a large congregation, and lifted up the hands that hung down and laboured to awaken the dead in sin. The minister seems a man of a simple heart, and surely not eager for preferment, or he would not be so content with his salary of £3 a year. Another neighbouring clergyman was present, who invited me to his

---

[19] Luke 15:11–32.
[20] Llansantffraed-in-Elwell, Radnorshire, Rev. Rice Williams's parish.
[21] Luke 14:15–24.
[22] Luke 7:36–50.
[23] Orig., "Thursday"; an error.
[24] Orig., "Acts 3:24"; an error.
[25] Cf. John 10:10.
[26] Rhayader, Radnorshire; 11 miles north of Builth Wells.

church, as have two or three others, whom I have not time to visit. At 5:00 rode onward to Llanidloes,[27] without calling on a faithful woman, at whose house were several waiting for me. We sent them notice and between 8:00 and 9:00 they came to us at our inn with many of the town, so that the house was suddenly filled. I pointed them to "the Lamb of God, who taketh away the sin of the world,"[28] and they received the word with all readiness of mind.

**Thursday, September 3.** At 6:00 went forth and cried near the townhall, "Ho, every one that thirsteth, come ye to the waters."[29] Their earnest attention convinced me God hath a work to do in this place. Took horse at 8:00 and rode hard to reach Machynlleth[30] by noon. Here they rang the bells to welcome us, but we had not time for preaching. Before night got to Dolgellau in Merionethshire. Here we left our dear friends, Mr. Gwynne and Phillips, next morning.

[**Friday, September 4**] reached Tan-y-Bwlch[31] by 9:00 and Aber Menai ferry[32] by 5:30. The wind was behind us, exactly fair for Ireland, but so high that there was no crossing the water from the other side till the tide was out. The boat attempted it several times and was driven back. We waited two hours, part of which time I slept on the ground, though not very comfortably. Then the boat came over and with much difficulty we got into it. It blew a hurricane; but we were soon out of danger, for the storm drove us to shore in a few minutes. We rode in the dark over the heavy sands, and in an hour got to the first small town in Anglesey. Stayed at a sorry public house till 10:00. Our guide talked of finding us another more experienced than himself to conduct us over the marsh—but he lived a mile off, we knew not where. While we were consulting, providence sent him to us. He called at our inn (by accident as the world speaks), and we set out with our convoy. The wind was now turned full against us, and brought the rain, which wetted us in a few minutes from head to foot. In half an hour's riding we got to a wash, or salt water, and our guide cried we were come too soon, for the flood was not out, and we should swim our horses. We committed them and ourselves to God and plunged in. The beasts just kept their feet. We passed through that and our other difficulties with a cheerful heart, and a little after midnight were brought safe to a brother's house. I took it for a stable while we were making our

---

[27] Llanidloes, Montgomeryshire; 11 miles southwest of Newtown.

[28] Cf. John 1:29.

[29] Isa. 55:1.

[30] Machynlleth, Montgomeryshire; 12 miles north of Aberystwyth.

[31] Tan-y-Bwlch, a hamlet in Llanfrothen parish, Merionethshire; on a hillside, 8.5 miles northeast of Harlech.

[32] Running from Caernarfon to Angelsey.

way in through the fern, of which it was full. But the fern stood us in good stead and made us a good fire to dry us. We lay for a short time and took horse again, and between 7:00 and 8:00 on **Saturday [September 5]** came to Holyhead, having been in our saddles near 25 hours. Sufficient unto this day is the labour thereof.[33]

Went to a public house, where the landlord told us he had no room for us. But upon our guide's insisting he should find us a lodging, he consented that we should stay. The wind continuing contrary, we lay down in the afternoon, and rose refreshed without feeling any ill effects of our journey.

At night we retired again to our garret and joined in prayer, when one came and told us the gentry (of which the house was full) desired to be admitted. We went down to the parlour, sang an hymn, and prayed, and gave a word of exhortation.

**Sunday, September 6.** Sent an offer of my assistance to the minister,[34] who was ready to beat the messenger, answering, "No such thing could be, and that I well knew but offered my assistance only to provoke him." I did not much wonder at his civility when I heard afterwards that he was an open persecutor of this way, had printed a book against us,[35] and driven the sincerest of his parish from the sacrament. One of them I have spoken with—a most notorious profligate that was, till he heard the gospel. His minister, seeing him coming to the Lord's Table, repelled him with bitter revilings. The poor man attempted to speak with him in private, but could not be admitted. At last he thought himself obliged to leave the Church and go over to the Dissenters, but our brother Jones[36] stopped him. I helped to confirm him in his calling, and now he seems resolved to obey the order of providence, and eat of occasion from them that seek occasion.

Just before church time some Irish gentlemen [[sent for me and desired, as [the] service of the church was in Welsh, that I would preach them a sermon in English. I promised them so to do when the prayer book service was over. Because of it the minister read in English. I durst not turn my back on the sacrament, although there was little likelihood of my being admitted. But I was en[couraged] to pray earnestly for the minister, and he was not suffered to reject me. He knew me by my band[37] and administered

---

[33] CW takes over writing for the next two paragraphs.

[34] Thomas Ellis served as curate of Holyhead 1737–58.

[35] Earlier this year Ellis had published *Byrr grynhôad eglur o'r grefydd Gristianogol, ynghyd a gair o gyngor ag addysg mewn perthynas i'r schismaticaid sy'n ymneillduo oddiwrth Eglwys Loegr*.

[36] William Jones, of Trefollwyn Blas, which is 1 mile west of Rhosmeirch; he was a convert of Howell Harris and traveled as a lay preacher around Angelsey.

[37] I.e., the clerical collar of his day.

to me in English. The same he did to Charles Perronet. Our friend Jones he stopped at and told him he ought not to come there while he drew people from the Church. He meant the poor man whom our brother had kept from leaving the Church, as he now assured him with meekness and submission. Mr. Ellis gave him the sacrament at last, and we all returned thankfully both on our own account and his.

[[When we came to our inn word was brought us from the gentlemen that they had been at church, and therefore would not give me the t[ime] for preaching. We perceived Satan had taken the alarm and was striving to hinder the word, but committed our case unto [the] Lord, and tarried his leisure. After evening service several wild people hovered about our inn, but did not promise[?] attention by their b[ehaviour]. Therefore we continued in our lodging till the gentlemen came to us requesting me again to preach. I went down and found many gathered together who even thrust me out to speak. I stood without and discoursed on the first words that offered, Acts 13:40[–41], "Beware therefore, lest that come upon you, [....]; Behold, thou despisers, and wonder, and perish, etc." The small vulgar were rude enough but offered <no[38]> violence. The gentlemen behaved like gentlemen. I continued speaking for near an hour and left the event[?] to God.

[[Two poor men followed us to our church[39] and joined in prayer and thanksgiving. The landlord soon gave us to understand that the ladies were offended at such fellows <coming> to the house, and I must not have them any more. We gave him little answer, but expect ere long to come to our m[ighty] Lord; [t st b[40]].

[[**Monday, September 7.** We continued waiting for a wind. **Tuesday, September 8.** We rose designing to ride to our brother Jones['s] when <news> was b[rought] us our captain would set sail d[irectly], against the wind. We entered the vessel at ten. The little wind we had was contrary. It increased in the evening, and at midnight was too high for us to sleep. My namesake[41] was neither so sick nor so burdened as I expected. By ten next morning [**September 9**] we were <taken> into the small packetboat, and by eleven [the] Lord brought us safe to Dublin.

[[Here the first news we heard from John Trembath was that the little flock stands fast in the storm of persecution, which arose as soon as my brother left them. The <popish mob> has broke open their room, destroyed all before them. Some of them are judged and sent to Newgate

---

[38] In this and the next four instances using angled brackets the right edge of the manuscript is torn away, the space of about one word. In some instances the missing item can be found in the MS Journal distillation.

[39] I.e., their room in the inn.

[40] The shorthand letters are clear; the expansion is not.

[41] Charles Perronet.

[prison], others bailed out. What will be the event we cannot tell, till we see whether the grand jury will find the bill.

[[In peril in the sea, in peril by the heathen, in peril among false brethren.[42] The day after my brother was embarked, Mr. Cennick made his appearance. John Trembath met him at Mr. Lunell's, and there he quite layed aside the mask, tending to all Count Zinzendorf['s] and the German errors, and railing most plaintively at my brother and me. I was grieved, even[?] sick, that poor John Cennick should ex[plicitly] call us slaves of sin and children of the devil. Though he has done his own business by it, and opened the eyes himself had blinded. Him that thinketh he standeth, let him take heed lest he fall.[43]]]

**September 9, Wednesday.** Walked at 5:00 in the evening to the shattered room in Marlborough Street,[44] where a few people were met, who did not fear what man (or devil) could do unto them. I find God has called me to a different work from what I expected here, even to bear the reproach of Christ and to suffer affliction with his people. This is our calling at present, and we see it. Since my brother's departure, the scene is entirely changed. Persecution is risen for the word's sake, and many are offended. The rain descends and the floods come, and the winds blow and beat upon the house.[45] All the fashionable hearers are swept away. Mr. Lunell[46] is gone to England. Every human support withdrawn. Even the poor soldiers who awed and restrained the mob are forbid by their wretched officers and confined from hearing the word. The popish mob, encouraged and assisted by the Protestants, are so insolent and outrageous that we can't pass through any street but it is immediately all up in arms. The mayor would still assist us,[47] if it was in his power, but the grand jury seem (most of them) to make no conscience of an oath, but rather determined we shall have no more justice than mercy shown us. The plainest evidence has been laid before them of the last riot—in which a mixed rabble of Papists and Protestants broke open our room and four locks; broke open a warehouse and stole and destroyed goods to a considerable value; beat and wounded several with clubs and trowels, etc.; tore away the benches, pulpit, window-cases, etc., and burnt them openly before the gate; and

---

[42] Cf. 2 Cor. 11:26.

[43] Cf. 1 Cor. 10:12.

[44] In 1747 Thomas Williams began to gather a Methodist society in Dublin. By the time JW visited them in August of that year, they were meeting in a rented room on Marlborough Street that had previously housed a Lutheran congregation. A week after JW left on Aug. 22, a riot broke out in Dublin; and this room suffered major damage.

[45] See Matt. 7:25.

[46] William Lunell (1699–1774), a wealthy cloth merchant in Dublin, who had welcomed JW earlier this year.

[47] Richard White was Lord Mayor of Dublin at that time.

swore they would murder us all. Notwithstanding, it is much doubted whether the jury will find the bill. But doth not the Most High regard!

I began making proof of my ministry amongst them in those words, "Comfort ye, comfort ye my people, saith your God. ...."[48] None made the least disturbance till I had concluded, and then we had the rabble attending us with the usual compliments to our lodgings.[49]

**Thursday, September 10.** At 5:00 in the morning declared again, "Jesus shall save his people from their sins."[50] Still all was quiet within doors. But the whole people, men, women, and children were upon us as soon as anyone appeared in the streets. One I observed crying, "Swaddler, swaddler!" (our usual title in this place), who was a young Ishmael indeed, a child who had not long learned to speak. I am sure he could not be above 3 years old.

We dined at a gentleman's who explained our name to me. It seems we are obliged to Mr. [John] Cennick for it, who abounds in such like expressions as, "I curse and blaspheme all the gods in heaven, but that babe that lay in the manger, that babe that lay on Mary's lap, that babe that lay in *swaddling* clouts,"[51] etc. Hence they nicknamed him "swaddler, or swaddling John." And the word ran through the town, and stuck to us all, not excepting the clergy of the place, some of whom are not at all easy under it.

At 5:00 I met the society, that they might depart by daylight, for there is no such thing as meeting at night while the violence of the storm continues. The Lord knit our hearts together in love stronger than death, and we both wept and rejoiced for the consolation. This work I perceive he has prepared for me to walk in. He has sent me hither to confirm the souls of the disciples, and keep them together in the present distress. The world rages and wonders at their steadfastness, for they expected the persecution would so scatter them that they would meet no more. Few indeed but the society venture, but of them not one is kept back by fear. May they daily increase in number, as well as grace; and seem all resolved to continue in the faith, and enter the kingdom through much tribulation.

**Friday, September 11.** Met the society at 1:00 for the first time, and spent an hour in prayer for our Church and nation. We shall hear of these prayers again another day—even the day of the great slaughter, when the towers fall.[52]

---

[48] Isa. 40:1ff.

[49] His lodgings were on Ship Street, near Dublin Castle; see Nov. 23, 1749.

[50] Cf. Matt. 1:21.

[51] "Clout" is here used in the sense of a rag or small, piece of cloth.

[52] Cf. Isa. 30:25.

Preached morning and evening, this and the following day [**Saturday, September 12**], no man forbidding me, although every man reviled us, both coming and going, with such fierceness of contempt as I have never seen in any other place or people.

**Sunday, September 13.** In the strength and name of the Lord, went forth this morning to Oxmantown Green. Stood under the wall of the barracks, and declared to near 1,000 people, "I am determined to know nothing among you, but Jesus Christ, and him crucified."[53] Here I found my Lord had business for me. I was in my calling. My heart was enlarged and my mouth opened. I preached Christ crucified with the manifestation of his Spirit and they all, both Protestants and Papists, listened quietly to words whereby they might be saved. Only an officer toward the end showed his readiness to fight for the devil, but his oaths and curses hurt none but himself.

Received the blessed sacrament at St. Patrick's [cathedral], and from evening prayers returned to the Green. Thousands were now assembled to hear the word, and many to hinder them. I called aloud, "Is it nothing to you, all ye that pass by? behold, and see if ever sorrow was like unto my sorrow, which is done unto me, wherewith my Father hath afflicted me in the day of his fierce anger!"[54] Our dying Lord applied his own word to many hearts. In vain did Satan <make> his poor blind tools the Papists rage, and shout, and cast stones. None were suffered to strike me, or hurt any of the hearers. After half an hour I dismissed the people (though they did not seem to regard the rain), and <removed> to a neighbouring house. The mob waited for me upon a bridge. We tried but could not get a coach, and were therefore forced, when it was dark, to walk home another way, without calling upon our Catholic friends.

**Monday, September 14.** Breakfasted at a serious Baptist's, who informed me of some of Mr. [John] Cennick's strange opinions, which he has heard him frequently declare without fear or wit, both in public and private. 1. He denies the trinity, excluding both the Father and the Holy Ghost from divine worship, wildly insisting that Christ is the trinity. 2. He maintains that God (literally, properly, not the man Christ, but God) died, or Christ in his divine nature; that God, or the Godhead was buried, mixed, blended, infused with the flesh of Christ in the grave; that the real blood of Christ literally was in the veins of a believer; that Christ's heart, flesh, bones are in him (without a figure) and his heart, flesh, bones in Christ. 3. That there are no means of grace, or channels appointed of God to transmit his grace to our souls. 4. That there is no growth in grace, but a man is entirely justified and entirely sanctified at once. In a word, that all brother Zinzendorff's and

---

[53] Cf. 1 Cor. 2:2.

[54] Cf. Lam. 1:12.

the German errors are infallible truths.[55] — I do not wonder now that the stream of prejudice runs so strong against us, seeing the people of Dublin, like the Bishop of London,[56] confound us all together.[57]

**Tuesday, September 15.** Woe is me now, for my soul is wearied because of murderers! I could not at first believe the description given me of this place by the most sober of its own inhabitants. It is full of stirs,[58] a tumultuous city! Violence is in the midst of her. The sons of Belial *show* their sin like Sodom, and there is no man to put them to shame.

As for murder, it is esteemed a very little thing. "He that sheddeth man's blood, by man shall *not* his blood be shed"[59]—in this city of refuge. Scarcely in Carolina[60] or Italy itself are murders so frequent, and so rarely punished. In their conflicts together, the Ormond mob and the Liberty mob[61] seldom part till one or more are killed. A poor constable was the last, whom they beat and dragged about till they killed him, and then hung him up in triumph. None was called in question for it, but the earth covered his blood. Last week a woman was beaten to death by the rabble; but that was all fair, for she was caught picking a pocket, and so there is an end of her. The difficulty of bringing any to justice is, I apprehend, the greater because almost all the constables are Papists and the magistrates, who should be a terror to evil doers, do themselves stand in awe of them.

No wonder if, in such a place, there should be no mercy nor justice for Christians. Our people have been treated with the utmost cruelty; and one of Mr. Cennick's society, a poor, weakly man, was so abused by his neighbour (who knocked him down and stamped upon his stomach) that he died a few days afterwards. The murderer was indeed brought to a trial; but acquitted, though the fact was proved by the clearest evidence, and even his own confession.

I preached in the evening without interruption, the mob being a little restrained, I suppose, for the present while our bill is depending. The jury have respited it till Friday. Meantime, the utmost application is made to them by the rioters, and none at all by us. We leave the matter to God. If they do us justice, it is more than we expect.

---

[55] Count Nikolaus Ludwig von Zinzendorf (1700–60), bishop of the Moravians (whom CW frequently calls the "Germans").

[56] Edmund Gibson (1669–1748) was Bishop of London; CW was referring, among other writings, to Gibson's *Observations on the Conduct and Behaviour of a Certain Sect, Usually distinguished by the Name of Methodists* (London: E. Owen, 1744).

[57] This last sentence is added in CW's hand.

[58] *OED*: "Commotion, disturbance, tumult; general excitement; fuss."

[59] Cf. Gen. 9:6; which CW specifically reverses.

[60] Orig., "Caroline."

[61] These were Roman Catholic and Protestant factions that had been battling one another in Dublin since 1726.

**September 16, Wednesday.** The gentlewoman who let us the room[62] was now very urgent with me to quit it, having suffered great loss by the last riot, and by a gentleman's this day throwing up an adjoining house of hers, which he had let for 2 years at £100 a year. I could not help promising to give up our right to the room, as soon as we could provide another.

The Lord was with us in the word. I carried Mr. Carmichel[63] (brought hither by providence) and his sister to our lodgings, where we passed the evening in prayer and thanksgiving. Her heart seems broken in pieces at the first hearing of the word.

We perceived the rioters were apprehensive that the bill would be found by the principal of them coming to us tonight and begging hard to be excepted out of it.

**Thursday, September [17].**[64] Got a particular account of the late riot, the material circumstances whereof have been proved upon oath by several witnesses before the mayor. After having frequently beat and threatened the lives of most of the society, breaking their windows, destroying the pulpit, etc. On Sunday, August 30, a mixed mob of Papists and Protestants assaulted the house in Marlborough Street, where the society were met after evening service. At first they threw in dead cats, etc., and made an uproar in the yard only. While the people were going out, the mob met them with sticks and stones, knocked down some of the men and women, and beat them in a barbarous manner. Others fled for their lives. Those that were yet in the house shut the door, to stop the stones cast at them. Then the rioters threw great <rocks> over the wall. But several of the society escaped the <back> way through a coach house. When the greater part were gone, the mob broke open the outward door and proceeded to the other, which they likewise broke open. Then they tore down the desk and forms, took two large counters with drawers, and carried them with several chairs, and a great part of the wainscot into the street, made a fire, and openly burned all which they did not steal.

There was a warehouse of Mrs. [Agnes] Felster over the preaching-room. It was locked but they broke open the lock, ransacked the room, took out several canisters of stuff (near £65) and other things of value amounting to about £100. Some of these they carried off as lawful prize, and committed the rest to the flame.

They have often openly threatened to take even our lives. Several they have beat and wounded, without the least provocation. Mr. Paterson in particular they knocked down, and when down cut him in several places,

---

[62] The owner of this room and an associated warehouse in the Strand at the corner of Great Marlborough Street was a widow, Mrs. Agnes Felster (d. 1769).

[63] It is unclear whether this is the Rev. John(?) Carmichael, former curate of Tarvin, whom JW mentions in a letter to Christopher Hopper, Feb. 6, 1750 (*Works*, 26:406).

[64] Orig., "September 18"; an error.

then threw him into a cellar and cast stones on him, that he might rise no more. His body was black by this usage and bruised all over. Mrs. Young was knocked down in the same manner and time, and her head cut. So were several others. About half hour past 9:00, the Lord Mayor came with his guard and saw with his own eyes the havoc which the mob had made. His coming at last dispersed them.

Upon application made, he readily granted warrants to apprehend the rioters. Several of the poorest and meanest of them (Papists mostly) were sent to Newgate. But the better sort made a mere mock of his authority and walked about the town, from alehouse to alehouse, with the constables whom, by drink and money, they had secured of their party.

Our hour of intercession was a solemn season, most present receiving a manifestation of the Spirit, even the spirit of contrition and prayer.

Dined at Mr. Powell's,[65] the printer, who informed us the conscientious gentlemen of the jury had thrown out all the bill, and very much surprised and enraged he was upon the occasion. It was no disappointment at all to me, who expected just so much justice. But my soul was filled with such comfort and faith as I have not felt before in Ireland. Now, thought I, God will take the matter into his own hands. The less of human help, the more of divine. *Dignus vindice nodus!*[66] All my trouble fled away and I was made willing to live and die with this people. My companions, J— and P[erronet?], with our friendly host and his wife, were partakers of the comfort. We continued long time singing unto the Lord, steadily rejoicing in the strength of our salvation.

Till now I have not met one open sinner in Dublin who would bear the least reproof. But today I stepped up <to some> well-dressed gentlemen who were mocking, and civilly desired them to leave that vulgar language to the vulgar. They begged my pardon, retracted their words, and we parted very good friends.

I expected now the blasphemy of the multitude, and that fear would be on every side. Charles Perronet seemed to be sure there would be nobody at the preaching, but there were more than I have seen yet, and deeply attentive they seemed to the scripture I enforced, "Who shall separate us from the love of Christ? shall tribulation, or persecution, ...."[67] We called on Mrs. Felster, and met Mr. Millar[68] the Lutheran minister, a simple, loving man, but not quite so bold as Martin Luther. She would fain have persuaded him to let me preach in his church, being terrified to death by

---

[65] Samuel Powell (d. 1772), whose print shop was on Crane Lane.

[66] "A knot [or difficulty] worthy [of God] to untie." Horace, *Ars Poetica*, 191.

[67] Cf. Rom. 8:35.

[68] JW spells the name "Miller" in his *Journal*, Apr. 20, 1748, *Works*, 20:219. The pastor there in 1754 was actually Rev. Olaf Mollen.

their not finding the bill, and in all haste for us to quit the house before it was pulled down. Indeed, she has some small ground for her fear, for the mob declare openly they will not leave one stone upon another. But the bridle is in their mouth, and till the permission comes from above, they can neither touch that, nor one hair of our heads.

**Saturday, September 19.** Breakfasted at Mr. Adjets[69] and found him full of indignation at the injustice (as he called it) of the jury. He did not yet seem to know that Christians are looked upon as outlaws in all times and places. Had the Papists, he said, brung like bill against the Protestants for assaulting one of their mass houses, it would have been found. This I granted, but observed that our good Protestants are infinite[ly] nearer the Papists than they are to us.

Our audience both morning and evening were larger than usual. Mrs. Felster, on whom we called in our way to the room, was violent for our giving it up immediately, and determined to shut it up and suffer us to preach no more. But before we parted, the Lord turned her heart, melted her into tears, and reconciled her to his cross. We expect the messengers of Satan will be with her again ere long. It is owing to one of them, a neighbouring curate, that she had resolved to turn us out before we can procure another place. Indeed Satan has given a general alarm, and now the pulpits ring with cautions and declarations against us. At night our sister Pitney[70] took leave of us with a heavy heart, hardly expecting to see us again in the flesh.

**Sunday, September 20.** After commending ourselves and [our] cause to God, we walked to the Green without doubt or fear. Indeed, if we took counsel with flesh and blood, all appearances are against us. The mob, who neither fear God nor regard man,[71] have the utmost encouragement and assurance of impunity, do what they will to us. They see there is no justice for Christians and have probably heard that open declaration of one of the jury that they were determined to find no bill for the Swaddlers, unless for murder.

I would verily believe that <G>od would now show himself the helper of the forsaken and make bare his arm in our defence.[72] Going out, I cast my eye on Hebrews 11:27[–29], "By faith he forsook Egypt, not fearing the wrath of the king: for he endured, as seeing him who is invisible. Through faith he kept the passover, and the sprinkling of blood, lest he that destroyed the firstborn should touch them. By faith they passed

---

[69] In MS Journal CW spells "Aggits."

[70] This is likely Mary Pitney, an active member of the Foundery in London since 1743, who was returning to London (CW would greet her in a letter to London dated Oct. 3).

[71] See Luke 18:4.

[72] Cf. Isa. 52:10.

through the Red sea as by dry land, which the Egyptians assaying to do were drowned."

When I appeared on the Green, it soon gathered the people, Protestants and Papists, to whom I called in the name of my Lord, "Come unto me, all ye that labour and are heavy laden, and I will give you rest."[73] The power of the Lord was upon them, keeping down all opposition. I saw before that he could take this way, and immediately turn the hearts of the fiercest persecutors, and it was so. I spake particularly, and with great freedom, to the Papists, urging them to repentance and the love of Christ crucified by the authority of their own Kempis[74] and their own liturgy. All listened with strange attention. None lifted up his hand or voice. Many were in tears. The word had free course and was glorified. I advised them to go to their respective places of worship, and appointed to preach again at 3:00 in the afternoon, it being too late and near dark when the evening service was over. They expressed general satisfaction, especially the Papists. This also hath God wrought.

Returning, we were assaulted before we got home by some rude boys who threw dirt at us. Others began to gather and join them, when a serious Baptist came by and desired us to take shelter in his house. We stayed and breakfasted, and left him quite happy in having protected us from the violence of the people.

Communicated at St. Patrick's [cathedral]—with Christ and his members. The ordination kept us till 2:00. I hastened to Marlborough Street, gave a short word of exhortation to the society, which was much blessed, and drove straight to the Green. The holiday folk were there before me, it being the scene of all manner of diversions on Sunday afternoon. I lifted up my voice and cried, "Ho, every one that thirsts, come ye to the waters, and he that hath no money ...."[75] Again the Lord fought for Israel, and refrained the fierceness of men. A great multitude of serious hearers encompassed me, while those who had not ears to hear withdrew on every side to the opposite hill, sat down in rows on the grass, and there continued quiet during the whole time. I never saw the hand of God more visible. The greatest rioters, who were ready to tear the ground last Sunday, now never offered to speak or move, but left me to invite the rest in strong constraining words to come and buy wine and milk without money and without price. Surely this day was that scripture fulfilled, "Behold, I have set before thee an open door, and no man can shut it."[76]

---

[73] Matt. 11:28.

[74] Thomas à Kempis (1379?–1471). Both Wesley brothers frequently drew upon his spiritual classic *The Imitation of Christ*.

[75] Cf. Isa. 55:1–2.

76 Rev. 3:8.

Finished my discourse just [in] time so that all might go to church. Went to our own and half heard a miserable essay on anger. I wished the preacher would have entertained us with a comment of Seneca's upon Solomon, rather than with his own.

Spent the evening at Mr. Powell's with a few serious well-wishers in songs of praise and thanksgiving.

**Monday, September 21.**[77] Began visiting the classes. Many have received the sense of God's pardoning love; one under the word last week. But all are in earnest, justified or unjustified, and seem made without fear. I have not met with such soldiers before—so young and yet so valiant.

Called in the afternoon on a gentlewoman of Mr. Cennick's society. There were four or five more of the sisters, who have known, as far as I can discern, the grace of the Lord Jesus. Mr. Cennick has forbid them to hear, or even converse with any of us—after all the outcry of the still Brethren against us in London for warning our children how they hearkened to *their* errors.

At the room I was directed to Zechariah 13:9, "I will bring the third part through the fire, and will refine them as silver ...." Many strangers were present: and it was a time of visitation; such as I have not known before in Dublin.[78]

**Tuesday, September 22.** Spent the evening at our printer's,[79] and met a lady who was deeply affected with our prayers and hymns on occasion of the news just come hither, that Bergen-op-Zoom is taken.[80] We had great faith that the Lord in the Day of Visitation will spare them who fear him now, and speak often one to another.

**Wednesday, September 23.** Heard that on Sunday last, after I was gone, the Popish mob fell upon the women as they were going home, but were beaten by the soldiers and driven off.[81] They vow revenge, and threaten to come with all their forces next Sunday. I now clearly saw the providence of God in not suffering the soldiers, though so generally well-disposed, to attend the preaching. For nothing else could prevent their killing some of the rioters. Nay, it is with the utmost difficulty that our own people are restrained. Some have said, since the jury will not, they will do themselves justice, and have carried arms to defend themselves. The society, I hope, are all at last persuaded to turn the other cheek. But

---

[77] The journal letter DCW 6/18 (in CW's hand) starts here and runs through Sept. 29.

[78] DDCW 6/88a omits "before."

[79] Samuel Powell.

[80] During the Austrian War of Succession a French army laid siege to and captured the strategic Dutch border fortress of Bergen op Zoom on the border of Brabant and Zealand in 1747. Britain was an ally with the Dutch, helping defend the fortress.

[81] DDCW 6/88a shortens to "beaten off by the soldiers."

there are many of our well-wishers who cannot be kept from resisting evil, so that what to do with them, I see not.

In our passage to the room (a mile distant from our lodgings) the mob gathered and insulted us. But we took shelter in the house of a pious Baptist, Mr. H., who was much scandalized at such treatment of a minister of the Established Church, and sure if a Popish priest were so persecuted he would soon be screened by the magistrates. I believe so too. Error of every kind will meet with favour, but the world never did nor every will *tolerate* true Christianity.

**Thursday, September 24.** Called on Mrs. Felster, our landlady, a messenger of Satan now to buffet us. Our enemies' threatenings have so terrified her that she seems resolved to get us out of her room by one means or another. Our only comfort is God will provide, but how or when is quite hidden from us.

We gave ourselves unto prayer with the society, who greatly strengthen my hands by their steadfastness and obedience of faith.

The people, in our return, gaped upon us with their mouths, as so many romping and roaring lions. What is it restrains them from tearing us to pieces? They want neither will nor power. The jury have taken off the reins from the many-headed beast, and our Protestant brethren have sold us into their hands. I can resolve our deliverance into nothing but the miraculous power of God. No man lays hands on us because our hour is not yet come. Therefore are we safe among multitudes who would think they did God service, nay and even merited heaven, by killing us.

**Friday, September 25.** Passed the evening very agreeably at a Baptist's, a woman of piety and understanding, although a great admirer of my father's *Life of Christ*.[82] She doubly honoured me for his sake, and would needs lend me the book. I have given it a reading and subscribe to the author's own judgment of it—that the verses are (some of them) tolerable, the notes good, but the cuts best of all.

**Sunday, September 27.** My text at the Green this morning was "Behold the Lamb of God, who taketh away the sin of the world."[83] Never have I seen a quieter congregation at the Foundery. The word seemed to sink into all their hearts. Several of the poor soldiers were within hearing, though out of sight behind doors and walls, for fear of their officers. I could not help asking, "And where is the fury of the opposer?" It is the Lord's doing, who maketh even our enemies to be at peace with us.

But the great execution was to be this afternoon. I began at 2:00, an hour before the mob expected us. Very many wild, wicked people were present, but all with the bridle in their mouths. The Papists stood like

---

[82] Samuel Wesley (1662–1735), *The Life of our Blessed Lord & Saviour, Jesus Christ; an heroic poem* (London: Charles Harper, 1693).

[83] John 1:29.

lambs. I spoke largely of late in the praise of Kempis, and quoted some of his sayings, which has won their hearts, it seems, for the present. At least God used this small circumstance to mollify them. Nay, several of them, I am credibly informed, are confident that I am a good Catholic.

I called on a large audience, "Wash ye, make you clean; put away the evil of your doings from before my eyes; ... saith the Lord: ...."[84] Not one offered to interrupt by deed or word, but all gave heed to the words which were spoken. After I had exhorted them for above an hour to repentance and faith, they all departed in peace.

**Monday, September 28.** Our landlady yesterday nailed up our room in Marlborough Street, but we had it broke open for preaching this morning. We are now come to close quarters with the enemy, who threatens hard to drive us out of *his* kingdom.

I had an hour's conference today with two serious, sensible Quakers, who hold the head, and perfectly agree with us as to the One Foundation.[85]

**Tuesday, September 29.** Through much and swift walking I have brought back my old lameness. My namesake[86] is not much stouter than me. Our other labourers have little to do, till the door is opened wider. Therefore I thought of writing for our horses to meet us a fortnight hence at Holyhead. In the midst of these thoughts we heard of an house to be let. Whether it is one of God's providing will soon appear. However, I have deferred our departure to October 26, finding no choice of my own, one way or the other. If the Lord has any work for us here, or elsewhere, his will be done, when and as he pleases![87]

**Tuesday, September 29.**[88] In the evening preached "the kingdom of heaven is at hand: repent, and believe the gospel."[89] I intended to speak mostly of the kingdom of grace, but was led unawares to describe the glorious appearing of our Lord, and the word was as an hammer breaking the rocks in pieces. The cries of the wounded almost drowned my voice. One, as I heard afterwards, received a cure.

Called at Mr. Powell's and found Mr. Edwards there,[90] landlord to Mr. Cennick's society. His sister had said before that he was much dissatisfied

---

[84] Isa. 1:16–18.

[85] See 1 Cor. 3:11.

[86] Charles Perronet.

[87] The journal section of DDCW 6/18 ends at this point; but a personal letter to JW is appended. In DDCW 6/88a there is here a copy of a personal letter to Hannah Dewell, dated Oct. 6. Both letters can be found below at the end of transcribing the journal portion of DDCW 6/88a.

[88] The journal letter DDCW 6/19 (in CW's hand) starts here and runs through Oct. 10.

[89] Mark 1:15.

[90] Samuel Edwards, a Baptist schoolmaster, was an executor of a former Baptist meeting house in Skinner's Alley, Dublin that had been rented to John Cennick and the Moravians.

with his tenants, having under let their room, and would be glad to be fairly rid of them. My answer, I remember, was I would not for all the world take any man's house over his head.[91] Mr. Edwards declared tonight that he should raise their rent and asked if we should be willing to take the room in case they refused it. "If they had the offer of it first," I said, "and did not accept of it, we should then be glad of the next refusal." But I found not the least temptation to covet my neighbour's good, or to do to others as I would not they should do to me.

**Wednesday, September 30.** Breakfasted with one of Mr. Cennick's society, who at my request invited *him*. He brought with him Mr. La Trobe,[92] his assistant, and three or four others, and *his wife*.[93] I congratulated him on his alteration of judgment so much for the better, felt much love in my heart towards him, and *covered his* late treatment of me and my brother.

After preaching at night I was very hungry but found nothing at home to eat. I know how to abound; it is time I should know how to be in want.

**Friday, October 2.** Passed two hours with Mrs. Powell[94] and another Baptist gentlewoman in close experimental discourse. Almost they were persuaded to give up their faith of adherence (so called) for the faith of the gospel—which works by love and necessarily includes peace, joy, power, the witness of God's Spirit.

**Sunday, October 4.** The rain prevented my preaching in the morning (time was when it would not have prevented[95] me). After sacrament it cleared up, and I found a few people waiting for me at the Green, who quickly increased to a great multitude. I invited them to Christ by that most comfortable promise, "Him that cometh unto me I will in no wise cast out."[96] All were quiet, and seemingly affected. Many received the word gladly and believingly. From St. Luke's [church] I hastened to Mary-bone[97] Lane and alarmed an attentive multitude with those awful words, "The Lord himself shall descend from heaven with a shout, with the voice of the archangel, and with the trump of God."[98] Many trembled, and some rejoiced in hope of the glory of God. Both his threatenings and promises found a way into their hearts. I find no such blessing in Dublin as at this place.

---

[91] DDCW 6/88a omits this sentence.

[92] Benjamin La Trobe (1727–86), a young Baptist ministerial student, who had become a Moravian and in Mar. 1747 organized the Skinner's Alley people into a Moravian society.

[93] While he had previously maintained that he preferred to remain single, in mid-July 1747 Cennick had married Jane Bryant of Clack, Wiltshire.

[94] Hannah (Edwards) Powell, Samuel's second wife, whom he married in 1742.

[95] DDCW 6/88a changes "prevented" to "hindered."

[96] John 6:37.

[97] CW spells as either "Mary-bone" or "Marybone." It is now called "Marrowbone."

[98] 1 Thess. 4:16.

One at first lifted up his voice in curses (a Papist behind the wall), whom I heard cry in the end, "The Lord bless you, sir!"

**Monday, October 5.** Mr. Cennick called at my request, and I expostulated with him on the behaviour of some of his society who have much reviled me for "taking their house over their heads" as they called it. He assured me he was entirely satisfied that neither I nor my brother could do an unjust or unkind thing to him, when I promised him before I left the place to tell him simply all I knew of the matter of his house.

At 4:00 took the field again, and declared to many quiet hearers on the Green, "Ye have sold yourselves for nought; and ye shall be redeemed without money."[99] I thought the present opportunity was not to be slipped, now that the Lord has appeared in our behalf and stilled in good measure the raging of the sea, and the noise of his waves, and the madness of the people. Our enemies concluded, when the jury refused us justice, that we should be immediately scattered and come to nought. But God frustrateth the tokens of the liars, and maketh diviners mad.[100] He takes the wise in their own craftiness,[101] and makes all these things work together for good and the furtherance of the gospel.[102] The rich indeed fled and escaped for their lives, but the poor, despised followers of Jesus were driven closer together by the storm, and stood as a rock in the midst of the waves. Not one turned back. A few, who at first were for standing in their own defence against the bloodthirsty Papists, were soon brought off their design of resisting evil, and committed their cause to him that judgeth righteously.[103]

We continued instant in prayer that God might touch the hearts of the magistrates and turn them towards us. The coming of the Lord Lieutenant,[104] on the very day when I first preached out, gave some check to the rioters though they were very sure "he would put us all down." But if any have applied to him for this purpose, I may be bold to say he did not give them such an answer as they desired. This, we find by the effects, for we can now walk the street without such manifest danger of our lives.

It was likewise of some service to us, the late Mayor's[105] sending so many of the vulgar rioters to prison. And the delay of the jury damped the principal rioters, or great vulgar, so that for want of their encouragement the mob grew heartless in the cause.

---

[99] Isa. 52:3.

[100] See Isa. 44:25.

[101] See Job 5:13.

[102] See Rom. 8:28.

[103] See 1 Pet. 2:23.

[104] The Lord Lieutenant of Ireland was the official representative of the British government; at that time, William Stanhope, 1st Earl of Harrington (1683–1756).

[105] William Walker's term as Lord Mayor ended on Sep. 29, 1747.

But the chief means God has used for restraining them was the Lord Chief Baron's[106] speech last week to the new mayor,[107] wherein he spake favourably of the Methodists as innocent, loyal people and severely of our persecutors, charging the Mayor to protect us from their violence; who thereupon issued out an order against riots, prohibiting in particular their kicking football in the Green on Sunday, while *any were preaching* there.

A Church minister likewise helped by preaching a severe sermon last Sunday against the persecutors, so that they say I hired him for the purpose. But surely God raised him up for the purpose, and to him be all the glory. The help that is done upon earth he doth it himself.[108] "Because thou hast been our helper, therefore under the shadow of thy wings will we rejoice."[109]

He hides us in the hallow of his hand *today*, and let him look to the morrow. When it is best that persecution should return, it will return—and not one moment sooner.

**Tuesday, October 6.** Preached again on the Green at 3:00, and walked away, the whole length of the city, to Marlborough Street. Great was the cry after Jesus, the Son of David, while I expounded blind Bartimaeus.[110]

**Wednesday, October 7.** In my way from the Green to the room called on Mrs. Dunn of Mr. Cennick's society and found her in much trouble through their violent treatment of her, merely for her love to us. Of all the Christians I have known, I have never met with any so straitened and bigoted as the Germans and their followers, so impotent of mind and so impatient of contradiction.

**Thursday, October 8.** Observed several soldiers in my congregation this afternoon, who venture to hear notwithstanding the prohibition. Now and then an officer comes by, and stops to see if any of their men are there, and then they skulk down kneeling or sitting on the ground behind the women. Near twenty of them were present today, and received the word with the utmost eagerness.

In Marlborough Street a brother met me with Mr. Crampton, one of the famous jury, who had openly declared, "If the mob threw all the preachers into the river, he would not find the bill." This gentleman is now come to help us to a preaching-house or a place to build one. The person who found it out for us is Mr. M—, one of the worst persecutors we had in Dublin, but who is now exceedingly set upon getting us a place *in his* neighbourhood. There is not in all the city a more convenient spot,

---

[106] The Lord Chief Baron was the senior judge in Ireland, a post held by John Bowes (1691–1767).

[107] Sir George Ripton was sworn in as Lord Mayor on Sep. 29, 1747.

[108] See Ps. 74:13 (BCP).

[109] Cf. Ps. 63:7 (BCP).

[110] Mark 10:46–52.

being in the center and inaccessible by a mob on all sides, and called "the Foundery." Mr. Crampton, when asked if he would let it to us, answered, "Yes; or to [the] Pope himself, if he will pay me well for it." It looks thus far as if the hand of God was in it, but time will fully show us his will concerning us.

Exhorted the society to walk as becometh the gospel, and in particular not to render evil for evil or railing for railing. To the reproaches cast upon one by the other society, I advised, "Answer them not a word, but leave the matter to God entirely."

**Friday, October 9.** Some days since there was not a man in Dublin who would let us a room, but now we have the offer of several houses. I saw one this morning, a new stone house and garden to be sold for a third of its worth, near Mary-bone Lane, where our greatest harvest is.

Called on Mr. Crampton, who will not let us the ground unless we take an adjoining house for the same term of years. If this be the place which God has designed us, all obstacles will be removed.

He is daily adding to our number, and will he not "enlarge our coast?"[111] This evening I admitted two more into the society; one of them a Papist, whom we caught in the Green.

**Saturday, October 10.**[112] Gave earnest for the brother's house, and dedicated it by prayer unto God.

Preached once more at the Green to many serious people. It has been remarkably fair weather all this week, and we have not had the least interruption by Protestant or Papist. All praise, all glory be to Jesus, the strength of Israel![113]

**Sunday, October 11.**[114] Preached on the Green to about 2,000 hearers, as quiet and well-behaved as any in Moorfields. At 2:00 the congregation was double, and equally serious. Only one Papist flung away in a rage, crying, "I ought to be stabbed for lumping them all together and telling them they might all be saved, of whatsoever church or party, if they would but go like the prodigal to their Father."[115] Many of the Church of Rome, as well as our own, seemed to be men of better spirit, and gave diligent heed to *their own* history, and will, I trust, occasion joy in heaven over them.

Went with the utmost reluctance to Mary-bone Lane, longing to find John Trembath or some other to preach in my place. It was so dark I could not see him, but heard his voice after I had begun and could not retreat.

---

[111] Cf. 1 Chron. 4:10.

[112] CW took over for Perronet, writing the entry for Oct. 10 in DDCW 6/88a.

[113] The journal section of DDCW 6/19 ends at this point; but a personal letter to JW (dated Oct. 13) is appended, which is placed below at the end of the transcription of DDCW 6/88a.

[114] DDCW 6/88a reverts to the hand of Charles Perronet.

[115] CW had apparently been preaching his sermon on the prodigal son (Luke 15:11–32).

What through weariness and aversion to the work I forgot to pray before I named my text, "Repent and believe the gospel."[116] I had scarce uttered the word when the Spirit of our Lord came down like a flood. The yard (containing above 500) and house were crowded with poor wounded sinners, whose cries compelled me several times to break off and give out a suitable verse or two. Almost every person present was in tears, either of sorrow or joy. We continued above an hour singing and crying. Such a time of refreshing I have not known since I left England. We expect to hear that the Lord has at this time restored the kingdom to some hearts and comforted his mourners.

Passed the evening with Mrs. Meecham,[117] a true mourner in Sion till Wednesday last, when the Lord put the new song in her mouth. She had been awakened by Mr. Cennick and in great doubt whether she ought not to continue hearing and following him *farther* than he followed Christ. Since he fell into the German errors, she has left him; but declared to the Lord in prayer that she would simply follow his will, and immediately her heart was quite set at liberty from Mr. Cennick, and a day or two after she found the pearl.[118] We rejoiced over her and with her, for she set us all on fire with the warmth of her first love. O that it may never cool! O that all who ever knew the grace of the Lord Jesus were fervent now as in the months that are past! Come, Lord Jesus, that we may have life, and that we may have it more abundantly.[119]

**Monday, October 12.** Called on Mr. Crampton, who will not let us have the ground for less than twice its value. How strange are we two met together—one who knows as much, the other as little of the world as most men in it! And yet a secret friend in whom I confide will see that he does me no wrong, nor the people through my ignorance.

**Tuesday, October 13.** Several who never heard the word send for us to pray by them when they are sick. I talked with one today who seemed throughly convinced of sin and desirous of a saviour. The neighbours flocked in, to hear the prayer and exhortation, to whom I had an opportunity of preaching Christ the justifier. Such seasons should never be lost.

Passed the afternoon at our house near Dolphin's Barn,[120] and was almost tempted to say "Soul, take thy ease!"[121] Prayed with some of the

---

[116] Mark 1:15.

[117] She was a widow, the sister of Ruth (Bertrand) Handy, and thus sister-in-law of Samuel Handy of Coolalough, whom she introduced into Methodism. See Crookshank, *Ireland*, 1:22–24.

[118] See Matt. 13:46.

[119] See John 10:10.

[120] Dolphin's Barn was a village on the southeast side of Dublin; the house was on Cork Street.

[121] See Luke 12:19.

brethren that our coming hither might be blessed to our new neighbours and could not help taking notice of the scripture that first offered, "They shall come, and the heavens shall declare his righteousness unto people that shall be born, whom the Lord hath made."[122]

Preached at Mary-bone Lane from Hebrews 13:14, "Here have we no continuing city, but we seek one to come." We received the never-failing blessing, even brought some steps on our journey toward the new Jerusalem.

**Thursday, October 15.** God, even our own God, gave us his blessing while we were assembled together with him in the midst. Great fellowship we had with all our absent brethren, particularly those at the Foundery. Our souls seemed one with theirs, and continued long time crying and following hard after God. Surely the word has taken root in this people's heart, and shall grow up in all the fruits of righteousness.

**Saturday, October 17.** Administered the sacrament to one who had received the grace of our Lord and lost it through pride. She now appeared deeply wounded, and inconsolable for Christ. Her sickness, we trust, will teach her not to blaspheme or rob God of his glory. The door of hope was opened again before we left her.

Passed the day at the house we have lately purchased [in Dolphin's Barn], writing and meditating. I could almost have said "Soul, take thine ease!"[123]—But I must not find rest in any garden except the garden of paradise.

Heard (as I do every day) of more souls who have received the atonement.

**Sunday, October 18.** Preached the gospel to the poor (and a rich man here and there intermixed) at 8:00 and 2:00. The rain swept away scarce any. It held up while I described at night our Lord's coming to judgment in his own words, Matthew 25. The yard and house was too narrow for the congregation, who all seemed all stirred up to wait for his appearing. Their earnest cries gave me great confidence of meeting them among the sheep at his right hand.

**October 19, Monday.**[124] Dined at a gentleman's whose heart, as it seems, God has turned towards us, so that he offers us a large convenient piece of ground to build on, at a very moderate price. We doubt not but our Lord will show us his will and direct us into every work which he has purposed for us to walk in. The time for building seems come, now that the magistrates are so favourable. The mayor has declared he will send

---

[122] Cf. Ps. 22:31.

[123] See Luke 12:19.

[124] CW took over for Perronet, writing the entry for Oct. 19 in DDCW 6/88a.

any man to Newgate[125] who only calls after us in the streets. Not that we are so vain as to think all the authority of man can long screen those who will live godly in Christ Jesus from suffering persecution.

In the evening explained (in Paul's) the commission of a gospel minister. A clergyman was of my audience and expressed his approbation of the truth.

**Tuesday, October 20.**[126] Waited, at her desire, on an aged gentlewoman who accosted me with "Sir, I sent for you to ask you a few questions, that if I find you wronged, I may be an advocate, otherwise an adversary." Her first interrogatory was whether I gave the sacrament to our people privately, and extorted a shilling from each every time of communicating. I easily and full satisfied her. She has read our books, she told me, and could not help believing that our design was to revive primitive Christianity; and therefore whosoever is on God's side, must be on ours. Our taking so much pains, she added, confirmed her in her opinion of us and the improbable stories our adversaries tell of us determined her to inquire of me and hear with her own ears. She desired me to go to prayers with the family, and to see her again, as she was confined by lameness, as often as I could.

**Wednesday, October 21.** I had promised Mrs. [Agnes] Felster our landlady (to make her easy) that the first time the mob came to make a riot I would go out to them, and thenceforth preach no more in her room. But the bridle has been so in their mouth that from my entrance into this day, not one rioter has appeared within the walls at the time of preaching. Yet, as her importunity increases, and she pleads a sort of promise of mine, and offers to excuse our making good the damage if we will quit the room directly, at last I have agreed with the advice of the church, to give it up. Accordingly, this evening I preached on the Good Samaritan[127] with divine assistance, and next morning, for the last time, on our Lord's appearing. Our hearts were greatly comforted together.

**[Thursday, October 22.]** Breakfasted with a serious Baptist who would fain make converts of Charles Perronet and me. I heard her arguments and accepted her books without the least inclination to contradict her. Suffice for the time past, that we laid the whole stress on externals. Let us settle *them* (still say I), but *first* become new creatures.

Met the society once more in Marlborough Street, and a greater blessing in the midst than ever. Our landlady was present and brought to her tears by my warnings against covetousness. Our friendly lawyer also and his wife, the first affected like the poor publican. They passed the rest

---

[125] Newgate prison, in Dublin.

[126] The journal letter DDCW 6/20 (in CW's hand) starts here and runs through Oct. 28. Perronet picks up again as the transcriber in DDCW 6/88a.

[127] Luke 10:29–37.

of the evening with us and our singers, and went away not a little pleased with their entertainment.

**Friday, October 23.** Met the few scattered sheep at our sister Crump's, just opposite to our old room, and had sweet fellowship with them in prayer and the word. She agrees to let us the upper floor to preach in, that the poor people may be kept together.

Soon after I got home she sent me word that she durst not let me the room, because her father threatened to cast her off upon hearing of it, and her landlord to turn her out of the house. I cannot but observe how hard Satan fights for his kingdom. We are forced to dispute every inch of ground with him. At present he seems to have got an advantage and driven us off that part of his ground, which is occupied by the rich.

Opened our house at the other end of the town[128] with solemn prayer. These are more noble than the gentry, being mostly poor and vulgar. Near 200 joined in earnest supplication for our Church, and the success of the gospel to be preached in this place.[129]

Visited a sick man who has been convinced, without hearing the word, by reading my brother's sermons and justified, as far as I can discern, by the immediate voice of Christ.

**Saturday, October 24.** John Trembath preached this morning at sister Crump's, which so alarmed our old landlady that she flew from her own proposals and refused to release us of our bargain. If we preached in the neighbourhood, she said, it was as bad or worse than preaching in her room. Therefore, she would compel us to keep it, which I am now resolved to do, being clear in my own conscience and before God and man. Accordingly, one preached there this evening and

**Sunday, October 25**, between 6:00 and 7:00 in the morning to a larger company than has been seen there for a long time. I spake meantime to the society assembled at my lodgings. Then to a great congregation at the Green from John, "And I, if I be lifted up from the earth, will draw all men unto me!"[130] The word took place, and many followed the drawings.

Passed three hours under my usual burden, among the dry bones of the house of Israel; at St. Patrick, I mean, in public prayer and the sacrament. How different the Spirit here from that in our chapel at London![131] I seldom enter this place, but the zealots are ready to drag me out, like that old profaner of the temple, Paul. Such murmuring, disputing, railing, and

---

[128] I.e., the house in Dolphin's Barn.

[129] DDCW 6/88a reads: "supplication for our Church, and the success of our Church, and the success of the gospel."

[130] John 12:32.

[131] CW is referring to the chapel at the intersection of West Street and St. Martin's Lane in London, just south of the "Seven Dials" intersection. It had been built by Huguenot refugees about 1700, at which time it was approved for full sacramental services. The Wesley brothers took a lease on the chapel in the mid 1740s.

loud abuse the very sight of me occasions that I can compare the house of God to nothing but a den of thieves and murderers.

The Dean indeed I must except and give honour to whom honour is due.[132] He has always behaved toward us with great courtesy and love; looks pleased to see us make the bulk of the communicants; appointed us a seat for ourselves (but the underling officers soon thrust us out); and constantly administers the sacrament to me first, as the order of our Church requires.

Stood our ground in the Green for half an hour in the rain. Gave the sacrament to a poor dying youth who seems not far from the blood of sprinkling. Went to church at St. Catherine and walked thence, at half hour past 5:00 in the dark and dirt to Dolphin's Barn. Mr. Perronet had by mistake given notice of my preaching there *after* evening service. I should never have chosen to *begin* in the night and before our windows were secured by shutters, but was now compelled to it, sorely against my will. The house, I found, would not hold a fourth of the congregation, and therefore stood in the garden under the house-wall. Between 1,000 and 2,000 stood in the open air and drank in the strange glad tidings. My text was "Comfort ye, comfort ye my people, saith your God."[133] He was sensibly present, as the God of all consolation. The neighbours, and those who had never heard the word before, received it with all readiness of mind. I found this is the place which God hath chosen and prayed in faith that here the gathering of the people might be!

John Trembath was preaching at the same time to a yard full [of] serious hearers in Mary-bone Lane. We met soon after 7:00 at our lodgings. I expected the society only, but hundreds were crammed together in all the rooms and stairs to hear the word. I was quite exhausted with preaching four times today already and walking several miles, but the Lord gave me fresh strength to expound his meeting with Zaccheus. I feared, one of our lodgers, a Papist, would be offended, but he was wonderfully pleased, and many others comforted together with me. Our brother Verney especially, who could truly say, "This day is salvation come to this house!"[134]

It was near 9:00 before the company went, and then I found myself as fresh and strong as in the morning.

**Monday, October 26.** Began visiting the classes. Took in several new members, and put out others who had been too hastily admitted by our helpers. It strengthened my hands to find some who have received forgiveness in hearing me, as well as the other preachers. One man especially, who on my declaring in the society I know our brethren in London are now praying for us, and the Spirit is come from them to us—in

---

[132] The current Dean of St. Patrick's cathedral was Rev. Francis Corbett (1688–1775).

[133] Isa. 40:1.

[134] Luke 19:9.

that instant he found the peace of God, and rejoiced with the unspeakable joy of faith and love.

Preached again in the evening at our old house, which was fuller than ever I saw it before. How wisely does God bring good out of evil! Through the covetousness of our landlady we have got our room again, and hope to stay in it till we have shaken Satan's kingdom.

**Tuesday, October 27.** Met, in visiting the classes, with one who received forgiveness, as he now informs me, while I was giving the society an account of the seven malefactors I attended to Tyburn, who all died in Christ and full assurance of faith that they should be with him that day in paradise.[135]

**Wednesday, October 28.** Dined at Mr. [John] Cennick's, who comes forward with his wife, if not *in*, yet *toward* the narrow way. At night he called upon us, to look over our writings and secure us against all fraud in our purchase of the house.[136] This also hath God wrought, and given us the heart of this man, both for his own good and ours.[137]

**Wednesday, October 28.**[138] Prayed by our sister Baker, whom I had late[ly] checked for her too great contempt of death, as it seemed to me. The trying time is come, yet she keeps her confidence.

**Friday, October 30.** Kept the intercession at Dolphin's Barn and preached to many attentive souls from Ezekiel 9. In our return we were stoned for the length of a street or two. Charles Perronet interposed his back to screen me. Here I received the first blow since I came to Dublin. Mr. Coates met us, once more, while the holiday folk were pursuing us, and encouraged us to go on, without regarding them. Near our lodgings they took their leave of us, without hurting either.

**Saturday, October 31.** Dined at Mrs. Gibson's, and heard the best news of any since our coming hither, namely that our sister Baker was just departed in full triumph. To one who asked her this morning how she did, she answered "bravely, bravely. Never better!" The pains of death had then got hold on her, but she smiled on the welcome messenger, took leave of her husband and children with calm joy, expressed great satisfaction at having chosen to suffer affliction with the people of God, confirmed them in the same happy choice, and soon after fell asleep and woke in paradise.

I called at the house, as well to exhort the mourners as to see the late temple of the Holy Ghost. The happy soul had left a smile on the clay

---

[135] See CW, MS Journal, July 13–19, 1738.

[136] The preaching house on Skinner's Alley.

[137] The journal section of DDCW 6/28 ends at this point; but a personal letter to JW (dated Oct. 29) is appended, which is placed below at the end of the transcription of DDCW 6/88a.

[138] The journal letter DDCW 6/21 (in CW's hand) starts here and runs through Nov. 6.

to tell where she was gone. We were all much comforted in prayer, and thanksgiving.

Preached for the last time in Mary-bone Lane from Revelation 7[:14], "These are they that came out of great tribulation, ...." It was a time of solemn rejoicing in hope of that day when all tears shall be wiped from our eyes.

**Sunday, November 1.** Met the society for the first time at 5:00 in Marlborough Street. Most of them were present and the Lord in the midst. I left our brethren to preach and walked to the Green, where I found a large and quiet audience.

At St. Patrick['s cathedral], Mr. K.[139] entertained us with a discourse so full of low pitiful lies and nonsense, as I have never heard from any except the ingenious Mr. Hoblyn.[140] I went from church to the Green; and from discoursing there half an hour, hastened to Dolphin's Barn. Our garden which holds near 3,000 was almost full. I called to many who had ears to hear, "The time is fulfilled, the kingdom of God is at hand: repent ye, and believe the gospel."[141] They heard with surprising attention. Not one disturbed us by deed or word; neither in departure through the city. It was half [an] hour past 5:00 when I came to my lodgings, and found them crowded with strangers, near 400 by computation, to whom I enforced our Lord's most gracious saying, "Behold, I stand at the door, and knock: if any man hear my voice, and open the door, I will come in to him, and sup with him, and he with me."[142] Many heard and opened, I am persuaded, in that hour. We continued in the word, and prayer, and rejoicing till near 8:00. As my day, so is my strength.[143] Preaching five times is no more than twice a day when the order of providence calls us to it. My strength do I ascribe unto thee, and all my success, and all my blessings!

**Monday, November 2.** Preached Jesus, Saviour from sin, at 6:00 in my lodgings, and he gave us a plain token that this is his will concerning us. We intend to continue the preaching here, morning and evening, till our new house is fitted up. I admitted five or six into the society and among them the soldier who was put under arrest last Sunday for the high crime and misdemeanour of *hearing a sermon* at the Green. The officers, after much threatening, let him go, but he continues refractory still, and resolved to work out his salvation.

---

[139] Most likely Rev. James King (d. 1759), Prebendary of Tipper at St. Patricks, 1737–59 (the only prebendary with a last name starting in "K").

[140] Rev. William Hoblyn, curate of St. Ives (see July 17, 1743 above).

[141] Mark 1:15.

[142] Rev. 3:20.

[143] See Deut. 33:25.

**Tuesday, November 3.**[144] Called in the evening on Mr. [Samuel] Powell, where I found Mr. [Samuel] Edwards, landlord to Mr. Cennick. He told me the German society had refused his proposals, which if I liked of, I might now have his house.[145] I consented that some of our society should talk with him about it. But the next day on second thoughts, and to cut off occasion from them <to> seek it, I sent Mr. Edwards word that I would have nothing to do with it till the time was up, and his old tenants had finally refused it. Not that I am so vain as to think they will not slander us (if we succeed them five years hence), and cry we have taken their house over their heads. All my concern is to do as I would be done by, to keep a conscience void of offence, and to avoid all appearance of evil.[146]

**Thursday, November 5.** Exhorted the society to walk as becometh the gospel[147] and rejoiced in their steady and orderly walking thus far. This day we set apart for seeking God in prayer and fasting, being utterly at a loss what to do? Whom to send to England, of our preachers, and whom to keep here. The reasons on both sides appear so equal that we have no way to determine but by lot. Accordingly, on

**Friday, November 6**, our family met at 5:00 as usual (after spending an hour each in private), and we prayed and cast lots. The lot fell on John Trembath, who entirely acquiesced with us all in the will of providence. Near a fortnight, the contrary wind has detained our brother Skelton,[148] that he might stay and take company with him.

The people have come before their time, every morning, some before 5:00, so that we shall be even forced to our old hour of preaching. I began at half hour past 5:00 this morning, and our hearts were melted down by the sight of Christ crucified.[149]

**Friday, November 6.**[150] Having tried all other ways in vain, at last we put it to the determination of lots who should go to England, and the lot fell upon John Trembath. Afterwards, it was made plain to us all by many concurrent providences that this was the thing to be done.

**Saturday, November 7.** Prayed by a young man near death. When we first visited him he was quite unawakened, but is now saved from fear of death and hell, and waits patiently for the great salvation of God. We had

---

[144] The text for Nov. 3, Nov. 5, and the first entry for Nov. 6 is found only in DDCW 6/21.

[145] The preaching house on Skinner's Alley.

[146] See Matt. 7:12, Acts 24:16, and 1 Thess. 5:22.

[147] See Phil. 1:27.

[148] Charles Skelton (c. 1725–98), a native of Ireland, had just offered himself as one of JW's traveling preachers. He soon chafed under JW's hand. He settled in Bury St. Edmunds as a Dissenting minister in 1754, and later was an Independent minister in Southwark.

[149] DDCW 6/21 ends here.

[150] The only text from this point through Feb. 6 is found in DDCW 6/88a.

several such instances of persons departing in the Lord, who never heard the gospel till we preached it to them on their deathbeds.

**Sunday, November 8.** Met the society at 5:00. Preached at 8:00 on the Green, at 2:00 to a great multitude in our garden, and in the evening to as many as our lodgings could contain. The Lord still giving testimony to the word of his grace.[151]

**Monday, November 9.** Many strangers flocked to the word in Ship Street. I spoke (never closer) from our Lord's words, "I am come that they might have life, and that they might have it more abundantly."[152]

**Tuesday, November 10.** Preached this evening at a new place in Hanbury Lane. The house was let us by a lawyer in prison. But as it is an hired house, and next door to a very warm antagonist of ours, the Rev. Mr. Nisbet, we do not expect to continue long unmolested. Three nights, however, we have preached the gospel, no man forbidding us, except the minister, who set on the boys to pelt us the first time.

**Thursday, November 12.** Hearing that the landlord and minister had procured a mob to hinder our preaching, I would not suffer any of the preachers or people to expose themselves at Hanbury Lane this evening. In the night our adversaries (who till then had waited for us in vain) broke into the house and took possession.

**Monday, November [23].** Preached after 2:00, and again after 5:00, at the [Dolphin's] Barn, where the word never returns void. We have now preaching twice a day at this place, and Marlborough Street, and our lodgings in Ship Street.

**Wednesday, November 25.** Rode six miles out of town with Mr. [Samuel] Powell to Mr. Smalley, a relation of his and one who greatly admired Mr. Cennick till he began preaching his peculiar doctrines. How many souls have been stumbled hereby, if not utterly turned out of the way! Therefore, they who perverted him have the greater sin.

**Thursday, November 26.** Having got our builder from London, and the prospect of another place just by us more promising than my other, I spent this day in walking about and taking subscriptions for the building. At night proposed it to the society, who were glad to give of their little. This and the day following was subscribed upward of £70.

**Friday, December 4.** Having purged out several from the society, which had been hastily taken in, I divided the rest into thee companies, to meet at the three preaching places on Monday, Friday, and Sunday night. I have met and spoke to the first several, and the Lord was with us of a truth.

**Monday, December 7.** Passed an hour at Mr. Millar's, the Lutheran minister who favoured me with a sight of Count [Nicholas] Zinzendorf's

---

[151] See Acts 14:3.
[152] John 10:10.

famous declaration against my brother and me,[153] (which shall I most admire, the weakness or the vanity of the man?) and likewise his translation of the New Testament.[154] We looked for St. James's epistle, but he was not to be found, the Count having thrust him out of the canon *by his own authority*.

At midnight I was raised by a dying child, brought into my room to be baptized.

**Sunday, December 13.** We had a large increase of communicants at St. Patrick's [cathedral]. They were mostly of the society, who came for example's, as well as the commandment's, sake. The good dean[155] expressed his approbation at the sight.

**Monday and Tuesday [December 14 and 15].** Had great rejoicing over our lately departed sister Witham.[156] Her dying prayers for me I found strengthening my hands, and confirming my hope of shortly following her.

**Wednesday, December 16.** Seldom have I been more alive than in the morning preaching, or more dead than in the evening.

**Saturday, December 19.** Spake at night from John 1[:12], "As many as received him, to them gave he power to become the sons of God." I was unavoidably led to warn the hearers against receiving Christ by halves, or so magnifying one of his offices, as to slight or deny the others.[157] The Priest must not swallow up the King, nor the Saviour the Lord. To dwell on his love *only*, without regarding his power and majesty, would make them turn the grace of Christ into wantonness, and talk of his blood in the most horrid, irreverent manner. I quoted that line of the German hymns,

> What is it that in all your meetings resounds?
> [...]
> Wounds, wounds, again wound-holes, and *nothing* but wounds:[158]

---

[153] This declaration was included in a letter that James Hutton published in The Daily Advertiser, Aug. 2, 1745 (letter dated July 24, 1745). A summary of Zinzendorf's comments, and JW's letter in reply can be found in Works 26:150–51.

[154] Nikolaus Zinzendorf, *Eines abermahligen Versuchs zur Übersetzung der historischen Bücher des Neuen Testaments unsers Herrn Jesu Christi* (Büdingen: J. C. Stöhr, 1739).

[155] Rev. Francis Corbett.

[156] Elizabeth (Harrison) Witham, an active member at the Foundery in London, died Nov. 29, 1747. See CW's published elegy, "On the Death of Mrs. Elizabeth Witham," *HSP* (1749), 1:282–86.

[157] See CW's hymn on this passage making the same point: *HSP* (1749), 2:181–84.

[158] Hymn 393, st. 4, in *A Collection of Hymns, With several translations from the Hymn-book of the Moravian Brethren* (London: Hutton, 1746) 2:735.

and heard how much wiser such writers are than the oracles of God. One or two who were too nearly concerned in my censure went away saying I spake against the blood of Christ and should certainly be damned unless I repented. The congregation seemed so affected as they ought to be.

**Wednesday, December 23.** A young man fetched me to his master's, a merchant with whom and his brother a clergyman I had much serious discourse. Another minister came in and heard me patiently in defence of this way, which they seemed almost to believe was no schism, n<or new> religion, but the very faith once delivered to the saints. One of the clergymen invited me to his lodgings in the college,[159] that we may have further conversation on this matter.

**Thursday, December 24.** We had much of the spirit of prayer in the society. O that the time were come when we shall pray always.

**Friday, Christmas Day.** The people met at my lodgings between 3:00 and 4:00. It was a day of rejoicing. So were the three following, suitable to the solemn occasion.

**Monday, December 28.** Prayed by a constant hearer of the word, who was walking through the valley of the shadow of death, and feared no evil. The next morning he departed in peace with that word, "Into thy hands I commend my spirit."[160]

A fortnight ago we sent a preacher[161] into the country, who now writes as follows:

> We reached Tyrrellspass, a little town about forty miles from Dublin on Thursday. I preached in an empty house to 500 or 600 people, who received the word with great attention. Next morning's audience was more numerous. They flocked from all parts to hear the glad tidings. Invited them to buy wine and milk without money and without price.[162] Their hearts were melted as before the fire, and many told me they would go ten miles to hear such comfortable doctrine. Surely a door is opened here for preaching the everlasting gospel.
> 
> Friday night I rode six miles farther, and preached at Mr. Handy's house.[163] The people looked at me as if I came from the clouds, being a mixed company of Churchmen, Dissenters, and Papists.
> 
> Saturday morning many more came to hear. They seem better reconciled than last night—but seem perishing for lack of knowledge.

---

[159] This is presumably Trinity College, Dublin.

[160] Luke 23:46.

[161] This was surely Thomas Williams (see CW's comment on Feb. 9, 1749 below), whom CW avoids naming due to distrust from the earlier episode where Williams treated CW falsely.

[162] Isa. 55:1.

[163] Samuel Handy (1713–79), who had been introduced to Methodism by his sister-in-law, Mrs. Meecham, owned a manor named Coolalough, just south of Horseleap, Co. Westmeath, Ireland; 6 miles west of Tyrrellspass.

In the next letter he informs us:

> I preach twice a day. About 600 came to hear me the first hour at Tullamore in the marketplace. Most behaved very careless at the beginning, but toward the middle of my discourse gave diligent heed. The mouths of gainsayers were stopped, or constrained to own it is the truth of God. The poor Papists are my constant attendants, and receive the word gladly notwithstanding the severe penances their priests lay upon them.
> The gentleman[164] where our brother is, sent word that he preaches with great success. My house is full of people, half of them Romans, who seem closely touched. Sunday morning he preached at Kilbeggan parish, to a great congregation of Churchmen, Presbyterians, Baptists, and Romans, to the satisfaction of all. The Romans in Kilbeggan parish are to fast three days in a week on bread and water for hearing mass, but they disobey the priest's order, and say, they will have him <killed?>.

**Tuesday, December 29.** Received another letter as follows:

> Tyrrellspass
> St. Stephen's Day [December 26]
>
> I have preached again in Tullamore. The harvest truly is great. About 2,000 attended yesterday. I met many, many attentive souls here at 4:00 in the morning and preached and sang and rejoiced truly. In the evening we had a large congregation of Romans, Churchmen, and Dissenters—many of them Quakers. The whole company was in tears. You would rejoice, dear sir, to see the work which is begun in this part of the vineyard. O for more labourers! We stand in great need of them. Lord send them speedily!

[[**Friday, January 8 [1748]**. Went mourning all the day long under b[urden] of s[uffering].[165] Mr. Cennick came and said he was satisfied I had acted fairly till now, but had just heard I had bidden Edwards £18 for our house. I simply denied it. Then he attacked [John] Haughton,[166] and said one was ready to make oath that he heard him make the offer to Edwards, Haughton answered he had never spoke to Edwards and offered to go face the man immediately. In talk Cennick said it was not fair in my

---

[164] Likely Samuel Handy.

[165] Shorthand indicates two words, beginning with "b" and "s," joined by "and" or "of." Other expansions are possible.

[166] John Haughton (d. 1781), a weaver in Chinley End, Derbyshire, became one of JW's early traveling preachers, mentioned as a special Assistant in Yorkshire in 1746. He had just been sent to assist CW in Ireland, and would spend the remainder of his ministry there. In 1755 he is listed as a Methodist local preacher in Dublin. In 1759 he secured episcopal ordination from the Bishop of Derry (William Barnard), and appointment as rector of Kilrea, Londonderry, where he "cordially received" JW in 1778.

brother to blame all the Brethren for the mistakes of a few, and soon after forgetting himself. When I would have excused the church, he said no, no; What one holds, all hold. They will agree to whatever their preachers have said. He said I had denied s[ervice] to all sects that commune in his hearing. I replied it was not the first lie he had told me to my face, and he unawares answered "And probably it would not be the last." He went and embittered Battersbys[?[167]] against us by lies. I granted his desire of staying till he should try all his interest with Edwards for the house. Saw Edwards soon after, who told me Cennick said I would have nothing to do with the house, therefore he might as well as let him have it. I told Cennick the very reverse.

[[Edwards called in the afternoon and would have engaged me to sign the writings immediately. I waived it till Cennick should make his last experiment[?].

[[**Friday, January [15**[168]**].** Heard more good news of the success of the gospel in the country. A Turk[169] returned.

[[**Wednesday, January 20.** Mr. [Charles] Perronet, without my knowledge, had told the society last night in Dolphin's Barn that he intended to go to Mr. [John] Cennick and ask if he had any farther pretensions to the house; and if not, he would take it himself for our society. Then went to Cennick with Edwards and heard all his ill-grounded complaints, which Edwards answered and finally refused him the house, lest he should keep possession when he had it.

[[Mr. [Samuel] Handy brought us glad tidings from the country, which made me eager to be with him.

[[In meeting the leaders found one or two of the steadiest shook by the foul slanders of the still Brethren. Seconded by honest John Healey, who fears I suppose if we take that house we shall not be in such haste to build.

[[**Thursday, January 21.** Met the society and expostulated with them on their many faults toward God and toward man. They were melted into tears, especially when I talked of leaving them. This evening Mr. Edwards and [Mr.] Wilkinson, another trustee who has given Cennick his final refusal.

[[**Friday, January 22.** In heaviness through the foul-mouthed treatment of false brethren, who have carried away one of our children, Mrs. Moore, by their still audaciousness in lying. Prayed for her in faith, and was relieved immediately. At night after pr[eaching[170]] the spirit of p[eace] and contrition fell mightily upon us.

---

[167] The consonant chain "btrsb" and final vowel sound "y" are clear in this and the following two cases. The other vowels are not indicated, so this is only one possible expansion.

[168] Orig., "14."

[169] I.e., Thomas Williams (see Dec. 28, 1747 above).

[170] Might also be "praying."

[[**Saturday, January 23.** Answer of prayer returned. Met Mrs. Moore, who humbled herself, begged my pardon and seemed quite recovered.

[[**Sunday, January 24.** Preached Christ crucified at the Barn,[171] from "They shall look upon me whom they have pierced, …,"[172] and this scripture was at the same time fulfilled in all their souls.

[[**Monday, January 25.** At Gurley's on purpose, had the blasphemies of [Mr.] Connor,[173] Christ in an error, the three-headed devil. Another brother came and confirmed the testimony. In the evening, at my desire Cennick called. I said I still desired he should have the house if he could get it. Expostulated, read his answer confirming Edwards.

[[**Tuesday, January 26.** Found a blessing in the evening preaching and among the society.

[[**Wednesday, [January 27].** Preached at Marlborough Street and met the society, with the great power and blessing in the midst.

[[**Friday, January 29.** Administered [the] sacrament to [an] old woman at Sophie Evans's. A solemn time!

[[**Thursday, February 4.** Mrs. Battersby our bitter slanderer came and was overcome by love.

[[**Friday, February 5.** Mr. Cennick came to return a book I lent him. I asked, Have you any further hopes of getting the house again. No. I am persuaded the trustees will never let it [to] us again. Now then, Mr. Cennick I will convince you I have no design of taking it over your head. You cannot have it from the Baptists, you shall have it if you please from us, and [on] the same terms we took it. He seemed surprised and pleased and answered That is ex[ceeding]ly kind. And then after some pause, But I think we had better have nothing more to do with the Baptists. Then said I, If we keep it, you shall preach there whenever you please. Again he testified thankfulness, and answered with great openness I am satisfied you have acted fairly throughout this affair, but I cannot acquit Mr. Holmes. I cleared him; and added I am convinced if either the Germans or we bear hard upon the other, God will avenge <.[174]> I was the more convinced this was right, because while I thought of it, he was sent p[romptly]? as on purpose.

[[**Saturday, February 6.** Mr. Battersby['s] wife and two daughters b[reakfast]ed with me and seemed all l[oving] friends. Preached at night on the Pool of Bethesda,[175] with greater power then I have found for some months past.]]

---

[171] That is, their new preaching house in Dolphin's Barn.

[172] Zech. 12:10.

[173] CW, MS Journal adds "of Mr. Cennick's society." He was teaching that Jesus made errors and that the doctrine of the Trinity turned God into a three-headed devil.

[174] Portion of page torn away containing one or more words.

[175] John 5:1–15.

*Annotation*: by CW, "Ireland. / Charles Perronett's transcribing. / Read it who can!"
*Source*: MARC, DDCW 6/88a (CW record copy, by amanuensis); collated with DDCW 6/18–DDCW 6/21 (holograph journal letters covering some portions of time period).

[Personal letters attached to various journal letters covered in this time period.[176]]

## To Elizabeth (Smith) Cart[177]

Dublin
October 3, [1747]

My Dear Friend,

All which has happened to you in your sickness I did fully expect, and glorify God in your behalf.

Pray on for your friend in distress of various kinds. It is well your heart is disengaged from one who is not worthy of your particular friendship. But I must suffer pain on every remembrance of that unhappy soul while mine is in the body.[178]

My love to sister Lewin,[179] brothers Perronet,[180] [John] Maddern, [Thomas] Maxfield, Reeves,[181] Reddel,[182] Moss,[183] whom I think of answering shortly.[184]

Farewell in the Lord Jesus.

---

[176] As was frequently CW's practice, he added short personal notes at the beginning or end of several of the original journal letters that are included in this transcription of his longer summary for his records. We present here each of these original personal notes.

[177] Elizabeth (Smith) Cart (c. 1700–1773), a widow of Quaker roots, had become attached to the Wesley brothers and assisted at the Foundery in London.

[178] They are possibly discussing Sarah Clavel; cf. CW's letter to JW of July 15, 1746.

[179] Sweet Lewin was a prominent early member at the Foundery, appearing on the Band lists, starting in Apr. 1742, as the leader of multiple bands for married women.

[180] Edward Perronet (1726–92), a younger brother of Charles, was also aligned and traveling with the Wesley brothers at this time.

[181] Jonathan Reeves (d. 1787) was drawn into the Methodist revival in Bristol in 1739, and became one of JW's earliest lay preachers.

[182] Likely John Reddall (or Riddal), who appears in the Foundery Band Lists for June 1745 in a single men's band (p. 94) and was a male leader there for over twenty years.

[183] Richard Moss (1718–84), born in Hurlston, Cheshire, was raised by his grandparents and apprenticed as a tailor. He came to London in 1737 and eventually heard JW preach. By 1744 he was not only a Methodist but living at the Foundery and accompanying JW on preaching trips. While mainly a servant, Moss preached occasionally on these trips.

[184] This list appears to be all persons who work and/or stay at the Foundery.

Remember me to friends Blackwells,[185] Dewell,[186] Rich,[187] Davy,[188] Withams,[189] Butts,[190] Clark,[191] [and Mary] Pitney.

*Address*: "To / Mrs Cart / at the Foundery / London."
*Postmarks*: "DUBLIN" and "9 / OC."
*Endorsement*: by JW, "Sept. 21—Journal to Sept. 29 / Ireland."
*Source*: holograph; MARC, DDCW 6/18.

## To Hannah Dewell

Dublin
October 6, [1747]

I waited till I could inform my good friends that our affairs here are somewhat settled and an effectual door opened for preaching the gospel. You may have heard that there are many adversaries, and these the fiercest and bitterest I have ever met with. We have indeed been as sheep in the midst of wolves, in danger every hour of being torn to pieces both by Papists and Protestants. But at last our Lord has appeared in our behalf and stilled in good measure the raging of the sea, and the noise of his waves, and the madness of the people.

Some time since a popish mob with some Protestants, so called, at their head and the Romish priests behind the curtains, broke open our preaching room, tore away the benches, pulpit, wainscot, etc., and burned them in the face of the sun, after they had cruelly abused and only not murdered several of the society. The riot in all its circumstances was laid in a bill before the grand jury, who were so wisely dealt with by the persecutors that they threw it out and thereby gave them full license to murder us all, if they were so minded. They concluded we should at least be broken to pieces hereby, and scattered, and come to naught. But

---

[185] Ebenezer Blackwell (1711–82), a London banker, and his wife Elizabeth (Molland) Blackwell (d. 1772), both friends and supporters of the Wesley brothers.

[186] Hannah Dewell (1700–62), who never married, settled in Lewisham, Kent, and became a member of the Methodist society there. She was a close friend of Elizabeth (Molland) Blackwell and frequent correspondent of CW.

[187] Priscilla (Wilford) Rich (c. 1713–83), the third wife of John Rich (1692–1761), who converted to Methodism shortly after their marriage in 1744.

[188] Almost certainly Mary Davey, a widow who was a leader at the Foundery at that time, but would later accept assignment as the housekeeper at Kingswood.

[189] Elizabeth (Harrison) Witham and her children Thomas and Sarah.

[190] Thomas Butts and his wife Hannah (Witham) Butts.

[191] Possibly Elizabeth Clarke, who appears in the Foundery Band Lists in 1745.

God frustrateth the tokens of the liars, and maketh diviners mad.[192] He turneth wise men backward, and maketh their knowledge foolish.[193] Nay, he takes them in their own craftiness,[194] and makes all these things work together for good and the furtherance of the gospel.[195] While the rich and half-awakened hearers fled away, and escaped for their lives, the poor despised followers of the Lamb stood firm as a rock in the midst of the waves. Not one fainted in the trial, or turned back. A few who were for standing in their own defence, against the bloodthirsty Papists, were soon brought off of their resolutions of resisting evil, and committed their cause to God that judgeth righteously.

We continued instant in prayer that he would be pleased to touch the hearts of the magistrates and turn them towards us. The coming of the Lord Lieutenant[196] on the very day when I first preached out gave some check to our persecutors, though they were very sure "he would put us all down." But if any have applied to him for this purpose, I may be bold to say he did not give them such an answer as they desired. This we found by the effects; for soon after, we could walk the streets without endangering our lives. I know likewise of some service to us the late mayor's[197] sending so many of the vulgar rioters to prison, and the deliberation of the jury, while the bill was in suspence, awed and damped the principal rioters or great vulgar, so that for want of *their* encouragement, the mob grew heartless in the cause. To complete all, the Lord Chief Baron,[198] in his speech to the new mayor,[199] spoke very favourably of the Methodists as innocent, loyal people, and severely of their persecutors, charging the mayor to protect us from their violence; who thereupon issued out an order against them, in particular prohibiting any to kick football, etc., on Oxmantown Green while *any were preaching*.

A Church minister likewise last Sunday preached a dreadful sermon against persecutors, so that they say *I hired him* for the purpose. But sure[ly] the Lord raised him up for that purpose. the help that is done upon earth, God doth it himself.[200] Because thou hast been our helper, therefore under the shadow of thy wings will we rejoice.[201]

---

[192] See Isa. 44:25.

[193] See Isa. 44:25.

[194] See Job 5:13.

[195] See Rom. 8:28.

[196] William Stanhope.

[197] William Walker's term as Lord Mayor of Dublin ended on Sep. 29, 1747.

[198] John Bowes.

[199] Sir George Ripton was sworn in as Lord Mayor of Dublin on Sep. 29, 1747.

[200] See Ps. 74:13 (BCP).

[201] See Ps. 63:7 (BCP).

Give God the glory that at present we have rest. Today he hides us in the hallow of his hand, and let him look to the morrow. This moment we live by faith, and by faith stand on the rock of ages. When it is most for his glory, and our good, that persecution should return, it will return: and not one moment sooner.

Our greatest trouble at present is that we have no place to meet in. But doth not our Father know this? And will not God provide? We humbly trust he will, and patiently tarry his leisure.

*Source*: manuscript copy for records; MARC, DDCW 6/88a, pp

## TO THE REV. JOHN WESLEY

Dolphin's Barn [Dublin]
October 13, [1747]

[[Dear Brother,]][202]

This is a dangerous place: so quiet and retired I could hide myself here for *my* time. *Hic gelidi fontes*, etc.[203] It is a thousand pities to spoil this pretty house and garden. You shall [[have it for your own if Miss Clark does not choose it. But you must send me money to pay for it, if it be not sent already. The bill I have received, and spent before it came, upon]] myself and companion.[204] His money, and three guineas of [John] Trembath's, and book-money borrowed, and five guineas, and four given me for printing, are to be paid out of it; besides money for keeping our horses two months, and two persons' travelling expenses to Bristol with the horses. All which I must furnish out of my £20, so that I don't expect so many shillings surplus.

John Trembath (and Charles Perronet most probably) will leave us October 26. At least the former, who you observe is to make a diversion in Wiltshire. John Cennick keeps the house another year.[205] Draw me him off, and his flock comes to us on course, to repair our loss at Kingswood. I [[may last show you my regimen. The second rule I have strictly observed, no thanks to me, but him who leads me not into temptation]]. I promised Mrs. [Agnes] Felster to quit the house before the time,[206] yet notwithstanding his [Cennick's] importunity, I cannot relinquish it till we got another.

---

[202] This and a few portions within the letter are in shorthand, which was expanded by Frank Baker and published in JW, *Works*, 26:266. A few corrections to the expansion are made here.

[203] "Here are cold springs ..."—Virgil, *Eclogues*, x.42.

[204] Charles Perronet.

[205] The preaching house on Skinner's Alley.

[206] The preaching house on Marlborough Lane.

Mr. Crampton demands £8 a year for the ground,[207] which is too much by 4. Here we stick at present, and I greatly doubt whether anything can be done unless you come yourself. Time you would have for writing sermons, much more than in London, and all things promise a great harvest. I will write just now to Jones of Anglesey[208] not to meet us with our horses till Monday fortnight, that I may first hear from you whether you will meet me at Garth on Wednesday, November 4. I could ride straight thence to London, or round by Bristol, as you choose. Bring John Healey[209] with you, if you have not sent him already. [[The Lord bless our good and gospel[?].

[[I do not care to tell you, lest it should not last, but I have had more love of late than for a long time past.

Farewell.]]

*Address*: "To / Mrs Lewin / at the Foundery / London."
*Postmarks*: "DUBLIN" and "OC / 13"; "19 / OC."
*Endorsement*: by JW, "Journal / fr[om] Sept. 29 to Oct. 10 / a[nswere]d Oct. 20 / in Dublin."
*Source*: holograph; MARC, DDCW 6/19.

## TO THE REV. JOHN WESLEY

[[Dublin]]<br>[[October]] 29, [1747]

[[Dear Brother,

[[Still I fear some after-stroke from [Samuel] Larwood, and should be easier if you could assure me all is safe. Commend to me [Thomas] Butt's contrivance as much as you please, only trust him not, for he has foully abused your confidence.]]

Whether Charles Perronet leaves me or not on Saturday is still undetermined. Charles Skelton carries our horses to Bristol, and returns by ship. [[John Trembath must stay with me. It is as much as his soul is worth to be left to himself till he is humbled so far as to see his danger.]]

---

[207] Crampton owned a property near the center of Dublin, called "the Foundery," (see journal letter, Oct. 8, 1747).

[208] William Jones, of Trefollwyn Blas.

[209] John Healey (fl. 1745–50) had aligned with Methodism in Newcastle by early 1743, when he served as a guide to JW (see JW, *Journal*, Apr. 1, 1743, *Works*, 19:321). He had a tendency to defend the cause physically, leading CW to send him out of Newcastle on Feb. 19, 1744 to avoid a mob (see CW, MS Journal). Healey moved to Nottingham and was arrested there on Mar. 10 as a Methodist sympathizer (ibid). He appears to have continued to assist the Wesley brothers from that point, though his name does not appear in the Minutes as a preacher. CW was expecting JW to send Healey to help in Ireland. CW consistently spells the last name "Healy."

[John] Haughton[210] I don't expect to see before our brethren go hence. It was inexcusable, his delay, when you wrote me word from Dublin that you had *then* sent him orders to set out.

Had you the thought to send me by John Healey as much of your volume as is printed? I would see it, if possible, before it be published.[211] Your answer to the bishop should not be lost.[212] Let the three passages be corrected with a pen, and then sell it privately. You *must* let brother Thornton[213] copy your new Oxford sermon in shorthand, and send it me for my approbation.[214]

We propose building a kind of booth in our garden to screen the hearers this winter.[215] John H[aughton]'s judgment determines us to Crampton's or Carr's ground[216]—unless the still Brethren should throw up their room in dudgeon;[217] then we succeed.

I set up my rest here for the winter. Toward February, I presume, you will relieve me yourself.

[[Mr. [Thomas] Williams is running into debt again, but take no notice of it to him. If my warning will stop him, well; if not, that will only happen which I expect, and we must part again. It cannot yet enter into my heart to conceive that God will ever join him and me in one work.

[[Your reasonings about tea do not appear conclusive.[218] "It is right and good for you and the people to leave it off, therefore for me." I never thought of tying up myself for life, neither shall I ever make any

---

[210] John Haughton (d. 1781), a weaver in Chinley End, Derbyshire, became one of JW's early traveling preachers, mentioned as a special Assistant in Yorkshire in 1746. He went to Ireland in Mar. 1748, and spent the remainder of his ministry there. In 1755 he is listed as a Methodist local preacher in Dublin. In 1759 he secured episcopal ordination from the Bishop of Derry (William Barnard), and appointment as rector of Kilrea, Londonderry, where he "cordially received" JW in 1778.

[211] JW published Vol. 2 of his *Sermons* at the end of the year.

[212] *A Letter to the Right Reverend the Lord Bishop of London* (1747), in which (as CW suggested) three passages were erased by hand, and omitted from later editions (see 11:327–51, 555, of this edn.).

[213] Henry Thornton (1710–63), an attorney, assisted the Wesley brothers with some legal matters through the mid 1750s. See Thornton to CW, Nov. 26, 1741.

[214] The last time that JW preached in Oxford was in Aug. 1744, and his sermon *Scriptural Christianity* (see *Works*, 1:159–80) was published shortly after. It was again his turn to preach the official university sermon, but Oxford officials chose to substitute another preacher (see *A Short History of the People called Methodists*, §30, *Works*, 9:440).

[215] At the property they had purchased in Dolphin's Barn.

[216] Crampton's property was near the center of Dublin; Carr may be the owner of the property on Mary-bone Lane (now Morrowbone Lane) where CW had preached several times in October.

[217] I.e., unless the Moravians walk away from the Skinner's Lane preaching house they had been renting in indignation.

[218] JW soon published his thoughts in *A Letter to a Friend Concerning Tea* (1748).

promise of drinking it no more. I am not fond of dispute, and therefore never opposed your arguments against it, though some of them appeared frivolous to me, such as the unwholesomeness, etc., and invented]] *ex post facto*.[219] [[In[deed] I have often heard you, though you now forget it, plead that argument on the other side [of] the case. But my two reasons for leaving it were: 1) example, that the poor people might leave off all they could not afford; 2) your desire. As to myself I must still insist upon my privilege either to use it or let it alone. Neither will I give up the liberty of ever having a friend to visit me, which I must do with tea, my only entertainment for him.[220]

[[As to my drinking it in Dublin, I have David's reason,[221] and were it sacred as the showbread I should not scruple it when I can get nothing else.

[[I find I must take care how I engage myself for the time to come, seeing]] *vestigia nulla retrorsum*,[222] [[and you make that a point of such importance, which you yourself lately told me was not the most excellent way. However, my example need not clash with yours. We are on different sides of the water, and may so continue. I am very well content to give up old England, and see it no more for ever. But if we should meet there again, my present mind is to abstain from tea there, merely to oblige you.

[[The above journal send to Mr. [Ebenezer] Blackwell and Mr. Perronet.[223]

[[Peace be with you.

Farewell ]][224]

*Address*: "To / Mrs Lewin / at the Foundery / London / single sheet."
*Postmarks*: "DUBLIN" and "OC 29"; "4 NO."
*Endorsement*: by JW, "J[ourna]l from Oct. 20, 1747 / Ireland."
*Source*: holograph; MARC, DDCW 6/20.

---

[219] "In retrospect."

[220] See CW's letter of July 15, 1746.

[221] See 1 Sam. 21:1–9.

[222] Horace, *Epistles*, I.i.74–75, "There is no retracing one's steps."

[223] CW likely means Rev. Vincent Perronet, of Shoreham; but could mean his son Edward Perronet.

[224] The shorthand in this letter was expanded by Frank Baker and published in *Works*, 26:266–68; a few corrections are made here.

## FEBRUARY 8–15, 1748[1]

**Sunday, February [7].** Met the society at 6:00 and continued with them in prayer and thanksgiving till 8:00. Then enforced to a crowded audience our Lord's dying command, "Do this in remembrance of me."[2] We had more than ever at the sacrament in St. Patrick's [cathedral]. Thence I hastened to administer it to a poor, dying sinner slowly awakening out of his natural state. At Marlborough Street, I explained Wrestling Jacob[3] and again at Dolphin's Barn, where many wept and made supplication with the angel. More especially at my exhortation afterwards. It was with great reluctance we parted, only for a few days.[4]

**Monday, February [8].** Between 4:00 and 5:00 our lodgings were filled with the society and others, whom I comforted (yet not I, but the Lord comforted both them and me) by that precious promise of preserving grace, Isaiah 43:2, "When thou passest through the waters, I will be with thee; and through the rivers, they shall not overflow thee. When thou walkest through the fire, thou shalt not be burned; neither shall the flame kindle upon thee."

Took horse soon after 6:00 with brother Watts[5] for Tyrrellspass,[6] baited[7] at Kilcock, 14 miles from Dublin, and again at Kinnegad, 10 miles short of the Pass. Within two or three miles of the place, we overtook a lad who we quickly found out by his *whistling* one of our tunes. He was a constant hearer of the word, although a Roman [Catholic], and joined with us in several hymns, which he had by heart. Near 7:00 we got, half choked with the fog, to Mr. Fouace's.[8] My cold was not a little increased by the journey, which I should not have undertaken on any other occasion. I had not been in the house half an hour when the whole town had taken the alarm and crowded in after me. The family dissuaded me from preaching after

---

[1] Only the original journal letter survives covering this week (DDCW 6/22). It is in CW's hand. It was the source of, and provides much greater detail than, the account of these days in CW, MS Journal.

[2] Cf. Luke 22:19.

[3] Gen. 32:24–31.

[4] In the left margin next to this paragraph, CW has written two separate lines in shorthand: [[Jameson with pitchfork / the men b[ought?] by judge.]] These notes relate to the incident described below on Feb. 10.

[5] JW describes brother Watts as "one of our stewards" in the early Methodist movement, in his letter to John Bennet, Dec. 7, 1749, *Works*, 26:395.

[6] Tyrrellspass, Co. Westmeath; CW spells "Teril's Pass."

[7] *OED*: "Of travellers: To stop at an inn, orig. to feed the horses, but later also to rest and refresh themselves."

[8] Stephen Fouace was the brother-in-law of Samuel Handy, married to his sister Anne. Fouace resided in Tyrrellspass; cf. Crookshank, *Ireland*, 1:25. CW spells "Fouce."

so fatiguing a journey, but I could not forebear—trusting in him whose strength is made perfect in weakness.[9]

I opened the book on "A certain man had two sons ...,"[10] and the Lord opened all our hearts. These are the publicans that enter the kingdom [of God] before the Pharisees. Never have I spoke to more hungry souls. They devoured every word. Some of them (in a way peculiar to themselves) *whistled for joy*. Such a feast I have not had since I left England. It refreshed even my body, more than meat and drink. I continued speaking till 9:00, and found we were then as well acquainted as if we had known one another all our lifetime.

God has surely begun a great work among them. The people of Tyrrellspass were wicked almost to a proverb. Swearing, drunkenness, sabbath-breaking, uncleanness, etc., reigned throughout the town from time immemorial. But now the scene is entirely changed. Not an oath is heard, nor a drunkard seen among them; but they are all (to one or two) turned from darkness to light, and from the power of Satan unto God. Near an hundred are already joined in a society, and following hard after the pardoning God.

I could not help asking in my heart, "Who hath begotten me these? My son Onesimus! —who in time past was unprofitable but now profitable; who therefore departed for a season, that we might receive him forever."[11]

I did not *feel* my body while preaching the gospel by *which I live*. But we had a sore night of it, both my companion and I, being in great pain and an high fever. At 7:00 when the people came, I could not lift up my head, or reach the next room without help. Yet was I held up, as it were, for three-quarters of an hour, to invite the labouring burdened sinners to Christ.[12] I then went to bed, and rose at noon, much refreshed and strengthened.

Mr. [Thomas] Williams and John Haughton came in the afternoon; the latter on his way to Dublin. We took horse at 4:00 for Mr. Jonathan Handy's; reached his house at Templemacateer,[13] seven miles from the Pass, by 6:00; and pointed several of his neighbours which he had got

---

[9] See 2 Cor. 12:9.

[10] See Matt. 21:28–32.

[11] Cf. Philem. 10–15. CW is reflecting on the irony that this vibrant early Methodist community was the product of the work of Thomas Williams! By the time CW incorporated this journal letter into his MS Journal, Williams had been expelled from the Methodist fold again, and CW leaves out of the latter document not only this paragraph but the multiple references to Williams in the next few paragraphs.

[12] I.e., his sermon on Matt. 11:28–29.

[13] Jonathan Handy (1704–59) was the older brother of Samuel, and Templemacateer was the name of his manor, which was about 2 miles northeast of Horseleap, Co. Westmeath (and his brother's manor named Coolalough). CW spells "Temple Macketeer."

together to the Lamb of God, who *beareth* away the sin of the world.[14] My continual coughing did not hinder my getting a little sleep in the night.

**Wednesday, February [10].** At 8:00 took horse for Athlone. We were seven in company, and rode mostly abreast (the road was so good) all the way. Some footmen overtook us, running in great haste, as we supposed that they might be time enough for the preaching. One horseman passed us, at full speed. We suspected nothing, and rode on singing, to within half a mile of the town. Mr. Samuel Handy and John Healey happened to be foremost two or three yards out of the line, though Mr. [Thomas] Williams and I had led the company till then. We were mounting a little hill, when three or four men appeared at the top and stopped us, taking up stones and bidding us go back. We thought them in jest, till the stones flew. John Healey was too far advanced to retreat, so he rode up to one of the ambush, who knocked him off from his horse with a stone. He fell backward, as dead, and lay without sense or motion. Mr. [Samuel] Handy, setting spurs to his horse, charged through the enemy, and turned upon them again. A large stone cast at him he caught in his hand. There were only four ruffians on the place as yet, but we saw several gathering to us from all sides. Mr. [Stephen] Fouace, Mr. Williams, and I were now at the spot where John Healey lay. I stood still and observed the man who knocked him down, striking him with a club on his face with the utmost violence. I cried to him to stop and thereby drew him on myself—which was the saving of poor John's life for that time. They had gathered great heaps of stones against our coming, any one of them sufficient to beat out a man's brains. How we escaped them God only knows, and our guardian angels. I stayed and Mr. Williams by me within four yards of them, before we retreated. All his care was for me. I had no apprehension of their hurting me, even when one struck me on the back with a large stone, which took away my breath for sometime. Mr. Fouace got a blow on his head with a stick; Mr. Williams one on the knee with a stone. Mr. Wache and Mr. Jonathan Handy escaped untouched. We were driven off by the showers of stones as often as we attempted to return. This seemed a prohibition to my preaching, and our company were for riding home. But I asked them whether a few of the devil's servants ought to stop the course of the gospel, and whether we *could* leave our half-murdered brother in their hands. This turned the scale.

We rode back again to the field of battle, which our enemies had now quitted, the Protestants beginning to rise upon them. It seems the Papists had laid the scheme for murdering us.[15] The man who wounded

---

[14] John 1:29.

[15] CW inserts here above the line a brief note in shorthand [[the woman risked]]. This is apparently a reminder added to the first draft to add the description of the woman who intervened to help Healey, which is found in the account in MS Journal.

John Healey so desperately was the priest's servant, and rode his master's horse. He and another were just going to finish the work with their knives, when a country fellow[16] came to his rescue, and ran one of the ruffians into the back with his pitchfork. It struck against the bone, and stopped, or the poor wretch had been probably hurried into eternity. The man made a second push at him, which Mr. Handy broke, and saved his enemy once more. He then rode after the priest's servant, and Mr. Williams joined in the pursuit, crying out, "Stop the murderer!" In the midst of a bog, they seized him and it was well for him Mr. Williams was by, or Mr. Handy (a leopard not yet laid down with the kid[17]) would have torn him to pieces. They carried him prisoner to Athlone, and charged the High Constable with him, who soon after let him go. But Father Farrell,[18] I presume, will answer for his forthcoming.

We found John Healey in his blood at a little hut whether the poor woman and her husband had carried him. We set him on a horse and led him to a public house in Athlone. He recovered his senses at hearing my voice in the hut and after he was blooded and his wounds dressed, seemed better, though in great pain. The surgeon would take nothing for his trouble. The people of the town expressed great indignation at our treatment. The soldiers flocked about us, declaring they were just coming out by their officer's order to guard us into town. But we came before our time, which prevented our enemies likewise, or we should have found an army of Romans ready to receive us; and how we *could* then have escaped being murdered, who can tell. The country, it seems, knew beforehand of the design, for the good Catholics made no secret of it.

We were advised to cross the water and preach in the barracks for our greater security. But at the Collector's desire, I walked down to the market-house in which Mr. Williams had preached last week for the first time. It was filled from end to end by a third of the congregation. I cast my eye on a ruined house just opposite and got up into a window, which commanded the marketplace. The space betwixt the market-house and me was crowded with the people. The gentlemen with the Collector and minister[19] sat in the room above it. There could not be so few as 3,000 hearers. I stood and cried, "Ho! every one that thirsteth, come ye to the waters!"[20] Neither my cold, nor pain in my shoulder hindered my lifting

---

[16] Remember the earlier shorthand note: [[Jameson with pitchfork]]. In MS Journal CW identifies the man as "Jameson, a Protestant."

[17] See Isa. 11:6.

[18] Rev. John Farrell (c. 1696–1753), was the priest at St. Mary's church, Athlone from 1723 to 1753. Charles spells "Farrel."

[19] A Rev. T— ; cf. CW, MS Journal, Sept. 25, 1748.

[20] Isa. 55:1.

up my voice like a trumpet. The Lord, I found, had set before me an open door, and I strongly invited poor desperate sinners to him. They gave diligent heed to the words which were spoken. Not one person behaved amiss. I urged and exhorted them for above an hour to repent and believe the gospel. My slightly mentioning the attempt to murder us excited a general pity and abhorrence. The congregation waited upon us to our inn and many of them out of town, with our trusty soldiers after our wounded man. The former got us to leave informations and promised to get us justice. The latter behaved like a servant of Christ, acknowledged the doctrine was the doctrine of our Church, accepted some of our books, and fairly bade us God's speed.

I got my back bathed with brandy, and after 2:00 took horse escorted by our troop of soldiers and others. Some of our company expected a fresh assault, but I believed the hour of darkness was passed and Satan's commission ended. He was only suffered to try our faith and hinder, if possible, the preaching [of] the gospel.

We marched very slow for the sake of John Healey, till we came to the field of battle. It was stained with blood abundantly. We halted there and sang a song of triumph and praise to God who giveth us the victory through our Lord Jesus Christ.[21] Here we sent back our guard, and went on our way rejoicing. None molested us till we reached Moate,[22] six or seven miles from Athlone. Brother [John] Haughton had preached there last week, and a little disturbance was made by beating a drum. I proclaimed in the street to about 1,000 tolerably quiet hearers, "This is the faithful saying, and worthy of ...."[23] These were *less* noble than those of Althone, yet most listened. A few stones were cast, and the drum beat, I suppose to entertain the ladies (Mr. Handy's family), who walked by us several times with great seeming contempt of Christ's gospel. They encouraged the drummer to interrupt us all they could, but he did not care to make his appearance. In spite of the genteel devil, some received benefit by the word, as their tears testified. We rode through the aliens to Mr. [Jonathan] Handy's and came safe thither with the night. The voice of joy and thanksgiving was heard in their dwelling-place, and we magnified the Lord our God, even the God of whom cometh salvation, the God by whom we escape death.

Between forty and fifty of the poor neighbours came to hear the word, several of them convinced and other[s] swiftly awakening out of their sins. I doubt not but these shall be the seed of a flourishing church. One of my

---

[21] CW wrote a hymn celebrating this deliverance, found in MS Miscellaneous Hymns, 5–7; and MS Richmond, 50–51. It seems unlikely that this was the hymn they sang the same day.

[22] Moate, Co. Westmeath, Ireland; 10 miles east of Athlone. CW spells "Moat."

[23] 1 Tim. 1:15.

hearers (mother to our host[24]) is, after a moral life of above eighty years, now convinced of unbelief and quietly waiting for the salvation of God.

**Thursday, February [11].** Our patient is in a fair way, feeling no inward bruises as we apprehended. I rose, after yesterday's labour, much better than I expected. Preached, and prayed by a sickly woman in the family, who lies on the brink of the pool.[25]

Rode to Tyrrellspass, and was received as alive from the dead. Our barn at night was crowded with high and low, rich and poor, whose curiosity brought them from all quarters. I showed them their condition and their cure in the wounded traveller and Good Samaritan.[26] They attended patiently for two hours, most were deeply affected. Counsellor Low[27] followed us to our lodging and had much friendly discourse with us. I passed another comfortable hour with the society, who, I verily believe, will stand when tribulation arises because of the word.

**Friday, February 12.** Preached at 7:00, and spake severely to the little, increasing flock. Spent the morning in conference with the strangers. One of them, a serious, understanding Roman [Catholic] seemed satisfied with my answers to his objections, and not far from the kingdom of heaven. Another who has been a grievous sinner, but a man of good sense and reading, went away in like manner, convinced and longing to be converted. The Counsellor (we heard today) had sat up all night searching the scriptures, if these things were so.

At noon took horse for Mr. Samuel Handy's, but rode past him first to Templemacateer and prayed with our sick woman, rejoicing over her in hope. Called in at our neighbour Booth's and prayed there. His wife expects her pardon every moment. By 5:00 we came to Coolalough,[28] where we met with more friends from the Pass and magnified the Lord together, till the people came. Our chapel was crowded with them that came from far. I invited them with strong importunity to the Great Supper,[29] and all seemed willing to accept of the invitation. Two hours passed away unperceived, before I could give over. Another [hour] we employed in singing, and at 11:00 parted in peace.

**Saturday, February 13.** Preached again to a few listening souls, one a poor publican, drowned in tears, who constantly attends the word of grace, on which all his hopes depend. Took horse before 1:00 with my

---

[24] Joan (Low) Handy (1675–1763).

[25] See John 5:3.

[26] Luke 10:29–37.

[27] This is likely John Low, of Cornaher House in Tyrrellspass, a relative of Samuel Handy's mother.

[28] The manor house of Samuel Handy; CW spells "Cullen-lough."

[29] Luke 14:15–24.

good friend Mr. Jonathan Handy, met Mr. [Thomas] Williams on the road, and came together to Tullamore. Here my spirit was much refreshed with five of our dragoons from Dublin. We spent an hour in prayer and singing. Then I called to many attentive sinners, "O Israel, thou hast destroyed thyself; but in me is thy help."[30] They received both the legal and the gospel saying as the truth of God. Several strangers and more of our beloved soldiers came into the house afterwards and talked with us of the things of the kingdom.

We then walked to our host and brother Allen's, half a mile out of town, and before 7:00 our house was filled with the people to whom I explained and informed with great enlargement, "The poor have the gospel preached [to] them."[31] It was a time of refreshment, like one of the former gospel-days. Surely our Lord hath much people in this place.

**Sunday, February 14.** Walked to Tullamore and enforced on a great multitude Isaiah 1:16, "Wash ye, make you clean; put away ...." It was piercing cold, yet the poor people stood close in an open yard and drank in the word of grace and reconciliation.

We rode to Philipstown,[32] five miles off, where at 2:00 I explained the Prodigal Son[33] to near 2,000 as listening souls as I have seen in Ireland. For an hour and an half I invited and pressed them to return to their Father, and they showed all the signs (which could then be shown) of sincere repentance. What most delighted me was the behaviour of near forty tall dragoons, with whom I spent some time in singing and conference, both before and after preaching. They are already turned from the power of Satan unto God—that they may receive forgiveness of sins. We fell into a sudden intimacy and were much comforted together. The whole people appeared a people ready prepared for the Lord. From the beginning they have received the word with all readiness, and cried out after the first sermon, "This day is salvation come to Philipstown."

Rode forward five long Irish miles to Tyrrellspass and cried to a crowded audience, "Is it nothing to you, all ye that pass by? behold, and see if ever sorrow was like unto my sorrow, ...."[34] For above an hour my voice and strength lasted, and Jesus Christ was evidently set forth before many eyes as crucified. Several strangers and gentlefolk were convinced and affected. Give God the glory, whose only Spirit convinces of sin, of righteousness, and of judgment.

Gave a word of exhortation to the society, before my strength was

---

[30] Hosea 13:9.

[31] Luke 7:22.

[32] Philipstown (now known as Daingean), Co. Offaly, Ireland; 8 miles east of Tullamore.

[33] Luke 15:11–32.

[34] Cf. Lam. 1:12.

quite exhausted.

[**Monday,**] **February 15.** Explained Isaiah 35, and gave the morning to conference with this simple-hearted people.

*Endorsement*: by JW, "Ireland."
*Source*: holograph; MARC, DDCW 6/22.

## SEPTEMBER 26–OCTOBER 27, 1748[1]

**Monday, September 26.** Came to Tyrrellspass by 3:00. Here the Lord is reviving his work. Mrs. Low[2] received her pardon under Robert Swindells[3] last night, and another this morning. I expounded the Pool of Bethesda,[4] and found great difference betwixt the hearers now and six weeks ago.[5] It is an extraordinary miracle of grace that they are not all scattered or fallen away through the fatal blunder of one of our preachers, who to cure their slackness told them, "They were no more a society." He broke them up. Accordingly, they have forbore assembling themselves for many weeks. I do not wonder now at their coldness, for how can one be warm alone! But I bless God that the wolf has not stole and killed and destroyed them all.

**Tuesday, September 27.** Found much life among them, while I applied those words, "Behold, I stand at the door, and knock: ...."[6] The first were become last. But I leave them with a comfortable hope that they will become first again.

I would have took horse immediately, but my beast was not forthcoming. Waited some time, and then set out on foot with my bags and gown. The horse was strayed (as I supposed), and therefore resolved to walk as much of the forty miles to Dublin as I could today and the rest tomorrow. Mr. Dean of Philipstown (lately become a brother through faith in Christ) would not suffer me to pursue my journey with such an equipage, and forced his horse upon me, going home himself on foot. Young Mr. Wade[7] bore me company three or four miles. His mother[8] died last week in peace. He is swiftly following her through the last stage of

---

[1] CW returned to Ireland for his second visit in mid-Aug. 1748. He likely mailed back to England biweekly journal letters, as he did during his first visit, but none are known to survive. What does survive is a secondary transcription (in the hands of an amanuensis, with CW making corrections and additions) that covers about half of this two-month visit (DDCW 6/23). The amanuensis was most likely Jonathan Reeves, who was assigned to Ireland (see JW, *Works*, 10:209) and traveling with CW (see MS Journal, Sept. 1, 1748). This transcription was the source of, and provides much greater detail than, the account of these days in CW, MS Journal.

[2] Likely the wife or mother of John Low, of Cornaher House in Tyrrellspass; see Feb. 11, 1748 above.

[3] Robert Swindells (d. 1782) became one of JW's traveling preachers in 1741. He accompanied JW to Ireland in 1748 and spent a large part of the next three decades itinerating there, along with the Rev. John Meriton.

[4] John 5:1–15.

[5] CW had visited Tyrrellspass on Aug. 17; see MS Journal.

[6] Rev. 3:20.

[7] This was a younger brother of Jeremiah Wade of Aughrim, he died within the year; see JW to CW, May 3–10, 1749.

[8] The widow (c. 1653–1748) of Jerome Wade; see MS Journal, Feb. 15, 1748.

a consumption; has not yet received the atonement, but cannot doubt the faithful mercies of his Saviour. He *knows* he shall not depart till his eyes have seen *his* salvation. I commended him to the Lord Jesus, and appointed to meet him in paradise. I rode on alone, yet not alone. The noon hour of prayer was very refreshing to my soul. My absent friends were never less absent. Soon after 7:00 I came safe to Dublin.

**Wednesday, September 28.** Breakfasted at Mrs. Folliard's, whom I left mourning and found rejoicing in Christ *her* Saviour. She has lately found his pardoning love in hearing Joseph Cownley,[9] as have several others, God having greatly owned and blessed both his public and private labours. The society is in a very flourishing way and grows daily both in grace and number. From 12:00 to 1:00 I spent as usual in our garden with my Christian friends, who never fail to meet me in my retirement at the throne of grace.[10] Unfolded the threefold promise of the gospel contained in Isaiah 35—that is, pardon, holiness, and heaven—and the Lord was in the midst and comforted our hearts together.

**Thursday, September 29.** Finished Isaiah 35 with a blessing, which attended the word in the evening also and at the society. It was a most tempestuous night. I was to have been on the sea at[11] this time, but blessed be God, who has ordered it otherwise.

**Friday, September 30.** At night our Lord pierced many hearts by that cry of his from the cross, "Is it nothing to you, all ye that pass by? ...."[12] The power continued or rather increased in the society. Two received the atonement, many a deeper sense of his love. None, I trust, were sent empty away.

**Saturday, October 1.** I have not had a more solemn hour in Dublin than that I passed this evening with the bands. It was my first time of meeting them. The Spirit of grace and supplication was poured out, and we rejoiced unto God with reverence.

**Sunday, October 2.** After sacrament, preached in our garden, but never with less life. In the evening discoursed from Isaiah 53, and God gave me utterance. One in that hour received faith and forgiveness. As soon as the society were met, the flame was kindled. One, and another, and another testified the grace of the Lord Jesus, which they then first

---

[9] Joseph Cownley (1723–92) was spiritually awakened under JW's preaching in Bath in 1743, and on returning to his native Leominster joined the Methodist society there and began to preach. By the 1746 Conference he was an Assistant, and JW described him as "one of the best preachers in England." JW had recently sent Cownley to Ireland to assist in the work there.

[10] I.e., he was in fellowship with his friends back in England, during prayer.

[11] Orig., "as at."

[12] Lam. 1:12.

experienced. A poor revolter, who like Demas[13] had forsaken us, stealing in this evening, found mercy unexpected. His servant at the same time felt her sins forgiven, and gave God the glory. So did two or three more. Eight or nine confessed their faith openly. Many more, I believe all present, received a manifestation of the Spirit and rejoiced either in hope, or in possession of their Saviour.

Slept at Mr. [William] Lunell's,[14] where I rejoiced to meet Mr. Balier, resolved to fight his way to heaven through wife, relations, and every friend he has in the world.

**Monday, October 3.** I had appointed yesterday for embarking, but the *fair wind* prevents me, by keeping all the packet[-boat]s on the other side. Hereby God gave me opportunity to talk with and (I hope confirm) several, and to preach the gospel again this evening. My text was Isaiah 52:[1], "Awake, awake; put on thy strength, O Zion; ...." The word was with unusual power. Many felt the weight of it. I was too easily discouraged from meeting the society afterwards by the slowness and perverseness of some of them. Went to my lodgings on the Key, and in the night my old companion—the toothache—paid me a visit.

**Tuesday, October 4.** The wind continued fair which kept me prisoner, or my toothache would not have detained me, though it was very troublesome all night.

**Wednesday afternoon, October [5].**[15] Ventured out to Mrs. Clement's, a violent persecutor when I has last in Dublin, but now a believer persecuted herself for the sake of the gospel. Preached and met the society this and the following evening, and was not a little comforted among them.

**Friday, October 7.** Met an old Quaker (at Mr. Lunell's), a Dutchman, who seemed to have great experience in the things of God. At two Mr. Lampe and his wife[16] called and were overjoyed to see me. I cannot yet give up my hope that they are designed for better things than feeding swine or entertaining the gay world.

A packet-boat, we hear, got as far as Wicklow, 30 miles off; and [being] unable to come nearer, is sailed back to the Head.

---

[13] Cf. 2 Tim. 4:10.

[14] William Lunell (1699–1774), son of a Huguenot refugee, became a wealthy cloth merchant (and sometimes banker) in Dublin. He lived in a large house at 15 Francis Street. He was apparently won for Methodism by Thomas Williams in early 1747. His second wife, Anne (Gratton) Lunell, had died Aug. 6, 1748 (see CW's epitaph in his letter to Lunell of Aug. 21).

[15] Orig., "6"; an error.

[16] John Frederick Lampe (1703–51), a musician and composer; and his wife Isabella (Young) Lampe (1715–95), an operatic soprano. Lampe composed settings for some of CW's hymns on the Christian year: *Hymns on the Great Festivals* (London: M. Cooper, 1746). See CW's elegy for Lampe in *Funeral Hymns* (1759), 30–31.

I took my leave of the flock, and left a blessing behind me, as I believe, giving God the[17] glory.

**Saturday, October 8.** The wind turned so as to bring a boat in, and then sunk away into a dead calm. However, we attempted at night to get out to sea. The particulars I sent in the following letter to Mr. Lunell.

Holyhead [Wales]<br>October 10 [1748]

My very Dear Friend and Brother,

I did not tell you what I felt at leaving you, but never had I a stronger apprehension of evil near. These sort of [fore]bodings or presages I rarely speak of till after their confirmation. On Saturday evening half hour past 8:00, I entered the small-boat. We were two hours making our way through the calm and fog to the vessel at the piles. There was not then water to cross the [sand]bar, so we took our rest till 11:00 on **Sunday morning**. Then God sent us a fair wind out of his treasuries, and we sailed smoothly before it, five knots an hour. All things promised of a speedy, prosperous voyage, yet still I found the *usual* burden upon my heart—usual, I mean, in time of extreme danger approaching.

Toward evening the wind freshened upon us, and we had full enough of it. I was called to account for a bit of cake I [ate][18] in the morning and thrown into violent exercise. The emptiness of my stomach made it so much the worse. All my sickness in my voyage to America, etc., were nothing like this. I expected it would throw me into convulsions. Up or down, cabin or deck, made no difference. Yet in the midst of it I perceived a distinct and heavier concern for I knew not what.

I[t] was now pitch dark, so that we could not see the Head, and no small tempest lay upon us. The captain had ordered in all the sails. I kept mostly upon deck till half hour past 8:00, when upon my inquiry he told me he expected to be in the harbor by 9:00. I answered we would compound for 10:00. While we were talking, the mainsail (as I take it) got loose and flew overboard, as if it would drag us all after it. The smallboat, at the same time, for want of fastening, fell out of its place. The master called, "All hands upon deck," and thrust me down into the cabin. Within a minute I heard a cry above, "We have lost the mast." A passenger ran up and brought us worse news, that it was not the mast but the poor master himself, whom I had scarce left when the boat, as they supposed, struck him overboard. But from that moment he was neither seen nor heard more. My soul was bowed before the Lord. I knelt down and commended his departing spirit to his mercy in Christ Jesus. I adored his distinguishing goodness. "The one shall be taken, and the other left."[19]

---

[17] Orig., "God in the."

[18] Orig., "eat."

[19] Cf. Matt. 24:40; Luke 17:34–36.

Why was not I rather than that poor soul so hurried into eternity without a moment's notice? It brought into my mind those lines of [Edward] Young, which I had read this morning:

> No warning given! unceremonious fate!
> A sudden rush from life's meridian joys!
> A plunge opaque beyond conjecture![20]

The sailors were so hurried and confounded they knew[21] not what they did. I thought it well for us that Jesus was at the helm. The decks were strewed with sails, boat, etc. The wind shifting about; the compass they could not get at; no, nor the helm for some time. We were just on the shore, and the vessel drove where or how they knew not. One of our cabin passengers ran to the helm, gave orders as captain and was very helpful in righting the ship. But I ascribe it to our invisible Pilot that we got safe to the harbour soon after 10:00.

The storm was so high that we doubted whether any boat would venture to fetch us. At last one answered and came. I thought it safer to lie in the vessel, but one in the boat calling, "Mr. Wesley, you must come." I followed, and by 11:00 found out my old lodgings at Robert Griffith's.

**Monday morning, October 3.** Blessed be God that I did not stay in the vessel last night. A more tempestuous sea I do not remember. It was just such another as that in Dublin a little before I embarked. I am brought hither in the very crisis by the power of faith. It blows an hurricane, while I write this. Commend me to the continual prayer of the brethren.

### Thanksgiving for our Deliverance from Shipwreck.[22]

1.   All praise to the Lord,
     Who rules with a word
     The untractable sea,
  And limits its rage by his steadfast decree:
     Whose providence binds,
     Or releases the winds,
     And compels them again
  At his beck to put on the invisible chain.

---

[20] This quote is from Night II, of Edward Young's *The Complaint, or Night Thoughts on Life, Death and Immortality* (London: Dodsley, 1742–45); but CW is quoting from the slightly abridged form that JW reprinted (without Young's permission!) in *Collection of Moral and Sacred Poems* (see 2:260).

[21] Orig., "know."

[22] CW later published this hymn in *HSP* (1749), 2:235–36.

2.     Even now he hath heard
    Our cry, and appear'd
    On the face of the deep,
And commanded the tempest its distance to keep:
    His piloting hand
    Has brought us to land,
    And no longer distrest,
We are joyful again in the haven to rest.

3.     O that all men would raise
    Their tribute of praise,
    His goodness declare,
And thankfully sing of his fatherly care!
    With rapture approve
    His dealings of love,
    And the wonders proclaim
Perform'd by the virtue of Jesu's name!

4.     Thro' Jesus alone
    He delivers his own,
    And a token doth send
That his love shall direct us, and save to the end:
    With joy we embrace
    The pledge of his grace,
    In a moment outfly
These storms of affliction, and land in the sky.

**Monday, October 10.**[23] At half hour past 9:00 took horse, etc. See the other paper.[24] [...]

[**Monday, October 24.** ...] full of glory."

My body was worn down though my spirit was quickened. Mr. Phillips[25] did not much admire our accommodations.[26] Our chamber looked very ghastly and could scarce afford a prophet's furniture.[27] But when we

---

[23] CW takes over for the amanuensis at this point, writing the final entries.
[24] CW is referring to a page that is now missing; see his account of Oct. 10–24 in MS Journal.
[25] Rev. Edward Phillips, of Maesmynis.
[26] In Coleford, Somerset.
[27] See 2 Kings 4:8–10.

came to the bed, we found but one thin quilt to cover us. I don't know what we should have done, if we could not have laid in our clothes.

**Tuesday, October [25].**[28] Explained Isaiah 35, and we had another gracious shower. Took our leave at 7:00 of our loving colliers, leaving one of our company, poor brother Crouch,[29] behind us ill of an ague. Rode as far as Paulton without any accident. Then my horse fell and cast me to the ground with such violence as if I had been shot out of an engine. I lay breathless for some time. Brother Phillips picked me up. It was several minutes before I could recover my breath. I found no bone broke or dislocated. My arm saved my breast, and was rendered senseless and useless. They set me up on my horse, and by noon we came well to Bristol. Got a surgeon to dress my arm and hand, which were only bruised; and my foot crushed by the horse falling on me. Let John Trembath preach and went early to bed.

**Wednesday, October [26].**[30] Woke with a stiff neck and aching bones, which did not interrupt my business, public or private. Preached at night with enlargement of heart, and was comforted among the women bands. Preached at 5:00 next morning; and feeling some pain in my breast, which wears off more and more.

*Source*: CW record copy, mainly by amanuensis; MARC, DDCW 6/23.

---

[28] Orig., "26"; an error.

[29] Likely Thomas Crouch, who had been serving as a local preacher since 1747 (see JW, *Works*, 10:206).

[30] Orig., "27"; an error.

## A COPY OF ELIZABETH STORY'S DECLARATION DECEMBER 9–20, 1748[1]

Elizabeth Story[2] hereby declareth that she has had no rest or peace in her soul since she reported certain things and afterward made affidavit thereof concerning Mr. Charles Wesley,[3] which report and affidavit were entirely false. That she has felt continual condemnation in her heart and has never prospered in soul or body since that time. That Mr. Broughton,[4] when she related those false matters, did caution her not to speak anything but what was the truth. That the cancer which she had in her breast she believes might be occasioned by her striking her breast against a chair.[5] That she freely and gladly maketh this declaration, hoping the Lord will forgive her this great sin, and desires Mr. Wesley's pardon for speaking and declaring such false things concerning him, being prompted thereto through the instigation of the devil.

This is the truth as witness my hand this ninth day of December 1748.

Elizabeth Story

Witnessed by
William Holland
Eliza[beth (Smith)] Cart
and
Sarah Verine

---

[1] In 1744 Thomas Williams sought ordination in the Church of England. CW chastised Williams for this attempt, since he lacked a university degree. Resentment over this matter inclined Williams to encourage a couple of young female supporters in the London Methodist society to accuse CW of immoral conduct. This charge was forwarded by Thomas Broughton to the Bishop of London, and CW refuted it directly to the Bishop at the time. Now, as CW was preparing to marry Sarah Gwynne, he (or his friends) apparently judged it prudent to get a written retraction from the main accuser. The location (or survival) of the original signed retraction is not known, but there is a longhand copy at the Moravian Archives in London, and a shorthand copy in CW's hand on the inside of a notebook cover at MARC. We transcribe the longhand copy, noting significant variants in the shorthand copy. For more information, see Randy Maddox and Timothy Underhill, "Untwisting the Tangled Web: Charles Wesley and Elizabeth Story," *Wesley and Methodist Studies* 8 (2016): 175–83.

[2] Little is known of Elizabeth Story other than that she is listed as a member of a single women's band in Apr. 1742 on the Foundery Bands list, but is absent from lists for 1744–45 after Thomas Williams had begun spreading dissent.

[3] In the shorthand copy CW is not named, the manuscript leaves a gap instead. This also happens with Story's subsequent reference to him.

[4] Rev. Thomas Broughton (1712–77), a student of University College, Oxford, became part of the "Oxford Methodists" in 1733. After receiving his degree and ordination he distanced himself from the Wesley brothers, serving as lecturer of All Hallows, Lombard Street.

[5] Story apparently had alleged that the cancer was judgment for her impropriety with CW.

[[To Mrs Hall[6] at Mrs Begrs[?] in Saint Thomas church yard Sarum]].[7]

Elizabeth Story told Mrs. Verine and her mother that it was through the persuasion of Mr. [Thomas] Williams and others that she had declared such false things concerning Mr. Charles Wesley, for that she had never seen an unhandsome action or heard a bad word from him in her life, was it the last word she was to speak. And when they asked her afterwards how she came to tell such lies of Mr. Charles Wesley, she replied that she had told a thousand lies of him in one week.

The mark of Sarah Verine X[8]

Elizabeth Story declared also to Mrs. Cart and William Holland that it was through the persuasion of Mr. [Thomas] Williams and others that she spoke, and afterwards made affidavit of such false things concerning Mr. Charles Wesley, and what greatly concerned her was that she had been the means of turning many souls out of the way thereby. And although others did persuade her to act so, yet they could not have made her done it unless she herself had been willing. That she did not hereby excuse herself, for she was bad enough and that God knew.

William Holland
Eliza[beth (Smith)] Cart[9]

A few days after that she[10] had made the declaration which was signed by William Holland, Elizabeth Cart, and Sarah Verine, she desired, with tears in her eyes, the said Sarah Verine, for God's sake, that when she went next time to Mr. Charles Wesley she would tell him that she had not felt such peace for five years past. Although she could not then say she felt the pardoning love of God as she had formerly, and was afraid as her sin was so great that she never should so experience it again, and in great anguish of soul cried out, "O God, how have I torn myself from thy people that would have been friends to me both in body and soul."

The mark of Sarah Verine X
[December 20, 1748[11]]

A Copy / January 31, 1748/9[12]

*Source*: London, Moravian Archives, AB91/WmHollandFolder/6 (longhand copy); collated with MARC, MA 1977/568 (CW shorthand copy).

---

[6] I.e., Martha (Wesley) Hall, CW's sister.

[7] This address information is found only in the shorthand copy.

[8] Shorthand copy omits "The mark of" but shows the "X," both here and below.

[9] Shorthand copy adds third signature "Sarah Verine X."

[10] Shorthand copy replaces "she" with "Elizabeth Story."

[11] Taken from heading.

[12] This comment is found only on the longhand copy in the Moravian Archives, indicating that it was a manuscript copy of the original affidavit.

## JUNE 29–JULY 20, 1751[1]

Journal to Newcastle

**Saturday, June 29, 1751.** I took horse [in Bristol] at 4:00 with Sarah Perrin, Francis Walker,[2] and Thomas Westell.[3] At Newport,[4] Thomas Westell left us. We lay at Ross[5] that night.

Reached Ludlow[6] next day [**Sunday, June 30**] by 2:00, having rode from 4:00 in the morning in almost incessant rain; yet none of us received the least hurt.

Preached at 6:00 to as many as the hall and parlour could hold. They seemed increased in earnestness, as well as number. I found *unexpected* life and comfort among them, and the following evenings had still more reason to hope that my labour has not been altogether in vain.

**Friday, July 5.** Between 6:00 and 7:00, set out with Sarah Perrin, my wife[7] and her sister,[8] and Francis Walker for Worcester. Arriving in the afternoon at our sister Blackmore's, we heard the rioters had been at their room on Monday evening in expectation of me, and made great disturbance. I doubted all along whether I had any business here at this time, yet at the desire of the poor people went to the preaching-house at 7:00. My wife and sister carried two ladies of their acquaintance, for whom I was in some pain. Almost as soon as I began to speak, the mob began to interrupt. But in spite of their lewd, hellish language, I preached the gospel, though with much contention. The fierceness of men God so far restrained that they had no power to beat or strike the people as usual. Neither did any molest us in our way home.

---

[1] A series of problematic cases in early 1751 led CW to challenge JW to exercise more control over the lay itinerant preachers. In response JW challenged CW to step out of his self-imposed sabbatical from itinerancy, and travel the northern circuit, with a particular eye to evaluating the lay preachers. This and the following three items trace this journey and CW's evaluation. They served as a source of, and provide much greater detail than, the account of this journey in CW, MS Journal. See Richard P. Heitzenrater, "Purge the Preachers: The Wesleys and Quality Control," in Kenneth G. E. Newport & Ted A. Campbell (eds.), *Charles Wesley: Life, Literature, and Legacy* (Peterborough: Epworth, 2007), 486–514.

[2] Francis Walker (1722–87), a native of Tewksbury, Gloucestershire, was serving as one of JW's itinerant preachers as early as 1744. He is listed as an Assistant in the *Minutes* starting in 1745 (*Works*, 10:159), until he married and settled in Gloucester, leading to his classification as a local preacher in 1755 (*Works*, 10:274).

[3] Thomas Westell (c. 1719–94) became one of JW's first traveling preachers within a few months of completing his apprenticeship as a joiner in Bristol in 1741. He retired in Bristol in 1778. CW spells "Westal."

[4] Newport, Gloucestershire; about 15 miles north of Bristol.

[5] Ross-on-Wye, Herefordshire.

[6] Ludlow, Shropshire; where Marmaduke and Sarah Gwynne had recently moved.

[7] Sarah (Gwynne) Wesley; they had been married in Apr. 1749.

[8] In MS Journal CW specifies this was Rebecca ("Becky") Gwynne (1724–99).

**Saturday, July 6.** It rained hard, but that did not hinder the few sincere hearers from attending the word at 5:00. Hitherto they have had quiet in the mornings, but now the sons of Belial were ready for us. While I was giving out a second hymn, they poured in upon us—some with their faces blacked, some without shirts, all in rags—and began to "stand up for the Church" by cursing and swearing, by singing and talking lewdly, and throwing dust and dirt all over us, with which they had filled their pockets—such as had any, I mean, to fill. I was soon covered from head to foot and almost blinded with bran, etc., thrown into my face. But I was well contented, since it was not lime or *aquafortis*,[9] which they sometimes threw among our people. Finding it impossible to be heard, I only told them I should apply to the magistrates for redress, and walked upstairs. They pressed after me, but Mr. Walker and some of the brethren blocked up the stairs and kept them down. I waited a quarter of an hour, but finding they stayed there, threatening and blaspheming, I went down through the midst of them (none being suffered to touch me) to my lodgings, and from thence to the mayor's. I passed an hour with him, pleading the poor people's cause. He said he had never before heard of their being so treated—that is, pelted, beat, and wounded, their house battered, the windows, partitions, and locks broken, etc. That none had applied to him for justice, or he should have granted it. That he was well assured of the great mischief the Methodists had done throughout the nation, and the great riches Mr. [George] Whitefield and their other teachers had acquired. That their societies were quite unnecessary, since the Church was sufficient, and he was for having neither Methodist nor Dissenter. I easily answered all his objections, and gave him (I hope) a more favourable opinion of them. He treated me with much civility and freedom, and promised at parting to do our people justice. Whether he does or no, I have satisfied my own conscience and leave the event to God.

At 10:00 we took horse for Tipton Green,[10] which we easily reached by 7:00. Our brother Jones[11] and his wife returned from Wednesbury[12] by 9:00. He gave me a melancholy account of the society, which from between 2[00] and 300 is dwindled away to about 70 weak, lifeless souls. Those who had borne the heat and burden of the day, and stood like a rock in all the storms of persecution, were removed from their steadfastness and

---

[9] "Strong water." *OED*: "The early scientific, and still the popular, name of the nitric acid or similar corrosive liquids."

[10] Tipton Green (now just Tipton), Staffordshire, England; 1 mile north of Dudley. CW spells "Tippen Green."

[11] James Jones, a man of some property, traveled for a time as one of JW's preachers, starting in 1743. He eventually restricted his work to Staffordshire where he was a greatly beloved and respected local preacher. Born in Tipton, he died in Birmingham in 1783.

[12] Wednesbury, Staffordshire. CW spells "Wensbury."

fallen back into the world through vain janglings and disputings. Well had it been for them if the predestinarians had never come here.

**Sunday, July 7.** Went to church and heard a very harmless sermon. What was once their one subject, the poor Methodists are now rarely mentioned from their pulpits. At 5:00 I preached out in Wednesbury to a very numerous congregation whom I could not look upon without tears. My text was Revelation 3:3, "Remember therefore how thou hast received and heard, and hold fast, and repent." Out of the abundance of my heart my mouth spake, and called them back to their first love and first works. It was a solemn season of sorrow. The Lord, I trust, knocked at many hearts which will hear his voice and open to him again.[13] He stirred up the faithful remnant to pray for their backsliding brethren; and the prayer of faith shall not return empty.

Another hour I employed in strongly exhorting the society to repentance. And my faith revived: and many, I believe, saw the door of hope opening.

Lodged at Mr. E——,[14] who did run well; but the world, that gulf of souls, has now quite swallowed him up. Still he acknowledges the truth and loves the witnesses thereof. O that he might strengthen the things that remain and are ready to die. His wife, sister, and a few neighbours, who had been my hearers at the beginning, seemed a good deal affected, and stirred up again to set their hand to the plough.

**Monday, July 8.** I preached at 5:00 with much freedom and hope of their recovery. In the afternoon the curate[15] met me at Mr. E——'s, a well-disposed youth just come from college, where his tutor, Mr. Bentham,[16] gave him an early prejudice for true religion. He invited me to his lodgings, joined with us in serious conversation and singing, and seemed ready for all good impressions.

At 6:00 I preached at Bromwich Heath[17] to a great multitude of the poor, who heard me gladly while I pointed them to the Lamb of God.[18] My mouth, as well as heart, was opened, and I hardly knew how to leave off. Many of them seemed just ready to lay hold on the Lord their righteousness.

---

[13] See Rev. 3:20.

[14] This may be John Eaton, a supporter of Methodism in the early 1740s; cf. Henry Herbert Prince, *The Romance of Early Methodism* (West Bromwich: J. G. Tomkins, 1925), 63–64.

[15] The current curate at Wednesbury was Henry Saunders (born c. 1728), who had received his BA from Oriel College, Oxford, in 1750.

[16] Edward Bentham (1707–76) had been tutor at Oriel College, Oxford, since 1732. He received his DD in 1749, was made a canon of Christ Church in 1754, and Regius professor of Theology in 1763.

[17] An open common in West Bromwich, Staffordshire; 4 miles northwest of Birmingham. CW spells "Bramidge Heath."

[18] Likely his sermon on John 1:29.

**Tuesday, July 9.** Preached at 5:00 in Wednesbury. Examined the society in Tipton Green at 3:00; then rode to Dudley [19]and preached to a quiet multitude who drank in every word of invitation to Christ. Returned to our brother Jones's and slept in peace.

**Wednesday, July 10.** Rode over with James Jones and preached again at Dudley on, "Him that cometh unto me, I will in no wise cast out."[20] Passed the day at our brother's and preached in the evening to many listening souls at Wednesbury, whom I exhorted to lay aside every weight and run the race, looking unto Jesus.[21] The word had free course and came with power to their hearts, as I have good cause to believe, giving God the glory. I then endeavoured to stir up the society and joined with them in earnest prayer for a general revival.

**Thursday, July 11.** My subject this morning was, "Him that overcometh will I make a pillar in the temple ...."[22] I then examined the classes and rejoiced to find them all orderly walkers, received in some backsliders on trial, and prayed by a sick sister who quietly waits for the salvation of God.

Dined in Darlaston[23] at our brother Jones's uncle. The master was gone to his house not made with hands and left a good report behind him. He was a good and hardy soldier of Jesus Christ, bold to confess him before men for whose sake he suffered the loss of all things and continued faithful unto death.[24] The people are a pattern to the whole flock,

> Meek, simple followers of the Lamb,
> They live, and speak, and think the same.[25]

By their patience and steadfastness of faith, they have conquered their fiercest adversaries. God gives them rest, and they walk in his fear and in the comfort of the Holy Ghost, increasing daily both in grace and number.

I preached at 7:00 to most of the town and pressed them to come boldly to the throne of grace.[26] My spirit was greatly enlarged and refreshed by theirs. Those without seemed all given into my hands. I never have spoken more convincingly.

---

[19] Dudley, Worcestershire (detached); 8 miles west of Birmingham.

[20] John 6:37.

[21] Heb. 12:1.

[22] Rev. 3:12.

[23] Darlaston, Staffordshire; 1 mile northwest of Wednesbury. CW spells "Darliston."

[24] Cf. Phil. 3:8; Rev. 2:10.

[25] "Primitive Christianity," st. 2, *HSP* (1749), 2:333. In the original the second line is in the past tense.

[26] Heb. 4:16.

At the society we were all in a flame of love. They made me full amends for my sorrow at Wednesbury. We commended them to the grace of our Lord and left them in body, not in spirit.

**Friday, July 12.** Took my leave of the flock in Wednesbury, exhorting them to continue in the apostles' doctrine, and in fellowship, and in breaking of bread, and in prayers.[27]

Sarah Perrin gave a good report of the women whom she has met and finds much grace among them. Half a dozen more of the wandering sheep I gathered in and restored to their brethren. Most of the rest, I believe, would return if they were looked after and pursued by faithful labourers.

Spent the hour of intercession at Birmingham. The room[28] was full of serious people, mostly of the society, which is increased as much as Wednesbury's is decreased.

Passed the afternoon, not unprofitably, at brother Rann's, and preached in the evening to as many as the society room could contain. There were several there of the better rank. All received the word with deep attention, and the Lord gave testimony thereto.

**July 13, Saturday.** I preached again at 5:00 from the same words, "Let us therefore come boldly to the throne of grace that we may obtain mercy and find grace to help in time of need."[29] The spirit of the congregation helped me much. I have found none like-minded, excepting those at Darlaston.

At night my mouth was opened again to make known the mystery of the gospel.[30] The word had free course into the hearers' hearts. "Thine is the kingdom, the power, and the glory!"[31]

**Sunday, July 14.** Preached at 6:00 with enlargement of heart, and examined the society afterwards. They do run well, blessed be God, and adorn the gospel of our Saviour. Heard a good sermon at Church upon using the world as not abusing him—but alas it supposed all the congregation to be Christians!

Being refused a field, I preached at 5:00 in the street, below brother Bridgens'[32] door. A great multitude flocked together, to whom I cried, "Ho! every one that thirsteth, come ye to the waters, and he that hath no

---

[27] Acts 2:42.

[28] This room was attached to a house owned by Thomas Walker, a barber-surgeon, on Steel House Lane; cf. W. C. Sheldon, *Early Methodism in Birmingham* (Birmingham: Buckler and Webb, 1903), 16.

[29] Heb. 4:16.

[30] See Eph. 6:19.

[31] Cf. Matt. 6:13.

[32] CW spells "Bridgen" here, and "Bridgins" in MS Journal. JW identifies as "George Bridgins" in his *Journal* on Mar. 18, 1768 (*Works*, 22:122). A George Bridgens was buried in Birmingham on Mar. 8, 1769. Based on CW's description here, he would have been nearly 100.

money; ....."[33] We apprehended some disturbance, but the power of God was over all that heard his word, and they seemed to receive it with all readiness of mind. Surely he hath much people in this place.

The cloud stayed on the society assembled together.[34] It was a time of refreshing and gracious visitation. The word of exhortation went from my heart to theirs. The spirit of prayer was poured out. Our friends (especially some at Bristol) were brought to my remembrance, whom we presented to the throne. And the God of all consolation made our souls as a watered garden, "but we shall see greater things than these."[35]

**Monday, July 15.** At 5:00 we took horse with our brother Bridgens, an old disciple, past 80. Lay at Duffield (three miles beyond Derby) at the pleasantest inn I ever saw. Set out at 6:00 next morning and by 2:00 reached Sheffield. Here my heart rejoiced to meet some of our dearest children in the gospel. I encouraged them by that word, "Behold, he cometh with clouds; and every eye shall see him."[36] The door has continued open, ever since Mr. Whitefield preached here and quite removed the prejudice of our fiercest opposers. Some of them were convinced by his word, some converted and added to the society. "He that escapes the sword of Jehu, let Elisha slay!"[37]

I met the society in great bodily weakness. Preached next morning (July 17) and inquired into their behaviour. None walks contrary to the gospel. Rode to Rotherham[38] and preached at the end of the town in a tanner's house, which he has opened with his whole heart to receive the gospel. Here I found several solid believers and was much comforted among them. Talked severally with the growing society, who flourish under the cross. Returned and preached in Sheffield Street without life or power to a wild, tumultuous rabble. I was still more dead at the society.

**Thursday, July 18.** Parted in great love and rode toward Barley Hall. Baited three hours at our sister Booth's[39] and laboured all the time to strip an old self-righteous Pharisee. At last our Lord got himself the victory. We left her in tears and deep convictions. A far greater miracle of grace than the conversion of a thousand harlots!

Dined at Barley Hall with our dear sister Johnson,[40] a widow indeed,

---

[33] Isa. 55:1.

[34] See Num. 9:15–23.

[35] Cf. John 1:50.

[36] Rev. 1:7.

[37] Cf. 1 Kings 19:17.

[38] Rotherham, Yorkshire; 6 miles northeast of Sheffield. CW spells "Rotheram."

[39] Elizabeth Booth (fl. 1740–65) was one of the earliest members of the Methodist society at Woodseats, about three miles south of Sheffield.

[40] Mrs. Johnson and her recently deceased husband owned Barley Hall, a farmstead half a mile north of Thorpe Hesley, Yorkshire. JW had first visited this farmstead in 1733 with his

and her six sons and daughter, all believers. I had heard at Sheffield that the society here was come to nothing, so that I came to them with reluctance. My congregation at night was as large and serious as usual, and the word was accompanied with the power which never fails me in this place. Surely, I said to myself, the Lord is not departed from this people. I was still more agreeably surprised in examining the classes, to find near seventy earnest souls, most of them believers and grown in grace. They walk in love and are a pattern to the flock, but who can stand against envy? The preacher who brought up an evil report of them to me had it from some of Sheffield, who through prejudice and jealousy would always hinder our preaching at this place. How cautious therefore and deliberate should we be in judging or believing any man without full proof! I marvel not now that my mouth was stopped at Sheffield.

**Friday, July 19.** Preached, before I set out, to this loving people and left them sorrowful yet rejoicing. We had a pleasant ride to Wakefield, where our brother [John] Johnson received us gladly. He himself was sick of a fever, but the Lord m<akes> his bed[41] and he waits upon him, without trouble, care, or choice.

Just at his door, our brother [William] Shent challenged us and another from Leeds, who eased our weary beasts of their burdens. Miss Norton[42] likewise, and a young gentlewoman of Oulton found us out and joined us in prayer and thanksgiving. At 3:00 we took horse again and in two hours got to our brother Shent's. Mrs. Hutchinson[43] was one of the first that found us there and with hearty love welcomed us to Leeds. At 8:00 I preached to many more than the house could hold, who were got together on so short notice. The Lord gave us token for good, and we came boldly to the throne of grace for mercy and grace to help.

**Saturday, July 20.** Finished my discourse from Hebrews 4, last,[44] to the house full of earnest souls, by whose faith both my mouth and heart were opened. Passed an hour with the leaders, examining into their state and that of their brethren. Each of 250 members can say to the world, "Which of you convinceth me of sin?"[45]—as I am informed, and hope to find it so, when I talk with them.

---

father, and CW had been mobbed there on May 27, 1743 (see MS Journal).

[41] See Job 17:13.

[42] Ann Norton (fl. 1750), a single woman of some means, was an early supporter of the Methodist work in Leeds. However, in 1755 she would side with those calling for separation from the Church of England and provided the property on which John Edwards would build White Chapel, as an independent congregation that drew away many of the Methodist society.

[43] Mary Hutchinson (b. 1695) of York married Timothy Hutchinson (1693–1747) of Baildon in 1715. They settled in Leeds, where Mary joined the Methodist society..

[44] I.e., Heb. 4:16 (the last verse).

[45] John 8:46.

At 4:00 visited a faithful brother, whose wife and sister were drawing back and in great danger of reconciliation with the world. We laboured to restore them in the spirit of meekness, and the Lord gave weight to our words. They were <press>ed down by the power of his love and have departed for a season, I trust, that we may receive them again forever.[46]

At 8:00 preached the gospel to a multitude of poor sinners, unfeignedly poor and hungering after righteousness. For above an hour I cried to them of a fearful heart, "Be strong, fear not; your God will come and save you."[47] "He that watereth shall be watered of the Lord."[48] So I found it of a truth. I seemed [to have] got among my Wednesbury or Newcastle colliers while in their first love, and by the general effect of the word was inclined to think I ought not to leave this willing people so soon as I proposed.

**Sunday, July 21.** Met the society at 5:00 and exhorted them to continue steadfastly in the apostles' doctrine, and in fellowship, and in breaking of bread, and in prayers.[49] At 7:00 preached in the shell of our new house, which contains above 3,000, but many were forced to listen without. My text was Zechariah 4[:9], "The hands of Zerubbabel have laid the foundation of this house; his hands also shall finish it." I was extremely weak in body, but the word was blessed to the hearers. Here is an open door indeed, and ought it not to be kept open by constant preaching?

We passed half an hour at our brother Ashe's and were much drawn out in prayer for the brethren. Took horse for Birstall,[50] where John Nelson comforted our hearts with his account of the success of the gospel in every place *except Scotland*. There he has been these three weeks, beating the air and spending his strength in vain. Twice a day he preached at Musselburgh[51] and another place to some thousands of *mere* hearers, without converting one soul.

His report upon the whole is that the Scotch are the most dead, most bigoted, most inaccessible people of any he ever saw or heard of.

I preached at 1:00 to men of a better spirit. Such a sight have I not seen for many months. They filled the valley and side of the hill as grasshoppers for multitude. Yet my voice reached the most distant, as I perceived by their bowing at the holy name. Not one, of so many thousands, appeared unconcerned. I pointed them to "the Lamb of God, who taketh away the sin of the world."[52] God gave me the voice of a trumpet and sent home the

---

[46] See Phil. 1:15.
[47] Isa. 35:4.
[48] Cf. Prov. 11:25.
[49] Acts 2:42.
[50] Birstall, Yorkshire. CW spells "Birstal."
[51] Musselburgh, Midlothian; 6 miles east of Edinburgh. CW spells "Musleburgh."
[52] John 1:29.

word to many hearts. "Not unto me, O Lord, not unto me!"[53]

After evening service, I met the same congregation but much increased, and lifted up my voice to comfort them by the precious promises. Our hearts were enlarged to receive the Saviour. The eyes of the blind were opened, and the ears of the deaf unstopped; the lame men leaped like harts, and the tongue of the dumb sang.[54] It was a time of most gracious visitation. We parted with fervent prayer for the universal conversion.

I found the burden of the Lord upon me, detaining me still in his work among this people, and could not help telling them I hoped to meet them once more on the next Lord's day.

The society collected from all parts filled their new room, above 800 of them, whom I earnestly exhorted to walk as becometh the gospel.[55] Great was our rejoicing before the Lord. We called upon our absent brethren to be partakers of our joy. One in particular was laid upon my heart and the heart of my fellow-travellers *before* I began praying for them. Several children seemed greatly affected. Upon my inquiry, John Nelson informed me that lately many of them had got together in the fields to sing and pray; that now they come every Sunday, near 300 of them, to be instructed by his wife; and some are converted, many under deep convictions, and all more or less awakened to work out their salvation. It is the Lord's doings! "Out of the mouth of babes and sucklings let him perfect praise!"[56]

[[Leeds]]
[[July]] 22, 1751

[[Dear Brother,

[[I see every day the wisdom of not limiting myself. Here is such an open door as compels me to stay; and my chief design for coming seems likely to succeed.]] Michael Fenwick[57] [[is here. I keep him with me, that I may fully prove him. I shall do nothing rashly; and believe nothing without full proof. Three more women I have found out whom the shepherd[58] has

---

[53] Cf. Ps. 115:1.

[54] See Isa. 35:6.

[55] Phil. 1:27.

[56] Cf. Matt. 21:16.

[57] Michael Fenwick (d. 1797) sought to became one of JW's helpers in 1751, but both JW and CW were doubtful of his gifts and discipline (see JW to CW, Aug. 3, 1751). In 1755 JW took Fenwick as his groom for a period, commenting that he was "upon occasion a tolerable preacher" (JW to E. Blackwell, Sept. 12, 1755). But by 1758 Fenwick had been encouraged by Conference to return to his career in business (*Works*, 10:283). He returned to itinerancy in 1767, serving until he was again asked to step aside in 1774.

[58] James Wheatley (d. 1775) became a traveling Methodist preacher about 1742, and attended the 1745 Conference. While JW initially thought highly of him, doubts began to surface in 1749. In 1751 JW and CW expelled Wheatley from the connexion in light of evidence

well-nigh devoured—rather I should call him a wolf in sheep's clothing. One woman is naturally turned back to the world, the flesh, and the devil. He will never have the impudence to show his face again in these parts. I fear I shall find his behaviour the same in all. Never, never must he hope to be received again amongst us! I pity those poor souls to whom he is now gone, but it is not in my power to hinder it.

[[Send me franks, or my journals will ruin you. The two Sarahs[59] join in love to your friend and you. Let us make a fourfold chord, and we shall not be easily broken. Our love to Friend]] Vigor[60] [[also. She must trust me a little longer for my answer; so must honest Thomas Westell. Pray for us publicly, and privately.

[[Send me direction where you are. Who looks to poor Ireland?
Farewell]][61]

*Address*: "To / The Revd. Mr Wesley / Bristol / by London / Single Sheet."
*Postmarks*: "LEEDS" and "24 / IY."
*Endorsement*: by JW, "Journal 1751 / to Jul[y] 20."
*Source*: holograph; MARC, DDCW 6/24–6/25.

---

of sexual improprieties with young women in his circuit. Wheatley immediately set up as an independent preacher in Norwich, where he gathered a significant following, but soon fell into his former ways and by 1756 had been found guilty of immorality in public court.

[59] Sarah (Gwynne) Wesley and Sarah Perrin; they are greeting JW and his new wife Mary (Goldhawk/Vazeille) Wesley.

[60] Mrs. Elizabeth (Stafford) Vigor (d. 1775), a widow of Quaker roots in Bristol, became a close friend of CW and his wife Sarah. See CW's mournful hymn composed on her death in MS Funeral Hymns, p. 73.

[61] The shorthand in this letter was expanded by Frank Baker and published in *Works*, 26:271–72; a few corrections are made here.

## JULY 22–AUGUST 13, 1751[1]

### Journal

**Monday, July 22.** I passed an hour of the afternoon at Miss Dodson's, a true mourner after Christ. The time of her departure seems at hand. But all her care is that her eyes, before they are closed, may see his salvation. We spake comfortably to her, and prayed for her fervently, nothing doubting but she will depart in peace.

I preached at 5:00 in the shell of the house and pointed a listening multitude to the Lamb of God.[2] The Comforter was present, as many hearts could testify. He continued with the society, and made the time a time of love and great refreshing.

**Tuesday, July 23.** At 5:00 I strongly warned the society from those words, "Ye are the salt of the earth. But if the salt hath lost its savour, wherewith shall it be salted? It is thenceforth good for nothing, but to be cast out, and to be trodden under foot of men."[3]

Visited a sister, sick and destitute of all things, yet triumphing over want, and pain, and death. I came rather to receive than minister consolation, for she herself was as full of comfort, and life, and love as the earthen vessel could hold. We did not lose the occasion of praying for our absent friends.

At 8:00 in the evening I preached "repentance and remission of sins"[4] in the name of Jesus to a vast multitude of high and low, rich and poor. They seemed *given into my hands*, and I had no respect of persons. The word was as a fire, and as an hammer. I am pure from the blood of all these sinners, for I have not shunned to declare unto them the whole counsel of God. But it should seem by their serious behaviour that they have ears to hear. The Lord send by whom he will send, to gather a people ready prepared for himself.

**Wednesday, July 24.** Proceeded at 5:00 to show the disciples how they ought to walk,[5] and then spake severally with the rest of the society. One only person, out of 250, have I met of a doubtful character. All the others have their conversation according to the gospel.

Walked to Woodhouse,[6] and preached at noon to many Dissenters in our brother [Benjamin] Stork's yard, but found myself very feeble

---

[1] See the introductory footnote for June 29–July 20, 1751, above.
[2] See John 1:29.
[3] Matt. 5:13.
[4] Luke 24:47.
[5] His sermon on Phil. 1:27–30.
[6] A village just north of Leeds.

and faint, just as I used to be before a fever. Returned with difficulty and administered the sacrament to our happy sister. Her words, so full of spirit and life, set us all on fire, confirming our souls and encouraging us to "enter the kingdom [of God] through much tribulation."[7]

Our little company adjourned to sister [Mary] Hutchinson's, where I laboured to hold up as long as I could—but was forced at last to follow their advice and lie down. Expecting to grow worse, I hastened first to disburden my soul by writing a dear friend who was grown slack and weary of the narrow way.[8] I warned and besought him with many tears to repent and do the first works.[9] Then the fever came and, being put to bed, I lay burning and restless (but not comfortless) all night.

**Thursday, July 25.** A sister had prayed by me last night in faith that Jesus might rebuke the fever, and this morning the answer came. While the fit was off, I was removed in a chair to a little quiet house of Miss Norton's, who with Sarah Perrin and my wife tended me as diligently as my guardian angel.

**Friday, July 26.** Had another fit, but nothing near so long or violent as the first. John Nelson called and refreshed me by his prayers and conversation. Above seventy, he informs me, have died of the Birstall society, in full triumph of faith.

**Saturday, July 27.** I had respite from pain, but continued all day in extreme weakness.

**Sunday, July 28.** I rose at 8:00, but was forced to bed again by ten. A shivering fit shook me most violently for two hours, but did not hinder my dictating to Sarah Perrin, who wrote my confused thoughts concerning the state of the church.[10] To me they seemed material, if to none else; and I could not deliver my own soul unless I left them behind me.

At noon Dr. Milner[11] came and ordered me the bark,[12] as soon as the hot fit was quite over. It lasted in full strength till between 6:00 and 7:00. In the midst of it, my old f<aith>ful friend and brother [Henry] Thornton called to see me and while he stayed suspended my pain <or> at least made me less attentive to it. At 8:00 I took the bark, and again at 12:00; but could not keep it in my stomach.

**Monday, July 29.** Continued the bark, the doctor having made some alteration in his prescription. He told me today that a foreign minister from

---

[7] Cf. Acts 14:22.

[8] In MS Journal CW specifies that this letter was to John Hutchinson; the letter is not known to survive.

[9] See Rev. 2:5.

[10] See below: July 28, 1751–January 16, 1752 (notebook on "The Preachers").

[11] Joseph Milner, MD (d. 1778), of Leeds.

[12] Cinchona, known popularly as "Jesuits bark" or "Peruvian bark," is a source of quinine.

Switzerland, now in town, was desirous to talk with me. In the afternoon Mr. Polier[13] came, and inquired thoroughly into all our affairs. I told him all I knew of the Methodists, with which he appeared fully satisfied. As far as I could judge, he seemed a man of great learning and piety, desiring nothing on earth <but> to save his own and his people's souls.

**Tuesday, July 30.** Expected the return of my fever, but God permitted it <not>. My little strength do I ascribe unto him, and to prayer as the means, rather than to physic. The poor people have borne my burden and have been heard at the throne of grace.

### August

**Thursday, August 1.** Was much refreshed in body by riding out. In the afternoon had another conference with Mr. Polier, and perceived I had entertained an angel unawares.[14] I cannot but believe him a chosen vessel, and rejoice that my fever detained me here to meet with him. Several of our books I gave him, and he designs to learn English, that he may read them. He promised to write to me from his own country, blessed God for our having met, and expressed great love at parting. In the evening we were strangely drawn out in prayer for him.

**Friday, August 2.** The purging returned and the fever threatened[15] all day, yet God <kept> it off.

**Saturday, August 3.** Was enabled to ride out again, and to confer with the preachers and others.

**Sunday, August 4.** Found my strength sensibly increase in the fresh air. Spent an hour with the women leaders, and appointed them to meet as a band once a week.

**Monday, August 5.** Went to the room, that I might hear with my own ears, one of whom many strange things had been told me. I attended diligently in a little room adjoining. But such a preacher have I never heard, and hope I never shall again! It was beyond all description! I cannot say he preached false doctrine or true, or any doctrine at all, but pure unmixed nonsense. Not one sentence did he utter that could do the least good <to> any one soul. Now and then a text of Scripture or a verse quotation was dragged in by head and shoulders. I could scarce refrain from stopping him. Many of the better sort we<re> present, from whom I could not conceal my uneasiness. He set my blood a-galloping, and threw me into such a sweat that I expected the fever to follow.

Some of the gentry as well as the leaders begged me to step up into the desk, and speak a few words to the poor, dissatisfied hearers. I did so,

---

[13] Rev. Jean-Antoine-Noé Polier (1713–83), who was a minister in Lausanne at that time.

[14] See Heb. 13:2.

[15] Orig., "threatened it."

taking no notice *of* the preacher, or *to* him.[16] But of this I am infallibly sure, that if ever he had a gift for preaching, he has now *totally* lost it.

**Tuesday, August 6.** I met the society in the afternoon, and prayed with them in solemn fear of God present. We did not forget the absent brethren and labourers. It seemed as if the Lord spake in an articulate voice, "Return unto me, and I will return unto you."[17] My faith was greatly strengthened *for the work*—as to the manner and instruments of carrying it on, I leave that entirely to God.

**Wednesday, August 8.** Took horse for Newcastle between 6:00 and 7:00. Miss [Ann] Norton was so obliging as to accompany us, with brother [William] Shent, and brother Lambertson.[18] The day seemed *made* for us— so cool, so calm, so bright. I renewed my strength by using it. In four hours we reached Knaresborough. Baited two hours and an half, and set out again; but my body failed through the length of the way. I rode slowly on in much pain, striving to reach Sandhutton,[19] but was constrained to stop short at Topcliffe.[20] Just ready to faint, I entered the house and <foun>d a very aged woman in the chimney-corner reading Thomas à Kempis. I fell into talk with her, and asked her the foundation of her hope. She simply answered, "A good life." I endeavoured to teach her better, and preached Christ the atonement, as the only foundation. She received my word with tears of joy. We joined in fervent prayer for her. All the family appeared much affected, and the landlady desired to know if I could not preach at their town. I found myself refreshed in body as well as soul, and easily rode on the few remaining miles to Sandhutton.

We were no sooner housed than it began to pour down, and continued raining till we set out next morning.

**Thursday, August 8.** From 5:00 to 8:00 we were riding to [Great] Smeaton. God stayed the bottles of heaven[21] and sent us fair weather out of the north. Soon after 2:00 we came safe to Ferryhill,[22] and by 6:00 to Durham.

---

[16] In MS Journal CW identifies this problematic preacher as Michael Fenwick. He goes on to say there: "I talked closely with him, utterly averse to working, and told him plainly he should either labour with his hands, or preach no more. He hardly complied, though he confessed it was his ruin, his having been taken off his business. He complained of my brother. I answered I would repair the supposed injury by setting him up again in his barber's shop. At last he yielded to work, so it might be *in private*."

[17] Mal. 3:7.

[18] John Lambertson (fl.1750), a clothier, was one of the original trustees of the Boggart House, the first Methodist Chapel in Leeds.

[19] Sandhutton is a small village about 3 miles north of Topcliffe, not to be confused with the village of Sand Hutton, located about 26 miles southeast of Topcliffe.

[20] CW spells "Toplift."

[21] See Job 38:37.

[22] Ferryhill, Co. Durham; CW spells "Fery Hill."

Some of the infant society found us out, and pressed me to preach at 8:00, the usual hour. I sent William Shent, and betook me to my rest, far less fatigued than I expected.

**Friday, August 9.** Jonathan Reeves was stopped in passing through the town to Yorkshire, by hearing of my being here. I was glad of his coming so providentially to my help. We took horse at 8:00 and rode leisurely to Newcastle. The Lord hath blessed our going out and our coming in,[23] and he shall still direct our paths if in all our ways we acknowledge him.[24]

My fellow travellers are better both in mind and body for their long journey, having seen in every place the hand and footsteps of the Almighty. Surely he hath been with us, and blessing he hath blessed us. We have received at his hands nothing but blessings, of which my fever is not the least. If he sent it to purge me that I may bring forth more fruit, his will be done; and if he send it again, as his messenger to summon me hence, I trust he will make me ready for himself, and finish by fitter instruments *the work*—for which alone I would desire to live.

I preached in the evening (but very feebly) on those words, "The third part will I bring through the fire."[25] Preaching, I plainly perceive, is not now my principal business. God knoweth my heart, and all its burdens. O that he would take the matter into his hand, and lay me aside as a broken vessel!

**Saturday, August 10.** Passed the day in conference with the preachers. Preached at night with a little life.

**Sunday, August 11.** Felt the fever hanging about me all day, notwithstanding the bark, which I continue taking.

In the evening I preached repentance and forgiveness[26] to a thin congregation, some of whom seemed to *feel* the word. The society appeared lively and solid. My mouth and heart was opened among them, and I vehemently exhorted them to watch and pray, as well for the labourers as themselves, that none of us might bring a reproach upon the gospel.

**Monday, August 12.** Had much talk with a brother from Scotland,[27] who has preached there, he tells me, many weeks (or months) and not converted one soul, "You may just as well preach to the stones," he added, "as to the Scots." Nevertheless to keep my brother's word, I sent William Shent to Musselborough. Before he went, he gave me this memorable account of their late trial at Leeds.

---

[23] See Ps. 121:8.

[24] See Prov. 3:6.

[25] Zech. 13:7–9.

[26] His sermon on Luke 24:47.

[27] This is apparently "J. J–n the drummer," a Methodist soldier stationed in Scotland; see Aug. 16, 1751 below.

## July–August 1751

At Whitecoat-Hill, three miles from Leeds, a few weeks since as our brother Maskew[28] was preaching, a mob arose, broke the windows and door, and struck the constable, Jacob Hawley, who was one of our brothers. On this, we indicted them for an assault, and the ringleader of the mob, John Hillingworth, indicted our brother the constable, and got persons to swear the constable struck him. The grand jury threw out our indictment, and found that against us. So we stood trial with them on Monday, July 15, 1751, and the Recorder (Richard Wilson, Esq.) gave it in our favour with the rest of the court.[29] But the foreman of the jury (Matthew Priestly) with two others (Richard Cloudsley and Jabez Bunnell) would not agree with the rest, being our bitter enemies. The foreman was the Rev. Mr. Murgatroyd's[30] great friend and champion against the Methodists.

However, the Recorder gave strict orders to a guard of constables to watch the jury, that they should have neither meat, drink, candles, nor tobacco till they were agreed in their verdict. They were kept prisoners all that night and the next day till 5:00 in the afternoon, when one of the jury said he would die before he would give it against us. Then he spoke closely to the foreman concerning his prejudice against the Methodists. God was pleased to touch his heart, and at last he condescended to refer it to one man. To this man (Joseph Inkersley) he who spake to the foreman directed his speech, and charged him to speak as in the presence of God, and as he would answer it to God in the day of judgment. The man turned pale, and trembled, and desired another might decide it. Another (Joseph Hardwick) being called on immediately decided it in favour of the Methodists.

After the trial, Sir Henry Ibbetson,[31] one of the justices, called a brother and said, "You see, God never forsakes a righteous man; take care you never forsake him."

While the trial lasted, hundreds of our enemies were waiting for the event, who showed by their fierceness and rage what they designed, had

---

[28] Jonathan Maskew (1718–93) was a Yorkshireman, born in Otley. He was drawn into revival efforts by William Grimshaw, and then introduced to JW. Maskew laboured as an itinerant preacher almost exclusively in the north, continuing to preach widely throughout the area even after he had married and settled down at Deanhead, near Rochdale.

[29] CW inserted a footnote at this point:
Judge of the Court: Richard Wilson, Esqr., Recorder of Leeds.
Justices: J. Frith, Mayor, Alderman [Thomas] Micklethwait, Alderman [Robert] Denison, Alderman [Thomas] Sawyer, Alderman [Robert] Smith[son], Alderman [John] Brooke, etc.
Jury: Matthew Priestley, Richard Cloudsley, Jabez Bunnell, Henry Briscoe, William Wormill, Richard Cockell, Joseph Naylor, Joseph Inkersley, George Dixon, Richard Sharp, William Upton, and Joseph Hardwick.
Four witnesses against; six witnesses for us.

[30] Rev. John Murgatroyd (1703–68), graduate of Cambridge, was curate of St. John's Chapel in Leeds.

[31] Sir Henry Ibbetson (d. 1761), baronet, would be elected mayor of Leeds the following year. CW spelled "Ibison" in MS Journal.

they got the trial. They intended to begin by pulling down the preaching house. But thanks be to God, who hath not delivered us over as a prey into their teeth! Thanks be to God, who giveth us the victory through our Lord Jesus Christ.[32]

*Source*: holograph; MARC, DDCW 6/29a.

---

[32] See 1 Cor. 15:57.

# August 13–October 3, 1751[1]

Journal

**Tuesday, August 13.** [in Newcastle] I had some conversation with one who thinks himself called to preach.[2] He told me himself that he had preached a long time in Scotland, and had not been instrumental in converting a single soul. "But you might as well preach to the stones," he added, "as to the Scots."

I could not find that he had had better success in other places, yet I would not judge of his gifts till I had heard him myself. This morning I did so, but not to my satisfaction. He made nothing out; spoke nothing that could either inform the understanding or affect the heart—but, to the best of my present judgment, *vox est praetereaque nihil*.[3]

At 9:00 I took horse with Sarah Perrin, etc., for Sunderland,[4] where an unexpected door was opened for preaching. I first met the society, 100 orderly walkers, and examined each. Most of them have received forgiveness, the greater part of them in meeting their classes. (An argument for classes, which I cannot get over!) At 7:00 I preached in a large convenient room built for the purpose and capable of [containing] 1,000 hearers. It was crowded with attentive souls, to whom I cried, "Behold the Lamb of God, who taketh away the sin of the world!"[5] For an hour and an half my strength held out and God gave strong testimony to his word. Then I was fit for nothing but to be carried to bed.

**Wednesday, August [14].**[6] At 9:00 took horse, and after half an hour's riding overtook a woman and girl standing by an horse. She begged us to help them up, and forward on their way; their beast having carried them quickly so far, but now refusing to go on. I stood by while Robert G[illespie][7] helped them up. The horse turned with them again, and rode back towards Sunderland. We had the riders to pick up again. I left them to Robert's care and rode forward, but my heart stopped and forced me back to their assistance. We got them up again, and put their beast between ours; but in vain. It broke through a gap into the field, and rode away with them toward home. As soon as it had shook them off, it stood still. I asked the woman whither she was going. She said to a

---

[1] See the introductory footnote for June 29–July 20, 1751, above.

[2] "J. J–n the drummer"; see Aug. 16 below.

[3] "[He] is only a voice, nothing more."

[4] Sunderland, Co. Durham; 11 miles southeast of Newcastle upon Tyne.

[5] John 1:29.

[6] Orig., "19"; an error.

[7] Robert Gillespie had been admitted on probation as an itinerant preacher in 1750 (see JW, *Works*, 10:237) and would be laid aside in Nov. 1751 (ibid, 246).

place nine miles off, in the road to Newcastle. I ordered Robert to take the girl up before him, hoping the horse would carry the woman alone; but still it was labour lost. We all beat the poor beast to drive him on, but he kicked and flounced till he had dismounted his rider. I then said, "Surely, good woman, God withstands you. You are going contrary to his will. I can compare your horse to nothing but Balaam's ass.[8] What can be the meaning of it?" She answered, "Sir, I will tell you all. That child I had by a gentleman who promised me marriage. He has since married another because [she is] richer than me. I am going to see if he will do anything for his child and me, but I fear it is not pleasing to God." I asked if she had aught to live upon. She told me she was married to a blacksmith and had a child by him; that it was but low with them. I advised her utterly to renounce that other wicked man (as God warned her to do) and to spend the rest of her days in repentance and working out her salvation. I gave her something, which she gratefully received with my advice. Her child and she then mounted their horse, who quietly carried them back to Sunderland.

**Friday, August 16.** I heard J. J–n, the drummer, again and liked him worse and worse. His false English and low vulgar ridiculous expressions I pass over. But with my strictest observation, I could not perceive one word that was accompanied with the power of God. Perhaps he might have done some good among the soldiers. But to leave his calling, and set up for an itinerant, seems as contrary to the design of God as to his own and the Church's interest.

At 7:00 I walked towards Ouseburn[9] to meet the classes, but my strength totally failed me by the time I got to Sandgate, and I was forced to call and rest me at a brother's till I recovered strength enough to return.

At 3:00 I was sent for by the gaoler's wife to a poor wretch under sentence of death for murdering his own daughter, a sick child of 14. Never have I spoken to a more stupid, ignorant, hardened sinner. I might as well have talked to the prison walls. He utterly denied the fact. I prayed with him, but with very little hope.

After preaching at the Orphan House,[10] I commended him to the prayers of the congregation. Yet at my next visit I perceived little change in him. Only he suffered me to speak, and said little himself of his own innocency.

---

[8] See Num. 22:21–38.

[9] Industrial area just outside the walls of Newcastle Upon Tyne, in the valley of the River Ouseburn where it enters the River Tyne. CW spells "Ew's Bourn."

[10] The Orphan House was the first Methodist building in the north of England, built in 1743 to serve as the principal base in that region. It stood just outside of the town walls in Newcastle, on the west side of what is now Northumberland Street.

**Sunday, August 18.** Rode to Sheep Hill[11] with Sarah Perrin, and Miss [Ann] Norton, to *see* the people at least, if I could not preach. Jonathan Reeves supplied my place and bade them, "Come boldly to the throne of grace."[12] During the hour that he was speaking, I recovered a little strength and went to a numerous congregation of our brethren and children. For a quarter of an hour I continued enforcing the apostle's words. We were all greatly comforted together, and I returned to Newcastle rejoicing.

Preached again in great weakness, and kept a love feast. Many believers from all parts were present, and I found the benefit of their faith. It was a solemn season of love and joy. The spirit of supplication was given, and the poor malefactor brought to our remembrance. Surely the Spirit made intercession. I have not been so refreshed this many a day.

**Monday, August 19.** Rode with my fellow travellers and Jonathan Reeves to Penshaw,[13] where I preached in the evening, and Jonathan next morning. Found when it was too late that they wanted reproof more than encouragement.

**Tuesday, August 20.** Preached in the afternoon at the prison upon, "Christ hath redeemed us from the curse of the law, ...."[14] Still I can perceive no deep repentance in the poor man, though he is to die tomorrow. He persists in his innocency, but confesses he deserves the severest punishment from God. I prayed over him with tears and took my leave of him, till we meet in eternity.

I was ready to wonder why the providence of God had directed me to him and engaged his people to pray for him, when one informed me that while I was praying for him in the congregation with great earnestness, a woman had received remission of sins. Many other good ends may be answered which yet we do not know, at least our prayers shall turn again into our own bosom.

At night I was drawn out again in fervent prayer for him, and continued therein near half an hour. The people were all affected greatly. It is impossible for so many prayers to return empty.

**Wednesday, August 21.** The first news I heard this morning from Jonathan Reeves was that he had been with John Down[e]s[15] and others, visiting the poor malefactor, and they verily believed he had found mercy. He told him his heart was so light he could not tell how to explain it,

---

[11] An area within Burnopfield, Co. Durham; 3 miles northwest of Stanley.

[12] Heb. 4:16.

[13] Penshaw, Co. Durham; 4 miles southwest of Sunderland. CW spells "Painsher," an archaic spelling reflecting pronunciation.

[14] Gal. 3:13.

[15] John Downes (c.1723–74) was one of JW's earliest and most trusted lay preachers. He was serving at the time in the Newcastle circuit as an Assistant (see *Works*, 10:233).

that he had been all night in prayer, that he was not in the least afraid to die. Two days before Jonathan [Reeves] had talked an hour and an half with him, and put him in great fear; but now he appeared quite calm and resigned, and so continued to the last moment. Surely if this sinner is saved, he is saved as by fire.[16]

Took horse at 9:00 for Horsley,[17] leaving Jonathan to attend the execution and bring us word. He overtook us in the afternoon with the same account of his convert, who showed all the marks of repentance and faith in death.

Passed the afternoon with Mr. Carr, a young minister from Scotland and some friends from Hexam.[18] Preached at 7:00 in our brother Smith's house, but the heat quite overcame me. Either the Lord will renew my strength or lay me aside like a broken vessel.

**Friday, August 23.** Had much talk with our brother Allen of Newcastle who has an office in the coal mines of £50 a year, and a gift of exhorting his colliers after their work is over, and every Sunday. He has been pressed, he told me, to throw up his business and give himself wholly to preaching, but he could never see it was the will of God concerning him. I confirmed him in his wise resolution not to reach himself beyond his measure.

Kept a watch-night, but left the lively congregation after 10:00 to honest, zealous Jonathan [Reeves].

**Saturday, August 24.** Rode to Durham and preached at night to as many as the society-house could contain. The word was with power, and the people in general seemed inclined to "repent and believe the gospel."[19]

**Sunday, August 25.** Received the sacrament at the Abbey,[20] where all things were indeed done decently and in order.[21] In the afternoon heard a tolerably good sermon at the parish Church, and then preached myself to a many quiet people in a yard; whom I pointed to the Lamb of God.[22] Here would be a great door opened, if there were *proper* labourers. Very great life I found in the society.

**Monday, August 26.** Set out at 6:00 with Miss Norton, Sarah Perrin, etc. Lodged at Thirsk,[23] and dined the next day at York. Preached at 6:00

---

[16] See 1 Cor. 3:15.

[17] Horsley, Northumberland; 2 miles west of Heddon-on-the-Wall. CW spells "Horseley."

[18] CW identifies the friends from Hexam as brother and sister Ord in MS Journal. In that setting he also spells the Scottish minister's name as above, while spelling it "Car" here.

[19] Mark 1:15.

[20] I.e., Durham Cathedral.

[21] See 1 Cor. 14:40.

[22] John 1:29.

[23] Thirsk, Yorkshire; 8 miles southeast of Northallerton.

to many deeply attentive hearers. Passed a restless night, expecting the return of my fever.

**Wednesday, August 28.** Received strength to preach in the afternoon, and meet the society. Next morning Miss Norton and Sarah Perrin set out with William Shent for Leeds, and we for Epworth.[24] It happened to be the fair day, which increased our evening congregation. I exhorted them to "come boldly to the throne of grace,"[25] and the word did not return empty.

**Saturday, August 31.** Rode with S[ally][26] to Misterton.[27] Prayed by an old believer who had saved all her house by prayer. Before the gospel came, she had in faith asked life for them; and as soon as the Methodists preached here her sons and daughters, brothers and sisters, and all her kin, who are the principal persons in the town, received the truth and entered into the society. I found a multitude of gracious souls who greedily drank the word, "I have blotted out thy transgressions as a thick cloud."[28] It was a time of great refreshing, both for them and me.

**Sunday, September 1.** Met the society from 6:00 to 8:00, and rejoiced over them as over our Kingswood colliers in their first love. Preached at 9:00, with double power. Many cried after Jesus. One fainted through vehemence of desire. I was forced to leave them and return to the dead souls in Epworth. There I preached at the cross,[29] and met the society, whom I endeavoured to stir up to the recovery of their former zeal.

**Monday, September 2.** Commended them to the quickening grace of God[30] and rode to Sykehouse.[31] Preached in the evening with a little life, but my bodily strength was exhausted. Took a vomit to keep off, if it please God, my fever.

**Tuesday, September 3.** Returned to Leeds, where our old companions in travel, Sarah Perrin and Miss Norton, with the rest received us gladly.

**Wednesday Morning, September 4.** Heard Michael Fenwick again— not without hearty pity for his poor audience. The next morning I heard Thomas Mitchell,[32] and could not help saying, "What is the chaff to the

---

[24] Epworth, Lincolnshire; 9 miles north of Gainsborough.

[25] Heb. 4:16.

[26] His wife Sarah (Gwynne) Wesley, who was traveling with him.

[27] Misterton, Nottinghamshire; 5 miles northwest of Gainsborough.

[28] Isa. 44:22.

[29] A small platform at the main city crossroad.

[30] See Eph. 2:5.

[31] Sykehouse, Yorkshire; 4 miles northwest of Thorne.

[32] Thomas Mitchell (1726–85), a native of Bingley, Yorkshire, joined the Methodists after a stint in the army, and served as an exhorter for a couple of years. He joined the ranks of traveling preachers in 1751, serving faithfully until his death.

wheat?"[33] *His* word was evidently the word of the Lord, notwithstanding the simplicity of the speaker, and the people seemed greatly quickened thereby.

Rode to Baildon[34] on purpose to see a very dear friend, who was quickened both soul and body at sight of me. Our satisfaction was mutual. At 3:00 I preached to many serious, lively souls at Windhill,[35] and got to Leeds with brother Towers[36] and the night.

**Friday, September 6.** Heard Michael [Fenwick]—for the last time. *Ohe! jam satis est!*[37] Although some things which he spake *were* very good, when my brother spake them, poor Michael made bold to borrow them out of the printed sermons, having got some paragraphs by heart. But the repeater made them all his own.

**Saturday, September 7.** Met by faithful Thomas Colbeck,[38] who gave me just such an account of Eleazer Webster[39] as I expected. Preached at night with life and comfort.

**Sunday, September 8.** Preached at noon to many thousands in Birstall, who *all seemed* ready prepared for the kingdom [of God]. At 5:00 found the new room[40] at Leeds crowded within and without. The Lord opened my mouth, and I humbly hope their hearts. His blessing continued with us, or rather increased at the society.

**Monday, September 9.** Preached with much freedom at Wakefield.[41]

**Tuesday, September 10.** Talked largely with Christopher Hopper[42]

---

[33] Jer. 23:28.

[34] Baildon, Yorkshire; 4 miles north of Bradford.

[35] Windhill, Yorkshire; 2 miles north of Bradford.

[36] Robert Towers, a class leader residing in Boar Lane; see JW's account of Towers in *Journal*, Feb. 1, 1748, *Works*, 20:206 (and errata in 24:714).

[37] "Now, that's enough." Horace, *Epistles*, I.v.12; Martial, *Epigrams*, IV.91.1.

[38] Thomas Colbeck (1723–79), a highly respected grocer and mercer, was steward of the Keighley Methodist society from 1746 until his death, and steward also of the Keighley or Haworth circuit. In 1748 JW accepted him as an Assistant among his traveling preachers, though in fact he was never stationed away from the West Riding of Yorkshire. He served (and attended Conference occasionally) as one of JW's major local preachers.

[39] See the account of Eleazer Webster on page 1 of the next document in this collection.

[40] The Methodist society in Leeds had been meeting at the cottage of Matthew Chippendale, a basket-maker of Boggart Close on Quarry Hill. When they outgrew the cottage they replaced it with a new meeting house on the same grounds. JW had preached in the emerging shell of this new room on May 14, 1751 (see *Journal*, *Works*, 20:389).

[41] Wakefield, Yorkshire; 8 miles south of Leeds.

[42] Christopher Hopper (1722–1802), a native of County Durham, was converted under Methodist preaching in 1743. That same year JW made him a class-leader, and he began to preach locally. About 1750 he become a full-time itinerant, and emerged as one of JW's longest serving and most trusted lay preachers.

concerning John Bennet[43] and Robert Swindells, David Trathen,[44] and Thomas Webb.[45] We were satisfied that there *is not* (as he apprehended) a formed design of confederating together, although the enemy may design it, and simple David would be glad of it. However, I resolved not to fix my judgment till I had talked to each party concerned.

In the afternoon John Bennet came. I carried him with me to Seacroft[46] and gave him an opportunity of telling me all his heart. He has been deeply prejudiced against my brother and kept warm or stirred up again by incendiaries and mischief-makers on every side. *Most* of them, I believe, *meant* well; but had far more zeal than discretion. *Some*, I am sure, were the devil's instruments, and told him of my brother *known* lies. No marvel if *such* menders of a bad matter have misinformed my brother also. But I trust the reign of Satan is over. One common friend, of a peaceable spirit, might have prevented all this evil.

I preached at Seacroft on those words of our Lord, "I do not condemn thee; go, and sin no more."[47] The Lord set to his seal, and I trust confirmed the souls of his disciples.

At night I talked with Robert Swindells, and felt great love for him as he did for me. Could my brother and I have him with us for a while, and lovingly reason the matter with him, I do in no wise despair of his coming entirely right.

Thomas Webb and David Trathen, I found in conversing, quite rooted in predestination, the spirit as well as doctrine, and resolved to preach it everywhere. These therefore, I cannot keep, for they will not stay with us, or from the Tabernacle.[48]

---

[43] John Bennet (c. 1715–59), of Chinley, Derbyshire, became associated with David Taylor and Benjamin Ingham after a dramatic conversion in 1742. Lady Huntingdon introduced him to JW in 1743; and he quickly became a lay preacher, creating his own "round" of Methodist societies in Derbyshire, Cheshire, and Lancashire. His relationship with JW was strained in Oct. 1749 when, through the instigation of CW, Bennet married Grace Murray, a widow whom JW believed was betrothed to himself. Moreover, Bennet was adopting more Calvinist views, which would lead him to part ways with the Wesleyan connexion in 1752. He received congregational ordination in 1754 and took charge of an Independent chapel at Warburton, Cheshire, where he served until his death.

[44] David Trathen was active among Methodists as a local preacher by 1747, and received as an itinerating preacher in 1748, but laid aside from this work in Nov. 1751 (see *Works*, 10:205, 214, 246). He subsequently disappears from Wesleyan circles. CW spells "Trathan."

[45] In this paragraph and four paragraphs later CW writes "J. Web." But in his manuscript "The Preachers 1751" he has correctly "Thomas Webb." Webb was accepted as a probationary itinerant in 1750, but laid aside in Nov. 1751 (see *Works*, 10:237, 246). This is not the same person as Capt. Thomas Webb who played a significant role in early American Methodism.

[46] Seacroft, Yorkshire; 4 miles east of Leeds.

[47] Cf. John 8:11.

[48] George Whitefield's preaching house.

**Wednesday, September 11.** Mr. [William] Grimshaw[49] came, and soon after Mr. [John] Milner.[50] At 10:00 we began our conference,[51] at which were present John Nelson, William Shent, Christopher Hopper, Thomas Colbeck, Jonathan Reeves, John Bennet, Paul Greenwood,[52] Michael Fenwick, Titus Knight[53] from Halifax, and Robert Swindells and Matthew Watson.[54] All these I had invited and given them notes. [Thomas] Webb and [David] Trathen came afterwards, but were not admitted. Brother Mortimer[55] [came afterwards] also, and William Darney,[56] whom I appointed to talk with before we met again in the afternoon.

Had anyone asked me the end of our conference, I could not have told him; only that I came to make observations, to get acquainted with the preachers, and [to] see if God had any thing to do with us, or by us.

We began with part of an hymn, as follows:[57]

---

[49] William Grimshaw (1708–63) matriculated at Christ's College, Cambridge in 1726, receiving his BA in 1730. He was ordained deacon and priest over the next two years. He held the curacy of St. Mary's Chapel, Todmorden for ten years; and in May 1742 became perpetual curate at Haworth, where he remained until his death. The Methodists also came to Haworth in 1742, and within five years both JW and CW had met Grimshaw. From the outset they were greatly attached, for Grimshaw was deeply religious and a boisterous evangelist. He became JW's right hand in the midlands and the north, and in Methodist trust deeds was named as the one responsible for the direction of Methodism in the event of the death of both Wesley brothers.

[50] John Milner (1710–77), a graduate of Jesus College, Cambridge in 1732, was vicar of Chipping, Lancashire. He was sympathetic to the Methodist movement, inviting JW to preach in his church in the face of significant opposition. See JW, *Journal*, Apr. 7, 1753 (*Works*, 20:450).

[51] While not quite of the status of earlier annual conferences, this meeting paralleled a regional meeting of JW with preachers near Bristol in May 1751 (see *Works*, 10:238–39).

[52] Paul Greenwood (d. 1767) began itinerating about 1747, serving for some years as one of "Grimshaw's men" in the Haworth round. The 1752 Irish Conference called him over to take care of Dublin. After this year he spent most of his ministry in the north of England. He was one of the preachers that started serving the Lord's Supper in 1760 without ordination, a practice that was soon quashed. Greenwood died in the Manchester circuit in March 1767.

[53] Orig., "Tho. Knight." Titus Knight (d. 1792) became an Independent minister at Halifax, but at the Conferences of 1753 and 1755 he was listed as a Methodist local preacher (see *Works*, 10:260, 275).

[54] A local preacher from Leeds; see *Works*, 10:206, 260.

[55] This was likely Samuel Mortimer, a local preacher in Leeds. See S. R. Valentine (ed.), *Mirror of the Soul: The Diary of an early Methodist Preacher, John Bennett: 1714–54* (Peterborough: Methodist Publishing House, 2002), 199.

[56] William Darney (d. 1774) became a pedlar-preacher on his conversion in the Scottish awakening in 1741 and formed religious societies in the West Riding of Yorkshire, which were secured for Methodism by the advocacy of William Grimshaw. At the 1747 Conference Darney was listed as a local preacher, and in 1748 he was received as an Assistant; but he proved so uncouth that he was laid aside in Nov. 1751 (see *Works*, 10:206, 214, 264). Through Grimshaw's continuing advocacy Darney was reinstated from time to time.

[57] This hymn appears (with a few changes in the last two stanzas) in MS Miscellaneous Hymns, 109–11; and MS Preachers Extraordinary, 1–3.

[1.] Arise, thou jealous God, arise,
    Thy sifting power exert,
Look thro' us with thy flaming eyes,
    And search out every heart.

2. Our inmost souls thy Spirit knows,
    And let him now display
Whom thou hast for thy glory chose,
    And purge the rest away.

3. Th' apostles false far off remove,
    The faithful labourers own,
And give *us* each himself to prove,
    And know as he is known.

4. Do *I* presume to preach thy word
    By thee uncall'd unsent?
Am *I* the servant of the Lord,
    Or Satan's instrument?

5. Is this, great God, my single aim
    Thine, wholly thine to be?
To serve thy will, declare thy name,
    And gather souls for thee?

6. To labour in my Master's cause,
    Thy grace to testify,
And spread the victory of thy cross,
    And on thy cross to die?

7. I once *unfeignedly believ'd*
    Myself sent forth by thee:
But have I *kept* the grace receiv'd
    In simple poverty?

8. Still do I for thy kingdom pant
    Till all its coming prove,
And nothing seek, and nothing want
    But more of Jesus' love?

9. If still I in thy grace abide,
   My call confirm and clear,
   And into thy whole counsel guide
   Thy poorest messenger.

10. Unite my heart to all that bear
    The burden of the Lord,
    And let our spotless lives declare
    The virtue of thy word.

11. One soul into us all inspire,
    And let it strongly move
    In fervent flames of calm desire
    To glorify thy love.

12. O may we in thy love agree
    To make its sweetness known,
    Thy love the bond of union be,
    And perfect us in one.

After prayer (in which I found much of the presence of God), I began without design to speak of the qualifications, work, and trials of a preacher; and what I thought requisite in men that acted in concert. As to preliminaries and principles we all agreed. This conversation lasted till 1:00.

I carried Mr. Grimshaw, Milner, and Bennet to dinner at Miss [Ann] Norton's.

At 3:00 we met again. But first I talked to brother Mortimer, whom I admitted, and to Darney, whom I rejected. His stiff-neckedness I knew of old, and was now resolved to bend or break him. The preachers had informed me of his obstinate behaviour toward my patient (too patient) brother at the last conference.[58] Besides his scandalous begging wherever he comes, and railing at his brethren or whomsoever he is displeased with. At Epworth he got more clothes than his horse could carry. They were ashamed to see the bags and bundles which he carried off. I told him these things in few words, for he soon took fire and flew out, as I expected, into such violence of behaviour that I thought he would have beat me. I left him raging like a wild bull in a net, and went to the preachers. Two hours more we spent in friendly, profitable conference. I told them my heart freely and fully concerning the work and the workmen. We parted in the spirit of love.

---

[58] A regional conference in Leeds led by JW on May 15, 1751 (see *Works*, 10:240).

At 6:00 I preached to thousands in the new house from, "Behold, he cometh with clouds; and every eye shall see him!"[59] We have not had such a time together since I came. The same power rested on the society. Our souls were as a watered garden. Thanks be to God for his unspeakable gift!

**Thursday, September 12.** I took a delightful leave of them at 5:00. Gave William Darney the hearing at Mr. Grimshaw's desire; Mr. Milner, Hopper, Bennet, [and] Shent were by. He denied everything, although William Shent proved it upon him. But I told him all past faults should be forgotten, on condition he refrained till the spring:

1. From railing.
2. From begging.
3. From printing any more of his nonsense. "Nonsense!" quoth he, "Nonsense. What, do you call my hymns nonsense! They are not mine but Christ's. He *gave* them [to] me, and Mr. John [Wesley] had nothing to say against them. And Mr. Grimshaw and Milner have recommended them. Here they are! What fault can you find with them?" With that he threw down his gauntlet—or book just printed—in an evil hour, his fate compelling. I opened it on those words:

> There's brother Toft, and Wrangle [...]
> When Satan souls do strangle[60]

(as near as I can remember) and read on till our brethren interrupted by the violence of their applause. Mr. Grimshaw and Milner were rather out of countenance and begged pardon for having recommended such a performance. But William [Darney] stood to it, that it was all divine. Neither would he promise not to print his own history,[61] which is almost ready for the press.

After I had turned him inside out, I agreed to his preaching among us, as a probationer, upon the aforesaid conditions. And he was compelled to say he would print no more books, without our imprimatur.

I would not admit him to the conference, that he might be humbled by perceiving I made a difference betwixt him and our preachers.

We passed the morning in prayer and conversation. I had hard work to keep all quiet, Mr. [William] Grimshaw and others urging John Bennet to explain his private opinions. I hardly staved them off, resolving to avoid a rupture at this time, and to divide the confederates. John Bennet

---

[59] Rev. 1:7.

[60] See William Darney, *A Collection of Hymns* (Leeds: James Lister, 1751), Hymn 1, st. 88 (p. 20): "There is Brother Toft and Wrangle, / of late they have begun / To seek, let them never strangle, / but thy Work carry on."

[61] William Darney, *The Progress of the Gospel in Great Britain* (Leeds: s.n., 1751).

indeed never had any design of setting up for himself or making a party, as he solemnly assured me. Of this John Nelson, [William] Shent, and [Christopher] Hopper were alike satisfied. Mr. Grimshaw many times advised me to keep fair with John Bennet, "as honest hearted a man," he called him, "as any among us." Trathen and Webb, I found, have complained heavily of Robert Swindells for deserting them. Him and John Bennet I have bound by love, and should not fear setting them both right, especially the latter, could I but part them and Satan's messengers.

We all agreed to postpone opinions till the next general conference, settled the affairs of the church the best we could, and parted *friends.*

At 3:00 took horse with Mr. Grimshaw, Milner, Shent, [and] Bennet for Birstall. Expounded Isaiah 35 with great enlargement and assistance. Rejoiced with the steadfast society and concluded the happy day with John Bennet in prayer.

**Friday, September 13.** I let him preach in the morning, which he did to the satisfaction of all. Rode with Jonathan Reeves to Bradford.[62] Preached repentance and remission of sins[63] in the street, to many seemingly serious people. Baptized a Dissenter's child. Picked up loving John Hutchinson[64] and rode on to Skircoat Green.[65] It was near sunset before I began there. The house would not contain a fifth part of the hearers. I stood out (the wall sheltering me, and an hill the people, from the high wind) and invited them to Christ, the justifier.[66] Great life I perceived among them, and very little in the society, whom I therefore sharply reproved. One cause of their backwardness is probably their many teachers. No less than four have sprung up from among themselves. To these I spoke very closely. One burst out into tears and offered to leave off preaching entirely. Another, Blacky Spenser, stood as hardened as William Darney. I set my mark upon him, as a stubborn, stiff-necked, mischievous man! He is continually quarrelling with one or other, and the impossibility of falling [away from Christ] sets him above all advice. I spake mildly and lovingly to him, not having time for breaking him. But if Satan does not serve himself upon him, I shall rejoice to be much mistaken.

**September 14, Saturday.** Heard John Bennet again. He spake sound words that could not be reproved, and they had a visible effect on the hearers. Took my leave of humble, modest J. Holywell, and bold audacious

---

[62] Bradford, Yorkshire; 8 miles west of Leeds.

[63] CW's usual summary for his sermon on Acts 2:37–39.

[64] John Hutchinson (1722–54) was the son of Timothy and Mary Hutchinson of Leeds. CW met John during his 1751 tour of northern England, and the fatherless John quickly became attached. John's health was fragile and CW helped care for him over the next couple of years. For CW's hymns on the occasion of Hutchinson's death see *Funeral Hymns* (1759), 6–12.

[65] Skircoat Green was an open area 1.5 miles south of Halifax, Yorkshire.

[66] See Rom. 3:26.

Blacky Spenser. Reached Keighley[67] by noon. Preached at 4:00 to about 1,000 as well-behaved hearers as I have lately seen, on whom I called with an opened mouth and heart, "Ho! every one that thirsteth, come ye to the waters."[68] Great life I also found in the society, now he that hindered is taken out of the way.[69]

**Sunday, September 15.** Bestowed an hour on the leaders, a dozen steady, solid men. Left Paul Greenwood to preach and hastened to Haworth.[70] Never saw a church better filled. But after I had prayed in the pulpit, the multitude in the churchyard cried out they could not hear and begged me to come forth. I did so, and preached Isaiah 35 from a tombstone. Between 3,[000] and 4,000 heard me gladly. At 2:00 I called again to above double the number, "Behold the Lamb of God, who taketh away the sin of the world!"[71] The church leads[72] and steeple were filled with clusters of people, all still as night. If ever I preached gospel, I preached it then. The Lord take all the glory!

Took horse immediately and followed our nimble guide, Johnny Grimshaw, to Ewood.[73] His father came panting after us. Sarah Perrin and her namesake[74] met us from Bristol, and brought Mr. Shent [[and Mr. [Thomas] Meyrick[75]]]. We passed a comfortable evening together. John Hutchinson still clave to us.

**Monday, September 16.** Preached at 9:00 in a convenient field to about 1,000 believers, all or conscious unbelievers; and again at 3:00 to about 3,000. *Their* spirit carried me beyond myself. Such a lively people I have not met with—so simple, loving, zealous. I could have gladly stayed to live and die with them.

Hitherto William Darney had attended us. I was willing for his own sake as well as his patron's to part friends, and therefore thought it sufficient to give William Shent a caution not to let Darney introduce *his* hymns in *our* societies. But re-considering [that] he might plead ignorance of my will, I ventured to tell him, as warily and gently as I could, that I would not have him make use of his own verses, unless in his own societies, or

---

[67] Keighley, Yorkshire; 13 miles northwest of Bradford.

[68] Isa. 55:1.

[69] See 2 Thess. 2:6–7.

[70] Haworth, Yorkshire; 2 miles southwest of Keighley. CW spells "Howorth."

[71] Cf. John 1:29.

[72] CW uses the archaic spelling "leeds." *OED*: "The sheets or strips of lead used to cover a roof; often collective for a lead flat, or lead roof."

[73] Ewood, Hall; William Grimshaw's estate, half a mile northeast of Mytholmroyd, Yorkshire.

[74] Sarah (Gwynne) Wesley.

[75] Meyrick had secured episcopal ordination in 1750 and was now curate of St. Ann's, Halifax (about 3 miles east of Ewood Hall).

Mr. Grimshaw's and Bennet's. But alas, what did my prudence avail! I "hit the cause that hurt his brain."[76] I wounded him in the most sensible part. He fell into his natural temper and roared so as utterly to astonish us. He railed on me most passionately, and did not spare Mr. Grimshaw himself. I told him we would let him make use of Watts's or Brady's [hymns[77]]—but not his own, upon any terms whatsoever. He insisted that he would sing his own hymns, and no other, seeing they were all given by inspiration, as was plain from his pouring out hundreds of them extempore, like John Cennick,[78] and *stans pede in uno*.[79] He behaved himself so outrageously on this trying occasion that his old friend [[and tamer]] Mr. Grimshaw gave him up for the most obstinate unpersuadable man he ever saw. *Infelix vales*,[80] away he flung from us *assuring* us, if we rejected his verses, we and all the work would come to nought.

Mr. Grimshaw now needed no farther proof of him, or of the necessity that he should be humbled and broken to pieces. He saw clearly that he had upheld him in his stubbornness and vanity, and resolved to resume his authority over him and join heartily with us to conquer him.

I shut up all with the following note—to William Shent.

Ewood [Hall]<br>September 16

Dear Brother Shent,

I leave this word of notice with you for our sons in the gospel as assistants or preachers in any degree.

At the desire of a very dear and faithful brother, I have consented to let William Darney preach among our children as *heretofore* although I believe his spirit is still whole and unbroken. But on these conditions, I consent:
1. That he does not rail or speak against anyone, much less any labourer [in the gospel]
2. That he does not beg of our people
3. That he does not print any more of his nonsense and
4. That he does not introduce the use of his doggerel hymns in any of our societies.

---

[76] Nathaniel Lee, *Caesar Borgia* (London, 1696), 59. The line describes madness.

[77] Isaac Watts(1674–1748) had published several volumes of hymns. Nicholas Brady (1659–1726) worked with Nahum Tate in producing *A New Version of the Psalms of David* (1698), and then published a *Supplement* (1700) giving new renderings of the "usual hymns" used in worship in the Church of England.

[78] CW spells "Cenwick." John Cennick published five booklets of hymns in rapid succession: *Sacred Hymns for the Children of God*, 2 parts (London: B. Milles, 1741–42); *Sacred Hymns for the Use of Religious Societies*, 3 parts (Bristol: Farley, 1743–44).

[79] "Standing on one foot." Horace, *Satires*, I.iv.10.

[80] "Unhappy farewells."

I cannot in conscience agree to his putting nonsense into their mouths. Indeed, they themselves would never consent to it. But he has utterly refused to promise forbearance; therefore, I have promised him that in whatsoever society of ours he uses his own verses, in that society *he shall preach no more.*
Witness my hand,

C. W.

**Wednesday, September 18.** Found much life in preaching to the morning congregation. Rejoiced to hear of my brother's longer stay in the west, whereby I am enabled to stay over Sunday here. Rode with John and Grace Bennet[81] to Bolton.[82] Preached there with much freedom and power. Found by the leaders that three or four have been hurt by [Thomas] Webb and [Robert] Swindell's preaching final perseverance. I warned them in the morning against dispute, and left them with regret.

**[Friday,] September 20.** My subject at Manchester[83] was Christ crucified, and crying from his cross, "Is it nothing to you, all ye that pass by?"[84] Many hearts, I trust, answered him in faith and love. Mr. [John] Milner was in the desk, partaker of our joy.

**Saturday, September 21.** John Bennet preached in the morning, with the demonstration of the Spirit, as several told me afterwards. Went on speaking with the society severally. A mystic brother I drove away in violent rage, by questioning his grace. The rest seemed very sincere and earnest. Several have found peace by hearing my brother, Christopher Hopper, John Bennet, etc. Passed an hour in useful conversation with Dr. Byrom,[85] who fairly and calmly told me what he thought amiss in us. Of such reprovers, how shy are we by nature? Yet such are our best friends.

---

[81] Grace Bennet (1716–1803) was born in Newcastle upon Tyne (maiden name unknown) and first married a Mr. Norman. Left a widow, in 1736 Grace Norman married Alexander Murray, a seaman, who also died six years later. She first heard JW preach in Moorfields on Sept. 9, 1739, and in the early 1740s was a member of bands for married women at the Foundery. After her husband's death, JW made her housekeeper at the Orphan House in Newcastle. She accompanied JW on a preaching tour in Ireland in 1748, during which JW suggested that they marry. This was not to be, largely through the intervention of CW, who solemnized the marriage of Grace to John Bennet on Oct. 3, 1749.

[82] Bolton, Lancashire; 10 miles northwest of Manchester.

[83] CW would have been preaching at the new Methodist meeting house just opened on Birchin Lane, off Church Street, in Manchester.

[84] Lam. 1:12.

[85] John Byrom (1692–1763), of Manchester, took degrees at Trinity College, Cambridge, and was elected fellow there in 1714. Shortly thereafter he went to France to study medicine. He returned to England in 1718, dividing his time between London, Cambridge, and Manchester. While he anticipated a career in medicine, this was soon abandoned. He turned his focus instead to poetry and developing a unique system of shorthand, gaining a reputation that led to election as fellow of the Royal Society in 1724. He also cultivated relationships with several leading non-Jurors. Both JW and CW used Byrom's shorthand. They were also influenced by him in the 1730s through their connection with John Clayton and other non-Jurors in Manchester.

A brother from Booth Bank[86] called and informed me that [Thomas] Webb and [David] Trathen have been preaching their favorite doctrines there, and much disturbed the flock. I wrote back by him to the stewards to stop them.

At night I preached Christ from Isaiah 61. Many Arians were present with their great apostle.[87] One openly contradicted. Great was the power and presence of our Lord in the midst of us. He answered for himself, and proved his commission to our hearts.

**Sunday, September 22.** Preached Christ crucified[88] at Stockport[89] to about 3,000. Some threatened hard, and threw dirt, etc., for a while, but the Lord restrained them. A mourning brother received the atonement. A great effectual door is opening, but there are many adversaries. The quietest place I have hither seen is Manchester, for the honour of High-Church[90] be it spoken.

Our house and yard were crowded at 5:00, and multitudes went away for want of room. The rest seemed given into my hand. I strongly urged them to repent and believe in him whom God sent to be their Saviour.[91] The Lord was with us of a truth, convincing, and converting. Met the loving society for the last time, and the last time proved the best.

**Monday, September 23.** Took my leave of the congregation, in love which never fails. Mentioned in my concluding prayer a brother in darkness, and God gave us strong faith for his recovery.

Left Mrs. Rider, our kind hostess, in tears; and poor, inconsolable John Hutchinson at sister Fanshaw's; and set out at 7:00 for Birmingham. Baited at Knutsford,[92] and Talk o' th' Hill,[93] and stretched as far as Newcastle.[94] I got little rest through my cough.

---

[86] Booth Bank, Yorkshire; 1 mile southwest of Slaithwaite. The brother was John Cross, who shared the letter from CW with John Bennet (see Bennet to CW, Oct. 4–12, 1751, MARC, MA 1977/130, p. 92.)

[87] CW is likely referring to members of the Cross Street Chapel in Manchester, a Dissenting congregation pastored by Rev. Joseph Mottershead (1688–1771), whose teaching had moved in a decidedly Arian direction, particularly under the influence of his co-pastor and son-in-law, Rev. John Seddon (1719–69).

[88] CW's usual title for his sermon on Lam. 1:12.

[89] Stockport, Cheshire; 6 miles southeast of Manchester.

[90] A reference to the non-Juror influence in Manchester.

[91] Likely his sermon on Acts 2:37–39.

[92] Knutsford, Cheshire; 14 miles southwest of Manchester.

[93] Orig., "Talk in the Hill." This village is now just Talke, Staffordshire; 4 mile north of Newcastle-under-Lyme.

[94] Newcastle-under-Lyme, Staffordshire.

**Tuesday, September 24.** Dined at Hednesford,[95] and came before 5:00 to Birmingham.

**Wednesday, September 25.** Robert Swindells, who had accompanied us thus far, took his leave and returned home. Had he gone on with me to London, I believe we never should have parted.

**Thursday, September 26.** Preached on the way to Wednesbury at noon; at Wednesbury in the evening with the *ancient* blessing. I suffered all the congregation to stay, while I strongly exhorted the society to do their first works. Returned by 10:00 to Birmingham.

**Friday, September 27.** Talked largely with C[harles] S[kelton]. He is very honest, or very false. I verily believe the former.

Kept the first watch-night at Birmingham. Our room was crowded with rich and poor. Many of both sort trembled at God's word; others rejoiced in hope of his glory.

**Saturday, September 28.** Took horse at 8:00 with our hearty old host, Mr. [George] Bridgens, and his daughter. (Sarah Perrin left us on Wednesday and went to Leominster.) It rained best part of the day, but not to hurt us. One or two other such days we have had on the road, but no rain to wet us throughout our journey. We dined at Studley,[96] and by 5:00 reached our brother Canning's in Evesham.[97]

I continued here till Wednesday. On Sunday afternoon the mayor lent us the town hall, which was thronged with quiet hearers, to whom I declared, "To us a son is born, to us a child is given."[98] Still there might be a great gathering in this place, if the society but agree among themselves. I laboured for peace once more, employed most of my time in reconciling them. Prevailed upon Mr. and Mrs. Canning to receive their daughter who had married without their consent, and left them on Wednesday morning in love (as it seemed) and peace with one another.

At night I expounded the Song of Simeon[99] at our brother Evans's in Oxford. Again here is the promise of a work, since he opened his house as well as heart to the gospel. Had much conversation with two serious scholars, who put me in mind of the first Methodists. They constantly attend the word, read by Mr. Evans's daughter with several of the townsmen. A little flock, which the Lord increase!

**Thursday, October 3.** Set out between 6:00 and 7:00. Called in passing on Mrs. Neal, and prayed with an earnest, gracious soul. We could not reach

---

[95] Hednesford, Staffordshire, 1.5 miles north of Cannock; CW spells "Hedgford," a 17th and 18th century spelling.

[96] Studley, Warwickshire; 3 miles southeast of Redditch.

[97] Likely Thomas Canning, who was headmaster of John Deacle's charity school, founded in 1736 on Port Street in Bengeworth.

[98] Isa. 9:6.

[99] Luke 2:25–32.

London till the next day. Our long journey ended there as prosperously as it began. The people were[100] ready, and joined heartily with us in prayer and thanksgiving.

*Endorsement*: by CW, "Journal in the North / June 29 to Oct. 3, 1751."[101]
*Source*: holograph; MARC, DDCW 6/26–6/27.

---

[100] Orig., "we"; an error.

[101] This endorsement, written on the blank backside of the final page of DDCW 6/27, is surely intended to cover DDCW 6/24–6/25, DDCW 6/29a, and DDCW 6/26–6/27, even though the pages of these various documents are not numbered consecutively.

## JULY 28, 1751–JANUARY 16, 1752[1]

[p. 1]

### The Preachers
### 1751

**I. Thomas Walker**[2]

In July I stopped Thomas Walker [at Worcester][3] from giving up his business. In October I found him at it in Evesham, where he preaches mornings and evenings, and thanks God and [me] for hindering him at Worcester.

Upon the strictest inquiry I cannot discover that he has much, if any, gift for preaching.

**II. Copy of my letter to the society in Nottingham [concerning Joseph Lee]**

I hear that Joseph Leigh[4] is among you. He is a weak man of little understanding, and less grace, I fear. But I *know* he is unstable as <wa>ter, therefore altogether unfit to direct and instruct others. Beware then how ye suffer him to speak, pray, or meddle at all with our society. He is not of us. I leave him to God, and advise you so to do.

**III. Aug. 4.**

Sent for **Eleazer Webster**;[5] talked with him fully, and silenced him! See papers, etc.

[p. 2]

---

[1] See the introductory footnote for June 29–July 20, 1751, above. The present document is not a journal letter. It is a manuscript notebook in which CW preserved notes both of his actions in silencing or restraining several Methodist lay preachers and of meetings held with his brother and others over this general concern.

[2] This heading appears below the two paragraphs on Walker in the manuscript; it is moved to provide consistency in format.

[3] It seems unlikely that this was Thomas Walker of Birmingham, a doctor-surgeon who had been converted under JW and hosted a society at his home (see JW, *Works*, 20:117n). In any case, no "Thomas Walker" appears as an approved itinerant in any surviving copy of Minutes, so CW's action had the effect he desired.

[4] An alternative spelling for Joseph Lee, whom JW had sent to help with the work in Newcastle—though not necessarily as a preacher (see CW letter to JW dated Oct. 3, 1742, attached to a journal letter above). He had subsequently moved to Nottingham.

[5] Eleazer Webster began preaching in Methodist settings about 1745. He appears as an official itinerant in the Minutes for 1747–48 (*Works*, 10:205, 208, 214). CW gives further details on his meeting with Webster in MS Journal, Aug. 5, 1751: "Thomas Colbeck brought Eleazer Webster to me. I spoke in vain to a self-hardened slave of sin, and silenced him." In Nov. it was agreed to drop Webster from the list of itinerants (see *Works*, 10:246). After that point he served as a local preacher around Keighley for several years.

### Written in the Interval of my Fever[6]

Unless a sudden remedy be found, *the preachers will destroy the work of God*. What has well nigh ruined many of them is idleness, the consequence of their having been taken from their trade. Most of them were as mere novices, as Michael Fenwick, without experience or stability, as fit to command an army as guide a Christian flock. Hence they quickly run themselves out of breath, losing first their grace, then their gifts and success. The unusual respect they met with turned their heads. The tinner, barber, thatcher, forgot *himself*, with his business, and immediately set up for a gentleman, and then—looked out for a fortune, having lost his only way of maintaining himself or family. Some have been betrayed by pride into still grosser sins; and are likely, unless stopped in time, to do the devil more service than ever they have done God. Some have fallen into grievous errors and must therefore be put away. What then will become of them? Will they not shut the door against us, in whatsoever new places they come? Will they not cause [p. 3] the same confusion that is now in Wales? Will not each, in time, set up for himself, like Kendrick, and make a new party, sect, or religion? Or supposing my brother and I have authority enough to quash them while we live, who shall stop them after our death? It does not satisfy my conscience to say, "God will look to that." *We* also must look to it ourselves, if we would not tempt God and act the part of rash enthusiasts. *We* must use all probable means of preventing so great an evil, as a *real schism entailed on the church*. *We* are justly answerable for the consequences of our own indiscretion and negligence. *We* are in conscience bound to hinder, as much as in us lies, our sons in the gospel from ruining their own souls and theirs that hear them.

The most effectual, the *only* way (in my judgment) is To SET THEM TO WORK AGAIN.[7] *All* of them, I mean, excepting a few, whom we can entirely trust. Hereby let the rest be proved: Which has grace, and which has not? Who is sent of God, and who of flesh and blood, of covetousness, sloth, pride, Satan? That man, who [p. 4] disdains to work with his own hands (after the great apostle [Paul]'s example), is no fellow-labourer for us. He seeks himself, not the glory of God and the salvation of souls. He has lost his single eye (if he ever had it) and because he will not work, he shall not preach.

The man who consents to labour at his calling approves his obedience and humility, both to us and the church. By being constantly employed, he escapes a thousand shams, stops the mouths of gainsayers, relieves the poor people of a grievous burden; and if God withdraws his gift, he is but where he was.

---

[6] Originally dictated to Sarah Perrin. See journal letter covering July 28, 1751 above.

[7] CW writes this out in printed capitals, to show extra emphasis.

If God continues to use him, like William Shent, John Nelson, Thomas Colbeck, etc., he has whereof to boast, that he makes the gospel of none expence. His trade leaves him no vacant time for sauntering, gossiping, fortune-hunting. And if he is inclined to marry, the church is secure against being burdened with his wife and children.

My counsel then is this:

1. That every preacher (excepting a very few) who has a trade return to it and labour with his own hands, like Thomas Westell, etc., by day and preach mornings [p. 5] and evenings at his own place of abode or the neighbouring societies. That now and then he may make an excursion, or perhaps take a journey to distant parts of the vineyard, and so return to his trade again.

2. That no future preacher be ever taken from his business or even permitted to preach till the point be settled, "How is he to be maintained?"

3. That no one be allowed to preach with us, till my brother and I have heard him *frequently* ourselves and talked largely with him, and each of us kept him with us, till *all the three are equally satisfied*.

[p. 6]

Agreed[8]

To lay aside:

>J[ames] Wheatley
>Elea[zer] Webster
>Rob[ert] Gillespie
>James Watson[9]
>Mich[ael] Fenwick
>J[ohn] Mad[d]ern
>D[avid] Trathen[10]
>T[homas] Webb
>W[illiam] Darney

[p. 7]

## Hints for Conversations, out of my Brother's Letters[11]

July 17, 1751

"I fear for Charles Skelton and Joseph Cownley more and more; I have heard they frequently and bitterly rail against the Church."

---

[8] This is a longhand listing of the names agreed upon in a meeting held Nov. 25, 1751, recorded in detail on p. 11 of this document.

[9] Both the longhand here and the shorthand repetition on page 11 below clearly give the first name as "James." But there is no other evidence anywhere that there was a James Watson serving as a preacher. CW may be misremembering the first name of Matthew Watson.

[10] CW spells "Trathan."

[11] None of JW's letters to CW during this trip have survived; CW's excerpts are the only trace of their content that remains (see *Works*, 26:470–76).

Q[uery]? What assurance *can* we have that they will not forsake it, at least when we are dead? Ought we to admit any man for a preacher *till we* can trust his invariable attachment to the Church?

July 20, 1751

"The church, that is the societies, both *must* and *shall* maintain the preachers *we send* among them; or I will preach among them no more. The least I can say to any of those preachers is, 'Give yourself wholly to the work, and you shall have food to eat, and raiment to put on.' And I cannot see that any preacher is *called* to any people who will not thus far assist him."

[Query]? How far do, or ought we to, send men to preach? How does this differ from ordaining?

If we take them from their trades [p. 8] and send them, ought we not to maintain them too?

Almost everything depends on you and me. Let nothing damp or hinder us. Only let us be alive, and put forth all our strength.

How is it that John Bennet cherishes all our malcontents?

July 24, [1751]

"As to preachers, my counsel is not to check the young ones, without strong necessity. If we lay some aside, we *must* have a supply, and of the two I prefer grace before gifts."

[Query]? Are not both indispensably necessary? Has not the cause suffered in Ireland especially through that insouciance, as well as gracelessness, of the preachers?

Should we not first regulate, reform, and bring into discipline, the preachers we *have*, *before* we look for more? Should we not also watch and labour to prevent the mischiefs which the discarded preachers may occasion?

"Let these things drive us two close together, and it is worth all the cost."

Amen, with all my heart, in the name of God! But *can* we unite [p. 9] unless it be given us from above? And must we not obtain the blessing through prayer?

July 27, [1751]

"What is it has eaten out the heart of half our preachers, particularly those in Ireland? Absolutely idleness—their not being constantly employed. *I see it plainer and plainer.* Therefore I beg you would inquire of each, 'How do you spend your time from morning to evening?' And give him his choice, 'Either follow your trade, or resolve before God to spend the same hours in *reading* which you used to spend in working.'"

Q[uery]: Has not God showed us both the disease and the remedy?

August 3, [1751]
"I heartily concur with you in dealing with all (not only disorderly walkers, but also) triflers, μαλακούς,[12] πολυπράγμονας,[13] as with Michael Fenwick.[14] I spoke to one this evening, so that I was even amazed at myself."

August 8, [1751]
["]We *must* have forty itinerant preachers, or drop some of our societies. ... You cannot so well judge of this, without seeing the letters I receive from all parts. ...["]

[p. 10]

August 15 [1751]
"If our preachers do not or will not spend *all* their time in study and saving souls, they *must* be employed close in other work, or perish."

August 21, [1751][15]
"I see plainly, the spirit of Ham,[16] if not of Korah,[17] has fully possessed several of our preachers. So much the more freely and firmly do I acquiesce in the determination of my brother that it is far better for us to have ten, or six preachers who are alive to God, sound in the faith, and of one heart with us, and with one another, than fifty of whom we have no such assurance."

August 17, [1751]
"C[harles] S[kelton] pleads for a kind of aristocracy, and says you and I should do nothing without the consent of[18] all the preachers, otherwise we govern arbitrarily, to which they cannot submit. Whence is this?"

I am told from Bristol you "rule the preachers with a rod of iron; they complain of it all over England," etc., etc. This must be considered. We want a general solemn fast.[19]

---

[12] Weak, effeminate, or infirm men.

[13] Busybodies.

[14] See CW, MS Journal, Aug. 5, 1751.

[15] The reference to CW in the second person suggests that this is an extract from a letter of JW to one of his trusted associates at Newcastle (who has shared it with CW). The most likely recipient is John Downes, assigned at the time as JW's Assistant in that circuit.

[16] See Gen. 9:20–27.

[17] See Num. 16:1–35.

[18] Orig., "to."

[19] This paragraph is inset because it is CW's response, not a quotation from JW's letter.

August 24, [1751]

"O that you and I may arise and stand upright![20] I quite agree with you. Let us have but six, so we are all one. I have sent one more, J. Loveybond,[21] home to his work. We may trust God to send forth more labourers.[22] [[Only be not unwilling to receive them, when there is reasonable proof that he has sent them.]]"

[p. 11]    [the remaining items are all in shorthand]

### [[On Monday, Nov.]] 25, 1751

[[I had a conference with my brother at Shoreham in the presence of Mr. [Vincent] Perronet. We both expressed our entire satisfaction in the end which both proposed, namely, the glory of God and the salvation of souls. We both acknowledge our mutual sincerity in desiring union between us as the means of this end; and after much conversation, we both agreed:

[[1. To concur or act in concert with respect to the preachers, so as neither to admit or refuse any but such as both of us admitted or refused;

[[[2.] More particularly that neither of us should receive any of the nine preachers underwritten:

James Wheatley
Eleazer Webster
Robert Gillespie
James Watson
Michael Fenwick
John Maddern
David Trathen
Thomas Webb
William Darney[23]

[[After our conference, I asked Mr. Perronet by himself whether I should not get my brother to sign the articles. He thought it better not to urge him further at present, lest I should appear too much to mistrust him, especially as he had himself proposed to have a book of the preachers and try to enter the names of received or regulated preachers, and when any one hereafter has to be put away, to put out his name with me in the place of all the others.]]

---

[20]    See Ps. 20:8 (BCP).

[21]    See CW, MS Journal, Apr. 15, 1751: "I heard Lovybond preach, most miserably. By how many degrees are such preachers worse than none!"

[22]    See Matt. 9:38.

[23]    All of the names are in shorthand.

**[[Wednesday, Nov.]] 27**
[[Called this morning on my sister,[24] who informed me that Michael Fenwick had been all day with my brother and asked pardon for his going to the Tabernacle,[25] and promised to go to his work, and so prevailed upon my brother to let him lay in the Foundery. Farther, that my brother told him he would buy his horse from him, and if his gifts should return by and by, he should have it again. It is, I thought, a direct breach of our articles and immediately rode to him at [Stoke] Newington,[26] and with all the address and gentleness I was master of, mentioned it to him, at the same time testifying my ardent desire of union and being with all confidence. He surprised me by his answer, wherein he did not in the least continue to excuse himself, but took advantage of my past dispassion and graciously told me he might have confidence in me—if I would [p. 12] do exactly as he did in London, and if I would be civil and good to his wife.]]

[[**Thursday, December]] 5, [1751].** [[[James] Wheatley told me he was obliged to leave the Church and carry away with him 1,000 more.

[[Query: Where will this end? Can I help saying this will be the case of every preacher whom we dismiss? And are we not therefore making a real schism?

[[Wheatley observed that all the lay preachers must do the same. Be sure, he will persuade them to it if he can (as the fool advised the rest to cut off their tails), and are they not too well inclined to follow such advice?

[[Query: If licensing our houses will not hasten the schism?

[[Query: If it came to this, should I leave the Church or the Methodists?

[[Query: Does not Mr. [William] Lunell rightly call the Methodists a seminary for Dissenters?]]

[[**For my Brother at our Next Conference**]]

[[• Could you stop a preacher if you would? [John] Maddern, [Michael] Fenwick.
[[• Was it not a breach of ar[ticles] or mo[rality], encouraging Fenwick, and taking him into our house?
[[• Do you look upon yourself as bound not to receive or reject singly?
[[• Will you release me of any farther concern for the preachers?
[[• If you knew of any scandalous behaviour of a preacher, would you not hide it from me? Would you not screen him with[?] an open enquiry?

---

[24] Emilia (Wesley) Harper; who was living in London, at the Foundery.
[25] George Whitefield's preaching house in London.
[26] While the shorthand is ambiguous, JW's sermon register confirms that he was presently in Stoke Newington, Middlesex.

[[• Why have you never mentioned Fellow[?[27]] to me? Is not the case for sparing him fair? The case for not communicating with us, pride?
[[• Have you seen the articles now?
[[• What single bishop ever took upon himself to ordain?]]

[p. 13]

### [[Sarah Perrin to Him [i.e., JW]]]

[[Bristol]]
[[December]] 2, 1751

[[Dear and Honoured Friend,

[[I was glad to find the people desirous of being visited and longing for faithful ministers. Their hunger for the sincere milk of the word is not all lost, but they can distinguish those who instead of bread give them a stone.

[[I am almost afraid to write all my mind, nevertheless I believe it is my duty.

[[I have long been afraid of the consequence of our suffering some preachers to go forth who have not gifts for the work; others who have not grace to adorn the gospel they preach, and whose passions are strong enough to lay waste God's heritage, wherever they come.

[[Who are answerable for the evils accompted[28] among us? Are not they whom the Lord has made overseers of the flock, if they do not, after they have been told of iniquity or have had examples of any kind proved upon those whom they send among the people, take every[?] means to prevent it for the time to come.

[[Has that been always done? How many servile accounts did I hear while I was in the north? How many sincere souls have been burdened above measure on the account of [Robert] G[illespie] and [James] Wheatley and Michael Fenwick? Some of them who labour in the word and doctrine were ashamed on their account, and their spirits ready to fail, because they, and some others such as they, were suffered so long to continue in the work.

[[Your brother was an ear witness to one discourse of Michael Fenwick, which I believe all present who could distinguish right from wrong thought more like a burlesque upon reason than preaching the gospel. Brothers [John] Nelson, [William] Shent, and others told me they had heard him after the same manner often to their sorrow. Should such a one be suffered

---

[27] Other options that might fit the shorthand include Farlow and Varlow; and a bit less plausibly, Farley or Varley. But there are no lay preachers with any of these names recorded.

[28] Archaic form of "accounted."

again to trouble the church ill[?] shall we say? Indeed, since I heard he is in London and endeavouring to get your consent, I fear it.

[[The next person I was desired to mention to you is brother]] Wells.[29] [[Sister Silby[30] came to my p[erso]n as I came away, and told me Richard Pearce[31] and she both begged you would put a stop to his being in that round, for they fear the consequence will be very bad. Their reasons are too many for me to write, but I hear you are not a stranger to his conduct though he has been suffered so long. Indeed a certain person some time ago on his way to London, being in company where they were speaking of James Wheatley, turned and smiled on brother Wells and said, This is not a time for Mr. Wesley to fall out with his preachers. A leader present replied, Is this a time for Mr. Wesley to allow of sin in his preachers?

[[O that God may give you wisdom liberally to try them which say they are app[ointed] and are not, and strength to put those from among you which are evil. And may the Lord also increase in you that tender fatherly care due to all those who are willing to spend and be spent for the gospel's sake. God will require this at your hands. He hath sent forth labourers and some there are, who deal under his anointings, who love you and seek his glory. Such you cannot encourage too much. But are there not also workers of iniquity, servants of sin corrupt in weakening your hands and sacrificing the flock. And is it not full as much required in seeking to withstand all such as it is to cherish those who are teachers sent of God?

[[Forgive if I do wrong, for I must now deliver my own soul. I verily believe unless you do with all your might strive to prevent false brothers, sons of Belial, going forth or continuing to labour with you, you will bring such a burden on your own shoulders as will crush you down. I am well assured nothing weakens your authority more than this. Oh may God give you to see it in the same light as many of us who long for our perfection see it in!

[p. 14]

[[Your brother greatly desires this regulation. Oh that your hearts might be closely united together in this work! I long to hear you are agreed on everything and are both resolved with all your strength to purge out the aggressors.

---

[29] This cannot be Samuel Wells (born c. 1745), who was first admitted on trial in 1769 (see *Works*, 10: 366). One possibility is a slight misspelling for Thomas Willis, of Bristol, who attended the 1746 Conference and appears to have preached in the surrounding area for a while (see *Works*, 10:184, n 483).

[30] A leader at Bradford-on-Avon; cf. JW, *Journal*, July 8, 1751, *Works*, 20:394.

[31] Pearce was landlord of the Cross Keys and a pillar of the society at Bradford-on-Avon; cf. *WHS* 6 (1908): 116.

[[I cannot help thinking to this very hour, if you had never joined hands in the work in Ireland with Thomas Williams you would have been much more blessed and much evil been prevented. God surely has had a controversy for that th[ing],[32] and I believe a curse has been upon the camp in Ireland for that very cause. I mention this because I think it not improbable the same sinner may be cast in your way again. All that labour with you and do not love the gospel, do much more hurt to the cause of God than any of the clergy can do, by turning the grace of God into wantonness they cause the enemies of Christ to blaspheme.

[[Perhaps my friend will say, "It is not your business to concern yourself so much about this thing. It is only about me." But my reasons for speaking verily are because I have been long afraid these heresies should spring up among us which caused so much sorrow to the churches in the beginning. And have we not lately heard doctrines[?] as ob[noxious] to the law of God as the Incas[33] or [belams[34]]. And as God changes not, I believe he will have a controversy with us for this, and whosoever has not c[alled] to our p[eople],[35] of what rank so ever, whether priest or publican in the church, for their testimony against the antinomian principles and all the evil practices that come to their con[troversy] w[ith] God.[36] The Lord will fight against them and they shall partake of the penalty of sin. I foresee tribulation for the abominations lately made amongst us.

[[But I praise God that you yourself have set us a pattern of self-denial and the daily cross. I am persuaded you thoroughly despise all the follies of life and cannot conform to the vain fashions and customs of this world either in food, furnishings, or dress. I believe you prefer relieving the poor before pleasing the eye or ear or any thing. And surely this is as much refined[?] a commandment as it is to do justice and walk humbly with God.

[[I long to find such ministers as are in all things en[couraging] to the flock, but where shall we find them and in the r[ight] w[ay]? Oh that the Lord may enable his sheep[?[37]] to repent and cleave to him with full p[urity] of heart, that he may bear us, though we have provoked him.]]

---

[32] Sarah Perrin had been deeply disturbed by Williams's role in encouraging Elizabeth Story's false accusations against CW (see the entry for December 1748 above).

[33] An account had recently been published in England attributing the formation of the Inca empire to a couple (the woman was both the man's sister and wife) who presented themselves as being of a rank superior to humans, etc. See "An Account of the Incas, or Emperors of Peru," *Gentleman's Magazine* 21 (1751): 533–35.

[34] These shorthand letters seem clear; the expansion or meaning is not.

[35] The shorthand indicates only the first letter of the first and last word in this four-word phrase; other expansions are possible.

[36] The last shorthand character might alternatively be expanded "the Church."

[37] The shorthand looks like "op," which could be expanded as "op[ponents]." The expansion given above, which seems to fit the context better, assumes that CW's pen made a slight skip in trying to form the loop for the shorthand symbol "sh."

[p. 15]

**[[Extract of a letter of Friend [John] Curtis to My Brother]]**

February 20, 1750/1

[[O permit me here one sigh on the ungrateful reflection that thou hast not left to thyself the half of the profits arising from thine labours on the books. But it is in vain to look back. Thy too great indenture[?] now straightens thee. Can no way be thought on to make this easy? Suppose thy brother was to accept of a living and to return his obligation to thee? Or I am persuaded in a little time the greatest part of the society love thee so well they would cheerfully consider this and assist, if it were mentioned to them by some proper person.]]

### [[January]] 16, 1752

[[With regard to the preachers, we agree:

[[1. That no one shall be permitted to preach in any of our societies till he has been examined both as to his gifts and grace, at least by the assistant, who, sending word to us, may by our answer admit him as a local preacher.

[[2. That such a preacher be not immediately taken from his trade but expected to follow it with all diligence.

[[3. That no person shall be received as a travelling preacher or taken from his trade by either of us alone, but by both conjointly giving him a note under both our hands.

[[4. That neither of us will readmit a travelling preacher laid aside without the consent of the other.

[[5. That if we should ever disagree in our judgment, we would refer the matter to Mr. [Vincent] Perronet.

[[6. That we will endeavour to be patterns of all we expect of our preachers, particularly of zeal, diligence, and punctuality in the work.

[[By constantly preaching and meeting the societies, by visiting yearly Ireland, Cornwall, and the north, and England; by superintending the whole work and every branch of it, with all the strength which God shall give.

[[We agree to the above written, till this day the next year.

John Wesley
Charles Wesley

In the presence of brother Perronet.]][38]

---

[38] This agreement included from this source in *Works*, 10:247–48.

[p. 16]

[[Letter to Mr. [Vincent] Perronet]]
[[November]] 23, 1751
[[The Foundery]]

[[Dear Sir,

[[On Monday our friend has promised to accompany me to Shoreham, but if Satan can hinder, he will.

[[Things are come to a crisis. Without a miracle I fear he will not hold to reasonable terms, and if he utterly refuses, I doubt my own p[atience] and r[easonable]ness.

[[Michael Fenwick, of whose fame you have heard, is come, and will in all p[robability] creep in with my brother again, and return to his post the rightened man as intended, etc. I shall stand in the gap as long as I can.

[[If our friend arrives to sign articles of my drawing up, he shall draw them up himself; only he must oblige himself to consult me in taking in or putting out. This is the whole of my demand, the one condition of my entire union with him. But this implies that he should not readmit those without my concurrence, whom at his desire I have put away.]]

Source: holograph; MARC, DDCW 8/5.

# MARCH 9–10, 1752[1]

[quoted material on the second and fourth pages of the bound pamphlet]

### The Rules of an Assistant[2]

1. Be diligent. Never be unemployed a moment. Never be triflingly employed. Never while away time; neither spend any more time at any place than is strictly necessary.

2. Be serious. Let your motto be "holiness to the Lord." Avoid all jesting[3] as you would avoid filthy talking,[4] and laughing as you would cursing and swearing.

3. Converse sparingly and cautiously with women.

4. Take no considerable[5] step toward marriage without first acquainting us.

5. Believe evil of no one. If you see it done, well. Else take heed how you credit it. Put the best construction on everything. You know the judge is always supposed to be on the prisoner's side.

6. Speak evil of no one; else *your* word especially would eat as doth a canker. Keep your thoughts within your own breast till you come to the person concerned.

7. Tell everyone what you think wrong in him, and as far,[6] and as soon as may be. Else it will fester in your heart. Make all haste to cast the fire out of your bosom.

8. Do not affect the gentleman.[7] You are the servants of all. Therefore

9. Be ashamed of nothing but sin—not of fetching wood, if time permit, or drawing water; not of cleaning your own shoes or your neighbour's.[8]

---

[1] The previous four items traced CW's attempt in 1751–52 to purge lay Methodist preachers that he judged to have neither the proper gifts nor grace. The response of some of those who were purged was to set up as independent ministers—for example, James Wheatley in Norwich. The present document marks a culmination of CW's effort as he encouraged the most gifted lay assistants to recommit themselves to the authority of the Wesley brothers and their relationship to the Church of England. Signed originally in 1752, the document was reaffirmed by the current cohort of assistants in 1756. The material is bound as a small manuscript pamphlet in a slightly intermixed order. It is presented here in its logical order.

[2] Quoting 1749 *Disciplinary Minutes*, [June 29, 1744] Q. 3 [§73] What are the Rules of an Assistant? (see *Works*, 10:809–10). Some variants reflect changes toward the version in 1753 *Large Minutes* (see ibid, 853–54).

[3] 1749 has "lightness" instead of "jesting."

[4] 1749 has "hell-fire" instead of "filthy talking."

[5] 1749 does not have "considerable."

[6] 1749 has "and that plainly" instead of "and as far."

[7] This brief sentence replaces two in 1749: "Do nothing as a gentleman. You have no more to do with this character than with that of a dancing-master."

[8] Item #10 in 1749 is omitted: "Take no money of anyone. If they give you food when you

10. Contract no debts without our knowledge.

11. Be punctual; do everything exactly at the time. And in general do not mend our rules, but keep them; not for wrath, but for conscience' sake.

12. Act in all things, not according to your own will, but "as a son in the gospel." As such, it is your part to employ your time in that manner which we direct: partly in visiting the flock from house to house (the sick in particular); partly in such course of reading, meditation, and prayer, as we advise from time to time. Above all, if you labour with us in our Lord's vineyard, it is needful you should do *that* part of the work which *we* direct, at *those* times and places which *we* judge most for his glory.

[then on fifth page]

**March 9, 1752**

We whose names are underwritten agree to these rules

John Wesley
Charles Wesley
Jonathan Reeves
Jos[eph] Cownley
John Jones
John Downes
C[harles] Perronet
Will[ia]m Shent
John Nelson[9]

[then on the very first page with text]

March 10, 1752

We whose names are underwritten, being clearly and fully convinced 1) that the success of the present work of God does in great measure depend on the entire union of all the labourers employed therein, [and] 2) that our present call is chiefly to the member of that Church wherein we have been brought up, are absolutely determined, by the grace of God:

1. To abide in the closest union with each other, and never knowingly or willingly to hear, speak, do, or suffer anything which tends to weaken that union.

---

are hungry, or clothes when you need them, it is good. But not silver or gold. Let there be no pretence to say we grow rich by the gospel." This item also omitted in 1753 *Large Minutes*.

[9] This list is a set of personal signatures.

2. Never to leave the communion of the Church of England, without the consent of all whose names are subjoined.

Charles Wesley<br>
Will[ia]m Shent<br>
John Jones<br>
John Downes<br>
John Nelson[10]

[then on third page, quoting from the London Conference, January 29, 1752[11]]

More particularly,[12] it is agreed by us whose names are underwritten:

1. That we will not listen, or willingly inquire into[13] any ill concerning each other.

2. That if we do hear any ill of each other, we will not be forward to believe it.

3. That as soon as possible we will communicate what we hear, by speaking or writing to the person concerned.

4. That till we have done this, we will not write or speak a syllable of it to any other person whatsoever.

5. That neither will we mention it, after we have done this, to any other person.

6. That we will not make any exception to any of these rules, unless we think ourselves absolutely obliged in conscience so to do.

N.B. these six particulars were subscribed to Jan. 29, 1752 by:[14]

John Wesley<br>
Charles Wesley<br>
John Trembath<br>
E[dward] Perronet<br>
Jonathon Reeves<br>
Jos[eph] Cownley

---

[10] This list is a set of personal signatures.

[11] Original signed memorandum preserved at Wesleyan University, Middletown, Connecticut; and given in JW, *Works*, 10:249–50.

[12] The first two words are added by CW, not part of the Jan. 29, 1752 original.

[13] The Jan. 29, 1752 original reads "after" instead of "into."

[14] This line is not part of Jan. 29, 1752 original.

C[harles] Perronet
Tho[ma]s Maxfield

and on March 9 1752 by —[15]

J[ohn] Downes
John Jones
John Nelson
Will[ia]m Shent[16]

[a reaffirmation on page 6, signed August 30, 1756, can be found below]

*Source*: holograph; MARC, DDCW 8/3.

---

[15] This clause is added by CW, either to indicate that Downes through Shent signed again, or that they did not sign the January original. The name of John Haime appears on the January original but is omitted in CW's copy.

[16] For this list only first and last initials are given, all in CW's hand.

## NOVEMBER 29–DECEMBER 11, 1753[1]

November 29, 1753

Between 9:00 and 10:00 Lady Huntingdon[2] surprised us by bringing Mrs. Gallatin[3] to see us. She had met her at Bath and conducted her to our house[4] with the mournful news of my brother's danger.[5] I concluded, from several letters last received and mentioning his recovery and design of officiating at the chapel, that he was out of all danger. But Mrs. Gallatin assured us she thought he would have expired at the altar last Sunday.[6]

Mr. Sims,[7] a clergyman, followed Lady Huntingdon—full of his first love. We joined in the Lord's Supper and found much power to pray, particularly for my brother.

At 2:00, as Mr. [John] Hutchinson and I were setting out, we were met by a letter from Mr. Briggs[8] informing me that I must make haste if

---

[1] There is no evidence that this fragment was intended as a journal letter. It was likely instead CW's personal record of this time of challenging health issues for his brother, his wife, and his young son (who died). This account was not included in CW, MS Journal.

[2] Selina (Shirley) Hastings, Countess of Huntingdon (1707–91), was the second daughter of Washington Shirley (2nd Earl Ferrers). In 1728 she married Theophilus Hastings (d. 1746), 9th Earl of Huntingdon. Their main home was Donington Park, Castle Donington, Leicestershire, though much of their time was spent in London and Bath. In part through the influence of her sister-in-law Lady Margaret Hastings (who married Benjamin Ingham in Nov. 1741), Selina came under the influence of the Methodists, probably in 1740. Lady Huntingdon's interaction with the Wesley brothers began the following year and was initially frequent. Within a few years the relationship had strained, in part over theological divergences (she was a moderate Calvinist). Relations with CW were restored after his marriage to Sarah Gwynne (in part because of social class, with Sarah's father having been a Member of Parliament). This would last until the early 1770s, when the Wesley brothers and Lady Huntingdon were split by controversy over the "anti-Calvinist" Minutes published out of a conference of JW with his preachers.

[3] Lucia (Foulkes) Gallatin (c. 1716–99), wife of Bartholomew Gallatin (1711–78), was a friend of Lady Huntingdon and correspondent with the chief leaders of British Methodism, both Arminian and Calvinist. Something of her own character and her travels as the wife of a field officer in the dragoons may be traced by means of the thirty-three letters written to her by William Grimshaw; cf. Frank Baker, *William Grimshaw* (London: Epworth, 1963), 217–30, 275–77.

[4] CW and his wife Sarah lived on Charles Street, in Bristol.

[5] JW fell into a serious illness on Oct. 20, 1751, that would last into the new year (see JW, *Works*, 20:479–84).

[6] JW rose from his sickbed to preach a promised charity sermon on Sunday, Nov. 25 (see ibid., 482).

[7] This is likely Richard Symes (born c. 1722), originally of Wells, Somerset, who received his BA from Hertford College, Oxford in 1744 and was ordained priest in 1747. He would be appointed rector of Bristol St. Werburgh in Sept. 1754.

[8] William Briggs (c. 1722–88) was the son of the Rev. Henry Briggs, DD, rector of Holt, Norfolk and Chaplain to George II. William worked at the custom house (and later the Ordnance Office) in London. He wrote CW on Nov. 22, 1742, seeking membership in the Methodist society. Speedily his natural abilities raised him to positions of responsibility. He was named a steward of the Foundery School in 1746 and attended the Conference of 1748 in that capacity. He served as a Book Steward 1753–59. In 1749 he married Elizabeth, daughter of the Rev. Vincent Perronet of Shoreham, with CW presiding. CW spells "Brigs" on this occasion.

I would see my brother alive. This made us all renew our entreaties to Mr. Hutchinson not to accompany me, lest he should retard me in my journey.[9] But he would not be dissuaded, resolving if I left him behind to follow me in a post-chaise. I was therefore forced to take him, but sorely against my will, in a chaise to Bath. We got to Mrs. Naylor's[10] with the night. He could not sleep for cold.

**Saturday, November 30.** We prayed with great earnestness for my brother. My heart was melted into warm desires of his recovery. Between 7:00 and 8:00 we set forward in a post-chaise and came safe to Newbury before night.

**Saturday, December 1.** My companion was strengthened to set out again before 7:00. Soon after 4:00 we were brought safe to Mrs. Boult's.[11] She had no expectation of us and was therefore quite unprepared. I had no other place to lodge my poor friend than the noisy Foundery. He had not more sleep than I expected.

**Sunday, December 2.** The first news I heard last night in Moorfields[12] was that my brother was something better. I rode at 9:00 to Lewisham,[13] found him with my sister[14] and Mrs. [Elizabeth (Molland)] Blackwell and [Hannah] Dewell, fell on his neck and wept. All present were alike affected. Last Wednesday he changed for the better while the people were praying for him at the Foundery. He has rested well ever since, his cough is abated, and his strength increased. Yet it is most probable he will not recover, being far gone in a galloping consumption just as my elder brother was at his age.[15]

I followed him to his chamber with my sister, and prayed with strong desire and a good hope of his recovery. All last Tuesday they expected his death every hour. He expected the same and wrote his own epitaph:

Here lyeth
The body of John Wesley

---

[9] John Hutchinson was suffering from both physical and mental ailments.

[10] Mary Naylor (1713–57) was a prominent member of the Bath society, with a home as well in Newington, who became a close friend of both CW and his wife Sally. When she died in Mar. 1757, CW honored her with a six- part eulogy; see *Funeral Hymns* (1759), 49–59.

[11] Susanna (Davis) Boult (d. 1774) and her husband John Boult (d. 1771) resided in Christopher's Alley in Upper Moorfields. Susanna appears in the Foundery Band Lists (1742–46) as a married woman, with her surname spelled "Bolt" (JW and others also use this spelling; but Boult is the spelling she and her husband use in their wills).

[12] The location of the Foundery in London.

[13] The location of the Limes, the home of the Blackwells and Hannah Dewell, where JW was convalescing.

[14] I.e., his sister-in-law, Mary (Goldhawk / Vazeille) Wesley.

[15] Rev. Samuel Wesley Jr. (1690–1739) died at the age of 49.

A brand, not once only, plucked out of the fire.[16]
He died of a consumption in the Fifty-first year of

his age.[17] Leaving (after his debts
were paid) not ten pounds behind him
praying, "God be merciful to me an
unprofitable servant."[18]

He desired this inscription (if any) should be put upon his tombstone.

He made it his request to his wife[19] and me to forget all that is past, which I very readily agreed to and once more offered her my service in great sincerity. Neither will I suspect hers, but hope she will *do* as she *says*.

I have been generally blamed for my absence in this time of danger. Several asked, "Does Mr. Charles know of his brother's illness?" and were answered, "Yes, yes; many here informed him." All my correspondents agreed in their accounts that my brother was much better, of which his ministering last Sunday at the chapel left me no doubt. Then they might have apprized me of his danger, but none thought of me till Tuesday when they looked for his death every hour. He had ordered letters to be wrote by Charles Perronet to the preachers to meet on the 21st instant, but not a word of notice was sent to me. Now I hear several letters were wrote me on Tuesday night, but I have left them unreceived at Bristol.

I attended my brother while he rode out for the air, and was surprised to see him hold out for three-quarters of an hour, and even gallop back the whole way.

In the afternoon I met the leaders and spoke them comfort; then called on my patient, John Hutchinson, whose journey has done him more good than harm.

My text at the Foundery was 1 John 5:14–15, "And this is the confidence that we have in him, that, if we ask anything according to his will, he heareth us. And if we know that he hear us, whatsoever we ask, we know that we have the petitions that we desired of him."

Whether the congregation received benefit I know not, being myself confused and overwhelmed with trouble and sorrow.

God made me to the society, I trust, a son of consolation.[20] I showed them the cause of my brother's danger, even our unprofitableness and the nation's rejecting his testimony. I strongly exhorted them to repent

---

[16] See Amos 4:11; Zech. 3:2. This was used in allusion to the time when the child JW was rescued from the burning rectory in Epworth.

[17] JW had turned 50 in June 1753; so he was living *in* his 51st year.

[18] Cf. Luke 18:13 and Matt. 25:30.

[19] Mary (Goldhawk/Vazeille) Wesley.

[20] See Acts 4:36.

and do their first works,[21] and *on no other condition* to hope for my brother's recovery. I told them I was persuaded his time was come, and he would have died now had not the prayer of faith interposed and God commended the shadow to go backward; that still his life was altogether precarious, and they must wrestle on before the decree brought forth for a full reverse of the sentence. In prayer God gave us strong cries and tears, and consolation of hope.

I told the society on Sunday night that I neither could nor would stand in my brother's place (if God took him to himself) for I had neither a body nor a mind, nor talents, nor grace for it.[22]

The whole society appear alive, so stirred up, so zealous, so prayerful, as I never knew.[23] Many backsliders are returning to us. Many secret friends now show themselves. The strangers stop us in the streets with their inquiries, and the people in general seem to find out the value of a blessing they are going to lose.

I carried Mr. Hutchinson to a quieter lodging, which the friendly Mr. Lloyd[24] offered us at his house. John Jones,[25] come post from Bristol, spent the useful evening with us, and then slept with me at the Foundery.

**Monday, December 3.** I was at a loss for a subject at 5:00 when I opened the Revelation and with fear and trembling began to expound it. Our Lord was with us of a truth and comforted our hearts with the blessed hope of his coming to reign before his ancients gloriously. Martin Luther in a time of trouble used to say, "Come, let us sing the 46 Psalm." I would rather say, "Let us read the Revelation of Jesus Christ." What is any private or public loss or calamity, what are all the advantages Satan ever gained, or shall gain over particular men or churches, when all things good and

---

[21] See Rev. 2:5.

[22] This paragraph stands in the manuscript as the second paragraph within the entry for Tuesday, Dec. 4. But CW marked it to be moved to this location.

[23] Orig., "as I never knew not"; an apparent unintended double negative.

[24] Samuel Lloyd (c. 1705–75) was a silk merchant in London, with his main office and residence on Devonshire Square. He was drawn into the Methodist revival in late 1748. He became particularly close to CW, but assisted both Wesley brothers in business matters over the next two decades.

[25] John Jones (1721–85), a native of Haverfordwest, Pembrokeshire, was one of JW's most scholarly lay helpers. He matriculated at Trinity College, Oxford in 1736, receiving his BA in 1739, his MA in 1742, and a B.Med. in 1745 (by virtue of this last degree he was known as Dr. Jones). Originally converted under Whitefield, Jones gravitated to the Arminianism of the Wesley brothers and began serving JW as an assistant in London in 1746. In 1748 JW appointed Jones languages master at Kingswood School, and on Feb. 8, 1749 solemnized Jones's marriage to Elizabeth Mann. Elizabeth died a year or two later; and on May 20, 1752 Jones was wed to Sarah Perrin. In 1758 Jones left Bristol and Kingswood School, but continued a staunch friend of the Wesley brothers, listed as one of their chief local preachers, moving to London to help care for the society there (since he was too frail for itinerancy). In 1770 Jones secured ordination from the Bishop of London. He ended his days as vicar of Harwich, Essex.

evil, Christ's power and antichrist's, conspire to hasten the grand event, to fulfil the mystery of God, and make all the kingdoms of the earth become the kingdoms of Christ.

I asked each of the select band[26] whether they could pray in faith for my brother's life. God has kept them all in darkness and suspense. Those who have most power with him have received no certain answer, being constrained to give him up *first*, if haply they may then receive him again as from the dead. Some have told me it was parting with a right eye, with one much dearer to them than their natural father. Many have found strong, increasing hope of his recovery; and a few, whose experience I less depend on, are confident of it.

I called on loving, faithful D[udy] P[erronet],[27] and then visited my patient at Mr. [Samuel] Lloyd's. With him I stayed [[wrongly]] till near 1:00, the time I had appointed for prayer at the Foundery. Many faithful souls then joined me in behalf of my brother, or rather of the Church and nation. Neither was our Lord absent. Great comfort and confidence we received that all shall work together for good,[28] even for the glory of God and furtherance of the gospel.

From intercession I waited on my sister to Dr. Fothergill,[29] who is much pleased with his patient's present case and greatly approves of his hastening to the Hotwells at Bristol. Tomorrow afternoon he promises to visit him at Lewisham.

The rest of the day I passed with John Hutchinson.

**Tuesday, December 4.** Proceeded in the Revelation and found the blessing promised to those who read or hear the words of that book.[30] From 6:00 to 7:00 employed with the preachers in prayer for my brother and the church.

This morning I got the long-wished for opportunity of talking fully to him [JW] of all which has passed since his marriage. And the result of our conference was perfect harmony.

Mrs. Dewell and Blackwall observed what a fair opportunity my wife might have had for inoculating with her sister.[31] I answered that I left every one to his own conscience; but for my part I looked upon it as taking the matter out of God's hands, and I should choose (if it depended on me) to

---

[26] The "select band" was a gathering of the most spiritually mature among the Methodists; in this case, the leaders at the Foundery.

[27] Duriah (Clarke) Perronet, wife of Edward Perronet (since 1748). They set up residence on King Street in upper Moorfield, London. This identification is confirmed in CW's letter to Sarah (Gwynne) Wesley on this day.

[28] See Rom. 8:28.

[29] John Fothergill (1712–80), a London physician.

[30] See Rev. 1:3.

[31] Rebecca Gwynne (1724–99), Sarah's sister, was living with CW and his wife at the time.

trust her entirely to him.

Before 5:00 I returned to the Foundery and found two letters from Lady Huntingdon, the first informing me they apprehended my wife was taken ill of the smallpox as soon as I left her; the second that it was come out and the confluent kind.[32] She had been frightened (after my departure) with one's abruptly telling her my brother was dead, and sickened immediately.

I immediately consulted Mr. Lloyd, who advised me to fly where my heart directed. "But what can I do with Mr. Hutchinson?" "Take him with you by all means." I went and made him the offer, [[but took care to tell him beforehand that as I should not leave my wife alone till she was out of danger, that therefore he could not be at my house. He flew out into a most outrageous passion, calling it turning him out of my house, as in vain I laboured to set him right, Mrs. Phillips and Felts assisting me. My mind and body were quite spent with travel. I left him at the height of his madness, met Mr. Lloyd who encouraged me to hasten to Bristol whether he would [ac]company me or no.]].

I preached on "Let not your hearts be troubled: .... In my Father's house are many mansions: ...."[33] Met good old Mr. [Vincent] Perronet and informed him of my journey.

[[Strove once more to reason with the whirlwind but increased my own burden thereby without lessening his. Lay down to rest with faithful John Jones, a man of a better spirit who knows to weep with them that weep.]]

**Wednesday, December 5.** At 5:00 found John Hutchinson, after a restless night, as the troubled sea. [[He had given a loose to his own thoughts and passions, and spent the night in thinking what bitter things would he say to me. All the devil could put into his heart to torment himself, or me, he uttered. Lady Huntingdon was the chief mark[?] of his malice, "that vile, wicked woman" as he called her, "that nasty baggage, that hypocritical goat," etc. etc. In vain I offered to receive him into my house if we found my wife out of danger or whenever she should be out of danger; that in the meanwhile he might lodge at Captain James's[34] who had invited him, or Mrs. [Elizabeth (Stafford)] Vigor's, or my own room in the Horsefair,[35] or Mrs. Wilson's next door to me. He was proof to all our entreaties.]]

... *tractabilis audit.*[36]

---

[32] These letters, dated Dec. 1 and Dec. 3, survive at MARC: MA 1977/504/1/25 and MA 1977/504/1/30.

[33] John 14:1–3.

[34] Captain [John] James was a supporter of Methodism in Bristol; see CW, MS Journal, June 19 and Aug. 7, 1749.

[35] I.e., a room set aside for CW at the New Room preaching house.

[36] Virgil, *Aeneid*, iv.439: "he listened to no words receptively."

*Nec magis ... quam si dura silex aut stet Marspasia cautes.*[37]

[[I told him the chaise would be at the door by 6:00, when he must determine whether to go or stay. He suffered me to go without him, and I sent for John Jones to accompany me. Just as we were setting out John Hutchinson came, thrust out by Mrs. Felt. My flesh shrank at taking him in, a miserable comforter to me in my lowest distress. Yet I durst not leave him in such a condition, a sure prey to Satan. The lightest consequence of his stay in London (where he grows worse every day) is bodily death. I therefore tried again to pacify him. But he was for quitting the chaise before we got through the city, and returning in a coach to his uncle's. There he said he would send for all his old friends, go to the alleys[?], and give a loose to his heart's desires.

[[I thought of poor Ignatius chained to his ten leopards.[38] I had all ten in one. At Hounslow[39] we got a fresh chaise and I sore persuaded him to go forward. At Salt Hill[40] we rested a while and rode thence to Reading.[41] There we had another desperate quarrel and he was again on the point of returning. Yet was he overruled to drive on to Newbury,[42] and instead of comforting me all the way [he] insulted my sorrow and spoke against my wife. I was so hindered and distracted by him that I could pray very little. As soon as I was released I took a walk by myself and poured out my heart in prayer, or my burden had been too heavy for me to bear. He was affrighted at my absence, and set upon the people of the inn to hunt after me. In under an hour I returned and he offered to go another stage to Marlborough.[43] On the way he acknowledged his fault and promised amendment. But at Marlborough he relapsed again and fell upon me for my weakness, etc. I ordered a bed to myself in another chamber. He followed me in a transport of rage, laid hold on me and began dragging me back to his room. I did not follow readily, which made him roar as if possessed and drew all the family to us. Had I put forth my strength he could not have prevailed, but I was afraid to hurt him and therefore let him drag me through a long gallery to his chamber. Then he locked me in. The servants without were frightened, fearing murder, and broke open the door. He made me sit down and I allowed him an hour to cool. Then he fell on his knees and begged my pardon for the violence he had offered me and for so exposing himself and me. I said all I could to soothe him and

---

[37] Virgil, *Aeneid*, vi.470–71: "no more altered than if hard flint stood there or Marpesian rock [i.e., marble]."

[38] See Ignatius, Epistle to the Romans, §5.

[39] Hounslow, Middlesex; about 10 miles west of London.

[40] Salt Hill, Berkshire, now a district of Slough, 21 miles west of London.

[41] Reading, Berkshire; about 40 miles west of London.

[42] About 60 miles west of London.

[43] Marlborough, Wiltshire; about 77 miles west of London.

then betook me to rest—in [an]other room.]]

**Thursday, December 6.** [[He had been sorely tempted in the night to cut his throat. When I came in he fell down again and asked my pardon, promising nevermore to grieve me.]] We set[44] out at 7:00 [[(but before we came to Bath his temper began to break out again; and before we reached Bristol, was as violent as ever. I resolved in myself nevermore to trust myself shut up with him, having passed two days as in hell)]] and came to Bristol by 4:00. I found my dearest friend on a restless bed of pain loaded with the worst kind of the worst disease. Mrs. Vigor and Jones[45] were ministering to her day and night. Sister Burges,[46] a most tender, skilful Christian woman, was her nurse. Dr. Middleton[47] has been a father to her. Good Lady Huntingdon attends her constantly twice a day, having deferred her journey to her son[48] on this account.

She had expressed a longing desire to see me just before I came, and rejoiced for the consolation. I saw her alive, but oh how changed! "The whole head faint, and the whole heart sick! From the crown of the head to the ...."[49] Yet under her sorest burden she blessed God that she had not been inoculated, receiving the disease as immediately sent from him.

I found the door of prayer wide open and entirely acquiesced in the divine will. I would not have it otherwise. God choose for me and mine in time and eternity!

[[My poor unhappy friend[50] vilely awaited as a messenger of Satan to buffet me. Mrs. Vigor offered him a bed at her house, but he flew out into the street, I followed and laid hold of him. He would needs go and proceed for himself. I reasoned with him but in vain. I told him there was but one bed in my house for me. He said I might lie out and leave it to him. I showed him the need of my never stirring from my wife till out of danger, and the great hurt he would do her if he should lodge in the house. His coughing would disturb and kill her. He answered "What was my wife more than another?" and "I made such a do with her, that she had more care than his sister would have, who was far better than her in fortune," and a deal of such stuff; and it is the greatest cruelty in me thus

---

[44] CW wrote these two words in shorthand, then repeated them in longhand.

[45] Elizabeth (Mann) Jones, the wife of John Jones.

[46] Possibly the wife of James Burges, of Bristol.

[47] John Middleton (c. 1680–1760), son of Patrick Middleton (1661–1736), a Scottish Episcopal priest well known for defending the nonjuring party, matriculated at Edinburgh in 1699, and studied medicine with Archibald Pitcairne. He moved to Bristol after completing his studies, serving as a physician (with a specialization in obstetrics) for over forty years. Middleton first attended CW when he became seriously ill in Aug. 1740, and became both his personal physician and good friend.

[48] Francis Hastings, 10th Earl of Huntingdon (1729–89).

[49] Isa. 1:5–6.

[50] John Hutchinson.

to turn him out of my house desolate after I had brought him from all his friends, not to let him lodge there one night till he could look about him. He desired me to leave him, which I absolutely refused dreading the consequences. He said he would go to Clifton. It was now dark. I went with him, leading him, and by the way told him our friends' fears that his sister was infected by the smallpox. Once or twice he softened but immediately relapsed again into his strange madness. I comforted myself that it was my last trial with him, and having delivered him to his sister, dropped down. The strength of nature could carry me no further. Mrs. Gallatin was there and ran to Lady Huntingdon for a cordial. I recovered myself in about an hour, and then Lady Huntingdon took me home in her coach. She joined with us in prayer for my afflicted partner, whom we found as I left her. I hastened to the [New] Room and stopped the people just as they [were] scattering. The men told me I rejoiced their hearts by "My brother lives." I gave a short account of him, joined in fervent prayer both for him and my wife, and the Lord greatly comforted us!]]

**Friday, December 7.** [[All this day she grew worse and worse, yet still the most threatening symptoms were kept off. We met at 7:00 and joined in mighty prayer for my brother and her. At 10:00 we had powerful prayer. My very soul was drawn out and the souls of all present. At 1:00 we wrestled again and could not doubt but our Lord heard us!]]

**Saturday, December 8.** [[We expect the child[51] to be taken every hour. I should be thankful if God spare him till his mother be out of danger. She draws nearer and nearer the crisis. God has [e]stablished[?] me in a "dreadful post of observation, darker every hour,"[52] yet after all this prayer ought I to doubt?]]

**Sunday, December 9.** [[The eleventh day [of her illness]. I ministered the sacrament at Kingswood and prayed with great feeling for my brother and her. She is now brought very low indeed, being often ready to faint and die under her burden. For about an hour in the afternoon I watched her while the glimmering lamp of life seemed every moment ready to go out. She got a little rest in the night.

[[I preached on "Let not your heart be troubled."[53]]]

**Monday, December 10.** [[The twelfth day. All day the pox began to turn in her face which is now a good deal sunk, and her feet began to swell and burn and be sore. She is not quite so low as she was, yet at times her fainting fits return, and she still lies struggling as in the toils of death. Who knoweth what another day and night will bring forth?]]

**Tuesday, December 11.** [[The thirteenth day. I was called up between 3:00 and 4:00. She lay fainting as before. On a momentous p[oint] the important

---

[51] CW and Sarah's first child, John, was born Aug. 21, 1752 and would die of smallpox on Jan. 7, 1754.

[52] Edward Young, *Night Thoughts*, Night 6, Pt. 1, ll. 32–33.

[53] John 14:1–3.

die of life spun doubtfully[?], ere it fell and turned up life! I prayed with her, and she revived. She has had a better night than we expected, and if she gets over another night we shall hope the worst is past.]]

[At] 6:00. [[She had a fit of coughing and feared being choked, but recovered, drank, and fell asleep till 11:00. She waked now and then, to drink, and lay quiet and composed after it. Lady Huntingdon called and was ...[54]]]

*Source*: CW record copy in his hand; MARC, DDCW 8/4.[55]

---

[54] The remainder of the manuscript is missing.

[55] An expansion of the shorthand sections starting at Dec. 4 was first published by John Tyson in *Quarterly Review* 4.1 (1984): 9–21. The expansion given here corrects Tyson at several points.

## JULY 8–31, 1754[1]

**Monday, July 8, 1754.** At 4:00 took horse for Norwich with my brother [JW], Charles Perronet, and Robert Windsor.[2]

On **Wednesday, July 10,** came to Attleborough[3] by 11:00 and were grieved more than surprised to read in the *Norwich Mercury* as follows:

[[I hope the public will suspend their censures of me, for my accusing myself thus in print, when I acquaint them that I look upon myself bound in duty to God and the world to acquit the innocent and detect the guilty. I do therefore hereby declare that T[imothy] Keymer[4] is innocent of adulterous practices with me, and J[ames] W[heatley] is guilty of the same, and that by his great pretensions to religion and holiness [he] deceived and ruined me, for which I hope for forgiveness of God and all the world. And as to the report of my ever denying it, it is entirely false. Witness my hand, Mary Mason, then Towler.[5]

[[N.B. in a few days will be published a faithful and true narrative of the whole affair, when the public will be the better able to make a right judgment.

---

[[The public are desired to suspend their judgments at present, as to what may be said, sworn, printed, or done in regard to the Rev. Mr.

---

[1] In 1751 the Wesley brothers removed James Wheatley as one of their lay preachers, due to sexual improprieties he had taken with women in the societies where he served. Wheatley moved to Norwich (where there was no current Methodist work) and began preaching, eventually gathering a society of his own. The Wesley brothers were troubled by this, in as much as Wheatley was characterized as a "Methodist." In December 1753 they publicly disavowed him, insisting Wheatley was an "Independent teacher." In addition, JW sent one of his lay preachers (Samuel Larwood) to initiate a proper Methodist work (See *Norwich Mercury*, Dec. 15–22, 1753, 3). Then, in early 1754 reports began emerging charging Wheatley with renewed sexual improprieties. This led the Wesleys to visit Norwich in July, to distinguish their Methodist work from Wheatley's society, and to nurture their own fledgling society. For a good survey of these various events, see Elizabeth J. Bellamy, *James Wheatley and Norwich Methodism in the 1750s* (Peterborough: World Methodist Historical Society, 1994). CW's account of this work in Norwich survives in two settings (the second comes next in this collection). This first setting is a manuscript in his hand that contains his initial journal notes (many in shorthand). There is little evidence that this document was mailed as a journal letter, beyond the interjection "O sir" in the July 29 entry. The period it covers is not included in CW, MS Journal.

[2] Robert Windsor (1704–90) was one of the first members of the Foundery society and served JW faithfully in various roles at the Foundery and City Road Chapel. See JW's reflections on Windsor's death in JW, *Journal*, Feb. 7, 1790 (*Works*, 24:165).

[3] Attleborough, Norfolk; about 15 miles southwest of Norwich.

[4] Timothy Keymer, a member of Wheatley's society in Norwich, became convinced of the truth of the charges against Wheatley and led the public attack upon him (perhaps out of a desire to gain control of the society himself). See Bellamy, *Wheatley*, 115–16.

[5] Mary Towler (bap. 1728) was not yet married the summer of 1753, at the time of her purported relationship with James Wheatley. She married Matthias Mason in Jan. 1754.

Wheatley—it being presumed that a proper reply will manifest a scene of villainy and wickedness, on the part of his accusers.]][6]

Here our brother Edwards[7] met us with a chaise, which brought us in the evening to Captain Gallatin's[8] at Lakenham, a small village a mile and half from Norwich.

The Captain brought us news that the whole city was in an uproar about poor James Wheatley, whose works of darkness are now brought to light; whereby the people are so scandalized and exasperated that they are ready to rise and tear him to pieces. We do not therefore wonder that the clergy are not forward to show their friendly inclination to us. Yet one has sent us a civil message excusing his not visiting us till the tumult is over.

**Thursday, July 11.** Captain Gallatin dined with the mayor,[9] a wise resolute man who labours for peace but greatly apprehends the rising of the people. We thought it best to lay by till the storm should a little subside. Still the waves rage horribly. The streets ring all day with James Wheatley's wickedness. From morning till night the mayor (as he informed our host) has been employed in taking the affidavits of the women whom he has tried to corrupt. These accounts are printed and cried about the city.[10]

What could Satan or his apostles do more to shut the door against the gospel in this place forever? Yet several came to us, entreating us to preach; and at night a great number were gathered together to hear us. The advertisement we had printed here last year[11] disclaiming Mr. Wheatley did much good and, with the blessing of God, helped the people

---

[6] CW transcribes word-for-word two advertisements, one underneath the other, that appeared in *Norwich Mercury* (June 29–July 6, 1754), p. 3.

[7] A Norwich bookseller, Mr. [J.?] Edwards owned a house and business near the Lamb Inn on Orford Hill (the present intersection of Red Lion Street and Orford Place).

[8] Bartholomew Gallatin (1711–78) and his wife Lucia lived in Lakenham, Norfolk. They we closely connected to Whitefield and Lady Huntingdon. Gallatin had been a Swiss army officer, who naturalized in 1737. He was commissioned captain in 1744, major in late 1754, and lieutenant-colonel in 1759, remaining in that rank until his retirement in 1771.

[9] The mayor of Norwich in 1754 was John Gay (d. 1787).

[10] These were apparently broadleaf sheets, not known to survive. The first pamphlet detailing the charges was published on July 17: Timothy Keymer, *The Wolf in Sheep's Cloathing; being a faithful and true narrative of the affair between Mr. James Wheatley, Mrs. Mary Mason, and T. Keymer* (Norwich: [William Chase], 1754). See the summary of the debate in Bellamy, *Wheatley*, 122–35.

[11] The following brief letter (dated Dec. 3) was published in the *Norwich Mercury* (Dec. 1–8, 1753), p. 3:
This is to certify whom it may concern that the Rev. Mr. James Wheatley, an Independent teacher, has not had for some years past any connection with us, or with the members of the Church of England, called Methodists, under our care.   John Wesley
   Charles Wesley

to distinguish. Our host also has assured the mayor [that] Mr. Wheatley is no Methodist or associate of ours. And the clergy, as well as people in general, are sensible of our attachment to the Church.

**Friday, July 12.** We continued in our retreat, leaving God to work and prepare our way at Norwich. A letter of Charles Perronet's to Wheatley they have printed there,[12] contrary to our express orders. It is not fit that our hand should be upon him. Fresh discoveries are daily made of his lewdness, enough to make the ears of all who hear to tingle. Yet is he quite insensible. Alas, who maketh us to differ?[13]

Robert Windsor was out of all patience at our delay, yet we could not believe the time for preaching fully come. We wait to let the ferment settle. We stand still to see the salvation of God.[14] The prayers offered up for us this day by our brethren in London will help us both to light and power and success.

Our host [Capt. Gallatin], who commanded last year at the riot at Leeds, confessed he dreaded the consequence of an English mob and should engage another officer to supply his place if the soldiers were called for. His great love for us heightened his apprehensions, but neither [he] nor I had the least presage of evil approaching *us*.

We passed our time till Sunday very quietly and comfortably in the pleasant house or garden with Mrs. [Lucia (Foulkes)] Gallatin and our books.

**Sunday, July 14.** At 5:00 we walked to brother Edwards's [house][15] in Norwich and at 7:00 took the field. I preached in a large adjoining triangle surrounded with houses (Hog Hill[16] they call it) to about 2,000 hearers, my brother standing by me. A drunkard or two were troublesome but more out of mirth than malice. In returning to our lodgings they pressed upon us so that it was hard work to keep our legs. My brother was greatly fatigued, but by church time he had renewed his strength. The people in the streets as well as the cathedral were surprisingly civil. The lessons, psalms, epistle, and gospel especially (the miraculous draught of fishes[17]), were very encouraging. The anthem made our hearts rejoice, "O pray for the peace of Jerusalem: they shall prosper that love her. Peace be within thy walls, and plenteousness within thy palaces. For my brethren and

---

[12] The pamphlet actually contained three letters, and a postscript dated Mar. 1754: Charles Perronet. *Letters to James Wheatley* ([Norwich:] 1754); see also Bellamy, *Wheatley*, 170–72.

[13] See 1 Cor. 4:7.

[14] See Exod. 14:13.

[15] Orig., "to Mr. Edwards"; i.e., CW leaves off the possessive ending here and throughout this document.

[16] Site of a prior swine market; now called Timberhill.

[17] Apparently the account in Luke 5.

companions' sake, I will wish thee prosperity. Yea, because of the house of the Lord our God I will seek to do thee good."[18]

We received the sacrament at the hands of the bishop.[19] Mrs. Gallatin carried away my brother. In the afternoon I went to St. Peter's[20] and at 5:00 to Hog Hill. There was computed to be present near 10,000. They filled all the place. Again I preached repentance towards God and faith in Jesus Christ. They listened with great seriousness; only whenever I mentioned such a scripture as "whoremongers and adulterers God shall judge,"[21] some cried out "What will become of Mr. Wheatley then?" Their hearts were plainly touched, as some showed by their tears. They all made way for me to depart. Who could have thought the people of Norwich would ever more have borne a field preacher? It is the Lord's doing, and it is marvellous in our eyes.[22] To him be all the glory who saith, "I will work and who shall hinder?"[23]

Several followed me to my lodgings where we spent another hour in conference and prayer.

**Monday, July 15.** At 5:00 the door was quite open. Multitudes heard with fixed attention. I did not spare them but marvelled at their patience while I strongly insisted, "Except ye repent, ye shall all likewise perish."[24] Afterwards they opened for me to pass home. What with my cold, and straining yesterday, I have lost my voice, and therefore retreated to Lakenham to lie by and be nursed.

**Tuesday, July 16.** At 4:00 walked with my brother to Norwich. He gave me my subject, "The grace of God which bringeth salvation hath appeared unto all men, Teaching us that, denying ungodliness and worldly lusts, we should live soberly, righteously,[25] and godly, in this present world."[26] My hoarseness hindered my being heard. My brother added a few strong words which were heard in their hearts. All expressed the utmost eagerness to hear him again. He appointed to meet them again the next morning.

---

[18] Ps. 122:6–9 (BCP).

[19] Thomas Hayter (1702–62) was Bishop of Norwich 1749–61. They would have been worshiping at Norwich Cathedral.

[20] The (parish) Church of St. Peter Mancroft.

[21] Cf. Heb. 13:4.

[22] See Ps. 118:23.

[23] Isa. 43:13.

[24] Luke 13:3, 5.

[25] Orig., "righteousness"; an error.

[26] Titus 2:11–12.

**Wednesday, July 17.**[27] The rain prevented our preaching. My usual stand is by the Bell Inn,[28] the people there showing all readiness of mind both to hear and make way for the gospel. The mistress attends constantly in the mornings. In the evening her house is crowded with gentlemen.

Yesterday she sent my brother an invitation to preach in her great room at the window, whence he might be heard by them without also. But today an alderman threatening her with a prosecution has made her draw back. I walked to Lakenham and stopped my brother.

**Thursday, July 18.**[29] Word was brought us that the gentlemen were much displeased at their disappointment last night. At 6:00 in the evening we went forth. My text was, "The kingdom of God is not meats or drinks; but righteousness, and peace, and joy in the Holy Ghost."[30] The people were amazingly serious. All behaved with the strictest decency. It is evidently the Lord's doing!

Some of the fiercest persecutors are our fastest friends, and constantly attend the word. Many appear affected under it. Not one dares open his mouth against it as yet. But when more good is done, then will be more opposition.

My brother re-capitulated and confirmed my sayings. Thus in the mouth of two witnesses every word was established.[31]

**Friday, July 19.**[32] At 4:00 my brother left us.[33] I preached at 5:00 from Hosea 13:9,[34] "O Israel, thou hast destroyed thyself; but in me is thy help." Still their patience of the truth continues, or even increases. Near a thousand we have every morning. One man, after I had concluded, spoke a rude word, which drew upon him the general indignation.

At night I had multitudes of the great vulgar and the small to hear me, with three justices and nine clergymen. The Lord opened my mouth to convince them of sin; and many, I am persuaded, felt the sharp two-edged sword.

**Saturday, July 20.** I declared to a more numerous audience (it being market-day), "Ye have sold yourselves for nought; and ye shall be

---

[27] Orig., "15"; an error.

[28] The Bell Inn was a public house on Orford Hill, just below the Castle; near both Hog Hill and Edwards's house.

[29] Orig., "17"; an error.

[30] Rom. 14:17.

[31] See 2 Cor. 13:1.

[32] Orig., "18"; an error.

[33] JW was headed to Bristol, by way of London, to see if the Hotwells could restore his health.

[34] Orig., "14:9"; an error.

redeemed without money."[35] The butchers were continually passing, yet all was quiet till I had done.

[[I forgot to mention that on Thursday morning James Wheatley overtook Charles Perronet and me in our way to Lakenham. I would hope he intended to pass by us. But Charles, looking back and spying him, forced him to stop and speak to us. He asked me how I did, to which I made no answer. Charles cried out, "Ride on, James, ride on; do not talk to us. I pray God give you repentance." He asked me then how my brother did, but still I said nothing. Then recovering himself, he said, "And God give you repentance, Mr. Perronet." I bade Charles turn back home and leave him; which he did, being grieved at the hardness of his heart.]]

**Sunday, July 21.** My audience at 7:00 was greatly increased. I discoursed on the three first verses of Isaiah 61, but dwelt on those words, "he hath sent me to preach glad tidings to the meek"[36]—or poor. I laboured (as all last week) to bring them to a sense of their wants; and for this end *I have preached the law*, which is extremely wanted here. The poor sinners have been surfeited with smooth words and flattering invitations. The greater cause have we for wonder and thanksgiving that they can now endure sound and severe doctrine.

Received the sacrament again from his lordship among a score of communicants. If the gospel prevails in this place, they will find the difference by and by.

Went to St. Peter's and thence to the street. It rained all the time that I was declaring the office of Christ in his own words, Isaiah 61; yet none departed. My congregation was lessened by the weather, but those who did attend were all serious and seemed to receive the word as a thirsty land the shower.

**Monday, July 22.** The rain hindered my preaching. [[I stayed at Mr. Edwards's all day writing. One Mrs. [Lydia] Bridgham,[37] a serious, sincere Baptist called to talk with me. She told me she had taken infinite pains with poor James [Wheatley] to bring him to confession and repentance; that he was forced to own the fact with Mrs. Mason, when confronted, but denied every thing else. She often urged him with that question whether he had not seduced other innocent women as well as her; to which he would answer by a th[orough] evasion. When she so drove and pent him about and he could not escape, he said "Well; whether I have done the same with ten or twenty or a hundred others, it is done now, and cannot be helped."

---

[35] Isa. 52:3.

[36] Cf. Isa. 61:1.

[37] First name given in Keymer, *Wolf in Sheep's Cloathing*, 9.

[[He has spared no pains to persuade his followers that all our preachers are such as himself.

[[Further she told me that Mrs. Mason had most explicitly confessed the effect to her; and that at first she was much ashamed, but afterward quite hardened; now a little dashed when she met his eyes in preaching; yet more [when] about him, lest he should be confounded, then herself.

[[I declared to her the reason why we had put him away from us.]]

God is providing us a place, an old large brew-house[38] which the owner, a justice of peace, has reserved for us. He has refused several, always declaring he would let it to none but Mr. John Wesley. Last Saturday Mr. Edwards, in my brother's name, agreed to take a lease for seven years; and this morning Mr. S–n has sent his workmen to begin putting it into repair. The people are much pleased at our taking it. So is not Satan and his antinomian apostles.

My brother's prophecy is come true, that all our caution and tenderness toward them will not hinder their saying all evil of us. The only curse I have had bestowed on me in Norwich was from a *good* woman of Mr. Wheatley's society—several of which are, I doubt not, gracious souls in whose shame and sorrow I sincerely sympathize. Others *show* what manner of spirit they are of by tearing their *supposed* enemies to pieces. They have already found out that it is I and our little society of eighteen members have set the people against poor Mr. Wheatley, and am come with my brother to execute the design *we* and Mr. [Timothy] Keymer laid against him in London. I trust our few children will [take] my advice and example not to answer them a word, not to meddle in their distractions, but to stand still and see the salvation of God.[39]

**Tuesday, July 23.** At 5:00 declared the end of our Lord's coming, even that they might have life, and have it more abundantly.[40] The seriousness of the people deepens at every discourse.

[[Some called on me to inquire after Mr. Cudworth's character,[41] concerning which I could say nothing. One of them has a relation of Mrs. Bryant[42] who has printed an account of James's immodest behaviour toward her; which it seems she was forced to do by Mr. Cudworth's

---

[38] This building had previously been a foundery, and was on Orford Hill, across the road from Mr. Edwards's house. CW will refer to it as a foundery later, echoing the Foundery in London.

[39] See Exod. 14:13.

[40] John 10:10.

[41] William Cudworth (c. 1717–63), a lay preacher from London, who was trained by George Whitefield but went independent. He had become connected with Wheatley in 1752. See Bellamy, *Wheatley*, 103–5.

[42] Fanny Bryant, a servant of Wheatley, had charged that he made advances toward her one evening when she was preparing his bed for the night; cf. James Wheatley, *A Reply to ... Keymer* (Norwich, 1754) 30–35.

threatening to prosecute her. This made her discover all to her father, and he to the Methodists, and so to the whole world. Thus does God take the wise in their own craftiness.[43]]]

Met Mr. S—n at the house, which at present is a mere heap of rubbish without windows, door, floor, roof, or walls. What will this chaos produce? I think it no bad omen that it was originally a foundery!

Wrote all day at Mr. Edwards's. I hear the blasphemy of the multitude. Their mouths are full of vile expressions: "Offence and torture to the sober ear!"[44] Woe unto that man who gives not occasion to the adversary to speak reproachfully! [[ But alas he is quite insensible of his evil. Nay, he makes lies his refuge, and openly shows a forehead that cannot blush.[45]

[[We walk on slippery ground. The antinomians shoot out their arrows—vain bitter words. They are out of all patience with Hughes[?]; so can discover[?] to James many assurances to him. "But Mr. Wesley and his preachers would never stay here." According to some, "I keep up a good correspondence with him, and have been thrice to drink tea with him." According to others, "I have offered to buy his [preaching] house over his head, and came down with my brother to execute the plot against him which he contrived."]]

At 7:00 expounded the barren fig tree[46] to a people who, notwithstanding all their stumbling blocks, can bear the truth which condemns them.

[[Some of the Tabernacle came,[47] to enquire if I had told an honest man they brought with them, that we had turned Mr. Wheatley out of our society, as George Whitefield had Mr. Cudworth. The latter I denied, the former I acknowledged; but spoke with tenderness and reserve of poor James, having often said "No one of his own society would more rejoice than I, if he could clear himself."]]

**Wednesday, July 24.** Preached the gospel from Isaiah 43:22ff. Three [[from the Tabernacle called with an insidious, vain design. I simply told them, "as to the charges here against Mr. Wheatley, I could neither affirm or deny them. But he had behaved indecently among us, which I never mention needlessly, that I no more speak against him than for him." One of them gave me an open letter from him. Mr. Edwards came in and took it, and burnt it before their face unread. They were much displeased at

---

[43] Cf. Job 5:13.

[44] Matthew Prior, *Solomon*, Book II, l. 121.

[45] Cf. Jer. 3:3.

[46] Luke 13:6–9.

[47] Wheatley (like Whitefield) called his preaching house the "Tabernacle." After an earlier building on Timberhill was damaged, he began construction in 1753 of a 1,000 seat building in Bishopgate (next to the present day Bishop's palace). It was officially opened in 1755. So the reference is to Wheatley's followers.

him. I said I did not choose either conversing or corresponding with him, but spoke mildly and calmed brother Edwards.

[[Poor James, I expect, will play us all his tricks and devices. The first we had this morning. Like a drowning man, he is catching at every thing and person near him, to save himself. From my heart I pity him; but without repentance how can he find mercy?]]

My congregation at night was considerably increased by the market-folk out of the country. I preached repentance from Revelation 1:7, "Behold, he cometh with clouds; and every eye shall see him!" The Lord opened my mouth to convince. His word begins to sink into their hearts. Many were in tears on every side. Toward the close of my discourse an huge man tried to ride up to me. But the people interposed again and again till a serious, stout man took and led his horse away and kept the poor drunkard at a due distance.

Some in the public-house behind me were noisy and troublesome, on whom I turned and recommended them to the prayers of the congregation. Satan often shows his willingness and inability to hurt or hinder us. In spite of all, the gospel has free course and gains daily ground on the hearers' hearts.

**Thursday, July 25.** The rain drove me into brother Edwards's. Only the serious followed. The poor have a right to the gospel. I therefore preached Christ crucified from Zechariah 12:10. They did in that hour look on him they had pierced and mourn, particularly [one] hardened rebel (that was) who was in tears the whole time.

Yesterday a woman came to ask me pardon for having railed on me, or rather on brother Edwards, in passing her. She belonged to the Tabernacle. I commended her ingenuousness, wished all the society like her, and gave her a book. From this, many stories are made. I think it best to have no communication at all with Mr. Wheatley or any of his followers; neither to mention him any more than if there was no such sinner upon earth.

[[Honest Mr. Cudworth (I could not help hearing) was yesterday with a gentlewoman who hears me, and asked her whether she had left the church of God? She put an end to his further trouble by answering him, " No; but when she could not find them in one place, she sought them in another."]]

At 7:00 preached, "The one thing needful,"[48] to a mixed multitude of good and bad. Some of the baser sort talked lewdly and blasphemously till I turned and set the terrors of the Lord in array against them. No wonder the slaves could not face me, when the master himself fled. The words directed to them made many a sincere heart tremble. I went on with more power than ever, so immediately did God bring good out of evil. The number of mourners increases. By and by they will be ripe for the gospel.

---
[48] Luke 10:42.

**Friday, July 26.** I enforced on many listening souls our Lord's most important words, "Ask, and it shall be given you; seek, and ye shall find; ...."[49]

At night I declared in the words and name of the Lord, "Blessed are the poor in spirit, for theirs is the kingdom of heaven."[50] Our congregation visibly increases both in number and seriousness. I was enabled to speak very close and convincing as we used to speak at the beginning. Many felt the sharp arrows of conviction, some raging and some mourning to feel them. But the fierceness of men God still turns to his praise.[51] None of last night's rebels showed their face. And when any attempts to disturb, some sober person (often a stranger to us) goes and quiets them. I seemed to find the prayers of our children at this time more than ever before. It is by dint of prayer and holy living we must prevail.

**Saturday, July 27.** The rain stopped me again this morning, but the people come to me. My text was, "Peace I leave you, my peace I give unto you."[52] All present, I believe, were stirred up to seek it; and their labour shall not be in vain.

*Just now* I hear from Leeds that my poor rebellious son has taken his flight! But God healed his backslidings first, and he is at rest! My poor John Hutchinson is at rest in the bosom of his heavenly Father.[53] O what a turn has it given my heart! What a mixture of passions do I feel here! But joy and thankfulness is uppermost. I opened the book of consolation and cast mine eye upon a word which shall wipe away all tears, "I will ransom them from the power of the grave; I will redeem them from death."[54]

[[This day was published in the *Norwich Mercury* the following advertisement of Mr. Paul,[55] a pious man, lately of Mr. Wheatley's society:]]

July 27

[[Whereas I am informed that on Sunday last, the 21st instant, Mr. John Richer did, in the Tabernacle, assert that I was not present as Mr. Wheeler's house when Mr. Wheatley is said (in a pamphlet called *The Wolf in Sheep's Clothing*) to have "fainted away," thereby to invalidate my evidence given against Mr Wheatley; this serves to inform the public that I never said I was there at *that time*. And I now, in a more public manner than I have yet done declare that , not long before the above-mentioned

---

[49] Matt. 7:7; or Luke 11:9.

[50] Matt. 5:3.

[51] See Ps. 76:10.

[52] John 14:27.

[53] John Hutchinson, CW's troubled friend, died July 23, 1754.

[54] Hosea 13:14.

[55] CW consistently writes in longhand the last names of Paul, Keymer, Richer, Towler, and Wheeler; but leaves Wheatley and Cudworth in shorthand, as is the rest of the text.

time, being at Mr. Wheeler's house, Messrs. Wheatley, Wheeler, and Keymer at the same time present, and after closely taxing Mr. Wheatley as having had criminal conversation with Miss Towler,[56] I heard the said Mr. Wheatley confess that he had been guilty of too great *indecencies or freedom* with Miss Towler; which confession we all understood to be a full acknowledgement of his having been *criminally* concerned with Miss Towler, and in this sense Mr. Wheatley himself very well knew we apprehended that confession.

[[This declaration Mr. Wheeler knows is truth, and I am always ready to appeal to God by the most solemn oath for the confirmation of what I have declared.

[[I also declare that Mr. Cudworth said at my house that Mr. Wheatley confessed the same, in substance, to him. I say "in substance" because of such a notorious spirit of prevarication among some persons that if one word should happen incautiously to be misplaced, the whole fact is confidently denied. The said Mr. Cudworth, I am well assured, understood this case in the same full and criminal sense that we ourselves did.

[[N.B. What I have here inserted is not out of any prejudice to Mr. Wheatley's person, or from any sinister view; for it was my determined purpose never to have divulged it, had I not the greatest reason to believe he still continued in the like practices, and that upon principle too; and also to clear my character of the scandalous aspersion virtually cast upon me by Mr. Richer.]]

Thomas Paul[57]

On Saturday the people leave work sooner; therefore I preached at 6:00. The street swarmed with drunkards who[58] gave us some trouble but were not suffered to interrupt us long. I preached the gospel of the kingdom from, "Fear not, little flock; it is the Father's good pleasure ...."[59]

**Sunday, July 28.** Met our little society, or rather candidates for a society, at 5:00 and read the Rules.[60] At 7:00 preached Christ Jesus, the Saviour of all men, to a numerous, quiet congregation from Isaiah 45:22, "Look unto me, and be ye saved, all the ends of the earth." The word seems to sink deeper and deeper.

Heard the bishop preach and received the sacrament from him. At 5:00, after prayer for an open door, went forth to such a multitude as we have not seen before in Norwich. During the hymn a pale trembling opposer

---

[56] Now Mary (Towler) Mason.

[57] CW transcribes word-for-word the advertisement found in *Norwich Mercury* (July 27–Aug. 4, 1754), p. 3.

[58] This sentence is written (with only slight variants) first in shorthand, which is then struck out, and then in longhand as given here.

[59] Luke 12:32.

[60] That is, the General Rules of the Methodist societies; see JW, *Works*, 9:69–73.

laboured to interrupt the work of God and draw off the people's attention. But as soon as I began reading the history of the prodigal,[61] his commission ended; and he left me to a quiet audience. Now the door was opened indeed. For an hour and an half I showed them themselves and invited them back to their Father's house. And surely he had compassion on them, inclining many hearts to return. God, I plainly found, had delivered them into my hand. He filled my mouth with persuasive words and my heart with strong desires of their salvation. I concluded and began again, testified my good will toward them and the sole end of my coming, which Satan had so long hindered. But if henceforth I see them no more, yet is my labour with my God. They have heard words, whereby they may be saved; and many of them, I cannot doubt, will be our crown of rejoicing in that great day!

Several serious persons followed me to Mr. Edwards's, desiring to be admitted into our society. I told them (as others before) to come among us first for some time and see how they liked it. We spent some time together in conference, praise, and prayer. I am in no haste for a society. First let us see how the candidates *live*.

**Monday, July 29.** All quiet and serious at the morning preaching. My subject, "God who spared not his own Son, but delivered him up for us all, how shall he not with him also freely give us all things?"[62] Several of the Tabernacle ventured to hear, notwithstanding the pains taken to deter them. But whether they hear or forbear, I see and follow my calling. The will and work of the Lord be done!

I feared my voice would have left me last night, but today I miss neither my voice nor strength.

After I was gone yester-evening, a well-dressed gentleman, I am informed, got as many as he could about him and warned them against me as one who came (he could assure them) with no other design than to rob and plunder them. I suspect the warning comes from one of the Romish persuasion. Several such have showed their "good will" towards us. But Mr. Edwards tells them, "We do not disturb *you*. If you do us, you know the laws and will expect what follows."

[[Never did I meet in any delays with so many hindrances to the gospel, O sir since poor James came hither, he and the devil have been labouring to shut the door against the true ministers and word of God. My brother and me, and every one of our sons in the gospel he and Cudsworth have represented as the vilest of men. But the grand stumbling block [consists] in his own life. He has made religion stink, and the truth to be evil spoken of, and the adversary to blaspheme. No one but the Almighty can make a way for his gospel in this city, and in spite of all obstructions he doth.

---

[61] Luke 15:11–32.

[62] Rom. 8:32.

[[Today is to be printed the Bishop of Exeter's scandalous letter to my brother;[63] but ten thousand such silly slanders will not make him black or Wheatley white. The world would rejoice to have it thought "We are all alike," but God who made the difference, will show it, and stand by his own messengers.]]

At 7:00 walked from Lakenham to Norwich where the Bishop of Exeter's letter to my brother had been all day hawked about the streets. The hill was covered with people waiting for me, notwithstanding the hard rain which confined me at Lakenham. It was near night, and I too hot to preach out, therefore we filled the house with as many as we could cram into it, and the rest stood in the street. I had double power to explain that glorious promise—"The redeemed of the Lord shall return, and come with singing unto Sion; and everlasting joy upon their heads."[64] The people more earnest, hearty, zealous than ever.

Another half hour I passed with some serious persons in conference and fervent prayer for the success of the gospel.

**Tuesday, July 30.** Preached at 5:00 from Isaiah 35 and found my mouth opened as well as people's hearts. The more Satan rages, the more our Lord will own and bless us. A poor rebel at the conclusion lifted up his voice; for whom I first prayed, and then turning full upon him preached repentance and Christ to his heart. I desired him to turn his face towards me, but he could not. However he felt the invisible chain, which held him to hear the offers of grace and salvation. I have great hopes that Satan has lost his slave. Some assured me they saw him depart in tears.

I began once more transcribing *mea sacra*[65] or Young's *Night Thoughts*.[66] No writings whatsoever are so useful to me but the inspired.

At St. Peter's I heard a very innocent sermon about public worship. There is no railing at present in any of the churches.

The Bishop of Exeter's letter was cried about the streets all day. We prayed and went forth at 7:00, expecting Satan's appearance. A multitude attended to Hosea 14:1, "O Israel, return unto the Lord; for thou art fallen by thine iniquity." My heart was greatly enlarged. A very few showed their willingness to disturb us, but were soon suppressed. I did not spare them, and the Lord gave weight to his word. I plainly perceive his work cannot be hindered, for there is no strength or counsel against the Lord.

---

[63] In 1752 George Lavington published *The Bishop of Exeter's Answer to Mr. J. Wesley's Late Letter to His Lordship* (London: John & Paul Knapton, 1752). He was republishing in Norwich: *Methodists Still the Same: or, two extracts out of the Bishop of Exeter's answer to Mr J. Wesley's late letter to his Lordship* (Norwich, 1754).

[64] Isa. 51:11.

[65] "My religion."

[66] CW was transcribing in shorthand; the transcription survives in MARC, DDCW 8/10.

Many persons there doubtless are in this licentious city who would fain stop the course of the gospel or drive it out. Several complain that their neighbours will not suffer them to persecute us. To say nothing of the clergy. Can Mr. Taylor's followers digest our doctrine of original sin?[67] Can either the Pharisees, with whom this place abounds, wish us success? Here are swarms of papists and antinomians, who bear us equal good will. And all Christ's enemies have a sword put into their hands by one wretched man! It is Satan's and *his* interest that the world should look upon us as all alike. And with this view, the Reverend Mr. [Lavington] republished those exploded scandals of my brother.[68] But he may find himself mistaken. It is too gross to pass even at Norwich. The clergy, I hear, declare they are satisfied of Mr. Wesley's unexceptionable character, and the generality of the people are much displeased at the nonsensical tale.

**Wednesday, July 31.** Expounded Isaiah 32:1 to my constant hearers who seem more and more to know their wants.

At night I laid the axe to the root and showed them their actual and original corruption from Revelation 3:17, "Thou sayest, I am rich, …; and knowest not that thou art wretched, and miserable, and poor, and blind, and naked." The strong man was disturbed in his palace and roared on every side. My strength increased with the opposition. A gentleman on horseback, among others, gnashed upon me with his teeth. But my voice prevailed, and they retreated to their stronghold, the alehouse.[69] There with difficulty they procured some butchers to appear in their quarrel, but they had no commission to approach till I had done. Then [during] the last hymn they made up to the table with great fury. The foremost often lifted up his stick to strike me, being within his reach, but he was not permitted. I stayed to pray for them and walked quickly to my lodgings. Poor Rabsheka[70] muttered something about the Bishop of Exeter, but did not accept of my invitation to Mr. Edwards's.

I am persuaded more good has been done this night than by any of my former discourses. The concern and love of the people is much increased by my *supposed* danger. We joined together in prayer and thanksgiving as usual, and I slept in peace.

*Source*: CW journal notes, in his hand; MARC, MA 1977/503, Box 5, file 5.

---

[67] John Taylor, (1694–1761) had been serving for some time as pastor of a Presbyterian congregation in Norwich. He was a prominent voice among the "rational dissenters," and JW's most extended apologetic treatise was a response to Taylor's *Scripture-Doctrine of Original Sin* (1740). For more details on Taylor and this work, see the editorial introduction to JW's *Doctrine of Original Sin*, Works, 12:117–54.

[68] I.e., Lavington, *Methodists Still the Same*.

[69] I.e., Bell Inn.

[70] See Isa. 36.

## JULY 8–AUGUST 13, 1754

(Thomas Jackson[1])

**Monday, July 8, 1754.** At 4:00 I took horse for Norwich with my brother [JW], Charles Perronet, and Robert Windsor. We were in fear for my brother, lest the heat of the journey should be too great for him. But the rain which God sent down all yesterday had laid the dust and cooled the air. The clouds also were ordered to attend us all the day, so that we had an easy and pleasant ride to Braintree.[2]

**Tuesday, July 9.** Still God in the weather favoured us, and brought us safe to Bury,[3] and ten miles beyond it.

**Wednesday, July 10.** Our leisurely travelling allowed us many hours for writing. Between 7:00 and 8:00 we set out, and by 11:00 reached Attleborough. Here our brother Edwards met us with a chaise, which brought us in the evening to Captain Gallatin's, at Lakenham, a mile and a half from Norwich.

The Captain brought us news that the whole city was in an uproar about poor Mr. [James] Wheatley, whose works of darkness are now brought to light; whereby the people are so scandalized and exasperated that they are ready to rise and tear him to pieces. We do not therefore wonder that the clergy are not forward to show their friendly inclinations towards us. Yet one has sent us a civil message, excusing his not visiting us till the tumult is over.

**Thursday, July 11.** Captain Gallatin dined with the mayor, a wise, resolute man, who labours for peace, but greatly apprehends the rising of the people. We thought it best to lay by till the storm should a little subside. Still the waves rage horribly. The streets ring all day with James [Wheatley]'s wickedness. From morning till night (the Captain informs us) the mayor has been employed in taking the affidavits of the women whom he has tried to corrupt. These accounts are printed and carried about the city.

What could Satan or his apostles do more to shut the door against the gospel in this place for ever? Yet several came to us, entreating us to preach; and at night a great number were gathered together to

---

[1] See footnote 1 to July 8–31, 1754 entry above. This entry covering July 8–Aug. 13, 1754 is found in Jackson, *CW Journal*, 2:100–113. Jackson was likely transcribing a journal letter (perhaps sent by CW to his wife) whose present location is unknown. The account is more polished, eliding or abridging parts of the July 8–31 manuscript above (see particularly July 10, 13–16, and 27–29). However, Jackson's text also adds some details through July and is the only source for material in August 1754. So we have included it as a separate entry (reformatting in keeping with our principles). Footnotes for persons and places given in the prior July 8–31 entry are not duplicated here.

[2] Braintree, Essex; about 35 miles northeast of London, Charing Cross.

[3] Bury St. Edmunds, Suffolk; about 25 miles north of Braintree.

hear us. The advertisement we had printed here last year disclaiming Mr. Wheatley did much good and, with the blessing of God, helped the people to distinguish. Our host also has assured the mayor [that] Mr. Wheatley is no Methodist or associate of ours. And the clergy, as well as people in general, are sensible of our inviolable attachment to the Church.

**Friday, July 12.** We continued in our retreat, transcribing the *Notes*,[4] and leaving God to work and prepare the way at Norwich.

**Wednesday, July 17.** Yesterday a lady sent my brother an invitation to preach in her great room, at the window, whence he might be heard by those without. But today an alderman, threatening a prosecution, has made her draw back. I walked to Lakenham, and stopped my brother. The rest of the day we spent in transcribing.

**Thursday, July 18.** Word was brought us that the gentlemen were much displeased at their disappointment last night. At 6:00 in the evening we went forth. My text was, "The kingdom of God is not meat and drink, but righteousness, peace, and joy in the Holy Ghost."[5] The people were amazingly serious. All behaved with the utmost decency. It is evidently the Lord's doing!

Some of the fiercest persecutors are our fastest friends, and constantly attend the word. Many appear affected under it. Not one dares open his mouth against it as yet.

My brother recapitulated and confirmed my sayings. In the mouth of two witnesses every word was established.[6]

**Friday, July 19.** At 4:00 my brother, by the advice of Charles Perronet, set out with him for Bristol. By how strange a providence has he been brought hither, that he might be sent hence to the Hotwells, the only probable means of restoring his health!

I preached at 5:00 from Hosea 13:9,[7] "O Israel, thou hast destroyed thyself; but in me is thy help." Still their patience of the truth continues, or even increases. Near a thousand we have every morning. One man, after I had concluded, spoke a rude word, which drew upon him the general indignation.

At night I had multitudes of the great vulgar, as well as the small to hear me, with three justices and nine clergymen. The Lord opened my mouth to convince them of sin; and many, I am persuaded, felt the sword of the Spirit in the word.

---

[4] CW was assisting JW in preparing *Explanatory Notes upon the New Testament*, which would appear in print in May 1755.

[5] Rom. 14:17.

[6] See 2 Cor. 13:1.

[7] Orig., "12:9"; a misprint.

**Saturday, July 20.** I declared to a more numerous audience (it being market-day), "Ye have sold yourselves for nought; and ye shall be redeemed without money."[8] The butchers were continually passing, yet all was quiet till I had done.

I forgot to mention that on Thursday morning James Wheatley overtook me and Charles Perronet in our way to Lakenham. I would hope he intended to pass by us. But Charles, looking back and spying him, forced him to stop and speak to us. He asked me how I did, to which I made no answer. Charles cried out, "Ride on, James, ride on; do not talk to us. I pray God give you repentance." He asked me how my brother did, but still I said nothing. Then recovering himself, he said, "And God give you repentance, Mr. Perronet." I bade Charles turn back and leave him; which he did, being grieved at the hardness of his heart. I passed the day at Lakenham, as usual.

**Sunday, July 21.** My audience at 7:00 was greatly increased. I spoke from the three first verses of Isaiah 61, but dwelt upon those words, "He hath sent me to preach the glad tidings to the meek,"[9] or poor. I laboured (as all the past week) to bring them to a sense of their wants; and to this end I have preached the law, which is extremely wanted here. They have been surfeited with smooth words and flattering invitations. The greater cause have we of wonder and thanksgiving that they can now endure sound and severe doctrine.

I received the sacrament again from the bishop's hands, among a score of communicants. If the gospel prevail in this place, they will find the difference by and by. I went to St. John's[10] and thence to the street. It rained all the time that I was declaring the office of Christ in his own words, Isaiah 61; yet none departed. My congregation was lessened by the weather, but those who did attend were serious and seemed to receive the word as a thirsty land the showers.

**Monday, July 22.** The rain hindered my preaching. God is providing us a place, an old large brewhouse, which the owner, a justice of peace, has reserved for us. He has refused several; always declaring he would let it to none but Mr. John Wesley. Last Saturday Mr. Edwards agreed to take a lease for seven years; and this morning Mr. S–n has sent his workmen to begin putting it into repair. The people are much pleased at our taking it. So is not Satan and his antinomian apostles.

My brother's prophecy is come true, that all our caution and tenderness towards them will not hinder their saying all manner of evil

---

[8] Isa. 52:3.

[9] Cf. Isa. 61:1.

[10] There is a small medieval church of St. John the Baptist on Timberhill; but note the account in CW's hand above says he went to St. Peter's (Church of St. Peter Mancroft).

of us. The only curse I have had bestowed on me in Norwich, was by a *good* woman of Mr. Wheatley's society—several of which are, I doubt not, gracious souls, in whose shame and sorrow I sincerely sympathize. Others *show* what manner of spirit they are of by tearing their *supposed* enemies to pieces. They have already found out that it is I and our little society of eighteen have set the people against poor Mr. Wheatley, and I am come hither with my brother to execute the design we and Mr. [Timothy] Keymer[11] laid against him in London. I trust our few children will take my counsel not to answer them a word, not to meddle with their distractions but to stand still.

**Tuesday, July 23.** At 5:00 I declared the end of our Lord's coming, even that they might have life, and have it more abundantly.[12] The seriousness of the people deepens at every discourse. Some called on me to inquire after Mr. [William] C[udworth]'s character, concerning which I could say nothing.

I met Mr. S–n at the house, which is at present a mere heap of rubbish, without walls, without roof, floor, doors, or windows. What will this chaos produce? I think it no bad omen that it was originally a foundery.

I wrote all day at Mr. Edwards's. I hear the blasphemy of the multitude. Their mouths are full of vile expressions:

Offence and torture to the sober ear.[13]

Woe unto the man that gives occasion to the enemy to speak reproachfully!

At 7:00 I expounded the barren fig tree[14] to a people who, notwithstanding all their stumbling-blocks, can endure sound doctrine.

**Wednesday, July 24.** I preached the gospel from Isaiah 43:22ff. Three from the Tabernacle[15] called with an invidious, vain design.

My congregation at night was considerably increased by the marketfolk out of the country. I preached repentance from Revelation 1:7: "Behold, he cometh with clouds; and every eye shall see him!" The Lord opened my mouth to convince. His word begins to sink into their hearts. Many were in tears on every side. Toward the close, a huge man tried to ride up to me. But the people interposed again and again, till a serious stout man took and led his horse away and kept the poor drunkard at

---

[11] Jackson spells "Keymar."

[12] John 10:10.

[13] Matthew Prior, *Solomon*, Book II, l. 121.

[14] Luke 13:6–9.

[15] I.e., James Wheatley's followers.

a due distance. Some in the public house behind me were noisy and troublesome, on whom I turned and recommended them to the prayers of the congregation. Satan often shows his willingness and inability to hurt or hinder us. In spite of all, the gospel has free course and gains daily on the hearers' hearts.

**Thursday, July 25.** The rain drove me into brother Edwards's. Only the sincere and serious attended. The poor have a right to the gospel. I therefore preached Christ crucified to them, from Zechariah 12:10. They did in that hour look on him they had pierced and mourn, particularly one hardened rebel (that was) who was in tears the whole time.

Yesterday a woman came to me to ask my pardon for having railed at me, or rather at Mr. Edwards, while passing her. She belonged to the Tabernacle. I commended her ingenuousness, wished all her society like her, and gave her a book. From this many stories were made. I think it best to have no communication at all with Mr. Wheatley or any of his followers; neither to mention, neither to think, of him, any more than if there was no such sinner upon earth.

I passed the day at Lakenham. At 7:00 I preached to a mixed multitude of good and bad. Some of the baser sort talked lewdly and blasphemously till I turned and set the terrors of the Lord in array against them. No wonder the slaves could not face me. The words directed to them made many a sincere heart tremble. I went on with more power than ever, so immediately did God bring good out of evil. The number of mourners increases. By and by they will be ripe for the gospel.

**Friday, July 26.** I enforced on many listening souls our Lord's most important words, "Ask, and it shall be given you; seek, and ye shall find."[16] I enjoyed my long-sought solitude all day at Lakenham.

**Tuesday, July 30.** I preached at 5:00 from Isaiah 35, and found my mouth opened, as well as the hearers' hearts. The more Satan rages, the more our Lord will own and bless us. A poor rebel, at the conclusion, lifted up his voice; for whom I first prayed, and then turning full upon him preached repentance and Christ to his heart. I desired him to turn his face toward me, but he could not. However he felt the invisible chain, which held him to hear an offer of grace and salvation. I have great hopes that Satan has lost his slave. Some have assured me they saw him depart in tears.

I began once more transcribing Dr. Young's *Night Thoughts*. No writings but the inspired are more useful to me. At St. Peter's I heard a very innocent sermon on public worship. There is no railing at present in any of the churches.

The Bishop of Exeter's letter[17] was cried about the streets all day. We prayed and went forth at 7:00, expecting Satan's appearance. A multitude

---

[16] Matt. 7:7; or Luke 11:9.

[17] George Lavington, *Methodists Still the Same: or, two extracts out of the Bishop of Exeter's answer to Mr J. Wesley's late letter to his Lordship* (Norwich, 1754).

attended to Hosea 14:1: "O Israel, return unto the Lord; for thou hast fallen by thine iniquity. Take with you words, ...." My heart was much enlarged. A very few showed their willingness to disturb, but were soon suppressed. I did not spare them, and the Lord gave weight to his word. I plainly perceive there is no strength nor counsel against the Lord.

Many persons there doubtless are in this great city who would fain stop the course of the gospel and drive it out. Several complain that their fellows will not suffer them to persecute. To say nothing of the clergy, can Mr. [John] Taylor's followers digest our doctrine of original sin? Can either the Pharisees or Sadducees, with which this place abounds, wish us success? Here are swarms of papists and antinomians, who bear us equal good-will. And all Christ's enemies have a sword put into their hands by that wretched man. It is Satan's and his interest that the world should look upon us as all alike. And with this view, no doubt, the Rev. Mr. [Lavington] published his scandals of my brother. But he may find himself mistaken. It is too gross to pass even at Norwich. The clergy, I hear, declare they are satisfied of Mr. John Wesley's unexceptionable character, and the generality of the people are much displeased at the nonsensical tale.

**Wednesday, July 31.** I expounded Isaiah 32:1–2 to a quiet, attentive congregation, who constantly attend, about two hundred of whom seem more and more to know their wants.

At night I laid the axe to the root, and showed them their actual and original corruption from Revelation 3:17: "Thou sayest, I am rich and increased with goods, and have need of nothing; and knowest not that thou art wretched, and miserable, and poor, and blind, and naked." The strong man was disturbed in his palace, and roared on every side. My strength increased with the opposition. A gentleman on horseback gnashed upon me with his teeth. But my voice prevailed, and they retreated to their strong hold, the alehouse. There with difficulty they procured some butchers to appear in their quarrel, yet they had no commission to approach till I had done. Then in the last hymn they made up to the table with great fury. The foremost often lifted up his stick to strike me, being within his reach, but he was not permitted. I stayed to pray for them and walked quietly to my lodgings. Poor Rabsheka[18] muttered something about the Bishop of Exeter, but did not accept my invitation to Mr. Edwards's.

I am persuaded more good has been done tonight, than by any of my former discourses. The concern and love of the people for me is much increased by my supposed danger. We joined together in prayer and thanksgiving, as usual, and I slept in peace.

---

[18] See Isa. 36.

**Thursday, August 1.** My morning congregation made me ample amends for last night's tumult; they were so serious, and so affected with the word, Matthew 11:5, "The blind receive their sight ...."

When I gave notice of preaching in the evening I did not know what a riotous day it is. Yet after prayer I went forth, to keep my word and see if the Lord had any work for me. The hill was covered with drunkards and rioters. But we saw the hand of God turning them aside and keeping them at a distance. My subject was, "What shall it profit a man, if he gain the whole world, and lose his own soul?"[19] The congregation looked like sheep in the midst of wolves. But the wolves had a bridle in their mouths and could not hurt or disturb the serious. Satan must rage, for his kingdom suffers loss. Many followed me home, with whom I spent some time in prayer.

By the time that the streets are too hot to hold us, we hope our house will be ready.

**Friday, August 2.** I spoke comfortably to the sincere from Matthew 5:3ff., "Blessed are the poor in spirit, for theirs is the kingdom of heaven. ...." A gentleman faced me while I brought all the threatenings of God's word to bear upon him. He often changed colour, in spite of all his diabolical resolution. The poor people were not ashamed to show their concern. They felt the word, if he did not, and were melted down through his obduracy.

I am at a loss for a church, Squire D— having sent his servant to forbid my preaching any more under his wall. I thought of removing my pulpit to Mr. Edwards's door. But providence ordered otherwise, by sending such violent rain today as flooded the street around us and filled it up with mud.

It being the fair day, we had a large company of drunkards to wait upon us at 7:00. I stood under a window of the Bell [Inn].[20] Satan quickly sent me two of his drunken champions, who did all in their power to interrupt me. Their heads were just as high as mine, and one laid his mouth to my ear and talked almost the whole time, I was forced, in my own defence, to speak as loud and as fast as I could. And they had no power to disturb me, while I applied the most blessed promise, Isaiah 35:10: "The ransomed of the Lord shall return, and come with songs unto Zion." Many experienced the power of the gospel, preached with much contention. The wild beasts of the people were quite tame, while I passed through the midst of them.

**Saturday, August 3.** I preached Christ the way, and the truth, and the life,[21] with great enlargement, the people assisting me. They seem a people ready prepared of the Lord. He was with us this morning of a truth.

---

[19] Mark 8:36 and parallels.

[20] Orig., "the Bull"; almost certainly a mistranscription.

[21] John 14:6.

**Sunday, August 4.** I met the society at 5:00, with some new members, or rather candidates—for such I esteem them all. I exhorted them to walk unblamable in all the commandments and ordinances.[22] We had sweet fellowship in singing and prayer.

At 7:00 I expounded blind Bartimaeus,[23] and the Lord bowed their hearts who heard. We never had so large a morning congregation, or so serious. The answers of prayer come back upon us. Surely God hath much people in this city.

I breakfasted at Mrs. Overton's, on whose ground Mr. Wheatley's first tabernacle[24] was built. She has offered herself as a candidate of society, having stayed in the other till sin forced her out. They are above measure displeased with her. She regards it not, but follows on to know the Lord.

I communicated at the cathedral. An elderly clergyman pointed me at the table to where the ministers were. The number of communicants begins to increase: a sign we do not make a separation, as a zealous advocate for the Church charged me in going home. I set him right and he was in a good measure appeased.

Poor James [Wheatley] has given them cause for suspicion. He too came to the cathedral at first, as my opponent told me, and pretended to bring others, till he had got so much hold of them as to take them all from it and turn them Dissenters. How has he increased our difficulties! But the power and blessing of God can set all right.

I met the society again after dinner, and strongly exhorted them to bring forth fruits meet for repentance.[25]

I was in great heaviness till 5:00, and then invited a huge multitude to the Great Supper, Luke 14:16ff., and gave an historical account of the Methodists. Some thought our congregation larger than any before and more serious. A few ragged drunkards stood at a distance, but were not suffered to make a noise till I had done. Then they lifted up their voice, which made me begin again. I exhorted, sang, prayed, and exhorted again. It was a glorious opportunity. Thanks be to God, who gives us the victory.[26]

Our house was crowded afterwards. For an hour I spoke, sang, prayed after God. A fair prospect we have of a flourishing society, such as shall not be ashamed to speak with their enemies in the gate. Every soul present, I am persuaded, felt the nearness of our Lord.

**Monday, August 5.** That scripture was fulfilled, "Behold, I stand at the door, and knock: if any man hear my voice, and open the door, I will

---

[22] Cf. Luke 1:6.

[23] Mark 10:46–52.

[24] Wheatley's first preaching house, or "Tabernacle," was on Timberhill. When it was damaged, he had built the larger replacement building in Bishopgate.

[25] Matt. 3:8; and parallels.

[26] See 1 Cor. 15:57.

come in to him, and sup with him, and he with me."²⁷ We knew not how to part, though we never part now without a blessing. Five more gave in their names as candidates for the society. Two had belonged to it formerly in London and Newcastle. Last night a poor backslider came to me with tears of sincere remorse. He had run well, been a leader in London, but forsaken the fountain of living water. The Lord has sent after the one lost sheep. I have a hope that he will rise again, to fall no more.

Today I heard that as soon as I had named my subject yesterday morning, blind Bartimaeus, some went away, crying they had heard enough of him from Wheatley. Poor James had attempted that history and made a lame piece of work, and many others, which straitens me much. I cannot yet preach of my favourite texts because he has. He has, as much as in him lay, poisoned the fountain, debased the language of God, hardened the people's hearts, palled their spiritual appetite, and made them even loathe religion and all that belongs to it. Their natural prejudices against the truth are increased. What mountains are these in the way to Christ! They can never flow down but at his presence.

I dined at Lakenham, and returned with Mrs. Gallatin to Norwich. Mrs. Overton, a sincere follower after Christ, drank tea with us. We had hardly time for a prayer before we went forth. A gentleman had been with me yesterday, desiring me to vindicate him from the aspersion of disturbing me in preaching. For his satisfaction I preached, contrary to my design, on the hill.[28] The rioters were there in great numbers. I called them to repentance, but they stopped their ears and ran upon me, casting dirt and stones, etc. I stood it for three quarters of an hour, but it was fighting with beasts. None of us were hurt by their violence, but several frightened. The rebels followed me departing. I turned and faced them. They fled when none pursued. The poor women had the worst of it. The lewd sons of Belial are furnished with weapons enough from the Tabernacle, and talk as inspired by their father. Our people were a good deal discouraged, fearing it will grow worse and worse. (We have a Butler here also, a ringleader of the rioters.[29]) I endeavoured to hearten them, and exhorted them to greater diligence in prayer. Prayer is our only refuge; and if our hands be steady, Israel shall prevail.

**Tuesday, August 6.** I was forced to rise at 2:00 by the cramp, and could not sleep afterwards. At 5:00 many sincere souls were comforted by the voice of the Good Shepherd: "Fear not, little flock: it is your Father's good pleasure to give you the kingdom."[30]

---

[27] Rev. 3:20.

[28] I.e., outside at Hog Hill (now Timberhill), rather than in the foundery.

[29] CW is alluding to Nicholas Butler, who had been the ring-leader of the anti-Methodist riots in Cork in 1749; see JW, *Journal*, July 20, 1749, *Works*, 20:285.

[30] Luke 12:32.

**Wednesday, August 7.** I preached from, "Wherewith shall I come before the Lord, and bow myself before the high God?"[31]

At 7:00 God, in answer to our continual prayer, opened the door in spite of all the powers of darkness. Preaching to this people is indeed threshing the mountains, yet several of them show great hunger for the word.

**Thursday, August 8.** Our morning hour is always peaceable and attended with the blessing of the gospel. The house is filled with the sincere, and the half-awakened listen without.

Mrs. [Lydia] Bridgham called, and warned me of the dear hearers (as Mr. Wheatley's society are called), some of whom she knew intended to come, pretending to condemn him, that they might ensnare me in my words.

I preached a little after 6:00 this evening, according to my notice in the morning, and so disappointed most of the rioters. One drunkard was sent to molest us, but the bridle was in his as well as his master's mouth. Many felt the meaning of those awful words, Philippians 2:9–10, "Wherefore God also hath highly exalted him, and given him a name which is above every name. That at the name of Jesus every knee should bow, of things in heaven, and things in the earth, and things under the earth." We afterwards returned thanks in the house, and earnestly prayed for the course of the gospel—as we always do, both before and after preaching.

**Friday, August 9.** I rose soon after 4:00. At 5:00 the Lord was mightily with us, to confirm his word, Matthew 1:21: "He shall save his people from their sins." Mrs. Bridgham, Mrs. Gallatin, with our brother and sister Edwards, joined me in praise and prayer till near 7:00 (a custom we hope, with God's help, to continue).

At 6:00 a tumultuous crowd surrounded me, while I cried aloud, "Let the wicked forsake his way, and the unrighteous man his thoughts; and let him return unto the Lord."[32] Satan visibly laboured in his children to hinder the gospel, which yet they could not hinder. A poor harlot shrieked out for the first quarter of an hour incessantly. I could hear no word but "Wheatley." I turned toward her and pressed her to enter the kingdom, with her sister harlots; but she did not care to show her face. We heard no more of her. Her allies stood motionless till I dismissed them.

A huge, black, grisly man followed me into the house, whom I took for a collier. He told me he was a tinker, T. Boult by name. [He] had been in all Mr. Wheatley's riots, and fought for him forty times. That, understanding I should settle here, he came to offer me his service and would henceforward fight for me. I thanked him for his non-necessary kindness, gave him a word of advice and a book, and he went away highly satisfied. I hear it was he that drove away the noisy harlot.

---

[31] Mic. 6:6.

[32] Isa. 55:7.

We rejoiced, as usual, in giving God the glory for his overruling providence.

I should not forget that this morning Mr. [Wheatley] had the modesty to pay us a visit. Mrs. Edwards opened the door and, seeing him, without speaking a word, bad or good, shut it again.

**Saturday, August 10.** The Lord prospered his word preached to many listening souls, from Hebrews 4:14–16.

**Sunday, August 11.** I walked to Norwich by 5:00 and met the society, to our mutual comfort. At 7:00 our street was filled from end to end. I strongly preached God in Christ, reconciling the world unto himself.[33] He stood by his ambassador, and bowed the hearts of all that heard. We never yet had so open a door. Two or three of the Tabernacle mocked at the beginning, but the stream carried them also away before it. This hour and a half has made us amends for our troubles and buffetings. We acknowledged God hearing prayer. Our brethren at London have surely wrestled for us, and prevailed.

We had double the number of communicants at the cathedral. All who are healed by our ministry show themselves to the priest, and enter into the temple with us.

I wonder we should miss so long so convenient a place for preaching as our own street is. The foundery shuts us up at one side, and Mr. Edwards's and his neighbours' houses on the other. Above three thousand may conveniently stand about the door, and twice as many at the end of Hog-hill. Every place was crowded in the evening, while I enforced the faithful and acceptable saying, that Jesus Christ came into the world to save sinners.[34] His power beat down all opposition and cleared his own way into their hearts. All seemed melted down or broken to pieces, either by the fire or the hammer.[35] The gospel had *free course*. The word was glorified and ran very swiftly. Let all who prayed for its success give God praise, and pray on; so shall it mightily prevail over this great wicked city.

Some of the best of the parish, as well as strangers, joined with us for an hour longer in prayer and thanksgiving. I enforced upon them, by particular and close application, both my morning and evening discourse. Such conversation, I find, is more useful than even preaching itself. The Lord was evidently with us in his convincing power.

**Monday, August 12.** The house was crowded, both within and without, while I expounded Mark 2:1ff., the Lord confirming his word.

**Tuesday, August 13.** I walked to Norwich. Many seem ready to close with Christ, and to come at his call, weary and heavy laden.[36] The more

---

[33] 2 Cor. 5:19.

[34] 1 Tim. 1:15–16.

[35] See Jer. 23:29.

[36] See Matt. 11:28.

disposed they are to receive the gospel, the more he opens my mouth to make it known.

At Lakenham I visited (with Mrs. Gallatin) a poor creature, lately delivered of a bastard child and now swiftly hastening to eternity. Neither she nor the woman who received her into her house can read. We talked much to little purpose. Only she seemed thankful for the pains we took with her, and desirous we should come and pray with her again.

I got a useful hour in the evening for conversation and prayer with our awakening neighbours.

*Source*: published transcription; Jackson, *CW Journal*, 2:100–113.

## OCTOBER 17–24, 1754[1]

[London]

**October 17.** Sister MacDonald first,[2] and then sister Clay,[3] informed me that Charles Perronet gave the sacrament to the preachers, Walsh[4] and Deaves,[5] and then to twelve at sister Garder's in the Minories.

**October 18.** I was with my brother, who said nothing of Perronet except, "We have in effect ordained already." He urged me to sign the preachers' certificates; was inclined to lay on hands; and to let the preachers administer.

**October 24.** Was with my brother. He is wavering; but willing to wait before he ordains or separates.

*Source*: published expansion; Luke Tyerman, *The Life and Time of the Rev. John Wesley, M.A., Founder of the Methodists*, 2nd edn., 3 vols. (New York: Harper & Brothers, 1872) 2:202.

---

[1] JW's published *Journal* records little over the winter of 1754–55; indeed, nothing at all from Oct. 28, 1754 to Feb. 16, 1755. But it is clear from letters and other sources that he was troubled about insuring access to the Lord's Supper among his Methodist people, and seriously considering (in his status as a presbyter) ordaining his lay preachers; while some of them were undertaking to officiate at the sacrament without ordination. One of the clearest glimpses at this growing crisis (at least in the estimation of CW) is an excerpt covering Oct. 17–24 from what Luke Tyerman identifies as a portion of CW's "shorthand diary." Unfortunately the current location of the source on which Tyerman is drawing is unknown. Thus we are limited to his excerpt and cannot verify the accuracy of his expansion.

[2] An Elizabeth MacDonald appears in the Foundery Band Lists as a married woman in the select society in Feb. 1745.

[3] Sarah Clay (c. 1717–83), an unmarried band-member at the Foundery from Apr. 1742, was a leader from Nov. 1742, and a member of the select society from its beginning in Dec. 1743. When JW buried her remains on Feb. 11, 1783, he spoke of her as "the last of those holy women who ... forty years ago devoted themselves wholly to God."

[4] Thomas Walsh (1730–59), raised Roman Catholic, was gifted in language study and for a while operated a school. Initially contemplating the priesthood, Walsh came to doubt some teachings of the Catholic church. In this time of questioning he found spiritual assurance among the Methodists. In 1750 he met JW, who convinced him to become a traveling preacher. Over the next nine years he would serve mainly in Ireland, but with stints in England and Wales as well.

[5] James Deaves appears in the *Minutes* as a traveling preacher first in 1753 (*Works*, 10:267), and remains listed through 1767 (10:344). He served mainly in Ireland.

## August 26–28, 1756[1]

[[Thursday. August 26, 1756. Both the travelling and local preachers, (about 50 of them were present) were called over and all objections which had been or were now made to any of them thoroughly considered. It was also considered which of the local preachers might be tried as itinerants. John Thorpe[2] and Cornelius Bastable[3] resigned.[4]

[[In the afternoon the rules of the society were read and considered one by one. The phrase was altered in one or two places, and a new rule added.[5]

[[We afterwards spoke largely of keeping united to the Church and using the clergy with tenderness. And there was no dissenting voice, but all were knit together in one mind and in one judgment.

[[Friday. [August] 27. The rules of the bands were read over and considered one by one, which, after some small alterations made, we all agreed to observe and enforce.

[[(Mr Charles said nothing.)[6]

---

[1] CW devoted significant energy in 1755–56 resisting efforts on the part of some of the lay preachers, and his brother JW, toward separation from the Church of England. His efforts are documented in a notebook in MARC (DDCW8/1) that contains several items:
 1) a longhand copy (in the hand of John Nelson) of a document drafted for discussion at the 1755 Conference in Leeds by JW (at CW's encouragement) entitled "Ought we to separate from the Church of England?" (see published transcription in JW, *Works*, 9:567–80);
 2) longhand copies (by CW) of several letters between JW, Samuel Walker, and Thomas Adam between Sept. and Nov. 1755;
 3) a longhand copy (in the hand of John Nelson) of those present at the 1755 Conference in Leeds and summary of the proceedings (see published transcription in *Works*, 10:270–276);
 4) a shorthand summary (by CW) of the proceedings of the 1756 Conference in Bristol (given here);
 5) a shorthand transcription (by CW) of a letter from JW to Nicholas Norton, Sept. 3, 1756; and
 6) shorthand copies (by CW) of several of his letters to others between Sept. and Nov. 1756.

[2] John Thorpe (c.1730–76), of Rotherham, had been drawn into the revival by Benjamin Ingham. He attended the 1753 Conference of JW's connexion in 1753, where he was listed as a "local preacher" in Staffordshire (see *Works*, 10:260, 268). He was never fully committed to the connexion with the Church of England, and became an Independent minister in Masbrough.

[3] Cornelius Bastable (c. 1725–1775), apparently a native of Middlezoy, Somerset, began "exhorting" in 1747 and came to JW's attention as a promising prospective preacher in Sept. 1748. He appears in the Minutes as a "probationary helper" in 1750, but did not advance to the regular itinerancy, likely because he married Catherine Stockdale (1726–86) in Cork in 1752 (see *Works*, 10:205, 237). Their time thereafter was split between Cork and Bristol.

[4] A record of the 1756 Conference in Bristol is included in *Works*, 10:277–78, built by correlating the brief report in JW's *Journal* (*Works*, 21:76–77) and a summary in a letter of CW to Samuel Walker of Sept. 6, 1756. The survival of CW's additional shorthand summary was not recognized at the time. The underlining here and following indicates material that is found only in this shorthand account, and thus supplements what is published in *Works*, 10:277–78.

[5] The revisions and addition did not appear until the next edition was published in Bristol (7th edn., 1762); see notes about changes in *Works*, 9:71 (line 1) and 9:72 (lines 1–2).

[6] This is surely a self-reference. CW was uncomfortable with many of the band rules. Cf. JW to CW, Aug. 8, 1752, *Works*, 26:498; and Randy L. Maddox, "Another Glimpse of the Divergent Wesley Brothers," *PCWS* 18 (2014): 99–100.

[[**Saturday. [August] 28.** The rules of Kingswood School were read and considered one by one. And we were all clearly convinced <u>that the objections which had been formerly made against it were removed</u>. In consequence of which it was agreed:

[[1. That a short account of the design and present state of the school be drawn up and printed.
[[2. <u>That every preacher should have a copy of this to be read in every society; and</u>
[[3. That a subscription for it should be begun in every place and a collection made <u>once or twice</u> a year.

[[Should not every preacher save the society the expense of unnecessary letters? Certainly he should write no more than are necessary himself. Nor encourage others to do it.

[[Are our preachers excusable in denying one another's letters? By no means, it is neither kind or honest.

[[Is it right to take another preacher's spurs, his horse bits, or whip without his leave? No more than it is to pick his pocket or rob him on the highway.

[[In the afternoon it was enquired have not several of our preachers been led unawares into Calvinism or antinomianism by reading Mr. Hervey's Dialogues.[7] It is to be feared they have. And the rather because those *Dialogues* were supposed to be strongly recommended by you. The letter to Mr. Hervey[8] was then read and a little enlarged upon.]]

*Source*: CW shorthand notes; DDCW 8/1, p. 89.[9]

---

[7] James Hervey, *Theron and Aspasio: or, a Series of Dialogues and Letters, upon the most important and interesting subjects*, 2 vols. (Dublin: Robert Main, 1755).

[8] This was apparently the first brief letter that JW sent to James Hervey, after reading *Theron and Aspasio*. This letter has not survived, but see the longer letter JW wrote in Oct. 1756 (and published in 1758), in *Works*, 13:323–44; the initial short letter is mentioned in the opening paragraph (13:323).

[9] An expansion of this shorthand record was published by Timothy Underhill in *WHS* 60 (2016): 244–45.

## AUGUST 30, 1756[1]

We whose names are underwritten, being clearly and fully convinced 1) that the success of the present work of God does in great measure depend on the entire union of all the labourers employed therein, [and] 2) that our present call is chiefly to the member of that Church wherein we have been brought up, are absolutely determined, by the grace of God:

1. To abide in the closest union with each other, and never knowingly or willingly to hear, speak, do, or suffer anything which tends to weaken that union.

2. Never to leave the communion of the Church of England, without first acquainting[2] all whose names are subjoined.

Tho[ma]s Johnson
Charles Wesley
James Jones
John Jones
John Nelson
John Downes
Will[ia]m Shent
W[illia]m Hitchens
Pet[er] Jaco
John Johnson
John Haughton
Thomas Mitchell
William Robarts
Rich[ar]d Lucas

*Source*: holograph; MARC, DDCW 8/3, p. 6.

---

[1] This is a reaffirmation of the covenant signed on Mar. 10, 1752 (given above). It reinforced the affirmations of staying in the Church of England taken at the 1755 and (just concluded) 1756 Conferences.

[2] Note that "first acquainting" has replaced "the consent of" in the 1752 original.

## SEPTEMBER 17–28, 1756[1]

**Friday, September 17, 1756.** At 7:00 I left Bristol with John Downes and came to Wallbridge[2] by 2:00. In the evening several attended the word and seemed stirred up to watch and pray.[3] I spoke to each of the little steady society. Forty-three have kept together for years under the care of our brother Watts. There is no disputes or disorders among them. I added a few words, exhorting them to continue steadfast in the communion of the Church of England. We were much refreshed and parted in great love.

**Saturday, September 18.** We set out again at 6:00, and in three hours came to Cheltenham. The twelve miles from thence to Evesham cost us near six hours for we rode the short—that is, the vale—way, and have taken our leave of it forever. By 4:00 we got weary enough to Mr. [Thomas] Canning's. The preaching room was full at so short a warning. I exhorted them to watch and pray always that they may be counted worthy to escape all these things which shall come to pass.[4]

Again at 7:00 next morning [**Sunday, September 19**] and 5:00 in the evening they received my saying, the Lord applying his word both to awaken and to confirm. Between church time I visited three or four of the society who were disabled by age and infirmity from assembling with their brethren and had therefore been neglected as not belonging to them. I found much of the life of God in conversing and praying with them. Wrote their names again in the society book with Mr. Canning's family and John Watson's, who seemed all resolved to do the first works.

I did not forget to confirm the brethren in their calling, that is, to live and die in the Church of England.

**Monday, September 20.** After commending them to God and to the word of his grace,[5] rode with our loving guide John Watson toward Birmingham. At Studley[6] he left us, full of his former zeal and resolved to carry fire among his neighbours in the village whither he is removed.

---

[1] CW had spent the last two years contesting every move among Methodists to separate from the Church of England. His efforts had culminated in a reaffirmation of this relationship at the August 1756 Conference in Bristol. To build on this momentum, CW took another preaching tour through the northern circuit of the Methodist connexion, where he intended to "confirm the Methodists in the Church," as he put it in a letter to Samuel Walker just before he set out. This journal letter is the source of, and is largely reproduced in, MS Journal.

[2] CW spells "Walbridge." An area in Stroud, Gloucestershire.

[3] Likely his sermon on Luke 21:36.

[4] Luke 21:36.

[5] See Acts 20:32.

[6] Studley, Warwickshire; about 12 miles south of Birmingham.

About 2:00 we got to Birmingham and soon after heard at the door Mr. I'Anson's voice.[7] He brought life with him, and we sharpened each other's countenance. The room was crowded at night. I warned them as a watchman of our Israel of the sword coming.[8] The word sunk into many hearts.

Had not time for meeting the society. But in conversation with several, I conceived fresh hope that they will at last become a lively settled people. Some who had forsaken us I received in again.

**Tuesday, September 21.** The Lord gave us a parting blessing. We kept pace with Mr. I'Anson's chaise to Ashby.[9] Our brother Adams received us joyfully. The wild beasts here are tamed, if not converted. None molested while I pointed them to "the Lamb of God, who taketh away the sin of the world."[10] We prayed earnestly for the conversion of these hardened sinners. I was comforted with the little company of twenty-one who meet to build up one another. Great life and love was in the midst of them.

**Wednesday, September 22.** Warned them of the impending judgments, and left them standing on the watch-tower.[11] We passed a profitable hour at Donington Park with Mr. H.[12]

Mr. I'Anson attended us five or six miles on our way to Nottingham, which we reached by 2:00. I spent the afternoon in taking down the names of the society and conversing with some of them. We rejoiced to meet once more after so long a separation. My subject, both at night and in the morning, was, "I will bring the third part through the fire."[13] It was a time of solemn rejoicing. There had been lately a great revival and increase of the society, but Satan was beginning again to sow his tares. My coming, I trust, was blessed at this season to the preventing a separation.

**Thursday, September 23.** It rained hard all night. John Downes's horse being lamed, detained him at Nottingham, by which the poor people got another sermon. I set out at 7:00 in the rain with a blind guide who at last blundered out his way to Sheffield. Here also I delivered my own soul, and the people seemed awakened and alarmed. I spoke plainly and

---

[7] This is likely Bryan I'Anson (1708–75), a solicitor at New Palace Yard, whom JW consulted for legal advice; or his older brother Sir Thomas I'Anson. See *WHS* 5 (1906): 230–37.

[8] Ezek. 33:1–6.

[9] Ashby de la Zouch, Leicestershire.

[10] John 1:29.

[11] Ezek. 33:1–6.

[12] Donington Park was the home of Lady Huntingdon, near Castle Donington, Leicestershire. Her husband died in 1746, so this was likely a conversation with her son Francis Hastings (1729–89), who became 10th Earl of Huntingdon in 1749.

[13] Zech. 13:7–9.

lovingly to the society of continuing in the Church; and although many of them were Dissenters or predestinarians, none were offended.

**Friday, September 24.** I had left William Shent sick abed in Charles Street.[14] But to my great surprise, entering brother Green's[15] at Rotherham this morning, the first person I set eyes on was William Shent himself. The Sunday after I left him he had had another fit of his ague, yet on Monday morning he would mount his horse and ride homeward as he was able. He had only one visit from his ague on the road, but grew stronger and stronger, more by virtue of prayer than physic.

I had advised the society (when last among them) to go to Church. They were then on the brink of a separation through a party for Mr. E[dwards][16] and [James] Wheatley, and proposed it to honest Mr. Cousins. His opposing quashed it for that time. The weak and wavering were then confirmed by my exhortation. Three or four of the others offended and said I made the Church Christ. I preached now as awakening as I could, and then declared before the society "that there was no salvation out of the church,"[17] that is, the mystical body of Christ, or the company of faithful people.[18] When I had fully explained myself on this head, we seemed all to be of one heart and one mind. Then they suffered the word of exhortation and were even glad when I said unto them, "Let us go into the house of the Lord."[19]

**Saturday, September 25.** I encouraged them by that precious promise, "I will bring the third part through the fire,"[20] and parted from them in great love. At 8:00 I preached on the same subject at Barley Hall.[21] I found there the never-failing blessing.

Rode on with William Shent, who had been threatened last night with the return of his fever, but we prayed and the fit was kept off. I was at a loss for a companion to York next week, when in passing through

---

[14] I.e., at CW's home in Bristol.

[15] William and Jane (Holmes) Green, of Rotherham, Yorkshire, were early converts and strong supporters of Methodism.

[16] John Edwards (1714–85) was converted under Whitefield in Ireland. He became a lay preacher in 1745 and a traveling preacher in 1747. He had successful ministries in Dublin and Limerick, and then in England. But by the mid 1750s he was chafing under JW's control of the itinerants, the restriction of lay preachers from the sacramental office, and JW's Arminian theology. Assigned the Leeds circuit in 1754, at the end of the 1755 Conference Edwards refused to move, taking many in society with him to form the independent congregation that built White Chapel in Leeds. He remained their pastor until his death.

[17] Cf. Cyprian of Carthage, *Unity of the Catholic Church*, 6.1.

[18] See BCP, Collect for Communion.

[19] Ps. 122:1.

[20] Zech. 13:9.

[21] A farmstead half a mile north of Thorpe Hesley, Yorkshire.

Hunslet,[22] one called after me. I turned and saw Mr. Crook,[23] who told me Dr. Cockburn[24] was at his house and had waited for me this week to carry me to York. We lighted and spent a delightful hour with the Dr. and him, both in their first love, both full of life, and zeal, and simplicity. Mr. Crook pressed me to assist him in the morning at the sacrament.

Passed the evening at Leeds in writing to my friends.

**Sunday, September 26.** At 7:00 I preached to the people of Leeds, who crowded our room, on "Thy kingdom come."[25] The disciples looked up and lifted up their heads. Walked with Dr. Cockburn to Hunslet. There Mr. Crook insisted on my preaching, which I did again from the same words. His congregation seemed to make no opposition to the truth, as a people ready prepared for the Lord. There were hundreds of communicants, mostly of Mr. Crook's awakening.

We passed an hour and an half at his house with the voice of joy and thanksgiving. Then I was for returning to Leeds when he pressed me into the service again. His chapel (which holds nearly as many as our preaching room) was filled from end to end. I preached at his desire on, "His blood be on us, and on our children."[26] The Lord confirmed the word and turned the curse into a blessing. His blood spake better things to us and for us. We looked upon him whom we had pierced and rejoiced as well as mourned.

I doubted my strength, yet set out for Leeds. Got to the room by a quarter after 5:00. It was crowded both within and without. I was very faint when I began explaining, "When these things begin to come to pass, then look up, and lift up your heads; for your redemption draweth nigh."[27] My little strength increased by using, and the word refreshed me both soul and body. The hearers were much but variously affected. O that they all may be found watching!

I could speak of nothing but love in the society for I felt nothing else. Great was our rejoicing over each other. Satan, I believe, has done his worst and will get no farther advantage by exasperating their spirits against their brethren who have forsaken them. They were all unanimous to *stay in the Church* because the Lord stays in it, and multiplies his witnesses therein, more than in any other church in Christendom.

**Monday, September 27.** I was surprised at the numbers that flocked to the morning preaching and eagerly received that saying of our Lord,

---

[22] Hunslet, Yorkshire; 1 mile south of Leeds.

[23] Rev. Henry Crook (1708–70), curate of Hunslet; CW spells "Crooke."

[24] Dr. Thomas Cockburn (d. 1768), who overlapped briefly with CW as a student at Westminster School. Cockburn later moved to Jamaica.

[25] Matt. 6:10; or Luke 11:2.

[26] Matt. 27:25.

[27] Luke 21:28.

"Behold, I come as a thief. Blessed is he that watcheth, and keepeth his garments."[28]

Breakfasted with Miss [Ann] Norton and found nothing in my heart but love towards her. She was not so evil affected towards the brethren she has left as I expected.[29] Nothing can ever bring such as her back but the charity which hopeth all things, beareth all things, endureth all things.[30]

Dined with Dr. Cockburn at brother Ashe's and passed the afternoon in conversing. Benjamin Stork I had great satisfaction with. While we were drinking tea at a brother's, Mr. [John] Edwards found me out. We talked freely and lovingly till the time of preaching. I walked with him to the house. Mr. Crook was also there. My text again was, "His blood be on us, and on our children."[31] The power of the Lord was present more than yesterday. I went to the Church prayers, with many others, who have all been dealt with to forsake them utterly. They will stand the firmer for their shaking.

**Tuesday, September 28.** We did not part in the morning without a blessing. At 7:00 set out with the Dr. [Cockburn] and William Shent for York. The rain brought back poor William's fever. I preached at night from Habakkuk 3:2, "O Lord, revive thy work in the midst of the years, in the midst of the years make known; in wrath remember mercy." The crowd made our low room excessively hot, but that did not hinder their attention. I had much life and faith for them.

Met the leaders, who gave me a good account of their brethren.

*Source*: holograph; MARC, MA 1977/503, Box 5, file 5.

---

[28] Rev. 16:15.

[29] After the Conference in 1755, Ann Norton joined John Edwards in withdrawing from the Wesleyan connection and setting up White Chapel, an Independent congregation in Leeds.

[30] See 1 Cor. 13:7–8.

[31] Matt. 27:25.

## October 1–10, 1756[1]

**October 1, Friday.** Preached again to the awakened, and believe the word took place. Breakfasted with T. Brooke,[2] who has once more left the Moravians. He accompanied me to the Minster,[3] which he constantly frequents. I met at his house Miss Th– earnestly seeking Christ. The means of her awakening was *Theron and Aspasio*.[4]

Heard that the woman who cried out last night was the same night delivered into the glorious liberty of God's children.

Passed an hour at Mr. D.'s and answered his candid objections. Had an opportunity of vindicating an old friend (Benjamin Ingham). It is hard a man should be hanged for his looks—condemned for the *appearance* of Moravianism. Their spirit and practices he has as utterly renounced as we have; their manner or phrase he cannot so easily shake off.

Found out Mercy Bell[5] and had sweet fellowship with her. I marvel not that *the Friends*, fallen as they are from their first love and simplicity, cannot receive her testimony, any more than our brethren can receive ours.

Had a most triumphant watch-night. We began between 7:00 and 8:00. The enemy did not like our employment and stirred up his servants without to interrupt us, but our voices prevailed. We sang the Hymns in a Tumult[6] with great consolation. Mr. Williamson's[7] maid was deeply wounded and expressed her inward compunction by strong cries for mercy. The shout of a king was in the midst of us,[8] and the people thought it full early to part at 11:00.

**Saturday, October 2.** The whole day was spent in singing, conference, and prayer. I attended the choir service. The people there were marvellously civil and obliged me with the anthem. I desired the Third of Habakkuk, "a feast for a king," as Queen Anne called it. Mr. Williamson walked with me to his house in the face of the sun. I would have spared him, but he was quite above fear. A pious sensible Dissenter clave to us all day and accompanied us to the preaching. I preached on my old terrible subject,

---

[1] See the introduction to the Sept. 17–28, 1756 journal letter above; this is a continuation of CW's preaching tour.

[2] T. Brooke and his wife were the pioneers of the society in Thirsk. CW spells "Brooks."

[3] The popular name for the Cathedral Church of St. Peter, York.

[4] James Hervey, *Theron and Aspasio* (Dublin: Robert Main, 1755).

[5] Ann Mercy Bell (c. 1707–76), raised Quaker in London, married Nathaniel Bell of York in 1731. About 1745 she took on a ministry role that included public exhortation among the Friends and in public settings.

[6] A set of four hymns at the end of *Hymns for Times of Trouble and Persecution* (London: Strahan, 1744), 43–47.

[7] Rev. William Williamson (d. 1758), vicar of St. Mary's Church, Bishophill Junior, York.

[8] See Num. 23:21.

"I will bring the third part through the fire."[9] We glorified God *in* the fires and rejoiced in hope of coming forth as gold.

**Sunday, October 3.** From 5:00 till near 8:00 I talked closely to each of the society. Then, at Mr. Williamson's request, preached on the ordinances from Isaiah 64[:5], "In those is continuance, and we shall be saved." I dwelt longest on what had been most neglected, family prayer, public prayers, and the sacrament. The Lord set to his seal and confirmed the word with a double blessing. I dismissed them at 9:00. Our preachers had often kept them till near 10:00 and thereby hindered their going to church.

Received the sacrament at the Minster. It was a solemn passover. They were forced to consecrate twice, the congregation being doubled and trebled through my exhortations and example. Glory be to God alone. I found great faith to pray for him that consecrated; and heard afterwards that it was Mr. B–, one who had known the Methodists from their rise at Oxford and was no enemy to them. I expect (unless I fall away myself) to meet that sort in paradise.

Went to Mr. Williamson's church. He read the prayers, as one that felt them, and then beckoned me. According to our private agreement, I stepped up into the pulpit when no one expected it, and cried to a full audience, "The kingdom of God is at hand: repent ye, and believe the gospel."[10] They were all attention and seemingly pleased to hear me. The word did not return void[11] but accomplished that for which it was sent. Neither is he that planteth anything, neither is he that watereth.

Dr. Cockburn drove me in his chaise to Acomb.[12] I lost my voice in the rain and could not without much straining cry, "Behold the Lamb of God, that taketh away the sin of the world."[13] A clergyman[14] and most of the gentry in the place were present. The rain dispersed us in half an hour. I attempted to meet the society at York, but could not speak to be heard. We got a longer evening at the hospitable doctor's. Mr. Williamson and his family, etc., were helpers of our joy.

**Monday, October 4.** Took my leave in the apostle's words to Titus, "The grace of God which bringeth salvation hath appeared to all men, teaching us that, denying ungodliness and worldly lusts, we should live soberly, righteously, and godly, ...."[15] From hence I strongly pressed the obedience of faith. We parted in body only.

---

[9] Zech. 13:7–9.

[10] Mark 1:15.

[11] See Isa. 55:11.

[12] Acomb, Yorkshire; 2 miles west of York.

[13] John 1:29.

[14] Likely John Coates (c. 1716–82), vicar of Acomb, 1740–65.

[15] Titus 2:11–12.

Through God's blessing on my week's stay among them, I hope: 1) peace and charity are restored; 2) they will recover their rising, both preacher and people, promising to meet again at 5:00; 3) they are brought back again to Church and sacrament and family prayer.

Dr. Cockburn and his wife attended us to Tadcaster,[16] where I found both voice and strength to point many earnest souls to the all-atoning Lamb of God.[17] The gentry listened as well as the poor; both dismissed me with many blessings.

It rained as soon as we took horse. We were soon wet to the skin, the high wind driving the storm full in our faces. I could hardly keep the saddle, was most concerned for poor William Shent, and forced him to stop at the first house. There I reproved a countryman for swearing and gave a word of advice, which was kindly received. We took refuge again at Seacroft[18] and enjoyed the last fair hour,[19] which brought us to Leeds by 2:00.

I renewed my strength against preaching time, after which I met the leaders and earnestly exhorted them to set a pattern to the flock.

**Tuesday, October 5.** At 5:00 preached in William Shent's shop. Breakfasted at Miss [Ann] Norton's. There Mr. [John] Edwards assured me, "He had never desired any one of our children to leave us." Doubtless they did it of their own mere motion. No one ever dealt with or took pains with them about it. No one ever spoke against the Church, etc., to unhinge them. They dropped into his mouth (as our first children into the Count's[20]) without his ever suspecting it.

Blessed be God, I found if he had robbed us of our children, he has not of our peace and love. He several times expressed his readiness to preach in our societies. I only answered the people could not trust him that he would not do in every place as he has done in Leeds. I endeavoured to treat him with due respect and love according to our rule, "If it be possible, as much as in you lieth, live peaceably with all men."[21]

Passed the day at Mr. [Henry] Crook's who told me his experience. I cannot doubt of his having known the pangs of the new birth. Our brethren question it because he does not use all their phrases and cannot follow all their violent counsels. I begged him to do nothing rashly, least of all to go from his post, preaching everywhere like us.

Drank tea at a sister's who has been as the troubled sea since the separation and as rough toward all, especially her husband, as Mr.

---

[16] Tadcaster, Yorkshire; 9 miles southwest of York.
[17] Likely preaching on John 1:29.
[18] Seacroft, Yorkshire; 4 miles east of Leeds.
[19] Orig., "house"; corrected in keeping with MS Journal.
[20] Count Nikolaus Ludwig von Zinzendorf.
[21] Rom. 12:18.

Edwards is smooth. I laboured to quiet her, and she was convinced of the great advantage Satan had gained. Alas, for the man by whom the offence came![22]

**Wednesday, October 6.** Walked to Hunslet with William [Shent] and heard Mr. Crook expound. Dined with him and were provoked by his zeal.

Returning I found Joseph Tucker[23] at my lodgings and threw away some words on one wiser in his own eyes than seven men that can render a reason.[24] [[He entirely justified Mr. Edwards. Therefore I can have no confidence in him, that he will not, if it was in his power, do just as Mr. Edwards has done.]]

Henry Thornton[25] came to spend an hour or two with us, and we sharpened one another's countenance.

At 6:00 I met the leaders and inquired into the behaviour of each member. Upwards of forty Mr. Edwards has carried off, but not by desiring any to leave us. I carried them all with me to prayers and wished them to follow my example by carrying the whole society to Church with them.

Returned to the room and encouraged many serious souls by that description of them, "Kept by the power of God through faith unto salvation."[26]

**Thursday, October 7.** After a most tempestuous night, I preached to a few whom the hurricane could not keep from the word.

[[Had more talk with Joseph Tucker, who frankly confessed if any of our societies should desire him to take charge of them, as a distinct body, he should not refuse them. I told him plainly that the ground of all such designs was pride. But my words were spoken to the air.]]

After church set out in a storm for Seacroft and rode on to Aberford.[27] My old friend, Mr. Ingham, was labouring in our Lord's vineyard, but I had the happiness to find Lady Margaret at home and their son Ignatius.[28] She informed me that his round of preaching reaches about 200 miles, that he has six fellow labourers, and above 1,000 souls in his societies, most of them converted. I sincerely rejoiced in his success. Ignatius could

---

[22] Cf. Matt. 18:7.

[23] Orig., "J. T."; name spelled out in shorthand in MS Journal. Joseph Tucker appears as a probationer in the 1749 Minutes (*Works*, 10:237), and as a "chief local preacher" stationed in Ireland in the 1755 Minutes (ibid, 10:274). He appears to have left the itinerancy about 1756.

[24] Cf. Prov. 26:16.

[25] Henry Thornton (fl. 1745–55), of Leeds, was a supporter of the Wesley brothers and assisted them on several legal matters, including CW's marriage settlement.

[26] 1 Pet. 1:5.

[27] Aberford, Yorkshire; 8 miles east of Leeds; the home of Benjamin Ingham.

[28] Lady Margaret Hastings (1700–68), sister-in-law of Lady Huntingdon, was the first of the Hastings family to befriend the Methodists, and married Benjamin Ingham in 1741.

hardly be pacified at my not preaching. We passed an hour and an half very profitably and set out again. The rain met and drove us to a tree for shelter. We narrowly missed many heavy showers and got safe back to Seacroft before night.

Soon after, our dearest brother [William] Grimshaw found us and brought a blessing with him. I preached from Luke 21[29] and farther enforced our Lord's warning on the society. I strongly exhorted them to continue steadfast in fellowship with each other and the whole Church of England. Our hearts were comforted and knit together as the heart of one man.

**Friday, October 8.** We had another blessed hour with them before we left this lively people. Continued till 1:00 in conference with my worthy friend and fellow labourer, a man after my own heart, whose love of the Church flows from his love of Christ. With such may my lot be cast in both worlds. Spent an hour in intercession for the Church and nation. I exhorted them to continue instant in this prayer and mark the end and the answer.

Rode with my faithful brother Grimshaw to Bramley.[30] Preached in a large barn (now a convenient chapel) to a multitude of serious souls who eagerly received my Lord's saying, "Look up, and lift up your heads; ...."[31] They all seemed to be broad awake when I called again in the morning (**Saturday, October 9**), "Watch ye therefore, and pray always."[32] Their spirit quickened mine. We had sweet fellowship together. I have no doubt but they will be accounted worthy to escape and to stand before the Son of man.

Returning to Leeds by 8:00, I met my brother [George] Whitefield and was much refreshed by the account of his abundant labours. Waited on him to our preaching house, and gladly sat under his word. Dined and preached at Rothwell.[33] Their large room was full, though it was an harvest day. I warned them of the impending storm,[34] with much freedom and faith for the sincere, concluding with a warm exhortation to continue in the ship.

**Sunday, October 10.** From Isaiah 64:5, "In those is continuance, and we shall be saved." I earnestly pressed the duties of constant communicating, of hearing, reading, practising the word, of fasting, of private family and public prayer. The society I stirred up to continue in fellowship and never

---

[29] MS Journal specifies Luke 21:34–36.
[30] Bramley, Yorkshire; 4 miles west of Leeds.
[31] Luke 21:28.
[32] Luke 21:34–36.
[33] Rothwell, Yorkshire; 5 miles southeast of Leeds.
[34] This was likely a sermon on Ezek. 33:1–6.

more give place to the sower of tares,[35] the divider of the brethren. I spoke tenderly and healingly of the breach, told them how to behave toward Mr. [James] Wheatley, Mr. [Charles] Skelton, and the rest who have rose up to draw away disciples after them, and insisted on that apostolical divine precept, "Let all your things be done in charity."[36] I did not mention the author of the late division, being convinced he left us for bread.

The spirit of love and union was in the midst of us. No more would be drawn away, I am confident, if an able, discreet preacher were stationed among them for a few months; and many of our departed brethren would be glad to come back.

My congregation at Birstall was lessened a thousand or two (as was supposed) through my brother Whitefield's preaching today at Haworth. However, between 4,[000] and 5,000 were left to receive my warning (yet not mine) from Luke 21.[37] After church we met again with a large increase. Every soul seemed to hang on the word. Two such precious opportunities I have not enjoyed this many a day. It was the old time revived; only a more weighty spirit ran through the congregation, and they stood like men prepared to meet the Lord.

I never fail to recommend the ordinances and communion with the Church.

[[Leeds]]
[[October]] 11, [1756]

[[Dear Brother,]]

Alex[ander] Coats[38] is [[come. He may have both sense and grace, but I wish he had a little more utterance. I am of George Whitefield's mind, that he will never do for Leeds. He is a barbarian to me, I am sure, for I can't understand one word in three which he speaks.

[[The worst of poor James [Rouquet] is his instability. If marriage helps to settle him, I shall much rejoice. <Your[39]> namesake also is far from being a pillar,[40] whatever he seems in his own eyes.[41]

[[I will read the *Notes*[42] as soon as I possibly can.

---

[35] Cf. Matt. 13:25.

[36] 1 Cor. 16:14.

[37] Likely preaching again on Luke 21:28.

[38] Alexander Coats (d. 1765) was a native of Scotland who became a traveling preacher in 1741.

[39] A small portion of the ms is torn away by the seal.

[40] CW wrote in "pillar" in longhand, under the shorthand sign.

[41] This is likely a reference to John Fenwick.

[42] JW had asked CW to review *Explanatory Notes upon the New Testament*, published the previous year, for corrections to make in the second edition.

[[By what I hear, brother]] Fisher[43] [[is little better than a false brother. He sent Mr. Edwards[44] a letter not much to your honour, soon after you left Ireland, which was read in Mr. Edwards's meeting. This should justify Mr. Edwards, [but] will not easily steal my confidence.

[[What passed between you and me about ordaining, if you have forgot, I will never remind you of it. Be it so, if you please. I have done you much wrong by supposing you capable of any wrong impression.[45] I shall never be so uncivil and so idle as to justify my suspicion.]] *Ipsa res nos reduxit in gratiam.*[46] [[Neither shall I dispute with you which is the greatest friend of the Church. You gave me great pleasure by insisting I am of the two [of us] the most likely to leave it. Most glad am I to believe you; and if you stand by it, it is no great matter whether I leave it or no.[47]

[[I hear from Bristol that you are far from well. If you are ill and send me no notice of it, you do me wrong. Some at London who dearly love you complain of your impotence of mind and unadvisableness[48] in preaching oftener than your strength can bear. For my part I shall last as long as I can, and spare myself (if my friends are pleased to call it so) that I may last the longer.

Farewell.]][49]

*Address*: "To / The Revd Mr J Wesley."
*Endorsement*: by JW, "Oct. 1756."
*Source*: holograph; MARC, MA 1977/503, Box 5, file 5.

---

[43] Likely John Fisher, who served as an itinerant from 1751 to 1760.

[44] John Edwards, a former itinerant who had become an Independent minister in Leeds.

[45] This expansion is a bit uncertain.

[46] "These things we will not repeat, out of grace."

[47] This paragraph also appears in shorthand by CW in MARC, DDCW 8/1e, p. 97.

[48] CW wrote out "impotence" and "unadvisableness" in longhand, under the shorthand signs.

[49] This expansion of the shorthand provided by Frank Baker and Richard Heitzenrater.

## October 11–23, 1756[1]

Mr. J[ohn] W[esley]:

**Monday, October 11.** After preaching at 5:00 to this solid stablished people, returned to Leeds and spent an hour with the leaders. They informed me that my late exhortations have stopped some who were on the point of going over to Mr. [John] Edwards's society and brought others back to the Church ordinances. A woman in particular after hearing me on Sunday morning went to Church (which she had long forsaken) and received a manifestation of Jesus Christ in the prayers. I earnestly pressed them to recommend to their brethren, both by advice and example, the neglected duties of family and public prayer and to watch over the flock with all diligence, that of those whom Christ hath given us we might lose none.

Hearing Mr. [George]Whitefield and Mr. [William] Grimshaw were returning to our watch-night, I waited for them at their lodgings with zealous, humble, loving Mr. [Henry] Crook. It rained so hard that Mr. Whitefield was agreeably surprised at 8:00 to find our house as full as it could cram. My brethren forced me to preach first, which I did from Zechariah 13[:9], "I will bring the third part through the fire." My brother George seconded me in the words of our Lord, "I say unto all, Watch,"[2] and spoke with a voice that raised the dead. The prayers and hymns were all attended with a solemn power. It was a most triumphant night. Few, if any, we hope, went unawakened away.

**Tuesday, October 12.** I took my leave of Leeds in earnest prayer at William Shent's. Some [[having asserted that the division was owing to him, I endeavoured impartially to examine the matter to the bottom; and have therefore talked largely not only to the leaders and several of the society, but more especially to]] Mr. [Robert] Towers, Miss Green, Benjamin Stork, Miss [Ann] Norton, and Mr. [John] Edwards. [[Upon the whole, I am convinced that the ground of all was Miss Norton's hatred of]] William Shent. [[This induced her to draw away Mr. Edwards from us. He could not resist the temptation of a certain provision for himself and family.[3] Interest blinded his eyes, so that the means to his end seemed right and honest to him, though base and treacherous to us. As for William Shent, I do not find that he did more than every upright man would have done on the occasion. He watched over the flock and counteracted them who were daily seducing our children. He gave early notice to my brother of

---

[1] See the introduction to the Sept. 17–28, 1756 journal letter above; this is a continuation of CW's preaching tour.

[2] Mark 13:37.

[3] Ann Norton donated the land for building White Chapel and obviously other support for John Edwards.

their design, and thereby drew all their resentment upon himself—as every honest preacher will]] *qui cum ingeniis conflictatur ejusmodi*.[4] [[Since the separation (Miss Green and others like-minded are my author[itie]s) he has behaved with such mildness and discretion as has kept the rest of our flock together, when violence or harsh treatment might have scattered them all.]]

Preached at 10:00 in Wakefield to a more quiet and serious congregation than I have ever met with there. The rooms and yard was crowded while I applied our Lord's saying, "Behold, I come as a thief. Blessed is he that watcheth, and keepeth his garments."[5]

[[Sent for Miss Norton, to John Johnson's, and asked her whether she had tried to draw away a young popular preacher of ours]] (E. H.) [[to Mr. Edwards. She desired he might answer me himself, which he did before her in the negative. She told me some of our ablest preachers were entirely in Mr. Edwards's sentiments and interest.]] *Nec nihil, nec omnia*.[6] [[We parted in love.]]

Rode to Joseph Bennet's near Dewsbury[7] and preached very awakening to a mixed crowd who gave diligent heed to what was spoken. My vehement exhortation to the society was on the usual subject, "steadfast continuance in the word,"[8] in fellowship, breaking of bread, and prayers, especially at Church and with their families.

Passed the evening with Jonas Eastwood,[9] stirred up himself and a great stirrer up of others. I would gladly part with 500 Methodists to be ordained and useful like him.

**Wednesday, October 13.** Rode with John Nelson to Birstall. The word at night was clothed with power, both to awaken and to confirm. My principal concern is for the societies, that their houses may be built upon the Rock before the rains descend and the flood come and the stream beat vehemently upon them.[10] I hear in most places of the effect of the word, but I hearken after it less than formerly and *take little notice* of them that say they receive comfort or faith or forgiveness. Let the fruits confirm it.

Preached at night and rejoiced in steadfast hope of our being brought through the fire.[11]

---

[4] "Who is involved with characters like that"; cf. Terence, *Andria*, 93.

[5] Rev. 16:15.

[6] "Neither nothing, nor everything."

[7] Dewsbury, Yorkshire; 8 miles southwest of Leeds.

[8] Cf. John 8:31.

[9] Jonas Eastwood (d. 1772) had been a headmaster at Kingswood school, but sought ordination and was now curate at Dewsbury; in 1757 he would be appointed curate of Cleckheaton, Yorkshire and serve there the remainder of his life.

[10] See Matt. 7:24–27.

[11] His sermon on Zech. 13:9.

**Thursday, October 14.** Baptized a Dissenter's child, and set out with faithful Titus Knight for Halifax. A mixed multitude listened to the word, "When thy judgments are in the earth, the inhabitants of the world will learn righteousness."[12] I have not found greater freedom than in this place, where I expected least. Set out in hard rain for Bradford. My subject there was Habakkuk 3:2,[13] "O Lord, revive thy work ...." The house was filled with Dissenters; some, I believe, were reached for I spoke in irresistible love to all and warned them to flee from the wrath to come.

**Friday, October 15.** After preaching, I gathered into the fold a wandering sheep whom [[John Whitford's[14]]] pride and folly had scattered. Having lost her first love, she married one who follows not with us, on which the society gave her up for lost. I rejoiced to find her miserable in prosperity and restless to recover the true happiness.

Found comfort at church in the first lesson, Wisdom 5. Could be glad, if the Lord gave opportunity, of constantly attending the public prayers for my own edification no less than for example's sake.

At 4:00 the preaching house was full of those that came from far. Our Lord did not send them empty away but fed many of them, I am persuaded, with the bread of life. D. Nelson, a girl of 14, who had walked from Birstall in the rain, told me she was carried under the word as out of the body. What to call the manifestation of the Spirit then given her, time and temptation will show.

Near two hours more we rejoiced at a primitive love-feast. My exhortation was, as usual, continue in the doctrine and in fellowship, etc.[15] We were met and dismissed by the consolation of Israel.

**Saturday, October 16.** Breakfasted again with my lost sheep that is found. Last night at the love-feast she recovered her shield. For her sake chiefly I believe myself sent to Bradford. Took my leave in that promise, "He that endureth to the end, the same shall be saved."[16]

Came with Thomas Colbeck to Keighley[17] before noon. John Nelson, Jonathan Catlow,[18] and Eleazer Webster completed our little band of preachers.

---

[12] Isa. 26:9.

[13] Orig., "3:1"; an error.

[14] John Whitford was listed as an "assistant in one place" in the 1747 Minutes (*Works*, 10:205), and received as a probationary assistant in 1748 (10:214). He left the connexion to become an Independent minister in Bolton in 1754 (see 10:270 n 947).

[15] Acts 2:42.

[16] Matt. 10:22; Mark 13:13.

[17] CW spells "Kighly."

[18] Jonathan Catlow appears first in the *Minutes* as a traveling preacher only in 1753 (see *Works*, 10:260, 268).

Found at 4:00 a large handsome room well filled. Did my office as a watchman and delivered my own soul.[19] Mr. Grimshaw assisted at the society. I recommended family-religion with all my might. The Spirit helped our infirmities, humbling and quickening us both in the word and in prayer. For near an hour and an half the cloud stayed on the assembly.

**Sunday, October 17.** We had no room to spare at 6:00 in the morning while I commended them to God and to the word of his grace.[20]

Preached the second time at Haworth (Mr. Grimshaw reading prayers) from Psalm 46:8–9,[21] "O come hither, and behold the works of the Lord; what destruction he hath brought on the earth. He maketh wars to cease in all the world." My mouth was opened to declare the approaching judgments and the glory which shall follow when the Lord is exalted over all the earth. The church, which had been lately much enlarged, could scarce contain the congregation, who seemed all either to tremble at the threatenings or rejoice in the promises of God.

We had a blessed number of communicants and the Master of the feast in the midst. I prayed and exhorted afterwards. Our hearts were comforted and lifted up to meet him in his glorious kingdom.

After an hour's interval, we met again, as many as the church walls could contain, but twice the number stood without till the prayers were over. Then I mounted a scaffold and, lifting up my eyes, saw the fields white unto harvest.[22] The churchyard, which will hold thousands, was quite covered. God gave me a voice to reach them all—their ears, I mean, and I hope the hearts of most. I warned them of those things which shall come to pass,[23] and warmly pressed them to private, family, and public prayer. Enlarged on the glorious consequences thereof, even deliverance from evil and standing before the Son of man. I concluded and began again, for it was an accepted time. The spirit of the congregation bore me up as in the days that are passed. I never remember when my mouth was more opened or my heart more enlarged. The help which is done upon earth God doth it himself.

A young preacher of Mr. Ingham's came to spend the evening with me at Mr. Grimshaw's.[24] I found great love for him and wish all our sons in the gospel equally modest and discreet.

---

[19] Likely preaching again on Ezek. 33:1–6.

[20] See Acts 20:32.

[21] Orig., "46:5"; an error.

[22] See John 4:35.

[23] Almost certainly preaching on Ezek. 33:1–6.

[24] He is identified as Mr. Allen two paragraphs later. James Allen (1734–1804) of Gayle, Yorkshire, became one of Ingham's chief preachers in 1752 and was ordained by Ingham in 1756.

**Monday, October 18.** He accompanied us to Heptonstall[25] where I preached at 10:00 on Isaiah 64:5, "In those is continuance, and we shall be saved." I was very faint when I began. The more plainly did it appear that the power was of God and not of man. I warned them against the wiles of the devil, whereby he would draw them away from the Church and the other means of grace. I spoke as the oracles of God, and God gave testimony bowing the hearts of all present except a few bigoted Baptists. Went on our way rejoicing to Ewood.[26]

There the hard rain interrupted us after I had spoke about half an hour from Ezekiel 9. Mr. Allen could not leave us yet but rode with us next morning (**Tuesday, October 19**) as far as Gauxholme.[27] I stood on a scaffold at the foot of an enormous mountain (the poor people facing me) and called, "Behold the Lamb of God, who taketh away the sin of the world!"[28] The word was a two-edged sword. I knew not then that several Baptists were present, a carnal, cavilling, contentious sect, who are always watching to steal away our children and make them as dead as themselves. Mr. Allen assured me they have carried off no less than fifty out of one society, and that several meetings are wholly made up out of old Methodists. I talked largely with Mr. Grimshaw how to remedy the evil. He agreed: 1) that nothing can save the Methodists from falling a prey to every seducer but close walking with God in all the commandments and ordinances, especially the word and prayer, private, family and public; 2) that the preachers should be allowed more time in every place to visit from house to house, after Mr. Baxter's manner;[29] 3) that a small treatise should be wrote to ground and preserve them, and lodged in every house.[30] Mr. Allen told me that none of their people, though lying in the thickest of the Baptists, are ever proselyted by them, so much pains is taken by the labourers to caution and confirm every soul.

We came to Bolton with the night. Above forty of this poor shattered people still keep together. Many of those without flocked to the word. In great bodily weakness I warned them to flee to the city of refuge, tried to heal the breach and quiet the minds of our children, and was comforted with them through hope of our Lord's last glorious appearing.

---

[25] Heptonstall, Yorkshire; half a mile northwest of Hebden Bridge.

[26] Ewood Hall, Grimshaw's estate; half a mile northeast of Mytholmroyd, Yorkshire.

[27] CW spells "Gawksholm." JW describes this as a lone house set on the side of an enormous mountain (*Journal*, July 20, 1759, *Works* 21:210). It was 1 mile southwest of Todmorden, Lancashire.

[28] Cf. John 1:29.

[29] Richard Baxter, *Gildas Salvianus, The Reformed Pastor; showing the nature of the pastoral work, especially in private instruction and catechizing* (London: Robert White, 1656).

[30] JW would attempt to meet this need in 1758 with his *Preservative Against Unsettled Notions in Religion*.

**Wednesday, October 20.** Talked kindly to poor John Whitford, who seemed quite sick of his separate congregation, so headstrong and untractable, so like their humble slave and teacher! His principles as well as spirit have cut off his retreat. *Vistigia nulla retrorsum*[31] when once a Methodist preacher has abused both ours and our children's confidence by setting up for himself. This he could never think of till the salt had lost its savour.

The rain quickened our pace to Manchester. I took up my lodgings at Mr. Philips. My subject at night was, "When these things begin to come to pass, look up for your redemption" (or Christ's kingdom) "is near."[32] Many Arian and Socinian Dissenters were present and gnashed upon me with their teeth while I preached the coming of Jesus Christ, the one eternal, self-existing God, to take vengeance on them and all his enemies who would not have him to reign over them. The large preaching house was filled with serious hearers who seemed both to hear and tremble at the rod.

**Thursday, October 21.** I finished my discourse to our Lord's disciples, parted with my right-hand, my bosom friend and brother Grimshaw. Breakfasted at Mrs. Fanshaw's and rejoiced, though she has left us, that she has not utterly forsaken God. Her soul has suffered loss yet her good desires remain. Here my old friend John Bolton found me out and confirmed his love to me. From church I went to dine with our sister Rider, still waiting for the consolation of Israel.

At night I discoursed on Titus 2:11. Spoke close and home on practical faith and relative duties, but more closely still to the society.

It seems the famous Mr. Roger Ball[33] is now among them picking up their pence and persons. They were smit with admiration of so fine a man (Thomas Williams himself was nothing to him) and invited him to settle with them. Another new preacher they have also got, a young Baptist, who is gathering himself a meeting out of them, like the Baptist preachers who have borrowed so many of Mr. Grimshaw's children. Our society in Manchester was upwards of 200, but their itching ears have reduced them to half the number.

To these I showed the melancholy state of the members of the Established Church who are the most unprincipled and ignorant of any that are called Protestants and therefore exposed to every seducer who thinks it worth his while to make them Dissenters, Moravians, or

---

[31] This is a proverb taken from Horace's Fable of the Fox and Lion (*Epistles*, I.i.74–75). It translates literally "no signs of returning." But it came to mean proverbially "There is no turning back."

[32] Luke 21:28.

[33] An immoral antinomian preacher, Roger Ball had insinuated himself into the Dublin society a few years earlier; see JW, *Journal*, Apr. 10, 1750, *Works*, 20:330.

Papists. I told them that of all the members of the Church of England, the poor Methodists are most exposed because serious and therefore worth stealing; and of all the Methodists, those of Manchester are in the greatest danger because the most unsettled and unadvisable. I challenged them to show me one Methodist who had ever prospered by turning Dissenter and asked what would become of them when my brother should die? Whether they would not then be scattered and broken into twenty sects, old or new. To prevent this I advised them: 1) to get grace, or the love and power of God, which alone could keep and stablish their hearts; 2) to continue in all the means of obtaining this, especially the word and prayers of all kinds, to read the scriptures daily, to go constantly to Church and sacrament.

I make more allowance for this poor shattered society because they have been sadly neglected, if not abused, by our preachers. The leaders of their own accord desired me *not* to let [[Joseph Tucker]] come among them again for he did them more harm than good by talking in *his witty way* against the clergy and the Church. As for poor [[John Hampson[34]]], he *could not* advise them to go to Church for he never went himself; but some informed me that he advised them *not* to go. When we set the wolf to keep the sheep, no wonder that the sheep are torn and scattered.

Our brother Johnson[35] tells me, since he sent the people back to church, two have lately received forgiveness there in the prayers and two more in the sermon of a Church minister. If he and brother Lucas[36] and Hacking[37] continue steadfast, they may undo the great evil which our unsound preachers have done and confirm the disciples in their calling.

I cannot leave them in so unsettled a condition, and therefore intend with God's help to spend another week among them. I talked with the leaders and earnestly pressed them to set an example to the flock by walking in all the commandments and ordinances blameless.

[[The people here groan under an heavy burden of debt, having John Hampson's family to keep and their building to pay for, etc., etc. Mr. Barlow gives me small encouragement; but will do what he can to obtain[?[38]] subscribers.]]

---

[34] John Hampson (c.1732–95) became a Methodist traveling preacher in 1752, took a hiatus between 1765–76, and withdrew entirely in 1784 in a dispute over how leadership would be structured on JW's death.

[35] Thomas Johnson (1720–97), a native of Wakefield, Yorkshire, was converted in 1748, and became a traveling preacher in 1752. He was appointed to the Leeds / York area at this time.

[36] Richard Lucas served as a traveling preacher 1755–65 (see *Works*, 10:273, 305).

[37] John Hacking is listed as a traveling preacher 1755–59 (see *Works*, 10:273, 287).

[38] The shorthand letters are clear: "obstn"; but a fitting word or phrase from these letters is not clear.

[[Manchester]]
[[October]] 23, [1756]

[[Dear Brother,

[[I talked fully with [Eleazer] Webster, and had great satisfaction in him.

[[What opportunity could I have at Bolton, which I came to late at night, and left early next morning? One subscriber I have got to the school, and two to the *Notes*.[39] I have mentioned both to every person I have yet met who was likely to subscribe.

[[Ask John Nelson and William Shent what good Joseph Tucker does in our societies. He is an unnecessary burden in every place. Let me entreat you not to keep him from returning home. I will speak to him again, fully and kindly, when I've come to Bath, and send you the result.

[[Surely John Whitford slandered you when he told me you pressed him at London to preach with us again. You then knew him to be a graceless predestinarian.

[[Mr. Walker's letter[40] deserves to be thoroughly considered.[41] Your answer I assent to. One only thing occurs to me now which might prevent in great measure the mischiefs which will probably ensue after our death, and that is *greater, much greater, deliberation and care in admitting preachers.* Consider seriously if we have not been too easy and too hasty in this matter. Let us pray God to show us if this has not been the principal cause why so many of our preachers have so lamentably miscarried. Ought any new preacher to be received before we know that he is grounded, not only in the doctrines we teach, but in the discipline also, and particularly in the communion of the Church of England? Ought we not to try what he can answer a Quaker, a Baptist, a Papist, as well as a Moravian or predestinarian? If we do not insist on that]] στοργή[42] [[for our desolate mother as a prerequisite,[43] yet should we not be well assured that the candidate[44] is no enemy to the Church?

[[I have but one thing more to offer at present. Is it not our duty to stop Joseph Cownley,[45] and such like, from railing and laughing at the Church? Should we not now, at least, shut the stable-door? The short remains of my life are devoted to this very thing, to follow your sons (as Charles Perronet

---

[39] I.e., the *Explanatory Notes upon the New Testament*.

[40] Samuel Walker (1714–61), rector of Truro; cf. his letter to JW, Sept. 5, 1755, in *Works*, 26:582–86.

[41] CW wrote "considered" in longhand, beneath the shorthand sign.

[42] "Affection," or "love."

[43] CW wrote "prerequisite" in longhand, under the shorthand sign.

[44] CW wrote "candidate" in longhand, under the shorthand sign.

[45] CW spelled his last name in longhand, under the shorthand sign.

once told me we should follow you) with buckets of water, to quench the flame of strife and division which they have or may kindle.[46]

[[You may send me another letter before I leave this place. Help us by your prayers.

Farewell in Christ.]]

[[I am glad James is so teachable.]]
[[And Charles so quiet.]] *Sed non ego credulus illi.*[47]
[[You do not tell me your opinion of the matter.]][48]

*Address*: "To / Mr Robert Windsor / in King street / Tower Hill / London."
*Postmark*: "25 / OC."
*Endorsement*: by JW, "Oct. 19, 1756 / a[nswere]d Nov. 4."
*Source*: holograph; MARC, MA 1977/503 Box 5.

---

[46] CW included an abridged longhand transcription of this and the preceding paragraph in his MS Journal (Oct. 21, 1756), with some slight variations from the shorthand letter given here.

[47] Cf. Virgil, *Eclogues*, ix.34; "But I do not trust him."

[48] Expansion of shorthand in closing letter provided by Frank Baker and Richard Heitzenrater.

## The Case of Magdalen Hunter
## November 1771

Two years ago,[1] on our coming to live in Chesterfield Street, Marylebone,[2] my wife and I came acquainted with Magdalen Hunter, a sober, modest, labourious woman with a very idle, drunken, wicked husband. She worked day and night to get bread for her two small children; but he often snatched it from them, and beat her cruelly. We have heard her shrieks quite cross the street, and she has been driven out in the night naked and took shelter under our door till the morning. She lived in continual danger of her life till for some petty robbery he was transported.

The parish then allowed her two shillings a week for some time; but about six months ago struck it off, supposing her able to provide for herself and children without it. She pleaded hard for its continuance, or part of it, but in vain. Many applications she made in her extreme necessities to the overseer of the poor, and met with as many harsh repulses. My wife employed her occasionally to wash or to clean the house, although she would never stay the whole day with us, often desiring leave to step home and look after her children, whom she seemed excessive fond of. My wife permitted her to go and bade her call at our house when she wanted anything. We sent her now and then the broken victuals;[3] but she seldom came for them, which made us think she was got into good business.

She now lodged at an house full of poor people within two doors of us.

We had recommended her as a charwoman to Mrs. Arnold, by the Middlesex Hospital, who was very kind and compassionate towards her. On **Tuesday, November 5**, at 9:00 in the morning, she went out to work there, having locked up her children, which none of the lodgers or neighbours would take care of in her absence. But she told one woman in the house. They were left, as usual, in her room, the kitchen.

It being a severe frost, they begged hard for a little fire. She complied and left a small bit of meat in the pot, promising to be back by 1:00. The youngest boy hung on her neck and begged her not to leave them. In turning the key upon them she felt great uneasiness, which continued all

---

[1] While the events in this account take place in Nov. 1771, CW apparently composed the final account (extracting from his manuscript journal) two years later. CW included a shorter version of this account in his funeral sermon for John Boult, preached Nov. 12, 1771; see *Westminster Journal and London Political Miscellany* (Nov. 9–16, 1771).

[2] In the late 1760s the growing demand for CW's presence in London to officiate in the chapels that allowed access to sacraments for the Methodists, as well as his concern to provide adequate musical instruction for his sons, led him to seek a permanent residence in London. In late 1770 he was offered a fully furnished house on Chesterfield Street in Marylebone by Martha (Meighen / Colvill) Gumley (1711–88), widow of Colonel Samuel Gumley. CW and his eldest son moved in Feb. 1771. CW spells "Marybone."

[3] *OED*: "fragments of food left after a meal."

the time she was at Mrs. Arnold's. At 1:00 she desired leave to go, but was kept a little longer to finish her work.

Soon after 2:00 I went out to bury a corpse.[4] I was scarcely gone when one of my children saw a smoke from Mrs. Hunter's house, and cried out, "Fire." My wife immediately cried, "Take care of Mrs. Hunter's children," and sent both maids to fetch them to our house. They met a woman with two children, which she told them were Mrs. Hunter's. My wife was not quite satisfied and went herself to the house. But the confusion and crowd in the street was so great that she could not get to it.

Though the house was full of lodgers, no one thought to save the children. They were too busy in saving their own rags. The kitchen was filled with smoke, occasioned, as it afterwards appeared, by some old rags which the children had set on fire to make a bonfire. Instead of immediately bursting open the door, they broke the window only and poured in water into the room, which increased the suffocation. A woman saw one of the [children] cross the room after the water was poured in. Even when the door was broke open, they forgot the children. At last a woman brought out the youngest and said she could find no more. [[Four servants passed by.]] Ten minutes afterwards a man went in and found the elder under the bed. He was alive, but the youngest just expiring.

They laid him upon a stone at the door of an house, cautiously shut for fear of trouble. Just then the mother came back. A woman met and bade her go to my house. She answered she must first go and see her children and then she would. The woman burst into tears and left her. The first sight she met was her child upon the stone. She ran about like a madwoman, in search of a surgeon. [[One sent for.]] One was found passing by, who attempted to bleed the boy in the street, but in vain. The other was blooded and sent to the hospital.

It was three o'clock. At 5:00, I returned and found my family in great distress. My daughter, seeing one of the children carried out half-dead, fell into fits. My wife and son were little better. At their desire, I went to the poor woman, who was carried to the adjoining alehouse. I saw her surrounded with women, all silent and in tears. She was hugging and rocking her dead child, and would not part with it. On sight of me, she exclaimed, "O Mr. Wesley. Mr. Wesley. God has found me out. God has punished me for my sins by taking away both my children." She went on with such deep heart-piercing complaints as I think I never heard, mixing bitter imprecations against the inhuman people of Marylebone. It was in vain to stop the torrent. I could only desire her to let go the dead child, which with difficulty I forced out of her arms. She then started up crying she would go see her other son, which she knew was dead. She had no

---

[4] I.e., to preside at a funeral.

strength to walk. I assured her he was alive and sent to the hospital, and I would see him myself in the morning. An humane baker helped her to his house, where she lay raving all night. [[Damn her, leave her laying in the common.]][5]

Next morning early I saw the child at the hospital. He had been in convulsions all night, but they hoped he might recover. I hastened to carry her the news, but she got my servant and another in the meanwhile to lead her to the hospital. Her violence there disturbed the patients in the ward; yet they could not refuse her request to stay and see the last of her son. He lingered till the afternoon before he expired. The doctors declared he died by suffocation. She could not bear to see him breathe his last, and even then contained herself within some bounds, only entreating them to let her have one kiss. As soon as she touched the dead body, she was quite outrageous and filled the ward with her cries and lamentations. To one of the governors offering her money, she answered, "I don't want money; give me back my children!" He tried to comfort her, as he himself told me, but he might as well have talked to one in Bedlam.[6]

At night I had a message from the hospital desiring me to come and get her away, if I could, for they knew not what to do with her. I sent my maid, with her kind friend the baker, who with much difficulty got her into a coach and brought her to his house. There I spent an hour endeavouring to assuage her. She renewed her bitter complaints of Marylebone; told me many particulars of her sufferings through want, such as I thought were not to be found in a Christian country. After parting with the last rag for bread, she had often nothing to give her children but cold water and a little oatmeal. Her only shift,[7] while it lasted, she used to wash and put on wet because she had no fire to dry it. As often as she applied to the overseer or beadle[8] for relief, she was repelled with the same answer, "You are not of this parish." She was invited to Scotland by her friends there, but ashamed to go till she had got clothes. All she desired to the parish was to continue her allowance till Christmas. Nay, if they would but have granted her one shilling a week, she said, she would never have left her poor children [[alone]].

I asked her why she did not inform us of her necessities. Pride, she answered, prevented her. "I knew Mrs. Wesley would have relieved me, but I was ashamed to come a-begging. O how gladly now would I go about begging from door to door with my two sweet babies if I could but get them back again. My cursed pride has killed both my children."

---

[5] These shorthand phrases are apparently some of her ravings.

[6] The Hospital of St. Mary of Bethlehem in London, used as an asylum for the mentally ill.

[7] A basic smock or dress.

[8] A lay helper in a church.

Farther she told me that she had had a religious education (as all the Scotch have), but had cast off the fear and service of God, and therefore he had justly cast off her. That she did not turn to him in her trouble, but forgot to pray or read her Bible or go to public worship. That she would not say God was severe, but God was righteous in taking away what she loved better than him. She often broke out into passionate clamours for death. Some of her words were, "O Jesus, wash me in thy blood, and take me to my children."

One thing very remarkable she informed me of, that some days ago when her children clamoured for bread and she had none to give them, she cried out in a fit of angry desperation, "O God, take me from these, or these from me." Immediately she said her heart smote her, but she could not call back the words. "And now," she added, "he has taken me at my word and taken perhaps the only possible way of bringing down my pride and saving my soul."

I asked her, "If God had taken her from them, instead of them from her, was she as fit to go? Where would she have been this moment." "In hell," was her ready answer; but God in the midst of wrath had remembered mercy and given her space to repent.

We prayed, and she was sensibly calmer and began to humble herself under the mighty hand of God, and even to see his mercy as well as his justice in the dispensation.

**November 7, Thursday.** At noon I called on Mrs. Arnold, who told me of Mrs. Hunter's coming to her house at 9:00 on Tuesday, working there till near 3:00, and then returning with victuals to her children.

In the afternoon I found the poor woman calmer, though she had not slept since her loss. Now and then she relapsed into passionate cries after her children, but less violent; and she desired to live, she said, only till she was ready to die and go to them.

**November 8, Friday afternoon.** The coroner's inquest sat upon the children at the next door alehouse. They sent for Mrs. Hunter (whom I had taken to my house by day, and Mr. Hill the baker lodged her at night). He ran into us, pale and trembling, and told us the jury were in doubt whether to bring it in accidental death or wilful murder; that only he and Mr. Sarson were for the first. I thought them not quite so wise as Solomon in distinguishing the true mother from the counterfeit.[9] He informed me that their doubt was occasioned by one Isaac who assured them, "She had set the house on fire on purpose to burn her own children." If I could think any parent capable of such villainy, it would be the man that could suspect another of it. But perhaps Mr. Isaac's only view was an innocent stratagem to keep the jury longer drinking at his house. He forced his way

---
[9] See 1 Kings 3:16–28.

into the room where the jury were. They turned him out and examined the poor woman who gave them a plain relation of the whole matter. Still they could not agree in their verdict, that honest man had so confounded them. Mr. Sarson left them to inform me they were nothing nearer a decision, having only the mother's word for her having been at Mrs. Arnold's. Soon after the jury desired my company, I went and confirmed her account, with which they were all entirely satisfied. I offer to confirm it by my oath. They said my word was quite sufficient, returned me thanks, and a few minutes after brought in their verdict [of] accidental death.

The coroner and most of the rest spake kindly to the distressed woman and made a small collection for her.

After the relation I had given them of her sufferings, I could not help adding, "Thus the parish have saved two shillings a week, but at the expense of two lives."

I was afraid that, if she heard of her being charged with the murder of her children, it would drive her quite distracted; and therefore kept her within the house. But on **Sunday, November 10**, at 7:00 in the morning, she got out of her lodging at Mr. Hill and "went to the grave to weep."[10] The poor children had been put into the earth on Saturday afternoon. I cannot say buried, for no service was read over them. And as they wanted bread when alive, they would have wanted a grave when dead, had not Mr. Hill bribed the sexton to dig them one instead of the shallow hole he would have put them into. He took two shillings of her to let her into the burying-ground. Two shillings more she gave for the loan of a Bible. She was locked in and lay upon the grave till noon. Mr. Hill hardly got her home. They put her to bed in an high fever and delirious. I carried a physician at night to see her.

I saw her the next day (**Monday, November 11**) in her senses, yet extremely ill, and asked why she had stayed so long in the burying-ground. She said she had been reading over the grave Ezekiel 37,[11] in hopes of praying her children alive again.

**Tuesday, November 12.** Two gentlemen called upon her and offered to take her into the workhouse. They assured me they knew nothing of her allowance being stopped, but thought she had it still. What pity, some charitable person could not look into the distresses of the poor!

I found Mrs. Hunter this morning in high spirits. She told me with great joy that she was to be tried for killing her children. So some people in Mr. Hill's shop had told her. She inquired of several when the trial would be and who would be sent to take her up. She asked my servant to carry her to the judge, and said to me, "As you know, Sir, I shall die innocent.

---

[10] Cf. John 11:31.

[11] See Ezek. 37:1–14, "the valley of the dry bones."

God, I hope, will have mercy upon me; and then I shall get my children again."

This brings to my mind what she told me soon after her children's death, that once in her extremity of want, seeing a baker set down his basket, she had a thought of stealing a loaf on purpose that she might be carried before the justice and have an opportunity of telling him her case. But the man being out of sight, she forbore.

*Annotation*: "Magd[alen] Hunter / Nov. 1771."
*Source*: holograph; MARC, DDCW 6/85.

## June 1772–April 1774
## The Case of Edward Davies[1]

Account of the
Conscientious and Christian Behaviour
of the Rev. Charles Wesley, when shamefully
treated by a hypocritical clergyman and cheated
in a horse.[2]

[p. 1]

On Saturday, June 27, 1772, I first rode out with Mr. Davies,[3] and frequently afterwards till July 16. He observed the windgalls[4] on my mare's legs, which he said would grow worse and worse, till in about a year she would be good for nothing.

He mentioned, as by accident, a most *"excellent mare of his, most easy, most sure, and the best in all Wales"*; which he valued at £11, being eleven years old, but would let me have his for my two mares. My little mare, he told me, was worth £4 or £5, my old one £4. Only he could not send me his, which had a foal, in less than three weeks after his return to Wales.

Having an entire confidence in him, I consented to give him both my mares in exchange for his—sight unseen[5]—and paid him £4, which my old mare sold for. But I was very loathe to part with my other mare before I received his, as he knew I could not *live* without riding.

July 16, [1772]. Mr. Davies told me at Mr. Evan's that he had borrowed brother Henderson's[6] little mare for me, till his mare should come, which he would send me in three weeks or *there abouts*. I had not the least doubt of her [page 2] answering the character given of her, but still I scrupled

---

[1] CW distilled this account of his dispute with Edward Davies over a horse into a small bound manuscript notebook. The account draws from his record copies of letters, and likely also from his manuscript journal.

[2] The title, on the outside cover of the notebook, is in the hand of Sarah Wesley Jr.

[3] Edward Davies (c. 1736–1812), originally of Rhyddlan, Flintshire, graduated from Jesus College, Oxford in 1759 and was ordained a priest in January 1760. He served as a perpetual curate at Bengeworth from 1767–72, where he once invited JW to preach (JW, *Journal*, Mar. 17, 1768). In 1768 Davies was also made rector of Coychurch, Glamorgan, Wales (though he was infrequently resident there). At the time of the dispute traced in this manuscript JW was trying to recruit Davies as another ordained leader for the Methodist work. CW abbreviates throughout the manuscript as "Mr. D."

[4] A soft swelling above the fetlock on a horse's leg.

[5] Orig., "unsight unseen."

[6] This is likely Richard Henderson, a native of Ireland who came to England about 1762 and soon entered the Methodist itinerancy (cf. *Works*, 10:296). Henderson ceased traveling about 1770 and settled near Bristol, where he ran an asylum for the mentally impaired.

parting with my only mare at an uncertainty. Then he said in displeasure he would be off his bargain, and I should not have his mare. I did not care to disoblige him, and therefore let him take mine.

I had soon cause to repent my easiness, and wrote pressingly to Mr. Davies for his mare. He answered, "I am exceeding sorry at your repeated disappointments and misfortunes, and much more so when I find it out of my power to relieve you in sending the mare immediately. And what grieves me more, I am apprehensive she will not be with you before the latter end of the month, of the 1st or 2nd of September. When she comes, she will fully please you I believe. *She will never throw you down; for I never rode so sure and so safe an one.*"

Mr. Henderson wanted his mare, having at Mr. Davies's pressing instance lent her, as he thought, for a few days only. I let him have her, and hired or borrowed, to my very great hazard and inconvenience, for the rest of the time.

In the beginning of September Mr. Davies sent me his mare, by some man we none of us knew, who delivered her to our man Joseph, telling him *she was lame*.

She was both lame and sick. I let her rest for some days and then walked her out. She could hardly drag her legs after her, went a little lame, and slipped behind almost continually. I had intended to ride her to Gloucester, but was forced to take a post-chaise. At my return I rode her the second time. [page 3] She fell and threw me over her head, with great violence. I ventured to ride her a few more times, but her legs swelled to so enormous a size through the fashions[7] that I was forced to let her lie by. Then she fell ill of the glanders, killed my son's horse, and a preacher's, and died herself.

Meantime my confidence in my friend was so great that I entirely acquitted him in my own thoughts of any design to overreach me or even knowledge of his mare's condition. Out of my concern for him I wrote to him as follows:

Bristol
December 10, 1772

My Good Friend,

I am sorry you heard of the mare's sickness. I never intended you should know it till it was past. Don't think me capable of an hard or unkind thought concerning you. You could not answer for events. Trusting

---

[7] *OED*: "'Fashions' is the 15–17th century spelling for the obsolete word 'farcin.' The modern spelling for this word is 'farcy,' which is defined as 'a disease of animals, *esp.* of horses, closely allied to glanders.'"

you will not make yourself uneasy, I am forced at last to inform you, that your mare has been sick ever since she came. The man who brought her told our man (a very careful, skilful fellow) that she was a little lame. After some days' rest I walked her out, and could but just perceive her lameness. Soon after she fell ill of the fashions. Our farrier is both a knowing and an honest man. No care, I assure you, has been wanting. In about a month's time I rode her again for a very few mornings. Still she refused her meat; till a week ago she was taken with the glanders; and so ill that our man expects her death every day.

Your offer of your only riding horse I take very kindly, but cannot be so ungenerous [page 4] as to accept of it. *If you can send me my own mare by the bearer*, I will thank you; for I need not *tell* you I am put to my shifts.[8]

In his answer he told me, "He would gladly send me my mare, but that she was lame." I had not the least doubt of his returning her, as soon as she was able to come. But fearing still lest he should be too much afflicted on my account, I wrote him another letter.

Bristol<br>January 1, 1773

Neither you nor I could help the inconveniences occasioned by that unfortunate beast. I did not tell you the worst of her because I did not desire that you should be troubled. I have not rode her twelve times in all. The first time she was led to water, she gave my son's little horse a kick which lamed him for above a month. Perceiving her to slip behind, I never rode her double. But the second time I rode her myself, she fell with such violence that it was next to a miracle I did not break my bones.

When, by her legs swelling to an enormous size, we found she had got the fashions, we kept her still in our stable, at the peril of the other horses. She had scarce recovered of that before she was seized with the glanders, which soon put an end to her life. Our horses escaped the glanders, but caught the fashions of her. Charles's horse is expected to die daily. The greatest care has been taken of them all. Our farrier thinks your mare's milk killed her.

What shall we say to these things? [page 5] With Ovid—*careat successibus, opto quisquis ab eventu facta notanda putat.*[9] I blame not you, nor myself, nor anyone. All that happens is providence to me; and if, for want of an horse, my short residue of days is made shorter, I find no inclination to complain.

I have been forced to hire an horse for several mornings, and sometimes I borrow.

I heard nothing more of my mare, till I saw her at the Foundery some months after. I supposed Mr. Davies had brought her up to London on

---

[8] OED: "'put to my shifts' means 'in the greatest difficulty.'"

[9] Ovid, *Heroides*, ii.85–86, "I hope that anyone who thinks what I did is wrong because of its result, also lacks success."

purpose to restore her to me, and ordered our servant to have her in readiness for my riding her to Bristol. I did not write and importune Mr. Davies for her (my brother having lent me his horse) purely out of tenderness toward and confidence in him. It never entered into my heart that he intended to keep her as his own, till our man at the Foundery forced me to know it. Then I wrote to Mr. Davies as follows.

Marylebone [London]<br>June 28, 1773

My Dear Sir,

John certainly mistook you. He tells me you forbid my riding my mare to Bristol, calling it yours. You know I was to give you two mares for one; and did pay you beforehand £4, the price my old mare sold for; and let you have my little mare (as you was then distressed for an horse), before I received your mare in exchange. I took your word assuring me, *"She was the best mare in Wales; would carry me and my wife all over England; and you believed would never fall with me."* At last, she was sent me lame and sick. I let her rest some days, and then [page 6] made the first trial of her. She slipped behind so frequently that I saw my wife could never venture upon her. One of my first times of gently riding her she fell down all at once and threw me over her head. Soon after it appeared that she had the fashions; and then the glanders, of which she died, after infecting my son's horse, and a poor preacher's, who both died.

The great inconveniences and dangers I ran all this time I made little, not much of, through fear of grieving you. You kindly offered to send me your own horse (as mine was lame), which I refused; choosing to be distressed rather than to distress you. But I made no doubt of your sending me my own mare when able to come. Mr. Horseman, when in town, promised to bring or send her back from Wales to Bristol. When I saw her here I concluded *you* had brought her up *for me*. On what you ground *your* claim to her I cannot conceive. I think both the mare and the £4 should be returned to me. Let any indifferent person judge.

The above letter I read to Mr. Davies before Mr. Ley[10] and Mr. Horton.[11] Mr. Davies answered "that as his mare was delivered to my servant *it was a bargain*, and my mare belonged to him." My reply was that Mr. Davies told me he would send me his mare by one of my brother's preachers or companions. Afterwards he said he would send it by some other man,

---

[10] William Ley (1739–1803), a native of Exeter, was a Methodist preacher 1758–63. He took a B.A. from St. Edmund Hall, Oxford in 1765 and was ordained deacon In 1769 he was ordained priest and appointed vicar of of East Tilsbury, a position he held until his death.

[11] Likely John Horton (1740–1802), of Islington, a Methodist, who would marry Mary Durbin in 1780 (see JW, *Journal*, Sept. 20, 1780, *Works*, 23:186).

some brother in those parts. Who the man or brother was, or what his name, I know not [page 7] to this day. How then could he be *my* servant or messenger? Besides, if I had sent my own servant to receive his mare, would that oblige me to have her untried, or rather entirely different from what he had vouched her to be? What reason that he should have my mare upon trial for almost a year, and I take his without any trial? Why must I be forced to buy a pig in a poke? Or how could a just or generous man take advantage of, or abuse the confidence of his friend? The most sharping[12] jockey could not do worse.

In our conference with Mr. Ley and Mr. Horton, Mr. Davies made an offer of referring our dispute to them. I knew them both to be entirely on my side and therefore told Mr. Davies "My necessity should give way to his extremity, and as he carried his wife out every day on my mare he was welcome to the use of her as long as his wife lived." Accordingly I left her to him although I designed to have rode her myself to Bristol, and returned home by the coach.

After her death I wrote to him to send back my mare by Mr. Snig. He sent her back, but with a very ill grace and the following letter:

London<br>August 7, 1773

Dear Sir,

The grey horse I have now come up, cost me £15.5s.0[d]., last May 12 month. From the time I had him he has not been well, and is at present not worth £5. Can I go to the seller [page 8] and complain? No. It is a casualty which he could not foresee. The mare I sent you from Wales, (had she been to be sold) two or three days before she set out I might have had £11 for. Was she sound when I left her at Cowbridge[13] on her way to Bristol? Yes, to the utmost of my knowledge, I can clearly make an affidavit. Was it my agreement to run all hazards to Bristol, or to send her on such conditions, or was I to defray her expenses on the way? No. I defrayed the expenses of that [mare] I had from you. It is true I had the little mare so much sooner than you had the other. According to the time of agreement I sent her. And now I will inform you what I did not intend. It cost me eleven shillings for you to have the use of Mr. Henderson's mare till near the time of yours coming, for I bought a silver spoon and made him a present of it.

In the Conference minutes Mr. Wesley has inserted, "Write him knave that would not do as he would be done by, in buying and selling of

---

[12] I.e., "swindling."

[13] Cowbridge, Glamorgan; about 4 miles southeast of Coychurch.

horses."[14] Have I in this instance with you? *To the searcher of hearts I appeal*, and to you I testify that I have to the utmost of my power, and all your letters acknowledge the same.

I did not answer this letter, because I had heard of the very unfair use he had made of my former letters, reading detached sentences out of them and putting his own construction on them. A few remarks I made on his letter as:

First, the cases are totally different. Was the seller of the grey horse his friend and brother? [page 9] And did he therefore take the horse upon *his* word, and pay for it before he had tried or seen it? Did the horse fall short in every respect for which the seller had warranted him? Did he receive him, from the first moment, visibly lame and sick, etc.?

Of his generous present poor sorrowful Mr. Henderson informed me at the beginning. Mr. Davies calls it (in a letter to me) "an ample recompense"! A spoon of 11s. for the use of his mare for seven weeks!

But "all my letters," he says "acknowledge" his honesty. All my letters demonstrate my obstinate *belief* of his honesty (at that time), and my unshaken confidence *in the word* of a Christian friend! Does this *extenuate* his making *such a use* of my credulity?

I expected to hear no more of the matter, when I received the following note:

No. 7 Winkworth Buildings
March 13, 1774

Rev. Sir,

As I shall now want my mare, you will please to send her by James's first wagon, a particular charge to take care of her. And in advising me of the day she is to be in London, you will oblige,
Your humble servant,

E[dward] D[avies]

[page 10]

I was less surprised than might be expected by this demand, which was soon followed by a second, more pressing. He could not hope for any more letters from me. But I wrote to Mr. Ley, desiring him to send Mr. Davies immediate word *that the mare was mine, and not his*. In his answer, April 5, he writes, "Your answer to Mr. Davies's letter came too late. He set out for Wales last Friday. I fear you will find him a k[nave] in grain.[15]

---

[14] 1766 Minutes, Q. 29, *Works*, 10:331.

[15] I.e., "a knave of the first rate."

He says he only lent you *his* mare, and if you do not deliver it up to him he will bring an action against you.

On Wednesday, April 6, I went with my family to spend a few days in Bath. On Saturday morning I was waked by a special messenger and letter from Mr. Davies. As it contains the merits of his cause, I transcribe the whole.

Bristol<br>Thursday Evening

Rev. Sir,

Your not answering my letters has caused me to disappoint a church ninety miles from town, and near as remote from Bristol, where I am come on purpose to demand my mare.

Which demand and right I draw from my purchasing of her, and the following consequences. In my agreement with you, you was to have my mare as soon as a person could be met with to take her after the 26th of August, and *you was to be* at the expense of the journey to Bristol. That very day I had the opportunity of delivering her into the care of your brother. And I, my servant, and several neighbours (if [page 11] required) will make affidavit that she went sound from me, to the utmost of my knowledge. I also believe that she would not have been ill, or died, if proper care had been taken to have had her milked on the road and in Bristol.

Such casualties I could not engage for, neither by law or equity. Now *what does Mr. Charles Wesley* think of the affair? Let us refer to his own letters for his sentiments:

First letter: "It must be near three weeks longer if you wait to send the mare by a preacher. A post-boy or a sailor you may as safely trust her to. I need not say I should be glad if you could sooner find a safe rider for her."

Second letter: "I am sorry you heard of the mare's sickness. I never intended you should know it till it was past. For believe me, my good friend, I am more troubled for you than for myself. Don't think me capable of an hard or unkind thought concerning *you*. You could not answer for events."

Third letter: "Neither you nor I could help the inconveniences arising from that unfortunate beast. Our farrier thinks the mare's milk killed her. What shall we say to these things? *Careat successibus, opto quisquis ab eventu facta notanda putat.*[16] I blame not you, nor myself, nor anyone. All that happens is providence to me."

From these letters I concluded you wrote in sincerity, and that you was fully satisfied. Therefore [page 12] it was to my utmost astonishment that you eight months after ordered my mare to be kept idle for days, because you intended taking her to Bristol, and this without consulting

---

[16] Ovid, *Heroides*, ii.85–86.

me. Did you imagine because I was in connection with you and [your] brother that you should use my property without my consent? I then let you know to the contrary.[17]

I expostulated with you, and your answer was, on the road to Islington, "We will not fall out about *meum* and *tuam*."[18] I informed you that I was willing to refer the matter to judges. You *declined it*, adding you should *mention her no more*.

Again at the Conference I was surprised that you should attempt to have the use of her, after treating me in the manner you did. But your brother, *begging her* as a favour, because he said his mare went another way. Yet, lest you should imagine you might expect her as yours, I wrote a letter to assure you of the contrary.

No answer came. Had you a shadow of claim remaining, why did not you *maintain it even then*? You have attempted effectually to bring the committee to recant their promise of allowing the trifle of ten guineas by your letters to them lately. But this I am well pleased with, as occurrences fall out.

Now, sir, without any farther altercations [page 13] from me, I have only this to desire, an answer, as short as you please, whether you will or not deliver up my mare to me this night or morning early. I am to set off near eighty miles by Sunday, if I have my mare; if not, I shall take two witnesses in the morning to demand her.

I am

Your humble servant,

E[dward] D[avies]

P. S. I have kept a copy of this.

I returned no answer to this because I now *knew* Mr. Davies, that he was not a man whom one could *safely* write to. Some stricture I did make on his letter:

"You was to be at the expense of the journey." Not a word of this was mentioned when I lent Mr. Davies my only mare for six weeks. But I should have gladly paid for *his* mare's coming, had she came such as he warranted her.

"I believe she would not have been ill or died, if proper care had been taken to have had her milked on the road and in Bristol." Why then did not Mr. Davies, who alone knew her condition, order his messenger to have her milked on the road, and to put us in mind of doing it? By his own confession it appears that through *his* neglect the mare died.

"Now *what does Mr. Charles Wesley* think of the affair? Let us refer to his own [page 14] letters for his sentiments." "When he wrote them" should be added; and "what *does* Mr. Charles Wesley think of the affair *now*" should be altered to "what *did* Mr. Charles Wesley think of the affair *then*."

---

[17] See CW's letter of June 28.

[18] "What belongs to me" and "what belongs to you."

I *then* thought Mr. Davies an *honest* man, a Christian brother, a faithful friend, and utterly incapable of taking *such* advantage of my unsuspicious, implicit *trust* in his honour and integrity. Would to God I *could so* think of him still!

"From these letters I concluded you wrote in sincerity."—Of love and confidence I surely did. But my sincerity did not meet with a suitable return.

"I concluded you was fully satisfied." Of Mr. Davies's honesty I *was then*; and therefore I had no doubt, when I wrote desiring him to send me back my mare, that he would send her as soon as possible.

"I expostulated with you on the road, and your answer was 'We will not fall out about *meum* and *tuam*.'" I well remember that after our conference at Mr. Horton's,[19] where I told him I would lend him my mare while his wife lived, I rode with him to Islington. And myself first mentioned the affair desiring we might not fall out about *meum* and *tuam*.

"I informed you that I was willing to refer the matter to judges." [page 15] He never mentioned anything like it to me, except once before Mr. Horton and [Mr.] Ley, to whom he slightly said he was willing to refer it. I did not immediately take him at his word, *because I knew they must have given it against him*, being entirely of my mind.

"Adding you should mention her no more." I remember no such words. If I did use any such, I could mean no more than that I should have my mare to him while his wife lived.

As for his *astonishment* that I should claim her at the Foundery, and his *surprise* that I should attempt to get her at the Conference, I cannot believe him sincere. He could not but know that I had not given up my claim. Let Mr. Horton and Mr. Ley bear witness. Did not they maintain my claim after I left London? Did not Mr. Ley bring him to his confession and tears, and almost persuade him to let me have my mare again? So Mr. Ley informed me, and that Mr. Davies had promised him to write to me, acknowledging my right.

"After treating me in the manner you did." From first to last I have treated him as a gentleman, a clergyman, and a friend.

"But your brother *begging* her as a *favor*." This cannot be true. I had told my brother the whole affair, and engaged him to get me back my mare. Mr. Davies did not think it prudent at *that time* to withhold her.

[page 16] "No answer came" (for the reason above mentioned). "Had you a shadow of claim remaining, why did not you maintain it even then?" Because I did not affect any farther correspondence with him. I knew both my words and my silence would be misinterpreted. So of two evils, I chose the least.

"You have attempted effectually to bring the committee to recant their promise of allowing the trifle of ten guineas, by your letters to them lately." This is like his other charges against me, the author of all his calamities. I have wrote no letter to any of the committee. One I wrote

---

[19] Horton lived at Highbury Place, in Islington.

Mr. Horton, advising them, if it was in their power, to make him a present of £40.

"Now, sir, I have only this to desire, an answer, as short as you please, whether you will or will not deliver up my mare—this night, or morning early. ... I shall take two witnesses in the morning to demand her." I dismissed his messenger, telling him I should return to Bristol that day.

I did return by the coach, visited a sick friend, and came home. There our man informed me that Mr. Davies had come, with one he called an evidencer, to our stable, and if Joseph had left it, as usual, on the latch, he verily believes the gentleman would have borrowed my mare, without any ceremony. That as it was, he could hardly hinder him, for he stayed a considerable time about the stable, looking [page 17] in at the window, which was open but not quite wide enough to get the man through it. Joseph bluntly told him "The mare was not his but mine; that the mare he had sent in exchange came both lame and sick, and so continued till she died, after killing two of our horses and costing us not less than £40.

I officiated on Sunday morning, and expected Mr. Davies till near 4:00 in the afternoon. Young Mr. Owen of Publow dined with us.[20] Till this very day I judged of Mr. Davies with the charity that hopeth all things.[21] Blinded by self-love and covetousness, he thought himself in the right and never *intended* to defraud me. So I obstinately hoped till Mr. Owen told me that *sometime before Mr. Davies sold me his mare he complained to him that "she was a very good beast, but every now and then was taken lame!"* If this was the case, alas and alas! What shall we think of his solemn appeals to God for his having done as he would be done by (calling him knave who would act otherwise), of his repeated offer to take his oath of her soundness, and his whole behaviour toward his unsuspicious friend!

Mr. Owen desired me to call upon him for his testimony when it came to a trial. I rode with him to Pensford,[22] intending to preach, but came too late; lodged at his father's house, and returned home the next day to dinner.

[page 18] During my absence Mr. Davies had frequently sent and called at my house. The last time my wife saw and *heard* him, his soft words made some impression upon her. His angry bitter words disturbed and frightened her, although she would not own it, because she laughed at his last threatening to print all my letters. He laid heavy things to my

---

[20] John Owen (1754–1824), the son of John Owen and Hannah Frances Owen of Publow, Gloucestershire. He was studying at this time for his BA at Worcester College, Oxford, and his mother ran a boarding school in Publow, which JW praised (see *Journal*, Sept. 15, 1772, *Works*, 22:348). Publow was five miles south of Bristol.

[21] Cf. 1 Cor. 13:7.

[22] Pensford, Gloucestershire; half a mile south of Publow.

charge; but the worst of all was that he had been £200 loser by me and he would immediately bring an action against me for his mare, unless I restored her by 5 o'clock.

My wife sent Mr. Stokes after him, who carried another gentleman. Mr. Davies read them my letters, to prove *my* judgment of his honesty. Mr. Stokes observed that those were only scraps, but he had seen my letters entire. After reasoning the case with him in vain, he assured him he should defend me, wherever legally attacked, and left him in great displeasure. "The trial," he told me, "should cost *me* nothing, but must cost Mr. Davies £40 or £50. That Mr. Owen's single testimony would cast him, and prove him a knave before all the world."

This, I confess, struck me. Here is a clergyman and a Methodist proved a knave before all the world—because *I* will not lose a few pounds to prevent it. Besides, how is this consistent with my own principles: "Let him have thy cloak also?"[23] *I soon came to a resolution*, followed Mr. Stokes to his own house, and made him write a note to Mr. Davies desiring [page 19] his company, that they might compromise the matter. After my return home I received the following, and last, letter from Mr. Davies.

Monday Night

Rev. Sir,

Had your treatment been in any measure Christian, or consistent, I should have had a real pleasure in compromising any affair, even to the injury of myself. But as you have shown no symptoms of sympathy for me in all my disappointments (though you was the great author of them) and have for want of common civility disappointed the church I was to officiate in for two Sundays past and brought me down to Bristol, I ought to expect a disbursement of all these consequences. Yet, sir, as I desire to be under the influence of that grace that will not permit me to return *par pari refert*,[24] if you choose to keep the mare, *it shall be* under one of these conditions: of your giving me £7 now, and I shall have her to ride to Studley and Wales, and return her to you in six weeks, as well as I have her in going out, or return you the money on consequence of accidents; or, to deliver me the mare tomorrow morning by 8:00.

Being but just come to the inn, I could not wait upon Mr. Stokes, neither will time admit it in the morning.

These are my ultimate proposals, therefore I expect the common civility of an answer.

Yours,

E[dward] Davies

---

[23] Matt. 5:40.

[24] "Like for like."

[page 20] My answer to his messenger was "He might come and take the horse tomorrow."

The next morning (Tuesday, April 12), he came to the stable and Joseph delivered my mare into his hands.

Thursday, April 14, Mr. Owen called and informed us that Mr. Davies had rode straight to his house. He thought it was my mare, but said nothing. Mr. Davies immediately began his complaints and produced his papers. Several of his own letters and of mine he read; but not a word did he say or read *concerning the mare*, though he laid many things to my charge. All he blamed my brother for was for promising more than he could perform.

While they were walking in the meadow, Mr. Owen pointed to an excellent horse of his own and said, "I must lose 15 guineas in selling this horse, because *at times he is taken lame*." Mr. Davies betrayed the utmost confusion, which the other was too generous and tender to take notice of.

At my house Mr. Owen informed me of a like bargain of Mr. Davies's in which he had jockeyed a man in the sale of two colts. But to excuse him at that time Mr. Owen laid it upon his wife's covetousness. He now gave me in writing these words:

> "April 10, 1774. Some time before Mr. Davies sold Mr. Charles Wesley his mare, he informed me that 'she was subject to be taken lame.'"

Captain [John] James assured me now that Mr. Davies was famous in Wales for such practices. [page 21] And Mr. Bold[25] (attorney and present mayor of Brecknock) informed me that he had been employed in a cause of Mr. Davies at Brecknock, but finding him totally in the wrong he got to the other counsel and made it up just before the trial should have begun, thereby preventing Mr. Davies—and religion through him—from being exposed in the face of the whole court.

*Source*: holograph; MARC, DDCW 7/111.

---

[25] Hugh Bold (1731–1809) was a lawyer in Brecon, Brecknockshire, and steward of the Wesleyan society in Brecon.

## c. 1784[1]
## SHORTHAND NOTES ON CONVERSATION WITH LORD MANSFIELD[2]

For Lord Mansfield

Ordination is separation.
I have stayed to prevent it.
The Methodists like the Jansenists *populus unius*[3] [a trts[4]].
All arguments used to make us separate.
Stayed out of principle, of Peronnet's judgment.[5]
Brother Sam's verse, wondrous memory.
Bishop pronouncement[?6], "You will never get them into the house again."
Your στοργή[7] with epistle, reasons,[8] and hymns.
Lenity[9] of government.
All rather wished[?] to be q[ueried].
I should have given my reasons and satisfied the bishops either by them or by my submission.
My brother rejoiced the wch[10] Act repealed–Cambray[?11] "I love my f[riends], etc."
What motive could we have but love? I was a deist[?], prsklo.[12]

---

[1] CW speaks of a conversation with Lord Mansfield in 1784 in a letter to Dr. Thomas Bradbury Chandler, Apr. 28, 1785. He quotes Mansfield saying "ordination is separation."

[2] Everything (including the title) but the one Greek word on this page is in shorthand. For ease of reading we have chosen not to begin each new line with double brackets.

[3] "One people."

[4] This shorthand is likely for Latin words as well, but no clear candidates identified.

[5] In 1756 Edward Perronet published *The Mitre*, a ferocious poetic attack on the Church of England, which led to a final break between him and the Wesley brothers.

[6] The shorthand is simply the three consonants "prn"; one might expect a name here; but no suitable name of a bishop has been identified.

[7] Love.

[8] Perhaps referring to the tract *Reasons Against Separation*.

[9] I.e., gentleness or softness; perhaps referring to JW's perceived leniency.

[10] The shorthand is clear; the expansion is not.

[11] François de Salignac de la Mothe-Fénelon, Archbishop of Cambray.

[12] The consonants are clear; the final vowel may be a "u."

No smuggling, no speaking against ministers or magistrates.
I b[eliev]ed Africans.[13]
Fear[?] to survive my country.

*Source*: CW shorthand notes; MARC, DDCW 4/8.[14]

---

[13] Likely referring to Little Ephraim Robin John and Ancona Robin Robin John, two members of an African family in Old Calabar involved in the slave trade who were themselves sold into slavery. Lord Mansfield was instrumental in their liberation in Bristol in the early 1770s, and CW helped care for them, calling them his "African children." He eventually helped arrange their return to Old Calabar, only to find out later that they resumed their role in facilitating slave trade. Cf. S T Kimbrough, Jr., "Charles Wesley and Slavery," *PCWS* 13 (2009): 35–52.

[14] These notes appear on the inside front cover of a manuscript notebook. On the top left corner of this page CW has written in longhand:
   Mem.
   Dec. 18, 1736 began my 27th year
      1776 began my 67th
      1782 began my 73
   At the bottom of this page, written upside down, is an early draft in shorthand of stanzas 4–6 of a hymn "On the Death of Mrs. Gwynne" noted in MS Funeral Hymns, 108.

## March 29, 1787[1]
## Shorthand Notes on Sarah (Perrin) Jones's Death[2]

While I was meeting the society on Sunday night she dropped down in a convulsive fit. After she came to herself she told me she found herself perfectly composed and happy; and if she had died in it, it would not have been a sudden death. Her sicknesses were all times of visitation; such resignation, comfort, happiness the Lord gave her therein!

Desirous to see her husband once more, but [igv[3]] it quite up.

One night when she saw she should die, she entered into a true examination of herself and state. Saw her whole life was a life of backslidings and had nothing to trust to but Christ alone.

Said the Lord hath laid me upon this bed to bless my friends; every friend and acquaintance has been brought to me by turns, and laid upon my heart, that I might offer them up, and bless them.

Her great faith for the work.

To me she said, "Faint not."

"I am turning my face to the wall like Hezekiah,[4] but blessed be God I do not desire any longer space."

Her union[?] with Mr. Whitefield.

His enlargement of heart.

The freeness of divine love.

Her message to friend Neal[?[5]].

To Mr. Bullard[?].

That night found no past experience would suffice, no faithfulness of man, but want out of myself to Christ; nothing of Christ's, no not any grace or any comfort would do, but mere naked whole Christ himself.

*Endorsement*: "Sarah Jones' Last."
*Source*: CW shorthand account; MARC, DDPr 2/30.

---

[1] Sarah (Perrin) Jones's husband, John Jones, died in Harwich (where he had been vicar) on Sept. 10. 1785. The only record of Sarah's death is on the monument for her husband in the parish church in Harwich, which indicates she died on March 29, 1787. She apparently moved back to London after her husband's death, to live near long-time Methodist friends. CW was in London through March 1787 and apparently recorded these notes.

[2] Everything except the endorsement in this document is in shorthand. For ease of reading we have chosen not to begin each new line with double brackets.

[3] The order of these shorthand letters is clear; the meaning is not.

[4] See 2 Kings 20:2.

[5] The shorthand might be instead "Dsl."

# CHARLES WESLEY'S BIOGRAPHICAL ACCOUNTS OF HIS MUSICAL SONS

For all of his poetic gifts, Charles Wesley was not particularly gifted with musical talent, either instrumental or vocal. The one whose melodic voice and performance on the harpsichord filled the Wesley home was his wife, Sarah (Gwynne) Wesley. At least, this was the case through the first decade of their marriage, until the first of two sons (who survived infancy) began to display extraordinary talent in music.

Charles Wesley's manuscript records of his sons Charles Jr. (1757–1834) and Samuel (1766–1837) and their musical gifts remain the main source of biographical information about their early years. The most polished of these records are accounts of each son that Wesley prepared and gave to Daines Barrington,[1] a member of the Royal Society, in hopes that he would publish them in the *Philosophical Transactions*.[2] Barrington chose to publish the material instead in a collection of his essays in 1781, and to focus most of his attention on Samuel.[3] Indeed, Barrington included in his published version only a third of the material that Wesley had sent him concerning Charles Jr. Thomas Jackson later published a more complete version of the account of Charles Jr.,[4] but he too omits some of the material that Wesley sent to Barrington (since it appears only in the shorthand account). Thus, this is the first setting in which all of Charles Wesley's surviving biographical records of his sons appear in their entirety.

---

[1] Daines Barrington (1727–1800) was an English lawyer, antiquary and naturalist; who served as a judge of Great Sessions for north Wales from 1757.

[2] CW's shorthand copy of his account of CW Jr. is headed "[[Copy to Judge Barrington, given him June 22, 1776]]." Where CW believed these accounts would appear is evident when he copies Barrington's version at the end of CW, MS Journal (DDCW 10/2) titled "Printed in the *Philosophical Transactions* of the year 1781." This heading is duplicated in Jackson, *CW Journal*, 2:151. In fact, the essay does not appear in this issue of the *Philosophical Transactions*.

[3] See Daines Barrington, *Miscellanies* (London: J. Nichols, 1781), 289–310.

[4] Jackson, *CW Journal*, 2:140–44.

In addition to the biographical records included below, there are other items related to the Wesley sons' early musical life that survive at the Methodist Archive and Research Centre and beyond. Most of these relate to a series of combined concert performances. This material has been collected and helpfully analysed in a recent article.[5] There have also been recent instructive pieces placing the Wesley sons in their musical context.[6]

---

[5] Alyson McLamore, "'By the Will and Order of Providence:' The Wesley Family Concerts, 1779–87," *Royal Musical Association Research Chronicle* 37 (2004), 71–220.

[6] See particularly Carlton R. Young, *Sacred Harmony: The Musical Wesley Family* (Dallas, TX: Bridwell Library, 2007), 28–32; Jonathan Barry, "Charles Wesley's Family and the Musical Life of Bristol," in *Music and the Wesleys*, edited by N. Temperley & S. Banfield (Urbana, IL: University of Illinois Press, 2010), 141–53; and Philip Olleson, "Father and Sons: Charles, Samuel, and Charles the Younger," in *Music and the Wesleys*, 175–82. See as well Olleson's masterful study *Samuel Wesley: The Man and His Music* (Woodbridge: Boydell Press, 2003).

# 1769–1772
## ACCOUNT OF JOSEPH KELWAY AND CHARLES WESLEY JR.[1]

Extracted out of my Journal

**Monday, August 14, 1769.** At 1:00 this day, Mr. Bromfeild[2] met us at Mr. Kelway's house,[3] having promised my son[4] the hearing of him. He highly entertained us with one of Handel's and one of his own lessons. Then he heard Charles play. Some of the words wherein he expressed his astonishment were, "I never saw one carry his hand so well. It is quite a picture! It is a gift from God. How would Handel[5] have shook his sides, if he could have heard him!"

He confirmed the advice Mr. Granville[6] had given him,[7] "Let him have no great master. B[ach[8]] or A[be]l[9] would ruin him."

"Come to me," he said,[10] "as often as you will, whenever you are in town; and I will assist you all I can." He stroked, embraced, praised him immoderately, and appointed him to come again on Monday.

---

[1] The original set of extracts (DDWes 7/105) that CW drew from this (no longer extant) portion of his manuscript journal was made in part at Kelway's request, as a record of his prized student (see entry for July 3, 1771). But CW extended the account as a record of a later dispute about whether Kelway originally intended to teach CW Jr. for no charge. CW appended a slightly refined copy of the positive portion of the account to his MS Journal (DDCW 10/2). Later he produced a more abridged and polished version of this positive portion that survives in two settings (DDCW 8/2, pp. 17–35; and DDCW 8/24, pp. 7–14).

[2] William Bromfeild (1712–92), a surgeon, was the founder of Lock Hospital in London, where Martin Madan (an organist and friend of CW) was chaplain. Madan likely introduced CW to Bromfeild. Like many others, CW consistently misspells the last name as "Bromfield."

[3] Joseph Kelway (d. 1782) was a prominent organist and harpsichord player in London in the mid-eighteenth century (his house was in King's Row, Upper Grosvenor Street). Kelway was organist at St. Martin's-in-the-Fields, where Handel and others often came to hear him play. In addition to Charles Wesley Jr., Kelway taught such prominent persons as Mary (Granville) Pendarves (later Mrs. Delany), and Queen Charlotte. He was known for his beautiful rendering of Scarlatti's difficult sonatas, and described by Charles Burney as the "head of the Scarlatti sect." Unfortunately for Kelway, Johann Christian Bach and his associate Carl Friedrich Abel introduced a new style, the pianoforte, in the 1760s. Kelway's musical sect did not survive the change in public taste.

[4] Charles Wesley Jr. (1757–1834) was born in Bristol on Dec. 11, 1757, as the third child (and second son) of Charles and Sarah (Gwynne) Wesley. He was the first child to survive to adulthood, and proved to be a gifted musician, particularly with the organ.

[5] George Frederic Handel (1685–1759).

[6] Bernard Granville (c. 1699–1775), brother of Mary (Granville) Pendarves, and close friend of Handel, who frequently stayed at Granville's estate of Calwich Abbey.

[7] DDCW 10/2 adds "at Bath."

[8] Johann Christian Bach (1735–82).

[9] Carl Friedrich Abel (1723–87).

[10] The other versions all add that Kelway made this offer "at parting."

439

**Monday, August 21.** Mr. Kelway gave him his first lesson (the first of Handel's[11]), and much commendation. "You have a better hand," said he, "than any of the masters.[12] B[ach] or A[bel] would ruin you in one month."

**Thursday, August 24.** Mr. Kelway was quite pleased with him; warned him against Handel's enemies and modern musicians; said to me, "If any great master taught him one year, it would cost me two to unteach him that man's lessons." He made him a present of his *Sonatas*,[13] with Handel's *Overtures*,[14] and Pergolesi's *Stabat Mater*.[15]

**Thursday, September 14.** Kelway to Charles, "You will be an honor to me. Handel's hands did not lie on the instrument[16] better than yours." [[His word was, "not so well."]]

**Monday, September 18.** Kelway to Charles, "Was you my own son, I could not love you better. Go on, and mind none of the musicians but Handel. You should not hear others. Come to me, and I will instruct you the best I can. You have a divine gift."

To me he said, "There are not two masters in town can play these two adagios. One cannot hear him play four bars without knowing him to be a genius. He has the very spirit of Scarlatti."[17]

**Thursday, September 21.** Cried out while Charles was playing, "It is here, in his heart, or he could not play thus." Then starting up, "I will maintain it before all the world that there is not a master in London can play this sonata as he does.

"The King would eat up this boy. I must carry him some morning to St. James's.[18] I am greatly obliged to Mr. Bromfeild for bringing him to me. He need not drudge[19] eight hours a day. Let him only go on, and he will excel[20] them all. There is no trouble in teaching him; it is pure pleasure."

To him, "My dear boy, let not the world debauch you. Some decry music for being old; they might as well object to an antique painting or statue. But B[ach], and A[bel], and G– have cut the throat of music. True music is lost!"

---

[11] I.e., Handel's first volume of *Suites de pièces pour le clavecin* (1720; HWV 462–33).

[12] DDCW 10/2 adds here: "They would hurt instead of helping you."

[13] Kelway's only major publication was *Six Sonatas for the Harpsichord* (1764).

[14] George Frederic Handel, *Six[ty] Overtures fitted to the Harpsicord or Spinnet* (London: Printed for J. Walsh, 1732–49).

[15] Giovanni Battista Pergolesi, *Stabat Mater* (1736).

[16] DDCW 10/2 specifies: "harpsichord."

[17] Domenico Scarlatti (1685–1757).

[18] St. James's Palace, the royal residence in Westminster, Middlesex.

[19] In place of "not drudge" DDCW 10/2 has: "not (as Mr. K[eebl]e told him) study." This is a reference to John Keeble (1711–1786).

[20] DDCW 10/2 reads: "on as he has begun, and he will soon excel."

**Monday, September 25.** "Handel once asked me, 'Mr. Kelway, why don't you keep company with other musicians?' I answered, 'Nay, Sir, why don't you?' He replied, 'Because I don't care to dirty myself.'"

Mr. Kelway to me, "You must take great delight in this boy. I am sure he is of a sweet disposition. His very soul is harmony." "All I can say of him, is," [said I,[21]] "that you have him uncorrupted." "Uncorrupted?" answered he; "he is purity itself. He is a miracle!" To him, "You will not be vain, my dear; it is a divine gift, and I hope you will make a proper use of it."

While he went on playing, Mr. Kelway said, "He teaches me my own music." To him, "My dear boy, *I will do for you all in my power; first, for Mr. Bromfeild's sake; then for your sake and my own. I am better pleased to teach you for nothing, than if I had ever so much money with you.*[22]

"You are to uphold music. Not one of my pupils could have learned that in a year, which you have learned in ten lessons."

A gentleman (Mr. Brown) coming in, and hearing him, cried, "Why, the boy feels every note!" He then shook him by the hand, with, "Go on, young gentleman; and you will be one of the first masters."

**Thursday, September 28.** Mr. Worgan[23] came to meet us at a friend's in the city (Mr. Birt's). After hearing Charles play, he generously said, "I will take him from this time under my own auspices, and freely teach him all I know myself." I should have thankfully accepted of his offer, had not Mr. Kelway been beforehand with him.

**Monday, October 2.** I mentioned this to Mr. Kelway, and asked his leave to tell Mr. Worgan the reason of my not closing with so advantageous an offer; namely, Mr. Kelway's having made it first. He gave me full permission to tell him, or whomsoever I pleased, *that he taught my son gratis.* With warm affection he again warned my son against the moderns.

**Thursday, October 12.** [Some of Mr. Kelway's words were,[24]] "Never have I met one who played with such spirit! Charming boy! I defy any master in London to play like him." For his greater encouragement, he promised to get a fine old harpsichord of Mahew's fitted up for him; [[and then to give him his choice of that or of his own, a Couchet;[25] the clearest and sweetest instrument I ever heard.]]

---

[21] "Said I" added in DDCW 10/2.

[22] CW's emphasis on this passage and that of Oct. 2 is related to Kelway's later complaint about not being paid.

[23] John Worgan (1724–90), a prominent London organist, appointed to play at Vauxhall Gardens in 1751.

[24] This preface added in DDCW 8/2, DDCW 10/2, and DDCW 8/24.

[25] The Couchet family of Antwerp comprised several generations of famous harpsichord builders. Kelway's harpsichord was made by Petrus Joannes Couchet (according to his will, which bequeathed it to a grandniece).

**Monday, October 23.** "Dear boy! He treats me with my own music. I wish Handel and Geminiani[26] were now alive. They would be in raptures with him."

**Thursday, October 26.** "He will bring my music into vogue. It cannot be played better."

**Monday, November 6.** "'Tis delightful! 'Tis admirable! 'Tis perfect singing! Dear jewel! Charming boy! I never heard any one play with such feeling." [[Then]] he talked of leaving him his successor—or words to that purport.

**Tuesday, November 21.** "Here sit I for my amusement. He makes me delight in my own music."

**Tuesday, November 28.** "Handel used to say, 'These ignorant fellows, after my death, will murder my music.' Geminiani made me swear to rescue his from them."

"'Tis the greatest pleasure to instruct this boy. He will keep up my music, when I am gone. I shall leave my stamp upon him. I shall make him the depositary of my skill."

**Tuesday, December 5.** "The King has asked after him a second time. I told His Majesty he had learned more in four months than any other could in four years. [[He asked me if he intended to make music his profession. I answered, 'No'.]] That he did not propose to make music *his profession*; that he did not want anything, etc."

To me [Mr. Kelway[27]] said, "He will keep alive my music. He will be *hated by all the masters*.[28] I loved music when young, but not so well as he does. One would think he had been the composer of this. He gives the colouring; the nice touches and finishing-strokes are his own. I love him better and better. He has it from God. He is an heaven-born child."

**Tuesday, December 12.** "This boy consoles me. He raises my spirits whenever I hear him. He has more taste and feeling than all our band."

**Friday, December 29.** "He plays this (Kelway's 6th Sonata) beyond all that I could have hoped." To my sister[29] he observed,[30] "It is the gift of God. No man in London can play like him. What colouring! What lights and shades! I could *cry* to hear him."

---

[26] Francesco Geminiani (1687–1762).

[27] DDWes 7/105 says simply "he"; the other versions give the name.

[28] DDCW 8/24 rewrites the first two lines: "To me Mr. K[elway] said (not prophetically, I hope), 'He will be hated by all the masters.'"

[29] Likely CW's sister-in-law Rebecca Gwynne, as specified on a later visit of Dec. 24, 1771 below. Other possibilities include Martha (Wesley) Hall or Emily (Wesley) Harper.

[30] DDCW 10/2: adds "(as before to others)."

**Tuesday, January 2, 1770.** "Handel told me, 'The musicians are all *impostors.*' Geminiani said he studied Corelli[31] every day of his life; and that one particular song in Otho[32] he could teach from morning till night."

**Friday, January 5.** "He is an old man at the harpsichord; he is not a boy." To Mr. Madan[33] he said, "He is the greatest genius in music I ever met with."

**Friday, January 12.** Charles was so transported in playing, that he told me afterwards, he did not know where he was, or that there was any person in the room but himself.

**Tuesday, January 16.** "Sir," [said Mr. Kelway to me,[34]] "you have got a Scarlatti in your house, as well as the King of Spain. Never have I heard a boy that plays with such spirit and feeling. Here sit I to hear myself. I never took such pleasure in my own music. His play is a cordial to me. He will be *the restorer* of music.

"Miss B– asked me, 'What shall I give him for playing to me?' I answered her, 'Yourself.' How would Handel and Geminiani have embraced him! I love him as well as you can do."

**Wednesday, February 7.** " He is Scarlatti all over. Play thus, my dear boy, and *revenge my quarrel.* He plays as well as me already."

**Wednesday, February 21.** Mr. Kelway coming to my house to teach Miss Hill and Charles. I paid him 45 guineas for an harpsichord of Mahew's. Miss B–, he told us, was to have given 50 [guineas] for it; but he bated 5 to Charles.

**Wednesday, March 7.** In walking with Mr. Kelway from my house, I asked him whether on "our return to Bristol I should not have Mr. Broderip[35] to teach my son?" His answer was, "No; he can learn nothing from Broderip, though Broderip may from him. If any man would learn to play well, let him hear that boy. Miss Hill does not know what an advantage she has in hearing him. When I sit by and listen, I can find no fault with him."

**[Saturday], April 7, 1770.** Took our leave of Mr. Kelway, who has now bestowed upon Charles 65 lessons.

---

[31] Arcangelo Corelli (1653–1713).

[32] This is likely the selection "Affanni del pensier" in the opera "Ottone: re di Germania" (English: "Otho: King of Germany"), by Handel.

[33] Rev. Martin Madan (1726–90) prepared for a career in law. He was goaded into listening to JW preach, as a means of improving his oratory style. But Madan was so moved by the sermon that he joined the Methodist cause. With the aid of the Countess of Huntingdon he secured ordination in 1757. An amateur organist, Madan served as chaplain and musician at the Lock Hospital, founded by William Bromfeild.

[34] This clarifying phrase added in DDCW 8/2, DDCW 10/2, and DDCW 8/24.

[35] Edmund Broderip (1727–79) was the organist at St. James's, the home parish of CW's family while in Bristol. CW uses only the first initial of his last name in all these texts. In other settings he consistently spells the last name "Broadrip."

**Thursday, February 7, 1771.** The day after my return to London, I waited upon Mr. Kelway, who received me with great kindness, and appointed Charles to come on Saturday.

**Saturday, February 9.** Charles played over his Sonatas. His master[36] was much pleased to find that in ten months absence he had forgot nothing.

**Friday, March 15.** While Charles was playing, his master surprised me by saying, "He plays my lessons better than I can."

**Tuesday, April 2.** "Now he never can be spoiled by *the fashionable music*.

"If they never should sell, yet I am glad I published my Sonatas for his sake. There is no man can play them like him."

**Friday, April 5.** Walking about, as delighted with his pupil, at last he stopped, made him a low bow, [and said] "Sir, you do me great honour. It puts me into a good humour to hear you."

**Friday, April 12.** "There it no music in London like this boy's play. There is not a man in Italy can play so well. It is not I, Charles, but *God who has given it to you*. And I heartily thank you for this lesson; it composes and makes me happy."

**Tuesday, April 16.** He was warm in his praise, adding a caution, "Charles, while you live, beware of Italians. They will poison you if they can, as they poisoned Pergolesi and Vinci."[37]

**Friday, May 24.** I paid Mr. Kelway 6 guineas for twelve of his new Sonatas,[38] which Charles impatiently expects.

**Tuesday, May 28.** Charles was happy in making his master so. But Mr. Kelway was very angry at G– for his cool approbation of his scholar. "G– does not so much as know what is in this boy: neither can any master in London know it."

**Wednesday, July 3.** Mr. Kelway gave him his 104th lesson, which makes a year complete. "No other," he assured me, "could have learned so much in many years. People," he said, "would not believe it, unless he had a particular account of the lessons." This, therefore, at his desire, I gave him extracted out of my journal.

Glorying in his scholar, he said, "They say I cannot communicate my skill; but I dare maintain, there is not such a player as this boy in England, no nor yet in France, or Spain, or Italy." He could carry it no farther, without repeating his former words to Mr. Bromfeild, "that there was not such another boy upon earth. *Abi, patrissas!*—more than even the father himself."[39]

---

[36] Orig.,"He"; changed to "His master" in DDCW 8/2, DDCW 10/2, and DDCW 8/24.

[37] Giovanni Battista Pergolesi (1710–36) and Leonardo Vinci (1690–1730); both were assumed by many musicians to have been poisoned.

[38] As DDCW 10/2 specifies, there was to be a "second set of" published sonatas. But these were never published.

[39] The last sentence appears only in DDCW 8/2, DDCW 10/2, and DDCW 8/24.

**Wednesday, July 10.** "It would be worth the masters' while to pay this boy for playing to them. If Manzuoli[40] was here, he would eat him up."

**Wednesday, August 7.** Mr. Kelway began teaching him Geminiani's lessons for the harpsichord,[41] having, he thinks, made him perfect in Scarlatti's music.

**Wednesday, August 28.** "Geminiani, if now alive, would carry this boy with him everywhere. He plays quite as well as I."

**Wednesday, September 11.** I carried Mr. Russell,[42] the painter, to Mr. Kelway's. He told me afterwards, that he knew the finest passages by the change of Charles's colour.[43] Mr. Kelway, being asked to play, said in jest, "How shall I play after my scholar." But he did play, and most inimitably.

**Saturday, September 28.** Again [he said[44]], "If Handel and Geminiani were alive, they would be mad at hearing this boy."

**[Wednesday],**[45] **October 9.** Pointing to Geminiani's picture, he said, "O what would that man have said, if he could have heard Charles! No man in London can play this prelude [[like him; no, not I myself]]."

**Wednesday, October 23.** "No one can play this lesson like him; no, not I myself." He added, as in a rapture, "This is too much to bear!"[46]

---

[40] Giovanni Manzuoli (c. 1720–82), an Italian opera singer, had performed in London's King's Theatre 1764–65, dramatically raising the quality of opera in London. CW spells "Mansoli."

[41] Francesco Geminiani, *The Art of Accompaniment; or, A new and well digested method to learn to perform the thorough bass on the harpsichord with propriety and elegance* (London: Printed for the author by John Johnson, 1753).

[42] John Russell [Jr.] (1745–1806), artist and son of the mayor of Guildford.

[43] Orig., "He marked his colour change at the finest passages of the music." The alternative sentence given in the text was written in shorthand above the line in DDWes 7/105 and adopted in the other three versions.

[44] This clarifying addition added in DDCW 10/2.

[45] Orig., "Saturday"; an error.

[46] The extract in DDCW 10/2 ends at this point. DDCW 8/2 and DDCW 8/24 add two sentences to this entry and then two paragraphs in closing; the text of 8/2 is given, with the most significant variants in 8/24 noted in [brackets].

… I have seen the tears run down his cheeks while Charles was playing one of Handel's lessons. "If I was without the door and did not know he was dead, I should swear it was Handel himself played."

To this plain narrative I shall only add that, as I am no judge of music myself, I cannot answer for the justness of Mr. Kelway's sentiments concerning the art and its professors. Much less do I subscribe to his high opinion of his pupil. Mr. Kelway's sincerity I do not doubt. His judgment also is unquestionable. But he might be under a secret bias. He had lately published his sonatas. They were ill received and even decried by the masters in general. Charles very highly esteemed them, as next to Handel and Geminiani. This naturally prejudiced Mr. Kelway in his favor, and accounts in some measure for his violent encomiums. I do not yet perceive that Charles is hurt either by Mr. Kelway's praises or prejudices.

Charles has now been some years under Dr. [William] Boyce's tuition, learning composition, and hopes to continue learning as long as the Dr. lives. At the same time he retains

**Saturday, December 21.** We called on Mr. Kelway. He was gone out and left no word (as he used to do) when we should come again. I had lately observed a great change in his behaviour towards us. Fretful and impatient at the least trifle, he plainly appeared unhappy in hearing Charles, sometimes flying out into extravagant passion at his "incredible stupidity," as he called it, and not always refraining from oaths and curses. Once he wished him at the devil[47] and sent him home in tears. I was amazed and could hardly bear it myself.

When I brought up my son in February, I told Mr. Kelway my intention of staying four months only. Then my wife came up and induced me to stay longer for the benefit of Charles. I acquainted his master with this, and he seemed quite satisfied. Yet still at times I was uneasy, lest he should think we stayed too long.

**Tuesday, December 24.** I found him at home in a very ill humour, of which I endeavoured to find out the cause. I did not yet suspect his repenting of his past generosity; yet conjectured he would be better pleased if paid for the time to come.

I had often wished to begin with him on a new footing, and oftener than twice or thrice proposed to pay him for the future. But he would never hear of it, or admit even of my thanks. Once when I introduced the subject, he stopped me with these words, "Never talk of paying me. The pleasure of teaching him is more to me than any money you could give me." My sister, Miss Gwynne,[48] was by and remembers the words.

I asked him when he pleased Charles should wait upon him again? He was not ready at an answer. Then apologizing for our long continuance in town, I asked him if he could blame Charles for making the most of his instructions? "No; by no means." Then I asked, "If he would teach him henceforward at his own price?" This he would not consent to "because he had received nothing hitherto." "But Sir," said I, "as you do not refuse scholars, why should you refuse him? Or what might be your meaning in lately telling my sister you would not have taught him what you have done for £500?"

I told him it was my resolution (if it should ever be in my power) to make his family amends for his generosity to my son. He answered short,

---

the most grateful veneration for his old master Kelway, and played to him while he was able to hear him, every week. He [neither speaks nor thinks disrespectfully of others, yet (added in 8/24)] believes he himself has had the two greatest masters in Christendom. Dr. Boyce and he seem equally satisfied. I hope he has caught a little of his master's temper as well as his skill. A more modest man than Dr. Boyce I have never known. I never heard him speak a vain or ill-natured word, either to exalt himself or to depreciate another. [the last four sentences are not present in 8/24]
    Chesterfield Street
    Marybone, 1777

[47] I.e., "to curse and swear, to send to the devil."

[48] Rebecca Gwynne.

"What right has my family to the reward of my labours?" and went on with a long relation of Handel's calling him fool for not insisting on 6 instead of 3 guineas earnest from Lady Chesterfield; and bidding him make her pay a guinea for every adagio he copied for her. I did not comprehend his meaning, unless it was *to get all he could out of everybody.*

My last request to him was that he would teach Charles according to his promise, the Third Lesson of Handel and one concerto of Corelli. "You know," said he, "the number of lessons he *has had.* Bring your son to me tomorrow fortnight."

Accordingly on **Wednesday, January 8, [1772]**, we waited upon him. Charles played over the first set of Geminiani's lessons. Mr. Kelway could not or would not find the least fault. Then he took me into the next room and asked, "Did Mr. [Bernard] Granville tell you I would teach your son gratis?" "No sir, what he told me was that no master in London but *you could* teach my son Handel's lessons, and you would *not.*" My last words he scarcely heard, saying himself at the same time, "You know how many lessons your son has had."

He hastily returned to the parlour, I following and asked, "Sir, would you have Charles come again?" He answered nothing. I went on, "Are you willing to teach him if I pay you from this time your own price?" He answered angrily, "You have paid me *nothing yet.* My education cost a great deal. Lord Essex paid several hundreds of pounds for it. This house cannot be maintained for nothing," etc. It was in vain to offer a reply. At last I understood his mind and silently withdrew with my son.

He was quite glad at his dismission, although Mr. Kelway had often said he could never learn from any master but himself. [[Even told him, "You can never learn from master but me."]]

**Monday, January 13.** Waited on Mr. [William] Bromfeild and told him all that had passed. He bade me refer Mr. Kelway to him.

**[Tuesday], January 21.** I wrote to him as follows, "Good Sir, I have taken the liberty to send you a short extract of my journal. It is undeniably plain that Mr. Kelway offered and intended to teach my son gratis; first, out of respect to you; then, for the pleasure of teaching him. Accordingly, he has instructed him for many months and never made the least mention of pay till now.

"What I wish to know through your kind assistance is whether Mr. Kelway is willing to teach my son *from this time* at his usual price, or on any terms whatsoever.

"As you are *the* proper and *the only* proper person I can apply to on this occasion, you will excuse my so earnestly entreating you to call, as soon as you can conveniently, on Mr. Kelway and allow me to wait upon you on Saturday morning to know the effect of your friendly interposition in behalf of," etc.

**Saturday, January 25.** Called on Mr. Bromfeild who told me he had been at Mr. Kelway's but missed of him; that then Mr. Kelway called on *him*. That Mr. Bromfeild began by asking, "What his pupil had done to displease him?" Mr. Kelway answered, "He will play and hear *other music*." Mr. Bromfeild then mentioned his teaching Charles gratis; this he allowed adding, "It was purely, Sir, out of respect to you. But there was no reason why I should always teach him on those terms. It cost my father and Lord Essex a great deal for my teaching." Mr. Bromfeild said, "Mr. Wesley is not a *beneficed* clergyman, yet of such a temper that he can never rest till he has made you some amends, not as a legal debt but as an *acknowledgment* of your kindness. What he takes ill is your *extorting* money from him after your *offer* to teach his son for *nothing*. If he had not trusted to that, he would have accepted Mr. [John] Worgan's offer to instruct his son gratis. 'Why let Mr. Worgan have him, but I know no man can teach him so well as I.'" "But on what terms," Mr. Bromfeild asked? "He is willing to pay from this time." Mr. Kelway offered to teach him still for nothing if Mr. Bromfeild desired it, purely to oblige him.

"That," said I, "I can never agree to, or to Mr. Kelway's teaching him at all, before we have struck off the old score." Mr. Bromfeild agreed that whatever I gave him by way of acknowledgment should go through *his hands*; and he would get me a full discharge, and also settle with Kelway the *terms* of his future instructions.

**Tuesday, February 4.** Mr. Bromfeild called and informed me he had been with Mr. Kelway and persuaded him "to put an end to a good man's distress," telling him that he himself, as well as Mr. Wesley had always understood that Mr. Kelway taught Charles for nothing. He answered that I was "50 guineas in his debt. Yet for your sake, Sir, I make his son a present of my past instructions. I know the poor boy will be miserable unless he learns of me; therefore, I will henceforward *give* him 3 lessons for a guinea. Let him come to me once or twice a week as he chooses."

Mr. Bromfeild said, "Mr. Wesley will then put a piece of plate[49] upon your table as a small expression of his gratitude." "There is no need of that," answered Mr. Kelway. "I freely give him all those lessons, to oblige you."

**Monday, February 10.** I called on Mr. Bromfeild and desired him to pay Mr. Kelway that £20 note (instead of plate) and get a receipt in full; for I could otherwise have no security that Mr. Kelway would not some time or other come upon me or my son for the whole 50 guineas.

**Thursday, February 27.** Waited again on Mr. Bromfeild. He informed me that he has paid Mr. Kelway, who *seemed* not to expect so much; told Mr. Bromfeild he hoped he had not *pressed* me to it, for he should be very *sorry* to distress me. As he gave no receipt, I was not quite satisfied, as

---

[49] I.e., a coin.

lying still at his mercy. Mr. Bromfeild kindly wrote him a letter desiring an acknowledgment, and the next day, **Friday, February 28**, brought me the following:

February 24, 1772

Received of Mr. Wesley by the hands of Mr. Bromfeild £20 for my instructions on the harpsichord to Master Charles Wesley and in full of all demands.

Joseph Kelway[50]

[[Fragments[51]

This is something, Look! He plays like a Christian not like a beast.
The harpsichord wire play[?[52]] is quite another instrument.
To my sister saying "it is a great addition to my nephew, your instruction, and what could not be procured[?] by any money."
He answered "Madam I would not have taken £500 tuition to teach[?[53]] him what I have.
Were I an uneducated man, I should desire nothing more than this boy for raising a brother.]]

*Source*: holograph; MARC, DDWes 7/105. Collated with abridged holograph versions: MARC, DDCW 8/2; MARC, DDCW 10/2; and MARC, DDCW 8/24.

---

[50] The actual receipt is also bound with the manuscript, and has CW's ironic annotation: "Febr. 24. 1772 / Mr Kelway's rect. for instructing Charles *gratis*! / £20."

[51] This set of shorthand notes appears on p. 16, the verso of the last page of longhand.

[52] Perhaps a reference to a pianoforte.

[53] The shorthand has eluded confident expansion, but this appears to be the idea.

## June 1776
## Biographical Account of Charles Wesley Jr.'s Childhood[1]

Charles was born[2] December 11, 1757. He was two years and three-quarters old when I first observed his strong inclination to music. He then surprised me by playing a tune[3] readily, and in just time. Soon after, he played several; whatever his mother sung, or whatever he heard in the streets.

From his birth, she used to quiet and amuse him with the harpsichord. But he would never suffer her to play with one hand only, taking the other and putting it on the keys, before he could speak. When he played himself, she used to tie him up by his backstring to the chair, for fear of his falling. Whatever tune it was, he always put a true bass to it. From the beginning, he played without study or hesitation; and, as the learned declared,[4] perfectly well.

Mr. [Edmund] Broderip[5] heard him in petticoats, and foretold he would one day make a great player.

Whenever he was called to play to a stranger, he would ask, in a word of his own, "Is he a musicker?" and if answered, "Yes," he played with all readiness.[6]

He always played *con spirito*.[7] There was something in his manner above a child, which struck the hearers, whether learned or unlearned.

---

[1] CW's account of the musical ability and training of Charles Jr. survives in four versions:
1) The earliest surviving version, and most complete through 1773, is now bound at the back of CW, MS Journal (DDCW 10/2).
2) In June 1776 CW prepared a polished version, with a few elisions and additional notes covering 1774–76, that he gave to Daines Barrington. Barrington published the first nine paragraphs of this version in *Miscellanies* (1781), 289–90. CW's shorthand copy of the version sent to Barrington survives in DDCW 7/105.
3) DDCW 8/2 is a manuscript pamphlet that contains a longhand copy reflecting the changes DDCW 7/105 made in DDCW 10/2, adding a few additional stylistic changes. However, it does not include the material for 1774–76 added in DDCW 7/105.
4) DDCW 8/24, another manuscript pamphlet, is in turn dependent upon DDCW 8/2 and characterized by more extensive rewriting and abridging of the text.
We transcribe here DDCW 10/2, adding the additional material in DDCW 7/105, and noting the most significant revisions or deletions of DDCW 10/2 in the other versions.

[2] DDCW 8/2 and DDCW 8/24 add: "at Bristol."

[3] DDCW 8/2 and DDCW 8/24 add: "upon the harpsichord."

[4] DDCW 7/105 and later versions substitute "masters told me" for "learned declared."

[5] DDCW 8/2 and DDCW 8/24 add: "first organist at Bristol." CW consistently spells in longhand versions as "Broadrip."

[6] DDCW 7/105 and later versions substitute "the greatest readiness" for "all readiness."

[7] "In a spirited manner."

At four years old, I carried him with me to London. Mr. Beard[8] was the first that confirmed Mr. Broaderip's judgment of him, and offered to get him admitted among the King's singing boys[9]; but I had then no thoughts of bringing him up a musician.

A gentleman carried him next to Mr. Stanley,[10] who expressed his pleasure and surprise at hearing him, and declared he had never met one of his age with so great a propensity to music. The gentleman told us he never before believed what [George Frederic] Handel used to tell him of himself, and his own love of music in his childhood.

Mr. [Martin] Madan presented my son to Mr. [John] Worgan, who was extremely kind to him and, as I then thought, partial. He told us he would prove an eminent master, if he was not taken off by other studies. He [i.e., Worgan] frequently entertained him on the harpsichord. Charles was greatly taken with his bold, full manner of playing, and seemed even then to catch a spark of his fire.

At our return to Bristol, we left him to ramble on till he was near six [years old]. Then we gave him Mr. Rooke[11] for a master; a man of no name, but very good-natured, who let him run on *ad libitum*,[12] while he sat by, more to observe than to control him.

Mr. Rogers,[13] the oldest organist in Bristol, was his first and very great friend.[14] He often set him upon his knee and made him play to him, declaring he was more delighted to hear him than any of his scholars, or himself.[15]

I always saw the importance (if he was to be a musician) of placing him under the best master that could be got, and also one who was an admirer of Handel, as my son preferred him to all the world. But I saw no likelihood of my being ever able to procure him the first master, or of purchasing the most excellent music, and other necessary means of acquiring so costly an art.

---

[8] John Beard (c. 1717–91), a tenor, was proprietor of Covent Garden Theatre in London.

[9] DDCW 7/105 and later versions specify that Beard offered to approach Dr. William Boyce about this entry into the King's boys' choir.

[10] John Stanley (1712–86), an organist and composer.

[11] Edward Rooke (d. 1773) was an organist in Bristol at All Saints from 1759–69, and at the cathedral from 1769 to his death.

[12] "At one's pleasure"; in music, at the discretion of the performer.

[13] Nelme Rogers (1697–1776) received his first post as organist at Bristol, All Saints, in 1715, and was organist at St. Mary Redcliffe 1727–72.

[14] DDCW 7/105 and DDCW 8/2 substitute "was one of his first friends" for "was his first and very great friend."

[15] DDCW 8/24 omits this paragraph. Barrington's published account ends here.

I think it was at our next journey to London that Lady Gertrude Hotham[16] heard him with much satisfaction and made him a present of all her music. Mrs. Rich[17] had before given him Handel's songs;[18] and Mr. Beard, Scarlatti's lessons and Purcell's.[19] Sir Charles Hotham[20] was particularly fond of him; promised him an organ, and that he should never want any means or encouragement in the pursuit of his art. But he went abroad soon after, and was thence translated to the heavenly country.

With him, Charles lost all hope and prospect of a benefactor.[21] Nevertheless, he went on with the assistance of nature, and his two favourite authors, Handel and [Arcangelo] Corelli, till he was ten years old. Then Mr. Rogers told me, "It was high time to put him in trammels"; and soon after, Mr. [Bernard] Granville at Bath, an old friend of Handel's, sent for him. After hearing him [play], he charged him to have nothing to do with any great master "who will utterly spoil you," he added, "and destroy any thing that is original in you. Study Handel's lessons, till perfect in them. The only man in London who *can* teach you them is [Joseph] Kelway; but he *will* not, neither for love nor money."

Soon after we went up to town,[22] Charles, notwithstanding Mr. Granville's caution, had a strong curiosity to hear the principal masters there. I wanted their judgment and advice for him. Through Mr. [William] Bromfeild's recommendation, he first heard Mr. Keeble[23] (a great lover[24] of Handel) and his favourite pupil, Mr. Burton.[25] Then he played to them. Mr. Burton said, "He had a very brilliant finger." Mr. Keeble, "That he ought to be encouraged by all the lovers of music; yet he must not expect it, because

---

[16] Lady Gertrude (Stanhope) Hotham (1696–1775), widow of Sir Charles Hotham (1693–1738), 5th Baronet of Scarborough, was a Methodist sympathizer and friend of CW's family, including him in her will.

[17] Priscilla (Wilford) Rich (c. 1713–83), the wife of John Rich (1692–1761), the actor and owner of a theatre in Covent Garden. She converted to Methodism shortly after their marriage.

[18] DDCW 8/24 specifies: "Handel's oratorio songs."

[19] CW compiled a list of the music donated to CW Jr. by 1768, which survives in MARC, DDCW 8/7. Cf. *PCWS* 14 (2010): 105–8.

[20] Charles Hotham (1735–1767), 6th Baronet of Scarborough, son of Sir Charles Hotham (1693–1738), 5th Baronet, and Lady Gertrude (Stanhope) Hotham.

[21] DDCW 7/105, DDCW 8/2: "hope and prospect of a patron and benefactor"; DDCW 8/24: "hopes of a patron."

[22] In late 1770 CW was offered use of a fully furnished house on Chesterfield Street in Marylebone by Martha (Meighen / Colvill) Gumley (1711–88), widow of Colonel Samuel Gumley. He and CW Jr. began to reside there in February 1771.

[23] John Keeble (1711–1786), a leading organist.

[24] DDCW 8/2 and DDCW 8/24: "great harmonist and lover."

[25] John Burton (1730–82), harpsichordist, organist, and composer.

he was not born in Italy." He advised him to pursue his studies of Latin, etc., till he was fourteen, and then to apply himself in earnest to harmony.

Mr. Arnold[26] treated him with the utmost affection; said he would soon surpass the masters;[27] and advised him "not to confine himself to any one author, but study what[28] was excellent in all."

Dr. Arne's[29] counsel was (like Mr. Keeble's), "To stay till he was fourteen, and then deliver himself up to the strictest master that could be got."

Vento[30] confessed, "He wanted nothing but an *Italian* master."

Giardini[31] (urged by Mr. Madan) at last owned, "That the boy played well"; and was for sending him to Bologna—or Paris!

They all agreed in this, that he was marked by nature for a musician and ought to cultivate his talent. Yet still I mistrusted them, as well as myself, till Mr. Bromfeild carried us to Mr. Kelway. His judgment was decisive and expressed in more than words, for he invited Charles to come to him whenever he was in London and generously promised to *give*[32] him all the assistance in his power.

He began with teaching him Handel's lessons; then his own, and Scarlatti's, and Geminiani's. For near two years, he instructed him gratis, and with such commendations as are not fit for me to repeat. Meantime, Charles attended the oratorios and rehearsals at both houses, through the favor of Mr. Stanley and invitation of Mr. Arnold. He also heard the best operas.

As soon as he was engaged with Mr. Kelway, his old friend Mr. Worgan kindly offered to take him without money, "under his auspices," (as he expressed himself), and to train him up in his art. Such a master for my son was the height of my ambition, but Mr. Kelway had been beforehand with him.[33]

Mr. Worgan continued his kindness. He often played and sung over to him whole oratorios. So did Mr. Battishill.[34] Mr. Kelway at one time played

---

[26] Samuel Arnold (1740–1802), organist and composer.

[27] DDCW 8/2 and DDCW 8/24 substitute "professors" for "masters."

[28] DDCW 7/105 and later versions render this: "any one author or style, but to study and adopt what."

[29] Thomas Augustine Arne (1710–78), theatrical composer.

[30] Mattia Vento (1735–76), a composer of Italian birth and training, spent his last decade in London.

[31] Felice Giardini (1716–96), an Italian violinist and composer who settled in London.

[32] See the debate over whether Kelway was offering to teach gratis, in the preceding item in this collection.

[33] This paragraph omitted in DDCW 7/105 and later versions; likely to avoid bringing up the earlier dispute with Kelway.

[34] Jonathan Battishill (1738–1801), composer and organist; CW spells "Battishil."

over to him the Messiah, on purpose to teach him the time and manner of Handel. For three seasons Charles heard all the oratorios, comparing the performers of either house with each other, and both with Mr. Worgan and Mr. Kelway.

He received great encouragement from Mr. Savage.[35] Mr. Arnold was another father to him. Mr. Worgan gave him many lessons in thorough bass and composition. Mr. Smith's[36] curiosity drew him to Mr. Kelway's to hear his scholar, whom he bade "go on, and prosper under the best of masters." Dr. Boyce[37] came several times to my house to hear him; gave him some of his own music; and set some hymns for us.[38] Asked if the King had heard him, and expressed much surprise when we told him, "No." His uncle[39] enriched him with an inestimable present of Dr. Boyce's *Cathedral Music*.[40]

It now evidently appeared that his particular bent was to church music. Other music he could take pleasure in (especially what was truly excellent in the Italian) and played it without any trouble, but his chief delight was the oratorios. These he played over and over from the score, till he had them all by heart, as well as the rest of Handel's music, and Corelli, and Scarlatti, and Geminiani.[41]

These two last years he has spent with his four classical authors, and in composition. Mr. Kelway has made him a player, that is certain; but he knows the difference betwixt that and a musician, and can never think himself the latter, till he is quite master of thorough bass.

Several have offered to teach it him. One eminent master (besides Mr. Worgan) equally skilled in Handel's and the Italian music told me he would engage to make him perfect master of harmony in half a year.[42] But as I waited, and deferred his instruction in the practical part, till I could find the very best instructor for him, so I keep him back from the theory. The only man to teach him that, and sacred music, he believes to be Dr. Boyce.[43]

---

[35] William Savage (1720–89), composer.

[36] Possibly John Christopher Smith (1712–95), close associate of Handel.

[37] William Boyce (1711–79), of London, a composer and organist. He became quite close with CW's family; cf. CW's *Ode on the Death of Dr. Boyce* [1779], published as a broadsheet and in *AM* 2 (1779): 606.

[38] This last clause is omitted in DDCW 7/105 and later versions.

[39] DDCW 8/2 adds the specification: "my brother"; suggesting this was JW, rather than one of Sarah (Gwynne) Wesley's brothers.

[40] William Boyce, *Cathedral Music: being a collection in score of the most valuable and useful compositions for that service, by the several English masters of the last two hundred years*, 3 vols. (London: for the author, 1760–73). See the playful poem by CW, in the voice of his son Samuel, asking Dr. Boyce for a gift of this collection in MS Nursery, p. 1.

[41] DDCW 8/24 ends here.

[42] This line is omitted in DDCW 7/105 and DDCW 8/2.

[43] DDCW 10/2 and DDCW 8/2 end here. The remaining material is found only in the shorthand version DDCW 7/105.

[[May 19, 1774 we returned to London. Two things Charles wanted to make him a musician, an organ and Dr. Boyce's instruction in composition. How to procure either I knew not, when by an unexpected providence a lady made him a p[resent] of both.[44]

[[Soon after he had the offer of an organist's place [paying] £54 a year, with scholars who would bring him between £100 and £200 more. I wanted him to do it[?[45]], though without any hesitation he refused it, because he was just beginning himself to learn of Dr. Boyce, neither would he c[are] for anything which must part him from his mother and me.

[[May 19, 1775. He has now attended Dr. Boyce for a 12 month, not less than two hours at a time and often more. The master and scholar seem equally satisfied. Once a week he has also waited on his old master Kelway at his desire, and entertained him with his play. His only object is personal improvement.

[[June 19, 1776. These seven last months he has again asked the boon of Dr. Boyce's in[struction], who has engaged to teach him so long as his pupil chooses to learn. His friends, especially Miss Madan, urge him to take scholars himself. He is afraid of commencing more, and if he did teach, would not undertake more than three or four at most. One scholar he has from his play made a musician of, without designing it, namely his brother [Samuel].

[[Many have wished the king might hear him. He never desired it himself, not even when His Majesty sent his old master Kelway to tell him he wanted to hear him.

[[He does not seek great things to himself, nor can we see or discover in him any signs of envy or naughty ambition or covetousness.]]

*Sources*: holograph: end section of CW, MS Journal (MARC, DDCW 10/2), pp. 1–7. Collated with CW shorthand copy at end of MARC, DDCW 7/105, pp. 17–18; and polished holograph copies in MARC, DDCW 8/2, pp. 1–8, and MARC, DDCW 8/24, pp. 2–7.

---

[44] The lady was Martha (Meighen / Colvill) Gumley, CW Jr.'s godmother; cf. George J. Stevenson, *Memorials of the Wesley Family* (London: S. W. Partridge, 1876), 404.

[45] This clause is difficult. The shorthand appears to be "I w/im to dt." The sense given above seems to fit the situation, but it could be something like "I warned him to distrust."

# November 1776
# Charles Wesley Jr. Performing for the King and Queen

While Charles was in petticoats, several of our friends offered to carry him to the King.[1] His mother and I could never consent to it, unless they could do it in a proper manner. At ten years old, he came under Mr. [Joseph] Kelway. He told us he often mentioned him to the King, and the King often inquired after him. He frequently said, "I must carry this boy some morning to St. James,"[2] or, "I must get him into the King's service. The King would eat him up." I never joined issue with him or said a single word to encourage him. It was indeed the only way of introducing him which we could approve of. One day he called at my house and told Charles the King desired to hear him and bade him look over such a concerto, which the King was fond of. But we heard no more of it and were content.

Sam[3] now began to draw the attention of the connoisseurs in music who were eager for introducing him to the Queen.[4] They put him upon writing an anthem for the chapel. It was performed there before Their Majesties, who did not stay to hear his voluntary after it.

Last year a prebend of Windsor[5] carried Charles thither and kept him three or four days. He played several times on the church organ, dined with the dean,[6] and with Lord Sandwich,[7] who much approved of his play. Their Majesties were there at Windsor but did not hear him.

The dean invited him down again when a swell was added to the organ, with other alterations. I insisted with Dr. Sh[eppard[8]] that he should not play before the King unless His Majesty had notice of it first. Charles, when at Windsor, did the same. The doctor did inform His Majesty, who was pleased to declare he would hear him after the evening service. Charles entertained Their Majesties with a voluntary for above half an hour. Their Majesties stood listening to it, the King beating time. They both expressed great satisfaction. He asked to speak with the player, but Charles was slipped away.

---

[1] George III (1738–1820), had been king since 1760.

[2] St. James's Palace, the royal residence in Westminster, Middlesex.

[3] Samuel Wesley (1766–1837).

[4] Queen Charlotte of Mecklenburg-Strelitz (1744–1818).

[5] I.e., St. George's Chapel at Windsor Castle, Berkshire.

[6] Frederick Keppel (1728–77) was Dean of Windsor.

[7] John Montagu (1718–92), 4th Earl of Sandwich.

[8] This is apparently Dr. Edward Sheppard (1737–1813), a native of Bristol, who had become the domestic chaplain of Agnes Erskine, Countess of Buchan in 1767. He resided in Bath and was friends with both Selina, Countess of Huntingdon and CW's family.

At their return to town on **Wednesday, November 6**, a message came from the King for Mr. Wesley (not the old gentleman) to attend Their Majesties at the Queen's house[9] at 7:00 in the evening.

Charles was there a quarter before 7:00 and found Mr. Atwood and Mr. Nicolay,[10] the King's pages, ready to receive him. They introduced him into the King's apartment, which opened into the Queen's, where Her Majesty and company could hear everything.

Soon after the King entered (with the Prince of Mecklenburg[11]), came up to Charles, smiling, said, "Sir, I am glad to see you," fell into familiar conversation, and with the greatest affability and freedom asked him a hundred questions, which Charles answered without any reserve or restraint.

"When did you first begin to play?"

"At three years old. Soon after, an organist at Bristol[12] taught me my notes."

"When did you come under Kelway?"

"At ten. After that, I learned composition of Dr. [William] Boyce."

"That was just right. I admired and loved Boyce exceedingly, as well as Kelway. Kelway was always in raptures when he spoke of you; he called you his jewel, was continually talking of you when he came to us, saying, 'Never did hands lay on the instrument like yours.' Then you was a boy; now you are a young man. Your father lived and preached at Bristol, but we will say no more of him. I believe all your family are musical."

"My mother," said Charles, "has a very fine ear."

It is a rule, it seems, with courtiers never to ask His Majesty a question or to begin a discourse. But Charles being ignorant of this, asked questions and started subjects without fear, or wit. His Majesty's condescension excluded fear.

The [King] made many remarks on music and its professors, with exact judgment and taste. "Kelway's extempore play was better than his composition. Arne's latter works fell far short of his first.[13] There is a famous player on the pianoforte whom I think nothing of.[14] Indeed, I hate his instrument. It is trifling and little better than a Jews' harp."

---

[9] Buckingham House (now Palace), which Charlotte preferred over St. James's Palace.

[10] Frederick de Nicolay (1728–1809) was a special confident of both the King and Queen, and her principal page. CW spells variously "Nicolai" and "Nicholai."

[11] CW apparently means Charles II (1741–1816), a cousin of the Queen, who was Duke of Mecklenburg and Prince of Mirow.

[12] Edmund Broderip (1727–79), the organist at St. James's in Bristol.

[13] Thomas Augustine Arne (1710–78).

[14] Johann Christian Bach (1735–82) had recently popularized the pianoforte over the harpsichord in London circles.

Charles said, "I have often heard Lord Mornington[15] speak of Your Majesty's exact judgment in music."

"Lord Mornington was a good musician himself. Don't you think so? He and I are old folks, and therefore love old music. He told me his family and yours are related."[16]

When the King signified his desire to hear him, Charles asked, "Which shall I play on first, the organ or the harpsichord?"

"Which *is* first? A king or a prince?" Charles bowed and went straight to the organ (the king of instruments).

He began with a voluntary. The King soon cried out, "Bravo"; and called to Nicolay, "Ay, Nicolay, this is the true organ-style—this is no water-gruel play. You hear how he makes the organ sing!"

To Charles, "Play that overture which you played at Windsor," the *Overture to the Occasional Oratorio*.[17] He made him play it a second time. Then called for several pieces of music (of Handel's chiefly), which Charles played by memory before Nicolay could bring the books. The King testified great delight and surprise, declaring he had never heard anything like it. "You have a most extraordinary memory. I never could get Kelway to play anything without a book. I have received no such pleasure since I heard him."

He observed that very few masters could play the organ. Owned he loved church-music beyond all other. Made Charles play several chants and services, and commended the finest passages with the nicest judgment.

"I should be obliged to you, sir, if you would play that a little slower."

"They play it so, in the cathedrals."

"I know that, but they play it too fast."

Sometimes Charles, in playing Handel's choruses, broke out unawares into singing, but immediately checked himself. The King encouraged and bade him sing on and joined with his voice himself.

In the short intervals of play, the King talked with the greatest condescension. "How do you like my room? I think nothing can be altered to improve the sound."

He frequently said, "I am afraid, I have tired you."

"Not in the least. I am extremely happy that I can give Your Majesty the least satisfaction."

---

[15] Garret Colley Wesley (1735–81), 1st Earl of Mornington.

[16] A genealogical link between the Wesley / Wellesley family in Ireland and CW's ancestors in England has not been conclusively demonstrated. There is a tradition that Garrett Wesley (1625–1728) of Ireland, who had no children, wrote to CW's father about the possibility of adopting CW; if true, this offer was declined. Garrett Wesley's estate went to his cousin Richard (Colley) Wesley (1690–1758), who was named 1st Baron of Mornington, and was the father of Garrett Colley Wesley.

[17] By George Frederic Handel (1685–1759).

The moment Charles touched the harpsichord, before he had played four bars, the King said, "That is [Domenico] Scarlatti. Is it not?" and made him play several of his sonatas, which he seemed greatly to enjoy.

Charles began a prelude of [Francesco] Geminiani. "This," said the King, "I never expected to hear again when I lost Kelway." He highly commended Purcell,[18] showed Charles some of his handwriting, and bade him play what he pleased. Charles played "Britons, Strike Home."[19] The Queen called from within, "Encore, encore!" The King, "Play it again, Mr. Wesley. Madam is coming over to our music."[20]

He often went in to her to communicate his remarks and wanted her to see how Charles's hands lay on the harpsichord. He stood by him while playing to observe his hands; turned over the leaves for him; patted him on the shoulder; and when he offered to rise, made him sit down again.

He desired him to play Handel's second coronation anthem, "My Heart is Inditing," which he preferred to the first,[21] and wondered that Charles could play so long a piece without the book.

He called for "Affanni del pensier" in Otho.[22] "This song Kelway could never play without tears, and I have often shed tears in hearing him. I now take more pleasure in hearing you play it than I should in hearing any person sing it. You make the harpsichord sing it in the most agreeable manner."

The last thing he called for was the old coronation anthem,[23] and was surprised that Charles remembered the long arpeggio with which it begins.

The servants came in more than once to call His Majesty to supper. He bade them begone and continued talking for half an hour when the music was over. When Charles spoke, he attended as unwilling to lose a word.

He asked several questions about Sam. "How tall is he? Of what age? Is he like you? They say he is modern in his music."

---

[18] Henry Purcell (1659–95); CW spells "Purcel."

[19] A British patriotic song, written for a theatrical production by Purcell in 1695.

[20] While of the house of Hanover, George III was born and raised in England; Charlotte was a native of Germany.

[21] In 1727 Handel was commissioned to provide music for the coronation of George II of England and Queen Caroline. He wrote four anthems. Within the original coronation ceremonies "Let thy hand be strengthened" was played first, then "Zadok the priest," then "The King shall rejoice," and finally "My heart is inditing" at the coronation of the Queen.

[22] The selection "Affanni del pensier" in the Italian opera "Ottone: re di Germania" (English: "Otho: King of Germany"), by Handel.

[23] This is possibly a reference to John Blow, "God Spake Sometimes in Visions," the coronation anthem he wrote for James II (1695). My thanks to Carlton Young for the suggestion.

"He plays in every style."

"I have been told he plays better than you. But I am content with you. It is impossible he should play better."

Charles said all he could in commendation of him, which the King seemed slow to believe. At last he said, "Well, since you tell me so, I will take your word."[24]

Charles expected to have been dismissed in an hour, but the King kept him till past 11:00, communicating his sentiments on various subjects. "I am no connoisseur in music; yet I have a judgment of my own. They tell me you are very shy of the professors. What think you of such, of such an one?"

"It does not become me to speak of so great masters."

"Right, you should not to others, but you may speak anything to me. Or I will tell you what I think; and when you are of my mind, give a nod."

Charles answered, not with a nod, but a *"Bon."*

"I find we think alike and believe we are of the same judgment in all things."

"What I know of music, I got from Mr. Kelway and Dr. Boyce. I had never the honour of seeing Italy."

"So much the better. But where have I been that I never heard you before? How have they kept you from me? In hearing you, I hear Kelway again. I had much rather hear you alone, than with my band."

"How did you like my organ at Windsor? The Queen, who is a judge, said it did not do you justice; and that you are the best organ-player she ever heard. I confess I never heard a finer voluntary than that you gave us. How do you like Windsor?"

"I confess I am partial to London."

"I don't wonder at that. But you must own Windsor is a pleasant place."

"It is strange that there was never yet a great master there."

*Source*: holograph; DDCW 6/50.

---

[24] This discussion of CW's son Samuel appears at the bottom on the last page of the manuscript, with instructions to insert it here.

# 1776–1777
## Biographical Account of Samuel Wesley's Childhood[1]

*Ore puer, puerique habitu, sed corde sagaci*
*AEquabat senium, atque astu superaverat annos.*
Silius Italicus[2]

Samuel was born[3] on St. Matthias's Day, February 24, 1766, the same day which gave birth to [George Frederick] Handel 82 years before. The seeds of harmony did not spring up in him quite so early as in his brother, for he was three years old before he aimed at a tune.[4] His first were, "God save great George our King," Fischer's minuet,[5] and such like; mostly picked up from the street organs. He did not put a true bass to them till he had learned his notes.

While his brother was playing, he used to stand by, with his childish fiddle, scraping and beating time. One observing him, asked me, "And what shall this boy do?" I answered, "Mend his brother's pens."[6] But

---

[1] CW's account of the musical ability and training of Samuel survives in two versions:
   1) The original and most complete version is in DDCW 8/2, pp. 20–32. This manuscript was created to send to Daines Barrington. Barrington's published version (*Miscellanies*, 291–98) reproduces it nearly word-for-word. CW does not date this particular manuscript, but it would come about the same time that he delivered the account of CW Jr. to Barrington (June 1776).
   2) The version in DDCW 8/24 (pp. 17–27) is derivative of DDCW 8/2, with scattered elisions and some editorial polishing.
   At the end of CW, MS Journal (DDCW 10/2), CW chose to transcribe Barrington's published account rather than his original. We transcribe here DDCW 8/2, noting only the most significant revisions or deletions in DDCW 8/24 and a couple of instructive footnotes in Barrington.

[2] Cf. Silius Italicus, viii.465–66. While this motto appears in both DDCW 8/2 and DDCW 8/24, it was squeezed at the top of the page after the fact. As CW notes, it is from Barrington's published account, where it marked the transition to Barrington's own comments on Samuel (p. 298). CW's suggested translation:
   In looks and garb, a boy; in judgment, sage
   Beyond his years, and wise as hoary age.

[3] DDCW 8/24 adds: "at Bristol."

[4] In *Miscellanies* (p. 291) Barrington added a footnote: His mother, Mrs. Wesley, however hath given me the following most convincing proof that he played a tune when he was but two years eleven months old—by producing a quarter guinea which was given to him by Mr. Addy for this extraordinary feat, wrapped in a piece of paper, containing the day and year of the gift, as well as the occasion of it. Mrs. Wesley had also an elder son, who died in his infancy, and who both sung a tune and beat time when he was but twelve months old.

[5] Johann Christian Fischer (1733–1800).

[6] Barrington (ibid., 291) adds an explanation: This alludes to a well-known story in the musical world. [Benedetto] Marcello, the celebrated composer, had an elder brother who had greatly distinguished himself in this science; and being asked what should be done with little Marcello, he answered, let him mend my pens, which piqued the boy so much that he determined to exceed his elder brother.

he did not resent the affront as deeply as Marcello did; so it was not indignation which made him a musician.

Mr. [Samuel] Arnold was the first who, hearing him at the harpsichord, said, "I set down Sam for one of my family." But we did not much regard him, coming after his brother [Charles], or suspect that the block contained a statue.[7]

The first thing which drew our attention was the great delight he took in hearing his brother play. Whenever Mr. [Joseph] Kelway came to teach him, Sam constantly attended and accompanied Charles *on the chair*. Undaunted by Mr. Kelway's frown, he went on. And even when his back was to the harpsichord, he crossed his hands on the chair, as the other did on the instrument, without ever missing a time.

He was so passionately fond of [Domenico] Scarlatti that, if Charles ever began playing him before Sam was called, he would cry and roar as if he had been beaten. Mr. [Martin] Madan, his godfather, finding him one day so belabouring the chair, told him, "He should have a better instrument by and by."

I have since recollected Mr. Kelway's words, "It is of the utmost importance to a learner *to hear the best music*." And, "If any man would learn to play well, let him hear Charles." Sam had this double advantage from his birth. As his brother employed the evenings in Handel's oratorios, Sam was always at his elbow, listening and joining with his voice. Nay, he would sometime[s] presume to find fault with his brother's play, when we thought he could know nothing of the matter.

He was between four and five years old when he got hold of the oratorio of *Samson* and by that alone taught himself to read. Soon after, he taught himself to write. From this time, he sprung up like a mushroom; and when turned of five, could read perfectly well; and had all the airs, recitatives, and choruses of *Samson* and *The Messiah*, both words and notes, by heart.

Whenever he heard his brother begin to play, he would tell us whose music it was, whether Handel, [Arcangelo] Corelli, Scarlatti, or any other, and what part of what lesson, sonata, or overture, etc.

Before he could write, he composed much music. His custom was to lay the words of an oratorio before him, and sing them all over. Thus he set (extempore for the most part) *Ruth, Gideon, Manasses,* and *The Death of Abel*. We observed, when he repeated the same words, it was always to the same tunes. The airs of *Ruth* in particular he made before he was six years old, laid them up in his memory till he was eight, and then wrote them down.

I have seen him open his prayer-book and sing the *Te Deum*, or an anthem from some Psalm, to his own music, accompanying it with the

---

[7] Barrington omits this clause, where CW admits they did not foresee Samuel as a prodigy.

harpsichord. This he often did, after he had learned his notes, which Mr. Williams,[8] a young organist of Bristol, taught him betwixt six and seven [years old].

How or when he learned counterpoint, I can hardly tell; but without being ever taught it, he soon wrote in parts.

He was full eight years old when Dr. [William] Boyce came to see us and accosted me with, "Sir, I hear you have got an English Mozart[9] in your house. Young Linley[10] tells me wonderful things of him." I called Sam to answer for himself. He had by this time scrawled down his oratorio of *Ruth*. The Dr. looked over it very carefully, and seemed highly pleased with the performance. Some of his words were, "These airs are some of the prettiest I have seen. This boy writes by nature as true a bass as I by rule and study. There is no man in England has two such sons as you," etc. He bade us let him run on *ad libitum*,[11] without any check of rules or masters.

After this, whenever the Dr. visited us, Sam ran to him with his song, sonata, or anthem; and the Dr. examined them with astonishing patience and delight.

As soon as Sam had quite finished his oratorio, he sent it as a present to the Dr., who immediately honoured him with the following note:

To Mr. Samuel Wesley,

Dr. Boyce's compliments and thanks to his very ingenious brother-composer, Mr. Samuel Wesley; and is very much pleased and obliged by the possession of the oratorio of *Ruth*, which he shall preserve with the utmost care, as the most curious product of his musical library.

For the short time that Sam continued under Mr. Williams it was hard to say which was the master and which the scholar. Sam chose what music he would learn; made his master learn the violincello to accompany him; and often broke out into extempore play, his master wisely letting him do as he pleased.

During this time, he taught himself the fiddle. A soldier assisted him about six weeks; and some time after, Mr. Kingsbury[12] gave him twenty lessons. His favourite instrument was the organ.

---

[8] David Williams succeeded Edward Rooke as organist of All Saints Church Bristol in 1772; he may be the David Williams baptized in Bristol in 1747, making him 25 years of age.

[9] Wolfgang Amadeus Mozart (1756–91), a renowned German musical prodigy.

[10] Thomas Linley the younger (1756–78) another musical prodigy and student of Boyce.

[11] "At one's pleasure"; in music, at the discretion of the performer.

[12] William Kingsbury (d. 1782), a violinist who would accompany CW's sons in their early public concerts. CW spells "Kinsbury."

He spent a month at Bath, while we were in Wales; served the Abbey on Sundays, gave them several voluntaries, and played the first fiddle in several private concerts.

He returned with us to London, greatly improved in his play. There I allowed him a month for learning all Handel's overtures. He got and played them over to me in three days. Handel's concertos he mastered with equal ease, and some of his lessons and Scarlatti's. Like Charles, he learned the hardest music without any pains or difficulty.

He borrowed his *Ruth* [from Dr. Boyce] to transcribe for Mr. Madan. Parts of it he played at Lord Le Despenser's,[13] who rewarded him with some of Handel's oratorios.[14]

Mr. Madan now began carrying him about to his musical friends. He played several times at Mr. Wilmot's[15] to the nobility, and some eminent masters and judges of music. They gave him music to play and subjects to pursue, which he had never seen. Mr. [John] Burton, Mr. Bates,[16] etc., expressed their approbation in the strongest terms. His extempore fugues, they said, were just and regular, but could not believe that he knew nothing of the rules of composition.

Several companies he entertained for hours together with his own music. As quick as his invention suggested, his hand executed it. The learned were astonished. Sir John Hawkins[17] cried out, "Inspiration, inspiration!" Dr. C– candidly acknowledged, "He has got that which we are searching after." An old musical gentleman, hearing him, could not refrain from tears.

Dr. Burney[18] was greatly pleased with his extempore play, and pursuing the subjects and fugues which he gave him; but insisted like the rest that he must have been taught the rules.

Mr. [John] Stanley and Mr. Burney[19] expressed the same surprise and satisfaction. An organist gave him a sonata he had just written, not easy, or very legible. Sam played it with great readiness and propriety, and better (as the composer owned to Mr. Madan) than he could himself.

---

[13] Francis Dashwood (1708–81), 11th Baron le Despencer.

[14] DDCW 8/24 omits this paragraph.

[15] CW is likely referring to Sir John Eardley Wilmot (1709–1792), a prominent London judge who twice refused the post of Lord Chancellor. He was already knighted, but not made a baron until late 1782, so the address of "Mr." might have been appropriate.

[16] Joah Bates (1740–99), a musician.

[17] Sir John Hawkins (1719–89), a music scholar and lawyer.

[18] Dr. Charles Burney (1726–1818), a celebrated music historian, composer, and musician.

[19] By the change of title CW may mean to be referencing Charles Burney Jr. (1757–1817).

Lord Barrington,[20] Lord Aylesford,[21] Lord Dudley,[22] Sir Watkin Williams-Wynn,[23] and other lovers of Handel were highly delighted with him, and encouraged him to hold fast his veneration for Handel and the old music. But old or new was all one to Sam, so it was but good. Whatever was presented, he played at sight and made variations on any tune; and as often as he played it again, made new variations. He imitated every author's style, whether Handel, Bach,[24] [Johann] Schobert, or Scarlatti himself.

One asked him how he liked Mozart's music. He played it over and said, "It was very well for one *of his years.*"

He went and played to Mr. Kelway, whom I afterwards asked what he thought of him. He would not allow him to be comparable to Charles; yet commended him greatly and told his mother, "It was a gift from God to both her sons; and as for Sam, he never saw so free and dégagé a gentleman." Mr. Madan had often said the same, "That Sam was everywhere as much admired for his behaviour as for his play."

Between eight and nine, he was brought through the smallpox by Mr. [William] Bromfeild's assistance, whom he therefore promised to reward with his next oratorio.

If he loved any thing better than music, it was regularity. He took to it himself. Nothing could exceed his punctuality. No company, no persuasion, could keep him up beyond his time. He never could be prevailed on to hear any opera or concert by night. The moment the clock gave warning for 8:00, away ran Sam, in the midst of his most favourite music. Once in the playhouse he rose up after the first part of *The Messiah* with, "Come, Mamma, let us go home, or I shan't be in bed by 8:00."

When some talked of carrying him to the Queen[25] and to try him, I asked if he was willing to go.[26] "Yes, with all my heart," he answered, "but I won't stay beyond 8:00."

The praises bestowed so lavishly on him did not seem to affect, much less to hurt him; and whenever he went into the company of his betters, he would much rather have stayed at home. Yet when among them, he was

---

[20] William Wildman Shute Barrington (1717–93), 2nd Viscount Barrington, the older brother of Daines Barrington.

[21] Heneage Finch (1715–77), 3rd Earl of Aylesford.

[22] Given the timing, this is likely John Ward (1725–88), 2nd Viscount Dudley and Ward; he had taken the title in May 1774, on his father's death.

[23] Sir Watkin Williams-Wynn (1749–1789), 4th Baronet, politician and patron of the arts.

[24] Likely referring to Johann Sebastian Bach (1685–1750); rather than his son Johann Christian Bach.

[25] Queen Charlotte of Mecklenburg-Strelitz (1744–1818), wife of George III.

[26] Orig., "willing go"; an error, corrected in DDCW 8/24.

free and easy; so that some remarked, "He behaved as one bred up in a court, yet without a courtier's servility."

On our coming to town this last time, he sent Dr. Boyce the last anthem he had made. The Dr. thought from its correctness that Charles must have helped him in it. But Charles assured him that he never assisted him, otherwise than by telling him, if he asked, whether such or such a passage were good harmony. And the Dr. was so scrupulous that, when Charles showed him an improper note, he would not suffer it to be altered.

Mr. Madan now carried him to more of the first masters. Mr. Abel[27] wrote him a subject and declared, "Not three masters in town could have answered it so well."

Mr. Cramer[28] took a great liking to him, offered to teach him the fiddle, and played some trios with his brother and him. He sent a man to take measure of him for a fiddle, and is confident a few lessons would set him up for a violinist.[29]

Sam often played the second fiddle, and sometimes the first, with Mr. Treadway, who declared, "Giardini himself could not play with greater exactness."

Mr. Madan brought Dr. Nares[30] to my house, who could not believe that a boy should write an oratorio, play at sight, and pursue any given subject. He brought two of the King's boys,[31] who sung over several songs and choruses in *Ruth*. Then he produced two bars of a fugue. Sam worked this very readily and well, adding a motet of his own, and then a voluntary on the organ, which quite removed the Dr.'s incredulity.

At the rehearsal at St. Paul's, Dr. Boyce met "his brother" Sam and, showing him to Dr. Howard,[32] told him, "This boy will soon surpass you all." Shortly after he came to see us, took up a jubilate, which Sam had lately wrote, and commended it as one of Charles's. When we told him whose it was, he declared, "He could find no fault in it"; adding, "There was not another boy upon earth who could have composed it"; and concluding with, "I never yet met with that person who owes so much to nature as Sam. He is come among us—dropped down from heaven!"[33]

---

[27] Carl Friedrich Abel (1723–87).

[28] Wilhelm Cramer (1746–99), violinist.

[29] DDCW 8/24 revises to: "… a fiddle, gave him a few lessons, and is confident he would not need more than 20."

[30] Dr. James Nares (1715–83), organist and composer.

[31] I.e., boy's in the King's choir.

[32] Dr. Samuel Howard (1710–82), organist and composer.

[33] DDCW 8/24 ends here. So does Barrington's published version of the material that CW sent, though Barrington then appends an extended account of his own observations of

Mr. Smith,[34] who assisted Handel in managing the oratorios, gave Sam two bars of a fugue composed for the organ, which Sam, though at the harpsichord, treated as a movement for the organ; and when he had worked it in a masterly manner for some time, fell into a second movement, which so naturally arose out of the former that Mr. Smith recognized his own notes, adding at the same time that composers were not from this instance to be hastily charged with plagiarism.

Some months before this Mr. Baumgarten[35] gave him the subject of a fugue, which Sam pursued a considerable time on the organ. Mr. Baumgarten declared it was almost note for note the same with a fugue which he had written and never showed to any one. He inferred from hence that his train of ideas and Sam's were very similar.

He has since declared that he verily believed there was not in Europe such an extempore player as Sam.

*Source*: holograph; MARC, DDCW 8/2, pp. 20–32. Collated with holograph polished version: MARC, DDCW 8/24, pp. 17–27.

Samuel Wesley (*Miscellanies*, 298–310; reproduced in Jackson, *CW Journal*, 2:158–66).

[34] John Christopher Smith (1712–95).

[35] Carl Friederich Baumgarten (1740–1824), born and trained in Germany, came to London at the age of eighteen. Working initially as an organist, violinist and teacher, he became the director of the Covent Garden orchestra 1780–94. CW spells "Bumgarden."

# Index of Persons

Abel, Carl Friedrich, musician, 439–40, 466
Acourt, John, 70, 73
Adams, brother, of Ashby de la Zouch, 396
Adams, Mr., of Devonshire, 202
Adams, John, of Tresmeer, 239–40, 242
Adjets [or Aggits], Mr., of Dublin, 257
Allen, brother, of Tullamore, 293
Allen, James, Inghamite preacher, 410–11
Allen, John, of Newcastle, 324
Annesley, Samuel Jr., 6
Armstead, Bridget, of Islington, 59
Arne, Thomas Augustine, composer, 453, 457
Arnold, Mrs., of London, 416, 419–20
Arnold, Samuel, musician, 453, 454, 462
Ashe, brother, of Leeds, 311, 399
Atwood, Mr., royal page, 457

B., Mrs., of Redruth, 221
B. Rev., in York Minster, 401
Bach, Johann Christian, 439, 440, 457n
Bach, Johann Sebastian, 465
Baker, sister, of Dublin, 271
Ball, John, Lollard preacher, 147
Ball, John, of London, 63
Ball, Roger, preacher, 412
Barber, Elizabeth, of Bristol, 122

Barcock, Edward, Newgate prisoner, 30–34
Barlow, Mr., of Manchester, 413
Barraby, Mary, of London, 63
Barrington, Daines, of London, 437
Barrington, William, 2nd Viscount Barrington, 465
Barrow, Hannah, of Kingswood, 106n
Bastable, Cornelius, itinerant, 392
Bates, Joah, musician, 464
Bath, sister N., of Bristol, 73, 76
Battersby, Mr. and Mrs., of Dublin, 279–80
Battishill, Jonathan, musician, 453
Baumgarten, Carl Friederich, musician, 467
Beard, John, London musician, 451–52
Bell, Ann Mercy, of York, 400
Bell, Richard, of London, 51, 54, 60, 65
Bell, Richard Jr., of London, 55, 71
Bennet, Edward, of Sheffield, 142, 150
(Murray) Bennet, Grace, 335
Bennet, John, of Chinley, 327–28, 330–32, 334–35, 342
Bennet, Rev. John, of Tresmeer, 211, 239–40, 242, 244
Bennet, Joseph, of Dewsbury, 408
Bennetts, John, of Trewellard, 224, 229, 233–34
Bentham, Edward, of Oxford University, 306

## Index of Persons

Bernard, Mr., of Bristol, 122
(Bentham) Berry, Ursula, 16
Bidgood, Hannah, of Sticklepath, 202
Biggot, Elisabeth, of Newcastle, 136
Birt, Mr., of London, 441
Bissicks, Thomas, of Bristol, 107
Blackmore, sister, of Worcester, 304
Blackwell, Ebenezer, of London, 281, 286
(Molland) Blackwell, Elizabeth, of London, 281, 356
Blatchley, Mr., 117
Blund, Mrs. of London, 53
Bold, Hugh, Esq., of Brecon, 433
Bolton, John, of Manchester, 412
Bond(?), Betty, of Bristol, 75
Booth, Mr. and Mrs., of Ireland, 292
Booth, Elizabeth, of Woodseats, 309
Borlase, Mr. (brother of next), 225
Borlase, Rev. Dr. Walter, of Madron, 225–26, 229n, 234
Bosher, Mary, of Bristol, 79, 84, 87
(Davis) Boult, Susanna, of London, 356
Boult, T., tinker of Norwich, 388
Bowers, George, of London, 51
Bowes, George, of Newcastle, 132–33
Bowes, John, Lord Chief Baron of Ireland, 264n, 282n
Bowmen, John, of Newcastle, 131
Boyce, Dr. William, musician, 445–46n, 451n, 454–55, 457, 460, 463, 464, 466
Bradshaw, sister, of Bristol, 70
Branford, Miss, of London, 62
Bray, John, of London, 31, 38, 41, 51–53, 60, 64
Bridgens, George, of Birmingham, 308–09, 337

Bridgham, Lydia, of Norwich, 370, 388
(Perronet) Briggs, Elizabeth, 355n
Briggs, William, of London, 355
Brimble, sister, of Bristol, 111
Briscoe, Henry, of Leeds, 319n
Broad, Ann, of London, 63
Broderip, Edmund, of Bristol, 443, 450
Bromfeild, William, of London, 439–41, 444, 447–49, 452–53, 465
Brooke, John, alderman of Leeds, 319n
Brooke, T., of Thirsk, 400
Broughton, Rev. Thomas, of London, 302
Brown, Mr., of London, 441
Brown, Catherine, of Newcastle, 137
Brown, John, of Tanfield Lea, 127
Brown, Peter, bookseller, 88
Brown, Robert ("Robin"), of Epworth, 8, 19, 24, 26
Bruce, Rev. George, of Newcastle, 133, 136
Bryant, Dean, Newgate prisoner, 30n
Bryant, Fanny, of Norwich, 371
Buckmaster, Mr., of London, 63
Bullard, Mr., 436
Bully, Mr., of Oxford, 48
Bunnell, Jabez, of Leeds, 319
Burges, sister, of Bristol, 362
Burney, Dr. Charles, music historian, 464
Burton, E., Justice of Peace, Wakefield, 174–78
Burton, John, organist, 452, 464
Butts (Witham), Hannah, 281
Butts, Thomas, of London, 185, 281
Byrom, Dr. John, of Manchester, 335

INDEX OF PERSONS

Cades, Mary, of London, 36
Calvin, John, reformer, 80, 89, 115, 118
Canning, Mr. Thomas, of Evesham, 337, 395
Canning, Mrs. Thomas, of Evesham, 337, 395
Canning, daughter, of Evesham, 337
Carr, Mr., of Dublin, 285
Carr, Rev., of Scotland, 324
Cart, Elizabeth (Smith), of London, 214, 280–81, 302–03
Castle, Mary, of Birstall, 178
Catlow, Jonathan, itinerant, 409
Cawdry, G., of London, 35n, 39–41
Cennick, Hannah, of Bristol, 69n
Cennick, John, 49, 85, 94–95, 104, 106, 108, 110, 113, 251–54, 259, 261–64, 266, 271, 273–74, 277–79, 283, 334
Charles II, Duke of Mecklenburg, 457
Charlotte, Queen of England, 456–60, 465
Cheney, John, of London, 36
Chenhall, William, of St. Just, 172n 230, 234
Clarke, Elizabeth, of London, 281n
Clavel, Sarah, of Deptford, 213–14, 280n
Clay, Sarah, of London, 391
Clement, Mrs., of Dublin, 297
Cloudsley, Richard, of Leeds, 319
Coates, Mr., of Dublin, 271
Coates, Rev. John, of Acomb, 401n
Coats, Alexander, itinerant, 405
Cockburn, Dr. Thomas, 398–99, 401–02
Cockell, Richard, of Leeds, 319n
Colbeck, Thomas, of Keighley and itinerant, 326, 328, 339n, 341, 409
Coldwall, Elizabeth, of Newcastle, 131–32

Connor, Mr., of Dublin, 279
Cook, brother, (of London?), 88
Corbett, Dr. Francis, Dean of St. Patrick's Cathedral, 270n, 275n
Corelli, Arcangelo, composer, 443, 447, 452, 454, 462
Cousins, Mr., of Rotherham, 397
Cownley, Joseph, itinerant, 296, 341, 352–53, 414
Cox, Hannah, of Bristol, 195
Cradock, Mrs., of Bristol, 121
Cramer, Wilhelm, violinist, 466
Crampton, Mr., of Dublin, 264–66, 284–85
Crisp, Tobias, author, 83
Crook, Rev. Henry, curate of Hunslet, 398–99, 402–03, 407
Crouch, Mr. Timothy, of Dowgate Hill, 56, 63
Crouch, Mrs. Timothy, of Dowgate Hill, 56
Crouch, Thomas, preacher, 301
Crump, sister, of Dublin, 269
Cudworth, William, Calvinist preacher, 371–75, 382

D., Mr., of York, 400
Darby, William, of Bristol, 69
Darney, William, itinerant, 328, 330–34, 341, 344
Dashwood, Francis, 11th Baron le Despencer, 464
Davey, Mary, of London, 281n
Davies, Rev. Edward, of Bengeworth, 422–33
Davis, brother, of Bristol, 77
Davis, brother, of Tavistock, 211
Davis, Mrs. Anne (d. 1775), of Bristol, 79–80
Davis, Kitty, of Bristol, 49n
Dawson, Mrs., of Plymouth Dock, 242
Dean, Mr., of Philipstown, 295

## Index of Persons

Deaves, James, itinerant, 391
Delamotte, Charles, 53n
Denison, Robert, alderman of Leeds, 319n
Dent, Jane, of Newcastle, 131
Dewell, Hannah, of London, 281–83, 356, 359
Dickson, Sarah, of Bristol, 123
Dixon, George, of Leeds, 319n
Dodson, Miss, of Leeds, 314
Doleman, John, of Bristol, 119
Downes, Mr., at Normandy, 19
Downes, John, itinerant, 323, 343n, 352–54, 394–96
Dunn, Mrs., of Dublin, 264
Dunton, John, London publisher, 13
Dupee, Margaret, of London, 59

Eastwood, Rev. Jonas, of Dewsbury, 408
Eaton, John, of Wednesbury, 306n
Edmonds, John, of London, 52
Edwards, [J.?], of Norwich, 366–67, 369–73, 376–79, 381–82, 388
Edwards, Mrs. [J.], of Norwich, 389
Edwards, John, itinerant, 275n, 397, 399, 402–03, 406–08
Edwards, Samuel, of Dublin, 261–62, 273, 277–79
Ellis, Anne, of London, 36
Ellis, Rev. Thomas, of Holyhead, 249–50
England, Rachel, of Bristol, 77, 91, 109, 117
English, Margaret, of Newcastle, 134
Errington, Matthew, of London, 139
Evans, Mr., of Oxford, 245, 337
Evans, daughter, of Oxford, 337
Evans, Sophie, of Dublin, 279
Ewsters, Mary, of London, 66

Fanshaw, sister, of Manchester, 336, 412
Farley, Felix, printer, of Bristol, 70, 72–73, 78, 88, 122
Felster, Agnes, of Dublin, 255–57, 260, 268, 283
Felts, Mrs., of London, 360
Fenwick, John, itinerant, 405n
Fenwick, Michael, itinerant, 312, 317n, 325–26, 328, 340–41, 343–46, 350
Finch, Heneage, 3rd Earl of Aylesford, 465
Fischer, Johann Christian, musician, 461
Fisher, John, itinerant, 406
Fluellen, Henry, Newgate prisoner, 30n
Folliard, Mrs., of Dublin, 296
Ford, Mrs., of Oxford, 67
Ford, Mr. James, of Bristol, 84
Ford, Mrs. James, of Bristol, 84
Fosset, John, Newgate prisoner, 30n
Fothergill, Dr. John, of London, 359
Fouace, Stephen, of Tyrrellspass, 287, 289
Fox, Mr. and Mrs., of Oxford, 67
Francis, Mary, of Bristol, 213–14, 218n
Frith, J., mayor of Leeds, 319n
Furth, Arthur, of Birstall, 175

G., A., of St. Ives, 158
Gallatin, Bartholomew, of Lakenham, 366–67, 379
(Foulkes) Gallatin, Lucia, of Lakenham, 355, 363, 367–68, 387–88, 390
Gambold, Rev. John, 64, 74
Garder, sister, of London, 391
Gardner, Mrs., 56
Gay, John, mayor of Norwich, 366

## Index of Persons

Gee, Mary, of Bristol, 122, 192
Geminiani, Francesco, musician, 442–43, 445, 447, 453–54, 459
George III, King of England, 456–60
Giardini, Felice, musician, 453, 466
Gibson, Mr., of Dublin, 271
Gibson, Mrs., of Dublin, 271
Gibson, Christian, of Newcastle, 131
Gibson, Edmund, Bishop of London, 254
Gillespie, Robert, itinerant, 321, 341, 344, 346
Golding, Charles, Newgate prisoner, 30n
Goodwin, Mr., of Exeter, 244
Gordon, Ensign, of Sheffield, 150
Goter, Richard, of London, 54
Graham, Anne, of London, 35–37, 39
Granville, Bernard, of Calwich Abbey, 439, 447, 452
Graves, Rev. Charles Caspar, 48, 67–68, 146, 149–50, 208, 225, 234
Green, Miss, of Leeds, 407–08
Green, [John?], of London, 214
Green, William, of Rotherham, 397
Greenfield, Edward, of St. Ives, 208, 225
Greenwood, Paul, itinerant, 328, 333
Gregory, sister, of Plymouth, 242
Gregory, Mary, of Bristol, 69
Gresley, Rev. Blinman, curate of Churchill, 182
(Whitefield) Grevil, Elizabeth, of Bristol, 70, 74n, 78, 88n, 89, 91
Griffith, Robert, of Holyhead, Anglesey, 299
Grimshaw, Johnny, of Haworth, 333

Grimshaw, Rev. William, of Haworth, 328, 330–32, 334, 404, 407, 410–12
(Meighen / Colvill) Gumley, Martha, 416n, 455
Gurley, Mr., of Dublin, 279
Gurney, Mr., 144–45
Guthrie, Rev. James, Ordinary Newgate prison, 32n
(Gwynne) Waller, Elizabeth, of Garth, 190n
Gwynne, Marmaduke, of Garth, 185, 246–48
Gwynne, Rebecca, of Garth and Ludlow, 304n, 442n, 446

H. Mr., Baptist of Dublin, 260
H., E., preacher in Leeds, 408
Hacking, John, itinerant, 413
Haime, John, itinerant, 201–02
Hales, Catherine, of Newcastle, 135
Hall, Mrs., of Newcastle, 136
Hall, Martha, see Martha (Wesley) Hall
Hall, Samuel Westley, 66
Hall, Rev. Westley, 36, 58–66, 69–70, 74, 133
Halyburton, Thomas, author, 188
Hamilton, sister, of London, 60
Hampson, John, itinerant, 413
Handel, George Frederic, composer, 438, 440–43, 445, 447, 451–54, 458–59, 461–62, 464–65, 467
Handy, Joan (Low), of Templemacateer, 292
Handy, Jonathan, of Templemacateer, 288–89, 291, 293
Handy, Samuel, of Coolalough, 276n, 277–78, 289–90, 292
Harding, James, of Bristol, 95, 195
Harding, Susanna, of Bristol, 116
Hardwick, Joseph, of Leeds, 319

*Index of Persons*

(Garding) Hardwick, Jane, of Brentford, 190
Hardwick, Thomas Sr., of Brentford, 190n
Hardwick, Thomas Jr., of Brentford and itinerant, 190n, 245
Hardy, Elizabeth, of Bristol, 81n
Hargreaves, Kitty, of Epworth, 49n
Harris, Mr., of Rosewarne, 220, 232–33
Harris, Howell, itinerant, 58–66, 74, 113, 115–19, 246
Harry, Richard, mayor of St. Ives, 154n
Harry, William, of St. Ives, 162
Haskins, Henry, of Siston, 112
Hastings, Francis, 10th Earl of Huntingdon, 362n, 396n
Hastings, Lady Margaret; wife of Benjamin Ingham, 403
(Shirley) Hastings, Selina, Countess of Huntingdon, 355, 359–60, 362–64
Hathy, sister, of Bristol, 122
Haughton, John, itinerant, 277, 285, 288, 291, 394
Hawkins, Sir John, music scholar, 464
Hawley, Jacob, constable of Leeds, 319
Hawthorn, Mr., 56n
Hawthorn, Mrs., 56
Haydon, John, of Bristol, 70, 122, 195n
Haynes, Mrs. Sarah, of Abson, 198–99
Haynes, Thomas, of Abson, 198–99
Hayter, Thomas, Bishop of Norwich, 368n
Healey, John, itinerant, 278, 284–85, 289–91
Hearle, Rev. Thomas, of St. Stithians, 212n
Henderson, Matthew, Newgate prisoner, 191n
Henderson, Richard, itinerant and Bristol, 422–23, 427–28
Hervey, James, Calvinist author, 393, 400
Heylyn, Rev. Dr. John, 197
Highnam, Esther, of Bristol, 79, 87
Hill, Miss, organ student of London, 443
Hill, Mary, of Bristol, 81, 83, 87
Hill, Mr., baker, of London, 419–20
Hilland, John, of London, 51, 54, 58
Hilland, Martha, of London, 51, 58
Hillingworth, John, of Leeds, 319
Hitchens, James, of Gwennap, 211, 231, 244
Hitchens, Samuel, of Gwennap, 244
Hitchens, William, itinerant, 394
Hoblyn, Rev. William, of St. Ives, 154n, 155n, 169–70, 173, 231–32, 243, 272
Hodges, Joseph, of London, 64–65
Hodges, Rev. John, of Wenvoe, 185, 196
Holland, William, of London, 61, 302–03
Hollaster, "Edy", of Bristol, 79, 82
Hollis, Isaac, of High Wycombe, 245
Holton, Anne, of Bristol, 85
Holywell, J., of Skircoat Green, 332
Hoole, Rev. Joseph, of Haxey, 6, 10, 19, 21, 25
Hooper, Mrs. Elizabeth, of Bristol, 69–70, 75–76, 88, 108–09
Hooper, William, of Bristol, 69n, 116, 118
Hopper, Christopher, itinerant, 326, 328, 331–32, 335
Horseman, Mr., 425
Horton, John, of Islington, 425–26, 430–31

## Index of Persons

Hotham, Sir Charles, 6th Baronet of Scarborough, 452
(Stanhope) Hotham, Lady Gertrude, 452
How[e], John, of Nottingham, 149
Hughes[?], of Norwich, 372
Humble, Frances, of Ryton, 136n
Humble, John, of Ryton, 136, 138
Humphreys, Joseph, itinerant, 77, 108–09
Hunter, Magdalen, of London, 416–21
Huntingdon, Lady – see Selina (Shirley) Hastings
Hutchings, Rev. John, in London, 41–42
Hutchinson, John, of Leeds, 332–33, 336, 355–62, 374
(Hutchinson) Hutchinson, Mary, of Leeds, 310, 315
Hutton, James, of London, 30n, 55, 60–61, 64–65
Hyde, Mr. and family, of Plymouth Dock, 208, 241–42

I'Anson, Bryan, of Westminster, 396
Ibbetson, Sir Henry, of Leeds, 319
St. Ignatius of Antioch, 361
St. Ignatius of Loyola, 65, 115
Ingham, Rev. Benjamin, 177, 211, 400, 403
Ingham, Ignatius, son of Benjamin, 403
Inkersley, Joseph, of Leeds, 319
Isaac, Mr., of London, 419

J., Mr., of Bristol, 195
J., Mrs., of Bristol, 195
J–n, J., Methodist soldier/drummer, 318n, 321n, 322
Jackson, Henry, of Newcastle, 126, 129, 131, 133, 138
Jackson, Mrs. Henry, of Newcastle, 128
Jackson, Herbert, of Plymouth, 237
Jackson, Mrs. Jane, of London, 56
Jaco, Peter, itinerant, 394
James, Captain John, of Bristol, 360, 433
Jameson, Mr., of Athlone, 287n, 290n
Jane, Mrs., of Bristol, 78n, 90
Jenkins, Herbert, itinerant, 185, 202, 240–42, 244
Jenkins, Mary, of Bristol, 121
John, William, of Heamoor, 217
Johnson family, of Barley Hall, 142, 309
Johnson, Isabel, of Newcastle, 132
Johnson, John, of Wakefield, 310, 408
Johnson, John, itinerant, 394
Johnson, Thomas, itinerant, 394, 413
Jones, Catherine, of Fonman Castle, 181
Jones, Edward, of Bristol, 123
(Mann) Jones, Elizabeth, of Kingswood, 362
Jones, James and wife, of Tipton, 305, 307, 394
Jones, John, itinerant, 353–54, 358, 360–61, 394
(Forrest) Jones, Mary, of Fonman Castle, 181
Jones, Mary Jr., of Fonman Castle, 181
Jones, Robert, of Fonman Castle, 181n, 199
Jones, Robert Jr., of Fonman Castle, 181
Jones, Sarah – see Sarah (Perrin) Jones
Jones, Thomas, Newgate prisoner, 30n

## Index of Persons

Jones, William, of Trefollwyn Blas, 249–50, 284

Keeble, John, musician, 440n, 452–53
Kelway, Joseph, musician, 439–49, 452–60, 462, 465
Kempthorn, W., of St. Ives, 162
Kendrick, William, of London and Yorkshire, 177–78, 340
Keppel, Frederick, Dean of Windsor, 456n
Keymer, Timothy, of Norwich, 365, 371, 375, 382
Kilpatrick, Margaret, of Newcastle, 135
King, sister, of Bristol, 122
King, Rev. James, of St. Patrick's, Dublin, 272
Kingsbury, William, musician, 463
Kinsman, Andrew, of Tavistock and Plymouth, 185n, 202, 204, 211, 240
Kitchin, John, of Newcastle, 128
Knight, [Mr. ?], of London, 61–62
Knight, Titus, of Halifax, 328, 409
Knowls, Lionel, of Birstall, 175
Labee, Francis, of Bristol, 69, 90–91, 114, 116–18
Labee, Sarah, of Bristol, 74, 80–81, 114
Lambert, Anne, see Anne (Wesley) Lambert
Lambert, John Jr., CW's nephew, 72–73, 77, 88
Lambertson, John, of Leeds, 317
Lampe, Isabelle (Young), 297
Lampe, John Friedrich, musician, 297
Larwood, Samuel, itinerant, 185, 205, 284
La Trobe, Benjamin, Moravian preacher, 262

Launder, Eleanore, of St. Ives, 162
Lavington, Mrs. [Mary?], prophetess, 35–42, 52
Lavington, George, Bishop of Exeter, 377–78, 383–84
Leigh (or Lee), Joseph, of London, etc., 339
Lewin, Sweet, of London, 280, 284, 286
Ley, William, itinerant, 425–27, 430
Line, Mr., of Malmesbury, 68
Linley, Thomas, musician, 463
Lloyd, Jenny, of Bristol, 86–87
Lloyd, Rev. John, of Ryton, 136, 138n
Lloyd, Samuel, of London, 358–61
Lodge, Edmond, of Whickham, 137n
Loveybond, J., itinerant, 344
Low, Mrs., of Tyrrellspass, 295
Low, Counsellor [John?], of Tyrrellspass, 292
Lucas, Richard, itinerant, 394, 413
Luther, Martin, 256, 358
Lunell, William, of Dublin, 251, 297–98, 345

M., Mr., of Dublin, 264
M., Mary, of Newcastle, 135
MacDonald, Elizabeth, of London, 391
Machell, John, Newgate prisoner, 30n
Madan, Miss, in London, 455
Madan, Rev. Martin, of London, 443, 451, 453, 462, 464–66
Maddern, John, of Zennor, 218n, 280, 344–45
Manzuoli, Giovanni, musician, 445
Marcello, Benedetto, musician, 461n, 462
Marshall, "Nanny," of Epworth, 5, 20, 22

## Index of Persons

Martin, William, of Bristol, 90
Maskew, Jonathan, itinerant, 319
Mason, Betty, of Bristol, 121
(Towler) Mason, Mary, of Norwich, 365, 370–71, 375
Mason, Samuel, London printer, 93
Massey, Elizabeth ("Betty"), of Epworth, 26
Maw, Mrs. Catherine, of Epworth, 27
Maw, John, of Epworth, 20, 27
Matthews, William, of London / Bristol, 89–91
Maxfield, Thomas, itinerant, 44–55, 70, 74, 128n, 139, 208, 280, 354
May, Edward, of St. Ives, 162, 167
Meecham, Mrs., of Dublin, 266
Meglow, Mr., of Sandhutton (?), 143
Meriton, Rev. John, 225
Meyrick, Thomas, itinerant, 121n, 185, 223, 333
Micklethwait, Thomas, alderman of Leeds, 319n
Millar, sister, of London, 58
Milner, Rev. John, of Chipping, 328, 330–32, 335
Milner, Dr. Joseph, of Leeds, 315
Mitchell, Mr., of St. Ives, 172n
Mitchell, Thomas, of Bristol, 72
Mitchell, Thomas, itinerant, 325, 394
Mollen, Rev. Olaf, of Dublin, 256, 274
Molther, Rev. Philip Henry, 51, 53, 55, 66
Montagu, John, 4th Earl of Sandwich, 456n
Montague, Edward Wortley, of Newcastle, 132
Moore, Mrs., of Dublin, 278–79
Morgan, Rebecca, of Bristol and Plymouth, 121–22, 205, 210

Morgan, Rev. William, of Idbury, 45, 47–48
Morgan, [Mrs. William], 46–47, 56
Morris, Daniel, of Bristol, 116
Moss, Richard, of London, 185n, 280
Mottershead, Rev. Joseph, of Manchester, 336n
Mozart, Wolfgang Amadeus, musician, 463, 465
Mudge, Rev. Zachariah, of Stoke Damerel, 209n
Murgatroyd, Rev. John, of Leeds, 319
Murray, William, 1st Earl of Mansfield, 434–35

(Jacket) Nance, Joan, of St. Ives, 162
Nance, John, of St. Ives, 154, 163–64, 166, 168
Nares, Dr. James, composer, 466
Naul, Mr., town clerk of St. Ives, 161n, 162
Naylor, Joseph, of Leeds, 319n
Naylor, Mrs. Mary, of Bath, 356
Neal, Mrs., 337
Nelson, D., of Birstall, 409
Nelson, John, of Birstall and itinerant, 179, 184, 311–12, 315, 328, 332, 341, 346, 352–54, 394, 408–09, 414
Nelson, William, of Isle of Portland, 200
Newton, Rev. William, of Sithney, 222n
Nicolay, Frederick de, royal page, 457–58
Nisbet, Rev., of Dublin, 274
Node, Mr., of Rode, 193
(Oxford) Norman, Mary, of Bristol, 70, 84, 116
Norton, Anne, of Leeds, 310, 315, 317, 323–25, 330, 399, 402, 407–08

## Index of Persons

Norton, Sarah, of Bristol, 122
Nowyers, Edward, of London, 214

Ockershausen, John, 177
Okeley, Francis, of London, 39n, 41
Okeley, John, of London, 39n, 41
Oldfield, Thomas, of Bristol, 84, 90
Oldfield, Ann, of Bristol, 81n
Ord, brother, of Hexam, 324n
Ord, sister, of Hexam, 324n
Overton, Mrs., of Norwich, 386–87
Owen, Esther, of London, 64
Owen, John Sr., of Publow, 431–33
Owen, John Jr., of Publow, 431
Oxlee, William, of London, 40, 54, 60–61

Page, Mary-Anne, of Bristol, 123
Paterson, Mr., of Dublin, 255
Patrick, Mrs., of Plymouth Dock, 241
Paul, Thomas, of Norwich, 374–75
Paul, Thomas, of St. Ives, 162, 165
Pearce, brother, of Sheffield, 152
Pearce, Richard, of Bradford-on-Avon, 198, 347
Pergolesi, Giovanni Battista, 440, 444
(Perrin) Jones, Sarah, 56n, 78, 304, 308, 313, 315, 321, 323–25, 333, 337, 340n, 346–48, 436
Perronet, Charles, itinerant, 231n, 245, 250, 256, 261, 268, 270–71, 278, 280, 283–84, 352, 354, 357, 365, 367, 370, 379–81, 391, 414–15
(Clarke) Perronet, Duriah, of London, 359
Perronet, Edward, itinerant, 280, 353, 404
Perronet, Rev. Vincent, of Shoreham, 286, 344, 349–50, 360
Perrot, Ann, of Bristol, 47
Philips, Captain, of Wales, 189

Philips, Mr., of Manchester, 412
Phillips, Mrs., of London, 360
Phillips, Rev. Edward, of Maesmynis, 246–48, 300–01
Pitney, Mary, of London, 257
Polier, Rev. Jean-Antoine-Noé, of Lausanne, 316
Ponting, Mr., of Malmesbury, 68
Poppelstone, sister, of Plymouth, 242
Porthouse / Portrees, Mr., of Bristol, 70, 78, 91
(Edwards) Powell, Hannah, of Dublin, 262
Powell, Samuel, printer, of Dublin, 256, 259, 261–62, 274–74
Poyntz, Strode, of Shepton Mallet, 187n, 200n
Priestly, Matthew, of Leeds, 319
Provis, Richard, of Brea, 216n
Purcell, Henry, composer, 452, 459
Purdy, John, of London, 123
Purnell, Elizabeth, of Bristol, 70, 84, 104

R., Mr., of Coleorton, 149
Raby, Thomas, Newgate prisoner, 30n
Rattenbury, Mr., of Tavistock, 243
Rawlins, Mr., of Whickham, 137
Reddall, John, of London, 280n
Redford, Sarah, of London, 63
Reed, Thomas, 111
Reeves, Jonathan, itinerant, 280, 318, 323–24, 328, 332, 352–53
Reynolds, George, of Kingswood, 57
Reynolds, John, of Kingswood, 57
Ricard, Mrs., of London, 63
Rich, Priscilla (Wilford), of London, 281, 452
Richards, Thomas, itinerant, 50n, 67n, 69–73, 77n, 83n, 88–89, 117–18, 122, 139, 238

Richardson, Ann ("Hannah"), of Bristol, 96–105, 111
Richer, John, of Norwich, 374–75
Rider, Mrs., of Manchester, 336, 412
Ridley, Richard, of London, 71
Rigby, Mrs., of London, 40
Rigby, Sarah, of Bristol, 121
Ripton, Sir George, Lord Mayor of Dublin, 264n, 282n
Robarts, William, itinerant, 394
Robertson, John, M.D., of Pitscombe, 200
Robinson, Mrs., of Newcastle, 126
Robson, John, of Oxford, 41, 67–68, 77
Rogers, brother, of Bristol, 195
Rogers, Rev. Jacob, 150
Rogers, Nelme, Bristol organist, 451–52
Rooke, Edmund, Bristol organist, 451
Rouquet, James, itinerant, 405
Rowdon, John, of Bristol, 122
Russell, John, of Guildford, 445
Rutter, Sarah, of Bristol, 82
Ryan, Elizabeth, of Bristol, 73

S., brother, of Bristol, 195
Sarson, Mr., of London, 419–20
Saunders, Rev. Henry, of Wednesbury, 306n
Savage, William, musician, 454
Sawyer, Thomas, of Leeds, 319n
Scarlatti, Domenico, 440, 443, 445, 452–54, 459, 462, 464–65
Scholey, Mr., of London, 40
Scholey, Mrs., of London, 40–41
Seaton, Mrs., of London, 56, 66, 73
Seddon, Rev. John, of Manchester, 336n
Sellers, Lydia, of London, 38
Sennet, John, of Bristol, 122

Seward, Benjamin, of Bengeworth, 43–46, 62
Seward, Mrs. Benjamin, of Bengeworth, 43–46
Seward, Henry, of Bengeworth, 43–46
Seward, Rev. Thomas, 45
Seward, William, of Badsey, 48, 72–73, 89–93, 115–17
Shafto, Elisabeth, of Newcastle, 131
Sharp, Richard, of Leeds, 319n
Sheen, sister, of Bristol, 122
Shent, William, of Leeds, 169, 310, 317–18, 325, 328, 331–34, 341, 346, 352–54, 394, 397, 399, 402–03, 407, 414
Shepherd, William, itinerant, 154, 156, 182, 184, 202, 224, 234, 239
Sheppard, Dr. Edward, of Bath, 456n
Shute, Lucy, of Bristol, 87
Silby, sister, of Bradford-on-Avon, 347
Simpson, John, of London, 51, 54, 58–60, 66–68, 72, 77
Sims, Peter, of London, 109
Skelton, Charles, itinerant, 273, 284, 341, 405
Smalley, Mr., of Ireland, 274
Smith, brother, of Horsley, 324
Smith, John Christopher, musician, 454, 467
Smith, Lucretia, of Bristol, 69, 73n, 76, 80n
Smith, Mary, of Bristol, 123
Smith, Nanny, of Bristol, 69
Smith, Sarah, of Bristol, 121
Smithson, Robert, of Leeds, 319n
Snig, Mr., 426
Soane, Martha, of London, 53
Sparks, Mr., of London, 31
Sparrow, Jane, of Lewisham, 64

*Index of Persons*

Spenser, Blacky, of Skircoat Green, 332–33
Spring, Elizabeth, of London, 58
Spring, Lucy, of London, 58
Stanhope, William, 1st Earl of Harrington, 263n, 282n
Stanley, John, musician, 451, 453, 464
Stanton, William, of London, 64
Star, Mr., of Way Wick, 183–84
Stedder, Mr. of Bristol, 90
Stephens, Mrs., of Plymouth Dock, 208, 241
Stephens, Kath., of Bristol, 122n
Stirt, Margaret, of Newcastle, 131
Stokes, Mr., of Bristol?, 432
Stone, William, of Shepton Mallet, 187, 200
Stonehouse, Rev. George, of Islington, 59
Stork, Benjamin, of Leeds, 314, 399, 407
Story, Elizabeth, of London, 302–03
Stretton, Mary, of London, 72
Sumpsion, Mr., of South Wraxall, 193
Swail, sister, of Bristol, 121
Swindells, Robert, itinerant, 295, 327–28, 332, 335, 337
Sylvester, William, Newgate prisoner, 30n
Symes, Rev. Richard, of Bristol, 355n
Symonds, Rev. William, of St. Ives, 154n, 159, 164, 171

Taylor, David, of Sheffield, 150
Taylor, Rev. John, of Norwich, 378, 384
Taylor, Mary, of Bristol, 122
Taylor, Rev. Samuel, of Quinton, 142, 144–45, 196
Taylor, Mrs. Samuel, of Quinton, 145

Th., Miss, of Thirsk, 400
Thomas à Kempis, 258, 261, 317
Thomas, Mr., of Sithney, 215
Thomas, Jonathan, Newgate prisoner, 30n, 31–34
Thomas, Mary, of Bristol, 123
Thomson, Rev. George, of St. Gennys, 184, 239, 244
Thornton, Henry, of Leeds, 285, 315, 403
Thorpe, John, of Rotherham, 392
Tillotson, John, author, 130
Todd, W., of Newcastle, 131
Tomlinson, Rev. Richard, of Whickham, 137n
Towers, Robert, of Leeds, 326, 407
Trathen, David, itinerant, 327–28, 332, 336, 341, 344
Treadway, Mr., violinist, 466
Trembath, John, itinerant, 187, 201, 211, 220, 223–24, 238, 244, 250–51, 265, 269–70, 273, 283–84, 301, 353
Trounce, Captain, of Tolcarn, 221
Tucker, Joseph, itinerant, 403, 413–14
Turner, Captain Joseph, of Bristol, 75n, 153
Turner, Mrs. Joseph, of Bristol, 75, 84
Turpine, Mr., of Epworth, 22

Upton, Joseph, Newgate prisoner, 30n
Upton, William, of Leeds, 319n
Ustick, Stephen, of Botallack, 225, 227, 229

Veal, sister, of Plymouth, 242
Vento, Mattia, composer, 453
Verine, Sarah, of London, 302–03
Verney, brother, of Dublin, 270
Vicary, sister, of Bristol, 122

## Index of Persons

(Stafford) Vigor, Elizabeth, of Bristol, 313, 360, 362
Viney, Richard, of London, 48, 69

W., Hanna, of Bristol, 87
Wache, Mr., of Ireland, 289
Wade, Mrs., of Killavalley, Tyrrellspass, 289
Wade, William, of Killavalley, Tyrrellspass, 289n, 295
Walker, Francis, itinerant, 304–05
Walker, Rev. Samuel, of Truro, 414
Walker, Thomas, of Birmingham, 308n
Walker, Thomas, potential itinerant, 339
Walker, W., of Birstall, 175
Walker, William, mayor of Dublin, 263n, 282
Waller, James, of London, 190, 199, 204n, 209–10, 215n, 220n, 222, 229, 239
Walsh, Thomas, itinerant, 391
Walters, Blanch, of Bristol, 121
Wanlas, Ann, of Newcastle, 131
Ward John, 2nd Viscount Dudley and Ward, 465
Watson, J., of Evesham, 395
Watson, James (?), itinerant, 341, 344
Watson, Matthew, of Leeds, 328
Watts, brother, in Ireland, 287
Watts, brother, of Wallbridge, 395
Watts, Isaac, hymn writer, 33–34, 334
Wayne, John, of Conham, 78, 84, 89
Webb, Thomas, itinerant, 327–28, 332, 335–36, 341, 344
Webster, Eleazer, itinerant, 326, 339, 341, 344, 409, 414
Wedmore, [sister?], of Bristol, 123
Wells, brother, of Bradford-on-Avon, 347

(Wesley) Harper, Anne ("Nancy"), of Epworth, 9–10, 17, 24–25, 72
Wesley, Charles Jr., 439–60, 462, 464–66
(Wesley) Harper, Emilia ("Emily"), of Epworth, 12–15, 16, 21–22, 345
Wesley, Garret Colley, 1st Earl of Mornington, 458
Wesley, Rev. John, 16–29, 30–34, 49, 57, 71, 76, 78, 82, 88, 91, 93, 94n, 101, 104, 106, 108–09, 116–17, 120, 127, 131, 135, 143, 146, 175, 185, 188, 195, 196, 205, 211, 214, 218, 221, 233, 238, 239, 244–47, 250–51, 262–63, 269, 275, 281, 283–86, 294, 313, 318, 326–27, 335, 340–50, 352–53, 355–63, 365–72, 376–84, 391–93, 406–07, 413, 415, 425–26, 428–30, 433, 434, 454
Wesley, Kezia ("Kezzy"), of Epworth, 14, 20, 24–25
(Wesley) Hall, Martha ("Patty"), of Epworth, 14, 36n, 66n, 303
Wesley, Mary ("Molly"), of Epworth, 20, 22–24
(Goldhawk/Vazeille) Wesley, Mary, 313, 356–57
Wesley, Mehetabel ("Hetty"), of Epworth, 9, 12, 14–15, 21, 24
Wesley, Rev. Samuel, father of CW, 6, 12–13
Wesley, Rev. Samuel Jr., brother of CW, 5–16
Wesley, Samuel, son of CW, 455–56, 459, 461–67
(Gwynne) Wesley, Sarah, 304, 313, 315, 325, 333, 355, 359–63, 416–17, 425, 431–32, 446
(Annesley) Wesley, Susanna, 5–9, 11, 16, 20–21, 71, 77
Wesley, Susanna Jr. ("Suky"), of Epworth, 9–11, 13, 15, 22–25, 28

## Index of Persons

Westell, Thomas, itinerant, 304, 313, 341
Whatley, George, Newgate prisoner, 30n
Wheatley, James, itinerant, 186n, 312n, 342, 344–47, 365–77, 379–83, 386–89, 397, 405
Wheeler, Mr., of Norwich, 374–75
White, Richard, Lord Mayor of Dublin, 251n
Whitefield, Rev. George, 35, 40, 52, 60, 62–63, 90–92, 104, 107–09, 113–18, 206, 208, 210, 240, 243, 305, 309, 372, 404–05, 407, 432, 436
Whitefield, Capt. James, 92
Whitehead, Esther, of Bristol, 123
Whitford, John, itinerant, 409, 412, 414
Wigginton, Ebenezer, of Bristol, 77, 188
Wildboar, Jonathan, of Bristol, 79, 81
Wilkinson, brother, of Newcastle, 128,
Wilkinson, Mrs., of Newcastle, 128
Wilkinson, Mr., of Dublin, 278
Wilkinson, Mr., of London, 63
Williams, Anne, of Bristol, 80n, 95, 121
Williams, Anthony, of Bristol, 72, 80n, 104n
Williams, David, Bristol organist, 463
Williams, Florence, of St. Ives, 162
Williams, Jane [Judith?], of Bristol, 122
Williams, Rev. Rice, of Llansantffraed-in-Elwell, 246
Williams, Thomas Sr., of Llanishen, 181
Williams, Thomas Jr., itinerant, 146, 154–57, 160–61, 164–71, 181, 251n, 276n, 278n, 285, 288–90, 293, 302n, 303, 348, 412
Williams, Willmot, of St. Ives, 162

Williams-Wynn, Sir Watkin, 4th Baronet, 465
Williamson, Rev. William, of York, 400–01
Willis, Thomas, of Conham/Bristol, 83n, 347n
Wilmot, Sir John Eardley, 464
Wilson, Mrs., of Bristol, 360
Wilson, Richard, of Leeds, 319
Wilson, Rev. Robert, of Tanfield, 139n
Windsor, Robert, of London, 365, 367, 379, 415
Winn, Rowland, 4th Baronet of Nostell Priory, 174, 17952
Winsor, [sister?], of Bristol, 121
Wise, Mr., French prophet, 35, 38, 40–41
(Harrison) Witham, Elizabeth, of London, 63, 275, 281n
Witham, Sarah, of London, 281n
Witham, Thomas, of London, 185, 281n
Woods, Joseph, of Birstall, 175–76, 178
Woolcock, James, of St. Ives, 162–63
Wooten, Elizabeth, of Bristol, 122n
Worgan, John, London organist, 441, 448, 451, 453–54
Worly, William, of Bristol, 72,
Wormill, William, of Leeds, 319n
Worth, Charles, of St. Ives, 163
Wynn, brother, near Painswick, 142

Y., Mr., of Newcastle, 137
Young, Mrs., of Dublin, 256
Young, Anne, of London, 55
Young, Edward, poet, 299, 363n, 377, 383

Zinzendorf, Count Nikolaus Ludwig von, 251, 253–54, 275–75, 402
Zouch, Rev. Charles, of Sandal Magna, 174–75, 178–79

# Index of Places

Aberford, Yorkshire, 403
Acomb, Yorkshire, 401
Ashby de la Zouch, Leicestershire, 396
Athlone, Co. Westmeath, Ireland, 289–90
Attleborough, Norfolk, 365, 379
Axminster, Devonshire, 201

Baildon, Yorkshire, 326
Bath, Somerset, 183, 190, 192, 194, 198, 240, 355–56, 362, 428, 439n, 452, 464
Bearfield, Wiltshire, 198
Bengeworth, Worcestershire, 43–46
Birmingham, Warwickshire, 142–43, 147, 308, 336–37, 395–96
Birstall, Yorkshire, 142–43, 175, 179, 311, 326, 332, 405, 408–09
Blackheath, Kent, 65
Bodmin, Cornwall, 153
Bolton, Lancashire, 335, 411, 414
Booth Bank, Yorkshire, 336
Bow, Devonshire, 153
Bradford, Yorkshire, 332, 409
Bradford-on-Avon, Wiltshire, 193
Braintree, Essex, 379
Bramley, Yorkshire, 404
Brentford, Middlesex, 185, 190, 245
Bristol, Gloucestershire, 67–71, 121–24, 142–43, 153, 181, 185–86, 190–98, 244, 301, 304, 355, 362–64, 392–95, 423–24, 428–33
  Baptist Mills, 114, 118, 181, 192, 194, 196, 199
  the Cupolas, 74, 83, 89
  the Downs, 196
  Horsefair (location of the New Room), 74n, 90, 190, 360
  Hotwells, 359, 380
  Malt-room (or Malt-house), 74, 81, 101
  Newgate prison, 191
  New Room (school house, the Room), 49n, 57, 74–75, 78–80, 87, 90–91, 109, 360, 363
  Rose Green, 83, 91
  Weavers' Hall, 190, 192
Builth Wells, Brecknockshire, 246–47
Burford, Oxfordshire, 245
Burnopfield, Co. Durham (Sheep Hill), 323

Castle Donington, Leicestershire, 149
Churchill, Somerset, 182
Coleford, Somerset, 199, 300n
Coleorton, Leicestershire, 149
Conham, Gloucestershire, 78, 84, 186 191–92, 194, 196–97
Coolalough (manor of Samuel Handy, Ireland), 292
Crockernwell, Devonshire, 202
Crowan, Cornwall, 215, 221, 223

Dolgellau, Merionethshire, 248
Donington Park (Huntingdon residence), 396
Downend, Gloucestershire, 104, 115

## Index of Places

Dublin, Ireland, 250–87, 296–98
   Dolphin's Barn, 266–72, 274, 278–79, 283–84, 285n, 287, 296–97
   Marlborough Street preaching room, 251, 255, 258, 261, 264, 268, 272, 274, 279, 283, 287
   Mary-bone Lane [now "Marrowbone"], 262, 265, 267, 270, 272
   Newgate prison, 250, 256, 268
   Oxmantown Green, 253, 258, 260, 262–65, 269–70, 272, 274, 282
   St. Patrick's cathedral, 253, 258–59, 272, 275, 287
   Skinner's Alley preaching room, 261–62, 271n, 273, 283, 285
Dudley, Worcestershire, 307
Duffield, Derbyshire, 309
Durham, Co. Durham, 317, 324

Epworth, Lincolnshire, 3–29 143, 325, 330
Evesham, Worcestershire, 46, 142, 144–45, 337, 339, 395
Exeter, Devonshire, 153, 202, 244

Ferryhill, Co. Durham, 143, 317
Frog Mill Inn, 245

Gauxholme, Lancashire, 411
Great Smeaton, Yorkshire, 317
Gwennap, Cornwall, 163, 211–13, 216, 220, 223–24, 229, 231–33, 235

Halifax, Yorkshire, 332, 409
Hanham Mount, Gloucestershire, 111
Haworth, Yorkshire, 333, 405, 410
Heamoor, Cornwall (Trewidden), 217
Heaton, Yorkshire, 174, 176
Hednesford, , Staffordshire, 337
Helston, Cornwall, 215–16, 222
Heptonstall, Yorkshire, 411

High Wycombe, Buckinghamshire, 245
Holyhead, Angelsey, 249, 261, 298
Horsley, Northumberland, 324
Hounslow, Middlesex, 361
Hungerford, Berkshire, 153
Hunslet, Yorkshire, 398, 403
Huntley, Gloucestershire, 245
Idbury, Oxfordshire, 47
Islington, Middlesex, 59, 429–30

Keighley, Yorkshire, 333, 409
Kendalshire (or Kendleshire), Gloucestershire, 95, 112, 118
Kenneggy Downs, Cornwall, 157, 167
Kilcock, Co. Kidare, Ireland, 287
Kingswood, Gloucestershire, 56, 74, 83, 94, 67, 103–04, 109, 111–12–14, 182, 186, 191, 195–96, 363
   Schoolhouse, 73n, 78, 84, 106–07, 109, 117, 393, 414
Kinnegad, Co. Westmeath, Ireland, 287
Knaresborough, Yorkshire, 143, 317
Knutsford, Cheshire, 336

Lakenham, Norfolk, 366–70, 377, 379–83, 387, 390
Land's End, Cornwall, 171
Laneast, Cornwall, 244
Launceston, Cornwall, 211
Leeds, Yorkshire, 142, 310–20, 325–32, 398–99, 402–07
Lewisham, Kent (home of the Blackwells), 64, 356, 359
Llandrindod Wells, Radnorshire, 246
Llanidloes, Montgomeryshire, 248
Llansantffraed-in-Elwell, Radnorshire, 247
London, 30–42, 50–66, 140–41, 143, 245, 338, 350–54, 356–61, 391, 416–21, 425–27, 439–67

## Index of Places

Foundery, 51–52, 54, 61–64, 66, 185, 245, 345, 350, 356–60, 424–25
Kennington Common, 53
Newgate prison, 30–34, 140
St. Paul's Cathedral, [50], 62, 466
Tyburn gallows, 32–34, cf. 271
Ludgvan, Cornwall, 212, 217, 222, 227, 232, 235

Machynlleth, Montgomeryshire, 248
Maesmynis, Brecknockshire, 246–47
Malmesbury, Wiltshire, 68
Manchester, Lancashire, 336–37, 412–15
Marshfield, Gloucestershire, 153
Melbourne, Derbyshire, 142, 148–49
Misterton, Nottinghamshire, 325
Mitchell, Cornwall, 153
Moate, Co. Westmeath, Ireland, 291–92
Morvah, Cornwall, 160–61, 217–18, 229
Mytholmroyd, Yorkshire (Ewood Hall), 333–34, 411

Nether Westcote, Oxfordshire, 46–48
Newbury, Berkshire, 356, 361
Newcastle-under-Lyme, Staffordshire, 336
Newcastle upon Tyne, Northumberland, 125–39, 143, 318–24
　Keelmen's Hospital, 132–34, 136, 138–39
　Newgate prison, 126, 133, 136–37, 322–23
　Orphan House, 126n, 322
　Sandgate, 128–29, 134, 137, 322
New Passage (near Pilning, Gloucestershire), 181

Newport, Gloucestershire, 304
Norwich, Norfolk, 365–90
　Bell Inn (on Orford Hill), 369, 378, 385
　Hog Hill (now Timberhill), 367–68, 377, 385, 387, 389
　Norwich Cathedral, 367, 386, 389
　Tabernacle (Wheatley's preaching house), 372–74, 376, 382–83, 386–87
Nottingham, Nottinghamshire, 142–43, 149–50, 339, 396

Oakhill, Somerset, 188, 199
Oxford, Oxfordshire, 49, 67, 72

Painswick, Gloucestershire, 142, 145
Paulton, Somerset, 301
Penponds, Cornwall, 220, 232
Pensford, Gloucestershire, 431
Penshaw, Co. Durham, 323
Philipstown, Co. Offaly, 293, 295
Pitcombe, Somerset, 200
Plymouth, Devonshire, 205–10, 220, 229, 237–38, 240–43
　Tabernacle (preaching house), 206–07, 240–41
Plymouth Dock, Devonshire, 207–08, 241–42
Pool, Cornwall, 157, 169
Portland, Isle of, Dorsetshire, 200–201
Publow, Gloucestershire, 199

Quinton, Worcestershire, 142, 144

Reading, Berkshire, 361
Redruth, Cornwall, 154, 163, 217, 221–23, 232
Rhayader, Radnorshire, 247
Rosewarne, Cornwall, 220n, 232n
Ross-on-Wye, Herefordshire, 304
Rotherham, Yorkshire, 309, 397
Rothwell, Yorkshire, 404
Ryton, Co. Durham, 135–36, 138

## Index of Places

St. Gennys, Cornwall, 238, 244
St. Hilary (Downs), Cornwall, 160, 172
St. Ives, Cornwall, 153–73, 213–20, 223–24, 231–235
Salt Hill, Berkshire, 361
Sandhutton, Yorkshire, 143, 317
Sandy Lane, Wiltshire, 190
Seacroft, Yorkshire, 327, 402–04
Sheffield, Yorkshire, 142, 150–52, 309–10, 396–97
Shepton Mallet, Somerset, 187, 199–200
Sherborne, Devonshire, 200
Shoreham, Kent, 344, 350
Siston, Gloucestershire, 112
Sithney, Cornwall, 215, 222, 232
Skircoat Green, Yorkshire, 332
Slough, Berkshire, 185
South Wraxall, Wiltshire, 193, 198
Southwell, Dorsetshire, 201
Sticklepath, Devonshire, 202, 211
Stithians, Cornwall, 212–13, 216, 221
Stockport, Cheshire, 336
Stoke Damerel, Devonshire, 209n
Stoke Newington, Middlesex, 345
Stroud, Gloucestershire, 142, 144, 395n
Studley, Warwickshire, 337, 395, 432
Sunderland, Co. Durham, 321–22
Swalwell, Co. Durham, 125, 132, 134
Sykehouse, Yorkshire, 325

Tadcaster, Yorkshire, 402
Talke ('Talk o' th' Hill), Staffordshire, 336
Tanfield, Co. Durham, 127, 139
Tanfield Lea, Co. Durham, 127n
Tan-y-Bwlch, Merionethshire, 248
Tavistock, Devonshire, 202, 204–05, 210, 220, 238, 240, 243

Teams, Co. Durham, 132
Thirsk, Yorkshire, 143n, 324
Thorpe Hesley, Yorkshire (Barley Hall), 142, 309, 397
Tipton (Green), Staffordshire, 305, 307
Topcliffe, Yorkshire, 317
Towednack, Cornwall, 154, 164
Trageare, Cornwall, 239
Tresmeer, Cornwall, 211, 244
Tullamore, Co. Offaly, Ireland, 277, 293
Tyrrellspass, Co. Westmeath, Ireland, 276–77, 287–88, 292–95

Wakefield, Yorkshire, 174–80, 310, 326, 408
Walsall, Staffordshire, 142, 146–48
Way Wick, Somerset, 183
Wednesbury, Staffordshire, 142–43, 145–48, 305–08, 337
Wendron, Cornwall, 216, 221
West Bromwich, Staffordshire, 306
Westerleigh, Gloucestershire, 94
Westminster, Middlesex,
   St. James's Palace, 440, 456
   Buckingham Palace, 457
Whickham, Co. Durham, 137
Whitecoat-Hill, Yorkshire, 319
Windhill, Yorkshire, 326
Windsor, Berkshire [castle and St. George's chapel], 456–60
Woolhampton, Berkshire, 190
Worcester, Worcestershire, 304–05, 339

York, Yorkshire, 400

Zennor, Cornwall, 159, 171, 218, 227

# Index of Scripture References and Allusions

## Old Testament

**Genesis**
6:5 .......................... 97
9:6 .......................... 254
9:20–27 .................... 343
19 ........................... 152
22 ........................... 114
28:16 ....................... 202
32:24–31 .................. 287
32:26 ....................... 101
32:28 ....................... 101

**Exodus**
3:2 .......................... 226
5:4–5 ....................... 139
13:21–22 .................. 165
14:13 .............. 161, 367, 371
14:19–20 .................. 206
40:35 ....................... 192

**Leviticus**
26:4–5 ..................... 200

**Numbers**
9:15–23 .................... 309
9:18 ........................ 192
13:30 ....................... 109

13:31 ....................... 109
16:1–35 .................... 343
22:21–38 .................. 322
23:10 ....................... 195
23:21 ................. 113, 400

**Deuteronomy**
29:29 ......................... 9
33:25 ................. 153, 272
33:26–27 ................... 171

**Joshua**
6 ............................ 113
7 ............................ 115
22:6 ........................ 227

**Judges**
17:6 ........................ 151

**Ruth**
1:16 ........................ 208

**1 Samuel**
1:15 ......................... 96
3:19 ........................ 193
21:1–9 ..................... 286

## Index of Scripture References and Allusions

**2 Samuel**
7:18 . . . . . . . . . . . . . . . . . . . . . . . 235
16:5–6 . . . . . . . . . . . . . . . . . 169, 230
16:7 . . . . . . . . . . . . . . . . . . . . . . . . 46

**1 Kings**
3:16–28 . . . . . . . . . . . . . . . . . . . . 419
8:22–61 . . . . . . . . . . . . . . . . . . . . 109
18:21 . . . . . . . . . . . . . . . . . . . . . . . 60
18:24 . . . . . . . . . . . . . . . . . . . . . . . 61
18:38 . . . . . . . . . . . . . . . . . . . . . . 106
19:17 . . . . . . . . . . . . . . . . . . . . . . 309
21–22 . . . . . . . . . . . . . . . . . . . . . . 115

**2 Kings**
2:9 . . . . . . . . . . . . . . . . . . . . . . . 196
4:8–10 . . . . . . . . . . . . . . . . . . . . . 300
18:17–37 . . . . . . . . . . . . . . . . . . . 160
20:2 436

**1 Chronicles**
4:10 . . . . . . . . . . . . . . . . . . . . . . . 265

**2 Chronicles**
6 . . . . . . . . . . . . . . . . . . . . . . . 109

**Esther**
9:29–32 . . . . . . . . . . . . . . . . . . . . 103

**Job**
5:13 . . . . . . . . . . . . . . . 263, 282, 372
6:4 . . . . . . . . . . . . . . . . . . . . . . . 135
17:13 . . . . . . . . . . . . . . . . . . . . . . 310
19:25 . . . . . . . . . . . . . . . . . . . . . . 104
23:8–9 . . . . . . . . . . . . . . . . . . . . . . 97
30:1 108
38:11 . . . . . . . . . . . . . . . . . . . . . . 161
38:37 . . . . . . . . . . . . . . . . . . 132, 317

**Psalms**
2:12 . . . . . . . . . . . . . . . . . . . . . . . 119
5:9 . . . . . . . . . . . . . . . . . . . . . . . . 97
5:13 (BCP) . . . . . . . . . . . . . . . . . . 166

8:2 . . . . . . . . . . . . . . . . . . . . . . . 139
18:32–34 . . . . . . . . . . . . . . . . . . . 129
20:7 . . . . . . . . . . . . . . . . . . . . . . . 120
20:8 (BCP) . . . . . . . . . . . . . . . . . . 344
22:31 . . . . . . . . . . . . . . . . . . . . . . 267
23:4 . . . . . . . . . . . . . . . . . . . . . . . 111
27:16 (BCP) . . . . . . . . . . . . . . . . . 101
29:1 . . . . . . . . . . . . . . . . . . . . . . . . 62
32:7 . . . . . . . . . . . . . . . . . . . . . . . 171
46 . . . . . . . . . . . . . . . . . . . . . . . 358
46:1 . . . . . . . . . . . . . . . . . . . . . . . 171
46:8–9 . . . . . . . . . . . . . . . . . . . . . 410
48:9 . . . . . . . . . . . . . . . . . . . . . . . 196
50:15 (BCP) . . . . . . . . . . . . . . . . . 172
55:14 . . . . . . . . . . . . . . . . . . . . . . 202
59:9 (BCP) . . . . . . . . . . . . . . . . . . 150
60:4 (BCP) . . . . . . . . . . . . . . . . . . 120
63:1 . . . . . . . . . . . . . . . . . . . . . . . . 97
63:7 (BCP) . . . . . . . . . . . . . . 264, 282
65:7 . . . . . . . . . . . . . . . . . . . . . . . 168
68:30 . . . . . . . . . . . . . . . . . . 168, 179
74:13 (BCP) . . . . . . . . . . . . . 264, 282
74:22–24 (BCP) . . . . . . . . . . . . . . 230
76:10 . . . . . . . . . . . . . . . . . . . . . . 374
77:13 . . . . . . . . . . . . . . . . . . . . . . 119
77:15 . . . . . . . . . . . . . . . . . . . . . . 108
80 . . . . . . . . . . . . . . . . . . . . . . . 196
93:3 . . . . . . . . . . . . . . . . . . . . . . . 206
93:4 (BCP) . . . . . . . . . . . . . . 147, 150
96:7 (BCP) . . . . . . . . . . . . . . 129, 166
100 . . . . . . . . . . . . . . . . . . . . . . . 156
106:2 . . . . . . . . . . . . . . . . . . . . . . 171
109:31 . . . . . . . . . . . . . . . . . . . . . 176
115:1 . . . . . . . . . . . . . . . 51, 232, 312
118:16 (BCP) . . . . . . . . . . . . . . . . 166
118:23 . . . . . . . . . . . . . . . . . . . . . 368
118:24 . . . . . . . . . . . . . . . . . . . . . 192
118:26 . . . . . . . . . . . . . . . . . . . . . 111
119:99 . . . . . . . . . . . . . . . . . . . . . 123
119:126 (BCP) . . . . . . . . . . . . . . . 170
121:8 . . . . . . . . . . . . . . . . . . . . . . 318
122:1 . . . . . . . . . . . . . . . . . . . . . . 397
122:6–9 (BCP) . . . . . . . . . . . . . . . 391

*Psalms (continued)*
124:1–7 (BCP) ............... 170
124:7 ........................ 88
130 ........................ 72n

**Proverbs**
1:20ff. ..................... 192
3:6 .................... 132, 318
6:18 ....................... 168
11:25 ...................... 311
26:5 ........................ 45
26:16 ...................... 403
27:1 ........................ 45

**Song of Solomon**
2:16 ....................... 100
8:7 ........................ 149

**Isaiah**
1:5–6 ...................... 362
1:14 ....................... 122
1:16 .................. 201, 203
1:16–18 .................... 261
4:3–4 ...................... 113
8:20 ........................ 42
9:6 ........................ 337
11:6 ............. 157, 223, 290
19:4 ....................... 122
26:3 ....................... 165
26:4 ....................... 119
26:9 ....................... 409
30:21 ...................... 114
30:25 ...................... 252
32:1–2 ................ 378, 384
35 ....184, 207, 200, 294, 296, 301,
            332, 333, 377, 383
35:1 ....................... 229
35:1–10 .................... 185
35:3 .................. 189, 193
35:3–4 ................ 199, 311
35:6 ....................... 312
35:91 ....................... 36
35:10 ................. 213, 385

36 .................... 378, 384
36:1–37:13 ................. 160
40:1 ........ 160, 173, 211, 246, 270
40:1ff. .................... 252
40:1–2 ..................... 221
40:8 ........................ 99
40:31 ............. 103, 153, 188
41:17 ....................... 97
42:3–4 ..................... 103
43:2 ....................... 287
43:13 ...................... 368
43:22ff. .............. 372, 382
43:25ff. ............ 62, 132, 156
44:22 ...................... 325
44:25 ................. 263, 282
45:8 ....................... 196
45:15 ....................... 97
45:22 .......... 104, 132, 157, 375
45:24 ...................... 157
49:2 ....................... 165
49:15 ...................... 104
50:1 ....................... 107
50:7–8 ..................... 107
51:11 ...................... 377
51:14 ....................... 99
52:1 .................. 94, 297
52:3 ............. 60, 263, 370, 381
52:10 ........ 30, 108, 137, 166, 257
52:12 ...................... 156
53 ......................... 296
53:6 ....................... 215
54 ......................... 136
54:3–4 ..................... 136
54:4149
54:16–17 ................... 136
54:17 ...................... 153
55:1 ........ 54, 149, 184, 199, 216,
            248, 258, 276, 290, 309, 333
55:7 ....................... 388
55:11 ... 164, 194, 199, 212, 235, 401
57:16 ....................... 99
59:1 ........................ 59
60:8 ....................... 125

*Isaiah (continued)*
| | |
|---|---|
| 61 | 336, 370, 381 |
| 61:1 | 133, 137, 198, 217, 370, 381 |
| 61:1–3 | 370, 381 |
| 61:3 | 152 |
| 63:1 | 127, 167 |
| 64:5 | 401, 404, 411 |

**Jeremiah**
| | |
|---|---|
| 1:8 | 223 |
| 1:18 | 206, 226 |
| 2:24 | 216 |
| 3:3 | 372 |
| 7 | 158 |
| 7:2–28 | 159 |
| 9 | 160 |
| 15:20 | 240 |
| 16:19 | 73 |
| 23:28 | 326 |
| 23:28–29 | 137 |
| 23:29 | 87, 129, 156, 183, 197, 201, 389 |
| 33:3 | 133 |

**Lamentations**
| | |
|---|---|
| 1:12 | 183, 201, 207, 208, 215, 232, 244, 247, 253, 293, 296, 335, 336 |

**Ezekiel**
| | |
|---|---|
| 9 | 271, 411 |
| 16 | 75 |
| 16:1 | 133 |
| 22:30 | 170 |
| 33:1–6 | 396 (2), 404, 410 (2) |
| 37 | 128 |
| 37:1–14 | 420 |
| 37:3 | 190 |
| 37:4 | 62 |

**Daniel**
| | |
|---|---|
| 6:22 | 156, 170 |
| 9:24 | 95 |
| 9:25 | 108 |
| 9:26 | 95 |
| 12:12–13 | 102 |

**Hosea**
| | |
|---|---|
| 2:14 | 96 |
| 6:1 | 194 |
| 6:1–3 | 94 |
| 6:3 | 98 |
| 11:4 | 85 |
| 13:9 | 125, 160, 209, 221, 232, 293, 369, 380 |
| 13:14 | 374 |
| 14:1 | 377, 384 |
| 14:4 | 192 |
| 14:6 | 100 |
| 14:8 | 231 |

**Amos**
| | |
|---|---|
| 4:11 | 357 |

**Micah**
| | |
|---|---|
| 6:6 | 388 |
| 7:8 | 39 |
| 7:18–19 | 158 |

**Habakkuk**
| | |
|---|---|
| 3 | 400 |
| 3:2 | 399, 409 |

**Zephaniah**
| | |
|---|---|
| 1:12 | 122 |

**Zechariah**
| | |
|---|---|
| 3:2 | 357 |
| 4:9 | 311 |
| 12:10 | 215, 241, 279, 373, 406 |
| 13:6 | 207, 233 |
| 13:7–9 | 211, 318, 396, 401 |
| 13:9 | 259, 397, 407, 408 |

**Malachi**
| | |
|---|---|
| 3:7 | 317 |
| 4:2 | 128, 221 |

# Apocrypha

**Wisdom of Solomon**
5 ........................ 409
5:14 ........................ 96

# New Testament

**Matthew**
1:21 .... 113, 154, 194, 198, 252, 388
3:7 ........................ 195
3:8 .................... 134, 386
3:12 ........................ 219
4:4 ........................ 135
5:1–12 .............. 47, 138, 173
5:3 .................... 233, 374
5:3ff. ........................ 385
5:4–6 ........................ 241
5:11 .................... 154, 159
5:13 ........................ 314
5:20 ........................ 55
5:25–26 ...................... 30
5:39 .................... 134, 148
5:40 ........................ 432
6:10 ........................ 398
6:13 .................... 113, 308
6:24 ........................ 151
7:7 ........ 198, 235, 244, 374, 383
7:8 ........................ 98
7:12 ........................ 273
7:15 .................... 40, 184
7:15–16 ................ 137, 155
7:16 ........................ 137
7:20 ........................ 40
7:22 ........................ 112
7:24–27 ...................... 408
7:25 ........................ 251
8:28 ........................ 154
9:1–9 ........................ 127
9:12 ........................ 241
9:20–22 ...................... 115
9:29 ........................ 30
9:36 .................... 131, 215
9:38 .................... 197, 344
10:14 ........................ 156
10:16–22 ................ 150, 168
10:22 .................... 229, 409
10:28 ........................ 162
11:5ff. ...... 149, 187, 204, 212, 350
11:12 ........................ 197
11:15 ........................ 187
11:28 .......... 134, 149, 155, 183,
    202, 207, 217, 246, 258, 389
11:28–30 ................ 218, 289
11:29 ........................ 182
13:25 ........................ 405
13:41 ........................ 219
13:46 ........................ 266
14:27 ........................ 221
14:30 ........................ 165
15:14 ........................ 191
15:22–28 ................ 125, 146
15:28 ........................ 125
16:24 ........................ 114
17:4 ........................ 192
17:21 ........................ 239
18:7 .................... 63, 403
19:6 ........................ 40
19:26 ........................ 129
19:30 .................. 46, 84, 221
20:12 ........................ 158
21:9 ................ 111, 144, 190
21:15 ........................ 144
21:16 ........................ 312
21:28–32 ...................... 288
22:1–6 ........................ 230

## Matthew (continued)

| Verse | Page |
|---|---|
| 22:21 | 172 |
| 23:2 | 83 |
| 23:39 | 111 |
| 24:15 | 221 |
| 24:27 | 99 |
| 24:30–33 | 160 |
| 24:40 | 298 |
| 25 | 267 |
| 25:6 | 109 |
| 25:1–13 | 197 |
| 25:30 | 357 |
| 27:25 | 200, 398, 399 |
| 27:46 | 99 |
| 28:20 | 39, 133 |

## Mark

| Verse | Page |
|---|---|
| 1:15 | 145, 147, 159, 239, 261, 266, 272, 324, 401 |
| 2:1ff. | 389 |
| 2:10 | 55 |
| 2:12 | 106 |
| 2:17 | 220, 240, 241 |
| 3:27 | 54, 60 |
| 5:1–13 | 152 |
| 5:15 | 85 |
| 5:25–34 | 115, 164 |
| 5:36 | 173 |
| 8:34 | 112 |
| 8:36 | 385 |
| 9:24 | 76 |
| 10:46–52 | 51, 157, 222, 264, 386 |
| 11:9 | 111 |
| 13:13 | 409 |
| 13:37 | 407 |
| 15:34 | 99 |

## Luke

| Verse | Page |
|---|---|
| 1:6 | 98, 386 |
| 1:46–47 | 132 |
| 1:77 | 146 |
| 2:25–32 | 201, 337 |
| 2:29 | 168 |
| 2:37 | 112 |
| 3:17 | 219 |
| 4:4 | 135 |
| 4:18 | 47, 137, 188 |
| 5 | 367 |
| 6:40 | 114 |
| 6:45 | 182 |
| 7:22 | 293 |
| 7:36–50 | 247 |
| 7:41–42 | 160 |
| 7:42 | 152 |
| 7:47 | 152 |
| 8:40–56 | 115 |
| 9:23 | 145, 224 |
| 9:50 | 154 |
| 9:55 | 112 |
| 10:29–37 | 48, 159, 160, 209, 223, 227, 246, 268, 292 |
| 10:37 | 98 |
| 10:42 | 74, 135, 186, 373 |
| 11:2 | 398 |
| 11:9 | 374, 383 |
| 12:8 | 149 |
| 12:12 | 147 |
| 12:19 | 266, 267 |
| 12:32 | 375, 387 |
| 12:49 | 95 |
| 13:3, 5 | 368 |
| 13:6–9 | 372, 382 |
| 13:11–17 | 231 |
| 13:30 | 122, 123 |
| 13:35 | 111 |
| 14:15–24 | 56, 126, 169, 186, 232, 247, 292, 386 |
| 14:17 | 138, 144, 186 |
| 14:21 | 138 |
| 14:23 | 159, 169, 204 |
| 15:7 | 126 |
| 15:11–32 | 163, 204, 247, 265, 293, 376 |
| 15:18 | 163 |
| 17:24 | 99 |
| 17:34–36 | 298 |

*Luke (continued)*
18:1–8 . . . . . . . . . . . . . . . . . . . . . 215
18:4 . . . . . . . . . . . . . . . . . . . . . . . 257
18:13 . . . . . . . . . . . . . . . . . . . . . . 357
18:22 . . . . . . . . . . . . . . . . . . . . . . 111
19:7 . . . . . . . . . . . . . . . . . . . . . . . 148
19:9 . . . . . . . . . . . . . . . . . . . . . . . 270
19:40 . . . . . . . . . . . . . . . . . . . . . . 191
21:15 . . . . . . . . . . . . . . . . . . . . . . 184
21:19 . . . . . . . . . . . . . . . . . . . . . . 164
21:28 . . . . . . . . . . . 398, 404, 405, 412
21:34–36 . . . . . . . . . . . . . 395, 404 (2)
22:19 . . . . . . . . . . . . . . . . . . . . . . 287
22:32 . . . . . . . . . . . . . . . . . . . . . . . 39
23:33–43 . . . . . . . . . . . . . . . . . . . . 31
23:42–43 . . . . . . . . . . . . . . . . . . . 111
23:43 . . . . . . . . . . . . . . . . . . . 32, 102
23:46 . . . . . . . . . . . . . . . . . . . . . . 276
24:47 . . . . . . . . . . . . . . . . . . 314, 318

**John**
1:12 . . . . . . . . . . . . . . . . . . . . . . . 275
1:29 . . . . . . . .157, 182, 188, 232, 248,
260, 289, 306, 311, 314, 321,
324, 333, 396, 401, 402, 411
1:50 . . . . . . . . . . . . . . . . . . . . . . . 309
3 . . . . . . . . . . . . . . . . . . . . . . . 137
3:9 . . . . . . . . . . . . . . . . . . . . . . . . 96
3:14 . . . . . . . . . . . . . . . . . . . . . . . 216
3:16 . . . . . . . . . . . . . . . . . . . . . . . . 79
3:29 . . . . . . . . . . . . . . . . . . . . . . . 152
4 . . . . . . . . . . . . . . . . . . . 126, 131
4:32 . . . . . . . . . . . . . . . . . . . . . . . . 47
4:35 . . . . . . . . . . . . . . . . . . . . . . . 410
4:35–36 . . . . . . . . . . . . . . . . . . . . 245
5:1–15 . . . . . . . . . 136, 152, 279, 295
5:3 . . . . . . . . . . . . . . . . . . . . . . . 292
5:25 . . . . . . . . . . . . . . . . . . . . . . . 135
5:40 . . . . . . . . . . . . . . . . . . . . . . . . 76
6:37 . . . . . . . . . . . . . . . . . . . 262, 307
6:44 . . . . . . . . . . . . . . . . . . . . . . . . 51
6:67 . . . . . . . . . . . . . . . . . . . . . . . 218
7:6 . . . . . . . . . . . . . . . . . . . . . . . 165

8 . . . . . . . . . . . . . . . . . . . . . . . 159
8:6 . . . . . . . . . . . . . . . . . . . . . . . . 74
8:11 . . . . . . . . . . . . . . . . . . . . . . . 327
8:31 . . . . . . . . . . . . . . . . . . . . . . . 408
8:39 . . . . . . . . . . . . . . . . . . . . . . . . 84
8:46 . . . . . . . . . . . . . . . . . . . . . . . 310
9 . . . . . . . . . . . . . . . . . . . . . . . 160
9:11 . . . . . . . . . . . . . . . . . . . . . . . 156
9:24 . . . . . . . . . . . . . . . . . . . . . . . . 63
10:4–5 . . . . . . . . . . . . . . . . . . . . . . 51
10:9 . . . . . . . . . . . . . . . . . . . 193, 215
10:10 . . . 192, 247, 266, 274, 371, 382
10:12 . . . . . . . . . . . . . . . . . . . . . . . 52
11:25 . . . . . . . . . . . . . . . . . . . . . . 100
11:31 . . . . . . . . . . . . . . . . . . . . . . 420
11:35 . . . . . . . . . . . . . . . . . . . . . . . 46
12:32 . . . . . . . . . . . . . . . . . . . . . . 269
14:1–2 . . . . . . . . . . . . . . . . . . . . . 210
14:1–3 . . . . . . . . . . . . . . . . . 360, 363
14:6 . . . . . . . . . . . . . . . . . . . . 74, 385
14:13 . . . . . . . . . . . . . . . . . . 145, 170
14:15 . . . . . . . . . . . . . . . . . . . . . . 208
14:27 . . . . . . . . . . . . . . . . . . 135, 374
15:18–27 . . . . . . . . . . . . . . . . . . . 171
16:7 . . . . . . . . . . . . . . . . . . . . . . . . 86
16:33 . . . . . . . . . . . . . . . . . . . . . . 101
19:30 . . . . . . . . . . . . . . . 34, 102, 127
20:25 . . . . . . . . . . . . . . . . . . . . . . . 37
21:6 . . . . . . . . . . . . . . . . . . . . . . . 138

**Acts**
1:4–5 . . . . . . . . . . . . . . . . . . . 78, 148
2:37–39 . . . . . .136, 148 (2), 181, 186,
206, 215, 216, 332, 336
2:40 . . . . . . . . . . . . . . . . . 164, 201, 230
2:42 . . . . . . . . . . . . . . . . . 308, 311, 409
2:42ff. . . . . . . . . . . . . . . . . . . 68, 79, 83
2:46 . . . . . . . . . . . . . . . . . . . . . . . . 79
3:19 . . . . . . . . . . . . . . 132, 197, 212, 235
3:26 . . . . . . . . . . . . . . . . . . . . . . . 247
4:36 . . . . . . . . . . . . . . . . . . . . . . . 357
5:34–36 . . . . . . . . . . . . . . . . . . . . 137
7:51 . . . . . . . . . . . . . . . . . . . . . . . . 87

# Index of Scripture References and Allusions

*Acts (continued)*
7:60 . . . . . . . . . . . . . . . . . . . . . . . 159
8:2 . . . . . . . . . . . . . . . . . . . . . . . 108
9:4 . . . . . . . . . . . . . . . . . . . . . . . 228
13:6–9 . . . . . . . . . . . . . . . . . . . . . 90
13:38 . . . . . . . . . . . . . . 134, 171, 198
13:40–41 . . . . . . . . . . . . . . . 100, 250
14:3 . . . . . . . . . . . . . . . . . . . 190, 274
14:22 . . . . . . . . . . . . . . . . . . 148, 315
16:20 . . . . . . . . . . . . . . . . . . . . . . 159
16:30 . . . . . . . . . . . . . . . . . . . . . . 222
17:6 . . . . . . . . . . . . . . . . . . . . . . . 146
17:11 . . . . . . . . . . . . . . . . . . . . . . 148
19:2 . . . . . . . . . . . . . . . . . . . . . . . 149
19:38 . . . . . . . . . . . . . . . . . . . . . . . 44
20:21 . . . . . . . . . . . . . . . . . . . . . . 246
20:24 . . . . . . . . . . . . . . . . . . . . . . 147
20:32 . . . . . . . . . . 201, 235, 395, 410
24:16 . . . . . . . . . . . . . . . . . . 172, 273
24:25 . . . . . . . . . . . . . . . . . . 135, 198
26:18 . . . . . . . . . . . . . . . . . . 134, 222
27:22ff. . . . . . . . . . . . . . . . . . . . . . 227
28:27–28 . . . . . . . . . . . . . . . . . . . 103

**Romans**
3:26 . . . . . . . . . . . . . . . . . . . . . . . 332
6 . . . . . . . . . . . . . . . . . . . . . . . . . . 38
6:8 . . . . . . . . . . . . . . . . . . . . . . . 112
7 . . . . . . . . . . . . . . . . . . . . . . 48, 68
7:13 . . . . . . . . . . . . . . . . . . . . . . . . 97
7:14 . . . . . . . . . . . . . . . . . . . . . . . 127
8:16 . . . . . . . . . . . . . . . . . . . 102, 131
8:26 . . . . . . . . . . . . . 54, 59, 102, 191
8:27 . . . . . . . . . . . . . . . . . . . 159, 192
8:28 . . . . . . . . . . . . . . . 263, 282, 359
8:31–32 . . . . . . . . . . . . . . . . . . . . 226
8:32 . . . . . . . . . . . . . . . . . . . . . . . 376
8:35 . . . . . . . . . . . . . . . . . . . . . . . 256
8:38–39 . . . . . . . . . . . . . . . . . . . . 242
9 . . . . . . . . . . . . . . . . . . . . . . . . . . 81
9:25 . . . . . . . . . . . . . . . . . . . . . . . 158
9:28 . . . . . . . . . . . . . . . 104, 112, 131
9:32 . . . . . . . . . . . . . . . . . . . . . . . . 96

11:20 . . . . . . . . . . . . . . . . . . . . . . . 75
12:18 . . . . . . . . . . . . . . . . . . . . . . 402
13:1 . . . . . . . . . . . . . . . . . . . . . . . 172
14:17 . . . . . . . . . . . . . . . . . . 369, 380
15:13 . . . . . . . . . . . . . . . . . . . . . . 128
16:20 . . . . . . . . . . . . . . . . . . . . . . . 39

**1 Corinthians**
1:12 . . . . . . . . . . . . . . . . . . . . . . . . 55
1:13 . . . . . . . . . . . . . . . . . . . . . . . 108
1:25 . . . . . . . . . . . . . . . . . . . . . . . 108
1:30 . . . . . . . . . . . . . . . . . . . . . . . . 53
1:31 . . . . . . . . . . . . . . . . . . . . . . . 194
2:1–2 . . . . . . . . . . . . . . . . . . 145, 146
2:2 . . . . . . . . . . . . . . . . . . . . 197, 253
2:5 . . . . . . . . . . . . . . . . . . . . . . . . 123
2:15 . . . . . . . . . . . . . . . . . . . . . 44, 55
3:4 . . . . . . . . . . . . . . . . . . . . . . . . . 55
3:11 . . . . . . . . . . . . . . . . . . . . . . . 261
3:15 . . . . . . . . . . . . . . . . . . . . . . . 324
3:22 . . . . . . . . . . . . . . . . . . . . . . . 100
4:7 . . . . . . . . . . . . . . . . . . . . . . . . 367
6:9–11 . . . . . . . . . . . . . . . . . 127, 129
7[:8] . . . . . . . . . . . . . . . . . . . . . . . . 37
7:16 . . . . . . . . . . . . . . . . . . . . . . . 111
9:12 . . . . . . . . . . . . . . . . . . . . . . . 164
9:27 . . . . . . . . . . . . . . . . . . . . . . . 101
10:12 . . . . . . . . . . . . . . . 75, 242, 251
10:13 . . . . . . . . . . . . . . . . . . . . . . 172
10:16 . . . . . . . . . . . . . . . . . . . . . . 186
10:31 . . . . . . . . . . . . . . . . . . . . . . 223
11:1 . . . . . . . . . . . . . . . . . . . . . . . 104
11:26 . . . . . . . . . . . . . . . . . . . . . . 186
12:6–9 . . . . . . . . . . . . . . . . . . . . . 136
13:7–8 . . . . . . . . . . . . . . 181, 399, 431
13:12 . . . . . . . . . . . . . . . . . . . . . . 112
14:40 . . . . . . . . . . . . . . . . . . . . . . 324
15:7 . . . . . . . . . . . . . . . . . . . . . . . 138
15:32 . . . . . . . . . . . . . . . . . . . . . . 147
15:52 . . . . . . . . . . . . . . . . . . . . . . 198
15:57 . . . . . . . . . . . . . . . 120, 320, 386
16:14 . . . . . . . . . . . . . . . . . . . . . . 405

## 2 Corinthians
4:7 ........................ 172
4:8–9 ........................ 98
5:1 ........................ 164
5:14 ........................ 155
5:17–18 ............ 68, 76, 84, 100
5:19 ........................ 354
5:20 ........................ 147
6:1 ........................ 112
6:4–10 ........................ 167
11:26 ........................ 251
12:7–9 ........................ 39
12:9 .............. 172, 188, 288
13:1 ................. 369, 380
13:5 ........................ 153

## Galatians
3:1 .................... 50, 135
3:13 ........................ 323
5:6 ........................ 54
5:7 ........................ 192

## Ephesians
1:7 .................... 65, 96
2:5 ........................ 325
4:1 .................. 196, 221
5:27 ........................ 219
6:10 ........................ 108
6:11–17 ........................ 107
6:12 ........................ 39
6:13 ........................ 167
6:17 ........................ 151
6:19 ........................ 308

## Philippians
1:15 ........................ 311
1:25ff. ........................ 56
1:27 ........ 145, 193, 233, 273, 312
1:27–30 ........................ 314
2:9–10 ........................ 388
2:12 .................... 74, 221
2:16 ........................ 146
3:8 ........................ 307

3:9–10 ........................ 50
3:14 .................. 152, 198
3:18–19 ........................ 79
4:7 ........................ 126

## Colossians
1:14 ........................ 96

## 1 Thessalonians
2:4 ........................ 168
4:16 ........................ 262
5:11 ........................ 189
5:22 ........................ 273
5:23 .................. 100, 233

## 2 Thessalonians
2:3 ........................ 97
2:6–7 ........................ 333
2:7 .................. 144, 170

## 1 Timothy
1:3–11 ........................ 155
1:15–16 ......... 95, 150, 158, 173,
                               291, 389
2:12 ........................ 145
4:10 ........................ 104
6:12 ........................ 193

## 2 Timothy
1:7 ........................ 191
2:11 ........................ 112
2:12 ........................ 162
2:15 ........................ 47
4:5 ........................ 176
4:10 ........................ 297
4:17 ........................ 168

## Titus
2:10 .................... 75, 134
2:11–12 ............ 368, 401, 412

## Philemon
3 ................... 46
10–15 ................ 288

## Hebrews
4:9 ............ 76, 78, 218
4:12 ...... 47, 137, 145, 189, 191
4:14–16 ............ 241, 389
4:16 ........ .212, 307, 308, 310, 323, 325
6:5 ............... 186, 234
6:11 ................... 197
9:12 ................... 191
10:9 ................ 67, 147
10:24 .................. 207
10:37 ................... 99
11:4 ................... 105
11:27–29 ............... 257
12:1–2 .............. 229, 307
12:2 ................ 58, 112
12:3 ................... 166
12:12 .................. 199
12:14 ................ 47, 97
12:24 .............. 190, 211
13:2 ................... 316
13:4 ................... 368
13:8 ................... 222
13:14 .................. 267

## James
1:4 .................... 44
1:22 ................... 197
1:18 ................... 137
5:7 .................... 185

## 1 Peter
1:5 ................... 403
1:8 ................... 105
1:13 .................. 126
2:3 ................... 150
2:17 .................. 151
2:23 .................. 263

3:9 ................... 146
4:7 ................... 186
4:10 .................. 120
4:11 ............... 50, 156
4:17 .................. 123
5:8 .................... 39

## 2 Peter
1:4 .................... 79
1:10 ................... 74
2:16 .................. 119

## 1 John
1 ..................... 74
1:3 ................... 181
1:7 ................... 145
1:8 ................. 38, 41
2:12ff. ................. 61
3:9 ................... 127
4:1 .................... 35
4:1–2 .................. 42
4:4 ................... 147
4:18 ............... 100, 131
5:14–15 ................ 357

## Jude
1:13 .................. 203

## Revelation
1 .................... 358
1:3 ................... 359
1:7 .......... 309, 331, 373, 382
1:16 .................. 103
2:5 .............. 219, 315, 358
2:10 ............. 200, 242, 307
2:20ff. ................. 37
3:2–3 .................. 191
3:3 ................... 306
3:8 ................... 258
3:12 .................. 307
3:14–16 ................ 227

*Revelation (continued)*
3:173 . . . . . . . . . . . . . . . . . . . . 78, 384
3:20 . . . . . . . . 197, 272, 295, 306, 387
5:12 . . . . . . . . . . . . . . . . . . . . . . . . 235
7:14 . . . . . . . . . . . . . . . . . . . . 234, 272
16:15 . . . . . . . . . . . . . . . . . . . 399, 408
16:18 . . . . . . . . . . . . . . . . . . . . . . . 104
19:7 . . . . . . . . . . . . . . . . . . . . . . . . 235
19:10 . . . . . . . . . . . . . . . . . . . . . . . 106
19:12ff. . . . . . . . . . . . . . . . . . . . . . . 78
19:13 . . . . . . . . . . . . . . . . . . . . . . . 135
22:17 . . . . . . . . . . . . . . . . . . . . 64, 234